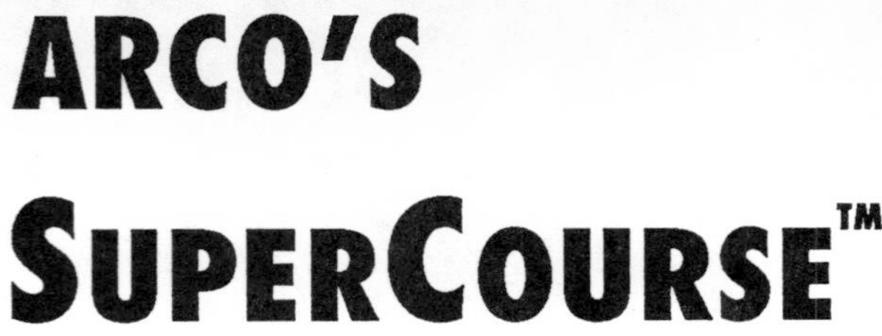

FOR THE TOEFL LISTENING COMPREHENSION CASSETTE TAPES

Get the tapes you need to take full advantage of this book. These two cassettes include the spoken parts of all the listening tests and will help you simulate an actual test-taking experience. Use the card below to order your tapes today.

Please detatch and return to:

Arco
Prentice Hall Mail Order
200 Old Tappan Road
Old Tappan, NJ 07675

❑ **YES, I want to get the most out of Arco's SuperCourse™ for the TOEFL. Please send me the LISTENING COMPREHENSION CASSETTE TAPES described above. I have enclosed $15.95 (plus local sales tax) for the set of 2 tapes.**

❑ **Check enclosed**

❑ **Please charge my credit card** ❑ **Visa** ❑ **Mastercard**

Acct.# .... **Exp. Date** ....

Signature ....
(All credit card orders must be signed)

Name ....

Address ....

City .... **State** .... **Zip** ....

Dept. R **92454-8 92494-4** **S1195Z1(2)**

SUPERCOURSE™ FOR THE TOEFL

SUPERCOURSE™ FOR THE TOEFL

Grace Yi Qiu Zhong
Patricia Noble Sullivan

New York London Toronto Sydney Tokyo Singapore

Dedicated to

Rebecca, Adam and Jessie

First Edition

PRENTICE HALL

Simon & Schuster, Inc.
15 Columbus Circle
New York, NY 10023

An Arco Book

Manufactured in the United States of America

3 4 5 6 7 8

Library of Congress Cataloging-in-Publication Data

Zhong, Grace Yi Qiu.
Supercourse for the TOEFL / by Grace Yi Qiu Zhong and Patricia Noble Sullivan.
p. cm.
ISBN 0-13-924531-6
1. English language—Textbooks for foreign speakers. 2. English language—Examinations—Study guides. I. Sullivan, Patricia Noble, 1942- . II. Title.
PE1128.Z47 1990. 90-1153
428.2'4'076—dc20 CIP

CONTENTS

Part One: Understanding the Test

Part Two: Understanding Yourself

Part Three: The Coaching Program

Part Four: Practice Tests

SYMBOLS

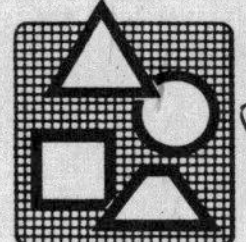
Types of Questions

strategy

testing point

scoring

guessing

fact

Dr. Watson

Sherlock Holmes

types of questions

= a specific type of question asked on the TOEFL

strategy

= a description of a strategy to increase your test-taking skills

testing point

= a list or description of a common testing point used on the TOEFL

scoring

= a system to use in estimating your TOEFL score

guessing

= a technique to help you guess at difficult questions

fact

= a fact about the TOEFL

Dr. Watson

= strategies and ideas of Dr. Watson

Sherlock Holmes

= strategies, ideas, and advice from Sherlock Holmes

A Letter to the Reader

Dear Reader,

The book you have just bought is worth hundreds of dollars. It is the first book to cover all forms of the TOEFL and include language skills, test-taking strategies, and five full-length practice tests. This book is the equivalent of an expensive test preparation course.

TOEFL preparation courses teach you test-taking skills and English language skills that will help you increase your score on the TOEFL. Those test-taking skills and exercises are in this book. You can learn them yourself by reading, studying, and practicing the exercises in this book.

In this book you will get:

- a diagnostic test to help you analyze your own strengths and weaknesses
- strategies that will help you identify the underlying testing points in each question
- charts to record your progress and point out areas for improvement
- hundreds of exercise questions that lead you through the steps of preparing for each part of the test
- five complete practice tests that are based on an analysis of questions taken directly from recent actual TOEFL exams.
- tests that are written in two forms: a long form and a short form, in order to give you practice no matter what form you are given when you take the TOEFL
- explanations of the answers for each test question and each answer choice
- lists that give you the most frequent vocabulary words, grammatical structures, topics, and types of questions that have been asked on recent TOEFL tests
- practice exercises for the TOEFL essay with sample student essays

There is no quick and easy way to increase your language skills. It takes time, work, and practice. This book gives you the advice and the practice exercises that will benefit you the most. This book contains essential English language skills and test-taking strategies to help you get your best score on the TOEFL.

We wish you the best in your future plans!

Grace Yi Qiu Zhong
Patricia Noble Sullivan

About This Book

This book has four parts. We encourage you to read the first two parts before you begin work on the exercises and practice tests.

Part One is a short introduction to the Test of English as a Foreign Language. It gives you basic information about the test itself and about how this book is organized. Lesson 6 introduces the detective Sherlock Holmes and his friend, Dr. Watson.

Part Two gives you information about figuring out your own level and skills. The charts and score analysis forms are introduced here.

Part Three is the most important working part of this book. Each of the sections of the TOEFL (Listening Comprehension, Structure, Vocabulary, and Reading) has two lessons. The first lesson begins with a pre-test to give you an idea of your own level. The lesson then gives you a list and a description of the most frequent words, structures, or topics in that section. In the second lesson of each section, you will practice exercises that will increase your test-taking skills for that section. Each of these lessons includes exercises and drills for you to practice the skills you are learning. There is a separate lesson on the Test of Written English.

Part Four includes five practice tests. Each of them is followed by complete explanatory answers. We encourage you to analyze your score after you take each test and keep a record of your improvement.

A cassette tape of all the listening comprehension tests and exercises is available for you to buy. Send in the form at the front of this book to order your cassette tape. We recommend that you buy the tape so that you get better listening comprehension practice, but if you choose not to buy the tape, you may read the tapescripts that are included here for each of the listening comprehension tests.

PART ONE

Understanding the Test

Lesson 1

Getting Started

Objectives

- To learn the meanings of some key terms
- To learn the answers to a few basic questions
  1. What is the TOEFL?
  2. What Institutions Require the TOEFL?
  3. What Is a Passing Score?
  4. How Many Times Can I Take the TOEFL?
  5. What Is the TWE?
  6. How do I Register for the TOEFL?

Lesson 1

What Is the TOEFL?

The letters T—O—E—F—L stand for Test of English as a Foreign Language. The purpose of this test is to measure your ability to read and understand North American English. The test is given approximately every month in many locations around the world, and it includes three sections: listening comprehension, structure and written expression, and vocabulary and reading comprehension.

What Institutions Require the TOEFL?

More than 2,300 colleges and universities in the United States and Canada require their applicants who are not native speakers of English to take the TOEFL. In addition, many other institutions, government agencies, and scholarship programs use TOEFL scores. In some countries the TOEFL is used to assess a person's knowledge of English for job purposes within that country. You must contact the institution or program you are interested in to see if it requires the TOEFL for your purposes.

What Is a Passing Score?

There is no single answer to this question. In general a score of 600 or more is considered excellent and a score of 400 or less is weak. The highest possible score anyone can get is 677. Some universities require a score of 550 or higher for entrance. Other schools may allow you in with a score of 450 or 500. In some schools you are required to take classes in English if your score is below a certain point. You must contact the schools or institutions that interest you to find out if it requires a particular score.

How Many Times Can I Take the TOEFL?

There is no limit to the number of times you can take the TOEFL. You can sign up to take it as often as you want.

What Is the TWE?

The letters T—W—E stand for Test of Written English. This is an essay test that is given several times a year with the TOEFL. It is not given on every test date. The purpose of the TWE is to give you a chance to demonstrate your ability to write in English. The TWE score is not added to your TOEFL score; it is a separate score that you receive with your TOEFL score report. Some universities require that applicants take the TWE; others do not. You can choose whether or not to take the TWE according to the date that you take the TOEFL. However, if you take the TOEFL on a day when the TWE is given, you must take the TWE. The Bulletin of Information for TOEFL tells you on which dates the TWE will be given.

How do I Register for the TOEFL?

To register for the TOEFL, you must fill out the registration form in the Bulletin of Information for TOEFL. The Bulletin is free and is given out at many colleges, univerities, and public libraries. If you cannot find a Bulletin of Information, you may write and request one from:

TOEFL/TSE Services
P.O. Box 6151
Princeton, New Jersey 08541-6151
USA

You may also telephone the above listed office at 609-771-7900 to request a Bulletin of Information. The number for general information is 609-882-6601. You must call between 8:30 A.M. and 4:30 P.M. Eastern time.

Lesson 2

An Overview of the TOEFL

Objectives

- To learn about the different kinds of questions on the TOEFL and TWE
- To learn the differences between different versions (long form and short form) of the TOEFL

1. TOEFL Questions
   - Listening Comprehension
   - Structure and Written Expression
   - Vocabulary and Reading Comprehension
2. TWE Questions
   - Comparison/Contrast
   - Chart/Graph
3. The Long and Short Forms

2

Lesson 2

TOEFL Questions

Listening Comprehension

The Listening Comprehension section has three parts:

Part A: Sentences
Part B: Conversations
Part C: Talks

The Listening Comprehension section is recorded on tape.
For each question, you have about 12 seconds to mark your answer.

Part A: Sentences

You will hear a sentence on the tape. After hearing it, you will choose the sentence in your test book that is the closest in meaning to the one you heard.

EXAMPLE:

You hear:
It's difficult to get all my work done in time.

Sample Answer

Ⓐ Ⓑ ● Ⓓ

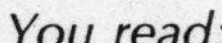

You read:
(A) My work is very difficult.
(B) All my work is finished now.
(C) It's hard to finish my work by the deadline.
(D) I work in a watch factory.

The answer is (C), which is a restatement of the recorded sentence. The word *hard* means *difficult,* and *in time* is similar in meaning to *by the deadline.*

Part B: Conversations

You will hear three voices. First, a man and a woman will have a short conversation. A third voice will then ask a question about the conversation.

EXAMPLE:

You hear:
Man: How about taking a break and getting some coffee?
Woman: Oh, that sounds great. I'm really exhausted.
Third Voice: What does the woman mean?

Sample Answer

You read:
(A) She wants to stop work for a while.
(B) She is going home to go to sleep.
(C) She has broken a coffee cup.
(D) She is too busy to get some coffee.

The answer is (A). You know that the woman wants to stop work because she tells the man that it sounds great to take a break. She says she is tired.

Part C: Talks

In this part you hear a talk by one person or a longer conversation between two people. You listen to the complete talk or conversation and then answer several questions about it.

EXAMPLE:

Questions 1 and 2 are based on the following talk.

You hear:
Good morning, students. Before we get started on our main topic for today, I'd like to make an announcement for all of you who are working on campus. We have a new rule that every person who is hired on campus must take a CPR course. CPR, as you probably know, stands for cardiopulmonary resuscitation. It's a simple procedure, but a lifesaving one. The classes will be held on Saturdays from 10 A.M. to 3 P.M. all through this month. You need to go to only one session. If you already have had CPR training during the last five years, you don't need the training course. Otherwise, sign up for a session at the end of this meeting.

1. *You hear:*
Who must take a CPR course?

Sample Answer

You read:
(A) Every student who is working on campus
(B) All graduate students
(C) All students who are in health classes
(D) Those who took it five years ago

2. *You hear:*
How long is each CPR session?

Sample Answer

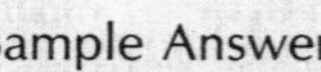

You read:
(A) One month long.
(B) Almost all day
(C) The whole weekend
(D) Five years

The answer to question 1 is (A). The speaker says that every person who is hired on campus must take a CPR course. The answer to question 2 is (B). The speaker says that the course is on Saturdays from 10 A.M. to 3 P.M., which is almost all day. The classes will be held every Saturday in the month, but students need to go to only one Saturday session.

Structure and Written Expression

The Structure and Written Expression section has two parts: sentence completion and error identification.

Sentence Completion

You must choose the word or phrase that correctly completes the sentence.

EXAMPLE:

A healthy meal ________ foods that give the body a variety of vitamins and minerals.

Sample Answer
Ⓐ Ⓑ ● Ⓓ

(A) that includes
(B) if it includes
(C) includes
(D) to be included

The answer is (C). This sentence is a statement that needs only a present tense verb to complete it.

Error Identification

You must choose the word or phrase that is written incorrectly.

EXAMPLE:

A fast-swimming (A) fish, such (B) as a trout or mackerel has (C) an ideal shape for move (D) through water.

Sample Answer
Ⓐ Ⓑ Ⓒ ●

The answer is (D). After the preposition *for* you must use a gerund, *moving.*

Vocabulary and Reading Comprehension

The Vocabulary section asks you to choose the word or phrase that would best keep the meaning of the original sentence if it were substituted for the underlined word.

EXAMPLE:

George Washington Carver gained international fame for his work in agricultural research.

Sample Answer

(A) prizes
(B) efficiency
(C) misfortune
(D) recognition

The answer is (D). The word *recognition* is the closest in meaning to *fame*.

In the Reading Comprehension section you will see several reading passages, followed by a few questions.

EXAMPLE:

Since sea coral is similar to human bone in its mineral content and its porous nature, it has been used effectively in bone grafts. It is especially useful in areas that are not weight-bearing. Traditionally, when human bone is defective it has been replaced with a graft from somewhere else in the person's body, usually the hips, ribs, or skull. This, however, requires surgery on two parts of the body and results in a longer operation and an increased chance of complications. In addition, bone grafts tend to be gradually absorbed by the body and they eventually need to be replaced. Using common sea coral from the South Pacific is an ingenious solution to this problem for plastic surgeons. When the coral is implanted in the body, the body's natural bone slowly begins to grow into the pores of the coral, making it stronger as the tissue grows.

1. What is this passage mainly about?

Sample Answer

(A) How sea coral grows
(B) An alternative replacement for damaged bone
(C) How a bone graft is made
(D) Problems that plastic surgeons have

2. According to the passage, what is one problem with using human bone in grafts?

Sample Answer

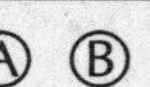

(A) It grows into the pores of coral.
(B) It is not strong enough.
(C) It becomes absorbed by the body.
(D) It is too porous.

The answer to question 1 is (B). The main topic of the passage is how sea coral can replace human bone in grafts.

The answer to question 2 is (C). The passage states that bone grafts tend to be gradually absorbed by the body.

TWE Questions

The Test of Written English has two types of questions: comparison/contrast and chart/graph.

Comparison/Contrast

EXAMPLE:

You are planning a trip to a country you have read a lot about but have not visited yet. Some of your friends think you should go on a guided tour with a group. Other friends think you should travel by yourself. Decide which of these two kinds of traveling is best for you. Give reasons to support your decision.

Chart/Graph

EXAMPLE:

The graph below shows the number of people driving cars to school as compared to the number of people who ride bicycles. Discuss this graph, explaining the relative changes in the use of the two methods of transportation over the year.

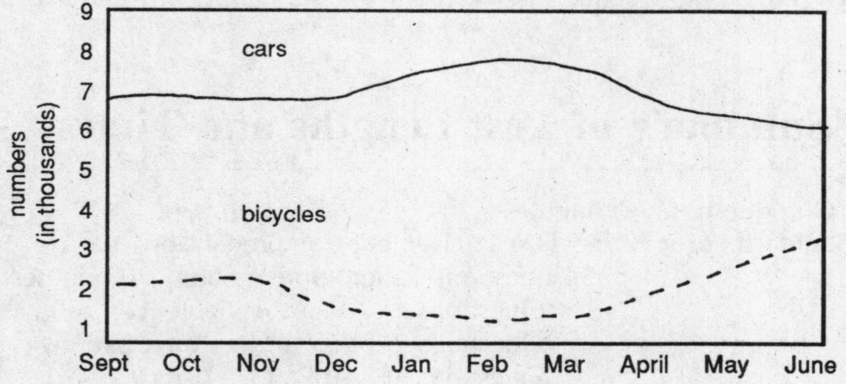

The Long and Short Forms of the TOEFL

There are two versions of the TOEFL: a long form and a short form. Either test version will occupy about two or three hours. For the first half hour of test time, you will be filling out all the pre-test information (names, addresses, institution numbers, etc.) The rest of the time is either the TOEFL alone or the TOEFL and the TWE. If you take the TWE you will get the standard (shorter) form of the TOEFL. If you take the test on a day when the TWE is not given, you may get a longer form of the TOEFL. Even though the tests are different in length, the converted score system assures that scoring will be uniform.

The table on page 14 shows you that the long form has 80 more questions than the standard form. You are given about 50 more minutes to complete the test in the long form, so you need to concentrate for a longer total period of time. In addition, you are given slightly fewer seconds per question. Remember, though, that the converted scores will give all the tests the same value, no matter how long or how hard they are.

TOEFL Tests: Comparison of Two Forms

Total Time in Testing Center

Standard (Short) Form	**Long Form**
Filling out forms = 30 minutes (approx)	Filling out forms = 30 min
TWE = 30 minutes	
TOEFL = 1 hour and 40 min	TOEFL = 2 hours and 30 min
Total = 2 hour and 40 min	Total = 3 hours

Number of Questions	**Standard**	**Long**
Section 1: Listening	50	80
Section 2: Structure	40	60
Section 3: Vocabulary/Reading	60	90
Totals:	150	230

Preparing for the Different Lengths of Tests

In order to do your best, you should psychologically prepare for the test you will take. Check the *Bulletin of Information* for the date you are taking the test. If the TWE is not given on that day you might get the longer form. This book helps you prepare by providing practice tests in both the standard form and the longer form.

Summary of Test Lengths and Times

TWE One question: 30 minutes

TOEFL: Standard Form

Section 1: Listening Comprehension
(50 questions-Time: approximately 30 minutes)
- Questions 1–20 Part A: Sentences
- Questions 21–35 Part B: Conversations
- Questions 36–50 Part C: Talks

Section 2: Structure and Written Expression
(40 questions—Time: 25 minutes)
- Questions 1–15 Sentence Completion
- Questions 16–40 Error Identification

Section 3: Vocabulary and Reading Comprehension
(60 questions—Time: 45 minutes)
- Questions 1–30 Vocabulary
- Questions 31–60 Reading Comprehension

TOEFL: Long Form

Section 1: Listening Comprehension
(80 questions—Time: approximately 50 minutes)
- Questions 1–30 Part A: Sentences
- Questions 31–55 Part B: Conversations
- Questions 56–80 Part C: Talks

Section 2: Structure and Written Expression
(60 questions—Time: 35 minutes)
- Questions 1–23 Sentence Completion
- Questions 24–60 Error Identification

Section 3: Vocabulary and Reading Comprehension
(90 questions—Time: 65 minutes)
- Questions 1–45 Vocabulary
- Questions 46–90 Reading Comprehension

Lesson 3

3

Basic Preparation

Objectives

- To learn about TOEFL instructions
- To learn important facts about marking your answers
- To understand how guessing helps you
- To learn a system of eliminating answers
- To learn what to do just before the test

1. Understanding the Instructions
2. Marking Your Answers
3. The Guessing Reward
4. Eliminating Answer Choices
5. What to Do If You Don't Know the Answer

Lesson 3

Understanding the Instructions

It is important that you carefully read the instructions for each part of the TOEFL before you take the test. While you are taking the test, you do not want to spend valuable time trying to figure out what to do. The instructions for each section of the TOEFL are given in Part Three, the Coaching Program, page 67. Read these carefully before you do the exercises. Be sure you understand every word. The instructions in this book are identical to those in the actual TOEFL exam.

As you read the TOEFL instructions reproduced here, notice the differences among the sections and parts. Then, as you do the practice tests and practice exercises in this book, follow the instructions carefully. Every practice test will help you prepare for the actual test if you have always done the practice questions exactly as you will do the actual questions. Studying the instructions before you take the test gives you several advantages.

1. You save valuable time during the real TOEFL.
2. You understand the TOEFL better.
3. You are more confident in yourself and your ability to take the TOEFL.
4. You avoid unnecessary errors.

In addition to instructions for answering questions in each section of the TOEFL, this lesson includes important general information about the test as a whole, some of which is listed below:

1. You are allowed to work on only one section of the TOEFL at a time. You are *not* allowed to work on the next section or go back to the section you just finished.
2. Do not try to cheat by looking at someone else's paper or by looking at your notes or books. If the examiner sees you doing this, your exam will probably be taken away. You will have to leave the test room immediately and you will get no credit for the test.
3. Do not make any marks in your test booklet. Do not take any notes or underline any words. Do not make any notes on your answer sheet.
4. When the examiner says that your time is up, stop work immediately. If you continue to work, your exam may be taken away from you and you will get no credit for the entire test.
5. You may not be allowed to get up and leave the room while taking the test. Be prepared to sit for about three hours.

Marking Your Answers

The TOEFL has a separate answer sheet for you to mark your answers. It is read and scored by machine so it is very important that you fill in the answer ovals in the correct way.

1. Bring two #2 pencils and a good eraser to the test center.
2. Fill in the complete oval. All your answer marks must be dark. Do not make any other marks on your answer sheet.
3. Do not mark two answers or put an X over an oval that you filled in by mistake. If the machine sees two answers marked for the same question, you will not get credit for either answer. If you make a mistake, erase the pencil mark completely.
4. Mark your answers like the correct example shown below.

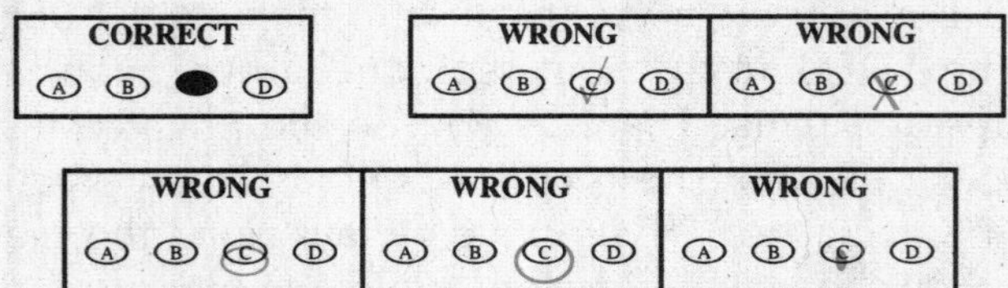

There are two kinds of TOEFL answer sheets. In one form, the letters for the answers are vertical, and in the other they are horizontal. When you are given your answer sheet, immediately notice which type you have so that you don't waste any seconds on your first questions. In this book, the answer sheets for Tests 1, 2, and 5 are in the vertical form, while the answer sheets for Tests 3 and 4 are in the horizontal form. Practice with both forms.

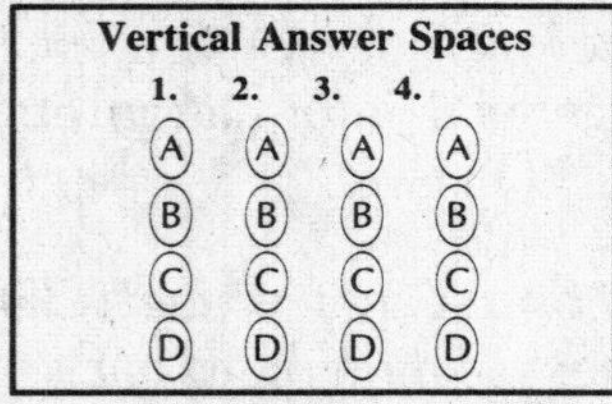

Horizontal Answer Spaces

1. A B C D
2. A B C D
3. A B C D
4. A B C D

One of the main difficulties of taking the TOEFL is the time pressure. You want to save time in every way that you can. Here are three suggestions that can save seconds for you.

1. When you begin to fill out the forms before the test begins, your pencil should be sharp. By the time you finish marking your name, address, and the necessary numbers, your pencil tip will be more dull. That is perfect for filling in the ovals. Don't sharpen your pencil during the test. With a wide, flat tip you can fill in the ovals more quickly.

2. If you hold your pencil straight up, with the tip flat against the paper, you can fill in the oval quickly with one or two strokes. This is quicker than going back and forth several times to fill in the oval. Practice this technique while taking the practice tests in this book.

3. If you use both hands to hold your place, you can save seconds. Since you have to read the questions in your test booklet and then mark your answers on a separate answer sheet, it is easy to lose your place on the answer sheet. It might take you an extra second to find the correct oval for each question. If you write with your right hand, put the answer sheet on your right and the booklet on your left. Keep your left hand on the question in the answer booklet, and keep your pencil on the corresponding line on your answer sheet. In this way you will always have your pencil on the correct answer line. You won't have to look for the line each time you look back and forth from the test booklet to the answer sheet. **Remember:** The more seconds you can save while marking your answer sheet, the more time you have for reading and choosing the answers.

The Guessing Reward

For your TOEFL score, only the correct answers are counted. There is no penalty for choosing an incorrect answer. Therefore, you should answer *every* question in each section of the test to maximize your chances for gaining points. But remember, only one answer for each question is allowed. If the machine sees two answers, you get no credit for that question.

Eliminating Answer Choices

At times you will not be sure which answer is correct. When this happens eliminate as many answer choices as possible before guessing in order to increase your chances of getting the answer right.

If you guess without eliminating any answer choices, your chance of getting the answer right is only 25 percent.

If you can eliminate one answer choice, however, you are guessing between three answers: now your chance of getting the right answer is 33 percent. That's a little better.

Of course, it is even better if you know that two answer choices are wrong. Then you are guessing between only the two remaining choices, so your chance is up to 50 percent.

What to Do If You Don't Know the Answer

You know that you should answer every question. But if you don't know the correct answer, what should you do? Try the following:

1. Eliminate any answers that you know are wrong.
2. Use your background knowledge to eliminate some answers.
3. Use any general "feelings" about English to help you eliminate other answers.
4. Choose between the answer choices that are left.
5. If you have no time to read the questions, choose one letter and mark all remaining spaces on your answer sheet with the same letter.

Lesson 4

Testing Points

4

Objectives

- To understand what is meant by *testing points*
- To learn how testing points are used in this book
- To learn how a knowledge of testing points can help you on the TOEFL

1. What is a Testing Point?
2. How Testing Points are Used in this Book
3. The Advantages of Learning to Recognize Testing Points
4. How To Apply Your Knowledge of Testing Points
5. Figure/Ground Theory

What Is a Testing Point?

Throughout this book you will see references to the words *testing points.* In this book, a testing point is the information on which you are being tested. Each of the questions on the TOEFL is written to test you on one or more particular items that are called testing points in this book. An example of an idiom testing point in Listening Comprehension is written below:

EXAMPLE:

You hear:
My sister always looks on the bright side of things.

Sample Answer

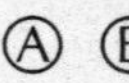  

You read:
(A) My sister is very intelligent.
(B) My sister always wears glasses.
(C) My sister has a positive attitude.
(D) My sister likes sunny days.

In the above example, the main testing point is the idiom "looks on the bright side of things." The answer is (C) since "looks on the bright side of things" means that a person has a positive attitude.

You will find examples of other testing points in each of the lessons in Part Three of this book, "The Coaching Program." The following list gives a few examples of common testing points:

Listening Comprehension
- a particular vocabulary word
- a particular idiomatic expression
- a grammatical structure
- a distinction between two similar-sounding words

Structure and Written Expression
- a correct verb tense
- a correct word form (e.g., adjective or adverb)
- the correct use of an adjective or adverb phrase
- agreement between subject and verb

Vocabulary and Reading Comprehension
- the meaning of a particular word
- the main idea of a passage
- understanding an inference
- understanding the author's point of view

How Testing Points Are Used in This Book

The most frequent testing points from actual TOEFL exams used between 1984 and 1989 are categorized for each section of the TOEFL. These lists are in The Coaching Program in Lessons 12, 14, and 18. You can use the lists to guide your study time.

The lessons on test-taking skills in The Coaching Program include exercises that help you practice using the testing points that are listed in the frequency lessons.

The practice tests were all developed based on testing points from actual TOEFL exams.

The explanatory answers for each question on the practice tests give the testing points and some testing point clues to help you in your pre-TOEFL study.

Advantages of Learning to Recognize Testing Points

Throughout this book, you are asked to think of the testing point as well as the correct answer to each question. At first, figuring out the testing points may take you extra time, but as you become more familiar with the process, you should find that it reduces the time necessary for you to choose answers.

The main advantage is this: *you learn to think like the test-maker as well as the test-taker!*

What are other advantages of learning to recognize testing points?

1. The TOEFL test is very broad. You can never know which questions and sentences will be used in each section. In contrast, the testing points are more narrow and consistent. They are repeated on tests from year to year.
2. If you know what testing points have been common on previous exams, you can concentrate on studying those key items, and therefore use your study time more efficiently.
3. If you understand the testing points, you can use the frequency lists in this book to give you an overall understanding of TOEFL exams.
4. When you take the real TOEFL, you can use your knowledge of testing points to help you make quick decisions about the answers. Some of the confusing parts of the TOEFL will also become more clear to you.
5. Understanding testing points gives you knowledge not only about the questions themselves but about how the questions are asked.
6. By using your knowledge of testing points you will have a new way to check your answers.
7. Your knowledge of testing points will ease your pre-test anxiety by giving you some confidence about what might be on your TOEFL exam.
8. By identifying testing points during your study time, you are building an organization in your mind that will help you retrieve the information more quickly while you are taking the TOEFL.

How To Apply Your Knowledge of Testing Points

Each lesson in Part Three, The Coaching Program, page 67, gives you strategies for using testing points in that section. The strategies are different in each section of the TOEFL since the testing points are different in each section.

The following example shows how your knowledge of the testing points in Section Two, Structure and Written Expression, can help you understand a question and answer it quickly. More information about these testing point clues is given in Lesson 15, page 183.

Test Sentence from Error Identification Part

My friend Jean, who is a virtuoso with castanets, are performing at the University
A (who) **B** (virtuoso) **C** (are) **D** (the)

Theater tonight.

Read the sentence, paying attention to the underlined words.

After you have studied the testing points in Lesson 15, pages 181–185, you will be aware of the following clues:

1. The commas show you that the part of the sentence beginning with *who* is a clause that can be omitted from the sentence without changing the grammatical correctness of the sentence.
2. One of the frequent testing points is agreement of subject and verb.
3. The word *Jean* is singular and therefore is not correct with the verb *are*.

Fill in (C) on your answer sheet.

In this sentence your knowledge of testing points will help you in four ways:

1. You gain knowledge by using a testing point clue (the commas).
2. Since you understand the use of the commas, you are not confused by the words *castanets are,* which might seem correct, but actually are not.
3. You gain time by checking particular testing points before trying to understand the whole sentence.
4. You realize that it is not necessary to understand the meaning of either *castanets* or *virtuoso,* so you do not waste time and energy wondering about these words.

You will find examples of testing points, ways to use testing points, and testing point clues in each of the lessons in Part Three, The Coaching Program.

Figure/Ground Theory

Our eyes are not like cameras; we don't always notice everything in front of them. We may see only what we are focusing on or what we want to see. Think of yourself in the following situations:

DAY 1:

You have a letter that you want to mail. While you are walking down the street, you see a mailbox, so you mail your letter.

DAY 2:

You are walking down the same street, but this time you are very hungry because you haven't had lunch. What do you see? The mailbox? Of course not. You see the restaurant where you can get a good lunch.

The two situations above give examples of Figure/Ground Theory, the concept of focusing only on certain objects in our environment. Even though there are many things around us at all times, we only remember the things that interest us. *Figure/Ground* refers to the different aspects of a picture or drawing: *Ground* refers to the background; *Figure* is the pattern or object of interest. Sometimes you focus on one object in a drawing, but at other times you focus on the background. By focusing on different parts of a picture, you see the picture in a different way.

Just as you can look at a picture in different ways, you can look at the TOEFL in different ways. You can teach yourself to focus on different parts of the TOEFL. The testing points and the clues for TOEFL questions are all in your test book. All these are right in front of your eyes. With your knowledge of testing points and your practice with testing points in this book, you will be able to pick out particular parts of questions. You will "see" the testing point clues that are in the sentence. You will be able to focus on important aspects of the questions which will help your test-taking skills.

Lesson 5

The Benefits of General Knowledge

5

Objectives

- To understand the benefits of having General Knowledge for the TOEFL
- To learn ways to develop your General Knowledge

1. What is General Knowledge?
2. The Benefits of General Knowledge
3. Developing General Knowledge

What is General Knowledge?

If you hear someone say, "I have some general knowledge about this topic," you can assume that he or she has a limited background that does not include many details or specific facts. For a college student, general knowledge is not enough; a more thorough understanding of concepts and facts in your major area of interest will be needed. For the TOEFL exam, however, general knowledge can help.

The Benefits of General Knowledge

The reading comprehension section and listening comprehension section of the TOEFL do not test you on specific facts or technical knowledge; they test your general reading and listening comprehension skills. You are asked to demonstrate skills such as understanding the main idea, making inferences, restating information, and identifying the author's purpose. In other words, you are being asked to demonstrate your skills in *comprehension,* not your knowledge of specific facts.

If you have at least a general idea of the topic you are reading about or listening to, your comprehension will be quicker. Look at the following examples of comprehension skills based on different levels of general knowledge.

Situation

The following people are planning to cook something. They are all reading the same recipe. Here are descriptions of their reading comprehension levels.

Person A: (Level 3 high)

The dish that Person A is cooking is often eaten in his own country. He has made the dish before so he knows the process. He knows what it will look like and taste like, but he doesn't know exactly how much sugar, salt, or flour to add. He is reading in order to *check* the details. This type of reading is quick; he understands easily.

Person B: (Level 2)

Person B has cooked before, but the dish she is cooking here is from another country. Although she knows how to cook in general, she is not familiar with the process for this particular dish. She is also not sure how the dish will look or taste. Since she has less general knowledge she has to read more slowly and carefully than Person A in order to understand the recipe.

Person C: (Level 1 low)

Person C has never cooked before. He is trying to cook this dish by following the recipe, but he is not sure of the meaning of most of the words in the recipe. He has to learn the meanings of the new vocabulary words in addition to learning the process of cooking itself. This is obviously the most difficult of the three types of reading. His reading is very slow; he has difficulty following the recipe.

How do these three levels relate to the TOEFL? Let's assume that the test includes a reading passage on a scientific topic.

Level 3

You have general knowledge about scientific concepts in your own language; you often read academic material. As you read in English, you are checking new information with your own background knowledge. You are able to predict some of the information in the passage because you are familiar with the general concepts, even though the information in the passage and some of the vocabulary words are new.

Level 2

You read well in your own language, but you are not familiar with scientific concepts. As you read you are learning the general concepts as well as the specific information in the reading passage. Your reading is slower than that of someone in Level 3.

Level 1

You don't read much in your own language. You are not familiar with any general scientific concepts and you rarely read academic material. It is very difficult for you to comprehend the information in the reading passages.

In Summary

The TOEFL is not trying to test your knowledge of specific facts; rather, it is testing your ability to comprehend information. Your comprehension skills will be greater if you understand the basic vocabulary and general concepts of the area you are reading about or listening to.

Developing General Knowledge

In Lessons 12 and 18 you will see lists of topics from Listening Comprehension talks and Reading Comprehension passages. Studying these lists can give you an idea of the areas that have frequently appeared on previous tests. It isn't worth your time to learn specific facts in these areas since you don't know what topics will be on your test. It can help your comprehension skills, however, to have some general knowledge and an understanding of vocabulary within this range of topics.

There is a benefit to reading in your own language as well as in English. You probably read faster in your own language, and as you read you are increasing your general knowledge, which can easily be translated into English. Your reading skills also improve as you read in your own language and the skills of understanding the main idea, inferring information, and restating ideas are similar in all languages.

The following suggestions will help you increase your basic vocabulary and your general knowledge. All of these will help your reading and listening comprehension skills.

1. Study the Reading Comprehension frequency list in the Coaching Program, pages 264 and 265, for a general idea of the topics used in previous TOEFL exams.
2. Use the frequency lists to guide you in your choice of reading material, but don't limit yourself to any particular kind of reading.
3. For general knowledge in areas such as science, music, or art, read in the lanuage that is easiest for you.
4. For topics in American history or American geography, read in English. This will help you learn American names.
5. Whenever you read in English, study the new vocabulary words, especially the ones that describe basic concepts in the field.
6. As you read in English, pay attention to the style of writing, especially if it seems very different from writing styles in your own language. Compare an English passage with a passage on the same topic in your own language in order to understand differences in style. This may help you to understand how English passages are written.
7. Your goal is to get a general background of the topics that are often used on TOEFL exams. Read for a broad understanding of general topics, not a deep and thorough understanding of a few topics. You are trying to broaden your background and increase your vocabulary.

Lesson 6

Understanding the Mystery

6

Objectives

- To learn about Sherlock Holmes and Dr. Watson
- To learn how Watson and Holmes are used in this book

1. Who Are Sherlock Holmes and Dr. Watson?
2. Why Are These Mystery Characters Used in This Book?
3. Test Patterns
4. Adventures of the TOEFL

Who Are Sherlock Holmes and Dr. Watson?

You may have read about about Sherlock Holmes, a fictional character created by the British author, Sir Arthur Conan Doyle. Sherlock Holmes is a famous detective who can solve even the most complex mysteries with his logical thinking, based on deductive reasoning. Dr. Watson, a medical doctor who is his friend and companion, is always fascinated by the way that Sherlock Holmes can use clues to lead him to the answers. Dr. Watson is obviously an intelligent person, but he does not use logical reasoning in the way Holmes does, and he cannot solve mysteries the way that Holmes can.

Why Are These Mystery Characters Used in This Book?

The TOEFL is often seen as a mystery. What questions will be in the Listening Comprehension section? What vocabulary words will be asked? What will the reading passages be about? This book uses Holmes and Watson to give you clues and strategies for answering questions. Put yourself in the role of detective so you can figure out clues that will help you answer TOEFL questions.

Test Patterns

The TOEFL is given almost every month of every year, and all of the tests are similar in many ways. Each test is statistically calculated to bring certain results, so every question must be written according to a special formula. All questions must fit a certain pattern. If the questions didn't follow a pattern, the tests would not be so similar.

What would happen if Holmes and Watson took the TOEFL (if they didn't speak English as their native language)? Probably, Watson would do fairly well; he is intelligent and educated, and he would probably study a lot and get a good score. Holmes, on the other hand, would probably do much better. While studying for the test, he would look for patterns and clues in the questions that would lead him to the answers. He would use logical reasoning to help eliminate answer choices.

The following illustrates what might happen if Holmes and Watson were to take the TOEFL.

Adventures of the TOEFL

The Case of the Missing Patterns

One day, while Dr. Watson and Sherlock Holmes were on a train on the way to solve a murder, Dr. Watson was amusing himself by preparing for the TOEFL. He was working in the Structure and Written Expression section. At first he felt quite confident because he was able to answer many of the questions correctly. However, as he continued reading the questions, marking the answers, and then checking the answer key he became upset because he thought he was missing too many questions.

"Oh dear," said Watson. "I don't know the answer again. I guess I'll just quit for now."

Holmes, who had been enjoying the views of the countryside, looked over at Watson and said, "Now Watson, don't stop without thinking about why you are missing those questions. Let me see your book."

Holmes saw three questions.

1. Wood, which (A) is used for cooking (B) food, heating homes, and construction (C) buildings, is extremely (D) important as a natural resource.

2. John Adams grew up (A) on his father's farm, doing the (B) usual country chores, including feeding (C) the horses, milk (D) the cows, and chopping wood.

3. Translated into (A) scientific terms, a host is a living plant or animal which provides (B) food, gives shelter, and to have (C) a profound effect on its parasites (D).

Watson's Answers

1. Ⓐ Ⓑ Ⓒ ● (correct)
2. Ⓐ Ⓑ Ⓒ ● (correct)
3. ● Ⓑ Ⓒ Ⓓ (incorrect)

Holmes saw that Watson had answered the first two questions correctly. "How did you know these?" he asked. "Oh, I'm not sure," said Watson. "It just seemed right to correct the sentence in Question 1 so that it would read (D) "constructing buildings" and the sentence in Question 2 sounded correct to say (D) "milking the cows."

"Certainly you are right," said Holmes. "But if you could get 1 and 2 correct, then you should get 3 correct also."

"But, why? I don't know what the sentence means. I picked (A) as the answer because I have never seen a sentence that begins with the word "translated."

"My dear Watson," said Holmes. "I have seen many sentences like this in Structure and Written Expression. You have forgotten to check the testing point clues and pay attention to patterns. In each of these sentences there are commas that signal you to check for parallel construction. Before you start worrying about whether you have seen a particular word before, you should be looking for general patterns. In each of these practice sentences there are three things that are listed together. Each of them must use the same form of speech. Look:

1....*cooking* food, *heating* homes, and *constructing* buildings...
2....*feeding* the horses, *milking* the cows, and *chopping* wood...
3....*provides* food, *gives* shelter, and *has* a profound effect...

"In the first two sentences the parallel words all end in /ing./ In the third sentence the verbs are all third-person singular. But the clues are the same. There are three phrases connected by commas and the word "and." Whenever you see this pattern, check to be sure that the words are all the same part of speech. When you read the sentence, focus on the words connected by commas before you spend time on the other difficult parts of the sentence."

"You are so right, my friend. Next time I study I will look for these patterns. But for now I think I will enjoy the scenery from the train window."

The more you are able to think like Holmes, the better your reasoning skills will be. In Part Three, The Coaching Program, page 67, you will read about basic strategies that are used by Watson. They are all good strategies, but they are not the only strategies. You will also learn about strategies that use patterns and clues. These "Holmesian" strategies take advantage of the information from previous TOEFL tests to help you understand patterns and follow clues.

PART TWO

Understanding Yourself

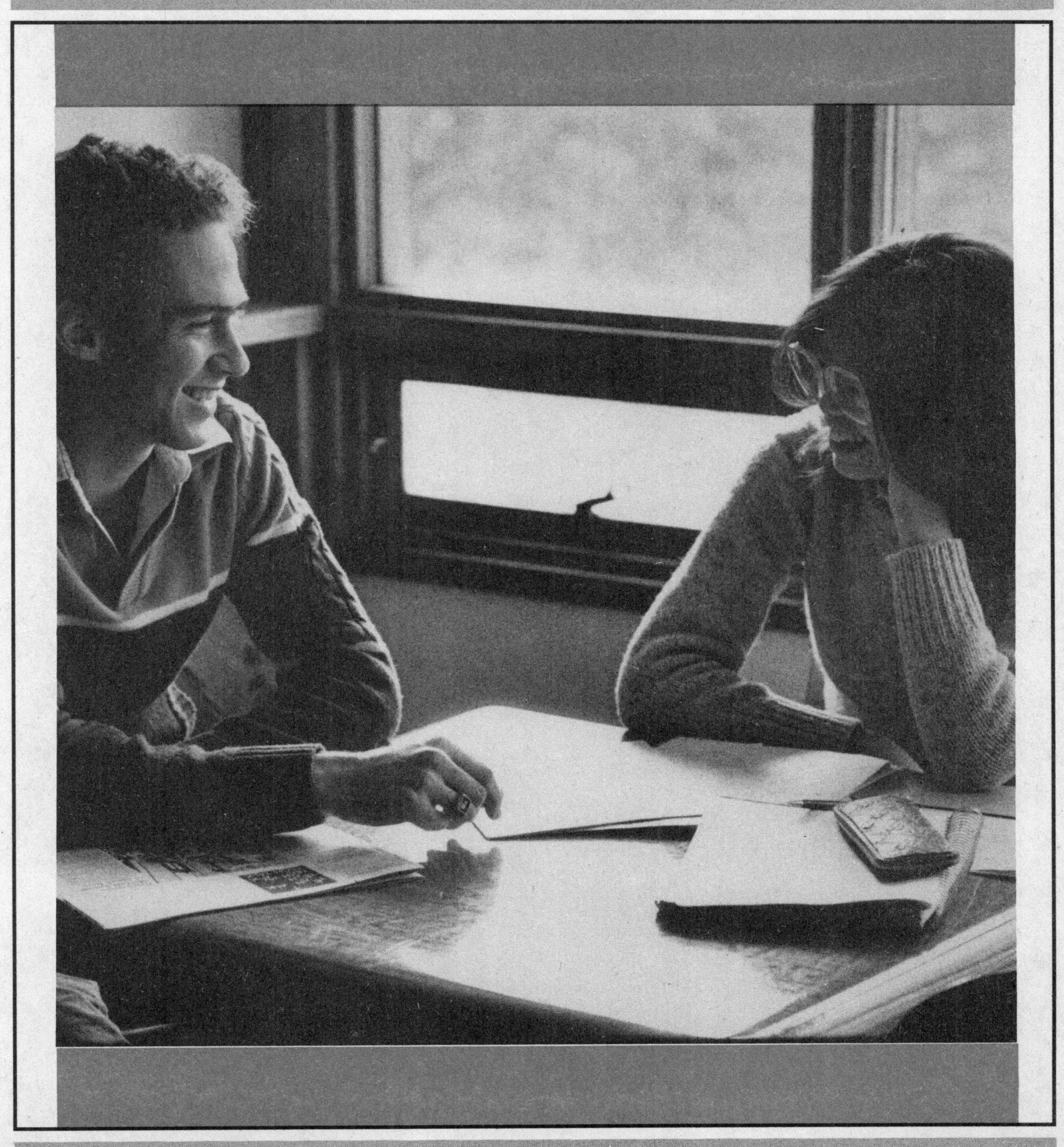

Lesson 7

Taking the Practice Tests

7

Objectives

- To give you information about taking the Practice Tests
- To remind you to simulate the real TOEFL as much as possible
  1. Taking the Diagnostic Test
  2. Taking the Other Practice Tests
  3. Imagine that the Practice Tests Are Real

Lesson 7

7

Taking the Diagnostic Test

Now that you have a general idea of the TOEFL, it is time for you to find out more about yourself. What is your general TOEFL level? What areas are you strong in? What areas are you weak in? What test-taking strategies do you use? How can you improve your test-taking strategies? This part of the book will help you answer these questions so that you can plan your study time wisely.

The first thing you need to do is take Practice Test 1, the Diagnostic Test, on page 359. Do this as soon as you finish reading this page, before you study the rest of this book. After you finish taking Practice Test 1, check your answers using the answer key on pages 381–382. Then figure out your approximate TOEFL score using the information in Lesson 8.

Taking the Other Practice Tests

This book has four other practice tests. Figure out how many weeks or months you have before you take the TOEFL, and plan to take each of the four remaining practice tests at regular intervals during that time. Take the final practice test a few days before you take the TOEFL.

Imagine that the Practice Tests are Real

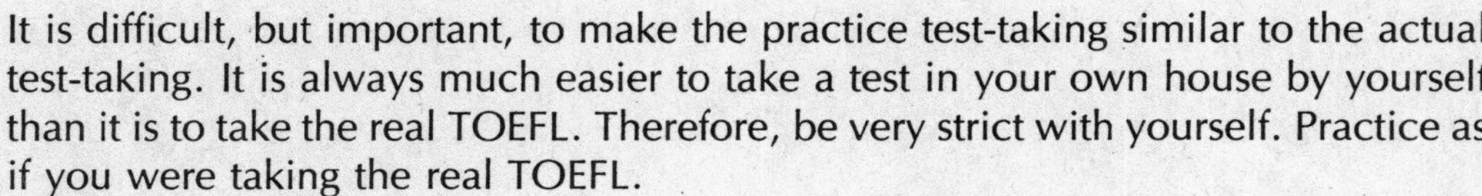

It is difficult, but important, to make the practice test-taking similar to the actual test-taking. It is always much easier to take a test in your own house by yourself than it is to take the real TOEFL. Therefore, be very strict with yourself. Practice as if you were taking the real TOEFL.

Don't answer questions after the time limit.
Don't look back and change answers in another section.
Don't stop the tape when you don't have time to mark your answer.
Do take the test in a place where you won't be bothered by the telephone, the doorbell, or people coming in to your room.
Do stay at your desk for the complete test. You will have no break during the real TOEFL exam.

Remember: Follow the time limits strictly as you take each practice test. Do not allow any interruptions.

Another way to prepare for the TOEFL is to train your mind to imagine that you are in a different situation. When you take a practice test pretend that it is the real TOEFL. Force yourself to work under the pressure of the real test. Then, later on, when you take the real TOEFL, pretend that it is only a practice test, and that you are taking it in your own home. In this way, you will be more relaxed during the actual TOEFL and therefore able to perform better.

Now turn to page 359 and take Practice Test 1. If you don't have the cassette that goes with this book, ask a friend to read the tapescript to you. The tapescript for Practice Test 1 is on page 633.

Lesson 8

Scoring and Analyzing Your Practice Tests

Objectives

- To learn the difference between raw scores and converted scores
- To learn how to compute your TOEFL score

1. What Is a Raw Score?
2. What Is a Converted Score?
3. Scoring Your Practice Tests
4. Score Conversion Table: Standard (Short) Form
5. Score Conversion Table: Long Form

Lesson 8

Read this lesson after you have taken Practice Test 1, the Diagnostic Test. Use the Answer Key on pages 381–382 to check your answers before you read this lesson. This lesson explains how to use the Score Analysis form on page 383 to figure out your approximate TOEFL score.

What Is a Raw Score?

A raw score is a count of the number of answers you have marked correctly on your answer sheet. When you take the real TOEFL, a computerized machine will count the number you have correct. Be sure to fill in the blanks completely. Make your marks dark enough so that the machine can read them easily.

What Is a Converted Score?

Your raw score is changed to a converted score before your total score is computed. For the actual TOEFL, this converted score is based on a statistical analysis of each test. The converted score system is used in order to insure that all TOEFL scores are equivalent, even if one particular test is easier or more difficult than another. The score conversion tables in this lesson are approximate tables; they give you only an estimate of your actual score.

Scoring Your Practice Tests

To find out your score, first count the number correct in each section. This is your raw score. Then change your raw score to an approximate converted score based on the tables in this lesson. Each time you take a practice test in this book, figure out your approximate TOEFL score by doing the following:

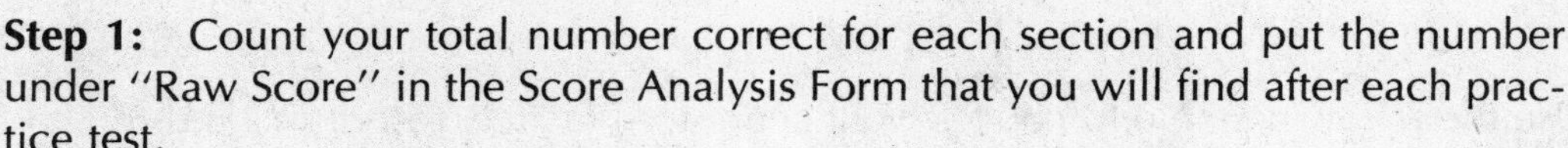

Step 1: Count your total number correct for each section and put the number under "Raw Score" in the Score Analysis Form that you will find after each practice test.

Step 2: Find the raw score range on Score Conversion Table on page 49.

Step 3: Find the converted score range on Score Conversion Table and put the two numbers in the Score Analysis Forms under "Converted Score Range."

Step 4: Multiply each of the score range numbers by 10.

Step 5: Divide each of the converted score numbers by 3.

Step 6: Add the columns of numbers to get your total approximate TOEFL score.

Example: This uses the Short Form conversion table:

	Raw Score	Raw Score Range	Converted Score Range	Approximate Score
Listening Comprehension	*30*	*30–32*	*(50–51)* × 10 ÷ 3 = *(500–510)* ÷ 3 =	*166–170*
Structure and Written Express	*25*	*24–26*	*(48–50)* × 10 ÷ 3 = *(480–500)* ÷ 3 =	*160–166*
Vocabulary and Reading Comp	*25*	*24–26*	*(42–43)* × 10 ÷ 3 = *(420–430)* ÷ 3 =	140–143
			Total Approximate Score	*466–479*

After you take each practice test, fill in the Score Analysis form that follows the test.

The forms allow you to analyze your own scores and use the information to guide your study time. Ask yourself the following questions:

1. What are your strong areas? What are your weak areas?
2. Do you think this test represents your knowledge of English accurately?
3. Are your scores on each test similar? Are your skills improving?
4. What are your strengths and weaknesses in each of the different parts of the test?

    Listening Comprehension Part A: comprehension of single sentences
    Listening Comrehension Part B: comprehension of short conversations
    Listening Comprehension Part C: comprehension of longer talks and conversations
    Structure, First Part: choosing a correct word or phrase
    Structure, Second Part: identifying an incorrect word or phrase
    Vocabulary: choosing a synonym for a word or group of words
    Reading Comprehension: reading a passage and answering questions

Use the following table to convert your score for Practice Tests 1, 2, and 5.

Score Conversion Table: Standard (Short) Form			
Number	Converted Scores		
Correct	Section 1	Section 2	Section 3
60			68
57–59			66–67
54–56			62–64
51–53			60–61
48–50	65–68		57–59
45–47	62–64		55–56
42–44	59–61		53–54
39–41	56–58		51–53
36–38	54–55	62–68	50–51
33–35	52–53	57–60	48–49
30–32	50–51	54–56	46–47
27–29	48–50	51–53	44–45
24–26	47–48	48–50	42–43
21–23	45–46	45–47	40–41
18–20	43–44	42–44	37–39
15–17	41–43	38–41	35–36
12–14	39–40	36–38	31–33
9–11	35–38	33–35	28–30
6–8	31–34	29–32	26–27
3–5	28–30	25–28	23–25
0–2	25–27	21–24	21–22

Use the following table to convert your score for Practice Tests 3 and 4.

Score Conversion Table: Long Form			
Number	Converted Scores		
Correct	Section 1	Section 2	Section 3
90			68
86–89			66–67
81–85			62–64
77–80	65–68		60–61
72–76	62–64		57–59
68–71	59–61		55–56
63–67	56–58		53–54
59–62	54–55	66–68	51–53
54–58	52–53	62–65	50–51
50–53	50–51	57–60	48–49
45–49	48–50	54–56	46–47
41–44	47–48	51–53	44–45
36–40	45–46	48–50	42–43
32–35	43–44	45–47	40–41
27–31	41–43	42–44	37–39
23–26	39–41	39–41	35–36
18–22	35–38	36–38	31–33
14–17	31–34	33–35	28–30
9–13	28–30	29–32	26–27
5–8	25–27	25–28	23–25
0–4	21–24	21–24	21–22

Lesson 9

Self-Evaluation Checklist

9

Objectives

- To get an understanding of your test-taking strategies
  1. What Is the Self-Evaluation Checklist?
  2. Checklist #1
  3. What Does Your Score Mean?

What Is the Self-Evaluation Checklist?

This checklist will help you understand your own test-taking strategies. It asks you about the way you answer TOEFL questions.

Answer the questions on this checklist right after you finish Practice Test 1, the Diagnostic Test. Go through the questions quickly, without thinking too much about any single question. Just mark your first response. If you can't remember something from the test, then look back at the test to get your answer. You may not understand some of the statements since you have not read about them yet. If you don't understand a statement, take a guess or leave it blank. You will understand it after you have read this book.

There are two checklists in this book. Both of them are the same. You should answer the questions on the checklists two times: once right after taking the Diagnostic Test and again after you take Practice Test 5. The second checklist begins on page 604, after Practice Test 5. The purpose of two checklists is to compare your test-taking strategies before you begin studying for the TOEFL and again after you have done the exercises in this book.

Self-Evaluation Checklist 1

Directions: Complete this checklist after you have taken Test 1, the Diagnostic Test. Read each statement and circle the number of the response you believe is most true right now. Do not spend very much time on any particular statement, but mark the first reponse you think of. Be honest. Only you will see the results.

Key: 1-Never 2-Rarely 3-Sometimes 4-Usually 5-Always

Circle your answers based on Listening Comprehension only.

1. I understood what the speaker said. 1 2 3 4 5
2. I read the four choices in Part A and B before I heard the tape. 1 2 3 4 5
3. I stopped thinking about a difficult question in order to focus on the next question. 1 2 3 4 5

Circle your answers based on Structure and Written Expression only.

4. I paid more attention to the grammar than to the meaning of each word. 1 2 3 4 5
5. I used my knowledge of testing points to help me choose the answer. 1 2 3 4 5
6. I didn't spend time trying to correct the incorrect words in the Error Identification part; I just identified them. 1 2 3 4 5

Circle your answers based on Vocabulary and Reading Comprehension only.

7. I paid close attention to the context of the vocabulary words before I marked the answers, even if the vocabulary words were familiar to me. 1 2 3 4 5

8. I paid close attention to the first and last sentences of each passage. 1 2 3 4 5

9. I used techniques of skimming and scanning to help me find answers quickly. 1 2 3 4 5

Circle your answers based on the entire Practice Test.

10. I left difficult questions unanswered and went back to them later. 1 2 3 4 5

11. I guessed at answers when I didn't know them. 1 2 3 4 5

12. I filled in all the answer blanks even if I didn't know the answers. 1 2 3 4 5

Add all your circled numbers.

YOUR TOTAL SCORE: ________

What Does Your Score Mean?

The higher your score is, the better you are using the test-taking strategies that are presented in this book. Answer this self-evaluation checklist again after you take Test 5. Then compare your two scores. If the second one is higher, it means that you have learned better test-taking strategies. By using better test-taking strategies, your score on the TOEFL should improve.

Lesson 10

Organizing Your Study

10

Objectives

- To learn a system for keeping your study notes
- To become aware of the effects of converted scores

1. Plan a Study Schedule
2. Personal Study Book
3. Finding the Most Profitable Way to Study
4. Practice Test-taking Skills
5. Remember What You Study

Lesson 10

Plan a Study Schedule

To make your study time the most efficient for you, you should plan a study schedule. Begin with an overall look at your daily schedule of work, school, or home activities. Then write down the answers to the following questions.

1. When do you plan to take the test? ______________________
2. How much time do you have until then? ______________________
3. How much time do you plan to spend preparing for the test?
____

Personal Study Book

Get a notebook just for TOEFL preparation, and as you study, keep notes about things you need to remember. This will be your personal study book. Keep notes for yourself on new words or grammar points that you want to remember. Write down new vocabulary words with your own personal definitions, and any cultural information that you are learning. Often only a few brief words will remind you of a specific grammar rule. To help you remember a rule or a new word, write an example using a sentence that is true for you. For instance, if you are always forgetting the use of "since" and "for," write two sentences that are true about yourself and memorize these sentences. (i.e., I began my English class last September. I have been studying English since September. I have been studying for nine months.)

When you begin writing your personal study book you may think this process takes too long, but it is important to take notes and to review those notes. If you don't continue to review what is in your memory, you may forget it.

Go through your personal study book from time to time. As you continue to review your notes, you will be reinforcing your memory about what is in the notes. Then on the day of the test all you need to do is quickly look at your review notes and you will remember what you studied.

Now that you have planned a study schedule and a personal study book, you need to plan what to study. If you have taken Practice Test 1 and have analyzed your score, you have an idea of the areas of your strengths and weaknesses. Read the following information for an overall idea of how the converted scores affect your scores.

Finding the Most Profitable Way To Study

As you know, there are three sections on the TOEFL: Listening Comprehension, Structure and Written Expression, and Vocabulary and Reading. The maximum converted score for each section is the same: 68 points. The formula that you learned in Lesson 8 gives you an approximate score for each section. The maximum score is 68 × 10 ÷ 3 = 227.

You can also calculate a score by using the percentage of correct answers. For example, in the short form, if you have 70 percent correct in each section, your TOEFL score will be:

1. Listening Comprehension—50 Questions
   70% of 50 = 35
   Converted Score for 35 is 53
   Score: 53 × 10 ÷ 3 = 177
2. Structure and Written Expression—40 Questions
   70% of 40 = 28
   Converted Score for 28 is 52
   Score: 52 × 10 ÷ 3 = 173
3. Vocabulary and Reading Comprehension—60 Questions
   70% of 60 = 42
   Converted Score for 42 is 53
   Score: 53 × 10 ÷ 3 = 177

Since each section has the same maximum score (68) but a different number of questions, it means that each section gives a different "weight" to the questions in that section. For example, in Listening Comrehension there are 50 questions, so each question is worth 1/50. It has a weight of 2 percent. In Structure and Written Expression, there are 40 questions, so each question is worth 1/40, for a weight of 2.5 percent. In the Vocabulary and Reading section, there are 60 questions, so each question is worth 1/60, for a weight of 1.67 percent. Therefore, one correct answer in Structure and Written Expression has a weight of 1.5 times that of one correct question in Vocabulary and Reading. Is this significant, in terms of your studying? Look at the following example of the difference in raising your score five points.

EXAMPLE 1:

Your raw score for Structure and Written Expression is 28 (70 percent). When you convert your score (520 ÷ 3) you get 173.
You get five more questions correct so your raw score is now 33, and your converted score is 190.

EXAMPLE 2:

Your raw score for Vocabulary and Reading is 42 (70 percent). When you convert your score (530 ÷ 3) you get 177.
You study hard and get five more questions correct. Now your raw score is 47. When you convert the score (560 ÷ 3) you get 187.

Compare the differences in the two converted scores above. If you get five more correct answers in Structure and Written Expression, your score is raised by 17 points, from 173 to 190. By contrast, if you get five more correct answers in Vocabulary and Reading, your score is raised by 10 points, from 177 to 187. The five extra points in Structure are worth a lot more than the five extra points in Reading and Vocabulary. If your preparation time is limited and your scores in Structure are low, it is more profitable for you to spend extra time on English structure.

Practice Test-Taking Skills

To demonstrate your knowledge well, it is important to study test-taking skills as well as language knowledge. By combining your study of the English language with the development of test-taking skills, you can improve both important areas. The lessons in the coaching section of this book guide you in using test-taking skills. By studying these lessons, you will learn to

1. Practice the skills of reading the answer choices before you hear the questions in the Listening Comprehension section;
2. Use the list of frequent testing points to guide you in the Structure and Written Expression section;
3. Figure out the meaning of new words and sentences by using your own logical thinking skills and context clues.

Remembering the Information You Study

One of the biggest difficulties with the TOEFL (as with most exams) is time: you need to get the information quickly. Here are a few things you can do to help you remember what you already know as well as what you are learning.

1. As you learn new information, think of the way you are categorizing it. In this book you will learn common testing points. These are categories that will help you remember new information. Continue to rehearse these categories by repeating the names to yourself and reviewing the meanings of the testing points as you study.
2. Make the new information very personal. Don't just use the book's examples of grammar rules. Write your own examples. They will be more meaningful to you; therefore, you will remember them better.
3. Categorize and review new vocabulary words. When you study new words, put them in situations that you will remember. Try to remember the new words by associating them with something you know. Use the system described in the vocabulary lesson in this book or use your own system. Use whatever system is meaningful to you to learn and continually review new words. Don't just read a list of words. Instead, practice using them. It is easy to forget things that you don't use and review.
4. As you learn new cultural information, think about its relation to your own culture. What is the same? What is different? How is it different? By spending a little time thinking about the answers to these questions, you will be reviewing the information. This will help you remember it and use it during the test.

Summary of Study Plan

1. Begin a Personal Study Book with your own examples and notes of things you are learning and want to remember.
2. Continue to review your personal study notes. Rehearse the information in your own mind so that you can remember the information quickly while you are taking the test.
3. Continue to practice the test-taking strategies in this book so that you feel confident in handling the time pressure on the test.
4. Spend extra time studying for the Structure and Written Expression section, both because it carries more "weight" and because the structures you learn to use will help you in the other sections of the test too.

Lesson 11

Before the Test

Objectives

- To learn some positive aspects of anxiety
- To learn what to do just before the test
  1. Anxiety Is Normal
  2. The Day Before the Test
  3. On the Day of the Test

Lesson 11

Anxiety Is Normal

Are you feeling anxious and nervous about taking the TOEFL? If so, you are not alone. Everyone who takes the TOEFL is anxious to some extent.

Anxiety is not all bad, however. In some ways, it can improve your performance. Part of your anxiety may actually be a feeling of anticipation and excitement that goes along with getting ready to demonstrate your skills. When you are this alert, your awareness increases. You may hear sounds more clearly; you may be able to concentrate more easily on the test questions.

Don't worry about your anxiety becoming greater as the test approaches. This is normal. The chart below demonstrates the "inverted V principle." This principle states that the closer you come to an event or activity that you are worried about, the more anxious you become. You might be aware of your heart beating faster or your hands perspiring. As soon as you begin the activity, your anxiety lessens. It will probably remain high during the activity, but it is less than it was before your began the activity. This state of anxiety will help you perform better.

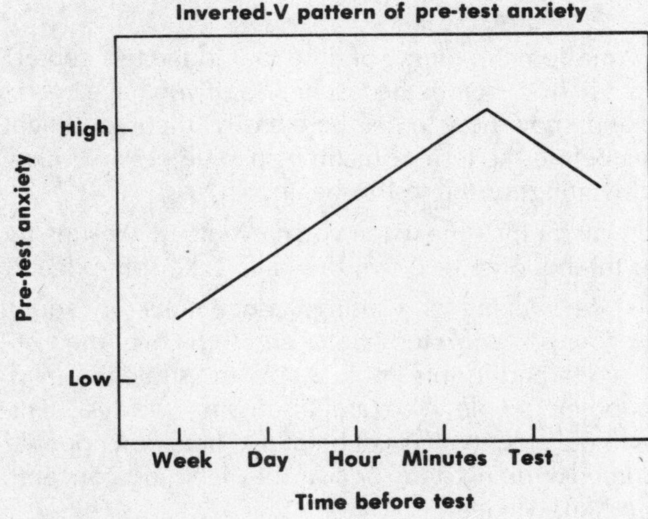

11

The Day Before the Test

1. Review your personal notes. Go through all your study notes so that you get an overall review of everything. Refresh your memory about the things you have learned so that you can apply that knowledge quickly. You want to be able to apply the knowledge you have without hesitation.
2. Do a mental walk-through of the test experience. Try to imagine where you will be sitting. "Feel" the time pressure as much as you can, and imagine how you will cope with it. Remember all the strategies you have learned and how they will apply to your situation.
3. DON'T begin to study new books or new grammar points or new vocabulary. You won't have time to learn how to apply the new knowledge, so it won't help you very much. It will probably just make you anxious about everything you don't know. Instead, focus on what you *do* know.
4. Take a walk or do some moderate physical activity to relieve anxiety.
5. Get a good night's sleep. DON'T stay up late studying; it won't help you at all. Go to bed at your usual time, neither later nor earlier.

On the Day of the Test

1. Eat a good breakfast so you will have enough energy for the test.
2. Don't drink too much coffee or tea since you are not supposed to leave the room during the test. You will be in the test center for about three hours.
3. Leave your home in plenty of time to find the test center. Try to get there about a half hour before the test begins. If you have been to the test center before and know how to get there easily, then you might arrive 10 to 15 minutes before the test. Sometimes people get anxious when they stand around waiting for the test to begin.
4. As you wait for the time when you can enter the testing room, relax. Walk around the building or down the hall. Take some deep breaths.
5. As you are walking or waiting, concentrate on your language skills. Review your personal study notes and think over the test-taking strategies you have learned in this book. Apply the strategies in your mind. Don't talk to other people who are discussing the test. That will probably increase your anxiety. It is not helpful to hear other people talk about what they studied or didn't study or how they feel. Just concentrate on your own skills and knowledge.
6. Give yourself a "self-talk" to build your confidence. Say the following sentences to yourself:
   - **a.** I have studied the frequency lists for all types of TOEFL questions. I am familiar with common testing points.
   - **b.** The testing point strategies I have learned will help me choose the answers quickly and correctly.

  c. By pre-reading the answer choices in the Listening Comprehension section I will get extra knowledge to help me understand the question quickly.
  d. The listening techniques I have practiced will help me keep up to the rhythm of listening, reading, and marking my answers.
  e. I have practiced the TOEFL under similar test conditions many times. I can deal with the time pressure and the difficult questions.
  f. This test will allow me to demonstrate my ability in English.
  g. This test is just a game. If my score is not high enough, I will take it again and do better.

7. After you sit down in the test center, relax. Calm yourself by taking a few deep breaths. If your shoulders feel tense, rub your neck and shoulder muscles. DON'T try to open your test booklet before the supervisor tells you to. Follow the supervisor's instructions *exactly*.

8. RELAX AND "PLAY THE GAME!"

PART THREE

The Coaching Program

Lesson 12

Listening Comprehension Topics and Questions

Objectives

- To learn the differences between Listening Comprehension questions
- To learn how often each type of question has been used on recent TOEFL exams
- To learn what topics recent TOEFL exams have used
- To practice the common kinds of questions

1. What Is a Listening Comprehension Question?
2. Listening Comprehension Pretest
3. Frequency of Types of Questions
4. Description and Examples of Questions and Categories

12

Lesson 12

The short form of the TOEFL typically contains 50 questions, 20 in Part A, 15 in Part B, and 15 in Part C. The long form usually has 80 questions, 30 in Part A, 25 in Part B, and 25 in Part C. You will hear the tape-recorded questions just one time, and then you will have about 12 seconds to mark your answer. You are not allowed to make any marks or notes as you listen.

What Is a Listening Comprehension Question?

Part A: Sentences

Below are the directions to Part A as you will read them in the TOEFL exam. You don't need to memorize the directions, but be sure that you understand them.

12

Directions: For each question in Part A, you will hear a short sentence. Each sentence will be spoken just one time. The sentences you hear will not be written out for you. Therefore, you must listen carefully to understand what the speaker says.
After you hear a sentence, read the four choices in your test book, marked (A), (B), (C), and (D), and decide which one is closest in meaning to the sentence you heard. Then, on your answer sheet, find the number of the question and fill in the space that corresponds to the letter of the answer you have chosen. Fill in the space so that the letter inside the oval cannot be seen.

Example:

You hear:
My friend Sam no longer smokes.

Sample Answer

  Ⓒ Ⓓ

You read:
(A) Sam has smoked for a long time.
(B) Sam doesn't smoke anymore.
(C) My friend doesn't like to smoke.
(D) My friend smokes less than he used to.

The answer to this question is (B) "Sam doesn't smoke anymore." In the recorded statement, the words, "no longer" mean that he has stopped smoking. We are not told anything about how long he has smoked, whether he likes smoking, or how much he smoked.

Part B: Conversations

In this section, you hear short conversations between male and female speakers. Read the directions below and be sure you understand them.

Directions: In Part B you will hear short conversations between two speakers. At the end of each conversation, a third person will ask a question about what was said. You will hear each conversation and the question about it just one time. Therefore, you must listen carefully to understand what each speaker says. After you hear a conversation and the question about it, read the four possible answers in your test book and decide which one is the best answer to the question you heard. Then, on your answer sheet, find the number of the question and fill in the space that corresponds to the letter of the answer you have chosen.

Example:

You hear:

Woman: I hope I can get into History 121 this semester.
Man: So do I. It's such a popular course.

What does the man mean?

Sample Answer

  Ⓒ ●

You read:

(A) He may not like the course.
(B) He doesn't know who will teach the course.
(C) He might not understand the lectures.
(D) He thinks many students want to take the course.

In this example, answer (D) is correct. The word "popular" implies that many students will want to take the course.

Part C: Talks

Part C consists of 2–4 short talks or conversations. As with Parts A and B, you cannot take any notes while the tape is on. After the talk is over, you will be asked approximately 4 to 8 questions about the talk. You will have about 12 seconds to mark your answer for each question. Read the TOEFL directions below.

Directions: In this part of the test, you will hear short talks and conversations. After each of them, you will be asked some questions. You will hear the talks and conversations and the questions about them just one time. They will not be written out for you. Therefore, you must listen carefully to understand what each speaker says. After you hear a question, read the four possible answers in your test book and decide which one is the best answer to the question you heard. Then, on your answer sheet, find the number of the question and fill in the space that corresponds to the letter of the answer you have chosen. Answer all questions on the basis of what is *stated* or *implied* in the talk or conversation.

Look at this sample talk:

You hear:

Questions 1 through 4 are based on the following talk.

As director, I'd first like to extend a welcome to all of you new students. I'm pleased to be able to explain some of the ways our office can help you. Today I'd like to give you some information about our child care programs.

On this campus we offer three different programs for students who have children. Enrollment in these child care programs is limited and early application is essential, since most programs have waiting lists. The Children's Center at Family Student Housing offers both part- and full-time day care while parents attend classes, study, or work. This center will take children between 2 and 8 years of age. Priority is given to low-income families. The center operates on weekdays and follows the academic calendar.

The University Infant Center is also located in the Family Student Housing complex. This center serves infants and toddlers from 3 months to 30 months. Fees are on an hourly basis.

Family Student Housing also sponsors a youth program for children of residents. This program operates a drop-in recreation center for school-aged children. It offers sports, crafts, outings, and tutoring during after-school hours.

If any of you new students need these services, please let me know right away so I can get you an application form. You can find me in the student services office from 9 to 5 every day.

Question 1: Who is the most likely speaker?

Sample Answer

Ⓐ ● Ⓒ Ⓓ

You read:

(A) The College President
(B) The Director of Student Services
(C) A Day Care Assistant
(D) A Faculty Member

Question 2: What is the main topic of this announcement?

● Ⓑ Ⓒ Ⓓ

You read:

(A) Child Care Programs
(B) Low-Income Families
(C) The University Infant Center
(D) After-School Sports

Question 3: When is the Children's Center open?

Ⓐ Ⓑ ● Ⓓ

You read:

(A) Every day of the week
(B) Every day of the year
(C) Monday through Friday only
(D) Summers only

Question 4: If you want to have child care, what should you do now? ● Ⓑ Ⓒ Ⓓ

You read:

(A) Go to the Student Services Center
(B) Go to the Child Care Center
(C) Go to the Family Student Housing complex
(D) Go to the Drop-In Recreation Center

The correct answer to Question 1 is (B) "The Director of Student Services." At the beginning of the talk the speaker says, "As director, I'd . . ."

The correct answer to Question 2 is (A) "Child Care Programs." The speaker begins by saying that the campus offers three different programs for students who have children.

The correct answer to Question 3 is (C) "Monday through Friday only." The speaker states that the center is open on weekdays.

The correct answer to Question 4 is (A) "Go to the Student Services Center." At the end of the talk, the speaker tells the audience to come to the office and let him or her know right away.

Listening Comprehension Pretest

Now that you have an idea of the different kinds of Listening Comprehension questions, take the following pretest to help you estimate your level and skills. The cassette tape for this book includes the listening part of this test. If you do not have the tape you can read the tapescript on page 627. Try to get a native English-speaking person to read it for you or to record it on your own tape. After you take the pretest, check your answers on page 76.

Directions: Listen to the cassette tape and circle the correct answers.

Part A: Sentences. Circle the letter of the sentence which is closest in meaning to the sentence you heard.

1. **(A)** I enjoy swimming.
(B) I'm putting in a new pool.
(C) I can swim very well.
(D) My pool has warm water.

2. **(A)** It's easy to pick up something light.
(B) Clean up before you leave.
(C) Don't leave the light on when you go out.
(D) Always wash the dishes after you eat.

3. **(A)** I'm very angry.
(B) I feel excited today.
(C) I'm going to the dump.
(D) I feel sad.

4. **(A)** Mary likes to throw sticks.
(B) Mary is a friend to many people.
(C) I will diet if Mary will.
(D) Mary has a lot of self-control.

5. **(A)** I'm not as well-prepared as I seem.
(B) I plan to return very soon.
(C) Please help me get ready.
(D) I can't find my suitcase even though I've been looking.

Part B: Conversations. Circle the letter of the sentence which is the best answer to the question you heard.

6. **(A)** It's not easy to find the right road.
   (B) The camping area is very far away.
   (C) It's a quick drive on a new highway.
   (D) The road is slow because it has many curves.

7. **(A)** In a florist shop
   (B) In a garden
   (C) In a post office
   (D) In a restaurant

8. **(A)** He is worried.
   (B) He is surprised.
   (C) He agrees with the woman.
   (D) He is disappointed.

9. **(A)** He went to the movie.
   (B) He didn't like the movie.
   (C) He didn't want to go to the movie.
   (D) He was too busy last night.

10. **(A)** Afraid
    (B) Worried
    (C) Happy
    (D) Sad

Part C: Talks. Answer questions 11 to 15 on the basis of what was stated or implied in the talk you heard.

11. **(A)** They are all interested in peace.
    (B) They are all taking writing classes.
    (C) They are all receiving scholarships.
    (D) They are all at the U.S. Institute of Peace.

12. **(A)** A member of Congress
    (B) A government employee
    (C) A student leader
    (D) A banker

13. **(A)** Information about a writing contest
    (B) Information about working for peace
    (C) Information about new campus rules
    (D) Information about applying for scholarships

14. **(A)** The international peace accord
    (B) Ways to apply for a scholarship
    (C) The economy of the nation
    (D) The new dorm rules

15. **(A)** At a contest
    (B) At a bank
    (C) At a university
    (D) At a government office

ANSWERS FOR LISTENING COMPREHENSION PRETEST

1. A	**6.** D	**11.** B
2. B	**7.** A	**12.** C
3. D	**8.** B	**13.** A
4. D	**9.** A	**14.** D
5. A	**10.** C	**15.** C

The pretest you just took gave you examples of questions from Parts A, B, and C. This next section tells you how common each type of question is.

Frequency of Types of Questions

Part A: Sentences

In Part A you hear a sentence on tape and you are asked either to choose a restatement of that sentence or to make an inference from that sentence. A study of 140 sentences taken from seven actual TOEFL tests given between 1987 and 1989 gives the following frequencies:

	Frequency	Approximate Percent
Restate a sentence	115	82
Infer from a sentence	25	18
	140	

Part B: Conversations

In Part B you hear one speaker and then a second speaker. You are then asked a question about what you have heard. A study of 105 of the questions following each conversation in seven actual tests given between 1987 and 1989 shows the following frequencies:

Questions:	Frequency	Approximate Percent
1. What does the second speaker (man or woman) mean? What does the second speaker (man or woman) imply? What does the second speaker (man or woman) suggest?	84	80
2. Where does the conversation take place? What are the man and woman doing?	8	8
3. What do we learn from the conversation? What do we learn about the situation?	7	7
4. What do we know about a third person who is named in the conversation?	4	4
5. How do the speakers feel?	2	2
	105	

Part C: Talks

In Part C you hear either a longer talk by one person or a longer conversation between two people. After the talk or conversation is over you are asked several questions about the talk. A study of 105 questions from 20 talks gives the following frequencies.

12

Kinds of Questions	Frequency	Approximate Percent
Restatement	67	64
Inference	27	26
Main Topic	8	8
Preceding or following possible topic	2	2
Location	1	1
	105	

Topics	Frequency	Approximate Percent
Conversation	8	40
Academic Lecture	6	30
Informative Talk	6	30
	20	

A "conversation" is a talk between two people. It might be about any topic. "Academic lecture" refers to a talk that is given by a professor, a teacher, or a teaching assistant to a class. An "informative talk" is also given by one person, but is not on an academic topic. It might be a report, an announcement, or advice about something.

Description and Examples of Questions and Categories

In this section you will see the same questions as in the pretest. This time, however, the categories and explanations are included. Read each question again, paying particular attention to the questions you missed in the pretest. Then turn to page 84 for the explanations of each answer.

Part A: Sentences

1. Restatement

This is the most common category for Part A. A restatement means that the correct answer is a sentence that gives the same meaning with different words.

EXAMPLE:

You hear:
It feels good to swim in the pool.

You read:
(A) I enjoy swimming.
(B) I'm putting in a new pool.
(C) I can swim very well.
(D) My pool has warm water.

2. Restatement

In this restatement, you are being tested mostly on your comprehension of the word *litter*.

EXAMPLE:

You hear:
Be sure to pick up the litter when you leave.

You read:
(A) It's easy to pick up something light.
(B) Clean up before you leave.
(C) Don't leave the light on when you go out.
(D) Always wash the dishes after you eat.

3. *Restatement*

This restatement tests you on your comprehension of the idiom *down in the dumps*. An idiom is a group of words used together to mean something that may be different from the meaning of each individual word. Some examples of idioms that have been used in previous TOEFL exams are:

down in the dumps	to look up to	in the first place
lend me a hand	to give up	to make up
side by side	to put off	to get along with
all too often	to keep in shape	to have a hand in

EXAMPLE:

You hear:
I feel down in the dumps today.

You read:
(A) I'm very angry.
(B) I feel excited today.
(C) I'm going to the dump.
(D) I feel sad.

4. *Inference*

In this kind of question, you must infer a logical response. The sentence is not simply a restatement of the same words. Sometimes the speaker's tone of voice helps you infer the meaning.

EXAMPLE:

You hear:
If anyone can stick to her diet, Mary can!

You read:
(A) Mary likes to throw sticks.
(B) Mary is a friend to many people.
(C) I will diet if Mary will.
(D) Mary has a lot of self-control.

5. *Inference*

This question is another example of inference. The correct answer is not just a restatement of the same words; it is an idea that is similar to the main idea of the sentence.

EXAMPLE:

You hear:
Although I look ready to go, I haven't packed yet.

You read:
(A) I'm not as well-prepared as I seem.
(B) I plan to return very soon.
(C) Please help me get ready.
(D) I can't find my suitcase even though I've been looking.

Part B: Conversations

6. Question: What does the woman mean?

In the following conversation, the words "narrow" and "winding" are the most important for understanding the woman's comment.

EXAMPLE:

You hear:

Man: Isn't it a long drive to the camping site?
Woman: It's not too far, but the road is narrow and winding.
What does the woman mean?

You read:

(A) It's not easy to find the right road.
(B) The camping area is very far away.
(C) It's a quick drive on a new highway.
(D) The road is slow because it has many curves.

7. Question: Where does this conversation take place?

In this conversation, you are also being tested on whether you understand the vocabulary words: *send flowers* and *arrangement.*

EXAMPLE:

You hear:

Man: Excuse me, ma'am. I'd like to send some flowers to my friend.
Woman: O.K. We have this arrangement on sale today.
Where does this conversation take place?

You read:

(A) In a florist shop.
(B) In a garden.
(C) In a post office.
(D) In a restaurant.

8. Question: What do we learn from the man's response?

In the following conversation it is particularly important to listen to the way the man says, "I did?" The speaker's tone of voice can emphasize his or her emotion.

EXAMPLE:

You hear:

Woman: Jim, you really did a good job on that report for the committee.
Man: I did?
What do we learn from the man's response?

You read:

(A) He is worried.
(B) He is surprised.
(C) He agrees with the woman.
(D) He is disappointed.

9. Question: What does the man say about Tom?

In this type of question, you must infer something about a third person. In this question, the man is contradicting the woman's comment.

EXAMPLE:

You hear:

Woman: It's too bad Tom couldn't go to the movie last night.
Man: But he did.
What does the man say about Tom?

You read:

(A) He went to the movie.
(B) He didn't like the movie.
(C) He didn't want to go to the movie.
(D) He was too busy last night.

10. Question: How does the woman feel?

For this kind of question, you must infer a feeling from one of the speaker's words.

EXAMPLE:

You hear:

Man: I've just heard the news!
Woman: Yes, I'm thrilled about getting accepted to the program!
How does the woman feel?

You read:

(A) Afraid
(B) Worried
(C) Happy
(D) Sad

Part C: Talks

11. Restatement

A restatement question uses words from the taped talk to answer the question.

EXAMPLE:

You hear:
Which of the following applies to all of the listeners of this talk?

You read:
(A) They are all interested in peace.
(B) They are all taking writing classes.
(C) They are all receiving scholarships.
(D) They are all at the U.S. Institute of Peace.

12. Inference

The answer to this kind of question is not stated directly in the talk.

EXAMPLE:

You hear:
Who is the most likely speaker of this talk?

You read:
(A) A member of Congress
(B) A government employee
(C) A student leader
(D) A banker

13. Main Topic

This kind of question asks for the main idea of the talk or conversation.

EXAMPLE:

You hear:
What is the main topic of this talk?

You read:
(A) Information about a writing contest
(B) Information about working for peace
(C) Information about new campus rules
(D) Information about applying for scholarships

14. Following or Preceding Possible Topic

This kind of question asks about what topic might follow or what topic might have come before the talk.

EXAMPLE:

You hear:
What will the speaker probably discuss next?

You read:
(A) The international peace accord
(B) Ways to apply for a scholarship
(C) The economy of the nation
(D) The new dorm rules

15. Location

This kind of question asks you where the talk most likely occurred.

EXAMPLE:

You hear:
Where did this talk most likely occur?

You read:
(A) At a contest
(B) At a bank
(C) At a university
(D) At a government office

Explanatory Answers

PART A: SENTENCES

1. (A) In this restatement the words "I enjoy..." have a similar meaning to "It feels good to..."

2. (B) This restatement is mainly a vocabulary question. The word "litter" means "garbage" or "pieces of paper on the floor or ground." When you "pick up the litter" you are cleaning up.

3. (D) The idiom "down in the dumps" means "feeling unhappy or sad."

4. (D) This is a logical conclusion. The statement implies that it is difficult to stay on a diet (to limit one's food in order to lose weight). Therefore, if Mary can stay on her diet (not eat foods that make her gain weight), then she must be strong in controlling her desires (have self-control).

5. (A) This is another kind of inference question. Since the speaker has not packed yet, he or she is not prepared, even though he or she seems (looks) ready to go.

PART B: CONVERSATIONS

6. (D) The most important word to understand in this conversation is the word *winding* which means that the road is not straight. It has curves in it. The woman implies that the trip will be slow because the car must go slowly on a winding road.

7. (A) This question may require some knowledge of United States culture. In a florist (flower) shop, people can send flowers by mail. The flowers themselves are not sent. The request is sent from one flower shop to another one, closer to the recipient, and the flowers are cut and delivered to the person. An *arrangement* is a vase of cut flowers.

8. (B) The woman is complimenting the man on his work. By raising his voice when he says,"I did?" the man shows that he is surprised. He actually means, "Did I really do a good job?" If his voice went down instead of up ("I did!"), he could mean that he agrees with her ("I really did do a good job.")

9. (A) When the man says, "But he did," he means "But Tom did go to the movie."

10. (C) It is clear that the woman is happy from the word *thrilled.*

PART C: TALKS

11. (B) Answer B is correct because the speaker says, "since you are all taking writing classes."

12. (C) Answer C is the most likely since he begins by saying he will talk about the new dorm rules. It is very unlikely that any of the other three people in the answer choices would talk about dorm rules, since dorms (dormitories) are where students live on a university campus.

13. (A) Most of the information in the talk is about the writing contest. Answer B is too general. Answer C is what will be talked about next, and answer D is too general.

14. (C) This is the most likely answer since the speaker mentions *dorms* and *writing classes.*

15. (D) The speaker begins by saying that he will discuss the new dorm rules after the announcement about the writing contest.

Summary

1. The frequency list for Part A (Sentences) shows that most of the sentences ask for a restatement. For some sentences, you are asked to infer something from the sentence.

2. The frequency list for Part B (Conversations) shows that most of the questions following each conversation ask you what the second speaker means.

3. The frequency list for Part C (Talks) shows that the most common kind of question is a restatement question. The answer to the question is stated directly in the talk.

4. The topic frequency list for Part C (Talks) shows that the talks are almost evenly divided between conversations between two people, academic lectures by a single person, and informative talks by a single person. The most common topic is something that might be spoken on a university or college campus.

Lesson 13

Listening Comprehension Skills

Objectives

- To learn common Listening Comprehension Testing Points.
- To identify similarities and differences after a quick reading of the answer choices.
- To develop techniques for increasing speed in answering listening comprehension questions.
- To establish a rhythmic work pattern.

1. Listening Comprehension Testing Points
2. Watson's Way: The Most Common Method
3. Holmes' Strategy: The Backwards Way
4. Look For Similarities in the Four Answer Choices
5. Look For Differences in the Four Answer Choices
6. The Talks
7. The Importance of Rhythm
8. How Does Repetition Prepare You for the Real TOEFL?
9. Listening Comprehension Improvement Charts
10. Shooting In The Dark
11. Listening Comprehension Drills

Listening Comprehension Testing Points

In Lesson 12, you saw examples of questions in Parts A, B, and C of the Listening Comprehension section and you read about the frequency of each kind of question. Within these kinds of questions, there are different testing points. Look again at the process you need to follow in each section:

Part A
: You hear a sentence.
: You choose a restatement of that sentence or you infer something from that sentence.

Part B
: You hear a conversation.
: You answer a question about that conversation.

Part C
: You hear a longer talk or conversation.
: You answer several questions about that talk.

In order to answer Listening Comprehension questions, you need to understand particular words or structures in each sentence, conversation, or talk. These are the testing points. Some common testing points are:

1. Grammatical structure.
2. General vocabulary.
3. Idioms or expressions.
4. Questions.
5. The use of a question word for making a statement.
6. Discrimination between similar sounding words.
7. Tone of voice for emphasis.
8. Location.

Examples of Testing Points

1. *Grammatical Structure*

Listening comprehension questions often use the conditional, the past perfect tense, a comparison, a negative, a modal.

You hear:
John said that if Jim won't go, he won't either.

Sample Answer

You read:
(A) John will go without Jim.
(B) John won't go without Jim.
(C) John doesn't want to see Jim.
(D) John thinks Jim will go.

The answer is (B).

2. *Vocabulary*

You hear:
Only half of the ten buses are running.

Sample Answer

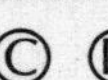

You read:
(A) The buses are running well.
(B) Five buses are working.
(C) There are twenty buses available.
(D) Only half of the people are well.

The answer is (B). You must know the meaning of "half" and you must be able to figure out that half of ten is five. You also need to know that *running* means *working* in this situation.

3. *Idiom*

You hear:
Woman: Are you going to the party?
Man: You bet!
What does the man mean?

Sample Answer

You read:
(A) He is going.
(B) He is not sure if he will go.
(C) He is not going.
(D) He thinks he will probably go.

The answer is (A). The words *you bet* mean *yes*.

4. *Question Formation*

Questions are often made by using tag questions or a suggestion such as "Why not go?" Sometimes statements are used as questions, such as, "You aren't ready yet?"

You hear:
He runs the marathon each year, doesn't he?

Sample Answer
Ⓐ Ⓑ ● Ⓓ

You read:
(A) It's been a year since the last marathon, hasn't it?
(B) Aren't they going to hold the marathon this year?
(C) Doesn't he always run in the marathon?
(D) The marathon is for everyone, isn't it?

The answer is (C).

5. *Question word used as a statement*

This kind of sentence begins with a word like *what* or *how,* but it is not a question.

You hear:
What an excellent job she did!

Sample Answer
   ●

You read:
(A) She didn't do the job well.
(B) What is excellent?
(C) What kind of job did she do?
(D) She did a very good job.

The answer is (D).

6. *Discrimination between similar sounding words*

Sometimes you are tested on whether you can hear the difference between two words that sound similar. The answer choices will have words that sound similar to the words on tape.

You hear:
She glanced at him through the door.

Sample Answer

You read:
(A) She threw away the door.
(B) She walked through the door.
(C) She looked at him.
(D) She danced for him.

The answer is (C). The word *glanced* sounds like *danced.* The word *through* sounds the same as *threw.*

13

7. *Tone of voice*

The tone of voice can emphasize or change the meaning of a statement. Sometimes it shows a contradiction or an opposite meaning.

You hear:

Man: I'll bet you really missed your family when they were gone.
Woman: Not much! Only every minute.
What does the woman mean?

Sample Answer

 Ⓑ Ⓒ Ⓓ

You read:

(A) She missed them a lot.
(B) She didn't miss them very much.
(C) She missed them for a few minutes.
(D) She doesn't have a very big family.

The answer is (A). When the woman says, *Not much,* she actually means *very much.*

8. *Location*

Sometimes a question in Part B will ask you where a conversation takes place. You must infer the location from the conversation.

You hear:

Woman: May I help you, sir?
Man: Yes, I'd like to open an account at this branch.
Where does the conversation take place?

Sample Answer

Ⓐ Ⓑ ● Ⓓ

You read:

(A) on a train
(B) in a home
(C) at a bank
(D) in a garden

The answer is (C). The words *open an account* refer to a bank account. The word *branch* refers to a *branch office* or *additional smaller office.*

When you do the listening comprehension drills and exercises, answer the question, of course. But also, make a note about what you think the testing point is for each sentence. Then organize your notes so that you have a list of grammar points, new vocabulary words, or similar-sounding words. Study these. Remember that no exact questions are ever repeated on TOEFL tests. Remember also, however, that the same grammatical point or vocabulary word can be repeated in many different kinds of questions.

How does Holmes work so well? He looks for logical patterns; he categorizes information; he eliminates unnecessary information. You can do the same.

EXERCISE 1

Determining Testing Points (Answers, pages 109–110)

Note: You will need to listen to the tape for this exercise. If you don't have the tape, you can read the tapescript on page 628.

Directions: In the following exercise, listen to the recorded statement and read the four answer choices. Then turn off the tape and write the testing point or points (some questions have two testing points). The testing points might be

Question

Listening discrimination (two similar-sounding words)

Vocabulary word or idiom

Grammatical structure

Tone of voice

The first question is done for you. Turn on the tape to Exercise 1 and listen to the example. When you hear the sound "beep," turn off the tape so you can write the answer.

EXAMPLE:

You hear:
"He ate too much."

Sample Answer

You read:
(A) Two of them ate.
(B) He overate.
(C) He is late to lunch.
(D) It was much too hot.

Answer: B. *He overate* means the same as *He ate too much.*
Testing Points:
Vocabulary: ate too much = overate
Listening Discrimination: *ate* sounds like *late*
much sounds like *lunch*
Now turn on the tape and listen to Exercise 1

1. **(A)** That's a bad error.
(B) I don't like this steak.
(C) Is he afraid of making mistakes?
(D) I took the wrong food.

Answer: _____

Testing Points:

____

____

2. **(A)** This book has the right date.
(B) Today is the due date.
(C) This book is very late.
(D) This book has the newest information.

Answer: ____

Testing Points:

____

____

3. **(A)** You ought to have completed the work by the deadline.
(B) It's time to finish your work.
(C) The clock in my workplace is broken.
(D) The work was finished before closing time.

Answer: ____

Testing Points:

____

____

4. **(A)** The train and the bus take the same time.
(B) Going by bus will take less time.
(C) Taking the train will get us there faster.
(D) You can take a bus to the train station.

Answer: ____

Testing Point:

____

____

5. **(A)** Don't ask me to manage your money.
(B) Please tell me where to find the manager.
(C) I suggest that you talk to the manager.
(D) Why didn't you get your refund?

Answer: ____

Testing Points:

____

____

6. **(A)** At a store
(B) At a bank
(C) At a post office
(D) At a school

Answer: ____

Testing Points:

____

____

7. **(A)** She is taking him far away.
(B) She is almost ready.
(C) She is worrying.
(D) She will take a long time.

Answer: _____

Testing Point:

____

____

8. **(A)** He agrees with the woman.
(B) He didn't like the speech.
(C) He is not sure about his feelings.
(D) He doesn't know how the woman feels.

Answers: _____

Testing Point:

____

____

9. **(A)** The play was too long.
(B) The play was funny.
(C) The play had many good scenes.
(D) The play was enjoyable.

Answer: _____

Testing Points:

____

____

10. **(A)** The buses are working.
(B) There are more buses than usual today.
(C) He agrees with the woman.
(D) The buses are broken down.

Answer: _____

Testing Points:

____

____

Watson's Way: The Most Common Method

Like many students, Dr. Watson thinks that the Listening Comprehension section of the TOEFL is very difficult. It is hard because of the time and the fact that it is tape-recorded. So, as other good students do, Watson reads the test directions carefully. For Part A, the test book says, "After you hear a sentence, read the four choices in your test book, and decide which one is closest in meaning to the sentence you heard." When Watson thinks through the process of what he is actually doing in this part of the test, he comes up with this:

1. Listen to the tape recording.
2. Analyze what I have just heard.
3. Locate the answer choices in my test booklet.
4. Read the four choices.
5. Compare what I have read to what I have just heard.
6. Search within myself for the best answer.
7. Select my answer.
8. Locate the correct place on my answer sheet.
9. Mark my answer.

Then Watson realizes that he has only 12 seconds for steps 2 through 9. No wonder he feels rushed and nervous! Watson's way works when he can quickly and easily understand the speaker. But often he is not sure what the speaker on the tape has said. He then feels like other people who have said things like:

"I'm nervous when I start the test and I don't hear all the things the speaker says."
"I understand the words when I read them, but I don't understand them when the speaker says them."
"It takes me too long to read the four choices, and I don't have time to mark my answer."
"The speaker says so much that I don't know what to listen for."
"I don't know what to study for."
"I can't remember the details without taking notes."

At this point, Watson asks for some help from his friend, Sherlock Holmes. Holmes thinks about the problems that Watson mentions and suggests a new strategy.

Holmes' Strategy: The Backwards Way

Because it helps your comprehension to know something about a topic before you hear it, Holmes has reversed the basic strategy that Watson uses; he has changed the order of listening and reading. In other words, he recommends that you

READ THE ANSWER CHOICES BEFORE YOU HEAR THE TAPE.

By a very quick reading of the four answer choices, you gain in several ways:

1. You get a clue about the topic of the question before you hear it so you can understand more quickly.
2. You read words before hearing them, which helps you identify new words when the speaker says them.
3. After hearing the speaker, you will have already read the answer choices, so you need less time to choose an answer.
4. Your anxiety is lessened since you have an idea about what the topic will be before you hear the speaker.

The difficulties of this method are easy to see, however. You must read very quickly and you must stop reading the instant the tape comes on so that you can concentrate on the speaker's voice. All of this takes practice. Let's look at some ways to increase your reading speed.

Look for Similarities in the Four Answer Choices

Look very quickly at the four sentences below. You don't need to read every word. In fact, don't even read in the normal way. Let your eyes travel DOWN the page, rather than across the page. Look for the words which are the same or similar.

(A) Tim usually sleeps late.
(B) Tim probably went to the show.
(C) Tim must have slept too long.
(D) Tim's show must have been canceled.

What similarities do you see? You can certainly see that the word *Tim* is repeated. You should also see that *sleeps* and *slept* are similar, and that *show* is repeated twice. It should take you only a few seconds to get this information, but even this amount of information can prepare you to understand the speaker. After noticing these similar words, take a quick guess about what the speaker will say. It will definitely be about someone named Tim. It will be about something that Tim did. Did he sleep? Did he go to a show? By asking yourself these questions before you hear the tape, you are getting a headstart on comprehension. You are listening for something specific.

Reading the answer choices before you hear the tape can provide clues for what to listen for. You also can choose an answer much more quickly after you hear the tape because you have already looked at the answer choices.

EXERCISE 2

Look For Similarities (Answers, page 110)

This exercise will help you develop skills for prereading the four answer choices in Listening Comprehension Parts A and B. Do it as quickly as you can, spending only a few seconds on each question. Let your eyes travel DOWN the sentences instead of reading each word across carefully. Put a line under each word that is repeated two or more times. Then answer the questions.

Part A

1. **(A)** There's a long line for the bus.
(B) The buses were lined up down the street.
(C) Many buses go down this street.
(D) The bus broke down on our street.

What words are repeated? ______________________________

What will the sentence probably be about? ____________________

2. **(A)** Susan remembered borrowing a biology lab manual.
(B) Susan was asked to return the lab manual.
(C) Susan is taking a biology lab.
(D) Susan wants to borrow her friend's lab manual.

What words are repeated? ______________________________

What will the sentence probably be about? ____________________

3. **(A)** They finished the test.
(B) They drank all the tea.
(C) They ate all the food.
(D) They forgot to add the "t."

What words are repeated? ______________________________

What will the sentence probably be about? ____________________

4. **(A)** I think she sings very well.
(B) I couldn't hear her voice well from the balcony.
(C) She should look up to the balcony as she sings.
(C) The seats up on top are very good.

What words are repeated? ______________________________

What will the sentence probably be about? ____________________

5. **(A)** I hope Tim calls us.
(B) Long-distance phone calls are very expensive.
(C) Did Tim call last night?
(D) I haven't gotten in touch with Tim yet.

What words are repeated? ______________________________

What will the sentence probably be about? ____________________

Part B

6. **(A)** In a department store.
(B) In a museum.
(C) In a camera store.
(D) In an art gallery.

What words are repeated? ______

What clues do you have about the conversation? ______

7. **(A)** An actor
(B) A seamstress
(C) A designer
(D) A model

What words are repeated? ______

What clues do you have about the conversation? ______

8. **(A)** She is not sure where it is.
(B) She agrees with the man.
(C) She can't find it.
(D) She doesn't know where to look.

What words are repeated? ______

What clues do you have about the conversation? ______

9. **(A)** She's in charge of the bookstore.
(B) She left the bookstore a few minutes ago.
(C) She'll be back in a little while.
(D) She's going to the bookstore soon.

What words are repeated? ______

What clues do you have about the conversation? ______

10. **(A)** How gardens affect people.
(B) Garden changes during the year.
(C) Why people enjoy gardens.
(D) The care of gardens.

What words are repeated? ______

What clues do you have about the conversation? ______

Look for Differences in the Four Answer Choices

When you are just beginning to practice reading before the tape comes on, you will find that you have only a few seconds of time. As you increase your skills, you will be able to work more quickly. Then, you may have time to read a little more and look for more than the similar words. If you have a few more seconds, noticing the differences in the answer choices can give you even more clues about what to listen for. Read the four answer choices below once more.

(A) Tim usually sleeps late.

(B) Tim probably went to the show.

(C) Tim must have slept too long.

(D) Tim's show must have been canceled.

Now notice what the differences are. You may see the difference between *sleeps late* and *slept too long*. You may also notice the difference between *went to the show* and *show was canceled.* Whatever differences you notice will help guide your listening but understanding these differences is more time-consuming and thus more difficult than just looking for similarities. Practice noticing differences only after you can quickly find the similarities.

EXERCISE **3**

Identifying Differences (Answers, page 111)

In the following exercise you see the same answer choices as in Exercise 2, except that the similar words have already been underlined. This time, as you quickly scan the sentences, note the important differences between them. Draw a new line under the most important differences.

PART A

1. **(A)** There's a long line for the bus.
(B) The buses were lined up down the street.
(C) Many buses go down this street.
(D) The bus broke down on our street.

What words show important differences? ____________________

2. **(A)** Susan remembered borrowing a biology lab manual.
(B) Susan was asked to return the lab manual.
(C) Susan is taking a biology lab.
(D) Susan wants to borrow her friend's lab manual.

What words show important differences? ____________________

3. **(A)** They finished the test.
(B) They drank all the tea.
(C) They ate all the food.
(D) They forgot to add the "t."

What words show important differences? ____________________

4. **(A)** I think she sings very well.
(B) I couldn't hear her voice well from the balcony.
(C) She should look up to the balcony as she sings.
(D) The seats up on top are very good.

What words show important differences? ____________________

5. **(A)** I hope Tim calls us.
(B) Long-distance phone calls are very expensive.
(C) Did Tim call last night?
(D) I haven't gotten in touch with Tim yet.

What words show important differnces? ____________________

PART B

6. **(A)** In a department store
(B) In a museum
(C) In a camera store
(D) In an art gallery

What is there in common in three of the four places? ____________

13

7. (A) An actor
(B) A seamstress
(C) A designer
(D) A model

These are all different people. What could they have in common?
____

8. (A) She is not sure where it is.
(B) She agrees with the man.
(C) She can't find it.
(D) She doesn't know where to look.

What are the important differences? ______________________________

9. (A) She's in charge of the bookstore.
(B) She left the bookstore a few minutes ago.
(C) She'll be back in a little while.
(D) She's going to the bookstore soon.

What are the important differences? ______________________________

10. (A) How gardens affect people.
(B) Garden changes during the year.
(C) Why people enjoy gardens.
(D) The care of gardens.

What are the important differences? ______________________________

The Talks

The talks in Part C take a different strategy. You have very little time to read the answer choices before you hear the tape. You can, however, look briefly at the answer choices before the tape comes on. Focus on very general ideas. Do you think the questions will ask "what," "where," "who," or "why?" Note whether you need to listen for names or occupations or dates. Listen carefully when the speaker tells you which questions will go with each talk or conversation. Below are two strategies for listening to the talks:

1. Close your eyes and concentrate totally on the speaker. Mentally visualize what you hear. Think of general things, like who might be talking, what relationship the speaker has to the possible listeners, or what the relationship is between the two speakers.
2. If you are a very advanced listener, and the topic seems easy to you, you might try looking at the answer choices as you listen to the tape. Since the questions usually follow the order of the talk, you may remember facts better if you look at the four answer choices while the tape is on. You don't need to try to guess the questions, just *look for words you hear the speaker say*. Keep your eyes moving down the test booklet as the speaker is talking. If you lose your place and are having difficulty comprehending, stop trying to read and just concentrate on the speaker. This is not an easy process, even for advanced listeners. It is difficult to read and listen at the same time. Try it during some of your practice tests to see if it helps you.

EXERCISE 4

Focusing On the Answer Choices (Answers, page 111)

In the following exercise, read the answer choices and then write a very general summary of the information you need to listen for. The focus of the question will usually be one of the following: a place, a time, an opinion, the name of a person, the main idea, a reason, a feeling, what someone does, or why something happens. Write the general focus on the line. This is only guessing. You do not know the question. The first one has been done for you.

EXAMPLE:

(A) Tired
(B) Happy
(C) Excited
(D) Lonely
Focus: How does someone feel?

1. **(A)** Taking a walk
(B) Sailing a boat
(C) Washing a car
(D) Looking at photographs

Focus: ______________________________

2. **(A)** By candlelight
(B) By electricity
(C) By a kerosene lamp
(D) By a wood fire

Focus: ______________________________

3. **(A)** A large family
(B) The museum workers
(C) A travel agent
(D) The crew of a ship

Focus: ______________________________

4. **(A)** She was an author
(B) She built her own cabin
(C) She saved people's lives
(D) She was the captain of a ship

Focus: ______________________________

5. **(A)** On an island
(B) In a small town
(C) At a hotel
(D) At a friend's house

Focus: ______________________________

6. **(A)** Marketing
(B) Languages
(C) Library Science
(D) Business

Focus: ______________________________

7. **(A)** They are brand-new.
   (B) They are heavy.
   (C) They cost a lot.
   (D) They are damaged.

   Focus: ____________________

8. **(A)** After class
   (B) After dinner
   (C) Tomorrow
   (D) Next week

   Focus: ____________________

9. **(A)** To study new varieties of plants
   (B) To visit a state forest
   (C) To have lunch in the woods
   (D) To enjoy nature

   Focus: ____________________

10. **(A)** Because she is the leader
    (B) Because the director is sick
    (C) Because the bus broke down
    (D) Because it's a holiday

    Focus: ____________________

The Importance of Rhythm

Rhythm is more important in the Listening section of TOEFL than in any other section. You must be able to keep up with the speaker on tape. You know that you have only about 12 seconds between questions. You should practice keeping within that time limit as you do the practice exercises in this book. The important thing to remember is to force yourself to concentrate completely on each question during your practice time. Don't turn off the tape or go back to repeat a question since it is the rhythm and timing that make this section so difficult. If you had time to listen over and over again to the questions, they would be much easier for you. Instead, if it is difficult for you, take the complete practice test over again.

To practice the rhythm of the TOEFL, do the following:

1. Read the answer choices.
2. Listen to the tape.
3. Choose and mark your answer.
4. Immediately read the answer choices for the next question.

Keep Up to the Rhythm of the Tape

One of the most difficult things to do is to stop thinking about one question after the next question comes on and YOU STILL HAVEN'T FIGURED OUT THE ANSWER YET! Everyone wants to answer every question correctly, of course; if you haven't finished a question, you will want to continue thinking about it. You cannot, however, because the tape continues. If you continue to think about the question you are working on, you will not be ready to listen to the next speaker. You can become lost in this cycle, which can continue and become very frustrating! You must force yourself to stop thinking about an unfinished question and concentrate on the next recorded question. Do this on every practice test: you must be willing to miss one question in order to keep up with the tape. Your ability to listen and work quickly will improve as you practice.

Repeat the Practice Tests to Improve Your Speed

When you are learning a new musical instrument or a new sport, you spend a lot of time going over the basic movements. You practice scales on the piano over and over again. You practice kicking the ball in soccer over and over again. Practice helps you learn a basic process so that you can do it quickly, correctly, and without thinking about each step.

In the same way, it can help you to repeat the same listening practice test several times. Each time you take the test your score will improve. Of course, part of the reason your score is getting better is that you are listening to material you have already heard. In addition, however, you are increasing your skills in keeping up to the rhythm of reading, listening, answering, and reading again. When you repeat a listening test, do not look up the explanatory answers in this book. Just use the answer key to see if your answer is correct or not. Then take the test again to see if you can improve your score by listening to the tape again. Continue to repeat a listening test until you can answer the questions quickly, without thinking about the process itself. After you have repeated each practice test several times, then look at the explanatory answers.

13

How Does Repetition Prepare You for the Real TOEFL?

1. If you read the TOEFL listening test instead of listening to it, you might say to yourself, "This material isn't hard! I know these words." The problem for most people is not the difficulty of the vocabulary or grammar; it is that you are listening to a tape. Your listening skill is what you need to practice.
2. When you read the explanatory answers, you are learning by reading. This helps you learn, but it will not help your listening skill as much as listening.
3. When you repeat a listening test, you are getting more practice in the process of taking the test.

The charts on page 107 give you a place to record your progress in listening skills.

Listening Comprehension Improvement Charts

You have already taken Practice Test 1, the Diagnostic Test. As you take Tests 2, 3, and 4, follow the procedure below.

Procedure

1. While you are taking Practice Test 2, put a check (√) by the questions you have to skip (which means "not answer") in order to keep up to the rhythm of the tape.
2. After you finish the test, check your answer sheet with the answer key and count the number of correct answers, but DON'T look up the explanation of the incorrect answers.
3. Write down your score (the number of correct answers) and the number of skipped questions in Chart A on page 107.
4. Repeat the SAME listening test. Check your score again and write it in Chart A, again without looking up the correct answers.
5. Continue this procedure at least three times or until you are satisfied with your improvement.
6. Do all three practice tests this way. Then fill out Chart B to see your improvement.

Remember: Never stop the tape during the test. You must continue to practice for the rhythm of the tape. As your score gets better, you should begin to feel more comfortable about working within the rhythm of the test. This will help relieve some of the anxiety about taking the TOEFL Listening Comprehension section.

After you have repeated one test three times, look up the explanatory answers; you can learn by studying your errors.

CHART A

Practice Test 2			
	Date	**Number Correct**	**Number Skipped**
First Time Taken			
Second Time Taken			
Third Time Taken			
Practice Test 3			
	Date	**Number Correct**	**Number Skipped**
First Time Taken			
Second Time Taken			
Third Time Taken			
Practice Test 4			
	Date	**Number Correct**	**Number Skipped**
First Time Taken			
Second Time Taken			
Third Time Taken			

CHART B

Step 1: Look at the three scores (the number correct) for each test on Chart A, and figure out your average score. Write the average for each test on Chart B, below.

Step 2: Look at the number of skipped questions on each test on Chart A, and figure out the average number of skipped questions for each test. Write that average number on the chart below.

Step 3: Compare your averages on the three tests. Is your average number correct higher for each test? Is your average number skipped lower for each test? If so, then you are working faster and better on each practice test.

	Average Correct	**Average Skipped**
Practice Test 2		
Practice Test 3		
Practice Test 4		

Shooting in the Dark

The phrase, "shooting in the dark" is an expression which means, "trying to do something when you don't understand how to do it." It comes from the idea of shooting a gun in the dark. You can't see the target.

What should you do if you don't understand everything you hear on the tape? First of all, don't give up. Remember Sherlock Holmes. Think like him. Eliminate one or two answers; this increases your odds for getting the answer right. Guess an answer from the limited information you have in your test booklet and from the words you have understood. As an example, read the four answer choices below.

(A) My aunt works in a travel agency.
(B) My aunt's dentist is traveling now.
(C) My aunt's dentist is working very hard this time of year.
(D) My aunt is traveling rather than working now.

Let's assume that you didn't understand the whole statement, but you got a few words. If you heard the word *dentist* or *tooth* or *extraction* or another word that relates to dentistry, then you should probably eliminate (A) and (D). If you heard the word *tickets* or *book tickets* or *airline,* or another travel word, you can probably eliminate (C). These elimination techniques do not always give you the right answer, but they increase your chances.

If you are having difficulty with Part C, the talks, you might be able to use your own background knowledge to help you eliminate some answers. Also, since you have a series of related questions and answer choices, you can sometimes compare answer choices within a section of one talk to make sure you don't contradict yourself in your answers.

Never leave a question unanswered. Your score is determined by a count of only the correct answers. Eliminate as many answers as you can by guessing. Then choose one of the leftover answer choices. If you are out of time, fill in all the remaining blanks with the same letter.

Summary

1. By learning to identify testing points, you can increase your speed in answering questions and also your ability to organize your study material.
2. To increase your comprehension of the recorded speech, read the four answer choices before the tape comes on, and then guess the topic.
3. To increase your speed in reading the four answer choices, read down the page, looking for similar words and phrases. After that, look for the differences in the answer choices.
4. It is important to practice the TOEFL rhythm. Read, listen, choose, mark, then read again quickly before the tape comes on. Keep strictly to the 12 seconds on your practice tapes. Don't turn off the tape while you are taking a practice test.

Explanatory Answers

EXERCISE 1

1. (A)
Testing Points:

Vocabulary: *Mistake* and *error* mean the same thing. *Bad* and *terrible* mean the same.

Listening Discrimination: *Mistake* and *steak* sound similar.

2. (D)
Testing Points:

Vocabulary: *Up-to-date* and *newest information* mean the same.

Listening Discrimination: *Up-to-date* and *due date* and *late* all sound similar.

3. (A)
Testing Points:

Structure: *Should* means the same as *ought to.*

Vocabulary/Idiom: *On time* means *by the deadline.*

4. (C)
Testing Point:

Structure: *Less time on the train* means *the train will be faster.*

5. (C)
Testing Points:

Question: *Why not . . .* or *Why don't you . . .* are other ways to say *I suggest that . . .*

Listening Discrimination: *Manager* and *manage* sound similar.

6. (A)
Testing Points:

Vocabulary: *Cash or charge* means *will you pay in cash (money) or will you use a credit card?*

Location: *Cash or charge* is asked when someone is buying something. Since the woman is buying a dress, it is most likely at a store.

7. (B)
Testing Point:

Vocabulary/Idiom: *In a minute* means *in a little while.* This implies that she is almost ready.

8. (A)
Testing Point:

Tone of voice: The phrase *wasn't it* is a positive agreement with the comment, *That was great!* It is a shortened version of the negative, *Wasn't it great!* Even though this looks like a question, it is actually a response. The speaker's voice goes down, rather than up, as in a question.

9. (D)
Testing Points

Structure: By saying *too,* the man indicates that he is agreeing with her and adding something else that was *fun*. His sentence could be lengthened to read, *Seeing the play was fun (enjoyable) too.*

Listening Discrimination: *Seeing* and *scenes* sound similar.

10. (A)
Testing Points:

Structure: The woman has made a negative statement: *The buses aren't running.* The man contradicts her by saying, *They are.* Therefore, you know the buses are coming at the regular time.

Vocabulary: *Running* and *working* mean that the buses are moving at their regular scheduled times.

EXERCISE 2

1. Repeated Words: line, lined up, bus, buses, street
The sentence will probably be about a bus on a street.

2. Repeated Words: Susan, borrow, biology, lab manual
The sentence will probably be about Susan and a lab manual or a biology class.

3. Repeated Words: they, tea, "t"
The sentence will probably be about some people who did something, maybe eating or drinking.

4. Repeated Words: I, sing, balcony
The sentence will probably be about a woman singing.

5. Repeated Words: Tim, call
The sentence will probably be about a man named Tim and a telephone call.

6. Repeated Words: in, store
You will be asked about where something happened or where someone is.

7. Repeated Words: An, a
You will be asked about someone's occupation. All the words have something to do with clothes.

8. Repeated Words: she, it
You will probably be asked about what someone did with something or where something is.

9. Repeated Words: she, bookstore
You will probably be asked about whether someone is or is not in the bookstore.

10. Repeated Words: gardens, people
You will probably be asked about the relationship between gardens and people.

EXERCISE 3

1. The important differences are between "go down" and "broke down." You also need to listen for whether the buses or the people are lined up.
2. The important differences are between "borrow" and "return." You also need to listen for whether the conversation is about a book (lab manual) or a class (lab).
3. The important differences are whether the conversation is about eating, drinking tea, or taking a test. Don't mistake "t" for "tea."
4. The important differences are the words "hear well" and "sing well." You need to think about who the sentence is focusing on: the singer or the listener.
5. The important differences are the words: "hope," "did," and "have . . . yet." The important question is the time of the action.
6. Answer choices B, C, and D have something to do with pictures.
7. All of these people work with clothes or wear special clothes.
8. The important differences are whether she has or has not looked for something: "not sure," "agrees with," "can't find," "doesn't know."
9. The important differences are the words "in charge," "left," "be back." You must listen for where she is. Is she in the store or not?
10. The important differences are "affect," "enjoy," and "care." Is the question about the garden itself or the people who care for the gardens?

EXERCISE 4

Your questions may not be exactly like these, but they should be similar. The underlined word is the most important.

1. <u>What</u> is someone doing?
2. <u>How</u> does someone get light or heat?
3. <u>Who</u> is doing something?
4. <u>Who</u> was she or <u>what</u> did she do?
5. <u>Where</u> are they or <u>where</u> is she?
6. <u>What</u>?
7. <u>What</u> about them?
8. <u>When</u> will (or did) something happen?
9. <u>Why</u> will someone go somewhere?
10. <u>Why</u> is someone doing something?

Listening Comprehension Drills

This part includes nine drills. The first three drills are "walk-throughs" of Parts A, B, and C. In the columns opposite the questions, you will find answers and explanations so that you can read through the steps of each question as you answer it. The sentences and conversations are written *after* the answer choices in order to help you practice looking for similarities and differences before you know the question.

The purpose of the walk-through drills is to help you to practice the process of listening comprehension as described in this lesson. The sentences, conversations, and talks for the walk-through drills are not recorded on tape. For these walk-through drills, just concentrate on the process of listening, not necessarily the speed.

In the walk-through drills, you are given two levels of thought processes: Level 1 and Level 2. Begin with Level 1 and follow this procedure:

1. Read through Level 1 to help yourself go through the process of finding similarities in the answer choices. In this level, you practice the process of guessing the topic before the tape comes on. (But for this drill there is no recorded tape; you will read the sentence.)
2. After you read Level 1, read Level 2. Level 2 is the same test, but this time you will practice looking for the differences in the answer choices. You will also practice guessing the testing point before you hear the tape (or read the sentence). You then check the testing point after reading the tapescript of the sentence or conversation.

Following the walk-through drills, you will find six drills with questions that are similar to those found in TOEFL exams. For these six drills it is important that you practice the skill of keeping up to the rhythm of the tape. DO NOT turn off the tape after a sentence or conversation that you do not understand. Instead, wait until the complete drill is over and then repeat the whole drill.

The recorded questions for the six drills are on the listening comprehension cassette tape that goes with this book. The tapescript is also written at the end of this book on page 628. If you do not have the cassette tape, try to get someone to read the tapescript to you. To save that person's time, you might ask him or her to read all the tapescripts on your own cassette tape, if possible. By doing this, you will be able to practice the drills several times on different days. The answers and explanations for these drills begin on page 139.

Walk-Through

Sentences

Part A (Level One)

Directions: Read the answer choices on the left side of the page, while also looking at the right side to see the process. Choose the answer that means the same as the sentence that follows.

1. (A) Julia knows that the computer class will begin soon.
   (B) Julia joined the computer class after she purchased a computer.
   (C) Julia knew how to use the computer before she bought it.
   (D) Julia developed a computer program for her class.

Julia bought a new computer, and *then* took a class to learn how to use it.

STEP 1: Look briefly at the answer choices for similarites.

Julia. . . computer class
Julia. . . computer class
Julia. . . computer
Julia. . . computer

STEP 2: Guess the topic.

Julia/computer

STEP 3: Listen to the tape.

STEP 4: Figure out testing point.
Time sequence: *and then*

STEP 5: Choose the answer: (B)

2. (A) There is a huge shopping center near the bicycle store.
   (B) The bicycle store is across the street.
   (C) The bicycle shop is a part of the shopping center.
   (D) Although the shopping center is big, the bicycle shop is small.

Across the street *from* the bicycle shop is a big shopping center.

STEP 1: Look briefly at the answer choices for similarities.

shopping center. . . bicycle store
bicycle store
bicycle shop. . . shopping center
shopping center. . . bicycle shop

STEP 2: Guess the topic.

shopping center/bicycle shop

STEP 3: Listen to the tape.

STEP 4: Figure out testing point.
Location identification:
across...from...

STEP 5: Choose the answer: (A)

13

3. **(A)** I should see my doctor earlier.
(B) I am taking Dr. Smith's class this semester.
(C) I could have known Dr. Smith earlier if I had had his class.
(D) Had I known Dr. Smith, I would have been enrolled in his class now.

STEP 1: Look briefly at the answer choices for similarities.

I...doctor
I... Dr. Smith's class
I... Dr. Smith...class
I... Dr. Smith...class

STEP 2: Guess the topic.

I/Dr. Smith/class

If I *had known* Dr. Smith earlier, I *would have taken* his class this semester.

STEP 3: Listen to the tape.

STEP 4: Figure out testing point.
Past conditional.

STEP 5: Choose the answer: (D)

4. **(A)** The occupation is respected but I don't like that kind of job.
(B) I created a new job for myself.
(C) Because the position was available, I applied for it.
(D) They opened a job position for me.

STEP 1: Look briefly at the answer choices for similarities.

occupation. . .I
I. . .a new job
the position. . .I
a job position

STEP 2: Guess the topic.

a new job

The position was open, *so* I applied for the job.

STEP 3: Listen to the tape.

STEP 4: Figure out testing point.
Structure: *so*

STEP 5: Choose the answer: (C)

5. **(A)** We need to take our clothes out of the dryer.
(B) The driver needs a quarter for a parking sticker.
(C) We probably need some money for the dryer.
(D) We don't need a dryer.

STEP 1: Look briefly at the answer choices for similarities.

dryer
—
dryer
dryer

STEP 2: Guess the topic.

drying clothes

We need some *quarters* for the *dryer* too, don't we?

STEP 3: Listen to the tape.

STEP 4: Figure out testing point.

Vocabulary: *quarter*
Similar sound: *dryer*/driver

STEP 5: Choose the answer: (C)

6. (A) The party was canceled because of the rain.
(B) Everybody was very polite at the party.
(C) The party was over before it began to rain.
(D) In spite of the rain, people came to the party.

STEP 1: Look briefly at the answer choices for similarities.

party. . .rain
. . .party
party. . .rain
rain. . .party

STEP 2: Guess the topic.

party/rain

STEP 3: Listen to the tape.

Everybody came to the party *although* it was raining.

STEP 4: Figure out testing point.

Structure: *although/party* and *rain* relationship

STEP 5: Choose the answer: (D)

7. (A) Fred likes the warm feelings of his classmates.
(B) Fred doesn't like to see worms.
(C) Fred doesn't like cold weather as much as warm.
(D) Fred prepared warm food for his classmates.

STEP 1: Look briefly at the answer choices for similarities.

Fred . . . warm . . . classmates
Fred
Fred. . .warm
Fred. . .warm. . .classmates

STEP 2: Guess the topic.

Fred/warm/classmates

STEP 3: Listen to the tape.

Fred *prefers* a warm climate.

STEP 4: Figure out testing point.

Vocabulary: *prefers* means *likes*. Opposite restatement: *prefers warm climate* means *doesn't like* cold weather.

Vocabulary: *climate* means *weather*.

STEP 5: Choose the answer: (C)

13

8. (A) I don't care if Jack likes Lisa.
(B) Lisa likes the jacket she has.
(C) I made up my mind to work with Lisa.
(D) I'd like to have a jacket like Lisa has

STEP 1: Look briefly at the answer choices for similarities.

I. . .Jack. . .Lisa
Lisa. . .jacket
I. . .Lisa
I. . .jacket. . .Lisa

Step 2: Guess the topic.

I/jacket/Lisa

STEP 3: Listen to the tape.

I *wouldn't mind having a jacket* like Lisa's.

STEP 4: Figure out the testing point.

Idiom: *wouldn't mind having* means *like to have*
Similar sounds: *jacket*/Jack

STEP 5: Choose the answer: (D)

9. (A) It's not good for him to get so tired.
(B) He should work harder.
(C) He should wear more clothes working at night.
(D) He doesn't know that he is a hard worker.

STEP 1: Look briefly at the answer choices for similarities.
. . .him
He. . .work
He. . .working
He. . .worker

STEP 2: Guess the topic.
he/work

He shouldn't work *so* hard *that* he *wears himself out*.

STEP 3: Listen to the tape.

STEP 4: Figure out testing point.
Idiom: *wears himself out* means *gets tired.*

STEP 5: Choose the answer: (A)

10. (A) Brenda used to type more quickly.
(B) Brenda studied regulations for a minute.
(C) Brenda improved her typing speed because of her regular practice.
(D) Brenda made a lot of mistakes because she typed too fast.

STEP 1: Look briefly at the answer choices for similarities.
Brenda. . .type
Brenda
Brenda. . .typing
Brenda. . .typed

STEP 1: Guess the topic.
Brenda/typing

Brenda has *practiced typing* two hours a day *regularly: now she can type* 65 words a minute.

STEP 3: Listen to the tape.

STEP 4: Figure out testing point.
Cause/result: *practiced typing. . .regularly. . . now she can type. . .* means *improved because of regular practice.*

STEP 5: Choose the answer: (C)

Sentences

Part A (Level Two)

If you are ready for Level Two, it means that you can see the similarities in the four answer choices quickly. It also means that you have extra time before the tape comes on.

Level Two adds two steps in addition to the steps in Level One.

1. Look for differences in the answer choices *after* you see the similarities.
2. Guess the testing point before you hear the tape, *in addition to* guessing the topic.

When you did Level 1 for the questions below you found the similarities and the topic. In this Level, only the differences are underlined.

1. (A) Julia knows that the computer class will begin soon
   (B) Julia joined the computer class after she purchased a computer.
   (C) Julia knew how to use the computer before she bought it.
   (D) Julia developed a computer program for her class.

Julia bought a new computer, and *then* took a class to learn how to use it.

STEP 1: Look briefly at the answer choices for the key differences.

soon
after
before

STEP 2: Guess the testing point.

Time sequence

STEP 3: Listen to the tape.

STEP 4: Figure out testing point.

Structure: *then*

STEP 5: Choose the answer: (B)

2. (A) There is a huge shopping center near the bicycle store.
   (B) The bicycle store is across the street.
   (C) The bicycle shop is a part of the shopping center.
   (D) Although the shopping center is big, the bicycle shop is small.

Across the street *from* the bicycle shop, there is a big shopping center.

STEP 1: Look briefly at the answer choices for the key differences.

near
across
a part of

STEP 2: Guess the testing point.

Location relationship between shopping center and bicycle shop *across. . from*

STEP 3: Listen to the tape.

STEP 4: Figure out testing point.

Structure: *across. . .from*

STEP 5: Choose the answer: (A)

13

3. (A) I should see my doctor earlier.
   (B) I am taking Dr. Smith's class this semester.
   (C) I could have known Dr. Smith earlier if I had had his class.
   (D) Had I known Dr. Smith, I would have been enrolled in his class now.

If I *had known* Dr. Smith earlier, I *would have taken* his class this semester.

STEP 1: Look briefly at the answer choices for the key differences.

should see
am taking
could have known
Had I known

STEP 2: Guess the testing point.

Verb tense

STEP 3: Listen to the tape.

STEP 4: Figure out the testing point.

Structure: Past conditional.

STEP 5: Choose the answer: (D)

4. (A) The occupation is respected but I don't like that type of job.
(B) I created a new job for myself.
(C) Because the position was available, I applied for it.
(D) They opened a job position for me.

STEP 1: Look briefly at the answer choices for the key differences.
but
—
because
—

STEP 2: Guess the testing point.
Transition

The position was open, *so* I applied for the job.

STEP 3: Listen to the tape.

STEP 4: Figure out testing point.
Structure: *so*

STEP 5: Choose the answer: (C)

5. (A) We need to take our clothes out of the dryer.
(B) The driver needs a quarter for a parking sticker.
(C) We probably need some money for the dryer.
(D) We don't need a dryer.

STEP 1: Look briefly at the answer choices for the key differences.
clothes
parking sticker
money
dryer

STEP 2: Guess the testing point.
Vocabulary

We need some *quarters* for the *dryer* too, don't we?

STEP 3: Listen to the tape.

STEP 4: Figure out the testing point.
Vocabulary: *quarter* as in money/*quarter* as in time;
Similar sound: *dryer*/driver

Step 5: Choose the answer: (C)

6. (A) The party was canceled because of the rain.
(B) Everybody was very polite at the party.
(C) The party was over before it began to rain.
(D) In spite of the rain, people came to the party.

STEP 1: Look briefly at the answer choices for the key differences.
because of
—
before
in spite of

STEP 2: Guess the testing point.
Reason or time

Everybody came to the party *although* it was raining.

STEP 3: Listen to the tape.

STEP 4: Figure out testing point.
Structure: *although*

STEP 5: Choose the answer: (D)

7. **(A)** Fred likes the warm feelings of his classmates.
(B) Fred doesn't like to see worms.
(C) Fred doesn't like cold weather as much as warm.
(D) Fred prepared warm food for his classmates.

STEP 1: Look briefly at the answer choices for the key differences.
likes/doesn't like

STEP 2: Guess the testing point.
Fred *likes* or *doesn't like* something.
Similar sounds: *warm/worms*

Fred *prefers* a *warm* climate.

STEP 3: Listen to the tape.

STEP 4: Figure out testing point.
Vocabulary: *prefers* means *likes; climate* means *weather.*
Opposite restatement: prefers *warm* climate means *doesn't like* cold weather;
Similar sounds: *warm/worm*

STEP 5: Choose the answer: (C)

8. **(A)** I don't care if Jack likes Lisa.
(B) Lisa likes the jacket she has.
(C) I made up my mind to work with Lisa.
(D) I'd like to have a jacket like Lisa has.

STEP 1: Look briefly at the answer choices for the key differences.
don't care
like

STEP 2: Guess the testing point.
Who likes what?
I/Jack(jacket)*/Lisa*

I *wouldn't mind having a jacket* like Lisa's.

STEP 3: Listen to the tape.

STEP 4: Figure out the testing point.
Idiom: *I wouldn't mind having* means *I'd like to have*
Similar sounds:
*jacket/*Jack

STEP 5: Choose the answer: (D)

9. **(A)** It's not good for him to get so tired.
(B) He should work harder.
(C) He should wear more clothes working at night.
(D) He doesn't know that he is a hard worker.

STEP 1: Look briefly at the answer choices for the key differences.
tired
work harder
wear more clothes
hard worker

STEP 2: Guess the testing point.
What should he do?

He shouldn't work *so* hard *that* he *wears himself out*.

STEP 3: Listen to the tape.

STEP 4: Figure out the testing point.
Structure: *so . . . that*
Idiom: *wears himself out* means gets tired.

STEP 5: Choose the answer: (A)

10. **(A)** Brenda used to type more quickly.
(B) Brenda studied regulations for a minute.
(C) Brenda improved her typing speed because of her regular prectice.
(D) Brenda made a lot of mistakes because she typed too fast.

STEP 1: Look briefly at the answer choices for the key differences.

used to
studied
improved . . . because of
made . . . mistakes because . . .

STEP 2: Guess the testing point.

Past tense? Reason?

Brenda has *practiced typing* two hours a day *regularly; now she can type* 65 words a minute.

STEP 3: Listen to the tape.

STEP 4: Figure out testing point.

Structure: has *practiced typing . . . regularly . . . now she can type . . .* means *improved . . . because of regular practice.*

STEP 5: Choose the answer: (C)

Conversations

Part B (Level One)

Directions: Read the answer choices on the left as you read through the thought process on the right side of the page.

1. **(A)** Applying for a job
(B) Dining at the cafeteria
(C) Studying at the library
(D) Asking for permission

STEP 1: Look briefly at the answer choices for similarities.

-ing
-ing
-ing
-ing

STEP 2: Guess the topic.

What is someone doing?

Woman: Are you interested in working in the library or in the cafeteria?
Man: Either place is fine, *as long as both positions are open now.*
What is the man doing?

STEP 3: Listen to the tape.

STEP 4: Figure out the testing point.

Vocabulary: *as long as* means *provided that* or *on the condition that. The position is open* means *the job is available*

Background Information: The question is most likely asked in a university job placement office.

STEP 5: Choose the answer: (A)

2. **(A)** Buying tickets for a show
(B) Shopping
(C) Ordering food at a restaurant
(D) Going on a walk

STEP 1: Look briefly at the answer choices for similarities.
-ing
-ing
-ing
-ing

STEP 2: Guess the topic.
What is someone doing?

Man: Do you want to *eat here or get it to go?*
Woman: To go.
What are the man and woman doing?

STEP 3: Listen to the tape.

STEP 4: Figure out the testing point.
Vocabulary: *to go* means *take the food and eat it outside the restaurant.*
Background Information: The conversation most likely takes place in a fast food restaurant after the people order.

STEP 5: Choose the answer: (C)

3. **(A)** The man expected a special lunch.
(B) The restaurant is closed on weekends.
(C) The man likes to make his own lunch.
(D) The restaurant is crowded.

STEP 1: Look briefly at the four choice for similarities.
man . . . lunch
restaurant
man . . . lunch
restaurant

STEP 2: Guess the topic.
lunch/restaurant

Man: *What?* You *don't* serve special lunches *on weekends?*
Woman: No, only on weekdays.
What do we learn from this conversation?

STEP 3: Listen to the tape.

STEP 4: Figure out the testing point.
Tone of Voice: The word *what* and the man's rising tone of voice show that he is surprised. The negative question and the man's tone of voice indicate that he is disappointed. He wants the special lunch.
Background Information: Location—The man is most likely in a restaurant on a weekend at noon speaking to a waitress.

STEP 5: Choose the answer: (A)

4. (A) The woman doesn't have to return the books.
   (B) He will return the books for the woman.
   (C) He wants the woman to borrow two books for him.
   (D) His books need to be returned, too.

STEP 1: Look briefly at the answer choices for similarities.

woman . . . books
He . . . books . . . woman
He . . . woman . . . books
books

STEP 2: Guess the topic.

He/woman/books

Woman: *Oh no!* My library books are *due today*.
Man: Well, *I am going over there* to study now.
What does the man imply?

STEP 3: Listen to the tape.

STEP 4: Figure out the testing point.

Structure: *going over there* means *going to the library.*

Implied meaning: Since the man has already made plans to go the library, he will take her books with him.

Background Information: This conversation most likely takes place between two friends on campus.

STEP 5: Choose the answer: (B)

5. (A) The woman is in the wrong classroom.
   (B) The woman is too late for class.
   (C) The professor is not Dr. Glen.
   (D) Physics 1A will begin soon.

STEP 1: Look briefly at the answer choices for similarities.

classroom
class
—
—

STEP 2: Guess the topic.
A university class

Woman: Excuse me. Is this the right room for physics 1A, Dr. Glen's class?
Man: You are in the right place, but the *class was* just *over*.
What does the man imply?

STEP 3: Listen to the tape.

STEP 4: Figure out the testing point.

Vocabulary: *class was over* means *class has already finished.*

Implied meaning: The woman missed the class because she was late.

Background Information: This conversation most likely takes place at a university classroom between two students or a student and a teacher.

STEP 5: Choose the answer: (B)

6. (A) She heard an accident.
 (B) She wants to go to a foreign country to learn its language.
 (C) It's hard to hear the accident.
 (D) Andrew speaks English almost like a native speaker.

STEP 1: Look briefly at the answer choices for similarities.
She heard . . . accident
She . . .
. . . to hear . . . accident
—

STEP 2: Guess the topic.
hear or *speak? accident?*

Man: It's amazing that Andrew has improved his English so much.
Woman: Yes, I *can hardly hear an accent*.
What does the woman mean?

STEP 3: Listen to the tape.

STEP 4: Figure out the testing point.
Vocabulary: *can hardly hear* means *can't hear very well.*
Similar sounds:
accent/accident

STEP 5: Choose the answer: (D)

NOTE: In the above choices, the repeated word *accident* leads you to an incorrect guess. Even though this happens occasionally, it is still a good idea to look for repeated words or ideas.

7. (A) He doesn't like the tape recorder.
 (B) He doesn't know where to buy it.
 (C) He feels that it is too expensive.
 (D) He thinks it is old fashioned

STEP 1: Look briefly at the answer choices for similarities.
He doesn't
He doesn't
He
He

STEP 2: Guess the topic.
He doesn't what?

Woman: Are you going to buy a tape recorder like Jean's?
Man: *With a price like that?*
What does the man mean?

STEP 3: Listen to the tape.

STEP 4: Figure out the testing point.
Tone of Voice: *with a price like that?* means that he doesn't like the price. The man's tone of voice in his question indicates that the price is too high; therefore, he doesn't want to buy it.
Background Information: This conversation most likely takes place between two friends talking about their friend Jean's tape recorder.

STEP 5: Choose the answer: (C)

8. **(A)** He doesn't like parties.
(B) He was tired last night.
(C) The flat tire made him late.
(D) He couldn't go to the party.

Step 1: Look briefly at the answer choices for similarities.

He . . . parties
He
. . . him . . .
He . . . party

STEP 2: Guess the topic.

He/party

Woman: Everybody at the party *expected you to come* last night.
Man: Sorry, I *had a flat tire* on my way to the party.
What does the man feel sorry about?

STEP 3: Listen to the tape.

STEP 4: Figure out the testing point.

Implied meaning: *We expected you to come* implies that he did not go.

Similar Sounds: *tired/tire*

Situation Background: This conversation most likely takes place between two friends on the day after a party.

STEP 5: Choose the answer: (D)

9. **(A)** Rose is a graduate student now.
(B) Karen is not working in the department.
(C) Karen's back was hurt.
(D) Rose and Karen are working together in the department.

STEP 1: Look briefly at the answer choice for similarities.

Rose
Karen . . . working
Karen's
Rose and Karen . . . working

STEP 2: Guess the topic:

Rose/Karen/working

Woman: Are Rose and Karen both secretaries in the Social Science Department?
Man: They were before, *but now Karen is back at school* finishing her degree.
What does the man mean?

STEP 3: Listen to the tape.

STEP 4: Figure out the testing point.

Implied meaning: *Now Karen is back at school* means that Karen is a student again. It implies that Karen has stopped working in order to finish school.

Similar words: *back* as an adverb in *back at school* and *back* as a noun in *hurt her back.*

Background Information: This conversation most likely takes place between two people at a university.

STEP 5: Choose the answer: (B)

10. **(A)** The woman can not return the blouse.
(B) It has been too long to return the merchandise.
(C) The woman can get some money back.
(D) The woman can exchange the blouse.

STEP 1: Look briefly at the answer choices for similarities.
The woman . . . blouse
—
The woman
The woman . . . blouse

STEP 2: Guess the topic.
The woman/blouse

Woman: This blouse doesn't fit me. May I return it?
Man: Yes you may. You can *have credit for something else* in the store, but *no refund.*
What do we learn from the man?

STEP 3: Listen to the tape.

STEP 4: Figure out the testing point.
Vocabulary: *have credit for something else* means *receive something else of the same value.* She can exchange the blouse for something else in the store. "No refund" means that she can not have the money back.
Background Information: This conversation most likely takes place between a shopper and a store worker in a store.

STEP 5: Choose the answer: (D)

Conversations

Part B (Level Two)

In addition to the steps listed in Part B, Level One, you have time to look for key differences between answer choices and guess the testing point.

13

1. **(A)** Applying for a job
(B) Dining at the cafeteria
(C) Studying at the library
(D) Asking for permission

STEP 1: Look briefly at the answer choices for the key differences.
job
cafeteria
library
permission

STEP 2: Guess the testing point.
What is someone doing?

Woman: Are you be interested in working at the library or at the cafeteria?
Man: Either place is fine, *as long as both positions are open now.*
What is the man doing?

STEP 3: Listen to the tape.

STEP 4: Figure out the testing point.
Idioms: *as long as* means *provided that* or *on the condition that. The position is open* means *the job is available.*
Background Information: The question is most likely asked in a university job placement office.

STEP 5: Choose the answer: (A)

2. (A) Buying tickets for a show
(B) Shopping
(C) Ordering food at a restaurant
(D) Going for a walk

STEP 1: Look briefly at the answer choices for the key differences.

tickets
shopping
food
walk

STEP 2: Guess the testing point.

What is someone doing?

Man: Do you want to *eat here* or to *get it to go?*
Woman: To go.
What are the man and woman doing?

STEP 3: Listen to the tape.

STEP 4: Figure out the testing point:

Vocabulary idiom: *to go* means *take the food and eat it outside the restaurant*

Background Information: The conversation most likely takes place in a fast food restaurant before the people order.

STEP 5: Choose the answer: (C)

3. (A) The man expected a special lunch.
(B) The restaurant is closed on weekends.
(C) The man likes to make his own lunch.
(D) The restaurant is crowded.

STEP 1: Look briefly at the answer choices for the key differences.

expected
closed
make lunch
crowded

STEP 2: Guess the testing point.

What is happening?

Man: *What?* You *don't* serve special lunches *on weekends?*
Woman: No, only on weekdays.
What do we learn from this conversation?

STEP 3: Listen to the tape.

STEP 4: Figure out the testing point.

Tone of Voice: The word *what* and the man's rising tone of voice show that he is surprised. The negative question and the man's tone of voice indicate that he is disappointed. He wants the special lunch.

Background Information: Location—The man is most likely in a restaurant in a weekend at noon speaking to a waitress.

STEP 5: Choose the answer: (A)

4. **(A)** The woman doesn't have to return the books.
(B) He will return the books for the woman.
(C) He wants the woman to borrow two books for him.
(D) His books need to be returned, too.

STEP 1: Look briefly at the answer choices for the key differences.

woman . . . return
He . . . return
He . . . borrow
returned

STEP 2: Guess the testing point.

He/woman
return books/borrow books

Woman: *Oh no!* My library books are due today.
Man: Well, I *am going over there* to study now.
What does the man imply?

STEP 3: Listen to the tape.

STEP 4: Figure out the testing point.

Structure: *going over there* means *going to the library*.

Implied meaning: Since the man has already made plans to go the library, he will take her books with him.

Background Information: This conversation most likely takes place between two friends on campus.

STEP 5: Choose the answer: (B)

5. **(A)** The woman is in the wrong classroom.
(B) The woman is too late for class.
(C) The professor is not Dr. Glen.
(D) Physics 1A will begin soon.

STEP 1: Look briefly at the answer choices for the key differences.

wrong
late
professor
physics 1A

STEP 2: Guess the testing point.

Something about a class

Woman: Excuse me. Is this the right room for physics 1A, Dr. Glen's class?
Man: You are in the right place, but the *class was* just *over*.
What does the man imply?

STEP 3: Listen to the tape

STEP 4: Figure out the testing point.

Vocabulary: *class was over* means *class has already finished.*

Implied meaning: The woman has missed the class because she is late.

Background Information: This conversation most likely takes place at a university classroom between two students or a student and a teacher.

STEP 5: Choose the answer: (B)

6. **(A)** She heard an accident.
(B) She wants to go to a foreign country to learn its language.
(C) It's hard to find the accident.
(D) Andrew speaks English almost like a native speaker.

STEP 1: Look briefly at the answer choices for the key differences.

heard
go
find
speaks

STEP 2: Guess the testing point.

She/Andrew
hear or *find* something?

Man: It's amazing that Andrew has improved his English so much.
Woman: Yes, I *can hardly hear an accent.*
What does the woman mean?

STEP 3: Listen to the tape.

STEP 4, Figure out the testing point.

Vocabulary: *can hardly hear* means *can't hear very well*

Similar sounds: *accent/accident*

STEP 5: Choose the answer: (D)

NOTE: In the above choices, the repeated word *accident* leads you to an incorrect guess. Even though this happens occasionly, it is a good idea to look for repeated words or ideas.

7. **(A)** He doesn't like the tape recorder.
(B) He doesn't know where to buy it.
(C) Feels that it is too expensive
(D) He thinks it is old-fashioned.

STEP 1: Look briefly at the answer choices for the key differences.

doesn't like
where to buy
too expensive
old-fashioned

STEP 2: Guess the testing point.

What does he think?

Woman: Are you going to buy a tape recorder like Jean's?
Man: *With the price like that?*
What does the man mean?

STEP 3: Listen to the tape.

STEP 4. Figure out the testing point.

Tone of Voice: *with a price* like that? means that he doesn't like the price. The man's rising tone of voice in his question indicates that the price is too high; therefore, he doesn't want to buy it.

STEP 5: Choose the answer: (C)

8. **(A)** He doesn't like parties.
(B) He was tired last night.
(C) The flat tire made him late.
(D) He couldn't go the party.

STEP 1: Look briefly at the answer choices for the key differences.

doesn't like
was tired
made him late
couldn't go

STEP 2: Guess the testing point.

He/verb/party

Woman: Everybody at the party *expected you to come* last night.
Man: Sorry, I *had a flat tire* on my way to the party.
What does the man feel sorry about?

STEP 3: Listen to the tape.

STEP 4: Figure out the testing point.

Implied meaning: *We expected you to come* implies that he did not go.

Similar Sound: *tired/tire*

Background Information: This conversation most likely takes place between two friends on the day after the party.

STEP 5: Choose the answer: (D)

9. **(A)** Rose is a graduate student now.
(B) Karen is not working in the department.
(C) Karen's back was hurt.
(D) Rose and Karen are working together in the department.

STEP 1: Look briefly at the answer choices for the key differences.

a graduate student
not working
was hurt
working together

STEP 2: Guess the testing point.

*Rose/Karen/*did what?

Woman: Are Rose and Karen both secretaries in the social science department?
Man: They were before, *but now Karen is back at school* finishing her degree.
What does the man mean?

STEP 3: Listen to the tape

STEP 4: Figure out the testing point.

Vocabulary: *Now Karen is back at school* means that Karen is a student again. It implies that Karen stopped working in order to finish school.

Similar words: *back* as an adverb in *back at school* and *back* as a noun in *hurt her back.*

Background Information: This conversation most likely takes place between two people at a university.

STEP 5: Choose the answer: (B)

10. (A) The woman can not return the blouse.
(B) It has been too long to return the merchandise.
(C) The woman can get some money back.
(D) The woman can exchange the blouse.

STEP 1: Look briefly at the answer choices for the key differences.
can not return
too long to return
get money back
exchange

STEP 2: Guess the testing point.
the woman/blouse
return/exchange/money back

Woman: This blouse doesn't fit me. May I return it?
Man: Yes you may. You can *have credit for something else* in the store, but *no refund*.
What do we learn from the man?

STEP 3: Listen to the tape.

STEP 4: Figure out the testing point.

Idiom: *have credit for something else* means *receive something else of the same value*. She can exchange the blouse for something else in the store.

"No refund" means that she cannot have the money back.

Background information: This conversation most likely takes place between a shopper and a store worker in a store.

STEP 5: Choose the answer: (D)

Talks

Part C (Level One)

Step 1: Before you hear the tape you may have a little time to pre-read the answer choices. You should look for two things: the type of question and the key words. This will help you anticipate the topic and help your listening comprehension. Practice by previewing the answer choices below.

1. (A) Hiking
(B) Skiing
(C) Fighting
(D) Working

KEY WORDS: all
POSSIBLE QUESTION:
What are they doing?

2. (A) Exhausted
(B) Afraid
(C) Worried
(D) Excited

KEY WORDS: all
POSSIBLE QUESTION:
How do they feel?

3. (A) At the fire lookout
(B) At someone's house
(C) At the ski lift
(D) At a cabin

KEY WORDS: *fire lookout, house, ski lift, cabin*
POSSIBLE QUESTION:
Where are they?

4. (A) The ones who sign up first
(B) The ones who pay
(C) Firends of the Forest Service
(D) Fire fighters

KEY WORDS: *sign up, pay, friends, fire fighters*
POSSIBLE QUESTION:
Who did something?

5. (A) Because she is very tired
   (B) Because she hopes for something she can't get
   (C) Because she doesn't believe the man
   (D) Because she wishes she were somewhere else

KEY WORDS: *tired, hopes, doesn't believe, somewhere else*
POSSIBLE QUESTION: Why?

Step 2: Concentrate on the taped talk or conversation, listening for any words that you remember from your preview.

Talks

Part C (Level Two)

Step 1: Preview the answer choices in the same way as you did in Level One. For more advanced speakers of English, an additional procedure is outlined here. You can try this method to see if it works for you.

Step 2: As you listen to the tape, follow the answer choices in the book looking for words that you hear. As soon as you see a word that the speaker says, then look at the next set of answer choices. Often the words that you see and hear are the ones that are the answers to the questions. If you get confused while trying to look for words, then stop reading and concentrate again on the speaker.

EXAMPLE:

Look for words you hear.

You read:

1. (A) Hiking
   (B) Skiing
   (C) Fighting
   (D) Working

2. (A) Exhausted
   (B) Afraid
   (C) Worried
   (D) Excited

You hear:

Woman: Boy, am I exhausted I didn't know that cross-country skiing could be such hard work!

Man: Yeah, but just think of how much exercise you're getting. And with cross-country skiing you don't have to fight the crowds. That's why I like it better than downhill skiing. I hate fighting the crowds and waiting for lifts.

Woman: Well, I agree with you there. And the price has really gone up for lift tickets. At least we don't have to pay anything for cross country skiing. But I'm still tired. How much farther to the cabin?

Man: We should be there in about an hour.

13

3. **(A)** At a fire lookout
   (B) At the man's home
   (C) At the skilift
   (D) At a cabin

4. **(A)** The ones who sign up first
   (B) The ones who pay
   (C) Friends of the Forest Service
   (D) Fire fighters

5. **(A)** Because she is very tired
   (B) Because she hopes for something she can't get
   (C) Because she doesn't believe the man
   (D) Because she wishes she were somewhere else

Woman: Good. I can make it. It'll be nice to have a place to rest. Who did you say owns this cabin?

Man: It's one of a series of cabins owned by the government. They're available on a first-come, first-served basis for summer hikers or winter skiers. I signed up for it a month ago.

Woman: Why were these cabins built?
Man: Some were originally built for fire lookouts and some for shelter for forest service workers. But the government doesn't use them anymore. We're lucky there is one near here for us to use.

Woman: What I'd love is a hot fire and some soup on the stove!

Man: You're dreaming. This cabin is primitive. Shelter only.

Woman: I know. And I'll enjoy anything at this point!

Man: Hey, I think I see it ahead. See that little place way over in the trees?

Questions:

1. What are these people doing?
2. How does the woman feel?
3. Where will they be in an hour?
4. Who can stay in the cabin?
5. Why does the man say that the woman is dreaming?

Answers to Walk-Through Talk

1. B
2. A
3. D
4. A
5. B

Drill 1: Sentences (Answers, page 140)

Directions: The recording for the following drill is on the cassette that goes with this book. If you don't have the tape you can read the tapescript on pages 628–629.

1. **(A)** Excuse me, are these mushrooms?
(B) I've tried most of these restaurants.
(C) I need more rest, as the doctor recommended.
(D) I need to know the direction to the ladies' room.

2. **(A)** Routine exercise helps David keep well.
(B) David is a good weather forecaster.
(C) The weather is getting colder gradually.
(D) David should put on more clothes since it's getting cold.

3. **(A)** You can find paper and pencils near the card catalog box.
(B) The paper in the card catalog is special.
(C) The card catalog box is on the table.
(D) The card catalog is classified alphabetically.

4. **(A)** Tom's sister spent a month with him.
(B) Tom lives in San Francisco.
(C) Tom's sister often visits San Francisco.
(D) Tom visited his sister in San Francisco.

5. **(A)** Bill is taking care of the chocolate cake.
(B) Cindy doesn't like either kind of cake.
(C) Bill and Cindy don't like chocolate cake.
(D) Both Bill and Cindy like chocolate cake.

6. **(A)** Let's buy some wine.
(B) Let's rest in the park for a little while.
(C) We've tried all those relaxation methods.
(D) Let's buy something in a grocery store.

7. **(A)** The wind caused Tony's earache.
(B) The wind is blowing over his head.
(C) Tony probably has a cold.
(D) Tony will go see his doctor.

8. **(A)** Judy didn't work in the machine shop.
(B) Judy thought the job had been completed already.
(C) Judy went to the library instead of the machine shop.
(D) Judy didn't go see about working in the machine shop.

9. **(A)** Pat is working rather quickly.
(B) Pat is wearing a red sweater.
(C) Pat is studying in a place that's not so noisy.
(D) Pat went home silently.

10. **(A)** I don't know what Lisa has sculpted.
(B) Lisa is confident about her ability as a sculptor.
(C) I can't decide which of Lisa's sculptures to buy.
(D) Lisa's sculpture is certainly better than the others.

Drill 2: Sentences (Answers, page 141)

Directions: The recording for the following drill is on the cassette that goes with this book. If you don't have the tape you can read the tapescript on page 629.

1. **(A)** I think the flowers were beautiful.
(B) She was wearing blossoming flowers.
(C) She is more beautiful when she wears flowers.
(D) I love beautiful flowers.

2. **(A)** The project fell apart before I completed it.
(B) My thesis includes this project.
(C) My thesis is a quarter finished.
(D) I have to finish this project before I start writing my thesis.

3. **(A)** Two women are nurses.
(B) Many cars were involved in an accident.
(C) Two people work in the hospital.
(D) Two people were hurt.

4. **(A)** Scientists have studied trains for twenty years.
(B) There have been problems because of lack of rain.
(C) The problem of acid rain has been studied for more than twenty years.
(D) Scientists have discovered a new way to make rain.

5. **(A)** We used to live in New York.
(B) We move every year.
(C) Los Angeles is better than New York.
(D) Our child likes Los Angeles better than New York.

6. **(A)** Gail is a scientist.
(B) Gail examined the leaf.
(C) Gail is a part of Ann's group.
(D) Gail learned how to use the microscope.

7. **(A)** I lost a lot of weight at the seminar.
(B) I waited at the hotel for my lost friends.
(C) I had a difficult time finding the hotel.
(D) The seminar began late.

8. **(A)** No one except Professor Smith knew the grades.
(B) Professor Smith rested in the afternoon.
(C) In the afternoon the students could find out their scores.
(D) Professor Smith wrote a letter to the students.

9. **(A)** They pointed to the treasure.
(B) Sam was appointed by the treasurer.
(C) The association had a meeting with Sam.
(D) Sam was chosen to be treasurer of the association.

10. **(A)** If you work hard, maybe you can finish reading it.
(B) You should read the book only once.
(C) You read so fast, you will forget everything.
(D) It's difficult to remember every word you read.

Drill 3: Conversations (Answers, page 142)

Directions: The recording for the following drill is on the cassette that goes with this book. If you don't have the tape you can read the tapescript on pages 629–630.

1. (A) Joan remembered to take her umbrella.
   (B) Joan's umbrella was no good.
   (C) Joan left her umbrella downstairs.
   (D) It's raining.
2. (A) Susan is a fast worker.
   (B) Susan did Jack's homework.
   (C) Susan didn't do all her own homework.
   (D) Susan has not finished her homework.
3. (A) He had some ice cream.
   (B) He had a piece of cake.
   (C) He had a piece of gum.
   (D) He had something to drink.
4. (A) The car looks fine.
   (B) The engine is good, but the brakes need work.
   (C) It looks old, but it runs well.
   (D) It needs a complete overhaul.
5. (A) To a storage room
   (B) To a classroom
   (C) To a store
   (D) To a library
6. (A) The painting is new.
   (B) It will be easy to sell the painting.
   (C) She didn't complete the painting.
   (D) She will not sell it.
7. (A) The travel agent is at the airport.
   (B) The theater is on Broadway.
   (C) The woman is going on a bus trip.
   (D) The woman bought an airplane ticket.
8. (A) A new shuttle bus
   (B) A regularly scheduled space flight
   (C) An airplane flight six years ago
   (D) A new church mission
9. (A) In a hospital
   (B) In a classroom
   (C) In an office
   (D) In a restaurant
10. (A) There are some other ways to do it.
    (B) This is the only way.
    (C) You should turn around.
    (D) Go straight ahead.

Drill 4: Conversations (Answers, page 142)

Directions: The recording for the following drill is on the cassette that goes with this book. If you don't have the tape you can read the tapescript on pages 630–631.

1. **(A)** The man was waiting to do something.
(B) The man was asking for directions.
(C) The man was making a turn.
(D) The man's car needs a tune up.

2. **(A)** Making an appointment
(B) Fixing a clock
(C) Discussing a price
(D) Going to class

3. **(A)** Alvin is not in at the moment.
(B) Hang up please.
(C) She will go and check.
(D) You called the wrong number.

4. **(A)** He'll recommend this book to his students.
(B) He enjoyed the book.
(C) He didn't like the pictures in the book.
(D) He didn't like the book at all.

5. **(A)** He doesn't see anything wrong with parking there.
(B) It will be OK for only a few minutes.
(C) The woman shouldn't park there.
(D) He wants to drive away fast.

6. **(A)** What the man told John.
(B) Why the man told John to come at 10:30.
(C) Where John was supposed to arrive.
(D) How John was coming.

7. **(A)** At a train station
(B) At a bus station
(C) At an airport
(D) At a travel agency

8. **(A)** At a dress shop
(B) At a barber shop
(C) At a grocery store
(D) At an airport

9. **(A)** She is not sure yet.
(B) She is going to apply.
(C) Her score is not high enough for her to apply.
(D) She is not going to apply.

10. **(A)** Mathematics
(B) Banking
(C) Credit
(D) Computers

Drill 5: Talks (Answers, page 143)

Directions: The recording for the following drill is on the cassette that goes with this book. If you don't have the tape you can read the tapescript on pages 631–632.

1. **(A)** To the cafeteria
(B) To the movie theater
(C) To her dorm room
(D) To the library

2. **(A)** The experiments take a lot of time to complete.
(B) She likes the reading, but not the labs.
(C) She can finish very easily.
(D) It is difficult for her to finish the reading and writing assignments.

3. **(A)** Term papers are easy for him.
(B) He has a lot of essay exams.
(C) He finds lab experiments easier than writing term papers.
(D) He is busier this semester than last semester.

4. **(A)** She doesn't like movies at all.
(B) She might go if it were a funny movie.
(C) She loves mystery movies.
(D) She will probably go to the movie with the man.

5. **(A)** The Student Activities Office will open.
(B) Seniors will measure their heads.
(C) Students will order new school hats.
(D) Seniors will graduate.

6. **(A)** All students
(B) All seniors
(C) All graduating seniors
(D) All faculty

7. **(A)** What kind of ceremony there will be
(B) How to order the graduation outfit
(C) How much to pay for the clothes
(D) Where to go for graduation

8. **(A)** Rent them.
(B) Buy them.
(C) Clean them.
(D) Measure them.

Drill 6: Talks (Answers, page 143)

Directions: The recording for the following drill is on the cassette that goes with this book. If you don't have the tape you can read the tapescript on page 632.

1. **(A)** To give the students new information
(B) To remind the students of something
(C) To warn the students of something
(D) To explain a new procedure

2. **(A)** By city bus
(B) In a school bus
(C) In individual cars
(D) Grouped in cars

3. **(A)** Handed out directions
(B) Went to the museum
(C) Wrote a report
(D) Studied Impressionism

4. **(A)** 1800–1850
(B) 1875–1900
(C) 1900–1950
(D) 1950–1975

5. **(A)** Yellowstone and the Grand Canyon are the most well-known national parks.
(B) It is important to try to visit small parks as well as large ones.
(C) The U.S. Park System is an important part of U.S. history.
(D) There are more than 300 parks, monuments, and historic sites in the National Park System.

6. **(A)** There were 37 parks.
(B) Yellowstone Park was established.
(C) The National Park Service was begun.
(D) Parks were classified into four groups.

7. **(A)** 37
(B) Less than 300
(C) More than 300
(D) Over 600

8. **(A)** Visit less well-known parks.
(B) Study the National Park System.
(C) Become a National Park Ranger.
(D) Go to Yellowstone and the Grand Canyon.

Answer Key for Drills

DRILL 1	DRILL 2	DRILL 3	DRILL 4	DRILL 5	DRILL 6
1. D	**1.** C	**1.** C	**1.** A	**1.** D	**1.** B
2. A	**2.** B	**2.** C	**2.** A	**2.** D	**2.** D
3. A	**3.** D	**3.** D	**3.** C	**3.** C	**3.** A
4. B	**4.** C	**4.** C	**4.** B	**4.** B	**4.** B
5. C	**5.** A	**5.** A	**5.** C	**5.** D	**5.** C
6. B	**6.** B	**6.** B	**6.** B	**6.** C	**6.** B
7. A	**7.** C	**7.** D	**7.** B	**7.** B	**7.** C
8. D	**8.** C	**8.** B	**8.** B	**8.** A	**8.** A
9. C	**9.** D	**9.** D	**9.** A		
10. C	**10.** D	**10.** A	**10.** B		

Explanatory Answers for Drills

DRILL 1: SENTENCES

1. **(D)** This is a restatement question. There are no repeated similar words in this question. The words "mushrooms" and "restaurants" are quite different. Before you heard the tape, you might have decided to listen for those two words. That is a good idea, but in this sentence the testing point is vocabulary: "restroom" and "ladies' room" both refer to a public toilet.

2. **(A)** This is a restatement question. The repeated words are "David" and "weather" and "cold." You might guess that the topic is about the weather or being cold. The testing points are structure and vocabulary ("it seems less likely...") and an idiom ("keeps on"). The phrase "keeps on" means "continues." In answer choice A, the word "routine" also refers to "a continuing or regular activity." The phrase "keeps on exercising regularly" means the same as "routine exercise." Don't be confused by the two meanings of the word "cold." The word "cold" as a temperature has a very different meaning from the word "cold" referring to having a virus that causes sneezing and a runny nose.

3. **(A)** This is a restatement question. The repeated words are "paper" and "card catalog. " If you know the meaning of "card catalog" you might guess that this sentence refers to a library or to alphabetical order. The main testing point is vocabulary/structure referring to location: "next to" is similar to "near." The phrase "scratch paper" refers to paper that is used for taking notes or writing rough drafts, not good paper for final written work. It is not necessary to know the meaning of "scratch paper" to get this question correct.

4. **(B)** This is an inference question. The similar words are "Tom's/Tom," "San Francisco," and "sister." You have many clue words in this sentence. You need to listen for what happens to Tom or his sister in San Francisco. The testing point is vocabulary and inference. *If* Tom's sister visited him in San Francisco, you can infer that Tom lives in San Francisco. You must read each answer choice carefully. Answer A is incorrect because we don't know how long Tom's sister stayed in San Francisco. Answer C is incorrect because we don't know how often Tom's sister visits San Francisco. Answer D is incorrect because Tom's sister doesn't live in San Francisco.

5. **(C)** This is a restatement question. The repeated words are "Bill," "Cindy," "chocolate," and "cake." You can guess that the sentence will refer to two people: "Bill" (a man's name) and "Cindy" (a woman's name.) The topic is chocolate cake. The testing points are structure ("neither...nor") and an idiom ("to care about.") The idiom "to care about" means "to like."

6. **(B)** This is a restatement question. The similar words are "Let's," "rest/relaxation," and "buy." You might guess that the sentence will be a suggestion about doing something because of the word "let's." The testing point is vocabulary: "shall we?" is a question form meaning "let's;" "relax" is similar to "rest." The phrase "for a while" is repeated as "for a little while."

7. **(A)** This is a restatement/inference question. The repeated words are "Tony" and "wind." You might guess that the sentence will be about being sick in some way because of the words "earache," cold," and "doctor." The testing point is structure: "XXX said that...." When you hear a sentence beginning in this way you might infer that what the person said is true. A second structure testing point is the passive voice: "X was caused by Y" means the same as "Y caused X."

8. **(D)** This is a restatement question. The repeated words are "Judy," and "machine shop." You might guess that the topic is about working because of the words "job" and "working." The testing point is vocabulary. The words "to see if" in this sentence mean the same as "to check" or "to ask." The meaning is the same as "to see about," which means "to check into," or "to find out about." The phrase "to see about" must be followed by a gerund; for example, "to see about going," "to see about working."

9. **(C)** This is a restatement question. The main repeated word is "Pat," which can be the name of a man or a woman. You can guess that the topic is about something that Pat is doing or did. The testing point is vocabulary. The phrase "doing her homework" is similar to "studying." The word "quiet" means the same as "not so noisy."

10. **(C)** This is a restatement question. The similar words are "Lisa," and "sculpted/sculptor/sculptures/sculpture." The testing point is vocabulary: the phrase "I don't know which one to choose" means the same as "I can't decide." We infer that "choose" in this sentence means "buy."

DRILL 2: SENTENCES

1. (C) This is a restatement question. The similar words are "flowers," and "beautiful," and "wear/wears." You should notice whether the statement focuses on "I" or "she" since both of these are repeated in the answer choices. The testing point is structure: "X makes her Y" can also be said as "she is more Y when X." Another example is this: *Rainy weather makes her sad means She is sadder when it rains.*

2. (B) This is a restatement question. The similar words are "project," "thesis," and "completed/finished." You might guess that this topic is about a university written project or a student thesis. The main testing point is vocabulary/structure: "X is part of Y" means the same as "Y includes X." In this sentence the word "project" might refer to a research or a study about any particular topic. A thesis is a formal written statement of a theory that is submitted as part of a university degree. It is not necessary to know what a thesis is in order to answer this question.

3. (D) This is an inference question. The repeated words are "two" and "people." You might guess that the topic is something concerning an accident, hospital, or being hurt. The testing point is inference. Since two people were sent to the hospital, you can infer that these people were hurt in the accident.

4. (C) This is a restatement question. The repeated words are "scientists," "problem," and "rain." The main testing point is vocabulary; the word "decade" means the same as "ten years." Two decades, then, is twenty years. An additional testing point is active/passive voice: "...have spent two decades studying" is the same as "...has been studied for twenty years." A third testing point is listening discrimination: the word "rain" sounds similar to "train."

5. (A) This is an inference question. The repeated words are "Los Angeles," "New York," and "better than." You might guess that this will be a comparison question, but actually it is not. You can infer from the sentence that "we used to live in New York" since "we moved to Los Angeles from New York." There is no mention of which city is better.

6. (B) This is a restatement question. The only repeated word is "Gail." Part of the sentence, "Gail examined the leaf," is repeated exactly in answer choice (B).

7. (C) This is a restatement question. The repeated words are "I" and "seminar." Two words that sound similar are "weight" and "waited." If a person has a "difficult time" finding a place, he or she probably does not know exactly where to go. The words then have a similar meaning to "I got lost."

8. (C) This is a restatement question. The similar words are "Professor Smith," "afternoon," and "grades/scores." The testing point is vocabulary. The word "to post" means the same as "to announce by putting up a notice on a bulletin board." Therefore, if the professor posted the scores, you can infer that the students can look at the board and find out their own scores.

9. (D) This is a restatement question. The similar words are "Sam," "association," and "treasure/treasurer." The words "pointed " and "appointed" also sound similar. The testing point is vocabulary. The word "selected" has a similar meaning to "chosen."

10. (D) This is a restatement question. The repeated words are "read" and "you." You might also notice the words "forget" and "remember" as clues. The testing point is vocabulary: "hard" and "difficult" have similar meanings.

DRILL 3: CONVERSATIONS

1. (C) If the umbrella is still downstairs, the man is implying that Joan left it there. The repeated words are "Joan" and "umbrella."

2. (C) This is a question about a third person: Susan. You must know the meaning of "copied." If Susan copied the homework, it means that she did not do all her own original work. She took someone else's work.

3. (D) For this question you must know the meaning of the word "lemonade," which is a sweet drink made from lemons, water, and sugar.

4. (C) To answer this question you must know the meaning of "needs a new paint job." If someone says that a car needs a paint job, he or she implies that the car doesn't look good the way that it is painted now. It probably looks old.

5. (A) For this question, you must know the meaning of the word "closet," which is a small room for storing things.

6. (B) To answer this question, you must know that "can sell it anytime" implies that the painting will be easy to sell. Whenever she decides to sell the painting, it will be easy to sell.

7. (D) From this conversation you can infer that the woman bought an airplane ticket since she says, "arrive at JFK airport."

8. (B) You know that the two speakers are discussing a space flight because of the words "space shuttle" and "taking off." The word "routine" refers to an activity that is completed in a regular and consistent way.

9. (D) To understand this question you must know that the speaker is a waitress or hostess who is taking customers to their table in a restaurant. She is asking how many people will be sitting at the table. The word "party" in this phrase means "group."

10. (A) The woman is using an idiomatic expression, "There is no way around it," which means, "There is no other way to do it." The man contradicts her by saying, "Yes, there is." He means that there is another way to do it.

DRILL 4: CONVERSATIONS

1. (A) The idiomic expression "to take a turn" or "to have a turn" refers to an occasion when two or more people do an activity in the proper order among themselves. Each person waits until the others have finished before doing the activity. Therefore, the phrase, "it's your turn" implies that the man has been waiting.

2. (A) You can infer that the two people are making an appointment to meet by the words, "are you free?" and "either time is all right."

3. (C) This is a telephone conversation. The woman is asking the man to wait on the telephone while she goes to see if Alvin is available to talk.

4. (B) The words, "I liked it overall" mean that the man liked the book in general. The words "nothing specific" mean that he didn't remember any parts that were extremely interesting. But since he liked it in general, you can infer that he enjoyed reading it.

5. (C) The man says, "No" because the place is a driveway. Other cars will need to use that space to drive in or out. It is not OK to park there; therefore, the woman should not park there.

6. (B) The words "how come" mean the same as "why." Answer B is the only answer that asks a "why" question.

7. (B) You can infer that this conversation takes place in a bus station because of the words "There is a bus leaving this station."

8. (B) You can infer that this conversation takes place in a barber shop because of the words "cut," "short," and "leave it long in front."

9. (A) The words "it all depends on....." mean that the woman doesn't know the answer yet. She won't know the answer until she knows what her test score is.

10. (B) You can infer that the people are discussing banking because of the words "savings account" and "checking account."

DRILL 5: TALKS

1. **(D)** This is a restatement question. In the beginning of the talk the woman says, "I'm going to the library."

2. **(D)** This is a restatement question. The woman says, "I feel like I'll never get through everything." The phrase "get through" means "finish" or "get to the end of something."

3. **(C)** This is a restatement question. The man says, "This semester seems easy now...I spend a lot of time in class....doing experiments."

4. **(B)** This is a restatement question. The woman says, "I might go to a comedy."

5. **(D)** This is an inference question. The speaker says, "Graduation ceremonies will be held on Saturday, June 10." From this statement, you can infer that seniors will graduate. The other answer choices all occur before June 10.

6. **(C)** This is a restatement question. The speaker says, "All graduating seniors must order their caps and gowns..."

7. **(B)** This is a main idea question. The information in the announcement gives the date for ordering caps and gowns, the way to measure your head, the rental fee, and the time to pick up and return the caps and gowns. The words "caps and gowns" refer to the graduation outfit that consists of a special type of hat and a robe.

8. **(A)** This is a restatement question. The speaker says that there will be a rental fee of $15.

DRILL 6: TALKS

1. **(B)** This is a restatement question. At the beginning of the talk, the speaker says, "I'd like to remind you of the field trip." The information in the talk is not new information, which is clear when she says, "I handed out directions ...yesterday," and "Remember, you can either do....."

2. **(D)** For this question you must know that a carpool is a group of people riding together in a car. This word can be used as a noun or a verb. The verb "to pool" means "to share in a resource or service." Therefore, "to carpool" is to share a car when people are going to the same place.

3. **(A)** This is a restatement question. The speaker says, "I handed out directions to the museum yesterday."

4. **(B)** This is a restatement question. The speaker says, "You'll see examples of art from the early period, around 1875 and up to the turn of the century." The "turn of the century" means the time around 1900.

5. **(C)** This is a main idea question. The speaker ends by saying that the national park system is an important part of our continuing history. All the other answers were mentioned, but the speaker mentions them as smaller information related to the importance of the parks.

6. **(B)** This is a restatement question. The speaker says, "Yellowstone, which was established back in 1872..." All of the other answers happened in 1916.

7. **(C)** This is a restatement question. The speaker says, "..we now have over 300 separate parks, monuments, sites, and memorials."

8. **(A)** This is a restatement question. The speaker says, "If you have time sometime, try visiting some of the less well-known parks..."

Lesson 14

Structure and Written Expression Questions

Objectives

- To learn differences between Structure and Written Expression Questions
- To learn common structures that recent TOEFL exams have used
- To practice the common structures
  1. What is a Structure and Written Expresson Question?
  2. The Frequency of Types of Sentence Completion Questions
  3. Description and Examples of Sentence Completion Questions
  4. Error Identification Pretest
  5. Frequency of Types of Error Identification Questions
  6. Description and Examples of Error Identification Questions

Lesson 14

In the short form of the TOEFL the Structure and Written Expression Section has 40 questions which include 15 completion sentences and 25 error identification sentences. The long form has approximately 60 questions, including 23 completion sentences and 37 error identification sentences.

What Is a Structure and Written Expression Question?

Sentence Completion

Sentence completion entails "fill in the blank" questions. Below are the instructions you will find when you take the TOEFL. You don't need to memorize them, just be sure that you understand them.

> ***Directions:*** Questions 1–15 are incomplete sentences. Beneath each sentence you will see four words or phrases, marked (A), (B), (C), and (D). Choose the *one* word or phrase that best completes the sentence. Then, on your answer sheet, find the number of the question and fill in the space that corresponds to the letter of the answer you have chosen. Fill in the space so that the letter inside the oval cannot be seen.

EXAMPLE:

Birds make nests in trees ________ hide their young in the leaves and branches.

(A) can where they
(B) where they can
(C) where can they
(D) where can

Sample Answer

Ⓐ ● Ⓒ Ⓓ

The answer to the example above is (B), "where they can." The answer begins an adjective clause that describes "trees." The other answer choices could not possibly fit in this sentence. Answer (A) is incorrect because of the verb "can," which could not follow "trees" in this sentence. Answer (C) would only be correct as the beginning of a question. Answer (D) is also the beginning of a question.

Error Identification

For error identification questions, you only need to identify the incorrect word or phrase; you don't need to correct the sentence. Below are the instructions you will find in the TOEFL test.

> ***Directions:*** In questions 16–40 each sentence has four underlined words or phrases. The four underlined parts of the sentence are marked (A), (B), (C), and (D). Identify the *one* underlined word or phrase that must be changed in order for the sentence to be correct. Then, on your answer sheet, find the number of the question and fill in the space that corresponds to the letter of the answer you have chosen.

EXAMPLE:

Aspirin is recommend (A) for many people for its (B) ability to thin (C) the (D) blood.

Sample Answer

● Ⓑ Ⓒ Ⓓ

The answer to the above example is (A). The phrase *is recommend* is incorrect. The correct answer would be "is recommended," a passive form of the verb. It is passive because it is impossible for *aspirin* to recommend anything. The sentence does not say who is recommending. You could make it an active sentence by writing, "Doctors recommend that many people take aspirin for its ability to thin the blood."

Sentence Completion Pretest

Now that you have an idea of the two kinds of questions in this section, take the following pretest to help you get an idea of your level and skills.

> ***Directions:*** Circle the letter of the best word or phrase to complete each sentence. Then check your answers on page 151.

1. In 1776, when the Declaration of Independence ________, the United States became a new country.

(A) signed
(B) that signed
(C) was signed
(D) that it signed

2. The union won benefits ________.
   (A) the members
   (B) for its members
   (C) its members for
   (D) members for its

3. In 1750 B.C., ________ the most famous collection of early laws.
   (A) then Hammurabi wrote
   (B) Hammurabi wrote
   (C) Hammurabi's wrote
   (D) Hammurabi, who wrote

4. ________ he got home last night is still a mystery to me.
   (A) How
   (B) Although
   (C) While
   (D) Since

5. New York is a major center ________.
   (A) at bank.
   (B) of bank.
   (C) of banking.
   (D) to banking.

6. Sleeping, resting, ________ are the best ways to care for a cold.
   (A) and that drinking fluids
   (B) and drinking fluids
   (C) which drank fluids
   (D) and one drink fluids

7. Impressionist artists tended ________ imagination and light more important than faithful reproduction of objects.
   (A) considering
   (B) be consider
   (C) consider to
   (D) to consider

8. A ray swims rapidly ________ broad winglike appendages.
   (A) by flapping its
   (B) its flapping
   (C) of the flapping
   (D) the flap

9. The greater ________ increase in population, the harder it is for people to find adequate housing.
   (A) of
   (B) is the
   (C) the
   (D) is of the

10. ________ nor animals can survive without oxygen.
(A) Plants can neither
(B) Neither can plants
(C) Plants, neither
(D) Neither plants

11. Excessive absenteeism results ________ problems for the schools.
(A) in
(B) with
(C) for
(D) to

12. ________ left Europe in 1492, he was unaware of the changes that would occur as a result of his voyage.
(A) From Columbus
(B) Because Columbus was
(C) That Columbus was
(D) When Columbus

13. Not until the late 1960s ________ on the moon.
(A) that Americans walked
(B) did Americans walk
(C) when did Americans walk
(D) when Americans walked

14. ________ AIDS has engaged many researchers in the last decade.
(A) By studying
(B) The study of
(C) Important study
(D) Now that the study

15. ________ during past centuries when people have come to the West seeking gold.
(A) Times
(B) Throughout times
(C) There have been times
(D) Times have been

16. Of all the national parks in the United States, Yellowstone is ________ visited.
(A) one of the most
(B) of the most
(C) one most
(D) the most one

17. Radio communication has changed ________ the rapid development of other communication media, such as television.
(A) because its
(B) is it because
(C) because of
(D) is because its

18. The day was ________ that people swarmed to the beach.

(A) such a hot
(B) so hot
(C) very hot
(D) hot

19. ________ felt hat is one of the symbols of a cowboy.

(A) A broad-brimmed
(B) Broad
(C) The brim, which is broad
(D) Broad brim

20. ________ the ozone layer were destroyed, most living things would disappear from the Earth in a few years.

(A) Besides
(B) If
(C) So
(D) For

21. ________ public schools, private schools charge tuition.

(A) Do not like
(B) No likeness to
(C) Dislike
(D) Unlike

22. ________ two fingerprints are identical.

(A) Nor
(B) No
(C) None
(D) Not

23. Silver nitrate dyes ________ it touches black.

(A) somehow
(B) there
(C) them
(D) everything

24. ________ of buying and selling occurs internationally.

(A) A great deal
(B) A great many
(C) Much greater
(D) Many

Answers to Sentence Completion Pretest

1. C
2. B
3. B
4. A
5. C
6. B
7. D
8. A
9. C
10. D
11. A
12. D
13. B
14. B
15. C
16. A
17. C
18. B
19. A
20. B
21. D
22. B
23. D
24. A

The Frequency of Types of Sentence Completion Questions

The following list of structures was compiled from a selection of actual TOEFL exams that were given between 1984 and 1989. These grammatical structures were taken from eleven tests; the list represents 165 questions from the first part of Section Two, Sentence Completion.

There are many different ways that these structure questions can be categorized; the list below represents only one way. The importance of this list is not the particular categories, but whether you understand the use of the testing points in the example questions that follow this list.

SENTENCE COMPLETION—165 QUESTIONS

Structure	Frequency	Approximate Percent
1. Verb	21	13
2. Word Order	16	10
3. Subject + verb	13	8
4. "Wh" word as subject/Noun clause	12	7
5. Prepositional phrase	11	6
6. Parallel Construction	11	6
7. Infinitive/gerund/participle	10	6
8. Adjective or adverb phrase	8	5
9. Comparison	8	5
10. Conjunction	7	4
11. Preposition	6	4
12. Adjective or adverb clause	5	3
13. Inverted verb	4	2
14. Subject/noun phrase	4	2
15. Expletive "there"	4	2
16. Superlative	4	2
17. Cause/result	4	2
18. Purpose/reason	3	2
19. Adjective	3	2
20. Conditional and contrary to fact	3	2
21. Like, unlike	3	2
22. No, not, none	3	2
23. Indefinite pronoun	1	1
24. Countable/non-countable	1	1
	165	

Description and Examples of Sentence Completion Questions

As you go through each of these examples this second time, focus on the structure categories. These are the testing points. You can check the explanatory answers on page 169.

1. Verb
The focus is on the verb. The specific testing point might be verb tense, verb agreement, or passive voice. You often have to decide whether the sentence needs a single verb or part of a clause.

EXAMPLE:

In 1776, when the Declaration of Independence ________, the United States became a new country.

(A) signed
(B) that signed
(C) was signed
(D) that it signed

2. Word order
The right words are in the answer choices, but three of the answer choices give the words in the wrong order.

EXAMPLE:

The union won benefits ________.

(A) the members
(B) for its members
(C) its members for
(D) members for its

3. Subject + Verb
Both the main subject and the verb are in the answer choices. You must decide between specific testing points such as possessive noun, order of words, verb tense, or parts of a clause.

EXAMPLE:

In 1750 B.C., ________ the most famous collection of early laws.

(A) then Hammurabi wrote
(B) Hammurabi wrote
(C) Hammurabi's wrote
(D) Hammurabi, who wrote

4. *Wh* word as subject or noun clause

The subject of the sentence is a clause beginning with "when," "what," "whatever," "how," "that," "why," or "where." The noun clause can also be the object of the sentence.

EXAMPLE:

_________ he got home last night is still a mystery to me.

(A) How
(B) Although
(C) While
(D) Since

5. Prepositional phrase

All the answer choices give prepositional phrases. You must choose the correct one.

EXAMPLE:

New York is a major center _________.

(A) at bank
(B) of bank
(C) of banking
(D) to banking

6. Parallel construction

Words are given in a series. They must all be written in the same form.

EXAMPLE:

Sleeping, resting, _________ are the best ways to care for a cold.

(A) and that drinking fluids
(B) and drinking fluids
(C) which drank fluids
(D) and one drink fluids

7. Infinitive/gerund/participle

The answer choices are words that end in *-ing, -ed, -en,* or begin with the word *to*.

EXAMPLE:

Impressionist artists tended _________ imagination and light more important than faithful reproduction of objects.

(A) considering
(B) be consider
(C) consider to
(D) to consider

8. Adjective or adverb phrase

The answer choice gives part of an adjective or adverb phrase. There may be one or several words in each answer choice.

EXAMPLE:

A ray swims rapidly ________ broad winglike appendages.

(A) by flapping its
(B) its flapping
(C) of the flapping
(D) the flap

9. Comparison

Any form of comparison is possible, either the form below or forms using *than, rather than,* or *as*.

EXAMPLE:

The greater ________ increase in population, the harder it is for people to find adequate housing.

(A) of
(B) is the
(C) the
(D) is of the

10. Conjunction.

These are words such as *and, both, either, or, neither, nor, but, for*. These words connect parts of sentences and show the relationship between words.

EXAMPLE:

________ nor animals can survive without oxygen.

(A) Plants can neither
(B) Neither can plants
(C) Plants, neither
(D) Neither plants

11. Preposition

The prepositions in this testing point are single words, not prepositions in phrases.

EXAMPLE:

Excessive absenteeism results ________ problems for the schools.

(A) in
(B) with
(C) for
(D) to

12. Adjective or adverb clause

The answer choices may begin or be any part of the clause. The clause might be the beginning, middle, or end of the sentence.

EXAMPLE:

________ left Europe in 1492, he was unaware of the changes that would occur as a result of his voyage.

(A) From Columbus

(B) Because Columbus was

(C) That Columbus was

(D) When Columbus

13. Inverted verb for emphasis

Adverbs such as *never, hardly ever, seldom, rarely, no longer, only recently, not only,* and *not until* often indicate an inverted verb. The auxiliary verbs *have* and *do* come before the noun. The sentences often begin in a form similar to *Not only did I... but also,* or *Rarely do I. . . .*

EXAMPLE:

Not until the late 1960s ________ on the moon.

(A) that Americans walked

(B) did Americans walk

(C) when did Americans walk

(D) when Americans walked

14. Subject/noun phrase

A single subject or a short noun phrase are the testing points.

EXAMPLE:

________ AIDS has engaged many researchers in the last decade.

(A) By studying

(B) The study of

(C) Important study

(D) Now that the study

15. Expletive *there*

The word *there* is usually followed by a form of the verb *to be*.

EXAMPLE:

________ during past centuries when people have come to the west seeking gold.

(A) Times

(B) Throughout times

(C) There have been times

(D) Times have been

16. Superlative

The testing point might be the word *the* or the construction, *one of the* ________....

EXAMPLE:

Of all the national parks in the United States, Yellowstone is ________ visited.

(A) one of the most
(B) of the most
(C) one most
(D) the most one

17. Cause/result

These sentences often use words like *because, because of, since,* or *for.*

EXAMPLE:

Radio communication has changed ________ the rapid development of other communication media, such as television.

(A) because its
(B) is it because
(C) because of
(D) is because its

18. Purpose/reason

These sentences often use words like *in order to, so, so that, such.*

EXAMPLE:

The day was ________ that people swarmed to the beach.

(A) such a hot
(B) so hot
(C) very hot
(D) hot

19. Adjective

This testing point might be single adjectives or hyphenated adjectives.

EXAMPLE:

________ felt hat is one of the symbols of a cowboy.

(A) A broad-brimmed
(B) Broad
(C) The brim, which is broad
(D) Broad brim

20. Conditional and contrary to fact

This might be a conditional beginning with *if,* or a sentence beginning with, *Had it not been for....*

EXAMPLE:

_________ the ozone layer were destroyed, most living things would disappear from the Earth in a few years.

(A) Besides
(B) If
(C) So
(D) For

21. Like/unlike

You must choose between words such as *like, unlike,* and *dislike.*

EXAMPLE:

_________ public schools, private schools charge tuition.

(A) Do not like
(B) No likeness to
(C) Dislike
(D) Unlike

22. No/not/none

You must choose between words such as *no, not,* and *none.*

EXAMPLE:

_________ two fingerprints are identical.

(A) Nor
(B) No
(C) None
(D) Not

23. Indefinite pronoun

These are words like *everyone, anyone,* or *anything.*

EXAMPLE:

Silver nitrate dyes _________ it touches black.

(A) somehow
(B) there
(C) them
(D) everything

24. Countable/non-countable

The specific testing points for this structure might be words such as *a great deal of.* or *many* or *much.*

> **EXAMPLE:**
>
> _________ of buying and selling occurs internationally.
>
> **(A)** A great deal
> **(B)** A great many
> **(C)** Much greater
> **(D)** Many

Error Identification Pretest

Directions: Take the following pretest to get an idea of your level and skills in Error Identification: Circle the word or phrase that is incorrect. Then check your answers on page 161.

1. The season (A) changes of weather cause (B) color changes in the leaves of (C) deciduous (D) trees.

2. Victims (A) of migraines are often unable (B) to tolerate ordinary (C) sights, sounds, odors, and press (D).

3. No (A) one was sure (B) how many (C) Americans suffer from chronic (D) fatigue syndrome.

4. Science (A) and technology (B) are (C) part of the knowledges (D) of educated people.

5. Some people believe that (A) humans will never (B) use away (C) all the (D) natural resources of earth.

6. Some artists like (A) their (B) art to be (C) shown in apart (D) museums.

7. The invention (A) of Alexander Graham Bell extremely (B) greatly extended the limits (C) of communication (D).

8. A delicious mixture (A) called a smoothee is a blend several (B) different (C) foods such as (D) milk, bananas, and vanilla.

9. The Medal of National Science is the highest (A) award scientific (B) that can be given (C) to any individual (D) in the United States.

10. A (A) milk can provide (B) protein for a cheap (C), nutritionally balanced (D) diet.

11. Scientists say (A) that (B) the color of the lake is a result (C) of his (D) unusual algae.

12. Three conditions critical (A) for growing (B) plants are soil temperature, chemical balance, or (C) amount (D) of moisture.

13. A technical (A) view of a new invention sometimes differ (B) from an (C) economic perspective (D).

14. Engines used (A) in space shuttles are much larger (B) and more strong (C) than the ones (D) used in jet planes.

15. When (A) there are low (B) sales, companies often decide developing (C) new products (D).

16. Elephants have so long (A) flexible trunks that (B) they seem clumsy (C) as (D) they walk.

17. Many people which (A) know the Missouri River well doubt (B) that (C) it can ever really be tamed (D).

18. Unlike another (A) schools, Fremont High School has a room and board (B) program to provide (C) assistance for (D) out-of-town students.

19. Garlic smells somewhat (A) alike (B) onion and is a flavorful (C) ingredient used in many dishes (D).

20. Many (A) people believe that New York is the (B) most great (C) city in (D) the United States.

21. New laws should be writing (A) to accomodate (B) changes in (C) our (D) society.

22. With reforestation now there are young (A) forests where (B) no long (C) ago the land was (D) gullied and bare.

23. Of the billions (A) of stars in the galaxy, how much (B) are suitable (C) for life (D)?

24. Victor served (A) as (B) president of (C) the school club since (D) fifteen years.

25. The majestic (A) Rocky Mountains stretch (B) each (C) the way from (D) Mexico to the Arctic.

26. In those (A) days of frequent (B) air travel, diseases can spread (C) around the world in a very short (D) time.

Answer Key For Error Identification

1. A	**6.** D	**11.** D	**16.** A	**21.** A	**26.** A
2. D	**7.** B	**12.** C	**17.** A	**22.** C	
3. B	**8.** B	**13.** B	**18.** A	**23.** B	
4. D	**9.** B	**14.** C	**19.** B	**24.** D	
5. C	**10.** A	**15.** C	**20.** C	**25.** C	

Frequency of Types of Error Identification Questions

The following list of structures was compiled from selected actual TOEFL exams given between 1984 and 1989. These grammatical structures were taken from eleven tests; the list represents 275 questions from the second part of Section Two, Error Identification.

The list below represents only one of the many possible ways to categorize testing points in error identification questions. The particular categories are not important; what matters is your understanding of how to use the testing points in the following example sentences.

ERROR IDENTIFICATION—275 QUESTIONS

Testing Point	Frequency	Approximate Percent
1. Word form	58	21
2. Parallel construction	28	10
3. Verb tense	28	10
4. Singular/plural noun	24	9
5. Preposition	17	6
6. Wrong word	16	6
7. Additional word	15	5
8. Omission of word	10	4
9. Word reversal	10	3
10. Article	9	3
11. Pronoun	8	3
12. Conjunction	8	3
13. Verb agreement	8	3
14. Comparative	7	3
15. Infinitive/gerund	4	1
16. So/such/ so that	4	1
17. Adjective/adverb clause	4	1
18. Other/another	3	1
19. Like/ unlike/ alike	3	1
20. Superlative	2	.7
21. Passive	2	.7
22. No/not/none	2	.7
23. Many/much	2	.7
24. Since/for	1	.3
25. Each/every/all	1	.3
26. These/those	1	.3
	275	

Description and Examples of Error Identification Testing Points

As you go through each of these examples this second time, focus on the descriptive categories. These are the testing points. You may check the explanatory answers on page 170.

1. Word form

Any word might be written incorrectly for this testing point: you might see a verb instead of a noun, or an adjective instead of an adverb, or any other form used incorrectly.

EXAMPLE:

The season (A) changes of weather cause (B) color changes in the leaves of (C) deciduous (D) trees.

2. Parallel construction

Parallel construction means that two or more words written in a series must be written in the same form.

EXAMPLE:

Victims (A) of migraines are often unable (B) to tolerate ordinary (C) sights, sounds, odors, and press (D).

3. Verb tense

Any verb might be written in the wrong tense.

EXAMPLE:

No (A) one was sure (B) how many (C) Americans suffer from chronic (D) fatigue syndrome.

4. Singular/plural noun

The noun form might need an *s* or it might have an unnecessary *s*. Mass nouns can be plural without adding an *s*.

EXAMPLE:

Science (A) and technology (B) are (C) part of the knowledges (D) of educated people.

14

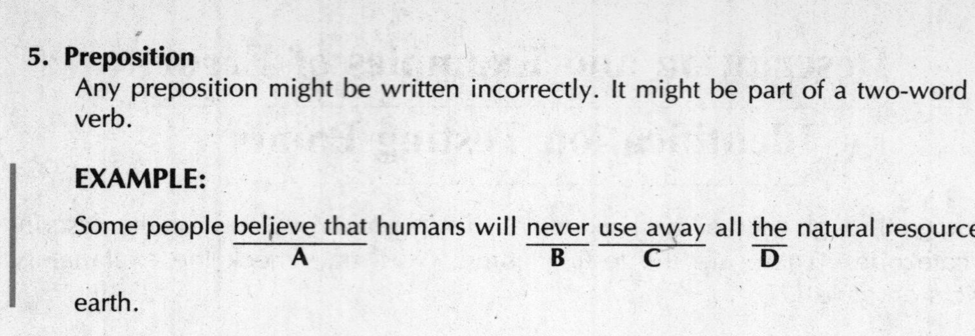

5. Preposition

Any preposition might be written incorrectly. It might be part of a two-word verb.

EXAMPLE:

Some people believe that humans will never use away all the natural resources of earth.

(A = believe that, B = never, C = use away, D = the)

6. Wrong word

In this type of sentence error, the wrong word is used. It might be *make* instead of *do;* or *big* instead of *great,* or *little* instead of *few,* or *separate* instead of *apart,* or any other similar words.

EXAMPLE:

Some artists like their art to be shown in apart museums.

(A = like, B = their, C = to be, D = apart)

7. Additional word

In this type of sentence there is a word which should not be in the sentence at all. It may be a double subject, a double negative, a repeated similar adjective or adverb, an unnecessary preposition, or any other unnecessary word.

EXAMPLE:

The invention of Alexander Graham Bell extremely greatly extended the limits of communication.

(A = invention, B = extremely, C = the limits, D = communication)

8. Omission of word

A necessary word is left out of the sentence. Any word can be left out.

EXAMPLE:

A delicious mixture called a smoothee is a blend several different foods such as milk, bananas, and vanilla.

(A = A delicious mixture, B = blend several, C = different, D = such as)

9. Word reversal

In this testing point, two words are reversed. It might be an adjective written before a noun or an adverb written before a verb or any other reversed words.

EXAMPLE:

The Medal of National Science is the highest award scientific that can be given to any individual in the United States.

(A = the highest, B = award scientific, C = can be given, D = individual)

10. Article

The words *a, an,* and *the* might be misused.

EXAMPLE:

A milk can provide protein for a cheap, nutritionally balanced diet.
A B C D

11. Pronoun

The focus is on any pronoun: subject, object, or possessive.

EXAMPLE:

Scientists say that the color of the lake is a result of his unusual algae.
A B C D

12. Conjunction

Conjunctions are words such as *both, and, or, but, either, neither, for, not only...but also.* Any of the words above might be substituted for another word.

EXAMPLE:

Three conditions critical for growing plants are soil temperature, chemical balance
A B

or amount of moisture.
C D

13. Verb agreement

The verb must agree with the noun, by being either singular or plural.

EXAMPLE:

A technical view of a new invention sometimes differ from an economic
A B C

perspective.
D

14. Comparative

The testing point might be the *-er* form or the word *more* or a construction like *as...as.*

EXAMPLE:

Engines used in space shuttles are much larger and more strong than the ones
A B C D

used in jet planes.

15. Infinitive/gerund

An infinitive might be used instead of a gerund (*-ing* form) or either word might be used incorrectly.

EXAMPLE:

When there are low sales, companies often decide developing new products.
A B C D

16. *So, such, so...that*

Any of the above words might be misused.

EXAMPLE:

Elephants have so long flexible trunks that they seem clumsy as they walk.
A B C D

17. Adjective/adverb clause beginning with *wh*

The clause begins with words such as *which, where, that, who,* or *when.*

EXAMPLE:

Many people which know the Missouri River well doubt that it can ever really
A B C

be tamed.
D

18. *Other/another*

One of these words might be used instead of the other.

EXAMPLE:

Unlike another schools, Fremont High School has a room and board program
A B

to provide assistance for out-of-town students.
C D

19. *Like/unlike/alike*

Any of the above words might be substituted for an incorrect form

EXAMPLE:

Garlic smells somewhat alike onion and is a flavorful ingredient used in many
A B C

dishes.
D

20. Superlative

The focus is usually on the word *the* or *most* or the ending *-est.*

EXAMPLE:

Many people believe that New York is the most great city in the United States.
A B C D

21. Passive

Sentences may use an incorrect form of passive or active voice.

EXAMPLE:

New laws should be writing to accommodate changes in our society.
A B C D

22. No/not/none

Any of the above words might be used instead of the correct word.

EXAMPLE:

With reforestation now there are young forests where no long ago the land was
A B C D

gullied and bare.

23. Many/much

Many is used with countable nouns and *much* is used with uncountable nouns.

EXAMPLE:

Of the billions of stars in the galaxy, how much are suitable for life?
A B C D

24. Since/for

The word *since* is used with a specific time, while the word *for* expresses a longer duration of time.

EXAMPLE:

Victor served as president of the school club since fifteen years.
A B C D

25. Each/every/all

Any of the above words might be used incorrectly. *Each* and *every* are singular. *All* is plural.

EXAMPLE:

The majestic Rocky Mountains stretch each the way from Mexico to the Arctic.
A B C D

26. *These/those*

The word *these* refers to something happening now or something close to the speaker; the word *those* refers to something in the past or something farther away.

EXAMPLE:

In those (A) days of frequent (B) air travel, diseases can spread (C) around the world in a very short (D) time.

Explanatory Answers

SENTENCE COMPLETION

1. **(C)** The correct answer is in the passive voice because the Declaration of Independence is not the actor; it cannot sign anything. People signed the Declaration of Independence.

2. **(B)** This is a prepositional phrase that describes who the benefits are for.

3. **(B)** A subject and verb are needed here. Answer A could not be correct because the word *then* refers to the time *1750 B.C.* and is an incorrect additional word.

4. **(A)** Only *how* is possible here since the other words would all begin dependent clauses.

5. **(C)** The word *banking* in this sentence is a noun form. It describes the process of using the bank, rather than the bank itself.

6. **(B)** The word *drinking* must be parallel with *sleeping* and *resting* by ending in *-ing*.

7. **(D)** After the verb *tend* you must use an infinitive in this sentence.

8. **(A)** The word *by* begins a description of how the fish swims.

9. **(C)** This is a proportional statement. It must always use the word *the* before the noun. You might memorize the following saying, "the bigger, the better."

10. **(D)** Neither/nor statements are connected with a noun or noun phrase: neither he nor I. . . . neither good nor bad . . .

11. **(A)** In this sentence, *results* is a verb. The word *in* follows the verb *results*. The other words could follow the noun form *results* but not the verb form.

12. **(D)** The correct answer begins an adverb clause. Answers B and C cannot be correct because *was left* is a passive form of the verb. This would mean, *someone left Columbus* instead of *Columbus left Europe*.

13. **(B)** The words *not until* will always be followed by the inverted verb form: "not until . . . will we have . . ." "not until . . . did they. . . ."

14. **(B)** You must use *the* before the noun *study*. Answer D is incorrect because it would begin a dependent clause and then another subject and verb would have to follow this sentence.

15. **(C)** The expletive *there* is followed by *to be* and refers to the existence of something. This form is similar to "There are books on the table."

16. **(A)** In a superlative, you must have the word, *the*. Answer D cannot be correct because *most* must be next to *visited*.

17. **(C)** The word *because* is followed by *of* when it comes before a noun.

18. **(B)** The clue in this sentence is the word *that*. The phrase *so hot that* gives a reason. Answer A is not correct because you must have a noun phrase after the words *such a* (i.e., *such a hot day*) Both C and D are incorrect because of the word *that* in the sentence.

19. **(A)** A hyphen is used when the two adjectives combine to make one idea. The word *broad* describes the *brim* (outside edge of the hat), not the hat itself. (The word *felt* in this sentence refers to material made of wool.)

20. **(B)** You can tell that this is a conditional needing the word *if* because of the verb, *would disappear*.

21. **(D)** The word unlike comes before a noun. The word *dislike* is a verb, e.g., "I dislike American hot dogs." Answer A could not be correct because there is no subject before the verb *do not like*. Answer C could not be correct because the word *likeness* means *resemblance* or *looks the same*.

22. **(B)** Before the noun *fingerprints,* you must use the word *no*. If you use the word *none,* you cannot have the noun in the sentence, e.g., "None are identical" is correct.

23. **(D)** In this sentence, the word *dyes* is a verb. You might also say, "Silver nitrate turns everything black," or "Good food makes everyone happy."

24. **(A)** The words *a great deal of* mean the same as *a lot of*. Because of the word *of* in the sentence you must choose answer A. Answer B is incorrect because *many* must be followed by a countable noun, e.g., "many of the books."

ERROR IDENTIFICATION

1. (A) The word *season* is a noun, but this sentence needs an adjective to describe the changes. The correct answer is *seasonal*. In this sentence *changes* is a noun, not a verb.

2. (D) The words *sights* and *sounds* are nouns. The third word must also be a noun: *pressure*.

3. (B) The verb must be in the present tense in this sentence because it is a general statement and because the verb *suffer* is in the present tense: *No one is sure. . . .*

4. (D) The word *knowledge* is a mass noun; it cannot take an *s* ending.

5. (C) The idiom *use up* is correct in this sentence; it means "use until nothing is left."

6. (D) The word that is necessary here is *separate*. It refers to several different places. The word *apart* refers to something that has been separated into pieces.

7. (B) The word *extremely* is not necessary because it has the same meaning as *greatly*.

8. (B) The words *blend* and *several* must have *of* between them, e.g., "a blend of several foods."

9. (B) The word *scientific* describes the award. The sentence must say, ". . . the highest scientific award."

10. (A) The word milk cannot be preceded by "a" since it is a mass (uncountable) noun.

11. (D) The pronoun *his* refers to male people or animals. To refer to a lake, the pronoun *its* must be used.

12. (C) Since all three conditions are required, they should be joined by *and*, not *or*.

13. (B) The verb must agree with the noun, e.g., "view . . . differs. . . ."

14. (C) Since *strong* is one syllable, you should write *stronger*.

15. (C) After the verb *decide* you need to use the infinitive form of the verb *to develop*.

16. (A) Since the word *trunks* is a noun, it must be preceded by the word *such*, e.g., ". . . such long trunks that. . . ."

17. (A) After the word *people*, use the pronoun *who*, e.g., "many people who know."

18. (A) The word *another* is used with singular nouns. In this sentence, the word *schools* is plural, so you must say, *other schools*.

19. (B) This sentence must use the word *like* instead of *alike* because there is a noun after the word. The word *alike* can't be followed by a noun.

20. (C) For this superlative adjective, you must say, "the greatest city" because the word *great* is only one syllable.

21. (A) This sentence needs the passive form of the verb, e.g., "new laws should be written . . ." because the laws themselves are not doing the writing.

22. (C) The phrase "not long ago" is correct because the word *not* gives the negative of *long ago*.

23. (B) Since "billions of stars" are countable, you must use *many*, instead of *much*.

24. (D) Because the sentence describes a duration of time (fifteen years) you must use the word *for* instead of *since*.

25. (C) The word *each* goes in front of a singular noun. This sentence describes a distance between two points, so it must use *all*.

26. (A) The word *those* refers to a past time or a distant time or object. This sentence is referring to the present time, so the word must be *these days*.

Summary

1. There are two types of Structure and Written Expression questions: Sentence Completion and Error Identification.
2. The frequency list for Sentence Completion shows that verbs, noun clauses, subjects and verbs, and prepositional phrases are the most common testing points. Many answer choices have all the correct words, but they are written in the wrong order.
3. The frequency list for Error Identification shows that most of the errors are incorrect forms of words, phrases that are not parallel, incorrect verb tenses, and incorrect nouns (singular or plural).

Lesson 15

Structure and Written Expression Skills

Objectives

- To practice using testing points
- To learn some testing point clues
- To establish a testing clock

1. Watson's Way: The Basic Way
2. Holmes's Advice: Use Testing Points
3. Further Advice From Holmes: Learn Testing Point Clues
4. Establish a Testing Clock
5. Shooting in the Dark
6. Structure and Written Expression Drills

Lesson 15

In Lesson 14 you practiced questions for the Structure and Written Expression section. In this lesson, you will practice test-taking skills for Structure and Written Expression.

Watson's Way: The Basic Way

Dr. Watson is an intelligent man, but he doesn't use logical skills to answer questions. He has studied English grammar so he usually gets a good score. He reads each question carefully, focusing on the answer choices, and he searches through his mind for information about English grammar. He doesn't think about the techniques he is using; however, he just goes through each test.

Sometimes, Watson comes to a question that he doesn't understand. It is then that he asks for help from his friend Sherlock Holmes.

Holmes' Advice: Use Testing Points

Holmes, as usual, looks for patterns and clues that lead him to the answers. He says to Dr. Watson, "Watson, my dear friend, you know that there are lists of frequently used grammatical structures. These are all the testing points. Why don't you use those lists to guide you in choosing your answers?" There are several ways that you can use testing points to help you.

Using Testing Points in Structure Questions

1. Look at the answer choices first.

Before you read the complete sentence, glance quickly at the answer choices. If they are short, make a quick guess about what the sentence needs. (The sentences are not written here.)

EXAMPLE 1:

(A) came
(B) coming
(C) has come
(D) will come

Guess: These answer choices are all verbs; the sentence must need a verb. Think about the verb tense while reading the sentence.

EXAMPLE 2:

(A) by asking
(B) to ask
(C) the asking of
(D) asking
Guess: This sentence might need a noun form or a verb form. You may need to choose between a gerund and an infinitive.

EXAMPLE 3:

(A) Not only is much of the history unwritten
(B) Although much of the history that is unwritten
(C) It is as much the unwritten history
(D) Much of the history is unwritten
Guess: These answer choices are too long to read quickly, so don't spend much time reading them now. First read the main sentence. When you read the sentence, look to see if it is a complete sentence with a main subject and verb. Then read these answer choices.

2. *Simplify the sentence*

Some of the sentences are long, but you may need to understand only part of the sentence in order to complete it. Focus on the most important parts. Sometimes you can leave out single words, like adjectives or adverbs; sometimes you can leave out prepositional phrases or complete clauses.

EXAMPLE 1

The scale of this 1264-mile coastline is ________ imposing that much of it is difficult to comprehend close up.
(A) as
(B) such
(C) so
(D) like
Guess: The sentence needs a connecting word.
Simplify: The scale of this XXXXX coastline is ________ XXXXXXX that much of it is difficult to comprehend XXXXXX XX.
Choose answer: (C) . . . so XXXXXXX that . . .

EXAMPLE 2:

A steady rate of growth occurs ________ the food intake remains the same throughout the peak period.
(A) according
(B) if
(C) with
(D) under
Simplify: A steady rate of growth occurs ________ the food intake remains the same XXXXXXX XXX XXXX XXXXXXX.
Choose answer: (B) . . . growth occurs if . . .

3. Think back over the list of frequent testing points. Ask yourself the following:

Is the verb tense correct?
Does the verb agree with the noun?
Does the sentence need a main subject and verb?
Does the sentence begin or end with a noun clause?
Are the adverbs, adjectives, and verbs in the right form?
Are the words written in parallel construction?

EXERCISE **1**

IDENTIFYING TESTING POINTS: Sentence Completion

(Answers, page 187)

Directions: Choose the answer that best completes each sentence and write the structure testing point for each question. Choose the testing point from the following list:

- Verb
- Word order
- *Wh* word as subject (when, where, why, how, what)
- Subject + verb
- Prepositional phrase
- Parallel construction
- Adjective or adverb phrase
- Comparison
- Infinitive, gerund, participle
- Conjunction (and, both, either, or, neither, nor, but)

Not all of the above testing points are used in the questions below, and some of the testing points are used more than once. If you are not sure which testing point to choose, guess. Sometimes a testing point fits more than one category.

1. An increase in population, without an increase in economic level, ________ result in a lower standard of living.

(A) tending to
(B) tends
(C) tends to
(D) will tend

Answer: ____

Testing Point: ________________________________

2. In some parts of the United States, it is common to get rain ________.

(A) of five days straight
(B) for five days straight
(C) on five days straight
(D) five days straight

Answer: ____

Testing Point: ________________________________

3. A shortage of workers ________ in certain areas of California this year.

(A) predicted
(B) is being predicted
(C) to predict
(D) predicting

Answer: ____

Testing Point: ________________________________

4. ________ impose a higher tax on cigarettes and other tobacco products.

(A) Voted by the State Board of Equalization .

(B) The State Board of Equalization voted to

(C) Voting by the State Board of Equalization

(D) Whereas the State Board of Equalization vote to

Answer: ____

Testing Point: ____________________

5. ________ if you are knowledgeable and well-prepared.

(A) The small are risks

(B) Are small the risks

(C) Small the risks are

(D) The risks are small

Answer: ____

Testing Point: ____________________

6. Once you know the pitfalls of certain acts, you ________ if they are worth the effort.

(A) be deciding

(B) can be decided

(C) can decide

(D) decided

Answer: ____

Testing Point: ____________________

7. ________ about the relationship between Thomas Jefferson and John Adams is inferred from their letters.

(A) What is known

(B) What is it

(C) Where are they

(D) When they lived

Answer: ____

Testing Point: ____________________

8. ________ the nation's overall weather patterns, meteorologists must constantly measure the changing conditions shown by satellite photos.

(A) Predicted

(B) To predict

(C) Unpredictable

(D) Of predicting

Answer: ____

Testing Point: ____________________

9. ________ through a telescope, the planets take on a new appearance.

(A) Seen
(B) To see
(C) Sees
(D) Seeing

Answer: ____

Testing Point: ____

10. The Rocky Mountain Goat eats sparse vegetation, lives in small herds, and can ________.

(A) crosses steep rock slides skillfully
(B) skillfully cross steep rock slides
(C) skillfully crossing steep rock slides
(D) steep rock slides are skillfully crossed

Answer: ____

Testing Point: ____

EXERCISE **2**

Identifying Testing Points: Error Identification

(Answers, page 187)

Directions: Choose the letter of the underlined portion of each sentence that is incorrect and write the structural testing point for each question. Choose the testing point from the following list:

Word form	Wrong word
Parallel Construction	Additional word
Verb tense	Omission of word
Singular/plural noun	Word reversal
Preposition	Article

Not all of the above testing points are used in the exercises below, and some of the testing points are repeated. If you are not sure which testing point to choose, guess. Sometimes a testing point fits more than one category.

1. A Bay Meadows jockey can be suspended (A) for (B) two years for carrying (C) an illegal electrical device while (D) a race.

Answer: ______

Testing Point: ______________________

2. For the first time in (A) three decades, Californians drank (B) less beer, winery (C), and hard liquor this year than they (D) did last year.

Answer: ______

Testing Point: ______________________

3. Many universities are calling for (A) additional ethnic studies (B) courses and changes in other courses give (C) more credit to (D) minority people.

Answer: ______

Testing Point: ______________________

15

4. A flammable liquid it (A) was used to ignite (B) a fire that (C) burned part of the (D) blighted Nairobi Shopping Center.

Answer: _______

Testing Point: ____

5. Twelve workers at a small semiconductor plant (A) were evacuated after (B) a container of gas poisonous (C) was accidentally disconnected (D).

Answer: _______

Testing Point: ____

6. Some politicians share (A) lunch and jokes after electing (B) even though a few weeks before (C) they may have been throwing insults at (D) each other.

Answer: _______

Testing Point: ____

7. To help (A) with the (B) waste disposal problem, many Americans had sorted (C) their garbage for (D) recycling.

Answer: _______

Testing Point: ____

8. A (A) strong economies (B) makes imports cheap (C) and exports more expensive (D).

Answer: _______

Testing Point: ____

9. While (A) a strong defend (B) is important to any country, it cannot be more important than the livelihood (C) of its (D) citizens.

Answer: _______

Testing Point: ____

10. In 1919 the California Assembly approve (A) plans to build Highway One through (C) the central coast region known (D) as Big Sur.

Answer: ______

Testing Point: ______________________________

Further Advice from Holmes: Learn Testing Point Clues

Dr. Watson approached his friend Sherlock Holmes one day. "Holmes," he said, "I'm very grateful to you for your advice. I've been writing down the testing points when I miss questions, and I have found that many of my mistakes in different sentences are actually the same testing point! It has helped me to organize my learning."

"I have another problem, however. It takes me a long time to read the questions. Often I don't know what they mean, and I have to look up new words in my dictionary."

"My dear Watson," answered Holmes. "I can understand how frustrating it is not to know all the words in this section of the test, but often you can choose the correct answers quickly by paying more attention to the structure than to the complete meaning of each sentence. Remember that your score is based only on how many questions you get right, not on how well you understand them.

"Look at the following sentence from your book:

The day was ________ that people swarmed to the beach.

(A) such a hot
(B) so hot
(C) very hot
(D) hot

In this sentence you probably stopped to look up the word, 'swarmed.'

"Yes, I did," answered Watson. "I found out that the word means that there were large numbers of people together and that the beach was crowded."

"Well," continued Holmes, "you won't be able to use your dictionary during the test. The word 'swarmed' is good to add to your vocabulary, but remember that you can answer the question without knowing the meaning of that word. Look at the clues in the sentence. They can help you concentrate on the structures."

Testing Point Clues

Some sentences have clues that can help guide you in choosing an answer. Some of the following clues are extra clues in sentences (like commas) and other clues are reminders of words that are often written together. This list has only ten clues.

15

You can probably think of many more. Add your own list of clues and reminders to this list. In the explanatory answers for the exercises and practice tests, you will also find other clues.

Clue 1. Commas

a. Look for commas that separate words in a series. The commas will remind you to check that the words are all written in the same part of speech. Don't just look for the endings, but look to see if the words are all nouns, adjectives, adverbs, verbs, gerunds, infinitives, or passive voice.

Example: *Sleeping, resting,* and *drinking fluids* are the best ways to care for a cold.

b. Look for a comma that tells you that part of the sentence is a dependent clause or a phrase. Then you will know that the main subject and verb is in another part of the sentence.

Example: *When Columbus left Europe in 1492,* he was unaware of the changes that would occur as a result of his voyage.

Clue 2. Gerunds/*-ing* form

a. After the word *by,* use the *-ing* form of the verb.

Example: *By traveling* with only one suitcase, you can move faster.

Some of the testing points consist of two words or phrases that often go together. If you see one of these words, look for the other one.

Clue 3. *Not until....did*

Example: *Not until* the late 1960s *did* Americans walk on the moon.

Clue 4. *Rarely...do/have*

Examples: *Rarely do* comets come close to the earth.
Rarely have I seen such a beautiful sunset.

Clue 5. *Not only...but... as well/also/too*

Examples: The president is *not only* the political leader *but* the military leader as *well.*
The president is *not only* the political leader, he is *also* the military leader.
The president is *not only* the political leader, he is the military leader *too.*

Clue 6. *Either...or*

Example: The seals will begin arriving on the beaches *either* in late fall *or* in early winter.

Clue 7. *Neither...nor*

Example: *Neither* plants *nor* animals can live without food.

Clue 8. *More...than*

Example: Studies show that it is *more* important to achieve happiness in life *than* it is to make money.

Clue 9. *One of the most ... is/was; one of the -est ... is/was*

Example: *One of the most* respected presidents of the U.S. *was* Abraham Lincoln.

Example: *One of the* rain*iest* places in the world *is* in Hawaii.

Clue 10. *So...that*

Example: The job was *so* difficult *that* many people couldn't finish the work.

Establish a Testing Clock

The Facts

If you have a test of 40 questions and you are given 25 minutes to complete the test, you have an average of 37.5 seconds for each question. This is what you have for the short form of the TOEFL. For the long form you may have even fewer seconds for each question. For many people, this is a very short time for each question.

Get the Most out of Your Practice Tests

To get the most out of your practice tests, be aware of how much time you are using for this part of the TOEFL. If you are working too quickly because you are worried about the time, you may make extra mistakes. If you are working too slowly, you may not finish the section and thus miss easy questions at the end.

Establish an internal testing clock before you take the test so that you feel comfortable with the amount of time you are spending on each question while you take the TOEFL. Use the following system to prepare yourself to follow your own testing clock.

1. During practice, allow yourself only 30 seconds for each question, but check yourself after you do 10 questions, not after each question. Give yourself five minutes to do 10 questions. This is because some questions are easier for you and will take less time while others are harder and will take more time.
2. Once you have developed a general sense of how long five minutes is, check the time after you do 20 questions. Give yourself only 10 minutes to do 20 questions.
3. Get used to this 10-minute time period so that you are able to "feel" the time. Plan on using this 10-minute checking time period while you take the real TOEFL.

If you run out of new material, take one of the old practice tests again in order to pace yourself. If you do this, give yourself less time, since you are already familiar with the questions. This approach is especially useful if the practice test was difficult for you.

Shooting in the Dark

What should you do if you can't pick out the answer?

1. First eliminate any answer that you know is not the right one; then guess among the answers that are left.
2. If there is one answer that you think might be correct, then choose that answer. Sometimes your first feeling is correct.
3. If you have no idea about what to eliminate and you have very little time left, choose one letter (possibly "B") and fill in all remaining blanks with that letter.

Summary

1. Study the lists of frequent structures in Lesson 14, so you can look for these frequent structures on the TOEFL test.
2. Many sentences have extra clues that can help you, such as commas or words that often go together.
3. When answering structure questions, you should concentrate more on the grammar than on the meaning of the sentence.
4. You can often pick out the correct answer even if you don't know all the vocabulary words or the complete meaning of each sentence.
5. Practice pacing yourself so that you can do about 20 questions in 10 minutes.

Answers to Exercises

EXERCISE 1: Identifying Testing Points: Sentence Completion

1. Answer: C

   Testing Point: verb

2. Answer: B

   Testing Point: prepositional phrase

3. Answer: B

   Testing Point: verb

4. Answer: B

   Testing Point: subject and verb

5. Answer: D

   Testing Point: subject and verb or word order

6. Answer: C

   Testing Point: verb

7. Answer: A

   Testing Point: *wh* word as subject. (This cannot be subject and verb because the main verb is not in the answer choice.)

8. Answer: B

   Testing Point: infinitive

9. Answer: A

   Testing Point: participle

10. Answer: B

    Testing Point: parallel construction

EXERCISE 2: Identifying Testing Points: Error Identification

1. Answer: D

   Testing Point: preposition or wrong word (The word should be *during*.)

2. Answer: C

   Testing Point: parallel construction or word form (The word should be *wine*.)

3. Answer: C

   Testing Point: omission of word or verb or infinitive (The correct answer is *to give*.)

4. Answer: A

   Testing Point: additional word (*It* should be left out.)

5. Answer: C

   Testing Point: word reversal

6. Answer: B

   Testing Point: word form (The word should be *an election* or *elections*.)

7. Answer: C

   Testing Point: verb tense (The verb should be *sort*.)

8. Answer: B

   Testing Point: singular/plural noun (The noun should be *economy*.)

9. Answer: B

   Testing Point: word form (The word should be *defense*.)

10. Answer: A

    Testing point: verb tense (The verb should be *approved*.)

Structure and Written Expression Drills

The next part of this lesson includes a "Walk-through" and five drills. The "Walk-through" gives you a chance to follow the thought process you go through as you answer the example questions.

The other five drills provide practice in answering Structure and Written Expression questions. These drills are similar to the actual TOEFL, but they contain fewer questions. After you finish the drills, check your answers on page 204. Then read the explanations on pages 205–206.

Walk-Through

Sentence Completion Directions: On the left side of the page are 10 incomplete sentences. Beneath each sentence you will see four words or phrases, marked (A), (B), (C), and (D). Choose the one word or phrase that best completes each sentence. Then read the step-by-step explanations in the box on the right side of the page.

1. As the atom is pumped with energy by a laser, ________ are excited into higher energy states.

(A) its electrons
(B) as its electrons
(C) it is electrons
(D) the electrons of its

STEP 1: Guess the problem from a brief glance at the choices: noun or noun phrase.

STEP 2: Simplify the sentence: As the atom is pumped ________ are excited . . .

STEP 3: Analyze: The sentence needs a noun or a noun phrase because the blank space is before a verb.

STEP 4: Identify the answer: (A) *its electrons* is correct. The sentence should be:
. . . *its electrons* are excited into . . . .
Additional information: Why others are wrong:
(B) *as* makes another dependent clause.
(C) adds a verb.
(D) *its* doesn't refer to anything.

STEP 5: Testing point: noun as a subject.

COMMENTS:
Be sure to check for agreement of the noun and verb: singular or plural.

2. A plant may be microscopic in size, such as one-celled algae, ________ large and complex, like a many-celled flower.

(A) or
(B) but
(C) and
(D) which is

STEP 1: Guess the problem from a brief glance at the choices: conjunction.

STEP 2: Simplify the sentence: A plant *may be* microscopic (small) . . . , ________ large . . . .

STEP 3: Analyze: The sentence needs a word to join two opposite ideas.

STEP 4: Identify the answer: (A) is a proper conjunction, because *or* connects the two opposite ideas.

STEP 5: Testing point: conjunction.

COMMENTS:
Other common connectors which often go together: both . . . and, not only . . . but also, so . . . that, such . . . that, neither . . . nor, either . . . or, as . . . as, so . . . as, i.e., When you see *both* in the sentence, it might be used as a hint for choosing and.

3. Except for a laser beam, diamond itself is the only material hard enough ________ diamonds.

(A) to cut
(B) cut
(C) cutting
(D) to be cut

STEP 1: Guess the problem from a brief glance at the choices: verb form.

STEP 2: Simplify the sentence: . . . diamond . . . is . . . hard enough ________ diamonds.

STEP 3: Analyze: An infinitive form follows *enough.*

STEP 4: Identify the answer: (A) is the correct answer. The sentence should be:
. . . diamond . . . is . . . hard enough *to cut* diamonds

STEP 5: Testing point: infinitive after *enough.*

4. Electricity has become ________ a vital part of American life that even a few seconds of shutdown will create chaos.

(A) thus
(B) so
(C) such
(D) very much

STEP 1: Guess the problem from a brief glance at the choices: connecting word.

STEP 2: Simplify the sentence: Electricity has become ________ a vital part . . . that . . .

STEP 3: Analyze: *that* indicates that the sentence needs *such* or *so* to fit in.

STEP 4: Identify the answer: (C) is the answer because *such* is followed by *a.*

STEP 5: Testing point: such/so.

COMMENTS:
Such is followed by a noun or an adjective + noun. If the noun is singular, *such* must be followed by "a." *So* is followed by an adjective or an adverb,
i.e., such good work
such a good job
so much work
so good
a doesn't follow *so.*

5. ________ a person feels appreciated, it is often because he or she has done something nice."

(A) Because
(B) What
(C) That
(D) When

STEP 1: Guess the problem from a brief glance at the choices: Beginning of an adjective or adverb clause or *wh* word as subject.

STEP 2: Simplify the sentence: ________ a person feels . . . , it is often

STEP 3: Analyze: Since *it is* . . . begins the main clause, the sentence needs a subordinating clause.

STEP 4: Identify the answer: (D) is correct. The sentence should be: *When* a person feels . . ., it is often because . . .

STEP 5: Testing point: Adverb clause.

COMMENTS:
More subordinating words: after, as, even if, because, since, although.

6. Ultraviolet rays are ________ induce sunburn and tanning of the skin.

(A) how
(B) who
(C) what
(D) why

STEP 1: Guess the problem from a brief glance at the choices: *wh* word

STEP 2: Simplify the sentence: . . . Rays are ________ induce sunburn . . .

STEP 3: Analyze: The word *what* means *the thing that.*

STEP 4: Identify the answer: (C) is the answer. *Ray* is a noun; *what* represents the noun.

STEP 5: Testing point: *wh* word as subject.

COMMENTS:
More sentences with *what* meaning *the thing that.*
1. What (the thing that) she lacks is time.
2. We must apply what we have learned.

7. The Louisiana territory, ________ more than four times the size of France, was purchased from France in 1803.

(A) the area
(B) an area
(C) the area has
(D) area with

STEP 1: Guess the problem from a brief glance at the choices: noun or noun phrase.

STEP 2: Simplify the sentence: Louisiana, . . . , was purchased . . .

STEP 3: Analyze: A phrase describes Louisiana.

STEP 4: Identify the answer. (B) is the proper answer. The sentence should be: The Louisiana territory, *an area* more than . . . , was purchased from . . .
Additional information: Why others are wrong:
(A) Incorrect article: there is not only one area that is four times the size of France.
(C) A verb can't be in this phrase.
(D) There is no article.

STEP 5: Testing point: Adjective phrase.

COMMENTS:
The commas indicate a phrase that describes the noun that came before it.

8. ________ was Charlie Chaplin admired as a first-class actor and comedian, but also he was well-known as a director.

(A) Now that
(B) Not that
(C) Never
(D) Not only

STEP 1: Guess the problem from a brief glance at the choices: negative.

STEP 2: Simplify the sentence: ________ was Charlie . . . admired as . . . , but also he was . . .
STEP 3: Analyze:
1. The inverted verb/subject form indicates that the sentence begins with a negative adverb.
2. The words *but also* indicate that you need to add something.
3. *Not only* goes with *but also.*

STEP 4: Identify the answer: (D) is the answer. The sentence should be: *Not only* was Charlie . . . admired as . . . , but also he was . . .

STEP 5: Testing point: not only . . . but also.

COMMENTS:
More examples of inverted verb forms:
Never had Joe stayed out so late means *Joe had never stayed so late.*

9. Capitalist society ________ profit as a valued goal.

(A) which regards
(B) regards
(C) was regarded
(D) regarded

STEP 1: Guess the problem from a brief glance at the choices: verb.

STEP 2: Simplify the sentence: . . . society . . . ________ profit as . . .

STEP 3: Analyze:
1. *Society* is a singular noun, the verb must agree
2. The verb form should be active voice.
3. Standard pattern: subject-verb-object.

STEP 4: Identify the answer:
(B) is the answer. The sentence should be: . . . society *regards* profit as . . .

STEP 5: Testing point: Verb form.

COMMENTS:
With questions about verbs, you should consider the following:
1. Singular/plural
2. Active/passive voice
3. Verb tense

10. Fathers are being encouraged to hold their newborns ________ develop a close relationship.

(A) therefore
(B) thus
(C) in order to
(D) in addition

STEP 1: Guess the problem from a brief glance at the choices: transition.

STEP 2: Simplify the sentence: Fathers are being encouraged to hold . . . develop . . .

STEP 3: Analyze:
The sentence needs a purpose or a reason connector.

STEP 4: Identify the answer:
(C) is the answer. The sentence should be: Fathers are being encouraged to hold . . . *in order to* develop . . .

STEP 5: Testing point: Subordinating conjunction/expression of purpose.

COMMENTS:
Other commonly used subordinating conjunctions: after, when, before, as, while, since, until although, even if, unless, lest, because, than, whether, so that, as soon as, as long as, as if, so . . . that, such . . . that, as . . . as.

Error Identification Directions: On the left side of the page are 10 sentences, each of which has four underlined words or phrases. The underlined parts of each sentence are marked (A), (B), (C), and (D). For each sentence, identify the one underlined word or phrase that must be changed in order for the sentence to be correct. Then read the step-by-step explanations in the box on the right side of the page.

1. *Jean-Christophe* is a two-thousand-page (A) novel original (B) published in (C) ten volumes (D).

STEP 1: Focus on underlined words.

STEP 2: Guess the testing point: word form. The answer is (B). Change *original* to *originally;* an adverb is needed to modify a past participle. (A) A hyphenated noun should be singular noun form. It is correct. (C) *in* is the correct preposition. (D) Plural noun is correct, agrees with *ten.*

STEP 3: Simplify sentence to check: . . . is a two-thousand-page novel originally published in . . . volumes.

COMMENTS:
1. Use adjective to modify noun.
2. Use adverb to modify verb, past participle, adjective, and present participle.

2. It (A) can take hundreds (B) of different experiments to achieve (C) a (D) ultimate solution.

STEP 1: Focus on the underlined words.

STEP 2: Guess the testing point: Article a/an/the.
(D) Change *a* to *an,* because *ultimate* begins with a vowel sound.
(A) The expletive *it* is followed correctly by an infinitive, *it . . . to achieve.*
(B) The plural noun is correct.
(C) *To achieve* is the correct infinitive form.

STEP 3: Simplify to check: *It can take hundreds . . . to achieve an ultimate solution.*

COMMENTS: Use *an* before a vowel sound, i.e., an umbrella, an umpire, an unhappy girl; *BUT:* a united country, a unified government, a unique spot. Use *an* before silent *h,* i.e., an hour.

3. Florence is a beautiful city which in people have successfully blended the modern with the ancient.
(A: a beautiful; B: which in; C: have successfully blended; D: with)

STEP 1: Focus on the underlined words.

STEP 2: Guess the testing point: word reversal.
(B) Change *which in* to *in which,* meaning *in the city* (Florence).
(A) *Beautiful* needs the article *a.*
(C) Correct present perfect tense. Use adverb to modify verb.
(D) The preposition after *blended* is correct.

STEP 3: Simplify to check: Florence is . . . beautiful city in which . . . people have successfully blended . . . with . . .

COMMENTS: *In whom* is used in a similar way, i.e., John is a man in whom I can put a lot of trust.

4. A certain amount of living space is important, but how many is enough?
(A: amount; B: is; C: but; D: many)

STEP 1: Focus on the underlined words.

STEP 2: Guess the testing point: many versus much; countable versus uncountable.
(D) *Many* doesn't agree with its antecedent *space.* Change *many* to *much* because *space* is an uncountable noun here. *Many* doesn't agree with the verb *is* either, so this is another way to identify the answer.
(A) This is correct since *space* is used as an uncountable noun.
(B) *Is* is correct because it agrees with the subject, *amount.*
(C) *But* is a correct transition.

STEP 3: Simplify to check: . . . space is . . . important but how much . . . ?

COMMENTS: Use *few* or *a few* for countable nouns; use *little* or *a little* for uncountable nouns.

5. When the night people's temperatures may drop, and it can be difficult to arouse them if their temperatures are still low in the morning.
(A: When; B: may drop; C: to arouse; D: low)

STEP 1: Focus on the underlined words.

STEP 2: Guess the testing point: Wrong word, when/in.
(A) The word *when* should begin a dependent clause, but in this sentence it doesn't, so the word is incorrect. It should be *in* or *during.*
(B) *May drop* is a correct verb that goes with the subject *temperatures.*
(C) The infinitive clause is correct.
(D) *Low* is the correct adjective.

STEP 3: Simplify to check: In the night . . . temperature may drop . . . it can be difficult . . .

6. Many psychologists today suggest (A) that we interpret dreams by compare (B) the dreams with (C) the reality of each person's life (D).

STEP 1: Focus on the underlined words

STEP 2: Guess the testing point: Word form; preposition + *-ing* form of the verb.
(B) Change *compare* to *comparing.* After a preposition, use a gerund form.
(A) This is a correct verb form.
(C) This is a correct preposition following *compare.*
(D) This is a correct singular possessive noun form.

STEP 3: Simplify to check: . . . psychologists today suggest that we interpret . . . by comparing . . . with the reality . . .

COMMENTS:
A preposition + *-ing* form commonly refers to the manner of doing something, i.e., *By working hard, you can learn quickly.*

7. Universities (A) in the United States can be supported either by government budgets (B) and (C) by private foundations (D).

STEP 1: Focus on the underlined words

STEP 2: Guess the testing point: conjunction, either/or.
(C) Change *and* to *or* because of the word *either; . . . either by . . . or by.*
(A) *Universities* is a correct plural noun.
(B) *Government budgets* is correct because *budgets* is a correct plural noun, and *government* as a noun modifies *budgets.*
(D) *Foundations* is a correct plural noun.

STEP 3: Simplify to check: Universities . . . either by government budgets or by . . . foundations.

COMMENTS: Other connectors that go together: neither . . . nor; both . . . and; as . . . as.

8. Mexico City (A) is definitely (B) one of the most large (C) cities (D) in the world.

STEP 1: Focus on the underlined words.

STEP 2: Guess the testing point: Superlative.
(C) Change *the most large* to *the largest.* Adjectives with one syllable form the superlative by adding *-est;*
(A) Both words are capitalized because both together are one name.
(B) This is a correct adverb modifying the verb.
(D) A plural noun must come after the phrase *one of . . . .*

STEP 3: Simplify to check: Mexico City . . . is one of the largest cities . . .

9. The monitor is used (A) with the IBM PC XT can be either (B) color or monochrome, but (C) it must have an adaptor installed (D) in the computer base.

STEP 1: Focus on the underlined words.

STEP 2: Guess the testing point: additional word.
(A) *Is used* is a passive verb form, but the main verb of the sentence is *can be*. Change *is used* to *used* which describes the monitor.
(B) This is a correct connector: *either . . . or*.
(C) *But* is a correct transition word; it introduces a contrasting idea.
(D) *Installed in* is a correct past participle modifying the noun *adaptor*.

STEP 3: Simplify to check: The monitor used with . . . can be either . . . or . . . but . . . .

COMMENTS: Use the past participle or present participle to modify a noun, i.e., *The shoes covered with mud are in the back room.*

10. The ingenuity of the Ban Chiang civilization which came (A) to China at less (B) 7000 years ago did not end with (C) bronze making (D).

STEP 1: Focus on the underlined words.

STEP 2: Guess the testing point: comparative.
(B) Change *at less* to *at least* or *less than*.
(A) This is the correct adjective clause describing *civilization*.
(C) This is the correct preposition.
(D) *Bronze making* is the correct gerund describing the act of making bronze.

STEP 3: Simplify to check: The ingenuity which came . . . at least 7000 years ago . . .

COMMENTS:
1. *Less* is followed by *than,* i.e., The civilization came less than 3000 years ago.
2. Quantifiers to tell how many or how much: for uncountable items use little, less, least, much, a great deal; for countable items use few, fewer, fewest, many, more, most

Drill 1 (Answers, page 205)

Directions: Choose the one word or phrase that best completes each sentence.

1. By measuring changing conditions in the atmosphere, ________ general weather patterns.
   (A) meteorologists who are predicting
   (B) meteorologists were predicted
   (C) predicting meteorologists
   (D) meteorologists can predict

2. Not until the end of the nineteenth century, ________ become a scientific discipline.
   (A) plant breeding had
   (B) did plant breeding
   (C) plant breeding have
   (D) have plant breeding

3. The cerebral cortex is ________ where the process of remembering faces takes place.
   (A) the area is brained
   (B) the area of the brain
   (C) and a brain area
   (D) brain area

4. By the end of the nineteenth century, Thomas Edison had invented the first practical light bulb, ________.
   (A) a source of cheap electrical light
   (B) the light of electricity cheap source
   (C) a source light cheap electrically
   (D) light with cheap electricity source

5. ________ about babies' feelings is inferred from their facial expressions.
   (A) What we know
   (B) To be known by us
   (C) Knowing
   (D) Known

6. ________, communities are formed in a variety of ways.
   (A) Created a division of labor
   (B) To create a division of labor
   (C) Create a division of labor
   (D) Creation of division of labor

7. Often weighing ________ 100 pounds, large dogs are used to pull sleds in the snow.
   (A) more than
   (B) just an
   (C) than it is
   (D) than

8. ________ some countries which have two seasons of the year instead of four seasons.
   (A) Are
   (B) Any
   (C) There are
   (D) There is

9. Approximately ninety per cent of the U.S. population will probably live in ________ near cities by the beginning of the year 2000.
   (A) or
   (B) for
   (C) so
   (D) by

10. Not until recently did scientists have enough data ________ to do a statistical analysis.
   (A) on animal life spans
   (B) life span on animals
   (C) difference about life animal spans
   (D) life span about animal difference

Drill 2 (Answers, page 205)

Directions: Choose the one word or phrase that best completes each sentence.

1. The conditions which are necessary ________ this project have not been met.
   (A) for the complete of
   (B) of completion of
   (C) for the completion of
   (D) of complete

2. ________ are found in virtually every country in the world.
   (A) Fruit flies and mosquitoes
   (B) Now that fruit flies and mosquitoes
   (C) When fruit flies and mosquitoes
   (D) Fruit flies and mosquitoes which

3. Successful salespeople ________ and understand the needs of the market.
   (A) products are thoroughly known
   (B) know their products thoroughly
   (C) thoroughly know their products are
   (D) their products are thoroughly known

4. The number of members of the executive board in a big corporation is fixed by the bylaws ________ by the president.
   (A) nevertheless
   (B) instead
   (C) despite
   (D) not

5. Lasers ________ steel by focusing an intense beam on the metal.
   (A) cutting
   (B) cut
   (C) to cut
   (D) of cutting

6. ________ common nuclear reaction, cold fusion does not require a high temperature.
   (A) Alike
   (B) It is unlikely
   (C) It is not like
   (D) Unlike

7. Native American people arrived on the North American continent _________ Europeans.
   (A) since
   (B) for
   (C) before
   (D) ahead

8. The ways of traveling _________ dramatically since the late nineteenth century.
   (A) will have changed
   (B) has changed
   (C) have changed
   (D) will change

9. How many of us _________ over complicated changes in the law!
   (A) not frustrated
   (B) not become frustrated
   (C) have not become frustrated
   (D) is not frustrated

10. A promissory note _________ anything without the trust deed.
   (A) does mean
   (B) is mean
   (C) have not mean
   (D) may not mean

Drill 3 (Answers, page 206)

Directions: Choose the one underlined portion of each sentence that must be changed in order for the sentence to be correct.

1. Leaves are believed (A) to be one of the best substance (B) to form (C) compost piles (D).

2. Wood is (A) an excellent resource (B) for heating (C) homes, cooking food, and build (D) houses.

3. River water pollution is (A) often indicator (B) by (C) algae distribution (D).

4. Modern farms (A) are much larger (B) than that (C) of former times (D).

5. It is (A) often not until the end of their lives that (B) famous people receive the recognize (C) they deserve (D).

6. Usually (A) the (B) climate in mountainous areas becomes much windy (C) at higher (D) altitudes.

7. A physical chemist (A) is required to (B) function (C) simultaneously as a physicist, chemistry (D), and mathematician.

8. A baby gorilla is a shy (A), friendly (B) animal that (C) like (D) attention.

9. Every liquid (A) has its own (B) threshold temperature which above (C) it becomes a gas (D).

10. After (A) being exposed to moist air, copper forms (B) a patina, the (C) thin green crust (D).

Drill 4 (Answers, page 206)

Directions: Choose the one underlined portion of each sentence that must be changed in order for the sentence to be correct.

1. Both (A) personality and external looking (B) vary (C) greatly even among (D) brothers and sisters.

2. Atomic units, the determinant (A) quantities of energy, time, length, charge, and to weight (B), are vital (C) to the functioning (D) of physical science.

3. A chemist's job often deals (A) with (B) the classify (C) of organic chemicals (D).

4. Trace contaminates can found (A) even (B) in purified gases (C) which are labeled 99.9999% pure (D).

5. Many scientists having (A) had their works (B) distributed by a scientific publishing (C) house based (D) in New York.

6. Some universities has (A) set up (B) small colleges for closer (C) relationships between (D) professors and students.

7. The number (A) of teaching assistants required meeting (B) undergraduate (C) course needs is rapidly (D) increasing.

8. Some skunks (A) can walking (B) briefly (C) on their hind (D) legs.

9. Franklin Delano Roosevelt, who (A) confined (B) to a (C) wheelchair, was (D) a very popular and successful U.S. president.

10. Not until (A) the electrolysis experiments of Michael Faraday, did the first ideas (B) about the nature of chemical bonding became (C) a serious (D) topic in chemistry.

Answer Key for Drills

Drill 1

1. D
2. B
3. B
4. A
5. A
6. B
7. A
8. C
9. A
10. A

Drill 2

1. C
2. A
3. B
4. D
5. B
6. D
7. C
8. C
9. C
10. D

Drill 3

1. B
2. D
3. B
4. C
5. C
6. C
7. D
8. D
9. C
10. C

Drill 4

1. B
2. B
3. C
4. A
5. A
6. A
7. B
8. B
9. B
10. C

Explanatory Answers

DRILL 1

1. (D) This sentence needs a subject and verb. The verb must be in the present tense (*can predict*) because the sentence is a general statement of fact.

2. (B) This is an inverted form for emphasis. Remember that *not until...did...* is a common structure. It means that plant breeding did not become a scientific discipline until the nineteenth century.

3. (B) This is a noun and prepositional phrase. It is necessary to use the word *the* two times because the sentence is referring to two specific items: the area and the brain.

4. (A) This phrase describes the light bulb with a noun plus prepositional phrase, *a source of cheap electrical light.*

5. (A) This sentence begins with a *wh* word in a noun clause as the subject of the sentence. The complete subject of the sentence is *what we know about babies' feelings*. The main verb is the word *is.*

6. (B) This sentence begins with an infinitive, *to create*. You could also say, *in order to create.*

7. (A) This is a comparison question. The weight of the dogs is compared to a measure of 100 pounds.

8. (C) This is a use of the expletive, *there are*. The verb must be plural to agree with the noun *countries.*

9. (A) The word *or* connects the words *in* and *near.* The meaning of the sentence is that the population might live either in cities or near cities.

10. (A) The prepositional phrase *on animal life spans* describes the data. The word *animal* describes the kind of life span. The words *life span* mean the length of time that a person or animal lives.

DRILL 2

1. (C) This sentence needs the noun *completion* to complete the prepositional phrase. Answer B is incorrect because the word *of* is incorrect and because the word *the* must come before the noun.

2. (A) This sentence needs a simple subject, not a phrase.

3. (B) The answer to this sentence must be a verb phrase with a verb in the present tense. Answers A and D are in the passive voice and answer C has two verbs so it does not combine with the rest of the sentence.

4. (D) This sentence uses the word *not* to begin a contrasting phrase.

5. (B) This sentence needs a plural present tense verb to go with the noun *lasers.*

6. (D) The word *unlike* shows a contrast between a common nuclear reaction and cold fusion.

7. (C) The word *before* is the correct time phrase. The word *since* is used to name the beginning of a time duration and the word *for* introduces a phrase of duration. The word *ahead* would be correct with the word *of.*

8. (C) This sentence needs a verb in the present perfect tense because of the phrase *since the late nineteenth century*. It must begin with *have* because of the plural noun *ways.*

9. (C) The word *have* is necessary in this sentence because the verb is in the present perfect tense, *have become*. Answer D is not correct because the verb is singular.

10. (D) This verb must be negative or use a modal because of the word *anything*. The answer cannot be answer C because if you use *have* then you must use the past participle form, *meant.*

DRILL 3

1. **(B)** The noun *substance* should be plural (*substances*) because it is in the phrase *one of the best substances.*
2. **(D)** This is a parallel construction sentence. The word *build* must be *building* to match *heating* and *cooking.*
3. **(B)** The noun *indicator* is incorrect. It should be a passive verb form: *indicated.*
4. **(C)** The word *that* should be *those* because it must be plural, referring to *farms.*
5. **(C)** The word *recognize* is a verb. In this sentence a noun is needed: *recognition.*
6. **(C)** This is a comparative sentence. The phrase *much windy* is incorrect. It should be *more windy.*
7. **(D)** This is a parallel construction sentence. Even though the three words in the series are all nouns, the word *chemistry* is a noun that describes a science. The other words are names of people. In this sentence you need a noun for the name for a person: *chemist.*
8. **(D)** The correct word should be *likes* because it must agree with the singular noun, *animal.*
9. **(C)** These two words are reversed. The correct answer is *above which it becomes a gas.* In this sentence, the word *which* refers to *threshold temperature.* The word *threshold* here means the point which produces a new response. Another way to say this sentence would be, *At a certain high temperature, every liquid becomes a gas.*
10. **(C)** This is an incorrect article. The correct word here is *a,* not *the* because the description *a thin green crust* is the definition of any patina.

DRILL 4

1. **(B)** This is an incorrect word form. The word *looking* should be *looks. External looks* refers to what people look like (hair color, eye color, tall, short, etc.)
2. **(B)** This is a parallel construction sentence. The correct word should be *weight,* the noun form. You could also classify this sentence as *additional word* since the sentence is correct without the word *to.*
3. **(C)** This is an incorrect word form. The correct word should be *classification,* the noun form.
4. **(A)** This is an omission sentence. The word *be* must be put between *can* and *found.* It is a passive verb.
5. **(A)** This is an incorrect verb form. The correct verb is a present perfect form, *have had.*
6. **(A)** The verb must agree with the plural subject *universities.* The correct answer is *have.*
7. **(B)** The necessary word here is an infinitive, *to meet.* The correct phrase is, *...required to meet course needs....* The word *needs* is a noun, not a verb. Another way to say this sentence is, *More teaching assistants are required to meet the needs of courses for undergraduates.*
8. **(B)** After the modal *can* the simple form of the verb must be used: *can walk.*
9. **(B)** This is an omission question. The word *was* must be added to make a correct passive voice: *was confined.*
10. **(C)** This is an incorrect verb tense. The correct word is *become.* It goes with the beginning of the sentence, *Not until..[time] ...did...[something]....become....*

Lesson 16

Vocabulary Questions and Skills

Objectives

- To learn about the types of questions in the vocabulary section
- To learn strategies for answering the vocabulary questions
- To learn what to do if you don't know the underlined word
- To learn two techniques for increasing your vocabulary

1. What is a Vocabulary Question?
2. Watson's Way: The Basic Strategy
3. Advice from Holmes
4. Increasing Your Vocabulary
5. Shooting in the Dark
6. Vocabulary Drills

16

Lesson 16

In the standard TOEFL, Section 3 contains 30 vocabulary questions. In the long form, there might be 45 vocabulary questions. Section 3 contains both vocabulary and reading comprehension, so you are able decide how much time to spend on each section. You can go back and forth between reading comprehension and vocabulary.

What Is a Vocabulary Question?

Below are the directions that are in the standard TOEFL exam. Read them to make sure that you understand them. You don't need to memorize them; these directions will be written in your exam when you take the test.

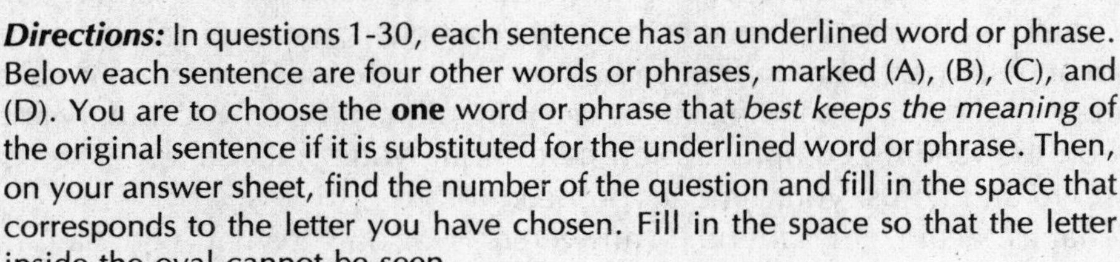

Directions: In questions 1-30, each sentence has an underlined word or phrase. Below each sentence are four other words or phrases, marked (A), (B), (C), and (D). You are to choose the **one** word or phrase that *best keeps the meaning* of the original sentence if it is substituted for the underlined word or phrase. Then, on your answer sheet, find the number of the question and fill in the space that corresponds to the letter you have chosen. Fill in the space so that the letter inside the oval cannot be seen.

EXAMPLE:

When the Titanic was sinking, very few people were evacuated.

(A) sheltered
(B) removed
(C) comforted
(D) frightened

Sample Answer

Ⓐ  Ⓒ Ⓓ

The best answer to this example is (B) *removed*. It is the one which best keeps the meaning of the word *evacuated*. The word *sheltered* means *protected*, the word *comforted* means *made to feel better*, and the word *frightened* means *afraid*. The preceding example is typical. The words chosen for the vocabulary section are standard written words. They are not usually idiomatic expressions, though sometimes they are short phrases like *in general* or *at the time of*.

Watson's Way: The Basic Strategy

Dr. Watson doesn't like to think about the vocabulary section of the test. After all, he says, "Nobody can learn all the words in the dictionary!" He has a fairly large vocabulary, however, so he usually does all right on the test. He is upset, though, because he doesn't know what words to study. And, since he feels that the reading comprehension section is more difficult, he doesn't spend much time preparing for the vocabulary section. His strategy is this:

1. Read the question.
2. Read the answer choices.
3. Look for a synonym for the underlined word.

Advice From Holmes

One day, as Dr. Watson was taking a practice test, Holmes stood behind him, puffing on his pipe. After a few moments, he said, "My dear Watson, you are making careless mistakes. Slow down."

"But Holmes," said Watson, "this vocabulary part is easier than the reading comprehension part. If I don't hurry, I won't have enough time to finish reading the passages in the next part."

"My dear man," said Holmes, "you do have a point, but remember this: you have an equal number of questions in each part and each question gets one point. We all know that reading comprehension takes longer and is more complicated, but you don't get any more points for it! Remember that your overall goal is to make points on this test. Since you might have a better chance of gaining points on this vocabulary part than on the reading part, slow down so you don't make any careless mistakes. Try spending about one third of the time on vocabulary and two thirds on the reading comprehension part during your practice test. Then check your score and adjust your time if you need to."

"Thanks again, my friend," answered Watson. "What you say makes sense."

Watson continued through the practice test. This time he did each question very thoroughly. Soon Holmes noticed that Watson was taking a very long time to take the practice test. He looked at Watson and asked, "Watson, my friend, why are you using your dictionary now?"

"I don't know the meaning of this word, 'artifacts,' " Watson answered.

"Let me have a look at your question," asked Holmes. He saw this:

Native American art and artifacts have been enthusiastically collected by admirers all over the world.

"Watson, I realize that you want to get all the answers correct, but during the test you can't use your dictionary. Try to figure out which words are the important ones to pay attention to. In this sentence you don't need to know the meaning of 'artifacts' to answer the question. You can skip over that word and focus on the underlined word."

"You've saved me time again," answered Watson. "I'll wait to use my dictionary until after I take the practice tests."

Watson continued with his test. This time he tried a new way to answer the questions quickly. He didn't even read the question; he just concentrated on the underlined word. He turned to Holmes, "Look at this word, 'house.' It's easy. I can save time by not even reading the whole sentence."

"Watch out, my friend," said Holmes. Easy words aren't always as easy as they seem. Read the whole sentence:

The museum is looking for a new building to <u>house</u> their modern art collection.

(A) build

(B) protect

(C) store

(D) establish

"The word 'house' is an easy noun, but in this sentence it is used as an verb. You have to read the whole sentence to know the meaning. If you don't know the verb form, you might pick 'protect' since a house will protect people. The correct answer, however, is 'store.' The word 'store' is also a verb, and it means 'to put away for the future.' The verb 'to house' means 'to put away in a house.' Both of these words are more commonly used as nouns, but you need to be familiar with their meanings as verbs too. You must read each sentence and check the part of speech of the underlined word."

Watson felt much more sure of his strategies now. He read each sentence, paying attention to the underlined word and skipping over the words that didn't seem necessary to the meaning of the underlined word.

Soon, however, Watson stopped again. He was puzzling over the next question. "Holmes," he called. "Here is another of those difficult questions. I know the meanings of the answer choices, and I have a general feeling of the meaning of the underlined word. I can eliminate two of the answer choices quite easily. But I can't choose between the other two choices. What should I do?"

"My dear fellow," answered Holmes. "Here we have another trick to use. Think of the relationship between the words. When you can't choose between two possible words, you may be mistaking 'cause and effect' for 'similar meaning.' Or you may be mistaking 'truth' for 'similar meaning.'"

"What do you mean?" asked Watson.

"Look at this example in your book:

Often before a storm breaks <u>an ominous</u> cloud appears overhead.

(A) a huge

(B) a rain

(C) a black

(D) a threatening

"I know that you have a good vocabulary and that you know the meanings of all the answer choices. Tell me the process that you go through to eliminate the wrong words." said Holmes.

"Well," said Watson. "I looked at the word 'huge' and I eliminated this one right away since I know that 'huge' means 'very large.' I figured that if 'ominous' meant 'very large,' I would probably have heard of it."

"That sounds good," said Holmes. "Continue."

"And then I eliminated the word 'rain' because, even though storms come from rain clouds, every rain cloud doesn't produce a storm. There are light, gentle spring rains and there are also snowstorms. So this answer didn't seem like it would be correct."

"You amaze me, my friend," responded Holmes. "You are using excellent skills. The words 'huge' and 'rain' make *true* sentences, but they are not synonyms for 'ominous.'"

"But now I have a problem," said Watson. "I can't decide between the next two words. I know the meaning of 'black' of course. Could 'ominous' be a synonym for 'black'?"

"Well, my friend," said Holmes. "this answer choice is more difficult. But it helps that you have a general feeling that 'ominous' means something negative. I'm sure you realize that storm clouds are dark, but even though this is true, the relationship is a cause/result relationship. The clouds are black because it is going to rain. But 'ominous' doesn't always mean 'black.' Here is another sentence: 'In the dark, I heard an ominous noise coming from alley.' In this sentence, 'ominous' does not have the meaning of 'black' at all. The answer to this question is (D) threatening. Use your logical thinking skills and the process of elimination to help you make that guess."

"Well Holmes, I'm almost finished with this practice test," said Watson, "but I have one more problem. Here is my last question. I know that I have studied this word before, but I can't remember the meaning. This one really bothers me since I feel that I can almost remember it, but not quite. What would you do in this case?"

Holmes thought for a minute and answered, "Think of the situation in which you remember hearing or seeing that word. If you can imagine the situation when you first heard or saw the word, you might have a clue about the meaning. I see the word that you are talking about: 'exotic.'"

> At the year-end gardener's sale, you have the chance to buy <u>exotic</u> plants at a good price.
>
> **(A)** unusual
>
> **(B)** ferocious
>
> **(C)** delicate
>
> **(D)** outdoor

"That's right," said Watson. "I know the meaning of 'unusual' and 'outdoor' and I think I know the meaning of 'delicate,' but I don't know anything about 'ferocious.' It's hard to eliminate any of the answer choices."

Holmes gave Watson this advice: "Try to think back to the time when you heard or saw the word, 'exotic.'" '

"Let me think," said Watson. "Oh, I remember. It was in an advertisement for vacations: I remember the phrase 'a trip to an exotic tropical beach.' "

"O.K," said Holmes. "Let's think about the meaning of that phrase. What kind of vacation would a travel agent want to advertise? Look at your answer choices. 'Outdoor' is possible, but all beaches are outdoors. 'Delicate' usually means 'needing careful attention' or 'easily broken.' That wouldn't be a good choice for this advertisement. 'Unusual' means 'uncommon.' That's the best guess! Wouldn't a travel agent want to advertise something that is not usual, something different from everyday life? My point is this: if you try to remember everything you can about where you saw a word, you get some clues to the meaning. Then you can use your logical thinking skills to help you guess an answer."

"Holmes, you have helped me immensely. I'm going to go take a walk now and consider all the clues you have given me."

Summary of Holmes' Advice

1. Read the question, focusing on the underlined word.
2. Work carefully so you don't make careless errors.
3. Don't spend a long time on other words in the sentence that you don't know. Sometimes these other words won't affect your answer, especially if they are the names of people or events.
4. Read the complete sentence and all the answer choices, even if you think you know the right answer.
5. Remember that you are looking for a synonym, not a cause and effect relationship or a true sentence.
6. Use logic to help you guess.

Increasing Your Vocabulary

We learn vocabulary in different ways, depending on what our purposes are and what the situation is. There are some words that we know but don't use actively. There are other words that we want to be able to use correctly in our everyday lives. When studying new words, sometimes a word will immediately become a part of our active vocabulary and we always remember it. At other times, however, we seem to forget new words very quickly. When studying new words, it is frustrating to spend a lot of time trying to memorize the words and then forget them all later. It seems like a waste of time.

In this section, you are given two methods for learning new words. In the first method, you only try to get a feeling for the meaning of the words without making them an active part of your vocabulary. To understand the purpose of this method, think of learning vocabulary like learning about new friends. When you are involved with new people, you get to know them little by little. When you first become acquainted you remember only their names and maybe their hairstyles, eye colors, or clothes. This is only a surface understanding. Later on, you get to know them better and they become friends. Method 1 describes a technique for getting acquainted with the meanings of new words. Method 2 is a way of learning words in order to make them an active part of your vocabulary.

Vocabulary Learning Method 1: Getting Acquainted

One way of learning new words is by playing with the words, rather than by memorizing the definitions. In this method, you are just getting acquainted with the words, not making them an active part of your vocabulary. You are getting a feeling for the meaning of the word. This method helps you prepare for the TOEFL exam because for the vocabulary section you don't need to write, spell, pronounce, or use the word correctly in a sentence. All you have to know is the meaning of the word so that you can pick out a synonym. You can use the words in Lesson 17 to practice this method.

Free Association

Choose a page of words from Lesson 17 or a list of any words that you want to learn and read through the list fairly quickly. Read the words, the explanations, and the example sentences. Then pick five or ten of the words you don't know and begin free association.

Free association means that you write any words that come to mind when you look at the new word and its definition. You might write a synonym, an opposite word, a word with similar spelling, a word from your own memory, or a word in your own language. Any word is OK. *Don't* copy a meaning from the dictionary. It is important that the words you write come from your own mind. Let your mind be free. Write anything you think of.

EXAMPLE:

mythical *(adj.)* a person or thing that is imagined or invented
Some cultures have old stories of *mythical* animals who came to Earth.

Free Association:
my
call
imagine
animal
story
unreal
unicorn
(You might add something in your own language)

When you have your list of words, you can do several things to help you remember the new words. The main point is for you to become familiar with the word. Even if your list of free associated words is not the same as the definition of the new words, the list will help you remember the new words. Write a free association for several words. Then try the activities below.

Activity 1: Cover your lists of free association and look only at the new words. Can you remember what words you wrote in your free association? Write them down again without looking at them. If you think of a new free association word, write it too.

Activity 2: Cover the new words and look at your lists of free association. Can you remember the new word for each list? Think of each of the new words. How does each one look? What is its shape? Try to remember the new word and write it down, even if you can't spell it correctly. Write it down in the way you think it looks. It doesn't matter if it is spelled wrong. Remember that this is only the first step in getting to know new words. You are not trying to know everything about the word yet.

Activity 3: Look at your new words again. Do another free association with the words that you forget. Sometimes a very strange picture in your mind will help you remember the words better. For instance, look at the following free association:

New Word: ambrosia
Free Association:
Asia
broken
ant
(I can't remember this word, so I look at the meaning again and see that it means something delicious to drink or eat. Now I picture in my mind a broken glass filled with delicious ants that I am drinking as I stand on map of Asia.)

Continue this free association technique, adding new lists of words every day. Go over the words four or five times. Keep reviewing the old words. Have fun with this method of learning. Write anything that you think of. You are not learning to *use* the words correctly yet, only to recognize them and remember a general meaning.

Vocabulary Learning Method 2: Becoming Friends

Method 1 helps you recognize new words, but it doesn't help you use them correctly. In order to actively use new words, you need to know a lot more about them.

Is the word formal or informal?
What kinds of situations is the word used in?
How is the word pronounced?
How is the word spelled?
What part of speech is this word?
Are there any prepositions that must follow the word?
Is there a common phrase that this word is used in?
What are the other forms of the word?

For the TOEFL it is usually unnecessary to use the words actively yourself. For your general knowledge of English, however, it is important to learn as much as you can about new words. The list below gives some ways to increase your active use of new vocabulary.

1. **Be an active reader.** Be aware of the new words you see, but don't stop reading to look up every new word in your dictionary. Instead, try to figure out the meaning of the whole passage that you are reading. To help you remember the new words, mark in pencil in your book beside the new words. Then when you are finished reading the whole passage, look up the words. Think about the meaning in the context of the passage you have just read. This will help you remember the meaning as well as the situation and the grammatical use.
2. **Keep your own list of words to learn and remember.** Get the words from your friends; from the radio or television; or from books, magazines, or newspapers. Every time you hear a word you want to know, write it down in a book that you always keep with you. Guess at the spelling. Try to write the whole sentence you heard. Also write down the situation that

you heard the word in. Then ask a friend to help you understand the meaning of the word. If there is no one to ask, then try to find the word in your dictionary. Then put it in your own "personal dictionary." Write the word, the meaning, and a sentence that makes sense to you. Add to this personal dictionary whenever you hear or see a word that you want to learn, and keep looking over your personal dictionary to remind yourself of the new words.

3. **Use the TOEFL word list in Lesson 17 as a guide.** In addition to free associating (Method 1), refer to the list whenever you get a chance. You don't have to go through the words in order, but just glance over any of the words. Notice whether any of these words are in other material you are reading. Learn to recognize other forms of these words (noun, verb, adjective, etc.).
4. **Practice your new words.** Try using them, even if you aren't sure that you are using them correctly. Ask your friends or teachers to correct you if you are using them wrong.

Shooting in the Dark

Some of the vocabulary questions may have words that you don't know at all. If that happens, try the following:

1. Use your knowledge of roots, prefixes, or suffixes to guess the meaning.

EXAMPLE:

Most recipients of the peace prize are given the award in person, but sometimes the award is given <u>posthumously</u>.

(A) when the person is out of the country
(B) after the person has died
(C) to political prisoners
(D) by mail

Let's go through each answer choice, with the assumption that you know that one meaning of *post* is *after* or *behind*.

(A) Eliminate this choice since it doesn't have a meaning of being after of behind something.
(B) A possible choice because *post* means *after*.
(C) A possible choice because if people are in jail, they are behind bars.
(D) A possible choice if the word *post* is about mail, rather than being a Latin prefix.

You now have three possible choices and one eliminated. If you know more about root words you might know that *humous* comes from the Latin word *humus*, meaning *the ground, the earth*. Now using your knowledge of Latin you should choose answer (B), by inferring that *after a person has died* could also be stated as *after a person is buried in the ground*. Answer (B) is the correct answer.

2. **Sometimes you can eliminate some of the answer choices because they look too similar.** A word that looks like the underlined word is sometimes put there just to confuse you.

EXAMPLE:

An important aspect of being a professor is the ability to work well with colleagues.

(A) students
(B) colleges
(C) business managers
(D) fellow workers

The words *colleges* and *colleagues* look similar, but have two very different meanings. *College* refers to a place; *colleague* refers to people that you work with. The correct answer is (D).

3. **If you are out of time or anxious to go ahead with the reading comprehension part, then be sure to fill in all blanks.** As a last resort, just fill in all the B ovals on your answer sheet. Never leave a question blank!

Summary

1. The underlined words are standard written English, not usually idiomatic English.
2. Half of your points in Section 3 come from the vocabulary part.
3. In the vocabulary section you only have to recognize the words and choose a synonym, not use them in sentences.
4. You don't need to spell the words or pronounce them correctly.
5. Your memory of the situation can help you guess at forgotten words.
6. Free association can help you remember the meanings of words.
7. Become an active reader and listener in order to add new words to your everyday use of English.
8. Sometimes a knowledge of prefixes, suffixes, and roots can help you guess a meaning.

Vocabulary Drills

This part contains five vocabulary drills. The first drill is called a "Walk-Through." Because it presents the answers and explanations right next to the questions, the Walk-Through can help you understand the thought process you need to go through to answer vocabulary questions.

The other four drills provide additional practice in answering TOEFL vocabulary questions. Most of the underlined words and answer choices in the drills are defined in the TOEFL Word List in Lesson 17.

Walk-Through

Directions: For each question, choose the one word or phrase which would best keep the meaning of the original sentence if it were substituted for the underlined word or phrase. Then read the right side for an explanation of each answer choice.

1. In order to remind people to drive safely, the police put up billboards with graphic displays of accidents.

(A) clear
(B) bloody
(C) dangerous
(D) colorful

1. (A) You might recognize the word *graph* as meaning a drawing or diagram. *Graphic* refers to being vivid or lifelike or clearly illustrated. Your knowledge of root words might help you with this question. The Greek root word *graph* means *write,* which you can associate with *clear.*

2. Seeing the Grand Canyon from the air is a sight to behold.

(A) hold on to
(B) remember
(C) anticipate
(D) gaze upon

2. (D) *To gaze upon* means to look intently upon something. Both *gaze* and *behold* have a feeling of wonder or love attached to them. We might say "gaze lovingly at the child," as though you are holding the child in your eyes. The words *hold on to* mean *to grab* or *attach on to.* There is no feeling of wonder in these words; in fact, there is the opposite feeling of fear or anxiety. You might use "hold on to a memory," but here you still have the feeling of anxiety because the memory might go away. Answer (B) might be a true statement, but it does not have the feeling of wonder. Answer (C) means to look forward to something that has not yet happened.

3. Ramps make public buildings more accessible to handicapped people.

(A) comparable to
(B) desirable for
(C) approachable for
(D) independent for

3. (C) If you have access to something, you can get it. *Approachable* is the closest meaning. Answer (A) is incorrect because nothing is compared. Answer (B) may be true, but this is a cause/result relationship: if it is accessible, it is probably desirable. Answer (D) is also a result: if the building is accessible, it allows the handicapped person to be independent.

4. The foremost item on the Congressman's agenda was the budget.

(A) only
(B) first
(C) most enthralling
(D) most perplexing

4. (B) Your knowledge of prefixes can help you here. *Fore* means *before* or *coming first.* Answer (A) means that there is no other. Answer (C) is close to *very interesting,* and answer (D) means *difficult to understand.*

5. There has been a lot of talk of rainfall as of late.

(A) recently
(B) today
(C) coming soon
(D) later this year

6. In some paintings, one color seems to dissolve into another.

(A) separate
(B) flow
(C) drive
(D) soar

7. Rabbits burrow in the woods and in other protected places.

(A) hunt
(B) reproduce
(C) sleep
(D) dig

8. Tapestries, carpets, and drapes can be damaged by too much glare.

(A) sunlight
(B) water
(C) mold
(D) mud

9. The elaborate detail on Victorian-style homes is known as "gingerbread."

(A) garages
(B) carriages
(C) houses
(D) roofs

10. Some studies indicate that exercise relieves stress.

(A) anxiety
(B) tension
(C) disharmony
(D) serenity

5. (A) *As of late* can mean at any time in the recent past. Answer (B) may be true in this sentence, but the time period (one day) is too short to be a synonym for *as of late*. Answer (C) refers to a future time, and answer (D) not only refers to a future time but also would refer to the rainfall itself instead of the talk about rainfall.

6. (B) *Dissolve* usually means *to become liquid,* but in this sentence it refers more to merging together. Answer (A) is the opposite of merging or flowing together. Answer (C) *drive* has no relationship to *dissolve,* and answer (D) *soar* means to fly or rise into the air.

7. (D) The word *burrow* can be a noun or a verb. As a noun, a burrow is a hole or tunnel dug by an animal for shelter. This sentence uses the verb form, meaning *dig a burrow.* An animal may go to its burrow after hunting (answer A), to reproduce (answer B), or to sleep (answer C).

8. (A) *Glare* is the strong light that comes from the direct sun. We wear sunglasses in order to keep the glare out of our eyes. The other answers might all be true, but they are not synonyms.

9. (C) There are usually a few questions on each exam that seem very easy, but be sure to read each complete sentence just to be sure the underlined word is actually used in the form you are familiar with.

10. (B) This is another question where you might get confused between cause and result. Answer (B) gives a synonym, whereas answer (A) is either a cause or result of stress. Answer (C) can also be a cause or result of stress. Answer (D) is the opposite of stress.

Drill 1 (Answers, page 224)

Directions: For each question choose the one word or phrase which would best keep the meaning of the original sentence if it were substituted for the underlined word or phrase.

1. A major portion of water in the United States is used for agricultural purposes.

(A) needs
(B) farmland
(C) innovation
(D) surveys

2. Young teenage boys are often shorter than girls their age.

(A) not as creative as
(B) not as tall as
(C) more aggressive than
(D) more active than

3. Scientists around the world are working on methods of predicting earthquakes.

(A) surmising
(B) foretelling
(C) verifying
(D) advocating

4. Mythical creatures have been a part of the folklore of many cultures throughout the centuries.

(A) Appealing
(B) Magical
(C) Legendary
(D) Fighting

5. From an airplane, farms dotting the countryside look like toys.

(A) scattered across
(B) bordering
(C) separating
(D) running into

6. One of the most celebrated holidays in the United States is Christmas.

(A) curious
(B) elaborate
(C) imitated
(D) famous

7. The precision of tools in a computer manufacturing company is critical.

(A) cleanliness
(B) accuracy
(C) temperature
(D) size

8. Everyone would like a panacea for health problems.

(A) protection against
(B) advice for
(C) a cure-all for
(D) a decrease in

9. People often marvel over the intense colors in tropical sunsets.

(A) vivid
(B) glowing
(C) harsh
(D) penetrating

10. Nonfat milk has slightly less fat than low-fat milk.

(A) even
(B) much
(C) a lot
(D) a little

11. It can be detrimental to your health to eat decayed food.

(A) rotten
(B) raw
(C) dirty
(D) ripe

12. Science researchers are looking into ways to extend human life.

(A) impeding
(B) anticipating
(C) dissecting
(D) investigating

13. In order to be a good cheerleader, one must be very enthusiastic.

(A) healthy
(B) excited
(C) limber
(D) strong

14. A new president tries to embody a new spirit during his first term in office.

(A) enjoy
(B) demonstrate
(C) expand
(D) gain

DRILL 2 (Answers, page 224)

Directions: For each question choose the one word or phrase which would best keep the meaning of the original sentence if it were substituted for the underlined word or phrase.

1. From the beginning of time, people have puzzled over the forces of the supernatural.
   (A) paid tribute to
   (B) wondered about
   (C) been frightened about
   (D) reported on

2. The surgeon general of the United States has warned against the consumption of alcohol and other addictive drugs.
   (A) cautioned
   (B) demonstrated
   (C) guarded
   (D) argued

3. At the end of each season, stores will often cut their prices to encourage sales.
   (A) review
   (B) reduce
   (C) do away with
   (D) make use of

4. Confined to a small space, a tree will not reach its natural height.
   (A) Attributed
   (B) Compared
   (C) Coupled
   (D) Limited

5. An aquarium often has a tube that releases oxygen into the tank.
   (A) pushes
   (B) loosens
   (C) emits
   (D) withdraws

6. During a drought there is hardly enough water to irrigate the fields.
   (A) scarcely
   (B) probably
   (C) variably
   (D) undeniably

7. In the fall it is gratifying to see stalks of wheat ready for harvest.
   (A) terrifying
   (B) satisfying
   (C) surprising
   (D) relaxing

8. Optimal weather conditions for fuschias include foggy mornings and temperatures above freezing.
   (A) Elaborate
   (B) Necessary
   (C) Most critical
   (D) Most advantageous

9. Buildings planned for earthquake zones need to allow for lateral movement.
   (A) incredible
   (B) violent
   (C) sideways
   (D) front to back

10. The exchange of goods for services is a concept that developed during primitive times.
    (A) influence
    (B) stockpiling
    (C) gathering
    (D) trade

11. Sometimes a haphazard event will stimulate scientific research.
    (A) a shocking
    (B) a forbidden
    (C) a chance
    (D) an inevitable

12. Plastic-ring holders used to carry cans and bottles can entangle fish and birds.
    (A) catch
    (B) guard against
    (C) patronize
    (D) rotate

13. The aim of the Montreal Protocol was to reduce chlorofluorocarbon emission in the atmosphere by 50 percent.
    (A) barrier
    (B) command
    (C) draft
    (D) goal

14. New machines have made duplication an easy job.
    (A) copying
    (B) typing
    (C) filing
    (D) writing

DRILL 3 (Answers, page 224)

Directions: For each question choose the one word or phrase which would best keep the meaning of the original sentence if it were substituted for the underlined word or phrase.

1. Before the explosion in the sale of personal computers, people spent a lot more time using typewriters.

(A) Suceeding
(B) Due to
(C) At the time of
(D) Prior to

2. Because of the work of brave astronauts, space exploration has achieved many of its goals.

(A) exciting
(B) courageous
(C) meticulous
(D) inventive

3. Babies work persistently at learning things such as hand-eye coordination.

(A) repeatedly
(B) occasionally
(C) intricately
(D) melodiously

4. The number of women working in mechanical jobs increases yearly.

(A) nourishes
(B) weighs
(C) grows
(D) varies

5. The widespread use of poisonous chemical fertilizers has been curtailed.

(A) secret
(B) general
(C) solitary
(D) rewarding

6. Dramatic changes have occurred in the earth's features since the Ice Age.

(A) appearance
(B) fossils
(C) functions
(D) pulp

7. In order to protect young children it is important to cover electrical outlets.

(A) batteries
(B) faucets
(C) sockets
(D) appliances

8. Gas stations are often situated on busy intersections.

(A) founded
(B) requested
(C) placed
(D) secluded

9. The smell of leaking gas easily penetrates a building.

(A) overlaps
(B) retreats from
(C) spreads through
(D) reaches

10. Among its other evils, a forest fire destroys the shelter used by thousands of wild animals.

(A) undomesticated
(B) shrewd
(C) savage
(D) undesirable

11. The world watched as Prince Charles and Lady Diana were wed.

(A) crowned
(B) married
(C) honored
(D) photographed

12. All information that is given in almanacs must be verified.

(A) unique
(B) informative
(C) checked
(D) interesting

13. Easter usually marks the advent of spring.

(A) disappearance
(B) festivities
(C) luck
(D) coming

14. Ralph Nader is an advocate of the people.

(A) a spokesperson for
(B) a fighter against
(C) a colleague with
(D) a commander of

DRILL 4 (Answers, page 224)

Directions: For each question choose the one word or phrase which would best keep the meaning of the original sentence if it were substituted for the underlined word or phrase.

1. Over the centuries there are gradual movements of the Earth's tectonic plates.
   (A) frequent
   (B) sudden
   (C) indivisable
   (D) small

2. Slow maturation in cool mountain air enhances the taste of coffee beans.
   (A) augments
   (B) attracts
   (C) arouses
   (D) acquires

3. A trickle of water over rocks can be very soothing.
   (A) An outburst
   (B) An explosion
   (C) A slow flow
   (D) A rush

4. Agent Orange has been linked to health problems of military veterans.
   (A) responsible for
   (B) connected to
   (C) used in
   (D) effective against

5. A misplaced billboard can totally obscure a scenic highway view.
   (A) hide
   (B) mar
   (C) damage
   (D) remove

6. Human fetal brain cells have been transplanted into the brains of adults.
   (A) copied
   (B) placed
   (C) pointed
   (D) fertilized

7. The Green Revolution was supposed to put an end to world hunger.
   (A) border
   (B) limit
   (C) stop
   (D) extend

8. The U.S. Congress office building is adjacent to the Capitol building.
   (A) next to
   (B) far from
   (C) within
   (D) behind

9. A truck driver must be alert at all times.
   (A) careful
   (B) astute
   (C) bold
   (D) awake

10. Charlie Chaplin was known for his comical performances.
    (A) polished
    (B) funny
    (C) poignant
    (D) clever

11. The caustic action of battery acid can destroy clothing.
    (A) burning
    (B) dangerous
    (C) explosive
    (D) debilitating

12. The U.S. government has special funds to offer to destitute people after major castastrophes.
    (A) lonely
    (B) sad
    (C) poor
    (D) sick

13. The inner areas of large cities often contain dilapidated buildings.
    (A) office
    (B) ruined
    (C) tall
    (D) important

14. "Mark Twain" is the fictitious name of Samuel Clemens.
    (A) middle
    (B) false
    (C) family
    (D) baptismal

Answer Key for Drills

Most of the underlined words and the answer choices are defined in the TOEFL Word List in Lesson 17.

Drill 1	Drill 2	Drill 3	Drill 4
1. A	**1.** B	**1.** D	**1.** D
2. B	**2.** A	**2.** B	**2.** A
3. B	**3.** B	**3.** A	**3.** C
4. C	**4.** D	**4.** C	**4.** B
5. A	**5.** C	**5.** B	**5.** A
6. D	**6.** A	**6.** A	**6.** B
7. B	**7.** B	**7.** C	**7.** C
8. C	**8.** D	**8.** C	**8.** A
9. A	**9.** C	**9.** C	**9.** D
10. D	**10.** D	**10.** A	**10.** B
11. A	**11.** C	**11.** B	**11.** A
12. D	**12.** A	**12.** C	**12.** C
13. B	**13.** D	**13.** D	**13.** B
14. B	**14.** A	**14.** A	**14.** B

Lesson 17

TOEFL Word List

Objectives

- To become familiar with the level of words that have been on previous TOEFL exams
- To provide a list of 570 words that are useful to know
- To give definitions and example sentences for each word

Lesson 17

TOEFL Vocabulary

Most of the words on the following list have been used in past TOEFL tests. Some of them have been the selected words in vocabulary questions and others have been used as answer choices. All of them represent the typical level of words used on TOEFL tests.

Use this list as a guide to your studying. As you probably know, the sentences used in the vocabulary section of the TOEFL are not repeated on future tests. Some of the words on this list have been repeated, however. Also, these words might be found in the reading section, the structure section, or the listening section of any TOEFL test.

As you know, words often have several different meanings; this list gives only one or two sentences for each word. When you come to a word that you are unfamiliar with, study the given meaning, but also look in your dictionary for other meanings. The underlined words and many of the answer choices in the vocabulary drills in Lesson 16 are defined in this TOEFL Word List. Use the vocabulary drills as practice tests to see how much you know from this list of words.

TOEFL Word List

abhor *(verb)* to hate or think of with disgust
The man abhorred the feel of snakes.

abject *(adj.)* poor or miserable; thought to be worthless
The family lived in abject poverty.
The woman gave an abject apology.

accelerate *(verb)* to increase the speed
This car accelerates quickly.

accentuate *(verb)* to give force to or draw attention to
Her blue scarf accentuated her blue eyes.

accessible *(adj.)* able to be reached; convenient
Elevators in tall buildings make the top floors accessible to everyone.

acclaim *(verb)* to give approval; to applaud
The man was acclaimed as a great actor.

accurate *(adj)*; accuracy (*noun*) exact; correct
In order to get 100 percent on the test, you must be accurate.

acrid *(adj.)* sharp, bitter smell or taste
The factory put out an acrid smell.

adjacent to *(adj.)* next to; near, but not necessarily touching
Our garage is adjacent to our house.

adjoin *(verb)* be next to or nearest to
The two houses are adjoining.

advantageous *(adj.)* profitable; helpful
Sometimes it is advantageous to own a car.

advent *(noun)* the arrival of an important development/season/person
Since the advent of nuclear power, there have been great changes in industry.

advocate *(noun/verb)* a person who supports or speaks in favor of something; to support
Our group is an advocate of equal opportunity for men and women.

affect *(verb)* to have an influence on
The cold climate affected the woman's health.

aforementioned *(adj.)* said or written before
The aforementioned topic is one of great interest.

aim *(noun/verb)* a purpose or goal; to point a weapon or direct a remark in order to hit something
The chairperson's remarks were aimed at graduating seniors.

alert/alertly *(adj./adv.)* fully awake and ready to act
The guard watched alertly as the people appeared.

alienate *(verb)* to cause a person to become unfriendly or indifferent
The candidate's angry speech alienated the listeners.

amass *(verb)* to collect or pile up
The rich man had amassed his fortune over several years.

ambition *(noun)* strong desire for success or fame
She works hard because of her great ambition to be a famous writer.

ambrosia *(noun)* food that has a delightful taste or smell; "food of the gods"
This fantastic dish tastes like ambrosia.

amend/amendment *(verb/noun)* improve; correct; a change made to a rule
Will the prisoner ever amend his behavior?
This new amendment to the law should bring justice to more people.

anomaly *(noun)* something abnormal or unusual
A bird that cannot fly is an anomaly.

anticipate *(verb)* to do something before someone else or before the right time; to see what is likely to happen in the future
The theater manager anticipated a large crowd for the performance.

anxiety *(noun)* an emotional condition of fear and uncertainty
Her family waited with anxiety for the news of her safe arrival.

apex *(noun)* the highest point; the top
The apex of the triangle faces to the north.

appall/appalling *(verb/adj.)* fill with fear; shock
The number of people who starved in the famine was appalling.

appeal to *(verb)* make a request; to call for help or sympathy; to attract
The organization for homeless people appealed to the county government for financial help.
That music appeals to me.

appear *(verb)* to come into view; to become visible
At dawn the sun appears on the horizon.

appliance *(noun)* a piece of equipment
A washing machine is an appliance I want to buy.

appropriate *(adj.)* suitable; proper
A wedding dress is not appropriate to wear to a beach party.

approximate *(adj.)* almost the same; more or less correct; close to
The approximate speed I was driving was 30 miles per hour.

apt *(adj.)* likely; appropriate; relevant
The mischievous child is apt to get into trouble.
Your statement is not apt to this conversation.

arduous *(adj.)* difficult; using much energy
Mountain climbing can be an arduous sport.

arouse *(verb)* to awaken; to cause to become active
My father used to arouse us at 6 A.M.

articulate *(verb)* to speak distinctly or clearly; to connect or be jointed
The speaker was able to articulate his words well.

as of late *(conj. + adj.)* recently
I've been feeling tired as of late.

aspect *(noun)* the particular way something appears; the look or appearance of something
To learn something well you must study it from all aspects.

astute *(adj.)* clever, quick
The astute student answered all the questions correctly.

attempt *(noun/verb)* the act of trying; to make an effort; to try
The prisoner escaped after three attempts.
The prisoner attempted to escape three times.

attribute *(verb)* to consider something as the result of something else
I attribute my success to my hard work.

augment *(verb)* to make something greater; to add to
I work at a weekend job to augment my income.

authoritative *(adj.)* having authority; commanding
The authoritative manner of the general made us respect him.

autonomy *(noun)* the right of self-government
The angry factory workers were demanding autonomy.

back and forth *(adv.)* movement: first one way and then the other
The anxious man walked back and forth across the room.

bare *(adj.)* without clothing or protection
Would you pick up live bees with your bare hands?

barely *(adv.)* only a bit; hardly
I barely know my new neighbors; they just moved in.

barrier *(noun)* something that prevents movement or progress
Mountains are a natural barrier between two valleys.

barter *(verb)* to exchange goods or property for other goods or property
Ancient societies bartered food before they had money.

beak *(noun)* the hard, horny part of a bird's mouth
The bird picked up a fish with its beak.

behold *(verb)* to look at, to observe
The clear blue-green lake is a lovely sight to behold.

bend *(verb)* to cause something to curve or be at an angle
Wire will bend easily, but steel will not.

beneficial *(adj.)* helpful
Fresh air and good food are beneficial to your health.

beyond *(prep)* farther than, later than, surpassing, exceeding
Don't stay out beyond midnight.
He lives beyond his income.

bind *(verb)* to tie or fasten, to hold to an agreement
The robbers bound the man's legs together so he couldn't escape (*past tense*).

bite, biting *(verb/adj.)* to cut with the teeth, the act of cutting with the teeth, an injury resulting from a sting or bite; a sharpness or sting.
We take bites when we eat.
In January we usually have a biting wind.

bizarre *(adj.)* very odd or unusual
The costumes for this play are bizarre.

bleak *(adj.)* cold, miserable, bare
The weather is bleak in December.

blunder *(verb)* to move with uncertainty; to make foolish mistakes
The candidate for president was careful not to blunder in his speech.

bold *(adj.)* without fear or shame
The bold explorers discovered new paths through the dangerous mountains.

border *(noun)* the edge, the line or boundary between two places
The lake is on the border of two countries.

brave *(adj.)* ready to face danger, having no fear, having courage
The brave soldier was ready to fight for his life.

breach *(noun)* a breaking or neglect of a rule or agreement
Fighting in the streets is a breach of the peace.

brink *(noun)* the edge of something, the upper edge of a steep place
He was on the brink of an emotional breakdown.

bump *(noun/verb)* a swelling; to move with a jerking motion
I have a bump on my arm from the bee sting.
The old car bumped down the dirt road.

burrow *(noun/verb)* a hole made in the ground by a small animal, such as a rabbit; to make a hole as a place of protection
The fox lived in a burrow in the woods.
The rabbit burrowed in its hole to hide from the dog.

bush *(noun)* a low-growing plant with many stems
The trees, bushes, and flowers in the park are beautiful.

bushy *(adj.)* growing thickly; rough and thick
That man has very bushy eyebrows.

by degrees *(adv.)* gradually
Their friendship grew by degrees.

by-product *(noun)* anything produced in the course of making something else; a secondary product
Molasses is a by-product of sugar.

by rights *(adv.)* if justice were done
This property is mine by rights.

campaign *(noun)* a series of planned activities intended to win votes for a candidate for public office
The man's campaign included months of traveling and giving speeches.

candid *(adj.)* frank, straightforward, truthful
I'll be candid with you; you did a poor job.

capacity *(noun)* the ability to hold or contain something
The movie theater has a capacity of 500 people.

care *(verb)* to feel interest or sorrow; to be willing; to look after someone by providing food, medical assistance, etc.
He doesn't seem to care whether he passes or fails.

carriage *(noun)* a vehicle for people, usually pulled by a horse
Before automobiles were invented, people traveled in carriages.

carve *(verb)* to form something by cutting away wood or stone
The statues by Michelangelo were carved from granite.

caustic *(adj.)* able to burn or destroy by chemical action
Acid is caustic.

celebrate *(verb)* to do something to show that a day or event is special
We celebrated my birthday by having a party.

celebrated *(adj.)* famous
Mark Twain is a celebrated author.

chart *(noun)* a map; a paper with diagrams, tables, or visual information
The sailors looked at their charts to find out where they were.

chore *(noun)* a duty; a piece of ordinary work; unpleasant work
Washing the car and taking out the garbage are two of my chores.

circulate *(verb)* to move from place to place freely
The teacher circulated around the room as the students studied.

circumstance *(noun)* the conditions or facts associated with an event or person
The suspect can't be judged guilty until the jury learns the circumstances of the crime.

classify *(verb)* to arrange in classes or groups
One of the secretary's jobs is to classify the new information.

clever *(adj.)* quick in learning and understanding things
The child was so clever that she was put ahead two years in school.

colleague *(noun)* a partner or associate working in the same profession
Her colleagues assisted her when she needed help.

collide *(verb)* to come together violently
The two cars collided as they turned the corner.

collusion *(noun)* a secret agreement or discussion for a dishonest reason
The robbers were in collusion before the robbery.

comic, comical *(adj.)* causing people to laugh
It was comical to see the dog do tricks.

command *(noun)* to be in a position of power
The general was in command of the army.

commence *(verb)* to begin
The program festivities commence at noon.

commonplace *(adj./noun)* normal, ordinary, obvious, not interesting
It is a commonplace event to eat dinner in the evening.

complexity *(noun)* something difficult to understand or explain
The complexity of the instructions made it difficult to play the game.

compromise *(noun/verb)* a settlement of a dispute by which each side gives up something it wants, an agreement
To settle the argument, each person compromised a bit.

compulsory *(adj.)* required
Is it compulsory to take an English class each semester?

conceal *(verb)* to hide, keep secret
The robber concealed a weapon under his coat.

confident *(adj.)* sure of oneself, certain
She was confident that she would pass the test.

confidential *(adj.)* secret
Some military information is confidential.

confined *(adj./verb)* restricted; to hold, to keep within limits
The prisoners were kept in a confined space.
The bird was kept confined to a cage.

conform *(verb)* to stay in agreement with rules
People who don't conform will be discharged from the group.

confront *(verb)* to meet or stand face to face, or to face defiantly
The prisoner confessed his crime when confronted with the evidence.

congregate *(verb)* to come together
After the speech, the audience congregated around the speaker.

conscript *(verb)* compelled by law, or to serve in the armed forces
The 18-year-old boy was conscripted into the army.

conserve *(verb)* to save, or to keep from destruction
During a drought, everyone needs to conserve water.

consider *(verb)* to think about
I'm considering taking a new job.

considerably *(adv.)* much, a great deal
I have considerably more work this year than I did last year.

considerate *(adj.)* thoughtful
It was considerate of my friend to send me a letter when I was sick.

conspicuous *(adj.)* easily seen
You look conspicuous in that large purple hat.

constrict *(verb)* to make tight or smaller
Wearing a tight band around your arm constricts your veins.

contemporary *(adj./noun)* belonging to the same time, of the present time, or modern
George Washington and Benjamin Franklin were contemporaries.
I live in a contemporary house.

contradictory *(adj.)* denying, opposing
These two accident reports are contradictory; they give different information.

contrast *(verb)* to compare so that differences are made clear
Her words contrast with her actions.

controversial *(adj.)* likely to cause an argument
There are many controversial topics that my father and I argue about.

convenient *(adj.)* easy to use, easy to get to, easy to do
It is convenient to have a washing machine in your house.

copious *(adj.)* plentiful, abundant, or wordy
This history class requires copious note-taking.

counter *(noun/verb)* a table or surface on which goods are shown or food prepared; to oppose, to return an attack
You can pick up your food from the counter.
My argument was countered by my friend's argument.

courageous *(adj.)* brave
Diving into the water to save a drowning person is a courageous act.

craggy *(adj.)* with high, steep, or sharp rocks
The mountain climbers slowly ascended the craggy slopes.

credible *(adj.)* believable
Her stories are rarely credible.

critic *(noun)* a person who gives judgment, usually about literature, art, or music
After his new play was performed, he was anxious to read what the critics said about it.

criticize *(verb)* to find fault with something or to judge something
People do not like to be criticized too much.

crush *(verb)* to press so that there is breaking or injury
His leg was crushed in an automobile accident.

culture *(noun)* advanced development of human powers; characteristics of a particular society, nation, or community
The culture of a group of people includes their food, clothing, rituals, and religious practices.

curious *(adj.)* eager to learn and to know; having an interest in something
Children are usually curious about the world.

curtail *(verb)* to shorten or reduce; cut back on
The amount of time we had to finish the project was curtailed.

cut *(noun/verb)* a reduction in size, amount, or length; a style of clothes or hair; a remark that hurts a person's feelings; to remove from something larger, to stay away from or be absent from class
I don't like the cut of that dress. (*style*)
The sharp razor made a cut in my cheek.

cycle *(noun)* a series of events taking place in regular, repeated order
Rain forms a cycle as it falls into rivers and then returns to the air.

damage *(adj./noun)* harm or injury
The insurance company will pay for the damages to your car.

debilitate *(verb/adj.)* causing weakness
Cancer is a debilitating disease.

decay *(verb)* to go bad, to lose power or health
Fruit decays quickly in hot weather.

deceptive *(adj.)* causing false beliefs, misleading
The test seemed deceptively easy, but actually it was very difficult. (adverb form).

defeat *(noun/verb)* to cause to fail
After five victories, the soccer team was defeated.

defect *(noun/verb)* an imperfection, a fault; to leave one's country for political reasons
If your new car has a defect, you can take it back.
She defected from her country and asked for political asylum.

deficit *(noun)* a condition of spending more than you have
The only way to decrease the budget deficit is to increase taxes.

delicacy *(adj.)* requiring special handling, a rare and choice kind of food
Some rare mushrooms are considered a delicacy.

den *(noun)* a secret place; an animal's hidden place, a room for studying
The fox's den is in the bushes.

design *(noun/verb)* a drawing or outline from which something is made; a pattern
A building with a poor design is not easy to work in.

desolate *(adj.)* ruined, barren, neglected, lonely, or sad
The small town looked desolate after the storm.

destitute *(adj.)* without food, clothes, or other necessities; needy
The war left many destitute people.

detachable *(adj.)* able to be removed, unfastened, or taken apart
The legs of this table are detachable.

detect *(verb)* to discover the presence of someone or something
The soldiers detected the enemy hiding in the valley.

deter *(verb)* to discourage
A locked door will deter thieves.

detrimental *(adj.)* causing damage or harm
Eating a lot of sugar is detrimental to your health.

dig *(verb)* to use a tool to move earth
To get ready to plant the tree, you must dig a big hole.

dilapidated *(adj.)* falling to pieces, in a state of disrepair, broken-down
No one wanted to live in the dilapidated old house.

dim *(adj.)* not bright, not seen clearly
A small light is too dim for reading.

diminutive *(adj.)* very small, tiny
A diminutive child can play the part of an elf in the school play.

discerning *(adj.)* able to see clearly, recognize
A discerning eye can tell the difference between planets and stars.

disconcerted *(verb)* upset
The boss was disconcerted to find that no one had locked the office.

discord *(noun)* disagreement, conflict
Quarrels over money have brought discord into the family.

disputed *(verb)* argued, debated, resisted
The exact boundary between the two countries was disputed.

disseminate *(verb)* to distribute, to spread widely
The news of the new king was disseminated over the whole country.

dissolve *(verb)* to become liquid, to melt, to disappear
Sugar will dissolve in water.

distinct *(adj.)* easily seen or heard, clearly marked, separate
She has a distinct accent.

dotting *(verb)* scattered, having a small round mark
From the air we could see houses dotting the landscape.

draft *(noun/verb)* an outline of something to be done, a current of air in a room; to select a person for the armed forces
Before I write an essay, I always write a first draft.
My brother was drafted into the army.

dribble *(verb)* to flow drop by drop
The baby dribbled his milk on his shirt.

due to *(prep.)* because of, caused by, attributed to.
The accident was due to slippery streets.

duel *(noun)* a fight, a contest
The duel between the two men began at dawn.

duplicate *(verb/adj./noun)* exactly alike, a copy
Please make a duplicate of this letter for me.

duration *(noun)* the time that something lasts
What is the duration of the school year in your country?

earmark *(verb/noun)* to set aside for a special purpose; an identification mark to show ownership
The boss has earmarked this money for Christmas decorations.

edifice *(noun)* a large building
To honor this great man we will build an edifice and dedicate it in his name.

elaborate *(verb/adj.)* worked out with much care, worked in detail
We have made elaborate plans for New Year's Day.

element *(noun)* a necessary or basic feature, a very small amount of something
Before learning physics you must know the elements of math.

eligible *(adj.)* suitable, having the right qualifications
Passing the TOEFL is one of the requirements for being eligible for entrance into a Canadian or American college.

17

elsewhere *(adv.)* at another place
He didn't like this school so he went elsewhere to college.

emancipate *(verb)* to set free
Abraham Lincoln is famous for having emancipated people from slavery.

embody *(verb)* to give ideas a definite form
Abraham Lincoln's ideas were embodied in his famous speeches.

embrace *(verb/noun)* to take someone into one's arms to show affection; to include
When the soldier saw his family after the war he embraced his mother and father.
This speech embraces all the major ideas of the president.

emerge *(verb)* to come out, to appear
The moon emerged from behind the clouds to shine on the water.

emit *(verb)* to give or to send out
A volcano emits fire from the earth.

emphasize *(verb)* to put force or stress on a word; to give a special value or importance
In our school we emphasize math and science.

encourage *(verb)* to give hope, confidence, or support
I encourage all my children to study hard in school.

enforce *(verb)* to cause something to be obeyed; to force or compel
A policemen enforces the law.

enhance *(verb)* to add to the value or importance of something
Keeping your house clean and well-cared for enhances its value.

enlist *(verb)* to voluntarily enroll in the armed forces; to get support
The boy enlisted in the army when he was 18 years old.

entangle *(verb)* to become caught or involved in something so that escape is difficult
The kitten cried when it got entangled in a ball of string.

enthusiast *(noun)* a person with enthusiasm, strong feelings of interest
My husband is a sports enthusiast; he watches sports on TV every day.

entitle *(verb)* to give a right to something
As a student here, you are entitled to use the services at the health center.

envy *(verb/noun)* to have feelings of disappointment because someone else has something which you want
The child envied her friend because the friend had a new bicycle.

epoch *(noun)* a period of time in history
Henry Ford's automobile began a new epoch in the history of transportation.

equipment *(noun)* things needed for a particular purpose
The tent, sleeping bags, and other equipment you need for your camping trip are already in the car.

erode, erosion *(verb/noun)* to wear away, usually by rain, wind, or acid
Acid eroded the metal under my car.
Water erosion from the heavy rains has caused damage to the land.

erratic *(adj.)* irregular, odd; likely to do unexpected things
The old man is dangerous on the road because he drives his car in an erratic manner.

essential *(adj.)* necessary
To enter many colleges, it is essential that you get 550 on the TOEFL exam.

establish *(verb)* to set up, to settle in a position
The governor wants to establish a new system of counting votes.

evacuate *(verb)* to leave empty, to withdraw
If there is a fire, evacuate the building quickly.

exaggerate *(verb)* to make something seem bigger, better, or worse than it is
I can never believe her stories; she always exaggerates the truth.

exceed *(verb)* to do more than enough, to go beyond, to be greater than
His success has exceeded all our hopes.

excel *(verb)* to do better than the others
In school, she excels in math.

excerpt *(noun)* a part of a book or article
In the magazine, you can read an excerpt of his latest book.

exchange *(verb/noun)* to trade one thing for another
This shirt doesn't fit; I'd like to exchange it for a smaller one.

exhilarating *(adj.)* filled with high spirits, lively, exciting
I have some exhilarating news: we won the national game!

exotic *(adj.)* unusual, coming from another country
In the north, you can keep exotic tropical plants in a greenhouse.

expanse *(noun)* a wide open area
To raise cattle, you need a large expanse of land.

explosion *(noun)* a loud noise caused by a sudden bursting
The bomb caused a huge explosion that was heard outside the city.

extravagant *(adj.)* wasting of money, excessive
Rich people are sometimes extravagant with their money; they spend a lot.

exquisite *(adj.)* of a high level of excellence, perfection
Your new emerald ring is exquisite.

extend *(verb)* to make longer
The teacher extended the deadline for our essays another week.

fabric *(noun)* cloth, textile material
What kind of fabric is your dress made of?

face *(verb/noun)* to meet confidently, to recognize, to turn in a certain direction
I don't want to face my friend after what I did to her.
Please face the front of the room.

fallible *(adj.)* likely to make an error
Everyone is fallible in some conditions.

fame *(noun)* the condition of being known or talked about, a good reputation
Unfortunately, his fame as a composer did not come until after his death.

fanciful *(adj.)* using creative images instead of reason and logic
He is a fanciful writer; I laugh at his stories.

fancy *(adj.)* very decorated, not plain
For the party, you should wear fancy clothes.

fastener *(noun)* something that ties or joins things together
A paper clip is a paper fastener.

faucet *(noun)* a device for controlling the flow of liquid (usually water) from a pipe or tank
To make the water come out, you must turn on the faucet.

favor *(verb)* to show support for, approval
Do you favor equal rights for women?

feature *(noun/verb)* the appearance of something; distinct or outstanding parts; an attraction or main part; to emphasize the main part
One of the main features of Yellowstone Park is Old Faithful.

feeble *(adj.)* weak or faint
The dying man had a feeble heart rate.

fellow *(adj)* having the same ideas or position; in the same condition; associated
My fellow workers and I are all going on a picnic together.

fertile *(adj.)* producing much, full of ideas, capable of developing
Our farmers are rich because our country has very fertile land.

fictitious *(adj.)* untrue or invented
The writer published under a fictitious name.

fiery *(adj.)* on fire, or angry, passionate
To persuade the people to fight for their rights, the man gave a fiery speech.

final analysis *(adj. + noun)* at the end, in conclusion
In the final analysis, the Northern team won the prize for "Team of the Year."

fitting *(adj.)* proper, suitable
It is fitting that you send a thank-you note after receiving a gift.

fizz *(verb/noun)* to make a bubbling hissing sound, as when gas escapes from a liquid.
Soft drinks like Coca-Cola fizz when they are poured into a glass.

flake *(noun)* a small, light, leaf-like piece
It is beautiful when snow falls like flakes from the sky.

flaw *(noun)* a fault, an imperfection
The store is selling clothes that have flaws at half price.

flexible *(adj.)* easily bent without breaking
A metal pipe is not flexible; soft plastic is flexible.

flicker *(verb)* to burn or shine unsteadily
The candle flickered in the wind and then went out.

flock *(noun)* a number of birds or animals together, a group
The bus had to stop for a flock of sheep.

forbidden *(adj./verb)* prohibited, to order not to be done
It is forbidden to enter the compound after dark.

foremost *(adj.)* first, most important
According to many people, Beethoven was the foremost composer of his period.

foster *(verb/adj.)* to help with the growth and development of an idea; to take care of someone else's child as if the child is your own
A relaxed environment can foster creative ideas.

found *(verb)* to establish, to start the building of something
Our organization was founded by a religious group.

fragrance *(noun)* a pleasing smell
I like perfume with the fragrance of fresh flowers.

frank *(adj.)* showing thoughts and feelings clearly
A frank person will tell the truth about how well your work is done.

frightening *(adj.)* filled with fear and alarm
A frightening nightmare can cause a child to wake up and cry.

frugal *(adj.)* economical, not wasteful
A frugal person saves more money than a person who shops without care.

fuel *(noun)* a material that produces energy or heat
Some cars run on diesel fuel and some on gasoline.

fully *(adv.)* completely
At 5 A.M. it is difficult for some people to be fully awake.

fund *(noun/verb)* a supply of necessary things, money; to provide money for support
Our group raised money for the scholarship fund.

fundamental *(noun/adj.)* basic, an essential part
The fundamentals of mathematics are learned in elementary school.

gain *(noun/verb)* an increase in power or wealth; to obtain something
The boss is only interested in gain. He wants to gain power.

gather *(verb)* to bring together
I like to gather flowers to put in the house.

gemstones *(noun)* precious, valuable stones or jewels
Some people keep gemstones in a safe.

glare *(noun/verb)* a strong, unpleasant light; to shine disagreeably
The light makes such a glare that I can't read my book.

glistening *(adj.)* shining brightly, sparkling
In the morning, the flowers are glistening with the dewdrops.

glow *(verb)* to send out light without flame
The horizon was glowing behind the mountains.

goods *(noun)* things which have worth or are valuable
After you count the goods, lock them in the warehouse.

gradually *(adv.)* very slowly, little by little
After studying hard, her grades gradually got better.

graphic *(adj.)* described in clear images
The man gave a graphic account of the fight.

gratifying *(adj.)* pleasing
It is gratifying to know I have friends to support me when I am sad.

grave *(adj.)* serious, requiring careful consideration
Her illness is grave.

grueling *(adj.)* severe, exhausting
The exam was grueling.

grumpy *(adj.)* bad-tempered
Grandpa is always grumpy when he first wakes up.

haphazardly *(adv.)* by chance, accidentally
The names for the committee were chosen haphazardly.

hardly *(adv.)* only just, scarcely
When I was sick I could hardly talk.

harmful *(adj.)* causing harm, damage, injury
Is it harmful to smoke cigarettes?

hatch *(verb)* to break out of an egg; to produce a plan
The chicks are hatching today.

head *(verb)* to move in a certain direction; to be at the head of
The parade is headed over to the other side of town.

hearty *(adj.)* strong, in good health
After a good breakfast, I feel hearty.

highlight *(noun/verb)* the most significant part; to emphasize
The highlight of the evening's performance was the piano concerto.

hostile *(adj.)* unfriendly
The enemies were hostile toward each other.

house *(verb/noun)* to provide a home or shelter for someone or something; dwelling
This room of the museum houses the special collection.

huge *(adj.)* very large
I just ate a huge dinner; I can't eat anything more.

humble *(adj.)* showing modesty; someone low in rank or unimportant
Though he had a humble upbringing, he became the chief officer of his business.

hybrid *(noun)* an animal or plant that is the offspring of two different parents or species
The mule is a hybrid animal, a cross between a donkey and a horse.

hygienic *(adj.)* free of disease germs
Doctors and nurses wash their hands well in order to be hygienic.

ignore *(verb)* to refuse to notice someone or something
When people are angry at each other, they sometimes ignore each other.

illicit *(adj.)* unlawful, forbidden
The illicit use of drugs is a problem in many countries.

imitate *(verb)* to copy something or use it as an example
By imitating great artists, young artists can learn good techniques.

impediment *(noun)* a physical defect or an obstacle
A lack of books and teachers is an impediment to learning.

imperceptible *(adv.)* slight, gradual, unnoticeable
The improvement, though imperceptible, was still there.

impress *(verb)* to have a strong influence on someone or something
I was very impressed by the speaker's presentation.

increase *(verb/noun)* to make larger; growth
There is an increase in the number of students in school this year.

incredible *(adv.)* something which cannot be believed, very surprising
The magician performed some incredible tricks.

indefinite *(adj.)* not fixed, vague
The factory will be closed for an indefinite period of time.

independent *(adj.)* not controlled by another, self-governing, thinking freely
Children often want to be independent as they grow older.

indicative *(adj.)* an indication or sign of something to come
The blossoms on the fruit trees are indicative of spring weather.

indiscriminate *(adj.)* having no care or taste
Our dog is an indiscriminate eater; he will eat almost anything.

induce *(verb)* to cause, to produce, to influence
Her illness was induced by a poor diet and overwork.

inevitable *(adj.)* something that is sure to happen, cannot be avoided
It is inevitable that the sun will rise tomorrow morning.

ingenious *(adj.)* very clever and skillful
The professor was ingenious at solving problems.

inherent *(adj.)* existing as a natural or permanent part of something
Problems are an inherent part of the job of president.

inhibit *(verb)* to restrain or suppress, to hinder
Being very tired inhibits studying.

innovation *(noun)* something new that is introduced
Each year the automobile industry comes out with innovations.

insatiable *(adj.)* something that cannot be satisfied
My father has an insatiable desire for candy.

inscription *(noun)* words that are marked, carved, or written on a surface
The inscription in the ring included my initials and our wedding date.

inspiring *(adj.)* uplifting thoughts
After the inspiring speech, the audience was filled with confidence.

instantaneous *(adj.)* immediate, happening in an instant
During the speech, there was instantaneous applause.

insult *(noun/verb)* speaking in a way that is intended to hurt a person's feelings
When the child was insulted, he cried.

intangible *(adj.)* that which cannot be touched or held; in one's mind
Ideas are intangible.

intense *(adj.)* deeply felt, high in degree
The explosion from the bomb caused intense heat for several miles.

intermittent *(adj.)* happening at intervals, stopping and starting
Today we will have intermittent rain.

intricate *(adj.)* complicated, difficult
The beauty of the painting is its intricate design.

intrusive *(adj.)* entering without invitation, unwanted
The loud noises outside the window were intrusive to my thoughts.

inundated *(verb)* flooded
The rains inundated the fields, washing away the crops.

invade *(verb)* to enter in great numbers; to attack
The army invaded the capital city.

invent *(verb)* to create or design something not already existing
The brilliant man invented a new technique to speed up his work.

jell *(verb)* to take shape, to hold shape
My scattered ideas are beginning to jell.
When the gelatin gets cool, it will jell.

landmark *(noun)* an object that marks the boundary of a piece of land, an object that is easily seen and can be used as a guide, an event that marks a turning point
The first hotel built in our city is still a landmark to progress.

largely *(adv.)* to a great extent
His success was due largely to his hard work.

lateral *(adj.)* From or at the sides of something, from side to side
Earthquakes usually cause a lateral movement in buildings.

laudable *(adj.)* deserving praise
Our president has accomplished many laudable acts.

legendary *(adj.)* from an old story told to people from generation to generation
The legendary travels of ancient Greeks are well known in literature.

lengthen *(verb)* to make something become longer
My skirt is too short; I need to lengthen it.

liberate *(verb)* to free
The victorious army liberated the prisoners.

ligament *(noun)* the tissue that holds bones together
While running, I tore the ligaments in my knee.

limited *(adj.)* restricted, narrow
There is a limited number of books on this topic for sale.

link *(noun/verb)* a ring or loop of a chain, something that unites or connects; to join together, to make a connection
The similar backgrounds of the two friends linked their lives together.

literally *(adv.)* exactly, corresponding word for word to the original, lacking in imagination
If you translate an idiom literally, you probably will not get the correct meaning.

loath *(verb)* to dislike strongly, to feel disgust for something
I loath snakes!

locale *(noun)* an area, the scene of an event
This is the locale of the accident.

look into *(verb)* to investigate, to examine
The computer technician will look into the computer problems.

ludicrous *(adj.)* ridiculous, absurd
It is ludicrous to say that it is easy to become fluent in all languages.

luminous *(adj.)* giving out light
Luminous paint is used on road signs so drivers can see them at night.

lyrical *(adj.)* full of emotion, like a song
The lyrical words of the poem made me feel almost like crying.

magnetic *(adj.)* having the properties of iron attracting iron, something that attracts
A compass needle is magnetic.
He has a magnetic personality.

magnificence *(noun)* splendor, imposing beauty
The palace is famous for its magnificence.

maintain *(verb)* to keep up, continue
By continuing to study the Russian language, I was able to maintain my proficiency.

mandatory *(adj.)* required
It is mandatory that you take basic science courses before entering college.

manually *(adv.)* by hand
The electricity went out so we operated the machinery manually.

mar *(verb)* to injure or damage
Nothing could mar the happiness of the newly wed couple.

master *(noun/verb)* a skilled person, one who has control over others; to become skillful in or knowledgeable about
By diligent study, I was able to master the English verb tenses.

mature *(verb/adj.)* to be fully grown, to be ready for use; perfected
A ten-year old child is not mature enough to leave her family.

melodious *(adj.)* having a musical quality
The songs of the birds are melodious to my ears.

merchandise *(noun)* things to buy or sell
The ships brought new merchandise in to the city.

meticulously *(adv.)* in a careful and detailed manner
She did her work meticulously.

minuscule *(adj.)* a tiny bit
There was a minuscule amount of iron in the chemical solution.

miserable *(adj.)* very unhappy, unfortunate
The starving people were cold and miserable.

misleading *(adj.)* causing a wrong impression; deceiving
The police were given misleading information about the crime.

mock *(verb/adj.)* to make fun of, insult; false
The rude children mocked the blind man.
The army held a mock battle to practice commands.

moderately *(adv.)* not extreme, reasonable, limited, medium
It is relaxing to swim in moderately warm water.

modern *(adj.)* of present times, up-to-date
Modern homes with new kitchen equipment are desired by many people.

motionless *(adv.)* still, having no movement
The bird stood motionless so that it could hardly be seen.

multiple *(adj.)* many, more than one
The woman received multiple injuries in the accident.

muscular *(adj.)* having many muscles, strong
The lifeguards on the beach were all muscular.

musty *(adj.)* having a stale or moldy smell
After being closed for a year, the house had a musty smell.

mutation *(noun)* a change, an alteration in the genes of a plant or animal which can be passed on to its offspring
The strong X-rays caused a mutation in the plant.

mythical *(adj.)* a person or thing that is imagined or invented
Some cultures have old stories of mythical animals who came to Earth.

naked *(adj.)* without clothes, bare, without protection
Babies are all born naked.
I can see it with my naked eye. (without a microscope or telescope)

nearby *(adv.)* close, not far
The school is so nearby that we can be there in five minutes.

nominal *(adj.)* a very small amount
A nominal fee is charged to enter the museum.

notorious *(adj.)* famous or known for doing something bad
A study of history can introduce you to many notorious people.

nourishment *(noun)* a source of strength and support, food
Food is nourishment for my body, but love is nourishment for my heart.

novelty *(noun)* something new or unusual; small toy or decoration
Some stores sell cheap novelty items for children to play with.

now and then *(adv.)* occasionally
Now and then I like to take a nap.

nutrient *(noun)* something that provides nourishment
To be healthy, our bodies must have proper nutrients.

oath *(noun)* a promise or vow to tell the truth
Before giving evidence before the court, you must take an oath.

obscure *(adj.)* hard to see or understand, hidden, indistinct, not well known
I know of an obscure restaurant that has delicious food.

obstacle *(noun)* a hindrance, something that prevents you from doing something
Arguments and fighting between nations are obstacles to world peace.

obvious *(adj.)* easily seen or understood
If you study hard, the answers on the test should be obvious.

ominous *(adj.)* threatening
Ominous black clouds on the horizon indicate a rainstorm.

omit *(verb)* to leave out
Please omit question number five on the test.

on the spot *(prep)* immediately, at the place one is needed
He was killed on the spot.

one by one *(adv.)* individually, one after another
To get your diploma, walk on the stage one by one.

operation *(noun)* a process of doing something, a surgical procedure
My father had an operation to remove his appendix.

optimal *(adj.)* the best; favorable; profitable
The optimal time to plant flower bulbs is in the fall.

option *(noun)* choice
You have the option of taking biology or chemistry.

outburst *(noun)* speaking out suddenly; anything that breaks out suddenly, usually violently
There was an outburst of violence after the new laws were passed.

outlawed *(verb)* made illegal
Guns are outlawed in many countries.

outlet *(noun)* a passage or vent for letting something out; the place in a wiring system where the electric current is available for use; an electrical socket
Before you can turn on the machine, you must plug the cord into the electrical outlet.

overlapping *(verb/adj.)* one thing covering part of another thing
The roof consists of overlapping tiles.
When building a roof, you overlap the tiles.

overthrow *(verb)* to conquer, to overturn, to upset
The army overthrew the old president and began a new system of government.

overwhelm *(verb)* to be defeated, to be exhausted, to cover completely
I was overwhelmed by all the work I had to do.

painstakingly *(adv.)* carefully, paying attention to detail
He does his work painstakingly; he is a great worker.

panacea *(noun)* a remedy for all troubles
There is no panacea that will bring everlasting happiness.

paramount *(adj.)* of primary importance
Eating well is paramount to your health.

particle *(noun)* a small piece, a part
Chew carefully so that you don't get a particle stuck in your throat.

particularly *(adv.)* especially
While wearing her new dress, the little girl was particularly careful not to get dirty.

passing *(adj.)* not lasting, going by
The passing years are becoming more difficult for the sick old man.

patch *(noun)* a piece of material used to cover a hole; a small area
The old clothes were covered with patches.

path *(noun)* a place made for walking
There is a path through the woods.

patronize *(verb)* to support, or to act in a condescending way
Many customers patronized the new store.
The woman was upset when she felt that her boss was patronizing.

penetrate *(verb)* to go into or through; to spread
The terrible smell penetrated the whole house.

perceive *(verb)* to become aware of something through the senses or mind
I perceive your meaning even though I can't understand your words.

perennial *(adv.)* continuing through the whole year
I like perennial plants because they don't die in the winter.

period *(noun)* a portion of time
I am interested in studying the period of the French Revolution.

perjury *(noun)* a false statement after giving an oath to tell the truth
The woman was put in jail for perjury.

perpendicular *(adj.)* at an angle of 90 degrees, upright
Trees grow perpendicular to the earth.

perplexing *(adj.)* confusing, complicated
It is perplexing to read the laws of the nation.

persistent *(adj.)* refusing to change, continuing for a long time, repeating again and again
With persistent work and study, she made great advances.

phenomenon *(noun)* something that can be perceived by the senses, something remarkable or unusual
If you're interested in a phenomenon like how mountains are made, take a class in earth science.

pierce *(verb)* to make a hole, to go through with a pointed instrument
The knife pierced a hole in the piece of wood.

plot *(verb/noun)* to plan secretly; the main story of a book or play; a small piece of ground
The enemies of the government plotted to overthrow the government.
I don't understand the plot of the play.
I planted my vegetable garden on a small plot of land by my house.

poignant *(adj.)* causing sad or painful feelings
The poignant part of the play made me feel like crying.

point out *(verb)* to show or call attention to something
The teacher pointed out my mistakes so that I could correct them.

pole *(noun)* a long slender round piece of wood or metal.
The flag was hung on a pole outside the office.

poll *(noun)* a survey of public opinion made by questioning people
The people took a poll to see which candidate might win.

popularity *(noun)* the quality of being popular, well-liked
The popularity of the candidate was apparent by the votes he got.

posthumously *(adv.)* after one's death
The poet was awarded the honor of "Best Poet" posthumously.

potentially *(adv.)* having the capability, the possibility
He is potentially the best artist ever born in our city.

praise *(noun/verb)* an expression of approval or esteem; to give approval, admiration, honor, or glory to someone
A teacher should praise students who do well.
We give praise to God.

pray *(verb)* to address God to give thanks or make requests, to ask earnestly
In church people pray to God.

precision *(noun)* the state of being exact, correct, accurate
A skilled engineer works with precision.

predict *(verb)* to foretell, to say in advance
I predict that it will rain tomorrow.

predominantly *(adv.)* having more strength, power, or numbers than others
The students in our school are predominantly from the north.

pressing *(adj.)* urgent, requiring immediate attention
There is a pressing need for reforms in the laws of our country.

prevail *(verb)* to gain victory over something, to be the usual thing, commonly seen or done
The south prevailed over the north in the last war.
The prevailing winds are from the west. (adj. form)

previously *(adv.)* before
Previously, our country had a king; now we have a president.

primitive *(adj.)* of early times, of an early culture, pretechnical culture
In primitive times, human beings lived in caves.

prior to *(adj.)* before
Prior to coming to the United States, I studied law in my own country.

private *(adj.)* concerning one person or group rather than for people in general; secret; secluded; isolated
I don't want my boss to know my private affairs.

proficient *(adj.)* skilled
I am proficient at using a personal computer.

profitable *(adj.)* useful; bringing in money or gain
We made a deal that was profitable to everyone.

prolonged *(adj.)* for a long time, made longer
After the lecture the students had a prolonged discussion.

promotion *(noun)* advancement to a higher rank or position
After working for two years in my company, I was given a promotion.

prone *(adj.)* lying down; to have a tendency to do something
After his illness he had to be in a prone position for two weeks.
Some people seem to be prone to accidents.

propagate *(verb)* to increase the number of plants or animals by natural means; to spread information
Some farmers and botanists propagate plants.

propel *(verb)* to drive something forward
An engine propels a boat.

prospect *(noun)* something hoped for or looked forward to
The prospect of getting a new job excites me.

prosperous *(adj.)* successful; rich
After winning the lottery, the woman became prosperous.

pulp *(noun)* the soft part of fruit; a mass of soft material such as wood fiber
To make paper, wood is soaked and mashed into a pulp.

purpose *(noun)* a plan or intention, something a person wants to do or get
My purpose in going to school is to get a degree and learn about my major field.

puzzling *(verb/adj.)* hard to understand or answer
I am still puzzled about why my friend quit his job.

radical *(adj.)* basic; extreme; fundamental
Advanced technology has caused us to make a radical change in the way we communicate.

range *(noun/verb)* a row of things; a large area; maximum distance; the limit; a stove with an oven; to travel over or roam
The Himalayas consist of a large range of mountains.
The cows feed on the range.
The range of colors in the rainbow is limited.
I bought a new range when I rebuilt my kitchen.
The deer ranged the woods in search of food.

rational *(adj.)* able to reason
When my mother had a high fever, she was not rational.

reach *(verb)* to stretch, to extend, to come to
The government wanted the new tax information to reach all citizens.

react *(verb)* to behave in response to a situation
When the people heard screams, they reacted in horror.

rebel *(verb)* to act against something; to show resistance; to fight
The child rebelled against his parents' demands by running away.

recall *(verb)* to remember; to ask to come back
The old woman couldn't remember much, but she recalled her childhood with pleasure.

recipient *(noun)* someone who receives something
I was a recipient of the award for best singer.

recovery *(noun)* getting well again; getting one's health back
His recovery after the illness was very rapid.

recycle *(verb)* to treat waste materials like paper, glass, or metal so they can be used again
We save all our old newspapers and take them downtown to be recycled.

reel *(noun/verb)* a roller for thread, wire, hose, or cable; to walk unsteadily
The fisherman had a reel on his fishing pole.
The drunk old man reeled as he walked.

refrain *(verb)* to stop from doing something
Please refrain from smoking while in the elevator.

refute *(verb)* to prove a person wrong or mistaken
My father always refutes my arguments.

regrettably *(adv.)* sadly
Regrettably, I won't be able to come to your wedding next month.

reimburse *(verb)* to give money back
The company will reimburse you for the money you spend on supplies.

relate *(verb)* to tell a story; to have a connection with something
Grandfather likes to relate stories from his childhood.
Scientists are trying to relate the illness to possible causes.

relatively *(adv.)* comparatively
Our family lives relatively comfortably compared to others in our town.

release *(verb)* to let go; to set free
The prisoners were released from the jail.

religiously *(adv.)* to do something conscientiously; devoutly; with faith
He does his physical exercises religiously every morning.

reluctantly *(adv.)* unwilling to do something
The man reluctantly admitted that he was guilty.

remains *(noun)* what is left; a dead body
The remains of the dinner were put in the refrigerator.
The remains of the saints are buried in the church cemetery.

remote *(adj.)* far away, distant; control from a distance
This new robot is operated by a remote switch.

renowned *(adj.)* famous, celebrated
The painter was renowned for his watercolor paintings of the ocean.

repair *(verb/adj.)* to restore to a good condition
When my bicycle broke I took it to a repair shop.

report *(noun/verb)* an account given of something heard or seen
She reported that she heard an explosion in the basement.

research *(noun)* an investigation to discover new facts or information
As a graduate student you are expected to do research.

resist *(verb)* to oppose an attack; not to give in to something
When the enemy forces advanced, the army resisted.
I can't resist eating chocolate; I love it too much.

resort *(noun/verb)* a place one goes to for fun, relaxation, or health; to turn to something for help to gain one's purpose
I'd like to visit a health resort on my vacation.
As a last resort, the policeman tied the prisoner's hands.

respect *(noun/verb)* honor, consideration, regard; to treat someone with consideration
We should all respect our grandparents.

restore *(verb)* to bring back to the original condition; to repair; to make well
A good carpenter can restore old furniture.

retreat *(verb/noun)* to move back, withdraw; a quiet and restful place
The army retreated when the enemy came.
On my vacation, I will visit a quiet retreat in the country.

revere *(verb)* to have a deep respect for; to regard highly
Some people revere their grandparents.

revision *(noun)* a corrected version of something
Please make the necessary revisions in this document.

rewarding *(adj.)* satisfying; giving pleasure in return for something
It was rewarding to see the smiles on the children's faces when they received their gifts.

rigorous *(adj.)* very hard, harsh, severe, very strict
To do well in this job, you must follow a rigorous system of work.

rise *(verb)* to appear, to get up, to come to life, to become greater in intensity or volume
After a heavy rainstorm, a river might rise several feet.

rolling *(verb/adj.)* turning over and over, swaying
The dog was rolling in the grass on its back.
During the storm, the boat was making a rolling motion.

rudimentary *(adj.)* elementary, undeveloped
In ages past, humans had rudimentary ideas of economics.

rumor *(noun/passive verb)* general talk, gossip, statement that may not be true
I heard a rumor that our business is closing; I hope it is false.
It is rumored that our business is closing.

run-down *(adj.)* not cared for, weak and exhausted, fallen into disrepair
That old vacant house has become run-down.
My watch is running down; it needs a new battery.

rural *(adj.)* in a country area
I live in a rural area with farms all around the houses.

scarcely *(adv.)* hardly, barely, almost not
We have scarcely any money left this month.

scattered *(adj.)* not situated together
The homes in the rural area are scattered around the hills.

scenery *(noun)* the general appearance of a place, features of the landscape
It's nice to stop while driving and look at the scenery.

scent *(noun)* smell, usually pleasant
The scent of flowers in a house gives me a nice fresh feeling.

scrupulously *(adv.)* done very carefully, paying attention to detail
He does his work scrupulously.

secluded *(adj.)* kept away from others, alone
The little house was secluded in the woods.

secretly *(adv.)* not known to others, quiet
My friend secretly told me that he was going to get married.

seed *(noun/verb)* the part of a flowering plant from which other plants grow; the origin of something; to sow a field with seed
The seeds in a peach are large; whereas the seeds in an orange are small.
The farmer seeded the field in the spring.

seek *(verb)* to look for
When it started to rain, the hikers began to seek shelter.

selection *(noun)* a collection, a group of chosen things
When eating in a cafeteria, you have a large selection of food to choose from.

sensible *(adj.)* reasonable, practical
It is sensible to dress warmly in cold weather.

serene *(adj.)* calm and clear
The ocean looks serene on a warm summer day.

shade *(noun/verb)* something that cuts off the sunlight; a screen or curtain; to protect from light or heat
It's cooler to sit in the shade.
On hot days I often close the shades.
An umbrella will shade you from the sun.

shaggy *(adj.)* hairy; rough, coarse or untidy hair
Don't let that shaggy dog come into my house!

sheer *(adj.)* complete or absolute; transparent cloth
It is sheer nonsense to listen for an echo in a crowded noisy place.
For her bridal veil, the woman chose a sheer lace.

shelter *(noun)* a place to be safe or protected
The political prisoners were looking for shelter in another country.

shield *(verb/noun)* to protect; a piece of metal, plastic, or other material that protects
Motorcycle riders wear leather jackets to shield themselves from the wind.

side by side *(adj.)* close together
The teacher asked the children to sit side by side for singing.

silently *(adv.)* quietly, making little sound
If you sit silently, you can hear the birds sing.

simultaneous *(adj.)* at the same time
The two heads of state signed the international agreement simultaneously.

single-story *(adj.)* a house or building with one floor
My friends live in a tall apartment building, but I live in a single-story house.

sinister *(adj.)* evil, unkind
The mean old man had a sinister look on his face.

site *(noun)* a place where something was or will be
This looks like a good site for a picnic lunch.

situated *(adj.)* placed, located
The Mississippi River is situated in the center of the United States.

sketch *(verb)* to make a rough, quick drawing or an outline; a rough plan
The artist made a sketch of the mountain so that he could paint it later.

slightly *(adv.)* to a small degree; slenderly
I am only slightly hungry now.

slim *(adj.)* small, insufficient, slender
She has slim hopes of getting the new job.
She should become slim if she eats less.

soak *(verb)* to become completely wet by absorbing liquid
Before you wash these very dirty clothes you should soak them in warm water.

socket *(noun)* a hole or space into which something fits
Before you can turn on the lamp, you must plug it into the socket.

sole *(adj./noun)* the only one; single; restricted; the undersurface of a person's foot or shoe
The jailer is the sole person to have a key to the prisoner's cell.
My old shoe has a hole in the sole.

solitary *(adj.)* living alone; without companions; seldom visited; lonely
The prisoner was put in solitary confinement.
Sometimes I like to take a solitary walk.

somewhat *(adv.)* to some degree, a little
I was somewhat surprised to find that I had passed the test.

sophisticated *(adj.)* a lack of simplicity or naturalness; cultured; with the latest improvements
After living abroad in a big city, she became quite sophisticated.

sort *(noun/verb)* a group or class of things which are similar in some way; to separate or arrange by class
I don't like this sort of music.

spacious *(adj.)* having a lot of space
In our new house we have a very spacious living room.

spectacular *(adj.)* grand, marvelous, remarkable
On the Fourth of July, we had a spectacular parade with fireworks.

split *(verb)* to break into two or more parts; divide
In order to eat a coconut, first you must split it.

sporadically *(adv.)* occasionally; inconsistently
Sporadically I get itchy red marks on my neck.

stain *(noun/verb)* a mark that doesn't wash out; to permanently change the color of something
Blood can stain your clothes if you don't wash it out.
In my house, I stained the wooden doors light brown.

stalk *(verb/noun)* to move quietly and cautiously toward something in order to get near; the part of a plant that supports the plant or flower
The cat stalked the unsuspecting mouse.
We eat the stalk of the celery plant.

static *(adj.)* in a state of balance, not increasing or decreasing; electric charges in the atmosphere; a crackling noise in radio or television
We could not listen to the radio because of all the static.

stem *(noun)* the stalk of a plant; the end coming up from the ground
Before you put the flowers in a vase you should cut the stems.

strengthen *(verb)* to make something stronger
If you add an introduction, it will strengthen your essay.

stress *(noun)* a condition causing depression or troubled thoughts
With all the work I have to do, I am under a lot of stress now.

strict *(adj.)* demanding obedience, clearly and exactly defined, precise
My boss is very strict; we have many rules to follow.

strip *(noun/verb)* a long narrow piece of material or land; to take off coverings
We have a small strip of land for growing vegetables behind the house.
We stripped off our clothes and jumped into the lake.

stripe *(noun)* a band of material of a different color, pattern, or material
My socks have three red stripes on them.

struggle *(verb/noun)* to fight; to make great effort for something; conflict
The prisoner struggled to be free of the handcuffs.

stubborn *(adj.)* obstinate; difficult to deal with; determined
The stubborn mule would not pull the farmer's plow.

stumble *(verb)* to hit one's foot against something and fall or almost fall
When I was running, I stumbled over a rock and fell.

style *(noun)* a manner of writing, speaking; a quality of being superior; a general appearance
The fashionable woman always bought clothes in the latest style.
I like Hemingway's writing style.

submarine *(noun)* a ship that is designed to operate under water
Many submarines were used in World War II.

subtle *(adj.)* difficult to perceive or describe
The subtle effects of the artist's use of color make her work fascinating.

superiority *(noun)* the state of being better than average
The superiority of your work gives you a good chance at being hired.

supernatural *(adj.)* spiritual, cannot be explained by physical laws
Ghosts and angels are supernatural.

surmise *(verb)* guess
Since the plane is delayed, I surmise that they won't be coming for dinner.

surpass *(verb)* to do better than someone or something else
On the last test, I surpassed my previous score.

survey *(verb)* to examine, to take a general view of
A builder surveyed the countryside to find the best place to build his house.

suspicious *(adj.)* having an idea that something bad is about to happen, thinking someone may be guilty
I have a suspicious feeling that he may be telling a lie.

swear *(verb)* to take an oath; to curse, to use bad language
The judge made all the people in the court swear to tell the truth.
The teacher was angry at the child for swearing in class.

swift *(adj.)* fast, quick
The swift runner won the race.

sympathetic *(adj.)* sharing the pain or troubled feelings of other people
I felt sympathetic toward my friend when her mother died.

symphony *(noun)* a long musical composition
Beethoven's symphonies are well known throughout the world.

tactfully *(adv.)* showing skill and understanding in dealing with other people
The boss tactfully told my friend that he didn't have the right skills for this job.

take place *(verb)* happen
The first scene of the play takes place before the hero and heroine have met.
The party will take place at my house.

tap *(verb/noun)* to make a light, quick, rhythmical touch on something; a faucet, a device for controlling the flow of liquid from a pipe
I like to tap my feet on the floor when I listen to music.
You waste water when you leave the tap open.

temperature *(noun)* a degree of heat or cold; a body fever
The child has a high temperature; she should stay in bed.

tend *(verb)* to be inclined to do something; to have a certain direction
Plants tend to turn toward the light.

tension *(noun)* strain; being tightly stretched
When my parents are angry with each other, there is a lot of tension in the house.

tentative *(adj.)* done as a trial to see what might happen
I made a tentative offer to buy the house.

terrifying *(adj.)* frightening
I had bad dreams after seeing that terrifying ghost movie.

theft *(noun)* the act of stealing
Did you read about the bank theft? The robbers got away with one thousand dollars.

theory *(noun)* an explanation of a general principle; an opinion, not necessarily based on logical reasoning
Darwin's theory of evolution is important in the study of botany.
My friend has a theory that rubbing the scalp will cause hair to grow.

thorn *(noun)* a pointed growth on the stem of a plant.
I love roses, but I don't like to pick them because of the thorns.

timid *(adj.)* shy, easily frightened
The timid child hid behind his mother's skirt.

tiny *(adj.)* very small
When I was sick I could only eat a tiny amount of food.

tolerate *(verb)* to put up with, to allow without protest
I can't tolerate loud, angry people.

tomb *(noun)* a place dug in the ground or carved out of rock to put a dead body, usually having a monument over it
The soldier's tomb is on top of the mountain.

touching *(adj.)* causing sympathy
It was very touching to receive letters from all my friends when I was in the hospital.

tough *(adj.)* hard to cut; difficult; not easily broken
The meat on my plate is so tough that I can't cut it.
I have a tough time doing all my math problems correctly.

trace *(noun/verb)* a very small amount; a mark showing someone has been in a place; to draw or sketch; to copy; to follow a line
There is only a trace of iodine in the water.
The archaeologists found traces of an ancient civilization.
By tracing the line in the sand, we could follow the path of the insect.

trade *(verb/noun)* to buy and sell; to give something for something else; means of earning one's living
My uncle is in the building trade.
Will you trade me your pen for my pencil?

transplant *(verb)* to transfer, to move to a new place
The tiny plants were transplanted from little pots in the kitchen to a sunny place in the yard.

trash *(noun)* something worthless; rubbish
When I cleaned up my desk, I threw a lot of old paper in the trash.

treasured *(adj.)* valued, loved
I keep my treasured jewels in the bank.

trial *(noun)* a test; an examination in a court of law
During this trial period the company will fix the new equipment without charge.
The woman was on trial for theft.

trickle *(verb/noun)* to flow slowly; to move little by little; a slow, small flow
The accident on the highway caused traffic to slow to a trickle.

trip *(verb/noun)* to stumble over something; a journey for pleasure
As he was walking, he tripped over the root of the large tree.

tropical *(adj.)* of the part of the earth around the equator
Many people like to spend their vacations on beaches that have tropical weather.

trunk *(noun)* the part of the tree that supports it; a large case to pack things in for traveling; the body of the person
To cut down a tree you must cut through the trunk.

turbulence *(noun)* the state of being violent, uncontrolled, disorderly
After the rainstorms, the turbulence of the water in the river caused damage to the farmer's fields.

ultimately *(adv.)* finally, in the end
At the end of the story, the hero and the heroine ultimately get married.

unaccustomed *(adj.)* not used to something; not usual
I am unaccustomed to eating dinner at midnight.

unauthorized *(adj.)* illegal
Unauthorized admittance will result in a fine or a jail sentence.

unbearable *(adj.)* not tolerable, causing much sadness
It is unbearable for me to see you go away for a year.

unbiased *(adj.)* impartial, giving each thing equal consideration
The judge and the jury must be unbiased as they listen to the testimony at a trial.

uncalled-for *(adj.)* undesirable, unnecessary, not justified
The man made a rude, uncalled-for remark to the woman.

unique *(adj.)* being the only one of its type
This handmade cloth is unique.

unquenchable *(adj.)* not able to be satisfied
I have an unquenchable thirst.

upgraded *(adj.)* raised in rank, made progress
I upgraded my work when I reviewed it a second time.

vacillate *(verb)* to waver, to be uncertain
I have a difficult time making decisions; I vacillate among all the options.

value *(noun/verb)* the quality of being useful or desirable; to estimate the monetary value of something; to have a high regard for something
The value of the things I love is more than the money I paid for them.
I value my friendships highly.

vandalism *(noun)* deliberate destruction of a work of art or private property
Because of possible vandalism, guards have been posted at the doors of the museum.

variable *(adj.)* changing
Tomorrow we'll be having variable winds from the north.
The variable standards at this school make it difficult to anticipate what will come next.

verify *(verb)* to test the truth or accuracy of something
Can you verify this answer?

view *(noun/verb)* that which is seen; a scene or prospect; to examine or consider
Have you viewed this problem from another point of view?

vigorous *(adj.)* having strength or energy
He works in a vigorous way.

virtually *(adv.)* in effect though not in fact, for all practical purposes
I am virtually done with writing this report.

vivid *(adj.)* lively; intense; bright; clear and distinct
I had a vivid dream last night about my parents.

warehouse *(noun)* a building for storing goods before distribution
The wheat will be kept in a warehouse until it can be distributed to the poor people.

warn *(verb)* to inform someone of possible danger
Fire alarms warn people that something is burning.

wary *(adj.)* to be in the habit of being careful about possible danger
I don't like to look over the cliff; I am wary of heights.

wed *(verb)* to marry
He will be wed next June.

weight *(noun)* the force or heaviness of something
It is important to consider weight when building furniture.

widespread *(adj.)* occurring over a large area
Widespread damage was caused by the earthquake.

wild *(adj.)* in an original or natural condition; not domesticated or cultivated; not civilized; uncontrolled
Most birds are wild, but some are kept in cages in the house.

willing *(adj.)* ready; agreeable
I am willing to help you finish your work.

withdraw *(verb)* to pull back or take out
I have to withdraw some of my money from the bank.

withhold *(verb)* to keep or refuse to give
Don't try to withhold the truth from me.

youthful *(adj.)* the state of being young
Even though he is old, the man has a youthful attitude about life.

Lesson 18

Reading Comprehension Topics and Questions

Objectives

- To learn about Reading Comprehension questions
- To learn what topics recent TOEFL exams have used
- To learn ten common types of Reading Comprehension questions
- To practice the ten kinds of questions

1. What is a Reading Comprehension Question?
2. Reading Comprehension Pretest
3. Answer Key for Pretest
4. Frequency of Reading Comprehension Topics
5. Frequency of Ten Kinds of Questions
6. Description and Examples of Questions

Lesson 18

The standard form of the TOEFL contains thirty reading comprehension questions. Usually there are five or six different passages, each one followed by four to six questions. On the long form of the TOEFL there may be seven or eight passages and forty-five questions all together. The vocabulary questions and the reading comprehension questions are both in Section 3. In the standard form, you have 45 minutes for all of Section 3. In the long form, you usually have 65 minutes. You can go back and forth between vocabulary and reading comprehension within this time limit.

What Is a Reading Comprehension Question?

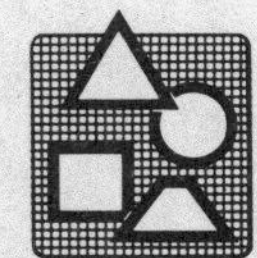

Below are the directions in the standard TOEFL exam. Read them to make sure that you understand them. You don't need to memorize them; these directions will be written in your exam when you take the test.

> ***Directions:*** In the rest of this section you will read several passages. Each one is followed by several questions about it. For questions 31–60, you are to choose the *one* best answer, (A), (B), (C), or (D), to each question. Then, on your answer sheet, find the number of the question and fill in the space that corresponds to the letter of the answer you have chosen.
>
> Answer all questions following a passage on the basis of what is *stated* or *implied* in that passage.
>
> Read the following passage:

Glaciers are ice fields that can be compared to slow-moving rivers of ice. They are formed when the amount of snow that falls during the year is more than the amount that melts. As the mass of snow builds up, it compresses and slowly turns to ice. As new layers of ice are formed, the layers on the bottom become more and more firmly packed down. Eventually, they begin to move. Glaciers move very slowly, rarely more than twenty-four inches a day. The top and center move more quickly than the sides, causing the ice to crack open and form large crevasses.

EXAMPLE 1

A glacier is

(A) a river
(B) packed ice
(C) a crevasse
(D) snow

Sample Answer

Ⓐ ● Ⓒ Ⓓ

According to the passage, snow turns to ice. As new layers form, old layers become "more firmly packed down." Therefore, you should choose answer (B).

EXAMPLE 2

How do glaciers move?

(A) Quickly
(B) Smoothly
(C) Unevenly
(D) Obviously

Sample Answer

 Ⓑ  

The passage states that "the top and center move more quickly than the sides." Therefore, you should choose answer (C).

Reading Comprehension Pretest (Answers, page 264)

Directions: Read the following passage and the questions that follow it. This passage is longer than most reading passages in TOEFL exams in order to give you practice with different kinds of questions. Answer each question on the basis of what is stated or implied in the passage.

A monkey is sitting expectantly in a laboratory, wearing earphones that keep its head in an upright fixed position. Its hand rests at its waist near a telegraph key that it can feel but cannot see. Soon a green light begins to blink and the monkey presses the key to signal that it is ready. Then it hears two syllables coming through the earphones, realizes that the syllables are different, and correctly lifts the key.

This is not an amazing event in the field of research on primate behavior. Scientific studies on animal behavior have been conducted for many years. Chimpanzees, gorillas, and monkeys have all been taught to comprehend messages from humans. What is new about this study is what the researcher noticed about the monkey's use of its hands. Although either hand could have been used for pressing the key, every one of the monkeys used its right hand. In other tasks, however, like grabbing food from a feeder or taking something that is offered to them, the monkeys seemed to have no preference for one hand over the other.

It has generally been assumed that only humans have the trait of favoring one hand. The right hemisphere of the brain controls the left arm and hand, and the left hemisphere of the brain controls the right arm and hand. Important mental abilities such as speaking and understanding language are handled by the left side of the brain, so it is thought that this produces a dominance of right-handed humans. However, a growing number of researchers are challenging this notion that nonhuman primates have no hand preferences. They argue that these traits can be traced back to primates living tens of millions of years ago. Their contention is that primates use their right hands to perform precise manipulations where they cannot clearly see what they are doing. And then why haven't researchers noticed this before? It is difficult to set up experiments that require the kind of task where handedness is important.

1. With what topic is this passage primarily concerned?

(A) The mental abilities of monkeys

(B) Hand preference in primates

(C) Hemispheres of the brain

(D) Experiments on nonhuman primates

2. Which of the following is the best title for this passage?

(A) Smart Monkeys

(B) Primates and Their Use of Language

(C) A Ten Million-Year History

(D) Humans and Primates: A Similarity?

3. In the first paragraph, what is the monkey expecting?

(A) A blinking light

(B) An earphone

(C) Some food

(D) A telegraph key

4. According to the passage, what do most scientists assume?

(A) Only humans have hand preferences.
(B) Only monkeys can learn to indicate their food choices.
(C) Speaking and understanding are more important than reading and writing.
(D) Setting up experiments for primates is difficult.

5. In what situation would a primate be most likely to use its right hand?

(A) Picking out a red block from a group of colored blocks
(B) Pushing a button that is hidden behind a black curtain
(C) Picking up a banana and peeling it
(D) Choosing a food after hearing the correct command

6. Why are scientists probably not very interested in the activity of the monkey as described in the first paragraph?

(A) The experiment has not followed a precise scientific format.
(B) The experiment is too easy for monkeys to do.
(C) Similar studies have been done many times.
(D) Scientists don't agree with the conclusions.

7. The word *grabbing* in line 11 refers to

(A) holding lightly
(B) taking quickly
(C) squeezing tightly
(D) picking up carefully

8. In line 19, the word *challenging* could best be replaced by

(A) accepting
(B) favoring
(C) claiming
(D) contesting

9. Which of the following did the monkeys in this passage NOT do?

(A) Signal their readiness
(B) Differentiate between two syllables
(C) Grab food from a feeding tray
(D) Use alternate hands to lift a key

10. Which of the following statements about the human brain is NOT mentioned?

(A) The left arm is controlled by the right hemisphere.
(B) Right-handedness is connected to stronger mental abilities.
(C) Speaking and understanding are centered in the left side.
(D) The left hemisphere contains the important oral language abilities.

11. Why does the author begin with the description of a monkey performing an experiment?

(A) To show the importance of the experiment
(B) To distinguish between two kinds of research
(C) To give a generalization of a concept
(D) To give an example of something to be discussed

12. What is the purpose of the final sentence of the passage?

(A) To give a reason
(B) To give a purpose
(C) To give a description
(D) To give an example

13. Which of the following would most likely be the topic of the next paragraph?

(A) A discussion of the differences between the hemispheres of the brain
(B) An example of a chimpanzee's ability to comprehend language
(C) Reasons that some scientists disagree with this hypothesis
(D) A discussion of experiments that indicate hand preference

14. What does the word *this* refer to in line 6?

(A) Correctly lifting a key
(B) Hearing two syllables through earphones
(C) The process that the monkey is able to carry out
(D) Pressing a key that the monkey cannot see

15. Which of the following best describes the organization of this passage?

(A) An example is given and then a new hypothesis is discussed.
(B) A concept is discussed before examples are given.
(C) A concept is discussed and reasons for it are examined.
(D) The contrasting views of scientists are compared.

16. Which of the following statements is best supported by this passage?

(A) Scientists disagree about the idea of handedness in primates.
(B) The right side of the brain is not as important as the left side.
(C) It is difficult to teach primates to comprehend human messages.
(D) Primates use both hands equally in carrying out precise tasks.

Answer Key for Pretest

1. B	**9.** D
2. D	**10.** B
3. A	**11.** D
4. A	**12.** A
5. B	**13.** D
6. C	**14.** C
7. B	**15.** A
8. D	**16.** A

Now that you have taken the pretest, look at the tables below to get an idea of how often different topics and types of questions are used.

Frequency of Reading Comprehension Topics

The following reading topics were taken from a sample of twelve TOEFL tests given between 1984 and 1989. Sixty-six paragraphs are represented.

Topic	Frequency	Approximate Percent
Sciences	31	47
Arts and Literature	17	25.5
United States History and Government	13	20
Other Social Sciences	5	8
	66	

1. Sciences

As you can see from the above list, almost half of the passages are science topics. Remember that you don't have to study science in order to answer the questions. All the answers are in the passage. The passage might be easier to understand, however, if you have a knowledge of the general vocabulary used in science. A variety of topics can be discussed in a scientific way. In the past there have been passages on topics such as the collection of maple syrup, the growth of fingernails, the use of robots, or a discussion of sound waves, echoes, or electricity. The following general areas are common:

Archeology	Botany	Ornithology
Astronomy	Environmental Science	Zoology
Biology	Geology	

2. Arts and Literature

The second greatest area for reading passages is Arts and Literature. Readings in this area have been on the following topics:

Music—You might find a topic about a particular instrument (trumpet, for instance), about a type of music (like jazz), or about singing or playing music in a group (an orchestra or choral group).
Biography—In this category you might read something about a person's life, possibly a famous writer, artist, or actor.
Literature—This category could include an analysis of a film or book or a discussion of a writer's literary style.
Art—This category includes passages on styles of painting (like cubism or realism) or a discussion of an artist's style or purpose.
Architecture—A passage in this category may be about a particular style of building, such as Victorian or renaissance.

3. United States History and Government

The next largest category of topics is United States history and government. This area could be included in general Social Science, but has been listed separately because of the large number of topics that are written about American history in the TOEFL. Though it will help you read faster if you already know something about American history, remember that the answers to each question are in each passage. Past TOEFL exams have had passages on the following topics:

Ancient America	Cowboys	War of Independence
Civil War	Native Americans (Indians)	Washington, D.C.
Colonial America	New York	

4. Other Social Sciences

This is the smallest of all topics. The most common topics have been economics and culture. Topics in economics have included monetary exchange and the barter system. Topics in culture have included cultural rules of societies.

Frequency of Ten Kinds of Questions

The following list gives you an idea of the kinds of questions that have been asked in the reading comprehension section. This list represents questions on twelve tests used between 1984 and 1989. You will find an example of each of these questions in this lesson.

Type of Question	Frequency	Approximate Percent
Restatement	117	31
Inference	108	29
Main Idea	49	13
Vocabulary	28	7
Negative Question	21	6
Author's Attitude, Opinion, or Purpose	21	6
Previous or Following Topic	9	2
Referent	8	2
Organization	7	2
Support	7	2
	375	

Description and Examples of Questions

This section describes each kind of reading comprehension question, using the examples from your pretest. As you go through these examples, pay particular attention to the questions that you missed in the pretest. Then check the explanatory answers on pages 274.

Main Idea

Almost every passage has one main idea question and it is often written first. Here are the most common forms for main idea questions:

What is the main topic of the passage?
With what topic is the passage primarily concerned?
What is the best title for this passage?

You usually have to understand the whole passage to choose the answer to these questions, but it also helps you to look carefully at the first sentence and the last sentence of the passage, where the main idea is often summed up.

To look for the main idea of the passage, look for an idea that is common to every sentence or paragraph or look for an idea that every sentence or each paragraph supports.

Incorrect answers to main idea questions are wrong for one of the following reasons:

The statement is too broad. (It encompasses more than the passage states.)
The statement is too narrow. (It relates only to some of the passage or only to one of the paragraphs.)
The statement is not relevant. (It contains information that was not discussed.)

EXAMPLES: Main Idea Questions

1. With what topic is this passage primarily concerned?
- **(A)** The mental abilities of monkeys
- **(B)** Hand preference in primates
- **(C)** Hemispheres of the brain
- **(D)** Experiments on nonhuman primates

2. Which of the following is the best title for this passage?
- **(A)** Smart Monkeys
- **(B)** Primates and Their Use of Language
- **(C)** A Ten Million-Year History
- **(D)** Humans and Primates: A Similarity?

Restatement

This is the most common kind of question on TOEFL exams. In a restatement, you can find the answer directly from the passage, though it may be expressed in different words. A restatement might use synonyms, opposite words, or a restructuring of grammar to express the same idea.

EXAMPLES: Restatement Questions

3. In the first paragraph, what is the monkey expecting?
- **(A)** A blinking light
- **(B)** An earphone
- **(C)** Some food
- **(D)** A telegraph key

4. According to the passage, what do most scientists assume?
- **(A)** Only humans have hand preferences.
- **(B)** Only monkeys can learn to indicate their food choices.
- **(C)** Speaking and understanding are more important than reading and writing.
- **(D)** Setting up experiments for primates is difficult.

Inference

Inference questions are the second most common question asked on TOEFL exams. In these questions, the answer cannot be directly read in the paragraph, and sometimes you must read several sentences in order to understand the inference. Sometimes the question begins with, "It can be inferred that..." or "The author implies that...," but other times there is no clue that this is an inference question.

EXAMPLES: Inference Questions

5. In what situation would a primate be most likely to use its right hand?

(A) Picking out a red block from a group of colored blocks
(B) Pushing a button that is hidden behind a black curtain
(C) Picking up a banana and peeling it
(D) Choosing a food after hearing the correct command

6. Why are scientists probably not very interested in the activity of the monkey as described in the first paragraph?

(A) The experiment has not followed a precise scientific format.
(B) The experiment is too easy for monkeys to do.
(C) Similar studies have been done many times.
(D) Scientists don't agree with the conclusions.

Vocabulary

It is very likely that you will get some questions on vocabulary in your TOEFL exam. In this question, you may need to use context clues to choose the best answer.

The questions might look like this:

In the third sentence, the phrase ________ most probably means that ________.
In the second paragraph, the author uses the phrase ________ to illustrate ________.
As used in line 6, the word ________ refers to ________.
In line 9, the word ________ could best be replaced by ________.

There are different kinds of vocabulary questions. Sometimes the question only requires knowledge of a general dictionary definition. Sometimes the vocabulary question requires you to understand a particular meaning in a particular passage. And sometimes the vocabulary question asks for the meaning of an illustration, example, or concept.

EXAMPLES: Vocabulary Questions

7. The word *grabbing* in line 11 refers to
- **(A)** holding lightly
- **(B)** taking quickly
- **(C)** squeezing tightly
- **(D)** picking up carefully

8. In line 19, the word *challenging* could best be replaced by
- **(A)** accepting
- **(B)** favoring
- **(C)** claiming
- **(D)** contesting

Negative Question

A negative question asks for something that is NOT in the passage. The questions usually begin like this:

Which of the following is NOT mentioned in the passage?
Which of the following would NOT be an example of ________?
All of the following were mentioned in the passage EXCEPT ________.

The answer choices for negative questions often give you words or phrases of things which are written in the passage, but which do not answer the question.

EXAMPLES: Negative Questions

9. Which of the following did the monkeys in this passage NOT do?
- **(A)** Signal their readiness
- **(B)** Differentiate between two syllables
- **(C)** Grab food from a feeding tray
- **(D)** Use alternate hands to lift a key

10. Which of the following statements about the human brain is NOT mentioned?
- **(A)** The left arm is controlled by the right hemisphere.
- **(B)** Right-handedness is connected to stronger mental abilities.
- **(C)** Speaking and understanding are centered in the left side.
- **(D)** The left hemisphere contains the important oral language abilities.

Author's Attitude, Opinion, or Purpose

In this question, you are not looking for a direct answer in the text; instead you must think of what the author is trying to do. Look at these examples:

What is the main purpose of this passage?
Why does the author mention ________?
The author uses an analogy of ________ in order to emphasize which of the following?
Which of the following lines indicates the author's attitude toward ________?
With which of the following statements would the author most likely agree?
Which of the following words best describes the author's tone?

Each of these questions asks for a different type of answer.

What is the author's purpose?

The answer choices might look like this:
To distinguish between ________
To cite examples of ________
To change ________
To trace the development of ________

Why does the author mention ________?

The answer choices might look like this:
To demonstrate that ________
To compare it to ________
To point out that ________
To give an example of ________

What is the author's attitude or tone?

The answer choices might look like this:
Disapproving
Confused
Impatient
Regretful

EXAMPLES: Author's Attitude, Opinion, or Purpose Questions

11. Why does the author begin with the description of a monkey performing an experiment?
    (A) To show the importance of the experiment
    (B) To distinguish between two kinds of research
    (C) To give a generalization of a concept
    (D) To give an example of something to be discussed

12. What is the purpose of the final sentence of the passage?
    (A) To give a reason
    (B) To give a purpose
    (C) To give a description
    (D) To give an example

Previous or Following Possible Topic

For this question you must use your understanding of the passage to infer what might have been written before or what might come next. The clues are often in the first or last sentences.

EXAMPLE: Following Possible Topic Question

13. Which of the following would most likely be the topic of the next paragraph?
    (A) A discussion of the differences between the hemispheres of the brain
    (B) An example of a chimpanzee's ability to comprehend language
    (C) Reasons that some scientists disagree with this hypothesis
    (D) A discussion of experiments that indicate hand preferences

Referent

The word *referent* comes from the verb *to refer*. For this question you must decide which word, phrase, or concept a pronoun is referring to. The questions often begin like the following:

In line XX, what does the word *it* refer to?
The word *they* in the first sentence refers to the ________.

For these questions, you look back to the previous noun or noun phrase to find the meaning. In some cases you must look ahead.

EXAMPLE: Referent Question

14. What does the word *this* refer to in line 6?
(A) Correctly lifting a key
(B) Hearing two syllables through earphones
(C) The process that the monkey is able to carry out
(D) Pressing a key that the monkey cannot see

Organization

The following questions ask for the general organization of the passage.

Which of the following statements best describes the organization of the passage?
How are the events of the passage presented?
Where in the passage does the author describe ________?
The ideas in the passage are divided into two paragraphs in order to contrast ________.

Typical patterns of organization include the following:

chronological order	definition and example	specific to general
comparison/contrast	statement and illustration	order of importance
cause/result	general to specific	alphabetical order

EXAMPLE: Organization Question

15. Which of the following best describes the organization of this passage?
(A) An example is given and then a new hypothesis is discussed.
(B) A concept is discussed before examples are given
(C) A concept is discussed and reasons for it are examined.
(D) The contrasting views of scientists are compared.

Support

This question is similar to a main idea question except that this kind asks about a detail rather than about the whole passage. The questions are similar to this:

Which of the following statements about ________ is supported by this passage?

For the answer, you usually must infer something about one person or one idea. As with the main idea and author's tone questions, be aware of statements that are too broad or too narrow, or that don't answer the question completely.

EXAMPLE: Support Question

16. Which of the following statements is best supported by this passage?

(A) Scientists disagree about the idea of handedness in primates.

(B) The right side of the brain is not as important as the left side.

(C) It is difficult to teach primates to comprehend human messages.

(D) Primates use both hands equally in carrying out precise tasks.

Explanatory Answers

Main Idea

1. (B) The major concern of this passage is the hypothesis that nonhuman primates have a preference for using their left or right hand.
2. (D) The author is writing about a similarity between humans and primates: hand preference. The other choices were mentioned, but are not the main point.

Restatement

3. (A) The only thing that the passage says is coming is the blinking green light. The earphones and telegraph key are already there. Nothing is mentioned about food.
4. (A) Lines 14–15 state that "only humans have the trait of favoring one hand."

Inference

5. (B) Lines 21–23 state that "primates use their right hands to perform precise manipulations where they cannot clearly see what they are doing." Answer (B) is the only choice where the monkey cannot see the object.
6. (C) The passage states (line 7) that studies on animal behavior have been conducted for many years and that this is not an amazing event. Therefore, one can infer that for that reason scientists are not very interested in the monkey experiment as described.

Vocabulary

7. (B) This is the best synonym for *grabbing* in any context.
8. (D) The verb *to challenge* means to *to question* or *to dispute*. Another synonym is the verb *to contest*.

Negative

9. (D) Answer (D) is the only one that the monkeys did not do. Lines 10–11 state that all the monkeys used their right hands to press the key.
10. (B) Nothing is mentioned about a connection between strong mental abilities and right-handedness.

Author's Attitude, Opinion, or Purpose

11. (D) The experiment is an example that introduces the topic that will be discussed. Even though the example does not mention the main point (hand preference), it introduces the idea of animal experiments.
12. (A) The final sentence explains why researchers haven't noticed the hand preference for nonhuman primates.

Following Possible Topic

13. (D) Since the final sentence mentions that it is difficult to set up experiments that require certain tasks, it is likely that the next paragraph would explain this in more detail.

Referent

14. (C) The word *this* refers to the entire process described in the first paragraph.

Organization

15. (A) The example of a monkey experiment is given and then the hypothesis of hand preference is discussed.

Support

16. (A) The fact that scientists disagree is supported by the statement in lines 14–15, "It has generally been assumed that only humans have the trait of favoring one hand, " and also lines 18–19, "...a growing number of researchers are challenging this notion..."

Summary

1. The frequency list of reading comprehension topics from selected TOEFL exams during the 1980s shows that the largest number of reading topics have focused on science.
2. A frequency list of questions asked on selected TOEFL exams shows that the two most common questions are restatement and inference. Almost all passages have one question about the main idea.
3. By practicing with the ten most common questions you will become familiar with the differences between questions. This will help you improve your reading skills and your speed in answering the questions.

Lesson 19

Reading Comprehension Skills

Objectives

- To analyze why reading comprehension is difficult
- To practice reading strategies
- To practice understanding the author's point of view

1. What Is Difficult?
2. What Can Help You with the Difficulties?
3. Improve Your Reading Strategies
4. What Is the Author's Point of View?
5. Advice from Holmes
6. Further Advice From Holmes
7. Reading Comprehension Drills

Lesson 19

What Is Difficult?

For some students the reading comprehension section is the most difficult part of the TOEFL. These students will often say that it is difficult because their reading is very slow. Often, however, it is not reading speed that makes this part difficult. It is the reading topics and vocabulary that create difficulty. Look at these three statements about reading comprehension passages.

1. Reading comprehension passages can be on any topic. It's true that since you can never know exactly which topics will be on the test you cannot prepare for specific topics. What you can do, however, is prepare in general. The frequency lists on pages 264 and 266 in Lesson 18 give you an idea of the topics and questions that have been used on recent tests. From these lists, you get an idea of the general level, the most common kinds of topics and questions that are asked. This gives you a lot of information to use in preparing for the TOEFL. You can practice reading short paragraphs that are similar to the passages on TOEFL tests. When you look at the list of topics in Lesson 18 you see that the majority of passages have been about topics relating to science. In addition, there are passages on United States history, United States government, literature, music, and art. By reading about these general topics, you become familiar with the vocabulary used in these areas. You also get more background information about the topics. Knowing the vocabulary used in a particular situation and having background knowledge about that situation are two of the most important aspects of improving your reading comprehension skills.

It is important to remember, however, that it is not necessary to have specific background knowledge to answer the reading comprehension questions. All the information you need is in each passage. The background information will help you understand more quickly, but it will not give you the specific answers. These passages are not testing you on your knowledge of factual information; they are testing you on whether you have the strategies to get the information from the passage.

Let's assume you begin to read a passage that looks like this:

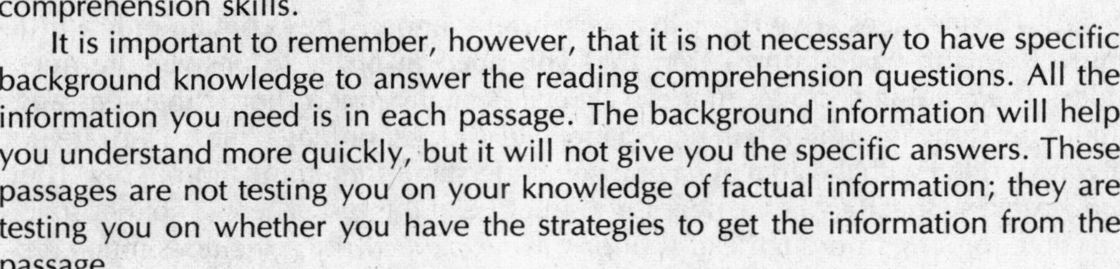

Fort Sill, a colonial outpost on the site of Rome, New York, controlled the principal route from the Hudson River to Lake Ontario.

You may read this sentence and say to yourself, "How can I understand this passage? I don't know what 'Fort Sill' means and I don't know what a 'colonial outpost' is." Never mind. You don't have to know anything about the topic. You should be saying to yourself: "OK. This is a passage I don't know anything about. But I know that all the information I need is right in the passage. In this case, if you have some background knowledge about early American history, the reading may be easier for you. But even if you don't know anything about the topic, your knowledge of test-taking strategies can help you answer the questions.

2. There are no titles and no pictures. Have you ever thought about how much titles and illustrations help your reading comprehension? Even vocabulary lists before a reading can help you prepare to read. However, titles, illustrations, and vocabulary lists, which help you focus on the topic and on what you already know about the topic, are absent on these reading passages.

Read the following short statement:

If it is oil-based, sponge it with turpentine. Then use very hot water. Otherwise, scrape off as much as possible and then use hot water.

Do you know what this short reading is about? It is hard to understand because you have no clues as to what the topic is.

Now read it again.

REMOVING A PAINT STAIN FROM CLOTHING

If it is oil-based, sponge it with turpentine. Then use very hot water. Otherwise, scrape off as much as possible and then use hot water.

The title gives you extra information that helps your comprehension. One of the reasons that short reading passages on the TOEFL are difficult to understand quickly is that they have no extra information. There is nothing you can do about this on the test, but you can prepare by reading other short passages that have no titles or illustrations and trying to guess the topic quickly.

3. The passages are written in a very brief manner. They contain only a little more than the basic information that you need in order to answer the questions. The reading passages in the TOEFL are usually much shorter than passages about the same information in newspapers, textbooks, or magazines. They are not always written with the goal of having you understand something thoroughly. They are written so that they fit the necessary structure of this test. There is neither space nor time for long, thorough explanations. Newspaper writing includes much repetition because the writer wants to interest and inform the reader quickly. In a comparable TOEFL reading passage, many repetitions and explanations may be left out. This makes the reading much more difficult.

Read the following two passages. Both give the same information.

Police say that one reason car vandalism has increased so much over the past three years is that fewer officers patrol the city's neighborhoods. This is partly because the hiring freeze that is supposed to fix the massive budget deficit has left the police with fewer officers. It is also because remaining officers are so busy responding to the other crises that they have no time to patrol the peaceful neighborhoods.

Police traditionally have divided their work into three parts—answering calls from citizens, filling out reports, and doing preventive patrolling in the neighborhoods. "We don't have time to do much patrolling now," the captain of one neighborhood station recently said after the residents complained that they never see patrol officers anymore.

Since there are fewer police officers because of a hiring freeze that is supposed to fix the budget deficit, and since those officers are busy responding to crisis situations, car vandalism has increased. Police have little time left for patrolling in neighborhoods since all their time is taken up by answering calls from citizens and filling out reports.

The shorter passage may be harder to understand because it uses fewer words and more complicated sentences. This kind of writing is typical in the TOEFL exam. Practice for the exam by reading this kind of condensed information. Do all the exercises in this book, of course, but also look in magazines and newspapers for short summaries of news items or reviews of scientific experiments. This reading will help get you prepared for TOEFL reading passages.

What Can Help You?

1. **You can predict something about the topics.** It is certainly true that you can never know exactly what will be on the TOEFL exam. You can, however, be guided by information from past tests. By studying the frequency list in Lesson 18 you can see that most of the topics concern science. On an average test there might be two out of five reading passages that are on the general topic of science. So, even though you can't prepare for a specific subject, you can prepare in general by reading scientific articles.

2. **You get a variety of passages.** Each TOEFL reading section has between four and six passages, and each of these passages might be written in a different style. Some of the styles are easier to read than others. So if one passage is very difficult for you, don't give up. You might find that the next one is easier.

3. **Much of the topic is revealed in the first and last sentences.** The topic sentence is often in the first or last sentence. When you read this you can get an idea of what the passage is about. Sometimes the topic sentence reveals the author's point of view. Often it will give you specific information to use in figuring out the main idea.

4. You don't always need to understand every word in the passage. Sometimes you only need to understand a small portion of the passage in order to answer all the questions. Of course, you need to read all of the passage quickly to get a general idea of the meaning of the passage. But if there is a part of it you don't understand, you shouldn't spend too much time trying to figure it out. That part may not be asked about in any of the questions.

Improve Your Reading Strategies

What Kind of Reader Are You?

Think about what you are doing as you read. Are you an auditory reader or are you a visual reader?

An auditory reader is *listening* to the words as he or she sees them. This reader may even actually say the words quietly while reading. Sometimes you can see the reader's lips moving. If you are this kind of reader, you are probably a slow reader. You need to increase your reading comprehension skills.

A visual reader does not say the words. Instead he or she makes a mental image of the meaning of the words. This reader is actively thinking ahead while reading, often predicting what will come next and is using the skills of prediction, reasoning, questioning, and summarizing to understand the meaning of the passages. This reader realizes that the underlying ideas are more important than each word.

A visual reader reads much faster and comprehends more quickly than an auditory reader. The following exercises in this chapter will help you increase these kinds of reading comprehension skills.

Read in Phrases

A fast reader does not need to read each word carefully. He or she looks over the page and groups words together. Try to train yourself to look at several words at one time. The following exercise will help you.

EXERCISE **1**

Reading In Phrases

1. Read the following passage in your normal way, timing yourself as you read. Check your watch.

   Beginning Time: 10.40

   The age of youth-oriented America is over. Now 25 percent of the people are over the age of 50, and this is the fastest growing segment of the population. Ideas of what constitutes an average lifestyle are changing. Now people go back to school at age 40, change careers at age 50, and fall in love at age 60. Because of these differences there must be changes in home and business design to incorporate the needs of older people. Lighting will have to be adjusted because of people's poorer vision. Doors will have levers rather than knobs. There will be a bigger demand for furniture designed for people with physical ailments. And the print used in magazines, newspapers, and books will have to be made bigger.

   Ending Time: 10.42
   Reading Time: 2

2. Now read the same words by phrases. Try to look at the whole line at one time, reading down the line as fast as you can. Check your watch again.

   Beginning Time: 10.42

The age of
youth-oriented America
is over.
Now 25 percent of the people
are over the age of 50,
and this is
the fastest growing segment
of the population.
Ideas of what constitutes
an average lifestyle are changing.
Now people
go back to school at age 40,
change careers at age 50,
and fall in love at age 60.
Because of these differences
there must be changes
in home and business design
to incorporate the needs
of older people.
Lighting will have to be adjusted
because of people's poorer vision.
Doors will have levers
rather than knobs.
There will be a bigger demand
for furniture
designed for people
with physical ailments.
And the print
used in magazines, newspapers, and books
will have to be made bigger.

Ending Time: 10.43

Reading Time: 1

3. Now try reading this same passage a third time. This time read the phrases as you just did, trying to let your eyes look at the marked phrases all at one time. Check your watch again.

Beginning Time: 10.44.50

The age of youth-oriented America / is over. / Now 25 percent of the people / are over the age of 50, / and this is / the fastest growing segment of the population. / Ideas of what constitutes / an average lifestyle / are changing. / Now people / go back to school at age 40 / change careers at age 50, / and fall in love at age 60. / Because of these differences / there must be changes / in home and business design / to incorporate the needs / of older people. / Lighting will have to be adjusted / because of people's poorer vision. / Doors will have levers / rather than knobs. / There will be a bigger demand / for furniture / designed for people / with physical ailments. / And the print / used in magazines, newspapers,and books / will have to be made bigger. /

Ending time: 10.44.30

Reading Time: 40 sec

Guess What Comes Next

A good reader is always thinking ahead. Your mind predicts what will come next in the reading, and then you check whether or not your prediction is true. The more you know about a topic, the easier it is to read because you can predict more accurately what will come next. Check your prediction skills in the following exercise.

EXERCISE 2

What Comes Next? (Answers, page 298)

Directions: For each of the following paragraphs, first read the paragraph quickly, just trying to get the general idea of the paragraph. Then go back and read each paragraph a second time, writing in the words that you think would fit the blank spaces. Then check your answers in the answer key. There may be other possible answers to the blanks in this exercise. The most important thing is not that you write down the exact word, but that you are able to figure out the overall meaning of the passage without each word in front of you.

READING 1

Are you prepared to save a life? You might be in a ______(1)______ sometime where you need the ______(2)______ to help someone live. You can carry everything you ______(3)______ with you: your hands, lungs, brain, and training in cardiopulmonary resuscitation. Cardiopulmonary resuscitation, usually called CPR, was first described by researchers in 1960. They found that by pushing on the chest of a person and breathing into the person's ______(4)______, they could sustain life until a ______(5)______ or ambulance came. CPR can be performed successfully by anyone who is ______(6)______.

READING 2

The fish are dying in the ______(1)______ of northern New York state. Fishermen are ______(2)______ about it since this ______(3)______ used to be a favorite place for fishing. Now each ______(4)______ there are fewer fish. Why? The problem is acid rain. This pollution comes from factories that burn coal or oil or gas. The wind carries the ______(5)______ into the ______(6)______ which can then come down as rain in an area hundreds of ______(7)______ away. Because of this, factories in the midwest of the United States are causing ______(8)______ in New York. The rain is full of acid chemicals which ______(9)______ the fish in the ______(10)______.

Use Transition Words and Phrases

Transition words and phrases guide your understanding of the overall organization of your reading. They can also help you answer the organization questions on the TOEFL test. Look at the following list of some transition words. Look for these words while you are reading, and make a mental note of what kind of paragraph organization the author is using.

Addition	Contrast	Result	Time
also	however	as a result	after a while
besides	on the other hand	consequently	afterward(s)
furthermore	in contrast	therefore	before
in addition to		in that case	later
moreover			meanwhile
too			then
			previously
			during
			as

EXERCISE 3

Transition Words and Phrases (Answers, page 298)

Directions: Read the following paragraphs and then circle the main transition words, using the list on the previous page (page 285). Then write the type of organization for each reading (Addition, Contrast, Result, or Time).

READING 1

Alexander Hamilton was an American statesman during the late eighteenth century. An illegitimate child, he was born in the West Indies, the son of James Hamilton (of Scottish descent) and Rachel Lavien (daughter of a doctor on the island). As a youth, he went to the North American colonies, and later studied at King's College (now Columbia University). During the Revolutionary War he wrote articles and pamphlets espousing the colonial cause. Later, he became a captain of artillery and, after attracting General Washington's attention, he worked as Washington's secretary and aide-de-camp. By 1780 he had outlined a plan of government with a strong central authority to replace the weak system of the Articles of Confederation.

Circle the words that give you a clue to the organization of this paragraph.
What kind of organization does Reading 1 have? ________

READING 2

The Metropolitan Museum of Art in New York City is the foremost repository of art in the United States. It opened in 1800 on its present site on Central Park facing Fifth Avenue. The museum's most outstanding collections include European paintings and sculpture of the Renaissance, Baroque, and modern periods. In addition, the Egyptian wing has the mastaba of Perneb (from around 2460 B.C.), which has been rebuilt in its original form. Besides the main building containing paintings and sculptures, the museum includes the Cloisters, a separate building devoted to medieval art which also contains an outstanding collection of armor.

Circle the words that give you a clue to the type of organization.
What is the organization of Reading 2? ________

READING 3

Since Vitamin K consists of substances that are essential for the clotting of blood, the human body can suffer without it. A consequence of insufficient Vitamin K is an abnormal length of time for the blood to clot. This may result in multiple hemorrhaging in various tissues. The deficiency occurs in hemorrhagic disease of the newborn infant, in liver damage, and in cases where the vitamin is not absorbed properly by the intestine. Though the deficiency is rarely of dietary origin, it is still prudent to include sources of Vitamin K in the normal diet.

Circle the words which give you a clue to the type of organization.
What is the organization of Reading 3? ________

Pick Out Important Words

When you are reading to get the main idea, you can eliminate many of the unimportant words. Here is one good way to practice reading for the TOEFL exam:

1. Read the first sentence carefully.
2. Skim over the next sentences, looking for the most important words.
3. Read the last sentence of each paragraph carefully.

Practice these skills in the following passage.
An outrigger canoe is a small boat with a wood or bamboo float attached to the side, extending out over the water. Outriggers are used throughout the **South Pacific and in the Indian Ocean**. Designed for **speed and stability**, the outrigger is usually **propelled by sail or paddle**. Some can reach speeds of over **20 miles per hour**. Usually the outrigger sails with the **float facing the wind** in order to **prevent capsizing**, although some outriggers have **two floats** to make them **more steady** in high seas. **These small boats are excellent for island traders.**

As you read the paragraph, it should look similar to this in your mind:
An outrigger canoe is a small boat with a wood or bamboo float attached to the side, extending out over the water. xxxxxxx xxx xxxx xxxxxxxx xxx **South Pacific and in the Indian Ocean.** xxxxxxx **speed and stability**, xxx xxxxxxxxx xx xxxxxxx **propelled by sail or paddle**. xxxx xxx xxxxx xxxxxx xx xxxx **20 miles per hour**. xxxxxxx xxx xxxxxxxxx xxxxx xxxx xxx **float facing the wind** xx xxxxx xx **prevent capsizing**, xxxxxxxx xxxx xxxxxxxxx xxxx **two floats** xx xxxx xxxx **more steady** xx xxxx xxxxx. **These small boats are excellent for island traders.**

Now look at the words which are in dark print:

An outrigger canoe is a small boat with a wood or bamboo float attached to the side, extending out over the water.
South Pacific and in the Indian Ocean
speed and stability
propelled by sail or paddle
20 miles per hour
float facing the wind
prevent capsizing
two floats
more steady
These small boats are excellent for island traders.

These words and phrases answer the main questions: Where? What? How much? How? Why? They are the major nouns, verbs, adjectives, and adverbs.

When you are looking for the important words, look for names of people and places; look for dates, times, and other numbers. Skim over the verb "to be" and the repeated words. There is no single answer to the question of how much you can skim over. Skimming depends on your ability, your background knowledge, and your purpose. Try skimming a little faster each time you practice, always checking to be sure that you are getting the main ideas.

EXERCISE **4**

Picking Out Important Words (Answers, page 298)

Directions: As you read the following passages, underline the words that you think are most important.

READING 1

A new sport has hit the ski slopes. If you're "cool" you call it "shredding." If you want to be technical, you call it "snowboard skiing." But most people call it "snowboarding." This sport has been gaining in popularity in the last few years. It's a combination of skateboarding and surfing, and is done on a board somewhat like a wide, short ski. The boards, which are often very colorful, are between 3-1/2 feet and 5 feet long and are about 11 inches wide. Special snowboard boots are clamped snugly into the bindings. Snowboarding is so popular in the United States, Europe, and Japan that there are now worldwide competitions with racing and freestyle events. Even though it's becoming common on the ski slopes, it is seen by some alpine skiers as frivolous. A common image of a snowboarder is one who is young and adventurous, of someone who takes risks and is rebellious.

READING 2

An exhibition of holograms is a strange sight. When you walk into the exhibition rooms, you may at first see only "empty" frames. But as you walk around, looking from certain angles and distances, you see the images appearing to turn off and on as you move. In addition, there are often tiny lamps suspended from the ceiling in dimly lit rooms. This adds to the eerie effect.

Holograms first became common in museums in the early 1970s. Since then they have undergone a multitude of breakthroughs and technological developments. Now they are much brighter and can be seen from a wide range of angles and distances. Whereas in the past, many holographers concentrated solely on technical concerns, now they are dedicating themselves to artistic concerns as well. Holography is definitely an important art form, one that will gain importance in the future.

Use Context Clues

As you practice reading for the TOEFL exam, don't use your dictionary while you are reading a passage the first time. After all, you won't be able to use your dictionary while you are taking the test and if you are stopping often to look up new words, your reading becomes slow. Instead of always looking up new words, concentrate on the whole meaning of the passage. Skip over the words that you don't know. Form an image in your mind of what the author is saying rather than trying to memorize each word. You will understand more of the passage if you remember the general meaning than if you concentrate on the meanings of individual words. Remember that you don't always need to know every word in order to understand the main idea.

As you practice reading skills, keep a pencil in your hand and underline the words you think are the most important (as you did in Exercise 4). Also make a mark beside the words you don't know. Then, after you are finished with the reading, go back and guess at the meanings of the new words. After that, ask someone or use your dictionary to see if your guess was right.

When you study new words, always think of them in the context of the reading. Visualize in your mind what the word means in that particular passage.

When you are trying to understand new words in context, there are several clues to use:

Your knowledge of roots, prefixes, and suffixes
Logical reasoning skills
Sentence punctuation
Sentence connecting words
Preceding and following sentences and words

1. ROOTS, PREFIXES, AND SUFFIXES

Common Roots and Their Meanings:

cide = kill	mort = death
cycle = wheel or circle	pend = hang
dent = tooth	phon = sound
dict = speak	psy = mind
fract = break	scope = see
graph = written, instrument	scrip = write
manu = hand	sect = cut
meter = measure	rupt = break
micro = small	

Common Prefixes:

•*Prefixes that mean no or not*

il	un
im	anti
in	dis
ir	mis

•*Prefixes that stand for numbers*

mono, uni = 1	penta, quint = 5
du, bi = 2	deca = 10
tri = 3	cent = 100
quad = 4	poly, multi = many

•*Prefixes that stand for relationships*

ante/anti = before	pre = before
circum = around	post = after
co, com = together	sub = under
inter = between	sur, super = above
peri = around	sym, syn = together, same

Common Suffixes:

•*Noun endings*

-ion -ment -ence
-tion -ness -ance
-sion -ity

•*Adjective endings*

-ic -ive -ous
-ish -y -al

•*Suffixes that stand for person*

-er -ier -or
-ist -cian

2. LOGICAL REASONING

Take a guess based on your own background knowledge and understanding of a particular situation.

> **EXAMPLE:**
>
> Feeling *satiated* after the delicious banquet, I lay down on the bed and went to sleep.

How do you feel after a big banquet? Full, not hungry. You can guess that *satiated* means *full*.

3. SENTENCE PUNCTUATION

Commas can help you guess at the meanings of words. Sometimes commas indicate words in a series. These words usually have a close relationship.

> **EXAMPLE:**
>
> Halloween night was a night for witches, *warlocks,* and ghosts.

The word *warlocks* is similar to the words *witches* and *ghosts*. It means a person who can do magic or can make an agreement with the devil.

Commas also indicate definitions within sentences.

> **EXAMPLE:**
>
> The old man was a *recluse*, living a life of religious solitude.

The word *recluse* means someone who lives apart from the rest of the world. Sometimes this is a chosen way of life for religious purposes.

4. SENTENCE CONNECTING WORDS

Some connecting words indicate an opposite or contrasting meaning in the sentence:

although	however
but	even though
in contrast to	

EXAMPLE:

Although he felt nervous as he walked up on stage, he felt composed after he began his presentation.

The word *although* indicates an opposite feeling. The two words which are opposite are *nervous* and *composed*. *Composed* means *calm* or *at ease*.

EXAMPLE:

In contrast to her quiet cousin, Florence was vivacious.

The words *in contrast to* indicate that *vivacious* will be the opposite of *quiet*. *Vivacious* means *lively, animated,* or *high spirited*.

5. PRECEDING AND FOLLOWING SENTENCES AND WORDS

Sometimes the sentences before or after the difficult words will give you a clue to the meaning.

EXAMPLE:

Spectators must stay behind the railing; only the participants are allowed on the floor.

The second part of this sentence gives you the clue that the word *spectators* means people who are not participants. *Spectators* are the people who are watching a performance, show, or game.

EXERCISE 5

Using Context Clues (Answers, page 299)

Directions: Guess the underlined words by using the context clues in each sentence. Do not use your dictionary. Check your answers after you guess.

How much are you influenced by the future? In some ways, we all are. Think about weather predictions. If there is a report of rain, we know what to wear or take with us. But some people also base their activities on premonitions. These thoughts are not necessarily based on fact, but on feelings. Sometimes they seem so strong that we postpone our immediate plans until these feelings pass. A business which can successfully anticipate changes in supply or demand can make a lot of money. On the other hand, if a business blunders by misjudging imminent events, it can go bankrupt.
Guess the meanings of the following words. Write the clues that helped you guess the meanings.

WORD	MEANING	CLUE
1. prediction	____________	____________
2. base	____________	____________
3. premonition	____________	____________
4. postpone	____________	____________
5. anticipate	____________	____________
6. demand	____________	____________
7. blunder	____________	____________
8. misjudge	____________	____________
9. imminent	____________	____________
10. bankrupt	____________	____________

What Is the Author's Point of View?

Many TOEFL reading comprehension exams have questions about the author's attitude, opinion, feeling, or tone. The question may be something like:
What is the author's tone in this passage?

(A) Pleased

(B) Disgusted

(C) Skeptical

(D) Amused

To find out the answer to these types of questions, skim through the passage looking for adjectives, adverbs, verbs, and nouns that give you clues to the author's feelings.

EXAMPLES:

1. Sentence: In such a situation, all of us lose a valuable piece of history that can never be retrieved.
Author's feeling: regret
Clue words: lose, never be retrieved

2. Sentence: She was admired for her common sense, her wit, and her compassion for those less fortunate.
Author's feeling: respect
Clue words: admired

3. Sentence: I couldn't believe that the mayor could actually make such a fool of himself as he did at the pie-eating contest.
Author's feeling: amusement
Clue words: couldn't believe, such a fool of himself

EXERCISE 6

Author's Tone of Voice (Answers, page 299)

Directions: For each sentence, guess the author's feeling. Choose from one or more of the following words:

amused	angry	pleased
regretful	respectful	worried
surprised		

1. His proposal contrasts sharply with the accepted views of most educated people.

   The author probably feels ________________________.
2. No one should be allowed to conduct such an experiment.

   The author probably feels ________________________.
3. The disappearance and reappearance of this constellation represents the most complete and arguably the fastest stellar eclipse yet seen.

   The author probably feels ________________________.
4. The radiation from intense solar disturbances could disrupt radio and telephone communications, damage electronic systems in satellites, and present radiation hazards to astronauts and aircraft passengers at high altitudes.

   The author probably feels ________________________.
5. The scientists wisely used the three results, plus further analysis of previous experiments, to confirm the validity of their earlier hypothesis.

   The author probably feels ________________________.

Advice From Holmes

When Holmes tries to solve a problem, he looks at the complete situation, not only the separate parts. For reading, he suggests that you think about each reading passage as a unit that includes the paragraph and the questions that follow it. Don't think of the passage as the first item and the questions that follow as the second item. Why? Because the questions can give clues about how to read. They often tell what information is important for understanding the passage and answering the questions.

Therefore, Holmes' words of advice are: *Use the questions as clues to help you read the passage quickly and efficiently.* There are two times that you can use the questions: 1) before you read the passage; 2) after you read the passage.

Before You Read the Passage:

A very quick look at the questions gives you an idea about what you need to know. Look at the following question stems from a passage that is NOT written here, and guess as much as you can about the topic of the passage.

1. In this passage, the author mentions the actor's birthplace in order to ________.
2. In line 6, the word *truant* can best be replaced by ________.
3. According to the passage, why does the actor support humanitarian causes?

Even without reading the passage at all, you can make several assumptions about the paragraph.

The passage is about an actor.
The actor's birthplace is important for some reason.
It is important to notice the word *truant*.
The actor gives money to (supports) some kind of humanitarian organization.

Reading quickly like this is called *skimming*. You are not reading to get the answers. You are only looking quickly to get a little information. Don't spend time reading the four answer choices. The answer choices will probably be too confusing because they give you too much information. Just skim over the questions. By reading the questions before you read the passage, you can get a brief idea of what the passage will be about.

After You Read the Passage

After you read the passage carefully (especially concentrating on the first and last sentences of each passage), you will probably be able to answer some of the questions without looking back. But there will probably be other questions that you can't answer. For those questions, the question stem can help you know what to look for.

The question stems give you an idea of what to scan for. Scanning is what you do when you are looking for some particular information. You scan, for instance, when you are looking up a number in a telephone book.

Sometimes the question stem will give you one word or phrase to scan for. In that case, you don't have to read the whole paragraph all the way through a second time. You can just concentrate on looking for one word. Some question stems give you information for scanning and some don't.

Look at the following question stems. Which ones give you information for scanning? What do they tell you to scan for?

1. With what topic is this passage primarily concerned?

This type of question doesn't give you any clues for scanning. You must understand the whole passage.

2. Who manages the 600 acres of wildlife preserve?

For this question, scan the passage for the word *manager* or *managing* or the number *600 acres*. Also, you know you are probably looking for the name of a person.

3. Why is the ancient gabbro rock now found only in isolated places?

Scan the passage for the words *gabbro rock* or the word *isolated*.

4. Which of the following statements is best supported by this passage?

This type of question does not give you any information to scan for.

5. The word *outcroppings* in line 9 refers to ________.

Scan through the passage, checking line 9 for the word *outcroppings*.

Further Advice From Holmes

In each TOEFL test there are five or six different reading comprehension passages, each one focusing on a different topic. As you know, the more background you have in a particular area, the easier it is for you to read and comprehend a passage in that area. Therefore, in order to be sure you have time to read the passages that are easier for you, glance at all the passages to get an idea of their topics. Don't spend such a long time on a difficult part that you don't have time to read and answer the questions in an easier part. Maybe the passage that is easiest for you is the last passage. Don't spend too long on hard questions. You can always come back to them after you finish all the passages.

Summary

1. The reading passages can be on any topic, but the most common are topics relating to science. Knowing something about the topic in general can make your reading faster, though this knowledge is not necessary for answering the questions.

2. The reading is made more difficult because it lacks titles and illustrations.

3. A visual reader, one who does not actually say each word, is faster than someone who is pronouncing each word.

4. Some strategies for improving reading comprehension are reading in phrases, guessing the words or ideas that come next, noticing the effect of transition words, being able to pick out the important words, and being able to use context clues to guess at the meanings of new words.

5. You can guess the author's tone by looking at adjectives, adverbs, verbs, and nouns in the passage.

6. Use the questions to help you skim for general meaning and scan for specific words.

7. Don't spend so much time on difficult questions and passages that you don't have time to read and answer the ones that are easier for you. Glance ahead at passages so you can get an idea of the topics in all of them.

Explanatory Answers

EXERCISE 1

(No answers are necessary for this exercise.)

EXERCISE 2, page 285

Some possible answers are given here. Others may be possible.

READING 1: (1) situation, place, problem, position
(2) knowledge, skills, equipment
(3) need, want, have to have
(4) mouth
(5) doctor, nurse, medical person
(6) trained, old enough, knowledgeable

READING 2: (1) lakes, rivers, ponds, waters (*Ocean* is incorrect because there is no ocean in New York State.)
(2) concerned, worried angry
(3) area, place
(4) year, month, season
(5) pollution, smoke, bad air, chemicals
(6) clouds, sky, air
(7) miles, kilometers
(8) problems, pollution
(9) kill
(10) water, rivers, lakes

EXERCISE 3, page 286

READING 1: This is a paragraph written in time (chronological) order.
The clue words are:
during the late eighteenth century
As a youth
later studied
During the Revolutionary War
Later he became...
after attracting...
By 1790

READING 2: This paragraph is adding information (addition).
The clue words are:
In addition
Besides
also

READING 3: This is a cause and result paragraph.
The clue words are:
Since
A *consequence* of...
may *result* in ...

EXERCISE 4, page 288

There are many different correct answers to this exercise. You must underline the words that are important to you. This is only one example.

READING 1: A new sport has hit the ski slopes. If you're "cool" you call it "shredding." If you want to be technical, you call it "snowboard skiing." But most people call it "snowboarding." This sport has been gaining in popularity in the last few years. It's a combination of skateboarding and surfing, and is done on a board somewhat like a wide, short ski. The boards, which are often very colorful, are between 3-½ feet and 5 feet long and are about 11 inches wide. Special snowboard boots are clamped snugly into the bindings. Snowboarding is so popular in the United States, Europe, and Japan that there are now worldwide competitions with racing and freestyle events. Even though it's becoming common on the ski slopes, it is seen by some alpine skiers as frivolous. A common image of a snowboarder is one who is young and adventurous, of someone who takes risks and is rebellious.

READING 2: An exhibition of holograms is a strange sight. When you walk into the exhibition rooms, you may at first see only "empty" frames. But as you walk around, looking from certain angles and distances, you see the images appearing to turn off and on as you move. In addition, there are often tiny lamps suspended from the ceiling in dimly lit rooms. This adds to the eerie effect. Holograms first became common in museums in the early 1970s. Since then they have undergone a multitude of breakthroughs and technological developments. Now they are much brighter and can be seen from a wide range of angles and distances. Whereas in the past, many holographers concentrated solely on technical concerns, now they are dedicating themselves to artistic concerns as well. Holography is definitely an important art form, one that will be gaining importance in the future.

EXERCISE 5, page 292

1. prediction = telling about the future
Clue: (root words) pre = before; dict = speak
The meaning here is similar to *decide on* or *choose.*
2. base = to make or form a foundation for
Clue: (logical reasoning) What verb might go with the word *activity?* Also you might guess the meaning of *base* as part of the word *basement,* the lowest part of a building, often underground.
3. premonition = thoughts telling or warning about something before it happens
Clue: (root words) pre = before; Clue: (following sentence) "These thoughts are not based on fact but on feelings."
4. postpone = do later
Clue: (root words) post = after
5. anticipate = hope for something in the future
Clue: (root words) anti = before
6. demand = what people want and can pay for
Clue: (logical reasoning) What does a business do to make money? Give people the things they want.
7. blunder = make a mistake
Clue: (sentence connecting words - "on the other hand") The word contrasts with "make a lot of money."
8. misjudge = give wrong decision about something
Clue: (root word) mis = wrong or not
9. imminent = coming soon
Clue: (logical reasoning) The whole paragraph is about the future.
10. bankrupt = going out of business, losing money
Clue: (root word) -rupt = break;
Clue: (previous sentence) A business can make a lot of money. On the other hand, it can go bankrupt.

EXERCISE 6, page 294

1. The author seems surprised or possibly angry or worried.
Clue words: contrasts sharply
2. The author seems angry. He could also be worried or surprised.
Clue words: no one should be allowed
3. The author seems surprised or respectful or pleased
Clue words: most complete and fastest yet seen
4. The author seems worried, or angry or surprised.
Clue words: could disrupt, damage, and present hazards
5. The author seems pleased or respectful.
Clue words: wisely used, confirm

Reading Comprehension Drills

The following pages contain five drills. The first one is a "Walk-Through" to help guide your thought process as you "walk" through each passage. On the left side of the page are the passages and questions. On the right side are the answers and explanations. Read it as you answer the questions to check on your reading strategies and skills.

The remaining drills each contain two passages and ten questions. They are in the same style as the TOEFL exam. The answers and explanations for all the drills begin on page 314.

Walk-Through

Directions: Each passage below is followed by questions based on its content. Answer all questions following a passage on the basis of what is *stated* or *implied* in that passage.

Pity the poor steelhead trout. As if it weren't risky enough dodging fishermen and hungry predators, some of the luckless fish fight their way miles upstream to mate, only to be stopped by a high waterfall or an impassable dam. Because of this problem, thoughtful water officials have installed special ladders and pools at their pumping stations. Now as the fish swim upstream they encounter a new series of low rock dams and pools instead of the 4-foot waterfall that made a difficult jump for the steelhead. And during the entire migrating season a fish ladder will allow fish to make it over the wooden dam, even when the company pumps are operating.

The first sentence of this passage gives the author's tone as well as the main topic. If you know what *trout* means, you know that this passage is about a type of fish. But even if you don't know what a trout is, you should be able to figure it out by the second sentence with the words *some of the luckless fish*. The word *luckless* also shows the author's tone.

1. This passage is mainly about
(A) a problem for fish
(B) waterfalls that are too high
(C) company pumps
(D) the mating season for trout

1. (A) This is a main idea question. The first two sentences tell you that the passage will be about a problem that fish have.
(B) is incorrect because it is only one example of the problem.
(C) is incorrect because this is only mentioned as the place where the problem occurs.
(D) is incorrect because it is mentioned as an example of when the problem occurs.

2. Why have special ladders been installed at some pumping stations?
(A) To help the fish mate
(B) To help the fish swim upstream
(C) To keep the fish from dying
(D) To protect fish from predators

2. (B) This is a restatement question. The passage states that as the fish are swimming upstream they are stopped by high waterfalls and dams. Then the passage states that because of *this* problem, special ladders have been installed. This question also tests your understanding of the word *this*.
(A) can be eliminated because it is not the best answer. The fish are swimming upstream in order to mate, but the ladders don't help them mate. They help them get to the place where they can mate.
(C) This answer may be true but it is not stated in the passage so it is not the best answer.
(D) is incorrect because the mention of predators is used as another example of the troubles that these fish have.

3. Which of the following words best describes the author's tone?
(A) Excited
(B) Saddened
(C) Amused
(D) Concerned

One of nature's richest, most productive habitats, riparian woodland once bordered more than 800,000 acres of waterways draining into the Sierra Nevada Mountains. Now this area has shrunk to about 12,000 acres because of the cutting down of willow and cottonwood trees. This decline in riparian woodland has resulted in the loss of habitat for a variety of species, including the yellow-billed cuckoo.

Around the turn of the century, the cuckoo population probably stood at about 70,000 breeding pairs in California. Today fewer than 300 of the birds exist in California. Their fate has been connected with the decline of riparian woodland, for when the cuckoos arrive each summer they rely on the willow and cottonwood trees for nesting and foraging. Each pair needs about 40 acres in order to forage for their food. Volunteers are now trying to expand the habitat for the yellow-billed cuckoo. So far, 75 acres of riparian woodland have been restored.

4. Which of the following would be the best title for this passage?
(A) Habits of Birds
(B) The Sierra Nevada Mountains
(C) Effects of Shrinking Woodlands
(D) Seeing Is Believing

3. (D) The author's tone is given with several words in this passage. The first word gives the first clue: *pity*. In the second sentence, the author mentions the *luckless* fish. Later the author says that the water officials are *thoughtful*. All of these words show that the author is concerned.
(A) is incorrect because no words specifically show that the author is excited.
(B) Even though the author may feel sadness about the plight of the fish, there is no general feeling of sadness expressed in this passage.
(C) Nothing in the passage gives any clues that the author thinks this situation is funny.

The first sentence of this passage tells you that the paragraph will be about a rich woodland area. Even if you don't know the meaning of *riparian,* you can guess that it has something to do with woodland or trees. The word *once* in the first sentence also tells you that something is not happening now. The last sentence of this first paragraph also gives you a main topic: the cuckoo. If you don't know the meaning of *cuckoo* you can guess that it is some kind of bird from the reference to building nests in the middle of the second paragraph.

4. (C) This is the best choice since the passage describes the connection between a declining cuckoo population and a decline in trees.
(A) is incorrect because the author does not discuss all birds.
(B) is incorrect because the Sierra Nevada Mountains are only mentioned to show the place.
(D) is incorrect because *seeing is believing* means that something is surprising. It means that you might not believe something unless you actually see it. That idea was not expressed in this paragraph.

5. According to the passage, which of the following is NOT true about riparian woodland?
(A) It has declined.
(B) It is rich.
(C) It is a waterway.
(D) It is a bird's habitat.

5. (C) This is a negative fact question. You can eliminate all the other choices because they are true. This answer is false because the area borders a waterway, but is not a waterway itself.
(A) is true because the second sentence of the passage states that, ". . . this area once bordered more than . . . ." And the third sentence begins with, "Now this area has shrunk . . . ."
(B) is true because the first sentence begins with, "one of nature's richest . . . ."
(D) is true because the first paragraph states that there is a "loss of habitat for a variety of species, including the yellow-billed cuckoo." And the last sentence says that the habitat has been expanded.

6. Which word is closest in meaning to the word "forage" as used in the second paragraph in the phrase, "in order to forage"?
(A) have babies
(B) nest
(C) search
(D) lay eggs

6. (C) *Forage* means *to search*. If you don't know this word you might choose by elimination.
(A) The sentence would not make sense if you say "have babies for food."
(B) must be incorrect because one sentence says, "nesting and foraging," therefore it cannot mean *nest*.
(D) must be incorrect because of logical reasoning. A bird does not need 40 acres to lay eggs.

7. What are volunteers trying to do?
(A) Plant trees
(B) Make nests
(C) Feed birds
(D) Breed cuckoos

7. (A) The last two sentences give you this information. "Volunteers are trying to *expand* the habitat . . . . 75 acres have been . . . *restored*." Expanding the habitat means to make more trees for the birds.
(B) must be incorrect because there is nothing said about volunteers making nests. Only the birds are making nests.
(C) is also incorrect because only the birds are searching for food.
(D) must be incorrect because nothing is said about volunteers trying to hatch bird eggs.

But is running really good for your health? A study done on marathon runners showed that runners increased their odds for infectious diseases such as colds and flu during heavy training periods and just after a marathon. Those runners who ran more than 60 miles a week doubled their odds for self-reported diseases over those who ran less than 20 miles per week. And of the marathoners who did not get sick before a race, 12.9 percent became sick during the week after the race. This compares to only 2.2 percent of similarly conditioned runners who did not run in that particular race.

By beginning with the word *but,* the author is showing that this whole passage is a response to an opposite idea. In this case the opposite idea is probably about the positive effects of running. Also, by beginning with a question, the author is telling us that the passage will be an answer to this question. We can see in the second sentence that it is a report of a scientific study, and furthermore, that it is probably important to pay attention to the numbers that are written.

8. From this passage, we can conclude that
(A) it is not healthy to run
(B) runners usually get sick after racing
(C) it is odd to get a cold during training
(D) runners who run a lot are more likely to get sick

8. (D) This is a restatement from the sentence that begins, "Those runners who ran more than 60 miles per week . . . ."
(A) is too general a statement. The study is only discussing how many people report sicknesses, not whether the whole sport of running is healthy.
(B) is also too general a statement. The study does not say that *usually* people get sick. It only says that the runners who participate are more likely to get sick than those who do not participate.
(C) uses the word *odd* to mean *strange.* In this passage, however, the word *odds* means *chances.*

9. The word *odds* in the second sentence can best be replaced by
(A) chances
(B) figures
(C) pieces
(D) triumphs

9. (A) The word *chances* is a synonym for *odds.* It is used to describe the probability of a particular event happening. This term is often used in betting.
(B) is incorrect because *figures* would most likely refer to *numbers* in this context. It is not a synonym.
(C) is incorrect because *pieces* refers to small bits of something.
(D) is incorrect because *triumphs* refers to something that one has done well; a success or victory.

10. What topic was the previous paragraph most likely about?
(A) A discussion of other diseases
(B) A discussion of the benefits of running
(C) A study about the effects of other types of exercises
(D) A way to cure colds and flu

10. (B) The word *but* shows that the previous paragraph must discuss a contrasting idea. Answer B is the only answer choice that indicates an opposition. The words "good for your health" indicate that the previous paragraph discussed something good about running. This passage discusses something bad about running.
(A) is incorrect because it shows an additional idea, not an opposite idea.
(C) is incorrect because it is an additional idea, not an opposite idea.
(D) is incorrect because curing colds is not the opposite of running.

Drill 1 (Answers, page 314)

Directions: Each passage below is followed by questions based on its content. Answer all questions following a passage on the basis of what is *stated* or *implied* in that passage.

The Iditarod sled race has once again woven its way across miles of barren country in Alaska. Inspired by a sled-dog relay of serum to Nome for a diphtheria outbreak in 1973, it has continued each year along the storm-raked coast. The mushers race across 1168 miles from Anchorage to Nome, stopping only to get food for themselves and their dogs, and to sleep in camps or homes along the way. Temperatures often hover around zero with the wind chill factor dropping the temperature to minus 20 degrees or more. The winner gets as much as $50,000, but only the hardiest competitors can enter this unique race.

1. What is the author's most likely feeling about this race and its competitors?
(A) Respect
(B) Fear
(C) Amusement
(D) Worry

2. The word *it* in line 3 refers to
(A) Nome
(B) diphtheria
(C) the race
(D) serum

3. Which of the following statements is NOT true according to the passage?
(A) There has been diphtheria in Alaska since 1973.
(B) The racers stop only to eat and sleep.
(C) The race is more than 1000 miles long.
(D) It can be very cold during the race.

4. The author implies that the coastal areas of Alaska
(A) have illnesses such as diphtheria
(B) are very stormy
(C) are never warm
(D) are places to make money

5. What word can be best substituted for the word *hardiest* in the last sentence?
(A) heaviest
(B) most outgoing
(C) friendliest
(D) strongest

Loved and admired by all who knew him, Tony Lazzeri became a victim of the passage of time. His marvelous achievements were known long before the advent of television, but it is only just recently that his name has been added to the Bay Area Sports Hall of Fame. Old-timers still insist that the 1927 Yankees were the best baseball team of all time. Besides Lazzeri, the famous names included Joe DiMaggio, Lefty Gomez, and Frank Crosetti. There are stories of how the opposing teams were reduced to jelly before the game even started, just by watching the Yankees take batting practice. It was Lazzeri who seemed to hold the team together. As one of his teammates recalled, "Tony not only was a great ballplayer, he was a great man. He was a leader. He was like a manager on the field." Lazzeri had a reputation as one of the smartest 15 players in baseball. He often called strategies, defensively as well as offensively. He would call the signals for such maneuvers as the hit-and-run. He took baseball very seriously. Tony's inauguration into the Bay Area Sports Hall of Fame was posthumous since Tony died of a heart attack in 1946 when he was only 42. For many who idolized Tony, this inauguration was nice, but not enough. "He should be in the big Hall of Fame, the one in Cooperstown," they say.

6. With which of the following subjects is the passage mainly concerned?
(A) The formation of a famous baseball team
(B) The death of Tony Lazzeri
(C) Maneuvers that make ballplayers great
(D) Why Lazzeri had such a reputation

7. DiMaggio, Gomez, Crosetti, and Lazzeri were all
(A) victims
(B) Yankees
(C) batters
(D) teams

8. The phrase *reduced to jelly* in line 6 most likely means that the opposing teams were
(A) nervous
(B) beaten up
(C) made to feel small
(D) very thoughtful

9. The author implies that Lazzeri was a man who
(A) provided strength to the team
(B) idolized baseball
(C) rarely got tired while playing
(D) enjoyed being famous

10. What is in Cooperstown?
(A) Tony Lazzeri's grave
(B) The Yankee stadium
(C) A Hall of Fame
(D) A baseball team

Drill 2 (Answers, page 315)

Directions: Each passage below is followed by questions based on its content. Answer all questions following a passage on the basis of what is *stated* or *implied* in that passage.

Edwin Forrest, often acknowledged as America's first national idol of American theater, was born in Philadelphia in 1806. He was only 14 years old when he played Young Norval in Home's *Douglas*. He gained experience supporting Edmund Kean in Shakespearean roles. In 1826 he established himself as one of the great tragedians of the century with his role as Othello in a New York debut. His acting was bold and forceful, though he was also criticized for his boasting and loud language. His violent temper did not injure his reputation as an actor, though, and his last appearance as Richelieu in Boston in 1871 was greeted with acclaim.

1. Which of the following statements is best supported by this passage?
- **(A)** Though Edwin Forrest was criticized, his reputation was not damaged.
- **(B)** Forrest was a great actor, but was brought down by his uncontrollable temper.
- **(C)** Though bold in his acting, in reality Forrest's life was a tragedy.
- **(D)** Forrest became a national idol at age 14, but was ruined later.

2. Which of the following roles was NOT one that Forrest played?
- **(A)** Young Norval
- **(B)** Edmund Kean
- **(C)** Othello
- **(D)** Richelieu

3. According to the author Forrest was
- **(A)** angry
- **(B)** temperamental
- **(C)** satisfied
- **(D)** creative

4. The word *injure* in line 7 could best be replaced by which of the following?
- **(A)** support
- **(B)** critique
- **(C)** damage
- **(D)** offend

5. According to the passage, what happened in 1826?
- **(A)** New York produced a new tragedian.
- **(B)** Forrest was in a New York play.
- **(C)** Forrest made his first debut.
- **(D)** *Othello* became known as a great tragedy.

What is the cause of chronic fatigue syndrome? Past research has suggested a link to the Epstein-Barr virus, but now many scientists are questioning that connection. New findings suggest that the Epstein-Barr virus is not a primary cause, but it may still trigger the illness. The symptoms may be due to a variety of things, rather than just one. Still, some researchers are sticking with the idea of Epstein-Barr virus causing the illness. They say that it is premature to make such a judgment.

Chronic fatigue syndrome has been dubbed the "yuppie disease" by some since it is often diagnosed in professional women in their twenties and thirties. It may be the result of never recovering completely from illnesses such as the flu. Though the cause is not clear, the symptoms are. To be called a chronic fatigue sufferer, one must have the debilitating illness for more than six months and must exhibit at least eight of the eleven symptoms, including sore throat, mild fever, and muscular aches.

6. With which of the following subjects is the passage mainly concerned?
(A) A disagreement between scientists
(B) Diseases affecting yuppies
(C) Causes and symptoms of an illness
(D) The relationship between a virus and an illness

7. Why is this illness often called the "yuppie disease?"
(A) It affects so many young professional women.
(B) It has so many symptoms.
(C) It is difficult to treat.
(D) No one knows for sure what causes it.

8. According to the passage, a sufferer of chronic fatigue syndrome
(A) will be sick for about six months
(B) will have had the flu
(C) will have eleven symptoms
(D) will have sore throat, aches, and fever

9. According to the passage, which of the following statements about chronic fatigue syndrome is best supported?
(A) A sufferer might never recover from it.
(B) Scientists don't agree on the cause.
(C) It is more common among women than men.
(D) The Epstein-Barr virus can cause premature effects of the illness.

10. Chronic fatigue syndrome will cause which of the following?
(A) Weakness
(B) Vomiting
(C) Rash
(D) Dizziness

Drill 3 (Answers, page 316)

Directions: Each passage below is followed by questions based on its content. Answer all questions following a passage on the basis of what is *stated* or *implied* in that passage.

Originator of the Montessori method of education for preschool children, Maria Montessori was the first woman to receive a medical degree in Italy. After receiving her degree in 1894, she worked with subnormal children as a psychiatrist at the University of Rome. It was there that she pioneered in the instruction of retarded children, especially through the use of an environment rich in manipulative materials. The success of Maria's program with retarded children led her to believe that the same improvements could be made in the education of normal preschool children. This led her to open the first day care center in Rome. With its success similar institutions were opened in other parts of Europe and in the United States. In the early part of this century, however, interest in the Montessori method declined because of those who argued that education should be more disciplined. But by the late 1950s the Montessori method experienced a renaissance, and in the 1960s the American Montessori Society was formed. The chief components of the Montessori method are self-motivation and autoeducation. Followers of the method believe that a child will learn naturally if put in an environment with the proper materials. The teacher acts as observer and only interferes if help is needed. Educators in this system are trying to reverse the traditional system of an active teacher and a passive class.

1. The best title for this passage is
(A) Self-Motivation
(B) The Montessori Method
(C) Educating Subnormal Children
(D) A New System of Education

2. In 1894 Maria Montessori
(A) opened a new day care center
(B) worked as a psychiatrist
(C) taught normal preschool children
(D) disciplined retarded children

3. The author implies that Maria Montessori believes that
(A) children need strong discipline
(B) it is important that teachers instruct children clearly
(C) teachers should be very active
(D) children will learn by themselves

4. With which phrase could the words *rich in* (in line 5) best be replaced?
(A) having an abundant supply of
(B) with a number of expensive
(C) containing deep and strong
(D) that amuses children with

5. The author implies that in this method of education, the most important things are
(A) teachers
(B) rules
(C) materials
(D) observers

19

Port-wine stains are distinctive birthmarks which cause red or purple stains on the skin. In the past physicians have tried to remove them with skin grafts or tatoo over them to hide them. Treatments such as these have never worked very well. A better treatment is argon-laser therapy, which has been useful with adults, but is unacceptable in children because of the scars it produces. A newer technique is gaining in popularity: dye laser. With dye laser, the average patient needs more than six sessions, but the results are dramatic. The treated skin is identical in texture and color to the adjacent normal skin in most people. Even in children, the treatment is amazing. The abnormal blood vessels that cause the disfiguring mark are slowly replaced by blood vessels of normal size and the skin color gradually fades to the normal tone. This treatment should bring relief to both parents and children who are worried about psychological development as well as disfigurement.

6. With which of the following subjects is this passage mainly concerned?
(A) Argon-laser therapy and its benefits
(B) Psychological problems among children with birthmarks
(C) The effects of dye laser treatment
(D) Birthmarks that disfigure children

7. Why is argon laser therapy *not* used on children as much as adults?
(A) It is too painful.
(B) It leaves another mark.
(C) It damages their immune systems.
(D) It is too dangerous for a young body.

8. What is the most likely reason that this particular birthmark is called a *port-wine* stain?
(A) Its size
(B) Its shape
(C) Its texture
(D) Its color

9. Why does the author say that the dye laser treatment is amazing?
(A) The treated skin is so much like the skin next to it.
(B) The treatment is so popular.
(C) Children will accept the treatment without problems.
(D) The treated children don't exhibit negative psychological effects.

10. What is the main purpose of this passage?
(A) To compare two techniques of treating port-wine stains
(B) To introduce the topic of port-wine stains and discuss its effects on children
(C) To analyze the cause of port-wine stains
(D) To describe the results of a new method of treating port-wine stains

Drill 4 (Answers, page 317)

Directions: Each passage below is followed by questions based on its content. Answer all questions following a passage on the basis of what is *stated* or *implied* in that passage.

Etching is a little like skating, some artists say. The needle glides across the ground, sometimes wobbling a little, but also moving gracefully. It is not easy. But a good etcher can capture not only the line but the light as well. At the end of the High Renaissance in Italy, etching allowed artists to throw fresh light on old images such as paintings of Raphael or Michelangelo. First used around 1510, etching became a medium favored for recording and copying designs used in paintings, to try out ideas, and to advertise concepts. The early masters combined the effects of painting and drawing in the genre of etchings. During the 17th century etching came into its own as an art style.

Etching involves scratching a needle through a ground of acid-resistant wax or varnish onto a copper plate. After the design has been etched into the ground, the plate is immersed in acid. The acid can bite into the metal plate but not into the surrounding area, which is still covered by the ground. When the acid has done its job, a decision made by the artist, the plate is withdrawn, the coating removed, and the plate inked for printing.

1. Why does the author mention a skater in the first sentence?
(A) To demonstrate that etching is not easy
(B) To compare a physical exercise with art
(C) To illustrate the movement of the etcher's needle
(D) To introduce the idea of adding to lightness in an etching

2. Etching was at its height in
(A) the 1500s
(B) the 1600s
(C) the 1700s
(D) the 1800s

3. How is this passage organized?
(A) A concept is defined and then a technique is explained.
(B) Specific techniques are explained and then a general conclusion is made.
(C) A cause is examined and the results are presented.
(D) Events are examined in order of importance.

4. In line 4, the author uses the word *throw* to mean which of the following?
(A) discard
(B) shape
(C) hurl
(D) put

5. How does the author present the events in the second paragraph?
(A) Chronological order
(B) Order of importance
(C) General to specific
(D) Cause and result

What made the Alamo famous was the battle. For thirteen days in 1836, the 188 Texan volunteers held off 4000 Mexican troops in one of the most violent dramas of American history. But the story began twelve years earlier. In 1824 Mexico won its independence from Spain and continued the colonization policy that had been initiated by Spain in 1821. Immigrants gladly took the oath of loyalty to Mexico in exchange for land, and they swarmed in. But then in 1824 Mexico redefined its territories, making them states. Texas was the only separate territory to lose its independence; it was joined to Coahuila and the capital was moved from San Antonio to Saltillo. The Texas residents felt a lack of representation in government affairs and they gathered in protest. By 1834 the rumbles of discontent grew louder and by 1835 they were fighting. The Texans felt that they were fighting for their rights, but in the eyes of the Mexican government the uprising was treasonous.

The Battle of the Alamo began on February 23, 1836 and lasted for thirteen days. It ended with every Texan fighter dying. The only lives which were spared were a few women and children. Though the fight was fateful for the men, it kindled the spirit of other fighters. Forty-six days after the fall of the Alamo, a furious counterattack by Texan and American volunteers began with the words, "Remember the Alamo!" The result of this fight was a free Texas, the beginning of a new republic.

6. Why is the Alamo famous?
(A) A fight took place there.
(B) Texans volunteered to live there.
(C) Americans came to join the Mexican Army.
(D) Mexico tried to annex it.

7. The author implies that people came to Texas in the 1820s to
(A) fight the Mexicans
(B) become farmers
(C) make Texas independent
(D) start a new government

8. According to the passage, what was the main reason that the Texans began fighting?
(A) They wanted more land.
(B) They weren't represented in the government.
(C) Their families were in danger.
(D) They wanted to move the capital.

9. Which of the following statements is NOT true according to the passage?
(A) All the Texan men were killed in the battle.
(B) The Mexicans won the battle.
(C) Texas was not an American state.
(D) The Texans died shouting, "Remember the Alamo!"

10. According to the passage, what happened after the battle?
(A) Texas became a part of the United States.
(B) Other men came to avenge the fight.
(C) The capital was moved back to San Antonio.
(D) The women and children were killed.

Answer Key for Drills

Drill 1	Drill 2	Drill 3	Drill 4
1. A	**1.** A	**1.** B	**1.** C
2. C	**2.** B	**2.** B	**2.** B
3. A	**3.** B	**3.** D	**3.** A
4. B	**4.** C	**4.** A	**4.** D
5. D	**5.** B	**5.** C	**5.** A
6. D	**6.** C	**6.** C	**6.** A
7. B	**7.** A	**7.** B	**7.** B
8. A	**8.** D	**8.** D	**8.** B
9. A	**9.** B	**9.** A	**9.** D
10. C	**10.** A	**10.** D	**10.** B

Explanatory Answers

DRILL 1, PAGE 305

1. (A) The author shows respect for the competitors of this race by the description of how difficult the race is. Also the word *hardiest* in the last sentence indicates her respect. There are no words that indicate either that she is afraid (B), that she thinks it is funny (C), or that she is worried (D) about the race or the competitors.

2. (C) This is a referent question. To see what *it* stands for, you must understand what the first part of the sentence stands for. The words "inspired by a sled-dog relay of serum to Nome for a diphtheria outbreak in 1973" all refer to the race. The race itself was inspired by this relay. Since all of the first part of the sentence refers to the race, the word *it* must also refer to the race. All of the other words are nouns in the sentence, but are not the referent for the whole phrase.

3. (A) This is a restatement question. The diphtheria outbreak occurred in 1973. Nothing in the passage says that it has continued. What has continued is the race, not the diphtheria outbreak. All the other sentences are true restatements.

4. (B) The is a restatement question. The author describes the coast as *storm-raked.* This means that many storms hit the coast. Answer (A) is not correct because it is written in the present tense. The author doesn't imply that there are always illnesses such as diphtheria. The passage states that diphtheria occurred once. We don't know if Alaska is an area where diphtheria occurs often. Answer (C) is also incorrect because of the tense. The passage mentions the cold weather during the race; this does not mean that it is always cold. Answer (D) is not correct because the only mention of money is the prize money for the race. This does not mean that it is necessarily a good place for anyone to make money.

5. (D) This is a vocabulary question. The ward *hardy* means *strong.*

6. (D) The is a main idea question. Most of the passage is about Tony Lazzeri and his reputation. The first sentence gives you a good clue, "Loved and admired..." Answer (A) would mean that the passage mainly discussed how the team was formed. This was not done. Answer (B) is mentioned, but only as a secondary fact. Answer (C) is too general. This passage is not about all ballplayers.

7. (B) The answer to this question is implied. All these members were mentioned as being a part of the 1927 Yankees baseball team. Only Lazzeri was mentioned as being a victim (A). The passage is not specific about who is a batter. And all the men are on the same team; they are not the names of different teams (D).

8. (A) This is an inference/vocabulary question. *Jelly* is a substance that shakes when moved around. If a person is like jelly, it probably means that he or she shakes, and shaking is a indication of being nervous. You could also use your own background knowledge to answer this question. How would you feel if you were about to play against a very good team? You would not be beaten up (B), though that may happen after the game. You may feel very small (C) or even thoughtful (D), but neither of those have the idea of shaking like jelly.

9. (A) This is a restatement question. The passage says that Lazzeri held the team together and that he was a leader. Anything that holds something together must be strong. Answers (B), (C), and (D) also may have been true, but nothing about these topics was mentioned.

10. (C) This is a restatement question. It can be answered with a knowledge of structure. The comma indicates that the phrase *the one in Cooperstown* refers to a big Hall of Fame.

DRILL 2, PAGE 307

1. **(A)** This is a support question. The final two sentences of the passage say that he was criticized for his boasting, but his reputation as an actor was not injured. Answer (B) could not be true because it is the opposite of Answer (A). Answer (C) could not be true because nothing was said about Forrest's life being a tragedy. Answer (D) must be false because he didn't become a national idol at age 14; he only played his first role on stage at age 14.

2. **(B)** This is a negative question. It says in the passage that he played the roles of Norval, Othello, and Richelieu. He did not play the role of Edmund Kean; he played the role of another person who was a support for Kean's role.

3. **(B)** This author implies that Forrest is temperamental by referring to his violent temper in the last sentence. One might infer the other feelings, but they are not stated by the author. Forrest's loud language, for instance, might have been because he was angry, but the author doesn't say this. He was also probably satisfied with many of his performances, but this is only a guess. And he was probably very creative since he was an acclaimed actor, but this answer comes from background knowledge, not the stated information.

4. **(C)** A reputation can be damaged by a person's actions. This means that a person then has a bad reputation. Answers (A) and (B) do not make sense in this sentence. The word *offend*, Answer (D), must have a person as the object, not a feeling. You could say, for instance, *I offended my friend,* which means you did something to make your friend feel bad.

5. **(B)** This is a restatement question. The sentence says that in 1826 Forrest played Othello in a New York debut. *Debut* is a French word that means *the first appearance*. In this case, the debut was his role in New York. Answer (A) is not correct because New York did not produce Forrest as a new actor. Answer (C) is not correct because we know that Forrest had been acting in other plays previously. Answer (D) is not correct because the passage does not say that this was the first time that the play *Othello* was performed in New York.

6. **(C)** This is a main idea question. The first paragraph discusses possible causes of chronic fatigue syndrome and the second paragraph discusses symptoms of the illness. Answer (A) is too narrow. A disagreement between scientists is discussed, but it is not the main topic. Answer (B) is too general. This passage is not about all diseases that affect yuppies. Answer (D) is too narrow. Though the relationship between the virus and the illness is discussed, this does not describe the second paragraph of the passage.

7. **(A)** This is a restatement question. The first sentence of the second paragraph gives this answer. Answer (B) doesn't show any relationship to yuppies. Answer (C) is not mentioned in the passage at all. Answer (D) is mentioned, but not in connection with yuppie women.

8. **(D)** This is a restatement question. The answer is in the last sentence of the passage. Answer (A) is incorrect because the passage says that a sufferer must have had the illness for at least six months. The person might be sick for much longer than six months. Answer (B) is incorrect because the passage only suggests that someone might have had the flu; it is not a requirement. Answer (C) is incorrect because the passage states that a person only has to have eight out of the eleven symptoms.

9. **(B)** This is a support question. In the first paragraph, it says that some scientists support the idea of Epstein–Barr virus causing the disease and some scientists don't support this. Answer (A) is incorrect because the passage states that some people might get this illness because they have never quite recovered from the flu. It doesn't say that they don't recover from this illness. Answer (C) is incorrect because there is no statement that compares men and women. You might assume that women get it more because only women are mentioned, but this answer is not the *best* supported. Answer (D) is incorrect because nothing is said about the Epstein–Barr virus causing premature effects. The word *premature* is used in connection with scientists making a judgment about the cause of the illness.

10. **(A)** This is a restatement/vocabulary question. The word *debilitating* in the last sentence means *causing weakness*. None of the other symptoms are mentioned.

DRILL 3, PAGE 309

1. **(B)** This is a main idea question. The passage is about the Montessori method in general. Answer (A), self-motivation, is too narrow. Self-motivation is a part of the philosophy of Maria Montessori, but the passage includes more than this. Answer (C) is also too narrow. The passage concerns more than the education of subnormal children. Answer (D) is incorrect because of the word *new*. This passage describes a system of education, but also mentions that it began in the early part of this century.

2. **(B)** This is a restatement question. The passage says that Maria worked as a psychiatrist after receiving her degree in 1894. Answer (A) is incorrect because she opened the day care center after she worked as a psychiatrist. We aren't told exactly when that was; it might have been after 1900. Answer (C) is incorrect for the same reason as Answer (A). We don't know the exact dates when she began working with normal children, but we know it was after she worked as a psychiatrist and it was after 1894. Answer (D) is incorrect because it is the opposite of what the Montessori method stands for. The passage states that people who opposed Maria Montessori wanted more discipline.

3. **(D)** This is an inference question. The final sentence implies that she believes that children will learn by themselves. The words *auto-education* and *learn naturally* imply learning by oneself. Answer (A) is the opposite of the Montessori philosophy, as evidenced by the opposition wanting more discipline. Answer (B) is incorrect because it is also opposite to the Montessori method. The passage states that teachers should act as observers, rather than active instructors. Answer (C) is incorrect for the same reason as Answer (B).

4. **(A)** This is a vocabulary question and may be an implication question. The word *rich* is often used to mean *having a lot, abundant,* or *plentiful*. Answer (B) is incorrect because *rich* and *expensive* are not synonyms. If you are rich you may be able to buy something that is expensive, but this is a cause and effect relationship, not a synonym. Answer (C) is incorrect because the meaning doesn't apply to this situation. In music, however, the word *rich* can mean *deep and strong*. (The music is rich; the tones are rich.) Answer (D) is incorrect because it is also a cause and effect idea. If the environment is well supplied with games (rich), the children will be amused. The words *rich* and *amused*, however, are not synonyms.

5. **(C)** This is an inference question. In the second paragraph, the author states that a child will learn if put in an environment with the proper materials. Answer (A) is incorrect because the opposite is stated. Teachers act as observers. The child may learn without the teacher, but not without the materials. Answer (B) is incorrect because the word *rules* implies a lot of discipline, and this is the opposite of the Montessori method. Answer (D) is incorrect for the same reason as Answer (A). Teachers should be observers, but children can learn without them.

6. **(C)** This is a main idea question. Most of the emphasis in this passage is on dye laser treatment. Answer (A) is incorrect because nothing is mentioned about the benefits of argon–laser treatment; the passage only states that it is better than skin grafts or tatoos. Answer (B) is incorrect because it is too narrow. The fact that some children have psychological problems is mentioned, but it is not a main point. Answer (D) is incorrect because it is too broad. This passage is not about all kinds of birthmarks, only port-wine stains.

7. **(B)** This is a restatement question. The passage states that argon–laser therapy leaves scars. Answers (A), (C), and (D) are all incorrect because the passage doesn't mention anything about pain, the immune system, or danger.

8. **(D)** This is an inference question. In the first sentence it says that port-wine stains cause red or purple stains on the skin. Therefore, you can infer that the color is important. You also might know that port is a wine which has a dark-red color. There is no mention of size or shape, answers (A) and (B), in this passage. The only mention of texture pertains to the change in the birthmark after the laser treatment.

9. **(A)** This is an inference question. The author says that the treatment is amazing after saying that the treated skin is identical in texture and color to the normal skin. Answer (B) is incorrect because it doesn't answer the question. The passage states that the dye laser treatment is gaining in popularity, but that alone isn't why the treatment is amazing. The popularity is a result, not a reason. Answer (C) is incorrect because nothing was said about how children accept the treatment. Answer (D) is also incorrect because psychological effects are mentioned as a possibility later in the passage.

10. **(D)** This is an author's purpose question. Most of the passage describes the dye laser treatment. Answer (A) is incorrect because the two laser techniques are not equally discussed. Answer (B) is incorrect because the discussion does not only concern the effects on children. Answer (C) is incorrect because the cause of port-wine stains is not discussed at all.

DRILL 4, PAGE 311

1. (C) This is an author's purpose question. After mentioning skating, the author mentions the artist's needle. The word *glide* in the second sentence implies moving smoothly over ice, like a skater. Answer (A) is incorrect because the sentence about not being easy is not right next to the sentence about skating. It is true that the author implies that it is not easy to skate or etch, but the sentence about the needle comes first and is therefore the best answer. Answer (B) is not correct because skating is mentioned as an example of an art form rather than a way to get exercise. Answer (D) is incorrect because the idea of light is mentioned to answer the question of what a good etcher can do, not what a skater does.

2. (B) This is a restatement question. The passage states that etching came into its own during the seventeenth century. The seventeenth century is the 1600s, and *came into its own* means that it became known publicly. Answer (A) is incorrect because the 1500s were when the art of etching was first developed; it was not at its height then. Answers (C) and (D) are both incorrect because nothing is mentioned about either of these two centuries.

3. (A) This is an organization question. The first paragraph gives a brief historical background of etching and the second paragraph describes the particular technique. Answer (B) is incorrect because the technique is not described first. Answer (C) is incorrect because there is no cause mentioned. Answer (D) is incorrect because there is no mention of which is the most important.

4. (D) This is a vocabulary question. The word *put* is a very general term, but in this case it is the best answer. *Throw fresh light* gives the idea of adding something new or seeing something in a new way. Answer (A) is incorrect because there is no implication of anything being discarded. The phrase *throw away,* however, means *discard.* Answer (B) is incorrect because *shape* as a verb means to change the shape of something. In this sentence, the old paintings are not reshaped; they are copied. Answer (C) is incorrect in this context, but the word *hurl* is often the synonym for *throw.* It means to cause something to go through the air violently.

5. (A) This is an organization question. The second paragraph describes the process of etching in the order that it is done. Answer (B) is incorrect because none of the parts of the process are mentioned as most important. Answer (C) is incorrect because there is no general principle mentioned first. Answer (D) is incorrect because the process is not described as one cause and one result, even though the results of the process are described.

6. (A) This is a restatement question. The first sentence states that the Alamo is famous because of a fight (battle). Answer (B) is incorrect because it is not the reason that the Alamo is famous. Answer (C) is incorrect because the Americans did not join the Mexican army; they were fighting the Mexican army. Answer (D) is incorrect because Mexico did not try to annex the Alamo; it annexed the whole territory of Texas.

7. (B) This is an inference question. The passage states that the people came to Texas for the land. This doesn't necessarily mean that they would be farmers, but it is the best choice of the answers. Answer (A) is incorrect because they didn't come in order to fight. The fight began years after they arrived. Answer (C) is incorrect for the same reason as Answer (A). They wanted to make Texas independent many years after they arrived in Texas. Answer (D) is incorrect for the same reason. Starting a new government is mentioned in the last sentence, many years after the people first arrived in Texas.

8. (B) This is a restatement question. The passage says that the people in Texas felt a lack of representation in government affairs. Answer (A) is incorrect because nothing is said about their land being taken away from them. Answer (C) is incorrect because no danger is mentioned. Answer (D) is incorrect because it is not the best answer. The passage states that the capital was moved away, and we might assume that they wanted the capital close to them. However, the lack of representation was stated as a direct reason so it is a better answer.

9. (D) This is a negative question. Answer (D) is the right answer because the Texans did not die shouting this. It was the new soldiers, who attacked 46 days later, who shouted this. Answers (A), (B), and (C) are all true according to the passage. Answer (B) is implied. Since all the Texans died, the Mexicans must have won. Answer (C) is also implied. The passage says that Texas was a territory, not a state, and that it lost its independence. Also the final sentence says that Texas became free and that it began as a republic. All of these words imply that Texas was not a state in the United States.

10. (B) This is an inference question. In the final paragraph, it says that there was a counterattack by Texan and American volunteers. This must mean that men came because they were angry at the news that all the men were killed. Answer (A) is incorrect because it is not stated. Even though you may know that Texas is a state now and in fact the sentence is true, it is not mentioned in the passage. The directions to this reading comprehension section say that you are only to answer questions based on what is stated or implied in the passage. There is no implication that Texas would later become a state in the United States. Answer (C) is incorrect because nothing was mentioned about moving the capital back. Answer (D) is incorrect because the opposite is stated. The women and children were not killed. (Their lives were *spared*).

Lesson 20

Test of Written English

Objectives

- To learn about the two types of essay questions
- To learn how the Test of Written English (TWE) is scored
- To learn four ways of organizing ideas before writing
- To understand key words and phrases used in essay questions
- To learn a step-by-step procedure for writing the essay
- To look at examples of student essays
- To practice reading charts and graphs
- To practice sample essays

Lesson 20

The Test of Written English (TWE) is a writing test which is given four or five times a year. It is not a required part of the TOEFL exam, but it is given at the same time as some TOEFL exams. If you want to take the TWE then you must sign up for the TOEFL on a day when the TWE is given. If you do not want to take the TWE then you must take the TOEFL on a day when the TWE is not given. Everyone who takes the TOEFL on a day when the TWE is given is required to write the essay. It is written first, before you open your TOEFL test book. You will have 30 minutes to read the question, plan your answer, and write your essay. Your score will be printed on your TOEFL score report form, but it is a separate score, not added to your TOEFL score. Check the Bulletin of Information for the specific dates that the TWE is given during the year you are taking the TOEFL.

What Types of Questions Are in the Test of Written English?

For the TWE you are asked to write about a topic in a way that is similar to what is required at a college or university. The examiners want to know the following:

1. Can you express and support your opinion?
2. Can you choose and defend a point of view?
3. Can you interpret a chart or graph?

In order to answer these questions, the TWE has two kinds of essays: a compare/contrast question and a chart/graph question.

Topics

The TWE essay questions ask you to write on something about which you are personally knowledgable. You do not have to study any special subjects to answer these questions.

The topics listed below have all been used on previous exams, so they will not be used again. They are summarized here to give you an idea of the kind of question you might be asked.

1. The advantages of spending time with a few friends as compared to spending time with a large group of friends
2. The good and bad effects of advertising

3. The advantages of visiting your country as a part of a tour group as compared to visiting as an individual
4. Whether technology creates problems or solves problems
5. Whether college should be available to all people or restricted to good students only
6. The value of objects in the home (as shown on a graph)

What Do The Score Numbers Mean?

The TWE is scored holistically. This means that you get one number as a score based on the total composition. The score is not divided into how many grammar mistakes or spelling mistakes you make. Your score is based more on how well you answer the question, organize your ideas, and support or defend your opinion.

The score is based on the following information:

Score	
6	You clearly demonstrate competence in writing, even though there may be occasional errors in your essay. Your essay is well-organized, you use details to support your ideas, you use different lengths of sentences, and you use a wide range of vocabulary words.
5	You demonstrate competence in your writing. You may have a few grammatical errors, but your essay is well organized. It does not have as many details as a number 6 essay. Some parts of your essay are written better than other parts. You demonstrate that you have a good range of vocabulary and that you can write sentences of varying lengths. This essay may have more grammar errors than a number 6 essay.
4	You demonstrate minimal competence in your writing. Your essay is adequately organized, but you may not cover all parts of the question clearly. You use some details, but not a lot. There may be some serious grammatical errors that confuse the reader.
3	You are developing competence, but your writing is difficult to understand. It is not organized clearly. You use little or no details. There are many errors in sentence structure, and you use incorrect words.
2	You may be incompetent in your writing. You are unable to organize your answer, there is little or no detail, there are serious errors in sentence structure, and your essay is not focused on the question.
1	You are incompetent in writing. There are many serious writing errors. The sentences are difficult to understand. Apparently you do not understand the question.

Based on the above list, a very good essay will:

1. answer the question clearly
2. be well-organized
3. use details and examples
4. have a variety of types of sentences
5. contain only a few grammar errors

Organization

From reading about the scores on page 322, you can see that organization is probably the single most important part of your score. The reader must be able to see that you understand the question and can write a clear response. In your 30 minutes of time, it is important to first *read* the question carefully, and then *write* a brief plan for yourself. You don't have time to write out your complete essay and then read it and copy it to improve it. You must learn to write some kind of organized notes, and then write your finished essay from the notes. Here are four possible ways for you to organize. Try them all and then use the method that is best for you.

The following examples of ways to organize your thoughts all use the question below:

Advertising is common throughout the world. Some people feel that advertising is generally helpful and others feel that it is generally harmful. Discuss your ideas of the good and bad effects of advertising, and decide whether you think it is generally helpful or harmful. Use specific examples to support your point of view.

---

1. Brainstorming

The following example of brainstorming is based on the above example question about advertising.

Step 1: After reading the question, write down all the ideas that come to your mind about the topic. Don't stop to think about whether you will use the ideas or not. Just write them down. Write quickly. Use single words or short phrases, not complete sentences. Don't try to organize anything yet.

EXAMPLE:

TV
bad
radio
newspapers—can help
songs and stories
too loud
funny pictures
learn about products
expensive to make
not true sometimes
signs—ruin the view
helps me know what's on sale
saves time choosing a store
the bicycle I bought
the things I bought that I don't need

Step 2: Look at your list, and then read the question again. Think again about what you are asked to discuss.

EXAMPLE:

Advertising is common throughout the world. Some people feel that advertising is generally helpful and others feel that it is generally harmful. Discuss your ideas of the good and bad effects of advertising, and decide whether you think it is generally helpful or harmful. Use specific examples to support your point of view.

Step 3: Make a system to classify your list.

EXAMPLE:

---

0 = places to advertise
▭ = helpful
[ ] = harmful
× = examples
– = can't use this in essay

Step 4: Classify your list

(TV)
[bad] (why?)
(radio)
(newspapers)—can help
~~songs and stories~~
[too loud]
~~funny pictures~~
▭ learn about products
expensive to make
[not true sometimes]
(signs)—[ruin the view]
▭ helps me know what's on sale
▭ saves time choosing a store
▭ helps me know prices on food
× the bicycle I bought
[the things I bought that I don't need]
× my boots and radio

Step 5: Make a brief outline or list of ideas in each of your categories. Add more details if necessary.

EXAMPLE:

Places to advertise
  TV, radio, newspapers, signs
Helpful Effects
  learn about the product (my bicycle)
  helps me know what's on sale (my boots)
  saves time in choosing a store (my radio)
  know prices on food
Harmful Effects
  too loud (TV and radio)
  ruins the view (signs)
  makes me buy what I don't need
Examples
  bicycle
  boots
  radio

Step 6: Use your list as a guide. Add an introduction and conclusion. Write your essay.

2. Clustering

The following example of clustering is based on the question about advertising.

Step 1: Write the major topic in the center of your paper. (For this question, you might start with two centers.) Then write any ideas that you think of on lines coming out from the center. Write examples or more specific ideas on lines coming out from the main lines. This is like brainstorming except that you are organizing more as you think of ideas.

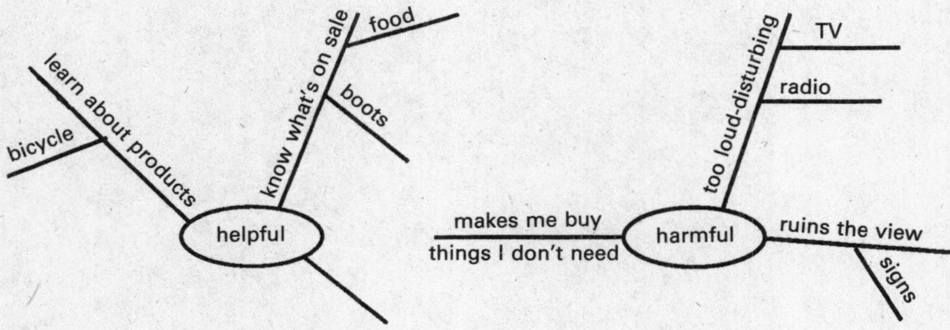

Step 2: Read back over the original question again and choose the "arms" of your cluster that best relate to your question.

Step 3: Begin your essay, keeping your ideas focused on the topic.

3. Using a Matrix

An organizational matrix gives you a space to write the main ideas and supporting details. Read the question carefully and analyze what the question is asking. What information does the question want you to describe, explain, compare, or interpret? Then write your main ideas on the left side of the page. Across from the main ideas, write the specific details or examples that you will use to support your main ideas. Use this matrix as a basis. Then add an introductory statement (or paragraph) and a concluding statement (or paragraph).

MATRIX	
Main Ideas	**Supporting Details**
Advertising comes in many forms.	TV, radio, newspaper, telephone books
Ads are helpful.	**1.** tell me what's on sale **2.** can save time in comparing prices **3.** give me information
Ads are harmful.	**1.** disturb me—too loud on TV **2.** feel like I'm being brainwashed **3.** sometimes buy what I don't need
I think they are generally helpful.	They give me information to make a choice.

4. Outlining

When you outline, you usually already have a good idea in your mind of how you will begin and what major points you plan to discuss. You write the outline to check your ideas, to make sure that they are well organized, and to use as a guideline to refer to as you write.

On the following page are two possible methods of outlining a compare/contrast question, using the question above about advertising.

Method 1

I. Places to advertise
 A. TV and radio
 B. Newspapers and signs
II. TV and radio
 A. Helpful
  1. learn about products
  2. know what's on sale
  3. save time
 B. Harmful
  1. too loud and disturbing
  2. feel like I'm being brainwashed
III. Newspapers and signs
 A. Helpful
  1. remind me of what I want
  2. I can read when I want to
 B. Harmful
  1. take too much space
  2. signs ruin the view outside
IV. My opinion

Method 2

I. Places to advertise
 A. TV, radio, newspapers, signs
II. Helpful
 A. learn about products
  example: TV, radio
 B. know what's on sale
  example: newspaper
 C. save time
  example: newspaper
 D. remind me of what I want
  examples: TV, radio, newspaper, signs
 E. I can read when I want to
  newspaper
III. Harmful
 A. too loud and disturbing
  TV and radio
 B. feel like I'm being brainwashed
  TV and radio
 C. take too much space
  newspaper and signs
 D. ruin the view outside
  signs
IV. My opinion

Organizing

(There is no answer key for this exercise. Check the previous pages for examples of how to organize.)

Directions: Write your own organization for the question below, using *one* of the methods previously shown. Use your own ideas; don't just copy the outlines in this book. *Don't* write the complete essay here. Just practice gathering your own ideas and organizing them by brainstorming, clustering, writing a matrix, or outlining.

Question:
Advertising is common throughout the world. Some people believe that advertising is generally helpful and others believe that it is generally harmful. Discuss your ideas of the good and bad effects of advertising, and decide whether you think it is generally helpful or harmful. Use specific examples to support your point of view.

Brainstorm	Cluster	Matrix	Outline
List Ideas 1. 2. 3. 4.		Main Ideas / Details	I. A. B. II. A. B.

Holmes' Advice: Pay Attention to Key Words

Understanding the Question

Holmes realizes the importance of planning and organizing before writing, but he also realizes that even if you plan well, it will not help unless you also answer the question completely. You must understand exactly what is meant by the clue words in the question. In some cases the organization is already outlined in the question. You just need to uncover the clues.

Word Clues

Each of the following words asks for something a little different.

discuss	describe	support
explain	analyze	give examples
state	compare	give reasons
interpret	contrast	

1. **Discuss**—Talk about a subject from more than one viewpoint. Sometimes the word *discuss* will be followed by more specific words.

   EXAMPLE:

   Some people say that people learn best by being competitive; others say that people learn best by being cooperative. *Discuss* these two positions.

2. **Explain**—Make something clear or interpret something. Sometimes it is important to give a cause/effect relationship or a step-by-step explanation of why something is happening or what something means.

   EXAMPLE:

   Look at the information about the cost of living in the above graph (not pictured here). *Explain* how the cost of living has changed in the past five years.

3. **State**—Say something briefly.

   EXAMPLE:

   Some people say that people learn best by being competitive while others say that people learn best by being cooperative. Discuss these two positions and *state* your opinion.

4. **Interpret**—Make the information clear or show the relationship between things. It is similar to *explain.*

EXAMPLE:

Look at the information about the cost of living in the above graph (not pictured here.) Explain how the cost of living has changed in the past five years by *interpreting* the information given for each year.

5. **Describe**—Give details of something. You might think of giving the reader a *word picture.*

EXAMPLE:

Some people believe that the best education is the formal education you get in school, while others think that the best education is real-life experiences outside school. Discuss these two positions and *describe* one experience that you have had, either in school or out of school, that has educated you in some way.

6. **Analyze**—Explain how or why something is happening. It is very similar to *explain.*

EXAMPLE:

Look at the information about the cost of living in the above graph (not pictured here). *Analyze* the differences between five years ago and today.

7. **Compare**—Look at two or more aspects of a situation and examine them to see how they are similar or different.

EXAMPLE:

Life has changed immensely with modern technology. Pick any one item, such as the telephone, computers, or satellites, and *compare* life today and life in the past as it relates to the item you have picked.

8. **Contrast**—Look at two or more parts of a situation and explain the differences between them.

EXAMPLE:

Life has changed immensely with modern technology. Pick any one item, such as the telephone, computers, or satellites, and *contrast* life today and life in the past without this item.

9. **Support**—Give evidence that what you say is true. You will often read, *support with details* or *support with examples.*

EXAMPLE:

Look at the information about the cost of living in the above graph (not pictured here). Explain your conclusions about today's cost of living, *supporting* them with details from the graph.

10. Give examples—Use your own experience to give the reader a *word picture* of your statements.

EXAMPLE:

Life has changed immensely with modern technology. Pick any one item in an area such as communication (telephones, television) or transportation (automobiles, airplanes) and *give examples* from your own experience that demonstrate how life has changed.

11. Give reasons—Give support for something with a statement about why it is true.

EXAMPLE:

Look at the information about the cost of living in the above graph (not pictured here). Explain your conclusions about today's cost of living, and *give the reasons* for your conclusions by using details from the graph to support your statements.

Transition Words

To *discuss, explain, analyze,* or *interpret* you might use some of the following words or phrases:

in general	every	some of
on the whole	usually	most of
in most cases	frequently	main
as a rule	rarely	major
all		

To *describe* a time you might use some of the following words or phrases:

when	subsequently	before
yesterday	during	eventually

To *compare* you might use the following words or phrases:

in a similar manner	not only. . .but also	similar to
both. . .and	as if	more
as. . . .as	as though	better
neither. . .nor	like	worse

To *contrast* you might use the following words or phrases:

yet	though	to the contrary
but	on the other hand	conversely
while	nevertheless	different from
however	at the same time	rather than
unlike		

For giving *examples* you might use the following words or phrases:

for example
for instance
as an example

Step-by-Step Procedure

Now that you have thought about organizing your thoughts, looking at the question, and using transition words, you need to put it all together. What should your essay include? What steps should you follow in writing your essay?

What Should Your Essay Include?

1. **A Beginning**
   Your first paragraph should give a brief statement about the question or problem. It should give your point of view or tell what you are going to discuss.
2. **A Middle**
   This part might be one or two or maybe three paragraphs. It should answer each part of the question with your reasons or examples.
3. **An end**
   The final paragraph should state your point of view clearly and summarize your ideas.

What Steps Should You Follow?

1. Read the question carefully, paying particular attention to clue words.
2. Decide on the main ideas that are needed.
3. Organize your ideas by brainstorming, clustering, outlining, or putting them in a matrix.
4. Add some explanatory details and examples in your organization.

5. Begin writing.
   Write an introduction that gives your main points and possibly some background information.
   Write a new paragraph to explain each part of your answer.
   Write a conclusion that gives a summary of your main point(s).
6. Go back over your essay, checking quickly for spelling and punctuation errors.

Looking at Student Essays

The following essays were written by students in English language classes. Each student wrote two essays. The first draft was written with 30 minutes for reading, planning, and writing. The second form of each was rewritten later. They are written here in the original form, with no corrections. The authors know that there are still errors in their essays, and that they could improve them with more time. Read each of the first drafts, and think of how you would improve them. Then read the author's improvements, and think again of what you would add or omit to improve them.

Essay Question:

Should the government have the power to censor material in books, plays, and films? Supporters say yes. The government should be able to prevent some material from being published for the good of the whole society. Opponents say that censorship destroys creativity and art, and that people should be allowed to read or see anything they choose. Discuss these two viewpoints. Which point of view do you agree with? Why?

First Draft by Heng Tan
Cabrillo College, Aptos, California

(The errors in the following essay have not been corrected.)

In the United States people are much freedom than the country all over the world. People are used all kind of concept or material. They produced books plays, films, and sprayed over the city. They didn't care about good or bad thing because they made business for a living. I disagree the concept above. The government should be destroy all bad things that made people hurt the feeling. And shouldn't allow people to see or read these articles.

The government should be choose a good concept to educate people from generation to generation. They have enough power to control, but maybe they want people to have experience about good or bad thing.

Rewritten Essay
by Heng Tan

(The following essay still contains errors.)

Censorship

Introduction/ Background information Example Point of View	In the United States people are much more free than many countries all over the world. People are used to publishing all kinds of concepts or materials. For example, people produce books, plays and films about pornography to attract people. If people look at pornography they will think about sex all the time. I think that the government should censor certain kinds of publication before they are released to the public.
Example Point of view	The government should have censorship over the books, plays, and films write about the girl forteen years old who has baby. That mean hurts others people feelings. The government shouldn't allow people to see or read these articles. I disagree with this attitude of not caring about what is good or bad material.
Conclusion	I don't think that censorship destroys creativity and art; it is a way of not giving people bad idea.

First Draft by Mario Espinosa
Cabrillo College, Aptos, California

(The errors in the following essay have not been corrected.)

A government that censor is a reaccionary government. Do you think that the government has the capacity to determine what is good and what is bad for the society that it's governing? I don't think so, the government's funtion is take care for the laws that the itself society chose for it and not to make the dessicion for itself toward that society.

Through the behavior, customs and culture society make its laws, and if at anytime these behaviors are consored, development and freedom are also censored.

I'm agree that censor destroys creativity, art and expression. so, people will not be able to express freely their thoughts, their art, their feelings due to dread to be censored.

So, censor is decadency.

Rewritten Essay
by Mario Espinosa

(The following essay still contains errors.)

Censorship

Introduction/ Background information

It is well known the fact that censorship has existed in the world from the beginning of humanity. In all stages of history it has manifested itself in one way or another. It is well known too that many people have had to leave their country because their thoughts have been against the established canons.

Background Information

Societies have always fought to their political regimes, their laws, and their rules regarding their culture and essential priorities. Even so, censorship is present in the world. In some places it is extreme, in others it is moderated or very subtle but it is there.

Example

In Mexico even if not openly, many books, plays and movies have been censored, as for example "Mexico Insurgente" by John Reed. In other Latinoamerican countries, many people and their work have been censored in the last years. And here in the United States, "the country of freedom" we have quite a few things to say about it. I know the case of an old woman who was stopped in Los Angeles International airport because she brought the book "La Muerte del Che Guevara." Finally she could enter the country but the book was confiscated. A ridiculous thing because this book may be bought in many bookstores here.

Conclusion

Point of view

Concluding, I think that the government's function is to take care of the law that the society itself chose, and not to take unilateral decisions for that society. When government censor the expressions of their societies, development and freedom are also censored. Censorship destroys creativity, art and expression.

Thus censorship is decadency.

EXERCISE 2

Student Essays (Answers, page 342)

Directions: Look back over the final drafts of the previous student essays and answer the following questions about each of them.

REWRITTEN ESSAY BY HENG TAN, PAGE 334

1. Does it begin with a short introduction of the question? ________
2. Does it discuss the two viewpoints given in the question? ________
3. Does it state the author's point of view clearly? ________
4. Does it give reasons for the author's point of view? ________
5. Does it give examples to support the author's statements? ________
6. Does it end with a short conclusion? ________
What score would you give it based on the score on page 322? ________

REWRITTEN ESSAY BY MARIO ESPINOSA, PAGE 335.

1. Does it begin with a short introduction of the question? ________
2. Does it discuss the two viewpoints given in the question? ________
3. Does it state the author's point of view clearly? ________
4. Does it give reasons for the author's point of view? ________
5. Does it give examples to support the author's statements? ________
6. Does it end with a short conclusion? ________
What score would you give it? ________

Now compare your answers with the answers on pages 342-343.

Three Sample Graphs

Circle Graph

Circle graphs are sometimes called "pie graphs." They are divided into parts, with the largest "piece of pie" showing the largest amount of something.

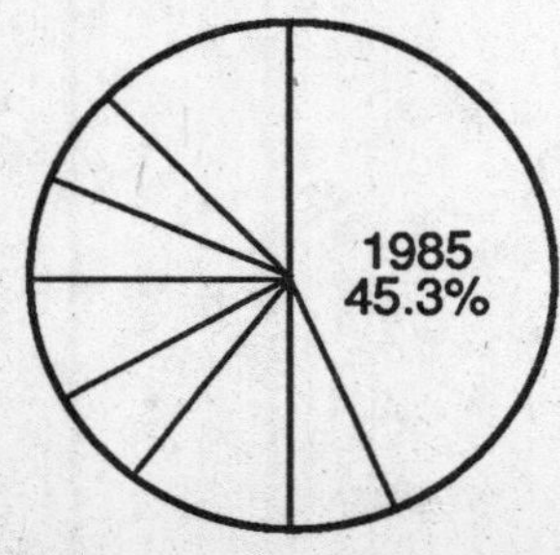

Bar Graph

Bar graphs give you information on two sides of the graph. You usually read them from left to right and from bottom to top.

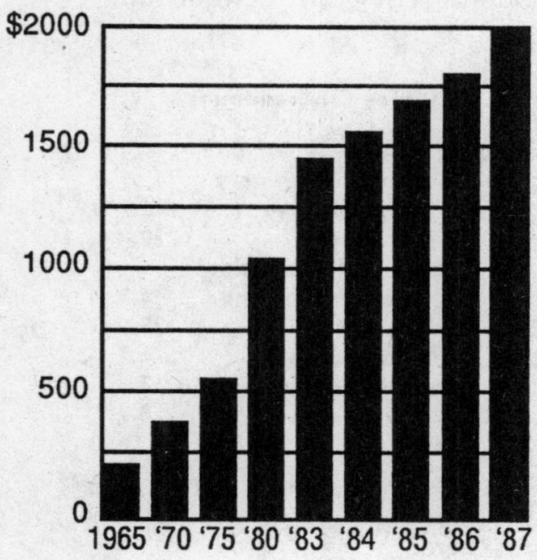

Line Graph

A line graph is similar to a bar graph except that points inside the graph are connected to show the information.

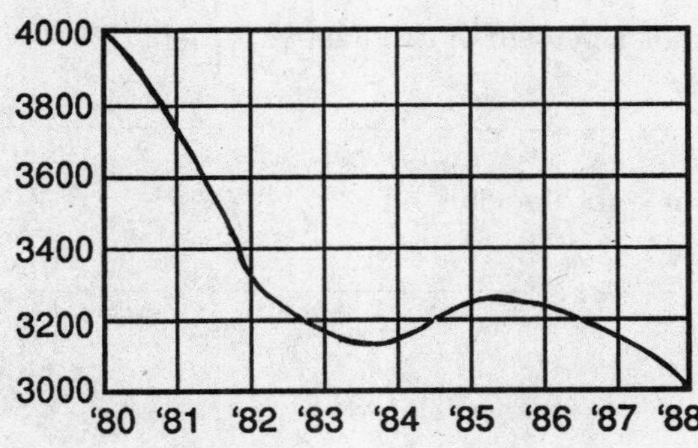

Reading a Circle Graph (Answers, page 343)

Directions: Read the following graph and answer the questions about it.

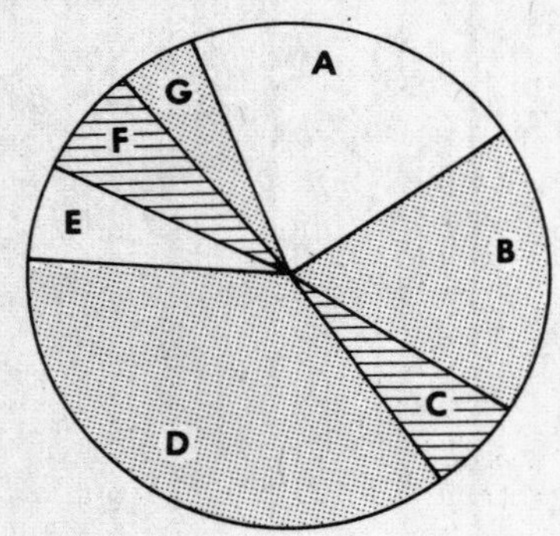

Valley City revenues

Total income — $4,091,000

A	**Garbage and waste disposal fees**	**22.7%**
B	**Water fees**	**20.4**
C	**Parks and recreation fees and income**	**4.9**
D	**Property tax**	**35.2**
E	**Interest earned**	**5.7**
F	**Contributions**	**7.4**
G	**Other income**	**3.7**

1. How much total income does Valley City receive?

____

2. From which source does Valley City get most of its income?

____

3. What percentage of income comes from garbage and waste disposal fees?

____

4. From what source does the city get about 5 percent of its income?

____

5. What are the three largest areas of income for the city?

____

Reading a Bar Graph (Answers, page 343)

Directions: Read the graph below and answer the questions.

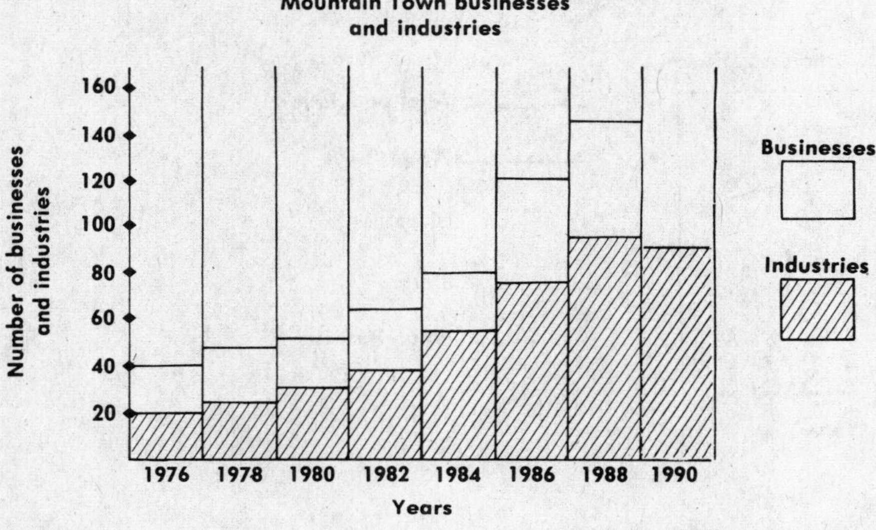

1. How many businesses and industries were there in Mountain Town in 1976?

2. In 1988, did Mountain Town have more businesses or industries?

3. In which years did Mountain Town have almost an equal number of businesses and industries?

4. In which year did Mountain Town have the least number of businesses in relation to the number of industries?

5. In what ways did the numbers of industries and businesses change in 1990 compared to 1988?

Reading a Line Graph (Answers, page 343)

Directions: Read the graph below and answer the questions.

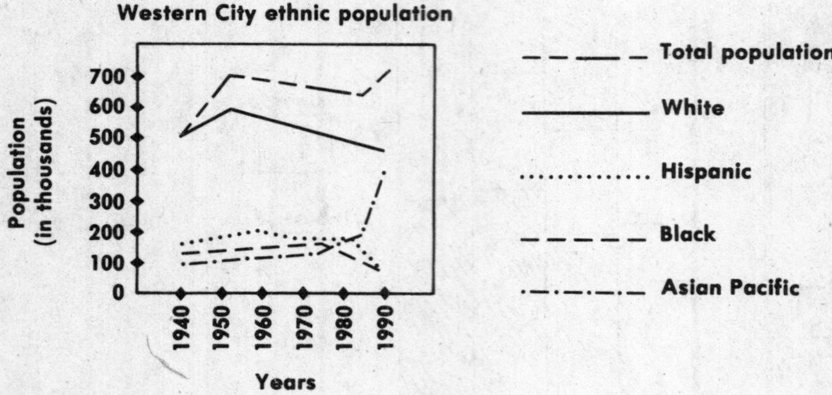

1. What is the population of Western City in 1990?

---

2. How would you describe the changes in the total population between the years 1950 and 1990?

---

3. What has happened to the white population of Western City since the year 1950?

---

4. What group of people has increased the most since 1940?

---

5. In 1990 what group of people has the greatest number?

Summary

1. The Test of Written English (TWE) is not a part of the TOEFL exam. It is a separate essay test, given on only some of the TOEFL test days.
2. The TWE is scored holistically wit[illegible]m 1 to 6. The score is not added to your TOEFL score.
3. For the essay question, you are asked to either write a compare/contrast essay or to interpret a chart or graph.
4. You have 30 minutes to read the question, plan your essay, and write the essay.
5. You should organize your ideas on a separate paper before you begin writing. Four kinds of organization are brainstorming, clustering, writing a matrix, and outlining.
6. Always read the question carefully and be sure to answer it completely.
7. Your essay should have a clear beginning, middle, and end.
8. Three common graphs are circle graphs, bar graphs, and line graphs.

Answers to Exercises

EXERCISE 1

There is no answer to this exercise. Refer back to the sample methods of organizing your thoughts on pages 323 to 327.

EXERCISE 2

These are general answers to the questions on page 336.
Heng Tan's essay:

1. Yes, it begins with a short introduction of *freedom,* but not a specific introduction of this particular question.
2. It discusses one side of the question.
3. Yes, the author's point of view is stated clearly.
4. The essay gives some reasons, but they are not written clearly. The writer's point of view is that government should censor certain kinds of materials. The reason for this point of view is that if people look at pornography they will think about sex. The writer later says that reading some things can hurt other people's feelings.
5. The writer gives two examples, though neither is very specific. The first example is about publishing all kinds of materials. The example is "people produce books, plays, and films about pornography." The second example is about what kinds of publications should be censored. The example is "books, plays, and films about the girl . . . who has a baby."
6. Yes, it ends with a short conclusion.

In the final draft of this essay, the writer improved the essay by adding an example, correcting some of the grammar and spelling, and strengthening the conclusion. The score for this essay might be a "3." The writer shows competence, but does not support the statement very well and does not give many details.

Mario Espinosa's essay:

1. Yes it begins with an introduction of the question.
2. It discusses only one side of the question.
3. Yes, the author's point of view is stated clearly.
4. Yes, it gives reasons to support the point of view. The writer's point of view is that government should not censor people's expression because that will also censor development and freedom and also creativity, art, and expression.

5. Yes, it gives good detailed examples about a book in Mexico, people in Latinoamerican countries, and a book in the United States (Los Angeles airport).
6. Yes, it ends with a short conclusion.

In the final draft, Mario developed the background material, added detailed examples, and rewrote the conclusion. He might receive a score of "4" or possibly "5," based on the examples and varied vocabulary. (A score of "4" and above is generally considered a "passing" score.)

EXERCISE 3

1. $4,091,000
2. Property Tax
3. 22.7 percent
4. Parks and recreation fees and income
5. Garbage and waste disposal fees
   Water fees
   Property Tax

EXERCISE 4

1. 40 (20 businesses and 20 industries)
2. It had more industries.
3. 1976 and 1978
4. 1984
5. The number of industries decreased and the number of businesses increased.

EXERCISE 5

1. A little more than 700,000.
2. The population decreased between 1950 and the early 1980s and then increased during the rest of the 1980s.
3. Since the early 1950s the white population has steadily decreased.
4. Since 1940 the Asian Pacific population has increased the most.
5. In 1990 the whites have the greatest number.

Written English Drills

The following pages contain seven drills. The first one is a Walk-Through which contains a completed essay along with a description of the thought process. There are six remaining drills that give you example essay questions. Write your own essays and then check the explanatory answers on pages 352 and 353 to see if you have included the important information.

Walk-Through

Directions: Read the following question and the completed essay. The right-hand side of the page gives the step-by-step thought process based on the procedure outlined on pages 332-333. The left-hand side of the page shows what the writer writes.

Essay Question:

Some people say that experience is the best way to learn something; others claim that the best way to learn something is by studying. Decide whether you think that experience or study is the best way to learn. Then discuss your position; why did you decide on this choice? Give examples to support your decision.

Clue Words

best way to learn
experience or study
discuss
why?
give examples to support

Step 1: Think of the clue words in the question. Underline them or write them down.

Main Idea

I think experience is the best way to learn.

Step 2: Think of your main idea.

Organization: Matrix

Topic	Support
experience	best for understanding best for remembering good way to judge
examples	computer swimming writing

Step 3: Organize your thoughts.

Additional Examples

Use all examples in matrix.

Step 4: Add examples and details.

Essay

My life has been affected more by my real experiences than by my studying. I have spent many years in school, and have read many books, but when I think of what is most important for learning, I think of the experiences that I have had.

STEP 5: Begin writing. Include the main point of view and some background information in the introduction.

It is only by experiencing something that I can really understand it. I remember when I was trying to learn to use a computer. I read the book over and over again and I read the information that my friends gave me, but it didn't make sense. It wasn't until I actually used the computer that I really understood it.

Explain a major point and give an example.

Experience helps me remember things also. When I was trying to improve my stroke in swimming, I listened to my instructor tell me how to improve, and I looked at some drawings of good swimming strokes. But I kept forgetting what to do. After I practiced in the pool, however, I could remember exactly what to do.

Give a second major point with an example.

There is another reason that I think that experience is a better way to learn. It helps me judge whether or not I have actually understood what I have studied. By acting instead of reading, I am able to prove to myself that I can do it correctly. A good example of this is my writing. I keep getting better at writing English, but it is only by actually doing the writing that I can judge my own improvement. It doesn't help me much just to read about it.

A third reason supporting experience.

I have no doubt about the superiority of experience as compared to study. I have tried both studying about things and actually trying them. I know that I understand and remember much better when I experience new things.

End with a conclusion that summarizes the main point.

STEP 6: Go back over the essay, checking for spelling and punctuation.

Drill 1: Compare/Contrast

(Answers: checklist, page 352)

Directions: Answer the following essay question. Use no more than 30 minutes to read the question, organize your thoughts, and write your essay. Write your organization notes on another paper.

Some people prefer the winter for its effect on activities and work. Others prefer the summer. Pick the season you like best (winter, spring, summer, fall) for work or activities you enjoy. Explain why you chose this season. Give reasons for your choice.

Drill 2: Compare/Contrast

(Answers: checklist, page 352)

Directions: Answer the following essay question. Use no more than 30 minutes to read the question, organize your thoughts, and write your essay. Write your organization notes on another paper.

Some people choose to live in a large city; others prefer living in a small town or village. What are some of the advantages and disadvantages of each? Which place would you prefer to live in? Why?

Drill 3: Compare/Contrast (Answers: checklist, page 352)

Directions: Answer the following essay question. Use no more than 30 minutes to read the question, organize your thoughts, and write your essay. Write your organization notes on another paper.

Some people prefer work or activities which mainly involve working with people. Others choose work or activities which mainly involve working with objects or machines. Compare the advantages of each choice. Which of these two ways of spending time do you prefer? Give reasons to support your answer.

Drill 4: Circle Graph (Answers: checklist, page 352)

Directions: Answer the following essay question. Use no more than 30 minutes to read the question, organize your thoughts, and write your essay. Write your organization notes on another paper.

The graph below shows the way that one college student spends her money. Describe her expenses, making some conclusions about her life, based on her expenses.

Where the Money Goes	
rent	32 percent
food	25 percent
entertainment	14 percent
health	10 percent
books	10 percent
transportation	7 percent
other	2 percent

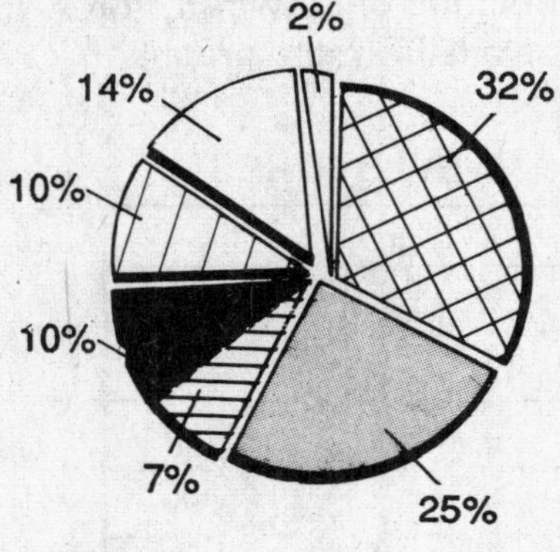

Drill 5: Bar Graph

(Answers: checklist, page 352)

Directions: Answer the following essay question. Use no more than 30 minutes to read the question, organize your thoughts, and write your essay. Write your organization notes on another paper.

The graph below shows the number of new fruit stores that opened between 1984 and 1989 in Central City. Discuss the information in the graph, making some conclusions about the opening of new fruit stores. Explain your conclusions, supporting them with details from the graph.

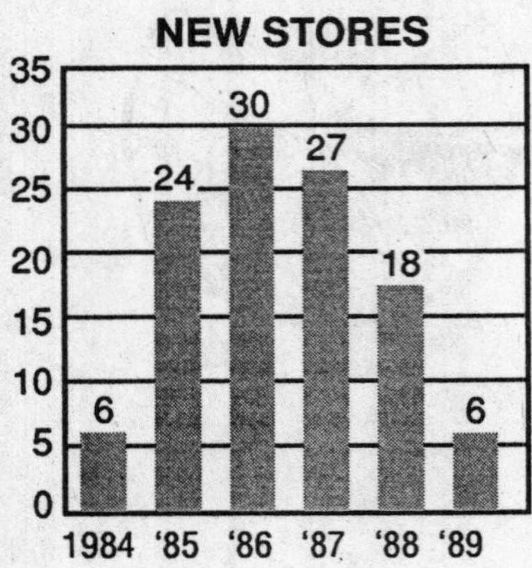

Drill 6: Line Graph

(Answers: checklist, page 353)

Directions: Answer the following essay question. Use no more than 30 minutes to read the question, organize your thoughts, and write your essay. Write your organization notes on another paper.

The graph below shows the number of students receiving scholarships in an eight-year period. Using information from the graph, compare the eight years. Form a conclusion about what is happening to the number of scholarships and explain your conclusions supporting them with details from the graph.

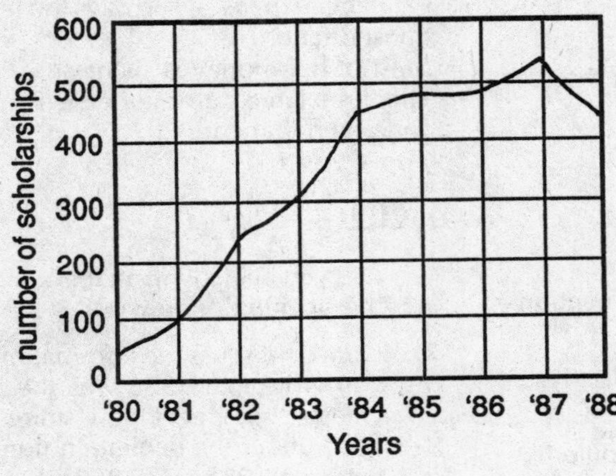

Explanatory Answers: Checklist

Instead of actual answers, these pages give you a checklist for each drill. Read your own essay and check to see that you have answered the questions here.

DRILL 1

1. Did you begin with an introduction that mentions the season you prefer and maybe the kind of work or activities you are discussing?
2. Did you explain what work or activities you do during the season you prefer?
3. Did you give reasons for why you prefer the season?
4. Did you end with a short conclusion?

DRILL 2

1. Did you begin with an introduction that mentions living in a town or city?
2. Did you mention *both* advantages *and* disadvantages of *both* large cities and small towns?
3. Did you state clearly which place you would like to live and give reasons?
4. Did you end with a short conclusion?

DRILL 3

1. Did you begin with an introduction that mentions activities or people?
2. Did you *compare* the advantages of both working with people *and* things?
3. Did you state clearly which of the choices you prefer and give reasons for your answer?
4. Did you end with a short conclusion?

DRILL 4

1. Did you begin with a short introduction that discusses the college student and her expenses?
2. Did you discuss *each* expense and its percentage?
3. Did you write about what you think the student's life is like, based on the graph? (She spends most of her money on rent and food)
4. Did you end with a short conclusion?

Some example sentences that you might use:

She pays more money for rent than for anything else.
Of all her expenses, she pays the least amount for transportation.
Most of her money is spent on rent and food.
The three largest areas of expense are rent, food, and entertainment.

DRILL 5

1. Did you begin with an introduction that mentions the opening of new fruit stores?
2. Did you discuss the information in the graph? Did you write that 1986 was the year in which the greatest number of new stores opened? Did you write about the decline in number of new stores between 1986 and 1989?
3. Did you conclude that there will probably be fewer than five new stores opening in the next year?
4. Did you end with a short conclusion?

Some example sentences that you might use:

The years 1984 and 1989 had the same number of new stores.
In 1986 there were 30 new stores.
The year 1986 had the greatest number of new stores.
Between 1986 and 1989 the number of new stores decreased.
There was a large jump in new stores between 1984 and 1985.
The three years between 1985 and 1987 had the greatest number of new stores opening.
The number of new stores decreased dramatically between 1986 and 1989.
It is likely that there will be fewer new stores opening in the next year.

DRILL 6

1. Did you begin with a short description of student scholarships?
2. Did you mention that the number of student scholarships given since 1980 rose every year until 1987? Did you mention that the number of students scholarships has declined since 1987?
3. Did you decide that the number of scholarships is probably going to drop more?
4. Did you end with a short conclusion about your ideas?

Some example sentences you might use are:

Between 1980 and 1987 the number of scholarships increased.
The number of scholarships given rose each year between 1980 and 1987.
Beginning in 1987, the number of scholarships decreased.
There was a steady increase in the number of scholarships given between 1980 and 1984.
Between 1984 and 1986, the number of scholarships remained almost the same.
There was a sharp decline in the number of scholarships given after 1987.

PART FOUR

Practice Tests

ANSWER SHEET FOR PRACTICE TEST I

Section 1: Listening Comprehension

1	2	3	4	5	6	7	8	9	10	11	12	13	14	15	16	17	18	19	20	21	22	23	24	25	26	27	28	29	30	31	32	33	34	35	36	37	38	39	40	41	42	43	44	45	46	47	48	49	50
A	A	A	A	A	A	A	A	A	A	A	A	A	A	A	A	A	A	A	A	A	A	A	A	A	A	A	A	A	A	A	A	A	A	A	A	A	A	A	A	A	A	A	A	A	A	A	A	A	A
B	B	B	B	B	B	B	B	B	B	B	B	B	B	B	B	B	B	B	B	B	B	B	B	B	B	B	B	B	B	B	B	B	B	B	B	B	B	B	B	B	B	B	B	B	B	B	B	B	B
C	C	C	C	C	C	C	C	C	C	C	C	C	C	C	C	C	C	C	C	C	C	C	C	C	C	C	C	C	C	C	C	C	C	C	C	C	C	C	C	C	C	C	C	C	C	C	C	C	C
D	D	D	D	D	D	D	D	D	D	D	D	D	D	D	D	D	D	D	D	D	D	D	D	D	D	D	D	D	D	D	D	D	D	D	D	D	D	D	D	D	D	D	D	D	D	D	D	D	D

Section 2: Structure and Written Expression

1	2	3	4	5	6	7	8	9	10	11	12	13	14	15	16	17	18	19	20	21	22	23	24	25	26	27	28	29	30	31	32	33	34	35	36	37	38	39	40
A	A	A	A	A	A	A	A	A	A	A	A	A	A	A	A	A	A	A	A	A	A	A	A	A	A	A	A	A	A	A	A	A	A	A	A	A	A	A	A
B	B	B	B	B	B	B	B	B	B	B	B	B	B	B	B	B	B	B	B	B	B	B	B	B	B	B	B	B	B	B	B	B	B	B	B	B	B	B	B
C	C	C	C	C	C	C	C	C	C	C	C	C	C	C	C	C	C	C	C	C	C	C	C	C	C	C	C	C	C	C	C	C	C	C	C	C	C	C	C
D	D	D	D	D	D	D	D	D	D	D	D	D	D	D	D	D	D	D	D	D	D	D	D	D	D	D	D	D	D	D	D	D	D	D	D	D	D	D	D

Section 3: Vocabulary and Reading Comprehension

1	2	3	4	5	6	7	8	9	10	11	12	13	14	15	16	17	18	19	20	21	22	23	24	25	26	27	28	29	30	31	32	33	34	35	36	37	38	39	40	41	42	43	44	45	46	47	48	49	50	51	52	53	54	55	56	57	58	59	60
A	A	A	A	A	A	A	A	A	A	A	A	A	A	A	A	A	A	A	A	A	A	A	A	A	A	A	A	A	A	A	A	A	A	A	A	A	A	A	A	A	A	A	A	A	A	A	A	A	A	A	A	A	A	A	A	A	A	A	A
B	B	B	B	B	B	B	B	B	B	B	B	B	B	B	B	B	B	B	B	B	B	B	B	B	B	B	B	B	B	B	B	B	B	B	B	B	B	B	B	B	B	B	B	B	B	B	B	B	B	B	B	B	B	B	B	B	B	B	B
C	C	C	C	C	C	C	C	C	C	C	C	C	C	C	C	C	C	C	C	C	C	C	C	C	C	C	C	C	C	C	C	C	C	C	C	C	C	C	C	C	C	C	C	C	C	C	C	C	C	C	C	C	C	C	C	C	C	C	C
D	D	D	D	D	D	D	D	D	D	D	D	D	D	D	D	D	D	D	D	D	D	D	D	D	D	D	D	D	D	D	D	D	D	D	D	D	D	D	D	D	D	D	D	D	D	D	D	D	D	D	D	D	D	D	D	D	D	D	D

Date Taken ____________________

Number Correct

Section 1 ________

Section 2 ________

Section 3 ________

Practice Test I
Diagnostic Test (Short Form)

NOTE: You will need the tape to do Section 1. If you do not have the tape, the tapescript for Section 1 is on pages 633 to 637. The answer key is on pages 381–382, and explanatory answers begin on page 385. Use the answer sheet for Practice Test I on page 357 to mark your answers.

1 1 1 1 1 1 1 1 1 1 1

SECTION 1
LISTENING COMPREHENSION
Time—approximately 35 minutes

In this section of the test, you will have an opportunity to demonstrate your ability to understand spoken English. There are three parts to this section, with special directions for each part.

Part A

Directions: For each question in Part A, you will hear a short sentence. Each sentence will be spoken just one time. The sentences you hear will not be written out for you. Therefore, you must listen carefully to understand what the speaker says.

After you hear a sentence, read the four choices in your test book, marked (A), (B), (C), and (D), and decide which one is closest in meaning to the sentence you heard. Then, on your answer sheet, find the number of the question and fill in the space that corresponds to the letter of the answer you have chosen. Fill in the space so that the letter inside the oval cannot be seen.

Example I:

You will hear:

Sample Answer

You will read:

(A) Mary outswam the others.
(B) Mary ought to swim with them.
(C) Mary and her friends swam to the island.
(D) Mary's friends owned the island.

The speaker said, "Mary swam out to the island with her friends." Sentence (C), "Mary and her friends swam to the island," is closest in meaning to the sentence you heard. Therefore, you should choose answer (C).

Example II:

You will hear:

Sample Answer

You will read:

(A) Please remind me to read this book.
(B) Could you help me carry these books?
(C) I don't mind if you help me.
(D) Do you have a heavy course load this term?

The speaker said, "Would you mind helping me with this load of books?" Sentence (B), "Could you help me carry these books?" is closest in meaning to the sentence you heard. Therefore, you should choose answer (B).

GO ON TO THE NEXT PAGE

1. (A) Is there a circular drive around the airport?
(B) How big is the airport?
(C) Is the airport close?
(D) Is this an international airport?

2. (A) The information won't come today.
(B) Bring me the information tomorrow.
(C) Mail it to me at your earliest convenience.
(D) Your speech is very informative.

3. (A) Jane is a teacher.
(B) Jane's mother doesn't want to teach.
(C) Jane takes care of her children herself.
(D) Jane's stepmother doesn't like her.

4. (A) The mother teaches the children at home.
(B) The children didn't go to school today.
(C) The school is nearby.
(D) Children should wear shoes.

5. (A) Sam shouldn't be cruel.
(B) Sam is calm.
(C) Sam is cooling himself down.
(D) Please make yourself comfortable.

6. (A) The road was not straight.
(B) It was windy.
(C) The road was just completed.
(D) The road was wide.

7. (A) Alan's rehearsal was canceled.
(B) Alan went to the rehearsal meeting.
(C) Alan slept through the performance.
(D) Alan always rehearses before a show.

8. (A) Diane is not getting better.
(B) It's bad enough to have a headache.
(C) Diane is completely satisfied.
(D) Bad weather doesn't affect Diane.

9. (A) All right, let's do it again.
(B) Turn to the right or left?
(C) You can't do it all correctly.
(D) Don't worry, everything will be OK.

10. (A) Did you like the class, too?
(B) Nobody can drop the class after today.
(C) Did both of you stop going to class?
(D) We, too, want to join the class.

11. (A) I mistook you for my friend.
(B) Excuse me, my friend.
(C) I feel sorry that you are not my friend.
(D) I don't think you are my friend.

12. (A) He doubts that he will become a junior high school student.
(B) Adults like him because he is active.
(C) He behaves like a junior high school student.
(D) Even though he is still in junior high school, he acts grown up.

13. (A) Dr. Stevenson earns a good salary as a department chair.
(B) Dr. Stevenson is fortunate this year, isn't she?
(C) Dr. Stevenson doesn't want to be involved in administration, does she?
(D) Do you think Dr. Stevenson will become the department chair this year?

14. (A) Have you been to this restaurant before?
(B) Are you certain you made a reservation?
(C) I am not sure you want to stay here.
(D) When did you make your reservation?

15. (A) Sam prefers apple pie to cheese cake.
(B) Sam ordered cheese cake for his friend.
(C) Apple pie is better for Sam than cheesecake.
(D) Sam ordered the one he likes the best.

16. (A) Success helps us learn.
(B) We can hardly learn anything from a bad experience.
(C) Failure usually gives us a good lesson.
(D) Success is the ultimate goal of learning.

17. (A) He usually dreamt that he ran very fast.
(B) He thinks that he can get along well.
(C) His ideas have helped him get ahead.
(D) His dreams are unrealistic.

18. (A) Simon should have studied every word that was on the test.
(B) The test will probably ask some questions that are difficult for Simon.
(C) Simon shouldn't take the test because he didn't study enough.
(D) The test will seem easy if Simon studies more.

19. (A) Why did you give me chocolate?
(B) I wish I had chocolate.
(C) You don't know what I like.
(D) Why don't you like chocolate?

20. (A) She will recover very fast.
(B) The doctor believed she would recover quickly.
(C) She didn't believe she would recover so fast.
(D) She improved more than her doctor expected.

GO ON TO THE NEXT PAGE

1 1 1 1 1 1 1 1 1 1 1

Part B

<u>Directions:</u> In Part B you will hear short conversations between two speakers. At the end of each conversation, a third person will ask a question about what was said. You will hear each conversation and question about it just one time. Therefore, you must listen carefully to understand what each speaker says. After you hear a conversation and the question about it, read the four possible answers in your test book and decide which <u>one</u> is the best answer to the question you heard. Then, on your answer sheet, find the number of the question and fill in the space that corresponds to the letter of the answer you have chosen.

Look at the following example.

You will hear:

<u>Sample Answer</u>

● Ⓑ Ⓒ Ⓓ

You will read:

(A) Present Professor Smith with a picture.
(B) Photograph Professor Smith.
(C) Put glass over the photograph.
(D) Replace the broken headlight.

From the conversation you learn that the woman thinks Professor Smith would like a photograph of the class. The best answer to the question "What does the woman think the class should do?" is (A), "Present Professor Smith with a picture." Therefore, you should choose answer (A).

GO ON TO THE NEXT PAGE

21. **(A)** He doesn't mind helping her.
(B) He has some problems.
(C) He is very busy.
(D) He had to help her.

22. **(A)** They are discussing a math contest.
(B) The woman is making a telephone call.
(C) A department store is having a sale.
(D) The post office is closed.

23. **(A)** He asked someone else to mow the lawn.
(B) Nobody mowed the lawn.
(C) He will wait until next week.
(D) He had a problem with his lungs.

24. **(A)** The law is too complicated to understand.
(B) It's good to have a dog around the house.
(C) No dogs are allowed in the area.
(D) Unfortunately, they don't have any dogs.

25. **(A)** This is the last one.
(B) The longer style is better.
(C) You should buy cheaper merchandise.
(D) It might not be of good quality.

26. **(A)** She fixed her friend's tape recorder.
(B) She tried to telephone her friend.
(C) She went to her friend's house.
(D) She arranged to meet her friend later.

27. **(A)** She is happy.
(B) She is joking.
(C) She is certain.
(D) She is busy.

28. **(A)** Give his approval.
(B) Buy a pen.
(C) Write an essay.
(D) Go back to work.

29. **(A)** No one lives there now.
(B) You'd better make an appointment.
(C) You can see it after your vacation.
(D) It's a beautiful place.

30. **(A)** The woman forgot that her lights were on.
(B) The woman needed more light.
(C) The man helped the woman carry a heavy load.
(D) The man picked up the woman's glasses.

31. **(A)** Tim has good study habits.
(B) Tim writes many papers.
(C) Tim lives in a dormitory.
(D) Tim's papers are often late.

32. **(A)** He cannot make a copy because of the copyright.
(B) He should wait until tomorrow.
(C) He can make his own copy.
(D) He cannot make a copy now.

33. **(A)** He is tired of using his new computer.
(B) He has just assembled the computer.
(C) He has used his new computer for writing his dissertation.
(D) He has found something wrong with the new computer.

34. **(A)** Dr. Martin didn't want so many students in his class.
(B) The students were supposed to buy the textbook earlier.
(C) The bookstore is going out of business.
(D) Dr. Martin didn't order enough textbooks for his students.

35. **(A)** Buying less expensive food
(B) Dining at the cafeteria
(C) Cooking more simply
(D) Studying harder

GO ON TO THE NEXT PAGE

1 1 1 1 1 1 1 1 1 1 1

Part C

Directions: In this part of the test, you will hear short talks and conversations. After each of them, you will be asked some questions. You will hear the talks and conversations and the questions about them just one time. They will not be written out for you. Therefore, you must listen carefully to understand what each speaker says.

After you hear a question, read the four possible answers in your test book and decide which one is the best answer to the question you heard. Then, on your answer sheet, find the number of the question and fill in the space that corresponds to the letter of the answer you have chosen.

Answer all questions on the basis of what is stated or implied in the talk or conversation.

Listen to this sample talk.

You will hear:

Now look at the following example.

You will hear:

Sample Answer

  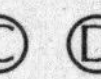

You will read:

(A) They are impossible to guide.
(B) They may go up in flames.
(C) They tend to leak gas.
(D) They are cheaply made.

The best answer to the question "Why are gas balloons considered dangerous?" is (B), "They may go up in flames." Therefore, you should choose answer (B).

Now look at the next example.

You will hear:

Sample Answer

 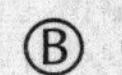 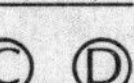

You will read:

(A) Watch for changes in weather.
(B) Watch their altitude.
(C) Check for weak spots in their balloons.
(D) Test the strength of the ropes.

The best answer to the question "According to the speaker, what must balloon pilots be careful to do?" is (A), "Watch for changes in weather." Therefore, you should choose answer (A).

GO ON TO THE NEXT PAGE

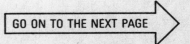

36. **(A)** Professor Smith
(B) A teaching assistant
(C) A specialist in chemistry
(D) A university technician

37. **(A)** Every day of the week
(B) One day a week
(C) Two days a week
(D) Once every two weeks

38. **(A)** To teach important safety rules
(B) To explain the grading procedures
(C) To demonstrate an experiment
(D) To tell students what safety equipment to buy

39. **(A)** Loose scarves
(B) Sandals
(C) Long necklaces
(D) Eyeglasses

40. **(A)** Buy a notebook
(B) Wash their lab equipment
(C) Do an experiment
(D) Put waste in the proper container

41. **(A)** The plays of Shakespeare
(B) The writer of Shakespeare plays
(C) The birthplace of Shakespeare
(D) The Earl of Oxford

42. **(A)** A visit to England
(B) An English literature test
(C) A discussion with a professor
(D) A discussion of a play

43. **(A)** A professor
(B) The Earl of Oxford
(C) A tourist
(D) An illiterate man

44. **(A)** Visit Shakespeare's house
(B) Visit Oxford
(C) Learn about the Earl of Oxford
(D) See Shakespeare's plays

45. **(A)** Reading about the Earl of Oxford
(B) Seeing a Shakespeare play
(C) Taking a class in Shakespeare
(D) Reading more plays

46. **(A)** Predators in the animal world
(B) Divisions of the food chain
(C) The loss of potential energy in predators
(D) A parasitic chain

47. **(A)** A bird eating a fish
(B) A rabbit eating grass
(C) A tapeworm living in an animal
(D) A plant using energy from the sun

48. **(A)** 2–3 percent
(B) 10 percent
(C) 12–15 percent
(D) More than 15 percent

49. **(A)** A plant uses energy.
(B) Animals kill other animals.
(C) Potential energy is lost.
(D) A microorganism feeds off dead matter.

50. **(A)** A green plant
(B) Dead matter
(C) A smaller animal
(D) A rabbit

THIS IS THE END OF THE LISTENING COMPREHENSION PART OF THIS TEST. The next part of the test is Section 2. Turn to the directions for Section 2 in your test book, read them, and begin work. Do not read or work on any other section of the test.

GO ON TO THE NEXT PAGE

2 2 2 2 2 2 2 2 2 2 2

SECTION 2
STRUCTURE AND WRITTEN EXPRESSION
Time—25 minues

This section is designed to measure your ability to recognize language that is appropriate for standard written English. There are two types of questions in this section, with special directions for each type.

Directions: Questions 1–15 are incomplete sentences. Beneath each sentence you will see four words or phrases, marked (A), (B), (C), and (D). Choose the one word or phrase that best completes the sentence. Then, on your answer sheet, find the number of the question and fill in the space that corresponds to the letter of the answer you have chosen. Fill in the space so that the letter inside the oval cannot be seen.

Example I:

Vegetables are an excellent source _________ vitamins.

Sample Answer

● Ⓑ Ⓒ Ⓓ

(A) of
(B) has
(C) where
(D) that

The sentence should read, "Vegetables are an excellent source of vitamins." Therefore, you should choose answer (A).

Example II:

_________ in history when remarkable progress was made within a relatively short span of time.

Sample Answer

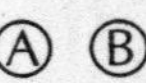   Ⓓ

(A) Periods
(B) Throughout periods
(C) There have been periods
(D) Periods have been

The sentence should read, "There have been periods in history when remarkable progress was made within a relatively short span of time." Therefore, you should choose answer (C).

After you read the directions, begin work on the questions.

GO ON TO THE NEXT PAGE

1. It's not easy for a casual observer to distinguish ________ genuine paintings and copies.

(A) between
(B) therefore
(C) for
(D) to

2. ________, all matter is formed of molecules.

(A) It doesn't matter if the complex
(B) No matter how complex
(C) How complex is not a matter
(D) It's not a complex matter

3. After World War I, automobiles, buses, and trucks became the most common ________.

(A) of transportation
(B) transport form
(C) forms of transportation
(D) transportation of form

4. Tears ________ anger and tension naturally.

(A) are relieved
(B) relieving
(C) relieve
(D) what they relieve

5. In a single day ________ are as many as thousands of people involved in business deals in one area.

(A) yet
(B) they
(C) ever
(D) there

6. Paper ________ from cellulose fibers.

(A) is produced
(B) producing
(C) produced
(D) which is produced

7. ________ an insurance agent it is necessary to pass the state examination.

(A) Become
(B) To become
(C) Having become
(D) One becomes

8. There are ________ art galleries in the city of Carmel.

(A) a great deal
(B) many
(C) much
(D) lots

9. One difficulty ________ at night is limited vision.

(A) to drive
(B) will drive
(C) with driving
(D) be driven

10. ________ the Pulitzer Prize in 1924.

(A) Edna Ferber won
(B) When Edna Ferber won
(C) With Edna Ferber's winning
(D) Edna Ferber's winning

11. All ________ of the world carry on breeding experiments to increase yield or to improve disease resistance.

(A) countries that grow wheat
(B) growth of wheat countries
(C) wheat-producing countries
(D) countries where wheat is grown

12. Throughout the United States ________ fast food restaurants where hamburgers are served.

(A) there are
(B) there is
(C) located
(D) are there

13. The human body contains water ________, bones, and muscles.

(A) is blood
(B) in its blood
(C) is in its blood
(D) it is in its blood

14. ________ covered by the sea, which occupies 71 percent of the earth.

(A) A huge unknown world is
(B) An huge unknown world
(C) How huge the unknown world
(D) So huge is the unknown world

GO ON TO THE NEXT PAGE

15. In his painting, "The Three Musicians" Picasso reached a climax in his use ________ geometric forms.

(A) to
(B) of
(C) on
(D) with

Directions: In questions 16–40 each sentence has four underlined words or phrases. The four underlined parts of the sentence are marked (A), (B), (C), and (D). Identify the one underlined word or phrase that must be changed in order for the sentence to be correct. Then, on your answer sheet, find the number of the question and fill in the space that corresponds to the letter of the answer you have chosen.

Example I:

A ray of light passing through (A) the center (B) of a thin lens keep (C) its original (D) direction.

Sample Answer

Ⓐ Ⓑ ● Ⓓ

The sentence should read, "A ray of light passing through the center of a thin lens keeps its original direction." Therefore, you should choose answer (C).

Example II:

The mandolin, a musical instrument (A) that has (B) strings, was probably copied from (C) the lute, a many (D) older instrument.

Sample Answer

Ⓐ Ⓑ Ⓒ ●

The sentence should read, "The mandolin, a musical instrument that has strings, was probably copied from the lute, a much older instrument." Therefore, you should choose answer (D).

Now begin work on the questions.

16. Not only cigarettes and too (A) alcohol is believed (B) to be (C) harmful to one's (D) health.

17. Approximately (A) 80 percent of (B) farm income in Utah it is derived (C) from livestock and livestock products (D).

18. The pleura that cover (A) the exterior (B) of the lungs (C) and the inner walls of the chest cavity is (D) a thin elastic membrane.

GO ON TO THE NEXT PAGE

19. Jays are more shorter and more colorful than crows.
A B C D

20. The first steps of scientific research is to decide how to gather data.
A B C D

21. Caffeine in coffee is relative harmless if people drink it moderately.
A B C D

22. Vibrating or shaking rapidly often cause noise.
A B C D

23. Soybeans can provides vegetarians with a nutritionally balanced diet for a low
A B C D
price.

24. The flotation process devised to separate minerals from other chemical
A B C D
compounds.

25. Of searching for underground deposits of oil, geologists often rely on
A B C D
magnetometers.

26. New York City, which is one of the largest cities in the world, is larger than any
A B C
other cities in the United States.
D

27. Radiation usual travels from a source in straight lines, but charged particles travel
A B C
in curved paths within magnetic fields.
D

28. One of the reasons that English-dubbed foreign movies often seem silly are that the
A B C
gestures don't match the speech.
D

29. Many young people lack the skills, good education, and financial to settle in the
A B C
urban areas where most jobs are found.
D

30. In geology, Earth's continents are classify by rock density and composition.
A B C D

31. People often seem anger when they don't get enough rest.
A B C D

32. Many modern families are finding ways to share household chores, works, and
A B C
care of children.
D

GO ON TO THE NEXT PAGE

33. Serotonin is produced in particular high concentrations in the hypothalamus,
A B
which joins the brain to the top of the spinal cord.
C D

34. Benjamin Banneker helped to produce the original architectural design that suc-
A B C
cessfully was use to build the city of Washington D.C.
D

35. The ancestors of some French Americans original came to the United States
A
because of the French Revolution, which broke out in 1789.
B C D

36. SPSSx is a computer program designed specific for statistical analysis with a large
A B C
amount of data.
D

37. Located on the frontally surface of the skull, the human eye is a spheroid organ in
A B C
a bony cavity.
D

38. Nicotine consumption is no diminished by pipe smoking; a causal relationship
A B C
exists between all forms of smoking and cancer.
D

39. Time is of few account in relation to great thoughts that are as vivid today as when
A B C
they first passed through their authors' minds, ages ago.
D

40. The advances in information technology are rapidly changing the nature at
A B C D
libraries.

THIS IS THE END OF SECTION 2. IF YOU FINISH BEFORE TIME IS UP, CHECK YOUR WORK ON SECTION 2 ONLY. DO NOT READ OR WORK ON ANY OTHER SECTION UNTIL YOUR TIME IS UP.	**STOP**

3 3 3 3 3 3 3 3 3 3 3

SECTION 3
VOCABULARY AND READING COMPREHENSION
Time—45 minutes

This section is designed to measure your comprehension of standard written English. There are two types of questions in this section, with special directions for each type.

Directions: In questions 1–30 each sentence has an underlined word or phrase. Below each sentence are four other words or phrases, marked (A), (B), (C), and (D). You are to choose the one word or phrase that best keeps the meaning of the original sentence if it is substituted for the underlined word or phrase. Then, on your answer sheet, find the number of the question and fill in the space that corresponds to the letter you have chosen. Fill in the space so that the letter inside the oval cannot be seen.

Example:

Passenger ships and aircraft are often equipped with ship-to-shore or air-to-land radio telephones.

(A) highways
(B) railroads
(C) planes
(D) sailboats

Sample Answer

Ⓐ Ⓑ ● Ⓓ

The best answer is (C) because "Passenger ships and planes are often equipped with ship-to-shore or air-to-land radio telephones" is closest in meaning to the original sentence. Therefore, you should choose answer (C).

Now begin work on the questions.

GO ON TO THE NEXT PAGE

1. Gradually, air conditioning and air travel have changed vacation habits.
   (A) Little by little
   (B) Recently
   (C) Suddenly
   (D) All at once

2. In ballet, Degas discovered the subject that was ideal for his talents.
   (A) representative of
   (B) perfect for
   (C) challenging for
   (D) old-fashioned for

3. A pamphlet will usually explain brief information about a new product.
   (A) A small booklet
   (B) A large sign
   (C) An advertisement
   (D) A slip of paper

4. The early 1930s were years of great hardship in North America.
   (A) famine
   (B) floods
   (C) commerce
   (D) suffering

5. Schools must protect children from the dangers of asbestos material.
   (A) threaten
   (B) promote
   (C) guard
   (D) mask

6. The first major effort to cope with soil erosion in the United States began in the 1930s.
   (A) select
   (B) advance
   (C) fund
   (D) manage

7. Sometimes a psychological problem will trigger a physical reaction.
   (A) release
   (B) initiate
   (C) perform
   (D) settle

8. The world is on the threshold of a new century.
   (A) realizing the importance of
   (B) at the beginning of
   (C) expecting
   (D) establishing goals for

9. The Freer Gallery of Art in Washington, D.C. presents a wide variety of Asian pottery and sculpture.
   (A) gives
   (B) sees
   (C) displays
   (D) preserves

10. Begonias are hardy and easy to grow under favorable conditions.
    (A) sunny
    (B) valuable
    (C) credit
    (D) advantageous

11. Since language is a cultural system, specific languages may classify objects and ideas in totally different fashions.
    (A) families
    (B) manners
    (C) levels
    (D) grades

12. The first spectacles were probably invented by Roger Bacon in the 13th century.
    (A) telescopes
    (B) eyeglasses
    (C) microscopes
    (D) binoculars

13. Fascinated with the idea of space travel as a child, Robert Goddard grew up to fire the world's first liquid-fueled rocket in 1926.
    (A) Studious about
    (B) Attracted by
    (C) Involved in
    (D) Attached to

14. Some doctors are not in favor of extending life, and they argue that people should have the right to die when they want.
    (A) creating
    (B) prolonging
    (C) hampering
    (D) redeeming

GO ON TO THE NEXT PAGE

15. Staring at other people can sometimes be impolite.

(A) Gazing steadily
(B) Glancing briefly
(C) Peeking carefully
(D) Winking privately

16. Even though there are many schools of martial art, one principle is common to all: training one's mind and body.

(A) colleges
(B) abilities
(C) types
(D) levels

17. The colors of the ocean and the sky merge into one on the horizon.

(A) blend
(B) maintain
(C) vanish
(D) alter

18. A map of Los Angeles and its vicinities is needed for new visitors to the L.A. area.

(A) facilities
(B) tourist spots
(C) vacant lots
(D) surroundings

19. Few scientific breakthroughs are discovered merely by coincidence.

(A) talent
(B) laymen
(C) chance
(D) imagination

20. Cottontail rabbits have large ears and short legs, and they move with a scurrying gait.

(A) jumping
(B) skipping
(C) scampering
(D) leaping

21. Being killed in a fight to protect one's rights is considered a supreme sacrifice by many people.

(A) an unusual
(B) the greatest
(C) a correct
(D) an abundant

22. Bison are characterized by huge heads and massive humps.

(A) novel
(B) flimsy
(C) large
(D) fat

23. The water of the Nile River supports practically all agriculture in the most densely populated parts of Egypt.

(A) ample
(B) eventual
(C) usual
(D) most

24. In 1863 President Lincoln proclaimed all slaves to be free.

(A) dedicated
(B) requested
(C) decided
(D) declared

25. Man's awareness of time is basically his consciousness of past, present, and future.

(A) innocence
(B) knowledge
(C) capability
(D) system

26. The bones of the very old are especially prone to fracture, although no age is exempt.

(A) infection
(B) cracking
(C) loosening
(D) degenerating

27. Thomas A. Edison was a celebrated American inventor in the 19th century.

(A) an ingenious
(B) a creative
(C) an eminent
(D) a successful

28. The faucets in this building were all replaced by the plumber.

(A) drains
(B) taps
(C) pumps
(D) pipes

GO ON TO THE NEXT PAGE

29. In the severe epidemic of the plague in Europe in the 14th century, the death toll was appalling.

(A) shocking
(B) weakening
(C) expanding
(D) demanding

30. Birds have a natural ability to fly.

(A) an innate
(B) a universal
(C) a real
(D) a native

Directions: In the rest of this section you will read several passages. Each one is followed by several questions about it. For questions 31–60, you are to choose the one best answer, (A), (B), (C), or (D), to each question. Then, on your answer sheet, find the number of the question and fill in the space that corresponds to the letter of the answer you have chosen.

Answer all questions following a passage on the basis of what is stated or implied in that passage.

Read the following passage:

The rattles with which a rattlesnake warns of its presence are formed by loosely interlocking hollow rings of hard skin, which make a buzzing sound when its tail is shaken. As a baby, the snake begins to firm its rattles from the button at the very tip of its tail. Thereafter, each time it sheds its skin, a new ring is formed. Popular belief holds that a snake's age can be told by counting the rings, but this idea is fallacious. In fact, a snake may lose its old skin as often as four times a year. Also, rattles tend to wear or break off with time.

Example I:

A rattlesnake's rattles are made of
(A) skin
(B) bone
(C) wood
(D) muscle

Sample Answer

●   

According to the passage, a rattlesnake's rattles are made out of rings of hard skin. Therefore, you should choose answer (A).

Example II:

How often does a rattlesnake shed its skin?
(A) Once every four years
(B) Once every four months
(C) Up to four times every year
(D) Four times more often than other snakes

Sample Answer

Ⓐ Ⓑ ● Ⓓ

The passage states that "a snake may lose its old skin as often as four times a year." Therefore, you should choose answer (C).

Now begin work on the questions.

GO ON TO THE NEXT PAGE

Questions 31–35

A new hearing device is now available for some hearing-impaired people. This device uses a magnet to hold the detachable sound-processing portion in place. Like other aids, it converts sound into vibrations. But it is unique in that it can transmit the vibrations directly to the magnet,and then to the inner ear. This produces a clearer sound. The new device will not help all hearing-impaired people, only those with a hearing loss caused by infection or other problem in the middle ear. It will probably help no more than 20 percent of all people with hearing problems. Those people, however, who often have persistent ear infections should find relief and restored hearing with the new device.

31. What is the author's main purpose?
(A) To describe a new cure for ear infections
(B) To inform medical personnel of a new device
(C) To urge doctors to use the new device
(D) To explain the use of the magnet

32. It can be inferred from the passage that
(A) this use of magnets is new
(B) infections are in the inner ear
(C) magnets can be dangerous for 80 percent of the people
(D) the new device is smaller than old ones

33. According to the passage, what does the device NOT do?
(A) Transmit sound to the inner ear
(B) Help all hearing-impaired people
(C) Produce clear sound
(D) Change sound into vibrations

34. The sound-processing unit
(A) is a magnet
(B) helps cure infections
(C) is placed in the middle ear
(D) can be removed

35. The word "relief" in the last sentence means
(A) less distress
(B) assistance
(C) distraction
(D) relaxation

GO ON TO THE NEXT PAGE

Questions 36–42

Potassium argon dating, which is used to calculate the age of ancient volcanic rocks, and, in turn, to reveal the age of early man, has caused anthropologists to revise their estimates of the age of some Stone Age cultures. In the 1960s the early hominid sites at Olduvai Gorge in East Africa were estimated to be 1.8 million years old. This was older than had been previously thought. Now another site in East Africa, of later hominid activity, has been estimated as older than was once thought. Layers of the volcanic ash in the Olorgesaillie river basin in Kenya were formerly estimated to be about 500,000 years old, but now are more accurately dated at 700,000 to 900,000 years old. Because of the many stone hand axes that have been uncovered, Olorgesaillie is considered a key site of Stone Age culture. Researchers are continuing to date other sites of early hominid remains. Many are now wondering whether other key sites might also be pushed back in time by potassium argon dating.

36. The best title for this passage is
(A) Early Hominid Sites
(B) Dating Early Sites
(C) Olduvai Gorge
(D) Stone Age Culture

37. The main purpose of this passage is to
(A) discuss new information
(B) inform reader of a new technique
(C) compare two places
(D) propose an idea

38. Olorgesaillie is a key site because of
(A) being very old
(B) having volcanic ash
(C) being near a river
(D) having many axes

39. It can be inferred from this passage that the age of early hominids is determined by
(A) the number of hand axes in the site
(B) the age of the rocks on the site
(C) the amount of activity shown by the site
(D) the number of layers of volcanic ash

40. The word "remains" in line 11 is closest in meaning to
(A) continues on
(B) parts not destroyed
(C) dead bodies
(D) stays behind

41. Olorgesaillie is
(A) older than Olduvai
(B) a hominid remain
(C) a hand axe
(D) a site

42. The age of the Olorgesaillie culture was determined from the
(A) hand axes
(B) volcanic ash
(C) hominid activity
(D) river basin

GO ON TO THE NEXT PAGE

Questions 43–48

Walt Whitman, born in New York in 1819, was one of America's unusual literary figures. An individualist, he rambled through the countryside seeing people and places, and making them his own. His experiences in earning a living were varied: at times he was a printer, a teacher, a carpenter, a nurse, and a newspaper editor. He was a big-hearted man, open and accepting. He gave freely of his time by caring for the wounded during the Civil War. Though he lived in the city, he often spent time in the country, developing his strong sense of nature, which carried through to his poems. In 1855 he collected the verses he had written, and published them in one thin volume, *Leaves of Grass*, a book which he revised and rewrote all the rest of his life. The book was ridiculed by some poets and generally ignored by others, probably because his verse forms were not traditional. He had felt that it was necessary to achieve a new poetic form in order to communicate his views. His reputation didn't grow until after his death, and it reached a high point in the 1920s. Since then, Whitman's style has greatly influenced modern poets.

43. The best title for this passage is
(A) *Leaves of Grass*
(B) Walt Whitman
(C) A Country Man
(D) Poetry: A New Form

44. The word "rambled" in line 2 is most similar to the meaning of
(A) stopped briefly
(B) marched excitedly
(C) traveled quickly
(D) walked slowly

45. In the phrase "making them his own" in line 3, he is
(A) owning them
(B) changing them
(C) understanding them
(D) working for them

46. Whitman's big-heartedness is shown by his
(A) visiting the countryside
(B) being an individualist
(C) caring for the wounded
(D) rewriting *Leaves of Grass*

47. The passage says that during Whitman's lifetime, other poets
(A) laughed at him
(B) communicated with him
(C) praised him
(D) accepted him

48. We can assume that Whitman was ignored because he
(A) rewrote his book
(B) rambled through the countryside
(C) published his poems
(D) wrote in a new form

GO ON TO THE NEXT PAGE

Questions 49–54

Reliable knowledge of early civilizations of the Americas is limited to archeological records, since so much of the original culture was destroyed by early conquerors. Nevertheless, evidence of impressive achievements in monumental architecture as well as in the art of healing, astronomy, mathematics, and engineering has been uncovered that commands respect as well as regret for the loss of this knowledge. In the field of agriculture, these civilizations left a heritage that has greatly enriched the food of today's planet. White potatoes, corn, beans, tomatoes, squash, chocolate, tapioca, vanilla, and turkey are just some of the foods that were originally developed by Indian civilizations. Lost, however, are the secrets of the Mayan astronomers and the Inca builders as well as many medicinal practices. Perhaps the greatest casualty, however, has been the Indian attitude toward life and the universe. Indians in these civilizations seldom warred with nature; instead, they adapted to it. Our present concern with ecology causes us to respect the people of these civilizations even more for this attitude.

49. The author's main point is that
(A) we have lost respect for the Indian attitude toward life and nature
(B) we have discovered new information about the early Indian civilizations
(C) archeology has given us reliable records of the great achievements of early American civilizations
(D) it is unfortunate that we have lost so much of the early American culture and knowledge

50. Which of the following has probably benefited the most from the discoveries of the early American civilizations?
(A) Research in astronomy
(B) Agriculture
(C) The building industry
(D) Environmental groups

51. Which of the following can NOT be traced back to these Indian civilizations?
(A) Tapioca pudding
(B) A vanilla bean
(C) A chocolate bar
(D) A strawberry

52. According to the author, the biggest loss has been
(A) an attitude toward nature
(B) knowledge of early astronomy
(C) techniques of early building
(D) early agricultural practices

53. Which can you infer that the people of these civilizations would be least likely to do?
(A) Build a monument
(B) Cook a turkey
(C) Cut down trees
(D) Use medicine

54. From the passage, you can infer that
(A) astronomers kept their art a secret
(B) builders built great structures
(C) conquerors kept early records
(D) doctors had little knowledge of medicine

GO ON TO THE NEXT PAGE

Questions 55–60

Another sign stimulus, of course, is sound. A male bird's song attracts females and repels competitors. Thus, it acts as a signal to birds of the same species. Male grasshoppers also attract females with a song. The *Ephippizzer bitterensis*, a grasshopper found along the Mediterranean coast of France, uses an organ borne on its back to produce a strident sound. Modified wing-like structures are scraped against each other to produce the sound, which is then amplified by a small shell. When females hear this sound, they scramble toward it, climbing over any obstacles that are in their way, and speeding up as they come close to their mates. Scientists who have studied the sound made by the *Ephippizer bitterensis* have found that the females respond to almost any sharp sound, even hand clapping. Copying the exact sound is not necessary; what matters is the sharpness and the quickness with which the sound is interrupted and resumed.

55. The author's main point is to
- **(A)** discuss ways in which males are attracted to females
- **(B)** compare *Ephippizer bitterensis'* sounds to bird songs
- **(C)** describe the sound produced
- **(D)** introduce sound as a sign stimulus

56. The author mentions bird songs in the beginning in order to
- **(A)** provide an illustration
- **(B)** point out a difference
- **(C)** argue a point
- **(D)** compare two animals

57. The previous paragraphs most likely discussed
- **(A)** how bird songs attract mates
- **(B)** how other grasshoppers produce sound
- **(C)** how competitors are repelled
- **(D)** how color and smell are attractions

58. The male *Ephippizer bitterensis* produces sound from a device on its
- **(A)** legs
- **(B)** back
- **(C)** head
- **(D)** wings

59. According to the passage, a female grasshopper
- **(A)** has a difficult time going over obstacles
- **(B)** flies to its mate
- **(C)** has tiny wings
- **(D)** goes faster when it gets close to the sound

60. It can be inferred that a female grasshopper might be most attracted to
- **(A)** a man crying
- **(B)** a cow mooing
- **(C)** a dog barking
- **(D)** a bee humming

THIS IS THE END OF SECTION 3. IF YOU FINISH BEFORE YOUR TIME IS UP, CHECK YOUR WORK ON SECTION 3 ONLY. DO NOT READ OR WORK ON ANY OTHER SECTION OF THE TEST. **STOP**

Answer Key for Practice Test I

SECTION 1: LISTENING COMPREHENSION

Part A

1. C	**6.** A	**11.** A	**16.** C
2. C	**7.** D	**12.** D	**17.** C
3. A	**8.** A	**13.** D	**18.** B
4. C	**9.** D	**14.** B	**19.** A
5. B	**10.** C	**15.** A	**20.** D

Part B

21. A	**26.** B	**31.** D
22. B	**27.** C	**32.** C
23. A	**28.** A	**33.** B
24. C	**29.** A	**34.** D
25. D	**30.** A	**35.** B

Part C

36. B	**41.** B	**46.** B
37. C	**42.** D	**47.** A
38. A	**43.** B	**48.** A
39. D	**44.** A	**49.** C
40. A	**45.** A	**50.** B

SECTION 2: STRUCTURE AND WRITTEN EXPRESSION

1. A	**11.** C	**21.** B	**31.** B
2. B	**12.** A	**22.** C	**32.** C
3. C	**13.** B	**23.** A	**33.** A
4. C	**14.** A	**24.** B	**34.** D
5. D	**15.** B	**25.** A	**35.** A
6. A	**16.** A	**26.** D	**36.** B
7. B	**17.** C	**27.** A	**37.** B
8. B	**18.** A	**28.** C	**38.** B
9. C	**19.** B	**29.** B	**39.** B
10. A	**20.** A	**30.** B	**40.** D

SECTION 3: VOCABULARY AND READING COMPREHENSION

1. A
2. B
3. A
4. D
5. C
6. D
7. B
8. B
9. C
10. D
11. B
12. B
13. B
14. B
15. A
16. C
17. A
18. D
19. C
20. C
21. B
22. C
23. D
24. D
25. B
26. B
27. C
28. B
29. A
30. A
31. B
32. A
33. B
34. D
35. A
36. B
37. A
38. D
39. B
40. B
41. D
42. B
43. B
44. D
45. C
46. C
47. A
48. D
49. D
50. B
51. D
52. A
53. C
54. B
55. D
56. A
57. D
58. B
59. D
60. C

Score Analysis Form for Practice Test I

Directions: Count the number of answers you have correct in Practice Test I, using the answer key on pages 381–382. Then use the example form on page 48 and the chart (Standard Form) on page 49 to figure out your converted score range. Fill in the rest of this form to help you plan your study time.

	RAW SCORE	CONVERTED SCORE RANGE (each)	APPROXIMATE SCORE RANGE (each)
Listening Comprehension	____	____–____ × 10 = ____–____	÷ 3 = ____–____
Structures and Written Expression	____	____–____ × 10 = ____–____	÷ 3 = ____–____
Vocabulary and Reading Comprehension	____	____–____ × 10 = ____–____	÷ 3 = ____–____
TOTAL APPROXIMATE SCORE (add 3 approximate scores)			____–____

What is your best section out of the above three? ____________

ANALYSIS OF EACH SECTION

1. Listening Comprehension

	Number Correct	Total	Percent Correct
Part A (Questions 1–20)	______	÷ 20	= ______%
Part B (Questions 21–35)	______	÷ 15	= ______%
Part C (Questions 36–50)	______	÷ 15	= ______%

Which part has the highest percentage of correct answers? ________

2. *Structure and Written Expression*

	Number Correct	Total	Percent Correct
Sentence Completion (Questions 1–15)	_______	÷ 15	= _______%
Error Correction (Questions 16–40)	_______	÷ 25	= _______%

Which section has the highest percentage of correct answers? ________

3. *Vocabulary and Reading Comprehension*

	Number Correct	Total	Percent Correct
Vocabulary (Questions 1–30)	_______	÷ 30	= _______%
Reading (Questions 31–60)	_______	÷ 30	= _______%

Which part has the highest percentage of correct answers? __________

Now that you have taken Practice Test I, the Diagnostic Test, fill out the Self-Evaluation Checklist on page 53.

Explanatory Answers

SECTION 1: LISTENING COMPREHENSION

These explanations begin with the sentence, "Glance at the choices and summarize." This means that you should have followed the pattern as discussed in Lesson 13. For maximum results you should have quickly read the four choices before you heard the taped sentence. Next, you should have tried to get a general sense of what the sentence might have been. At a lower English level, you could probably see some similar words that helped you prepare for the taped sentence. At a higher English level, you might have been able to guess a topic from the answer choices. You will see both repeated words and general topics in the explanatory answers below. They are given as examples of one way to summarize. You may see other words that help you guess the topic. Practice guessing the topic as much as you can. The more you practice, the better you will become.

The Listening Comprehension Tapescript for this test is on pages 633 to 637.

Part A

1. Is the airport located around here?
(A) Is there a circular drive around the airport?
(B) How big is the airport?
(C) Is the airport close?
(D) Is this an international airport?

(C) Glance at the choices and summarize: question, airport. Testing point: restatement. "Is . . . located around here?" means the same as "Is . . . close?"

2. Send me the information as soon as possible.
(A) The information won't come today.
(B) Bring me the information tomorrow.
(C) Mail it to me at your earliest convenience.
(D) Your speech is very informative.

(C) Glance at the choices and summarize: information, today, tomorrow. Testing point 1: restatement. "Send me" means "mail it to me." Testing point 2: vocabulary. "As soon as possible" means "at your earliest convenience."

3. Jane followed in her mother's footsteps by teaching disabled children.
(A) Jane is a teacher.
(B) Jane's mother doesn't want to teach.
(C) Jane takes care of her children herself.
(D) Jane's stepmother doesn't like her.

(A) Glance at the choices and summarize: Jane, teacher. Testing point: inference. "Jane followed ... footsteps by teaching..." implies "Jane is a teacher."

4. The kids can go to school by foot.
(A) The mother teaches the children at home.
(B) The children didn't go to school today.
(C) The school is nearby.
(D) Children should wear shoes.

(C) Glance at the choices and summarize: children, school. Testing point: inference. "... can go to school by foot" implies "The school is nearby."

5. Sam looks cool and confident.
(A) Sam shouldn't be cruel.
(B) Sam is calm.
(C) Sam is cooling himself down.
(D) Please make yourself comfortable.

(B) Glance at the choices and summarize: Sam, cruel, calm. Testing point: inference. "Sam looks cool and confident" implies "Sam is calm." You may notice the words that sound similar: cruel, cool.

6. It was a winding and muddy road.
(A) The road was not straight.
(B) It was windy.
(C) The road was just completed.
(D) The road was wide.

(A) Glance at the choices and summarize: road, straight, windy. Testing point: restatement (opposite). "It was a winding ... road" means "The road was not straight." Testing point 2: vocabulary. "Winding" means "curving" or "not straight."

7. Alan never neglects to rehearse before his performance.
(A) Alan's rehearsal was canceled.
(B) Alan went to the rehearsal meeting.
(C) Alan slept through the performance.
(D) Alan always rehearses before a show.

(D) Glance at the choices and summarize: Alan, rehearsal. Testing point 1: vocabulary. "... never neglects rehearsing ..." means "... always rehearses ..." Testing point 2: vocabulary. A "performance" can be a "show."

8. Diane's allergy has gone from bad to worse.
(A) Diane is not getting better.
(B) It's bad enough to have a headache.
(C) Diane is completely satisfied.
(D) Bad weather doesn't affect Diane.

(A) Glance at the choices and summarize: Diane, feeling. Testing point: idiom. "... has gone from bad to worse" means "... is not getting better."

9. It's going to be all right.
(A) All right, let's do it again.
(B) Turn to the right or left?
(C) You can't do it all correctly.
(D) Don't worry, everything will be OK.

(D) Glance at the choices and summarize: right, left, wrong. Testing point: restatement. "It's going to be all right" means "Everything will be OK."

10. Did you two give up the class?
(A) Did you like the class, too?
(B) Nobody can drop the class after today.
(C) Did both of you stop going to class?
(D) We, too, want to join the class.

(C) Glance at the choices and summarize: too, two, to, class. Testing point 1: idiom. "Give up" means "stop doing something." Testing point 2: restatement. "You two" means "both of you."

11. I'm sorry; I thought you were a friend of mine.
(A) I mistook you for my friend.
(B) Excuse me, my friend.
(C) I feel sorry that you are not my friend.
(D) I don't think you are my friend.

(A) Glance at the choices and summarize: I, friend, sorry. Testing point: restatement. "I thought you were a friend of mine" means you are not the person I thought you were. "I mistook you for my friend."

12. He acts like an adult, but he is only a junior high school student.
(A) He doubts that he will become a junior high school student.
(B) Adults like him because he is active.
(C) He behaves like a junior high school student.
(D) Even though he is still in junior high school, he acts grown up.

(D) Glance at the choices and summarize: He, student. Testing point 1: restatement. The words "but" and "even though" are both connectors. Testing point 2: vocabulary. "Adult" means "grown up."

13. Dr. Stevenson will probably be elected as the department chair this year, won't she?
(A) Dr. Stevenson earns a good salary as a department chair.
(B) Dr. Stevenson is fortunate this year, isn't she?
(C) Dr. Stevenson doesn't want to be involved in administration, does she?
(D) Do you think Dr. Stevenson will become the department chair this year?

(D) Glance at the choices and summarize: Dr. Stevenson, department chair. Testing point: restatement. "Dr. Stevenson will ... be elected as ..., won't she?" is a tag question, which means "Do you think she will become the department chair?"

14. Are you sure you have a reservation for dinner?
(A) Have you been to this restaurant before?
(B) Are you certain you made a reservation?
(C) I am not sure you want to stay here.
(D) When did you make your reservation?

(B) Glance at the choices and summarize: restaurant, reservation. Testing point: restatement. "Are you sure ...?" means "Are you certain?"

15. Sam ordered cheese cake for dessert this time, although he likes apple pie better.
(A) Sam prefers apple pie to cheese cake.
(B) Sam ordered cheese cake for his friend.
(C) Apple pie is better for Sam than cheesecake.
(D) Sam ordered the one he likes the best.

(A) Glance at the choices and summarize: Sam, likes, cake. Testing point: restatement. "... he likes apple pie better" means the same as "... prefers apple pie."

16. Often we learn more from failure than from success.
- **(A)** Success helps us learn.
- **(B)** We can hardly learn anything from a bad experience.
- **(C)** Failure usually gives us a good lesson.
- **(D)** Success is the ultimate goal of learning.

(C) Glance at the choices and summarize: success, learn. Testing point 1: restatement. "Learn more from failure ..." means "failure gives us a good lesson." Testing point 2: vocabulary. "Often" means "usually."

17. If he were not a dreamer, he wouldn't have gone this far.
- **(A)** He usually dreamt that he ran very fast.
- **(B)** He thinks that he can get along well.
- **(C)** His ideas have helped him get ahead.
- **(D)** His dreams are unrealistic.

(C) Glance at the choices and summarize: He, dream. Testing point 1: conditional, inference. "If he were not a dreamer, he wouldn't have gone this far" implies that he has gone this far because he is a dreamer. Testing point 2: inference. "Dreamer" implies "a person with ideas." "Have gone this far" implies "has gotten ahead" or "has had success."

18. Simon shouldn't expect to know everything on the test.
- **(A)** Simon should have studied every word that was on the test.
- **(B)** The test will probably ask some questions that are difficult for Simon.
- **(C)** Simon shouldn't take the test because he didn't study enough.
- **(D)** The test will seem easy if Simon studies more.

(B) Glance at the choices and summarize: Simon, test, study. Testing point: inference."Simon shouldn't expect to know everything on the test" implies "The test will ask some questions that are difficult for Simon."

19. You know I don't like chocolate.
- **(A)** Why did you give me chocolate?
- **(B)** I wish I had chocolate.
- **(C)** You don't know what I like.
- **(D)** Why don't you like chocolate?

(A) Glance at the choices and summarize: question or negative, chocolate. Testing point: inference. "You know I don't like chocolate" implies "Why did you give me chocolate?"

20. She recovered faster than the doctor predicted.
- **(A)** She will recover very fast.
- **(B)** The doctor believed she would recover quickly.
- **(C)** She didn't believe she would recover so fast.
- **(D)** She improved more than her doctor expected.

(D) Glance at the choices and summarize: She, recover, fast. Testing point: restatement. "Recovered faster" means "improved more." Testing point 2: vocabulary. "Predicted" means "expected."

Part B

21. Woman: Thanks for the help.
Man: No problem.
What does the man mean?
(A) He doesn't mind helping her.
(B) He has some problems.
(C) He is very busy.
(D) He had to help her.

(A) Glance at the choices and summarize: he does what? Testing point: idiom/inference. The phrase "no problem" means that he has no difficulty with helping the woman.

22. Woman: I can't get through to this number.
Man: You must first dial one.
What do we learn from this conversation?
(A) They are discussing a math contest.
(B) The woman is making a telephone call.
(C) A department store is having a sale.
(D) The post office is closed.

(B) Glance at the choices and summarize: What is happening? Testing point: cultural knowledge/vocabulary. "Get through to this number" and "dial one" are phrases used when making a telephone call. The words "dial one" mean that you must dial number "1" before you dial other numbers. "Get through to" means "make a connection."

23. Woman: Did you mow the lawn?
Man: I had the neighbor boy take care of it.
What does the man mean?
(A) He asked someone else to mow the lawn.
(B) Nobody mowed the lawn.
(C) He will wait until next week.
(D) He had a problem with his lungs.

(A) Glance at the choices and summarize: he, lawn, mow. Testing point 1: idiom. "Take care of something" means "to do something"; "I had somebody take care of it" means that he asked somebody to do the job for him. Testing point 2: vocabulary. "To mow" means "to cut." "A lawn" is an area of grass in a garden, park, or yard.

24. Woman: Are there any dogs around?
Man: No, they're not allowed in this complex.
What do we learn from the conversation?
(A) The law is too complicated to understand.
(B) It's good to have a dog around the house.
(C) No dogs are allowed in the area.
(D) Unfortunately, they don't have any dogs.

(C) Glance at the choices and summarize: dogs, law. Testing point: inference. In the sentence "They are not allowed in this complex," "they" refers to "dogs"; "Dogs are not allowed in this complex" means "No dogs are allowed in this area."

25. Man: This one is much cheaper.
Woman: But it may not last as long.
What does the woman imply?
(A) This is the last one.
(B) The longer style is better.
(C) You should buy cheaper merchandise.
(D) It might not be of good quality.

(D) Glance at the choices and summarize: better, cheaper, merchandise. Testing point 1: inference. "May not last long" implies that it is not made well; the quality is poor. Testing point 2: vocabulary. "To last" means "to remain in good condition."

26. Man: Did you ever get in touch with your friend?
Woman: No, when I called, all I got was a recorded message.
What did the woman do?
(A) She fixed her friend's tape recorder.
(B) She tried to telephone her friend.
(C) She went to her friend's house.
(D) She arranged to meet her friend later.

(B) Glance at the choices and summarize: she, friend. Testing point 1: idiom. "Get in touch with somebody" means to contact somebody. Testing point 2: inference. "Did you ever get in touch with your friend?" implies that you were trying to talk to your friend. "When I called" implies the use of the telephone.

27. Man: Are you sure?
Woman: Of course I am.
What does the woman mean?
(A) She is happy.
(B) She is joking.
(C) She is certain.
(D) She is busy.

(C) Glance at the choices and summarize: She, is what? Testing point: inference. "Are you sure?" is another way of saying "Are you certain that your information is correct?"

28. Woman: Could you OK this request for me?
Man: Sure, may I use your pen?
What does the man need to do?
(A) Give his approval.
(B) Buy a pen.
(C) Write an essay.
(D) Go back to work.

(A) Glance at the choices and summarize: do something. Testing point: idiom. "To OK something" means "to give approval."

29. Woman: Is it possible to see the apartment before we rent it?
Man: You bet, it's vacant.
What does the man mean?
(A) No one lives there now.
(B) You'd better make an appointment.
(C) You can see it after your vacation.
(D) It's a beautiful place.

(A) Glance at the choices and summarize: live, appointment, place. Testing point: vocabulary. "Vacant" means "no one lives there." The phrase "you bet" means the same as "sure" or "OK" or "of course."

30. Man: You left your lights on!
Woman: Oh, thanks a lot.
What do we learn from the conversation?
(A) The woman forgot that her lights were on.
(B) The woman needed more light.
(C) The man helped the woman carry a heavy load.
(D) The man picked up the woman's glasses.

(A) Glance at the choices and summarize: left, lights on. Testing point: inference. "You left your lights on!" implies "you forgot to turn off your lights." Because of the word "your," the implication is that they are referring to lights in the woman's car.

31. Woman: Tim missed the deadline for the assignment again.
Man: He's got to adjust his study habits in order to survive at the university.
What do we learn about Tim?
(A) Tim has good study habits.
(B) Tim writes many papers.
(C) Tim lives in a dormitory.
(D) Tim's papers are often late.

(D) Glance at the choices and summarize: Tim, papers. Testing point: vocabulary. "Miss the deadline" means "be late." "An assignment" can be a "paper" required by a class.

32. Man: Is there anyone available to help make a copy of my VCR tape?
Woman: No, not until tomorrow. But you can do it yourself by following the instructions on the machine.
What does the woman mean?
(A) He cannot make a copy because of the copyright.
(B) He should wait until tomorrow.
(C) He can make his own copy.
(D) He cannot make a copy now.

(C) Glance at the choices and summarize: he, copy, wait. Testing point: restatement. In the phrase "you can do *it* yourself," "it" refers to "make a copy of the VCR tape."

33. Woman: How do you like your new computer?
Man: I've just put it together, but I really haven't tried to use it yet.
What does the man mean?
(A) He is tired of using his new computer.
(B) He has just assembled the computer.
(C) He has used his new computer for writing his dissertation.
(D) He has found something wrong with the new computer.

(B) Glance at the choices and summarize: he, computer. Testing point 1: idiom. "Put it together" means "assemble." Testing point 2: restatement. In the phrase "put *it* together," "it" refers to "computer."

34. Woman: The bookstore has runout of the textbook assigned by Dr. Martin.
Man: He didn't expect so many students to take his class this semester.
What do we learn about this situation?
(A) Dr. Martin didn't want so many students in his class.
(B) The students were supposed to buy the textbook earlier.
(C) The bookstore is going out of business.
(D) Dr. Martin didn't order enough textbooks for his students.

(D) Glance at the choices and summarize: Dr. Martin, student, textbook. Testing point 1: idiom. "Run out of the textbook" means that the textbooks are all sold out; there are no more left. Testing point 2: inference. Dr. Martin (the professor) didn't expect so many students, so he didn't ask the bookstore to order enough books.

35. Woman: It takes too much time to cook; I wish I had more time to study.
Man: Why don't you eat at the university cafeteria? It's not too expensive.
What does the man suggest?
(A) Buying less expensive food.
(B) Dining at the cafeteria.
(C) Cooking more simply.
(D) Studying harder.

(B) Glance at the choices and summarize: food, comparative. Testing point: question. *"Why don't you* eat . . . cafeteria?" means "I suggest you eat at the cafeteria."

Part C

See Listening Comprehension Tapescript on page 635 for a written version of the talks for this test.

36. Who is the speaker of this talk?
(A) Professor Smith
(B) A teaching assistant
(C) A specialist in chemistry
(D) A university technician

(B) This is a restatement question. The speaker says, "I'm your teaching assistant."

37. How often does this class meet?
(A) Every day of the week
(B) One day a week
(C) Two days a week
(D) Once every two weeks

(C) This is a restatement question. The speaker says, "It's a required meeting, twice a week."

38. What is the main purpose of the speaker's talk?
(A) To teach important safety rules
(B) To explain the grading procedures
(C) To demonstrate an experiment
(D) To tell students what safety equipment to buy

(A) This is a restatement question. The speaker says, "But the most important information I want to give you today is about the safety procedures." He also mentions two safety procedures about wearing clothes and cleaning up.

39. Which of the following can be worn in the lab?
(A) Loose scarves
(B) Sandals
(C) Long necklaces
(D) Eyeglasses

(D) This question can be answered by elimination. The speaker mentions that students cannot wear loose scarves, sandals, or long necklaces. He does not mention eyeglasses. Even if you didn't remember these items, you might guess the answer to this question.

40. What must the students do before the next class?
(A) Buy a notebook
(B) Wash their lab equipment
(C) Do an experiment
(D) Put waste in the proper container

(A) This is a restatement question. The speaker ends his talk by telling the students to be sure to get a lab notebook.

41. What is the main topic of this conversation?
(A) The plays of Shakespeare
(B) The writer of Shakespeare plays
(C) The birthplace of Shakespeare
(D) The Earl of Oxford

(B) This question is best answered by elimination. Answer (A) is too general. The discussion is not about all the plays of Shakespeare. Answer (C) is too narrow. The birthplace is only mentioned once; it is not a main topic. Answer (D) is possible, but it is also not the major topic. The most important topic of this conversation is that there is some doubt who actually wrote Shakespeare plays.

42. What led to this conversation?
(A) A visit to England
(B) An English literature test
(C) A discussion with a professor
(D) A discussion of a play

(D) This is an inference question. The conversation begins with the two people discussing a play.

43. According to the conversation, who might have written the Shakespeare plays?
(A) A professor
(B) The Earl of Oxford
(C) A tourist
(D) An illiterate man

(B) This is a restatement question. The man says that his teacher mentions the Earl of Oxford as one likely candidate for being the writer of Shakespeare's plays. The male speaker also mentions that the man called Shakespeare might have been illiterate, but if that is true, then he isn't the writer of the Shakespeare plays.

44. According to the conversation, what do tourists do?
(A) Visit Shakespeare's house
(B) Visit Oxford
(C) Learn about the Earl of Oxford
(D) See Shakespeare's plays

(A) This is a restatement question. The man says that tourists go to the house in Stratford.

45. What is the woman interested in doing now?
(A) Reading about the Earl of Oxford
(B) Seeing a Shakespeare play
(C) Taking a class in Shakespeare
(D) Reading more plays

(A) This is a restatement question. The woman ends the conversation by saying that she will go read more about the Earl of Oxford.

46. What is the major topic of this lecture?
(A) Predators in the animal world
(B) Divisions of the food chain
(C) The loss of potential energy in predators
(D) A parasitic chain

(B) In the beginning of the talk, the speaker says that she will introduce the food chain. The other topics are not major topics; they are examples of one aspect of the food chain.

47. Which of the following is an example of a predator chain?
(A) A bird eating a fish
(B) A rabbit eating grass
(C) A tapeworm living in an animal
(D) A plant using energy from the sun

(A) This is an inference question. The speaker says that a predator chain is when a larger animal feeds on a smaller animal. Answer (A) is the only answer that fits this category.

48. How much of the potential energy from the sun can a plant use?
(A) 2–3 percent
(B) 10 percent
(C) 12–15 percent
(D) More than 15 percent

(A) This is a restatement question. The speaker says that a plant can use only about 2 or 3 percent of the energy that falls on it.

49. What happens at each step of the food chain?
(A) A plant uses energy.
(B) Animals kill other animals.
(C) Potential energy is lost.
(D) A microorganism feeds off dead matter.

(C) This is a restatement question. The speaker says that in each type of chain, potential energy is lost at each level. The other answers do not apply to all types of food chains.

50. What is eaten in a saprophytic chain?
(A) A green plant
(B) Dead matter
(C) A smaller animal
(D) A rabbit

(B) This is a restatement question. The speaker states that in a saprophytic chain a microorganism feeds off dead matter.

SECTION 2: STRUCTURE AND WRITTEN EXPRESSION

1. It's not easy for a casual observer to distinguish ________ genuine paintings and copies.

(A) between
(B) therefore
(C) for
(D) to

(A) Testing point: preposition. "Between" (or "among") must follow the verb "distinguish."

2. ________, all matter is formed of molecules.

(A) It doesn't matter if the complex
(B) No matter how complex
(C) How complex is not a matter
(D) It's not a complex matter

(B) Testing point: word order. The complete sentence should read, "No matter how complex it is . . ." The words "it is" have been omitted in (B), but grammatically, the sentence is still correct. One of the difficulties with this sentence is the word "matter." The word "matter" has two different meanings. The first definition is a part of a phrase meaning "It doesn't matter" or "It's not important." The second definition of "matter" is "the substance of a physical thing."

3. After World War I automobiles, buses, and trucks became the most common ________.

(A) of transportation
(B) transport form
(C) forms of transportation
(D) transportation of form

(C) Testing point: noun + prepositional phrase. The noun "forms" needs to be plural and in the correct order: "common forms of transportation."

4. Tears ________ anger and tension naturally.

(A) are relieved
(B) relieving
(C) relieve
(D) what they relieve

(C) Testing point: verb. The sentence needs a present tense verb to agree with a plural noun.

5. In a single day ________ are as many as thousands of people involved in business deals in one area.

(A) yet
(B) they
(C) ever
(D) there

(D) Testing point: Expletive "there." The words "there are" refer to the existence of "thousands of people."

6. Paper ________ from cellulose fibers.

(A) is produced
(B) producing
(C) produced
(D) which is produced

(A) Testing point: passive voice. The sentence should be "Paper is produced from . . ." In the active voice it would be, "People produce paper from . . ."

7. ________ an insurance agent it is necessary to pass the state examination.

(A) Become
(B) To become
(C) Having become
(D) One becomes

(B) Testing point: infinitive phrase. An infinitive is commonly used to express purpose. In this sentence the examination is necessary for the purpose of becoming an insurance agent.

8. There are ________ art galleries in the city of Carmel.

(A) a great deal
(B) many
(C) much
(D) lots

(B) Testing point: many/much. The word "galleries" is plural, and the word "many" is used before a plural noun.

9. One difficulty ________ at night is limited vision.

(A) to drive
(B) will drive
(C) with driving
(D) be driven

(C) Testing point: prepositional phrase. The sentence needs a prepositional phrase to modify the noun "difficulty."

10. ________ the Pulitzer Prize in 1924.

(A) Edna Ferber won
(B) When Edna Ferber won
(C) With Edna Ferber's winning
(D) Edna Ferber's winning

(A) Testing point: subject + verb. The sentence needs a subject and a past tense verb.

11. All ________ of the world carry on breeding experiments to increase yield or to improve disease resistance.

(A) countries that grow wheat
(B) growth of wheat countries
(C) wheat-producing countries
(D) countries where wheat is grown

(C) Testing point: noun. "All ________ of the world" indicates the sentence needs a noun or a noun phrase, not a clause.

12. Throughout the United States ________ fast food restaurants where hamburgers are served.

(A) there are
(B) there is
(C) located
(D) are there

(A) Testing point: expletive "there." The sentence should read, ". . . there are . . . restaurants where . . . are served." The verb must be plural because of "restaurants."

13. The human body contains water ________, bones, and muscles.

(A) is blood
(B) in its blood
(C) is in its blood
(D) it is in its blood

(B) Testing point: prepositional phrase. The sentence needs a prepositional phrase to describe where the water is. The commas indicate that the nouns are part of a series that must be written in parallel construction. Answers (A) and (C) are incorrect because they add another verb. Answer (D) is incorrect because it adds another complete sentence.

14. ________ covered by the sea which occupies 71 percent of the earth.

(A) A huge unknown world is
(B) An huge unknown world
(C) How huge the unknown world
(D) So huge is the unknown world

(A) Testing point: subject + passive voice verb. The sentence needs a subject and a passive voice in the present tense. The verb is "is covered."

15. In his painting "The Three Musicians" Picasso reached a climax in his use ________ geometric forms.

(A) to
(B) of
(C) on
(D) with

(B) Testing point: preposition. The preposition "of" follows the noun "use." The prepositional phrase "of geometric forms" describes the type of use.

16. Not only cigarettes <u>and too</u> (A) alcohol is <u>believed</u> (B) <u>to be</u> (C) harmful to <u>one's</u> (D) health.

(A) Testing point: conjunction. "Not only . . ., but also . . ."; Note: "not only" is a clue.

17. <u>Approximately</u> (A) 80 percent <u>of</u> (B) farm income in Utah <u>it is derived</u> (C) from livestock and <u>livestock products</u> (D).

(C) Testing point: additional word. "It" is an unnecessary extra subject.

18. The pleura that <u>cover</u> (A) the <u>exterior</u> (B) of the <u>lungs</u> (C) and the inner walls of the chest cavity <u>is</u> (D) a thin elastic membrane.

(A) Testing point: verb agreement. "The pleura" is a singular noun, so "cover" should be "covers."

19. <u>Jays</u> (A) are <u>more shorter</u> (B) and more <u>colorful</u> (C) <u>than</u> (D) crows.

(B) Testing point: comparative. "More shorter" is not correct; it should be "shorter."

20. The first <u>steps</u> (A) of scientific <u>research</u> (B) is <u>to decide</u> (C) how to <u>gather data</u> (D).

(A) Testing point: singular/plural noun. "Steps" should be changed to "step," because the verb is singular.

21. Caffeine in coffee is relative harmless if
A B

people drink it moderately.
C D

(B) Testing point: word form. The adverb form is used to modify the adjective "harmless." "Relative" is an adjective; therefore, it should be changed to "relatively."

22. Vibrating or shaking rapidly often cause noise.
A B C D

(C) Testing point: verb agreement. "Vibrating *or* shaking" is singular. The verb "cause" should be changed to "causes."

23. Soybeans can provides vegetarians with a nu-
A B C

tritionally balanced diet for a low price.
D

(A) Testing point: verb tense. After "can" the verb should be "provide."

24. The flotation process devised to separate
A B

minerals from other chemical compounds.
C D

(B) Testing point: passive voice. "Devised" should be changed to "was devised."

25. Of searching for underground deposits of oil,
A B

geologists often rely on magnetometers.
C D

(A) Testing point: preposition. "Of searching" is not correct. The correct answer is "In searching," "While searching," or "During their search."

26. New York City, which is one of the largest cit-
A B

ies in the world, is larger than any other cities
C D

in the United States.

(D) Testing point: singular/plural noun. After "than any other," a singular noun should be used. "Cities" should be changed to "city."

27. Radiation usual travels from a source in
A

straight lines, but charged particles travel in
B C

curved paths within magnetic fields.
D

(A) Testing point: word form. An adverb is used to modify a verb. "Usual" should be changed to "usually."

28. One of the reasons that English-dubbed for-
A

eign movies often seem silly are that the ges-
B C

tures don't match the speech.
D

(C) Testing point: verb agreement. The subject is "one," not "reasons." Since it is a singular form, "are" should be "is."

29. Many young people lack the skills, good edu-
A

cation, and financial to settle in the urban ar-
B C

eas where most jobs are found.
D

(B) Testing point: parallel construction. "Skills" and "education" are nouns, but "financial" is an adjective. A noun should be used: "finances."

30. In geology, Earth's continents are classify by
A B

rock density and composition.
C D

(B) Testing point: word form. The verb is in the passive voice. The correct answer is "classified by."

31. People often seem anger when they don't get
A B C

enough rest.
D

(B) Testing point: word form. After "seem" an adjective should be used. "Anger" should be changed to "angry."

32. Many modern families are finding ways to share household chores, works, and care of children.
A: are finding — B: to share — C: works — D: care of

(C) Testing point: parallel construction. The word "works" refers to products of the intellect or imagination, as in "works of art." It should be changed to "work," which is a mass noun (uncountable), meaning "employment."

33. Serotonin is produced in particular high concentrations in the hypothalamus, which joins the brain to the top of the spinal cord.
A: particular — B: concentrations — C: which joins — D: to

(A) Testing point: word form. An adverb is used to modify the adjective, "high." "Particular" should be changed to "particularly."

34. Benjamin Banneker helped to produce the original architectural design that successfully was use to build the city of Washington D.C.
A: helped — B: architectural — C: that — D: use to

(D) Testing point: passive voice. The word "use" should be changed to "used."

35. The ancestors of some French Americans original came to the United States because of the French Revolution, which broke out in 1789.
A: original — B: because of — C: which — D: broke out

(A) Testing point: word form. An adverb is used to modify the verb, "came." "Original" is an adjective; it should be changed to "originally."

36. SPSSx is a computer program designed specific for statistical analysis with a large amount of datum.
A: designed — B: specific — C: with — D: amount of

(B) Testing point: word form. "Specific" is an adjective. The sentence should have the adverb "specifically," which modifies "designed."

37. Located on the frontally surface of the skull, the human eye is a spheroid organ in a bony cavity.
A: Located — B: frontally — C: spheroid — D: bony

(B) Testing point: word form. An adjective is needed to modify the noun "surface." The correct word is "frontal," meaning "on the front."

38. Nicotine consumption is no diminished by pipe smoking; a causal relationship exists between all forms of smoking and cancer.
A: Nicotine — B: no — C: pipe smoking — D: exists

(B) Testing point: No/not/none. Use "no" before a noun; use "not" to form a negative; use "none" as a negative noun. Here, the correct word is "not."

39. Time is of few account in relation to great thoughts that are as vivid today as when they first passed through their authors' minds, ages ago.
A: of — B: few — C: as vivid today — D: ages ago

(B) Testing point: wrong word. Use "few" with a countable noun; use "little" with an uncountable noun. Here the correct word is "little."

40. The advances in information technology are rapidly changing the nature at libraries.
A: The advances — B: in — C: the nature — D: at

(D) Testing point: preposition. "At libraries" should be changed to "of libraries." The phrase "the nature of ..." means "the quality or characteristics" that are a natural part of something.

SECTION 3: VOCABULARY AND READING COMPREHENSION

1. Gradually, air conditioning and air travel have changed vacation habits.

(A) Little by little
(B) Recently
(C) Suddenly
(D) All at once

(A) The word "gradually" refers to something happening slowly over a long period of time.

2. In ballet, Degas discovered the subject that was ideal for his talents.

(A) representative of
(B) perfect for
(C) challenging for
(D) old-fashioned for

(B) The word "ideal" means the same as "perfect."

3. A pamphlet will usually explain brief information about a new product.

(A) A small booklet
(B) A large sign
(C) An advertisement
(D) A slip of paper

(A) A pamphlet is a small thin book, which is often stapled together and bound in a paper cover.

4. The early 1930s were years of great hardship in North America.

(A) famine
(B) floods
(C) commerce
(D) suffering

(D) The word "hardship" means "difficult time" or "time of suffering or discomfort."

5. Schools must protect children from the dangers of asbestos material.

(A) threaten
(B) promote
(C) guard
(D) mask

(C) The word "protect" means "to guard or defend from harm or danger."

6. The first major effort to cope with soil erosion in the United States began in the 1930s.

(A) select
(B) advance
(C) fund
(D) manage

(D) If you can cope with something it means that you can successfully live with or manage the difficulties of it. The meaning of this sentence is that the United States government tried to control the problems of soil erosion.

7. Sometimes a psychological problem will trigger a physical reaction.

(A) release
(B) initiate
(C) perform
(D) settle

(B) The verb "trigger" is often used in scientific writing. It means that one event is the immediate cause of another event.

8. The world is on the threshold of a new century.

(A) realizing the importance of
(B) at the beginning of
(C) expecting
(D) establishing goals for

(B) As a single noun, one definition of a "threshold" is a stone or piece of wood under a doorway. In this sentence the word refers to the beginning or the start of something new.

9. The Freer Gallery of Art in Washington, D.C. presents a wide variety of Asian pottery and sculpture.

(A) gives
(B) sees
(C) displays
(D) preserves

(C) In this sentence, the word "present" means to show or display something.

10. Begonias are hardy and easy to grow under favorable conditions.

(A) sunny
(B) valuable
(C) credit
(D) advantageous

(D) A favorable condition is one that is helpful. The word "advantageous" means the same.

11. Since language is a cultural system, specific languages may classify objects and ideas in totally different fashions.

(A) families
(B) manners
(C) levels
(D) grades

(B) In this sentence, the word "fashion" refers to the manner or style of doing or making something.

12. The first spectacles were probably invented by Roger Bacon in the 13th century.

(A) telescopes
(B) eyeglasses
(C) microscopes
(D) binoculars

(B) "Spectacles" is an old-fashioned word for "eyeglasses."

13. Fascinated with the idea of space travel as a child, Robert Goddard grew up to fire the world's first liquid-fueled rocket in 1926.

(A) Studious about
(B) Attracted by
(C) Involved in
(D) Attached to

(B) "Fascinated" means "being charmed or very attracted." If you are fascinated by something, you may also be involved in it or studious about it, but these are cause/effect relationships, not synonyms.

14. Some doctors are not in favor of extending life, and they argue that people should have the right to die when they want.

(A) creating
(B) prolonging
(C) hampering
(D) redeeming

(B) "Extending" and "prolonging" both mean to make something become longer or make something last longer.

15. Staring at other people can sometimes be impolite.

(A) Gazing steadily
(B) Glancing briefly
(C) Peeking carefully
(D) Winking privately

(A) "To stare" is to look directly at someone or something for a long time. The word "gazing" gives the same idea.

16. Even though there are many schools of martial art, one principle is common to all: training one's mind and body.

(A) colleges
(B) abilities
(C) types
(D) levels

(C) The word "school" has many meanings. In this sentence it refers to a particular type of teaching, based on a particular way of thinking.

17. The colors of the ocean and the sky merge into one on the horizon.

(A) blend
(B) maintain
(C) vanish
(D) alter

(A) "Merge" means to come together as one. "Blend" also means to come together so that you cannot tell the difference between two things.

18. A map of Los Angeles and its vicinities is needed for new visitors to the L.A. area.

(A) facilities
(B) tourist spots
(C) vacant lots
(D) surroundings

(D) Both "vicinities" and "surroundings" refer to the area around a place.

19. Few scientific breakthroughs are discovered merely by coincidence.

(A) talent
(B) laymen
(C) chance
(D) imagination

(C) Both "coincidence" and "chance" refer to something happening by luck, rather than by planning.

20. Cottontail rabbits have large ears and short legs, and they move with a scurrying gait.

(A) jumping
(B) skipping
(C) scampering
(D) leaping

(C) Both "scurrying" and "scampering" refer to a movement that consists of short, quick steps. A "skipping" movement is a quick jump or a movement with a quick step and jump. "Leaping" is a longer jump.

21. Being killed in a fight to protect one's rights is considered a supreme sacrifice by many people.

(A) an unusual
(B) the greatest
(C) a correct
(D) an abundant

(B) "Supreme" refers to something that is the highest in rank or degree or quality; something that is above all the rest. "Abundant" means "more than enough."

22. Bison are characterized by huge heads and massive humps.

(A) novel
(B) flimsy
(C) large
(D) fat

(C) The word "massive" means "large," "heavy," or "solid."

23. The water of the Nile River supports practically all agriculture in the most densely populated parts of Egypt.

(A) ample
(B) eventual
(C) usual
(D) most

(D) "Practically all" means the same as "almost all" or "most." The word "ample" means "enough for all."

24. In 1863 President Lincoln proclaimed all slaves to be free.

(A) dedicated
(B) requested
(C) decided
(D) declared

(D) To "proclaim" is to "announce officially," which is the same as to "declare."

25. Man's awareness of time is basically his consciousness of past, present, and future.

(A) innocence
(B) knowledge
(C) capability
(D) system

(B) To "be aware" means to be conscious of something through the senses, i.e., seeing, hearing, feeling, or touching. This means the same as "having knowledge."

26. The bones of the very old are especially prone to fracture, although no age is exempt.

(A) infection
(B) cracking
(C) loosening
(D) degenerating

(B) A fracture is a break or crack in something.

27. Thomas A. Edison was a celebrated American inventor in the 19th century.

(A) an ingenious
(B) a creative
(C) an eminent
(D) a successful

(C) The words "celebrated" and "eminent" both mean famous, outstanding, or remarkable.

28. The faucets in this building were all replaced by the plumber.

(A) drains
(B) taps
(C) pumps
(D) pipes

(B) A faucet or tap is the device you turn to regulate the flow of water from a pipe.

29. In the severe epidemic of the plague in Europe in the 14th century, the death toll was appalling.

(A) shocking
(B) weakening
(C) expanding
(D) demanding

(A) "Appalling" and "shocking" both mean "terrible" or "horrifying." Often this word is used in the passive voice, e.g., "I was appalled to learn that so many people died in the plague."

30. Birds have a natural ability to fly.

(A) an innate
(B) a universal
(C) a real
(D) a native

(A) "Natural" in this sentence means that something comes from nature; it does not need teaching or training.

31. What is the author's main purpose?

(A) To describe a new cure for ear infections
(B) To inform medical personnel of a new device
(C) To urge doctors to use the new device
(D) To explain the use of the magnet

(B) The author is giving information in this passage, so (B) is the best answer. The passage mentions relief for ear infections but not a cure. There are no words that are strong that would indicate urging, such as "Do this," or "Use this now," or "You should . . ." The magnet is only mentioned as the way the device is used, not as a main purpose.

32. It can be inferred from the passage that

(A) this use of magnets is new
(B) infections are in the inner ear
(C) magnets can be dangerous for 80 percent of the people
(D) the new device is smaller than old ones

(A) This is an inference question. The passage states that the device is unique because of the magnet. There is no mention of infections in the inner ear, just in the middle ear. Also there is no mention of danger or of the size of the device.

33. According to the passage, what does the device NOT do?

(A) Transmit sound to the inner ear
(B) Help all hearing-impaired people
(C) Produce clear sound
(D) Change sound into vibrations

(B) This is a negative question that is also a restatement. The passage states that the device helps only 20 percent of people with hearing problems, so it can't help all people.

34. The sound processing unit

(A) is a magnet
(B) helps cure infections
(C) is placed in the middle ear
(D) can be removed

(D) This is a restatement question. The passage states that the device is detachable, which means "removable."

35. The word "relief" in the last sentence means

(A) less distress
(B) assistance
(C) distraction
(D) relaxation

(A) This is a vocabulary question. It can be inferred that people who have ear infections and loss of hearing are distressed or uncomfortable. Therefore, "relief" would mean less distress. Answer (B) is incorrect, because "relief" only means "assistance" when it is referring to financial help. Answer (C) means "something annoying or unwelcome." Answer (D), "relaxation," may be a result of relief, but it is not a synonym.

36. The best title for this passage is

(A) Early Hominid Sites
(B) Dating Early Sites
(C) Olduvai Gorge
(D) Stone Age Culture

(B) The first sentence of the passage states that potassium argon is used for calculating the age of rocks, and the rest of the passage mentions dates of sites several times. Answers (A) and (D) are too broad; the passage is not discussing all early hominid sites or all Stone Age culture. Answer (C) is too narrow. Olduvai Gorge is mentioned only one time.

37. The main purpose of this passage is to

(A) discuss new information
(B) inform reader of a new technique
(C) compare two places
(D) propose an idea

(A) This is an author's-purpose question. The author first mentions that anthropologists are revising their estimates. The passage then discusses new information about the date of Olorgesaillie. There is no mention of this technique as being new, and the passage does not compare the key sites.

38. Olorgesaillie is a key site because of

(A) being very old
(B) having volcanic ash
(C) being near a river
(D) having many axes

(D) This is a restatement question. The passage states that "because of the many stone hand axes ... Olorgesaillie is considered a key site . . ."

39. It can be inferred from this passage that the age of early hominids is determined by

(A) the number of hand axes in the site
(B) the age of the rocks on the site
(C) the amount of activity shown by the site
(D) the number of layers of volcanic ash

(B) The first sentence gives the answer to this question. "Potassium argon is used for calculating the age of . . . rocks, and in turn, for revealing the age of early man."

40. The word "remains" in line 11 is closest in meaning to

(A) continues on
(B) parts not destroyed
(C) dead bodies
(D) stays behind

(B) All of these words are synonyms for "remains" in some context. Answer (B) is the best answer here, since the passage is referring to a site that is over 500,000 years old. Most objects from that period have been destroyed. The term "dead bodies" is too narrow. The remains may include more than bodies.

41. Olorgesaillie is

(A) older than Olduvai
(B) a hominid remain
(C) a hand axe
(D) a site

(D) This is a restatement question. The passage states that "Olorgesaillie is considered a key site . . ."

42. The age of the Olorgesaillie culture was determined from the

(A) hand axes
(B) volcanic ash
(C) hominid activity
(D) river basin

(B) This is a restatement question. The passages states that "layers of volcanic ash . . . were estimated to be about 500,000 years old, but now are more accurately dated at 700,000 to 900,000 years old."

43. The best title for this passage is

(A) *Leaves of Grass*
(B) Walt Whitman
(C) A Country Man
(D) Poetry: A New Form

(B) "Walt Whitman" is the best answer for this question. The best way to decide on this answer is by elimination. Answers (A) and (C) are too narrow. They refer to only part of the information mentioned in the passage. Answer (D) is too general. The passage does not discuss very much about a new form of poetry.

44. The word "rambled" in line 2 is most similar to the meaning of

(A) stopped briefly
(B) marched excitedly
(C) traveled quickly
(D) walked slowly

(D) To "ramble" describes the act of walking or strolling, or roaming without any special goal.

45. In the phrase "making them his own" in line 3, he is

(A) owning them
(B) changing them
(C) understanding them
(D) working for them

(C) This is a vocabulary/inference question. The best guess for this question is "understanding them." It will help you to eliminate answers in this question. Answer (A) is a possible meaning of "making them his own" in another context. But in this paragraph he is not taking or adopting anything. Answers (B) and (D) can be eliminated, since there is no mention of changing or working for people in the countryside.

46. Whitman's big-heartedness is shown by his

(A) visiting the countryside
(B) being an individualist
(C) caring for the wounded
(D) rewriting *Leaves of Grass*

(C) This is an inference question. The passage states that he cared for the wounded just after stating that he was "big-hearted." The word "big-hearted" means "generous and caring." The other answer choices do not show generosity.

47. The passage says that during Whitman's lifetime other poets

(A) laughed at him
(B) communicated with him
(C) praised him
(D) accepted him

(A) This is a restatement question. The passage says that other poets ridiculed him. "Ridiculed" means "laughed at" or "made fun of." The other answer choices are not mentioned.

48. We can assume that Whitman was ignored because he

(A) rewrote his book
(B) rambled through the countryside
(C) published his poems
(D) wrote in a new form

(D) This is an inference question. The passage states that Whitman's verse forms were not traditional. We can assume then that the form was new.

49. The author's main point is that

(A) we have lost respect for the Indian attitude toward life and nature
(B) we have discovered new information about the early Indian civilizations
(C) archeology has given us reliable records of the great achievements of early American civilizations
(D) it is unfortunate that we have lost so much of the early American culture and knowledge

(D) This is a main-idea question. The author infers that it is unfortunate that we have lost so much by the words "regret for the loss . . ." and "the greatest casualty . . ."

50. Which of the following has probably benefited the most from the discoveries of the early American civilizations?

(A) Research in astronomy
(B) Agriculture
(C) The building industry
(D) Environmental groups

(B) This is an inference question that may be best chosen by elimination. Answers (A) and (C) are incorrect because the passage states that secrets about Mayan astronomy and Inca builders were lost. Answer (D) is incorrect, because there is no reason to infer that environmental groups have benefited. It is possible to infer that environmental groups might be interested in the discoveries because of the Indian attitude toward life and the universe, but there is no mention of how they would benefit. The passage does name many foods that were originally developed by Indian civilizations. The development of these foods benefited the agriculture industry.

51. Which of the following can NOT be traced back to these Indian civilizations?

(A) Tapioca pudding
(B) A vanilla bean
(C) A chocolate bar
(D) A strawberry

(D) This is a negative question. It can be answered by elimination. Tapioca, vanilla, and chocolate are all mentioned as being originally developed by Indian civilizations.

52. According to the author, the biggest loss has been

(A) an attitude toward nature
(B) knowledge of early astronomy
(C) techniques of early building
(D) early agricultural practices

(A) This is a restatement question. The author states that the greatest casualty has been the Indian attitude toward life and the universe.

53. Which can you infer that the people of these civilizations would be least likely to do?

(A) Build a monument
(B) Cook a turkey
(C) Cut down trees
(D) Use medicine

(C) This is an inference question. It seems least likely that these people would cut down trees, because that would be "warring with nature."

54. From the passage, you can infer that

(A) astronomers kept their art a secret
(B) builders built great structures
(C) conquerors kept early records
(D) doctors had little knowledge of medicine

(B) The passage states that there is impressive achievement in monumental architecture. From this you can infer that people built great structures. Nothing is mentioned about astronomers keeping secrets or about conquerors keeping records. The passage states that doctors knew the art of healing, so they must have had a lot of knowledge about medicine.

55. The author's main point is to

(A) discuss ways in which males are attracted to females
(B) compare *Ephippizer bitterensis's* sound to bird songs
(C) describe the sound produced
(D) introduce sound as a sign stimulus

(D) This is a main-idea question. In the first sentence, the passage mentions sound as a sign stimulus. This is a general topic that covers both paragraphs. The other answer choices are mentioned as smaller topics.

56. The author mentions bird songs in the beginning in order to

(A) provide an illustration
(B) point out a difference
(C) argue a point
(D) compare two animals

(A) This is an author's-purpose question. The bird songs are an illustration of sound as a stimulus. There is no indication that the author is comparing or pointing out differences between two animals or two types of sounds. The two animals are both mentioned as examples.

57. The previous paragraphs most likely discussed

(A) how bird songs attract mates
(B) how other grasshoppers produce sound
(C) how competitors are repelled
(D) how color and smell are attractions

(D) This is a previous-topic question. Answer (D) is the most likely answer, since "sound" easily follows "color" and "smell." The first word of the passage, "another," indicates that the topic is an addition to a similar topic. Answers (A) and (B) cannot be correct since they both discuss sound and therefore would not be introduced with "another sign." Answer (C) is an opposite topic and would therefore not be introduced with "another sign . . ."

58. The male *Ephippizer bitterensis* produces sound from a device on its

(A) legs
(B) back
(C) head
(D) wings

(B) This is a restatement question. The passage states that the sound is produced using an organ borne on its back.

59. According to the passage, a female grasshopper

(A) has a difficult time going over obstacles
(B) flies to its mate
(C) has tiny wings
(D) goes faster when it gets close to the sound

(D) This is a restatement question. The passage states that females speed up as they come close to their mates.

60. It can be inferred that a female grasshopper might be most attracted to

(A) a man crying
(B) a cow mooing
(C) a dog barking
(D) a bee humming

(C) This is an inference statement. The passage states that the important characteristics of the sound are sharpness and quickness. Only answer (C) would be a sharp, quick sound. The others are all longer and steadier.

Practice Test II
(Short Form)

Note: You will need the tape to do Section 1. If you do not have the tape, the tapescript for Section 1 is on pages 637 to 641. The answer key is on pages 427–428, and explanatory answers begin on page 431. Use the answer sheet for Practice Test II on page 405 to mark your answers.

ANSWER SHEET FOR PRACTICE TEST II

Section 1: Listening Comprehension

1	2	3	4	5	6	7	8	9	10	11	12	13	14	15	16	17	18	19	20	21	22	23	24	25	26	27	28	29	30	31	32	33	34	35	36	37	38	39	40	41	42	43	44	45	46	47	48	49	50
A	A	A	A	A	A	A	A	A	A	A	A	A	A	A	A	A	A	A	A	A	A	A	A	A	A	A	A	A	A	A	A	A	A	A	A	A	A	A	A	A	A	A	A	A	A	A	A	A	A
B	B	B	B	B	B	B	B	B	B	B	B	B	B	B	B	B	B	B	B	B	B	B	B	B	B	B	B	B	B	B	B	B	B	B	B	B	B	B	B	B	B	B	B	B	B	B	B	B	B
C	C	C	C	C	C	C	C	C	C	C	C	C	C	C	C	C	C	C	C	C	C	C	C	C	C	C	C	C	C	C	C	C	C	C	C	C	C	C	C	C	C	C	C	C	C	C	C	C	C
D	D	D	D	D	D	D	D	D	D	D	D	D	D	D	D	D	D	D	D	D	D	D	D	D	D	D	D	D	D	D	D	D	D	D	D	D	D	D	D	D	D	D	D	D	D	D	D	D	D

Section 2: Structure and Written Expression

1	2	3	4	5	6	7	8	9	10	11	12	13	14	15	16	17	18	19	20	21	22	23	24	25	26	27	28	29	30	31	32	33	34	35	36	37	38	39	40
A	A	A	A	A	A	A	A	A	A	A	A	A	A	A	A	A	A	A	A	A	A	A	A	A	A	A	A	A	A	A	A	A	A	A	A	A	A	A	A
B	B	B	B	B	B	B	B	B	B	B	B	B	B	B	B	B	B	B	B	B	B	B	B	B	B	B	B	B	B	B	B	B	B	B	B	B	B	B	B
C	C	C	C	C	C	C	C	C	C	C	C	C	C	C	C	C	C	C	C	C	C	C	C	C	C	C	C	C	C	C	C	C	C	C	C	C	C	C	C
D	D	D	D	D	D	D	D	D	D	D	D	D	D	D	D	D	D	D	D	D	D	D	D	D	D	D	D	D	D	D	D	D	D	D	D	D	D	D	D

Section 3: Vocabulary and Reading Comprehension

1	2	3	4	5	6	7	8	9	10	11	12	13	14	15	16	17	18	19	20	21	22	23	24	25	26	27	28	29	30	31	32	33	34	35	36	37	38	39	40	41	42	43	44	45	46	47	48	49	50	51	52	53	54	55	56	57	58	59	60
A	A	A	A	A	A	A	A	A	A	A	A	A	A	A	A	A	A	A	A	A	A	A	A	A	A	A	A	A	A	A	A	A	A	A	A	A	A	A	A	A	A	A	A	A	A	A	A	A	A	A	A	A	A	A	A	A	A	A	A
B	B	B	B	B	B	B	B	B	B	B	B	B	B	B	B	B	B	B	B	B	B	B	B	B	B	B	B	B	B	B	B	B	B	B	B	B	B	B	B	B	B	B	B	B	B	B	B	B	B	B	B	B	B	B	B	B	B	B	B
C	C	C	C	C	C	C	C	C	C	C	C	C	C	C	C	C	C	C	C	C	C	C	C	C	C	C	C	C	C	C	C	C	C	C	C	C	C	C	C	C	C	C	C	C	C	C	C	C	C	C	C	C	C	C	C	C	C	C	C
D	D	D	D	D	D	D	D	D	D	D	D	D	D	D	D	D	D	D	D	D	D	D	D	D	D	D	D	D	D	D	D	D	D	D	D	D	D	D	D	D	D	D	D	D	D	D	D	D	D	D	D	D	D	D	D	D	D	D	D

Date Taken ____________________________

Number Correct

Section 1 _________

Section 2 _________

Section 3 _________

1 1 1 1 1 1 1 1 1 1 1

SECTION 1: LISTENING COMPREHENSION
Time—approximately 35 minutes

In this section of the test, you will have an opportunity to demonstrate your ability to understand spoken English. There are three parts to this section, with special directions for each part.

Part A

Directions: For each question in Part A, you will hear a short sentence. Each sentence will be spoken just one time. The sentences you hear will not be written out for you. Therefore, you must listen carefully to understand what the speaker says.

After you hear a sentence, read the four choices in your test book, marked (A), (B), (C), and (D), and decide which one is closest in meaning to the sentence you heard. Then, on your answer sheet, find the number of the question and fill in the space that corresponds to the letter of the answer you have chosen. Fill in the space so that the letter inside the oval cannot be seen.

Example I:

You will hear:

Sample Answer

Ⓐ Ⓑ  Ⓓ

You will read:

(A) Mary outswam the others.
(B) Mary ought to swim with them.
(C) Mary and her friends swam to the island.
(D) Mary's friends owned the island.

The speaker said, "Mary swam out to the island with her friends." Sentence (C), "Mary and her friends swam to the island," is closest in meaning to the sentence you heard. Therefore, you should choose answer (C).

Example II

You will hear:

Sample Answer

   Ⓓ

You will read:

(A) Please remind me to read this book.
(B) Could you help me carry these books?
(C) I don't mind if you help me.
(D) Do you have a heavy course load this term?

The speaker said, "Would you mind helping me with this load of books?" Sentence (B), "Could you help me carry these books?" is closest in meaning to the sentence you heard. Therefore, you should choose answer (B).

GO ON TO THE NEXT PAGE

1. (A) I want to go early.
   (B) I like to be late.
   (C) I hope you won't be early.
   (D) I prefer to be late.

2. (A) I want to go less than you.
   (B) I'll go if you can't go..
   (C) I won't go even if you go.
   (D) I'll go if you go.

3. (A) It's raining.
   (B) It's likely to rain.
   (C) It looks wet.
   (D) It likes rain.

4. (A) I had an argument with my old friend yesterday.
   (B) I passed my friend in town.
   (C) I met my friend in town by accident.
   (D) My friend and I had an accident yesterday.

5. (A) Ann is very intelligent.
   (B) Ann doesn't like her brother.
   (C) Ann is willing to listen to new ideas.
   (D) Ann is like her brother.

6. (A) I'd like to go running with you after class.
   (B) Please run down to the class for me.
   (C) Let's meet after class.
   (D) Let me tell you about the class.

7. (A) She missed one class this semester.
   (B) She hasn't missed any classes this semester.
   (C) She's missed only a few classes this semester.
   (D) She's missed many classes this semester.

8. (A) Bill forgot to pay the bill, and the phone is not working.
   (B) Bill paid the bill on time, but the phone is still not working.
   (C) Bill forgot the phone was not working when he paid the bill.
   (D) Bill forgot to connect the phone before he paid the bill.

9. (A) She's keeping a secret.
   (B) She doesn't want to tell anyone about the accident to her nose.
   (C) She doesn't know anything.
   (D) She doesn't like to talk about her ideas.

10. (A) It takes a long time to run.
    (B) It's worth it to run a long time in training.
    (C) Your work will be worth the time eventually.
    (D) An old well gets worse in time.

11. (A) The information is old.
    (B) The book is sold out.
    (C) The quality is poor.
    (D) There is no date on the book.

12. (A) It seems cheap to buy a car.
    (B) Cheap cars do not run well.
    (C) It's convenient to have a car.
    (D) It's expensive to have a car.

13. (A) He isn't growing anymore.
    (B) He seems younger than eighteen.
    (C) He is short for his age.
    (D) He is almost eighteen.

14. (A) Randy likes pizza better than tacos.
    (B) Randy doesn't like tacos.
    (C) Randy would like a piece of pizza.
    (D) Randy likes to talk about pizza.

15. (A) Jim is used to smoking.
    (B) Jim likes to smoke when it's hot.
    (C) Jim does not smoke anymore.
    (D) Jim smoked more before.

16. (A) Exercising can reduce depression.
    (B) Exercise can cause depression.
    (C) Depression helps you exercise better.
    (D) Depression can remind you to exercise.

17. (A) They are different books, but they look alike.
    (B) The covers are different.
    (C) They cover different material.
    (D) Some of the books have soft covers.

18. (A) Mary asked the salesman to be present.
    (B) Mary presented the wrapping.
    (C) The salesman dropped the present.
    (D) The salesman put paper around the present.

19. (A) I am really hungry!
    (B) I have never been hungry!
    (C) I am very angry!
    (D) I'm never angry!

20. (A) Jenny is younger than Jane.
    (B) Jane is smaller than Jenny.
    (C) Jane is older than Jenny.
    (D) Jane is bigger than Jenny.

GO ON TO THE NEXT PAGE

1 1 1 1 1 1 1 1 1 1 1

Part B

Directions: In Part B you will hear short conversations between two speakers. At the end of each conversation, a third person will ask a question about what was said. You will hear each conversation and question about it just one time. Therefore, you must listen carefully to understand what each speaker says. After you hear a conversation and the question about it, read the four possible answers in your test book and decide which one is the best answer to the question you heard. Then, on your answer sheet, find the number of the question and fill in the space that corresponds to the letter of the answer you have chosen.

Look at the following example.

You will hear:

Sample Answer

You will read:

(A) Present Professor Smith with a picture.
(B) Photograph Professor Smith.
(C) Put glass over the photograph.
(D) Replace the broken headlight.

From the conversation you learn that the woman thinks Professor Smith would like a photograph of the class. The best answer to the question "What does the woman think the class should do?" is (A), "Present Professor Smith with a picture." Therefore, you should choose answer (A).

GO ON TO THE NEXT PAGE

21. **(A)** She's hungry.
(B) She's tired.
(C) She's bored.
(D) She's thirsty.

22. **(A)** He wishes the professor would talk more.
(B) He doesn't always understand the professor.
(C) He thinks the professor has an accent.
(D) He thinks the professor talks too quietly.

23. **(A)** She wants to pay the bill.
(B) She wants Bill to pay for the meal.
(C) She wants to pay for her meal.
(D) She wants the man to pay.

24. **(A)** Her drink tastes sour.
(B) Her throat hurts.
(C) She hasn't sold anything.
(D) She is very busy.

25. **(A)** She has had a nice day.
(B) She is sick.
(C) The daylight hours are long.
(D) She is tired.

26. **(A)** He will mail a check for her.
(B) He will pick up her mail.
(C) He will put a check in his mailbox.
(D) He will take a check from her mailbox.

27. **(A)** She will take it because she likes it.
(B) She will take it even though she doesn't like it.
(C) She won't take it because she doesn't like it.
(D) She won't take it even though she likes it.

28. **(A)** She does not like cake.
(B) She is going to dive.
(C) She is afraid to diet.
(D) She wants to lose weight.

29. **(A)** In a dressing room
(B) In a bedroom
(C) In a department store
(D) In a restaurant

30. **(A)** Buying a computer
(B) Getting directions
(C) Buying books
(D) Registering for classes

31. **(A)** He will pay for a call from Lisa.
(B) He will make a call to Lisa.
(C) He is collecting money for Lisa.
(D) He is correcting a call from Lisa.

32. **(A)** It is expensive to buy life insurance.
(B) Everyone should have health insurance.
(C) The man wants to buy car insurance.
(D) The man had an accident.

33. **(A)** She thinks it will be fine.
(B) She says it is impossible.
(C) She has to ask for permission.
(D) She doesn't know yet.

34. **(A)** She misplaced her contact lenses.
(B) She finds her old glasses better.
(C) She couldn't contact her optometrist.
(D) Her contact lenses are better.

35. **(A)** One should write down anything important.
(B) Nobody can be the best.
(C) Do as well as you can.
(D) It's difficult to write correctly.

GO ON TO THE NEXT PAGE

1 1 1 1 1 1 1 1 1 1 1

Part C

Directions: In this part of the test, you will hear short talks and conversations. After each of them, you will be asked some questions. You will hear the talks and conversations and the questions about them just one time. They will not be written out for you. Therefore, you must listen carefully to understand what each speaker says.

After you hear a question, read the four possible answers in your test book and decide which one is the best answer to the question you heard. Then, on your answer sheet, find the number of the question and fill in the space that corresponds to the letter of the answer you have chosen.

Answer all questions on the basis of what is stated or implied in the talk or conversation.

Listen to this sample talk.

You will hear:

Now look at the following example:

You will hear:

Sample Answer

You will read:
(A) They are impossible to guide.
(B) They may go up in flames.
(C) They tend to leak gas.
(D) They are cheaply made.

The best answer to the question "Why are gas balloons considered dangerous?" is (B), "They may go up in flames." Therefore, you should choose answer (B).

Now look at the next example

You will hear:

Sample Answer

You will read:
(A) Watch for changes in weather.
(B) Watch their altitude.
(C) Check for weak spots in their balloons.
(D) Test the strength of the ropes.

The best answer to the question "According to the speaker, what must ballon pilots be careful to do?" is (A), "Watch for changes in weather." Therefore, you should choose answer (A).

GO ON TO THE NEXT PAGE

36. **(A)** In a doctor's office
(B) In an exercise class
(C) In a dentist's office
(D) In a biology class

37. **(A)** How to stretch
(B) How to change ideas
(C) How to pull a tooth
(D) How to exhale

38. **(A)** Gaining new concepts
(B) Releasing stress
(C) Stretching
(D) Pulling teeth

39. **(A)** It is difficult to learn something new.
(B) It always hurts to exercise.
(C) It hurts more to have a tooth pulled than it does to exercise.
(D) If you don't feel the pain of stretching, you need to stretch more.

40. **(A)** The woman will pull a tooth.
(B) Everyone will go home.
(C) The woman will demonstrate a new way to exercise.
(D) The woman will discuss difficulties of learning.

41. **(A)** Ana
(B) Ana's friend
(C) A clerk at the social security office
(D) A person from Spain

42. **(A)** Because she couldn't speak Spanish.
(B) Because her friend wasn't there to help her.
(C) Because she couldn't write very well.
(D) Because she didn't realize it wasn't English.

43. **(A)** It was in Spanish.
(B) She couldn't read enough English.
(C) She hadn't been in the country long enough.
(D) She was too embarrassed.

44. **(A)** Because he couldn't help Ana.
(B) Because it was so difficult to understand the form.
(C) Because Ana's friend was not there.
(D) Because he gave her the wrong form.

45. **(A)** Jealous
(B) Angry
(C) Pleased
(D) Concerned

46. **(A)** A doctor
(B) A mechanic
(C) A professor
(D) A chemist

47. **(A)** Ultraviolet light
(B) The use of spray cans
(C) Air-conditioning systems
(D) Fluorocarbons and the ozone layer

48. **(A)** Providing fluorocarbons
(B) Shielding the sun
(C) Protecting the earth
(D) Destroying chemicals

49. **(A)** Fluorocarbons
(B) Oxygen
(C) Shields
(D) Ultraviolet light

50. **(A)** How to Make Air Conditioners with Fluorocarbons
(B) Harmful Effects of Ultraviolet Light
(C) The Makeup of the Ozone Layer
(D) The Sun as a Cause of Ozone Layer Depletion

THIS IS THE END OF THE LISTENING COMPREHENSION PART OF THIS TEST. The next part of the test is Section 2. Turn to the directions for Section 2 in your test book, read them, and begin to work. Do not read or work on any other section of the test.

2 2 2 2 2 2 2 2 2 2 2

SECTION 2
STRUCTURE AND WRITTEN EXPRESSION
Time—25 minutes

This section is designed to measure your ability to recognize language that is appropriate for standard written English. There are two types of questions in this section, with special directions for each type.

Directions: Questions 1–15 are incomplete sentences. Beneath each sentence you will see four words or phrases, marked (A), (B), (C), and (D). Choose the one word or phrase that best completes the sentence. Then, on your answer sheet, find the number of the question and fill in the space that corresponds to the letter of the answer you have chosen. Fill in the space so that the letter inside the oval cannot be seen.

Example I:

Vegetables are an excellent source ________ vitamins.

(A) of
(B) has
(C) where
(D) that

Sample Answer

● Ⓑ Ⓒ Ⓓ

The sentence should read, "Vegetables are an excellent source of vitamins." Therefore, you should choose answer (A).

Example II:

________ in history when remarkable progress was made within a relatively short span of time.

(A) Periods
(B) Throughout periods
(C) There have been periods
(D) Periods have been

Sample Answer

Ⓐ Ⓑ ● Ⓓ

The sentence should read, "There have been periods in history when remarkable progress was made within a relatively short span of time." Therefore, you should choose answer (C).

Now begin work on the questions.

GO ON TO THE NEXT PAGE

1. The population of cities in the Eastern and Northern areas of the United States is declining, while ________ Southern cities is growing.
   (A) that in
   (B) that of
   (C) those of
   (D) those in

2. Some people find it surprising ________ his career as an actor in California.
   (A) when Ronald Reagan began
   (B) Ronald Reagan began
   (C) that Ronald Reagan began
   (D) to know Ronald Reagan

3. The travels of Marco Polo in the twelfth century would not have been so well known ________ for the book he wrote while in jail.
   (A) it not have been
   (B) is not been
   (C) had it not been
   (D) has not been

4. The Caspian Sea, a salt lake, is ________ any other lake in the world.
   (A) largest
   (B) the largest
   (C) larger than
   (D) the larger than

5. At 3,810 meters above sea level in Bolivia stands Lake Titicaca, ________ in the world.
   (A) the highest large lake
   (B) highest large lake
   (C) high largest lake
   (D) the high largest lake

6. ________ in an electric typewriter is the ability to correct spelling errors.
   (A) There are many new features
   (B) New features
   (C) The new features
   (D) One of the new features

7. Ballet dancers, ________ actors, must spend many hours a day practicing before a performance.
   (A) like
   (B) the like
   (C) the same
   (D) same as

8. It is a sign ________ fall when the leaves on the trees begin to change color.
   (A) for
   (B) at
   (C) to
   (D) of

9. Bees have compound eyes ________ almost 6,000 tiny lenses.
   (A) made of
   (B) made in
   (C) made on
   (D) made up

10. ________ the reactions of people with amnesia, scientists are learning more about the process of memory in the brain.
   (A) By studying
   (B) To study
   (C) They study
   (D) They're studying

11. The White House is where the president lives, and the Capitol Building is where ________.
   (A) laws made
   (B) the laws are making
   (C) the laws are made
   (D) are making the laws

12. High levels of hazardous waste ________ in soil near many nuclear defense facilities.
   (A) have been measured
   (B) has been measured
   (C) is measuring
   (D) are measuring

13. Bigamy is a situation in which a man ________ two women at the same time.
   (A) marries to
   (B) is marry to
   (C) married
   (D) is married to

14. ________ the rainfall was adequate this year, the apricot trees still did not produce a high yield.
   (A) Since
   (B) However
   (C) Although
   (D) Due to

GO ON TO THE NEXT PAGE

15. Ludwig van Beethoven is considered one of the greatest composers ________.

(A) who ever lived
(B) he lived
(C) when living
(D) while he lived

Directions: In questions 16–40 each sentence has four underlined words or phrases. The four underlined parts of the sentence are marked (A), (B), (C), and (D). Identify the one underlined word or phrase that must be changed in order for the sentence to be correct. Then, on your answer sheet, find the number of the question and fill in the space that corresponds to the letter of the answer you have chosen.

Example I:

A ray of light passing through (A) the center (B) of a thin lens keep (C) its original (D) direction.

Sample Answer

Ⓐ Ⓑ ● Ⓓ

The sentence should read, "A ray of light passing through the center of a thin lens keeps its original direction." Therefore, you should answer (C).

Example II:

The mandolin, a musical instrument (A) that has (B) strings, was probably copied from (C) the lute, a many (D) older instrument.

Sample Answer

Ⓐ Ⓑ Ⓒ ●

The sentence should read, "The mandolin, a musical instrument that has strings, was probably copied from the lute, a much older instrument." Therefore, you should choose answer (D).

Now begin work on the questions.

16. The (A) research works (B) of paleontologists comes to life with (C) paintings and sculptures of (D) dinosaurs.

17. According to (A) a *Newsweek* magazine poll taken (B) in 1986, 77 percent of Americans want the U.S. and the Soviet Union to sign an arms (C) agreement limits (D) nuclear weapons.

GO ON TO THE NEXT PAGE

18. In 1963, the Beatles, with their haircuts, clothes, and joking, drew crowds of
A B C
shrieking teenagers.
D

19. Conditions that are necessary for a successful business includes consumer demand
A B C D
and adequate supply.

20. On New Year's Day, most Americans watch football on TV, visiting friends, and
A B C
relax around the house.
D

21. Scientists have been studying the effects of aspirin on lower the instances of heart
A B C D
attacks in people.

22. The more you pull on a square knot, the tightest it gets.
A B C D

23. The koto, a Japanese string instrument, consists in a long wooden body and seven
A B C
to thirteen strings.
D

24. Much of the beautifully spring color in the mountain meadows comes from the
A B C D
flower of the wild lupine plant.

25. The earliest suspension bridges in the United States were built by American
A B C
building James Finley.
D

26. Caterpillars have three pairs of legs, two row of eyes, and strong jaws.
A B C D

27. Cro-Magnon man, a human being who lived about 35,000 years ago, was about
A B
six feet tall, stood straight, and with a large brain and a high forehead.
C D

28. The boll weevil, a cotton-eating insect, was a major reason for the change from a
A B
one-crop economy to diversified agricultural in the U.S.
C D

29. Scientists predict that there would be an earthquake of great magnitude in Califor-
A B
nia within the next few years.
C D

GO ON TO THE NEXT PAGE

30. The number of wild condors, an endangered species of bird, have been increasing steadily this year because of the work of scientists and environmentalists.
(A: species of; B: have been; C: steadily; D: because of)

31. Since the last explore voyage into space, we have increased our knowledge about the planet Jupiter.
(A: Since; B: explore; C: increased; D: about)

32. Mahogany wood, what is used for making furniture, is resistant to termites, and is a beautiful color.
(A: what; B: making; C: resistant to; D: is)

33. Muscular dystrophy is a disease of the muscles, which commonly afflicting boys more than girls.
(A: the; B: commonly; C: afflicting; D: more than)

34. Yellowstone National Park is well known for its beautiful canyon, its amazed geysers, and its wild life.
(A: beautiful; B: canyon; C: amazed; D: wild life)

35. Have red leaves in the fall, the poison oak plant is easy to see.
(A: Have; B: the; C: plant is; D: easy)

36. A planetarium, with his domed ceiling and many projectors, is capable of showing the position of the stars in any season.
(A: A; B: his; C: capable of; D: the position of)

37. Both scientists and treasure seekers are interesting in uncovering the mysteries of the sunken ship, the *Titanic*.
(A: Both; B: treasure seekers; C: interesting in; D: uncovering)

38. Harvard University, that is the oldest American college, was founded in 1636.
(A: that is; B: the oldest; C: was; D: founded)

39. Franz Schubert, the famous Austrian composer, was first taught to play the violin and piano from his father.
(A: was; B: taught to play; C: the; D: from)

40. A few of the works in art of the French painter Cezanne are part of the permanent collection of the Museum of Modern Art in New York City.
(A: A few of; B: works in art; C: part of; D: collection of)

THIS IS THE END OF SECTION 2. CHECK YOUR WORK ON SECTION 2 ONLY. DO NOT READ OR WORK ON ANY OTHER SECTION OF THE TEST UNTIL YOUR TIME IS UP. **STOP**

3 3 3 3 3 3 3 3 3 3 3

SECTION 3
VOCABULARY AND READING COMPREHENSION
Time—45 minutes

This section is designed to measure your comprehension of standard written English. There are two types of questions in this section, with special directions for each type.

Directions: In questions 1–30 each sentence has an underlined word or phrase. Below each sentence are four other words or phrases, marked (A), (B), (C), and (D). You are to choose the one word or phrase that best keeps the meaning of the original sentence if it is substituted for the underlined word or phrase. Then, on your answer sheet, find the number of the question and fill in the space that corresponds to the letter you have chosen. Fill in the space so that the letter inside the oval cannot be seen.

Example:

Passenger ships and aircraft are often equipped with ship-to-shore or air-to-land radio telephones.

(A) highways
(B) railroads
(C) planes
(D) sailboats

Sample Answer

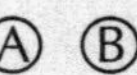   Ⓓ

The best answer is (C) because "Passenger ships and planes are often equipped with ship-to-shore or air-to-land radio telephones" is closest in meaning to the original sentence. Therefore, you should choose answer (C).

Now begin work on the questions.

GO ON TO THE NEXT PAGE

1. Vincent Van Gogh is renowned for his post-impressionist paintings.

(A) regarded
(B) applauded
(C) accomplished
(D) famous

2. Extreme sunburn can cause small blisters on the skin.

(A) spots
(B) swellings
(C) wounds
(D) bites

3. Natural occurrences such as hurricanes, earthquakes, and tornadoes can have catastrophic effects on people.

(A) disastrous
(B) killing
(C) categorical
(D) unimaginable

4. Jane Goodall has written a new, comprehensive book on her study of the chimpanzees in Africa.

(A) complete
(B) factual
(C) festive
(D) illustrated

5. The earthworm is a segmented worm found in almost all parts of the world.

(A) plated
(B) round
(C) long
(D) sectional

6. Ammonia is a chemical with a penetrating odor.

(A) smell
(B) flavor
(C) sting
(D) burn

7. After the American Civil War, the Southern armies were granted amnesty.

(A) punished
(B) frightened
(C) pardoned
(D) separated

8. Amphibians like frogs and toads have moist skin.

(A) wet
(B) slimy
(C) sticky
(D) tough

9. The Bay of Pigs invasion in 1961 resulted in severe criticism of President Kennedy by the American people.

(A) deep
(B) special
(C) tight
(D) harsh

10. Coral is made by a small, sedentary animal that lives in the ocean.

(A) secluded
(B) hard-working
(C) immobile
(D) lively

11. Charles Darwin formulated his famous theory of evolution during his five-year cruise on the *Beagle*.

(A) expanded
(B) developed
(C) critiqued
(D) finished

12. By the end of the Crimean War, the name of Florence Nightingale was legendary.

(A) imaginary
(B) novel
(C) gratifying
(D) famous

13. A devastating earthquake in North America occurred in Alaska in 1964.

(A) damaging
(B) divisive
(C) crushing
(D) shocking

14. In many coastal areas of the U.S. there is a deficiency of sand, causing an erosion problem.

(A) quality
(B) propagation
(C) movement
(D) lack

GO ON TO THE NEXT PAGE

15. The increase in world population was negligible until around 1900.
(A) unimportant
(B) needless
(C) average
(D) misleading

16. A credit card allows the user to receive credit at the time of a purchase.
(A) donate
(B) arbitrate
(C) reject
(D) obtain

17. Credit card holders can postpone payment on their purchases by accepting a monthly interest charge.
(A) provide
(B) decrease
(C) mail
(D) defer

18. William Faulkner, a brilliant American novelist, was awarded the 1949 Nobel Prize in literature.
(A) intelligent
(B) starry
(C) captive
(D) well-known

19. When frost appears on a window, it often has a delicate and curious pattern.
(A) special
(B) strange
(C) fine
(D) cute

20. The American Dental Association cautions people not to neglect their teeth during their growing years.
(A) abuse
(B) damage
(C) disrupt
(D) disregard

21. When the earth turns, the moon appears to rise in the east and set in the west.
(A) refers
(B) seems
(C) is likely
(D) is supposed

22. One goal of a physical fitness program is to maximize a person's strength and endurance.
(A) split
(B) distinguish
(C) increase
(D) combine

23. Among the dangers of drilling for oil in the ocean is the problem of potential leaks.
(A) serious
(B) dangerous
(C) influential
(D) possible

24. Kangaroos give birth to babies that develop within their mothers' pouches.
(A) abdominal sacks
(B) tender care
(C) range of hearing
(D) concealed nests

25. Unicorns, dragons, and centaurs are all imaginary animals.
(A) magic
(B) unimportant
(C) pictorial
(D) unreal

26. The Milky Way consists of about a hundred billion stars.
(A) is conscious of
(B) surrounds
(C) is composed of
(D) makes

27. Blizzards in the high mountains can be dangerous for hikers and skiers.
(A) Snow storms
(B) High winds
(C) Avalanches
(D) Slippery ice

28. To make raisins, the ripened grapes are usually picked by hand, placed on trays, and set in the sun for several days.
(A) dried
(B) cleaned
(C) crushed
(D) mature

GO ON TO THE NEXT PAGE

29. Of all the Olympic ski events, ski jumping is the most spectacular.

(A) striking
(B) dangerous
(C) appealing
(D) difficult

30. The central states in the U.S. are noted for their production of wheat and corn.

(A) applauded for
(B) informed of
(C) known for
(D) described by

Directions: In the rest of this section you will read several passages. Each one is followed by several questions about it. For questions 31–60, you are to choose the one best answer. (A), (B), (C), or (D), to each question. Then, on your answer sheet, find the number of the question and fill in the space that corresponds to the letter of the answer you have chosen.

Answer all questions following a passage on the basis of what is stated or implied in that passage.

Read the following passage:

The rattles with which a rattlesnake warns of its presence are formed by loosely interlocking hollow rings of hard skin, which make a buzzing sound when its tail is shaken. As a baby, the snake begins to form its rattles from the button at the very tip of its tail. Thereafter, each time it sheds its skin, a new ring is formed. Popular belief holds that a snake's age can be told by counting the rings, but this idea is fallacious. In fact, a snake may lose its old skin as often as four times a year. Also, rattles tend to wear or break off with time.

Example I:

A rattlesnake's rattles are made of

Sample Answer

   Ⓓ

(A) skin
(B) bone
(C) wood
(D) muscle

According to the passage, a rattlesnake's rattles are made out of rings of hard skin. Therefore, you should choose answer (A).

Example II:

How often does a rattlesnake shed its skin?

Sample Answer

   Ⓓ

(A) Once every four years
(B) Once every four months
(C) Up to four times every year
(D) Four times more often than other snakes

The passage states that "a snake may lose its old skin as often as four times a year." Therefore, you should choose answer (C).

Now begin work on the questions.

GO ON TO THE NEXT PAGE

Questions 31–34

The American architect and engineer, Buckminster Fuller, was born in 1895 in Massachusetts. He devoted his life to the invention of revolutionary technological designs to solve problems of modern living. He is best known for his development of the geodesic dome, which is an extremely light and yet enormously strong spherical structure composed of triangular pieces. The geodesic dome is an application of his principle of deriving maximum output from a minimum input of material and energy. In the 1950s many of these domes were built for military and industrial uses. A considerable number of homes also have been built using geodesic dome structures. Fuller was also a controversial writer. Among his many books are *Nine Chains to the Moon* (1938), *Ideas and Integrities* (1963—an autobiography), *Utopia or Oblivion* (1970), and *Earth, Inc.* (1973).

31. Which of the following would be the most appropriate title for this passage?
(A) The Geodesic Dome
(B) An American Architect
(C) American Architecture
(D) Revolutionary Designs

32. Which statement best describes the dome?
(A) It uses a lot of material, but takes less energy to construct than traditional structures.
(B) It takes a lot of energy to build.
(C) It is very spacious.
(D) It takes less material and energy than traditional structures.

33. A geodesic dome is closest in shape to
(A) a tube
(B) the end of a box
(C) a half of a ball
(D) the tip of a triangle

34. Fuller wrote about his life in his book
(A) *Ideas and Integrities*
(B) *Utopia or Oblivion*
(C) *Nine Chains to the Moon*
(D) *Earth, Inc.*

GO ON TO THE NEXT PAGE

Questions 35–40

Water on the earth is being recycled continuously in a process known as the hydrologic cycle. The first step of the cycle is the evaporation of water in the oceans. Evaporation is the process of water turning into vapor, which then forms clouds in the sky. The second step is the water returning to the earth in the form of precipitation: either rain, snow, or ice. When the water reaches the earth's surface, it runs off into the rivers, lakes, and the ocean, where the cycle begins again.

Not all water, however, stays on the surface of the earth in the hydrologic cycle. Some of it seeps into the ground through infiltration and collects under the earth's surface as groundwater. This groundwater is extremely important to life on earth, since 95 percent of the earth's water is in the oceans and is too salty for human beings or plants. Of the 5 percent on land, only .05 percent is above ground in rivers or lakes. The rest is underground water. This groundwater is plentiful and dependable, because it doesn't depend on seasonal rain or snow. It is the major source of water for many cities. But as the population increases and the need for water also increases, the groundwater in some areas is getting dangerously low. Added to this problem is an increasing amount of pollution that seeps into the groundwater. In the future, with a growing population and more toxic waste, the hydrologic cycle we depend on could become dangerously imbalanced.

35. Clouds are formed from
(A) water vapor
(B) evaporation
(C) the hydrologic cycle
(D) groundwater

36. Water returns to the earth by
(A) infiltration
(B) pollution
(C) precipitation
(D) evaporation

37. Groundwater
(A) depends on seasonal rain
(B) comes from toxic waste
(C) is .05 percent of all water
(D) collects under the earth

38. The amount of groundwater is
(A) about 95 percent of all water
(B) less than 5 percent of all water
(C) .05 percent of above-ground water
(D) 95 percent of above-ground water

39. The supply of groundwater is getting low because of
(A) conservation
(B) toxic waste
(C) pollution
(D) population increase

40. The best title for this passage is
(A) Water Conservation
(B) The Hydrologic Cycle
(C) Underground Water
(D) Polluted Groundwater

GO ON TO THE NEXT PAGE

Questions 41–47

The Library of Congress in Washington, D.C., which houses the largest collection of books in the world, is fighting a battle against paper deterioration. The pages of old books, often yellowed and torn, sometimes crumble when they are touched. The main culprit in the battle is the acidic paper that has been used for making books since the nineteenth century.

Air pollution and moisture have added to the problem. Strangely, the books that are most in danger of destruction are not the oldest books. The paper in books produced before the last century was made from cotton and linen rags, which are naturally low in acid. And the Gutenberg Bible, printed five centuries ago, was made of thin calfskin, and is in remarkably good shape. But in the nineteenth century, with widespread literacy bringing a demand for a cheaper and more plentiful supply of paper, the industry began using chemically treated wood pulp for making paper. It is the chemical in this paper that is causing today's problem.

This problem of paper deterioration is one of global concern. France, Canada, and Austria are all doing research into new methods of deacidification. A new technology has been developed recently, in fact, that allows for mass deacidification of thousands of books at the same time. It costs less than microfilming and still preserves books in their original form. It is hoped there will soon be treatment facilities all over the world to preserve and deacidify library book collections.

41. The Library of Congress
- **(A)** is headed for destruction
- **(B)** is fighting a battle
- **(C)** is causing paper deterioration
- **(D)** was built in the nineteenth century

42. According to this passage, libraries are trying to stop
- **(A)** the tearing of books
- **(B)** the yellowing of pages
- **(C)** the problem of air pollution
- **(D)** the deterioration of paper

43. Before the nineteenth century,
- **(A)** most books crumbled
- **(B)** the industry used wood pulp
- **(C)** paper had less acid
- **(D)** thousands of books were deacidified

44. We can assume from this passage that
- **(A)** cotton and linen rags are not good for making paper
- **(B)** calfskin is low in acid
- **(C)** wood pulp is expensive
- **(D)** microfilming is an inexpensive way to preserve old books

45. Some countries in the world are
- **(A)** using calfskin for book production
- **(B)** producing books from cotton and linen rags
- **(C)** doing research into methods of mass preservation
- **(D)** building treatment facilities

46. A new technique in deacidification
- **(A)** uses microfilm to save books
- **(B)** will save the Gutenberg Bible
- **(C)** uses chemically treated wood pulp
- **(D)** can treat thousands of books at a time

47. The best title for this passage is
- **(A)** Paper Deterioration
- **(B)** The Gutenberg Bible
- **(C)** Microfilming vs. Deacidification
- **(D)** Types of Paper Used in Bookmaking

GO ON TO THE NEXT PAGE

Questions 48–53

Impressionism in painting developed in the late nineteenth century in France. It began with a loosely structured group of painters who got together mainly to exhibit their paintings. Their art was characterized by the attempt to depict light and movement by using pure broken color. The movement began with four friends who met in a cafe: Monet, Renoir, Sisley, and Bazille. They were reacting against the academic standards of their time and the romantic emphasis on emotion as a subject matter. They rejected the role of imagination in art. Instead, they observed nature closely, painting with a scientific interest in visual phenomena. Their subject matter was as diverse as their personalities. Monet and Sisley painted landscapes with changing effects of light, and Renoir painted idealized women and children. The works of impressionists were received with hostility until the 1920s. By the 1930s impressionism had a large cult following, and by the 1950s even the least important works by people associated with the movement commanded enormous prices.

48. Impressionism began with a small group of artists who wanted to
(A) use light colors
(B) fight the government
(C) become scientists
(D) show their paintings

49. The first impressionists
(A) supported the academic standards
(B) began a new academy
(C) did not like the academic standards
(D) developed new official standards

50. The early impressionist artists painted
(A) with imagination
(B) different subject matter
(C) landscapes
(D) diverse personalities

51. What subject matter did Monet and Sisley usually paint?
(A) Country scenes
(B) Portraits
(C) Skyscrapers
(D) Animals in nature

52. Which of the following typifies the early impressionists?
(A) They had a romantic emphasis
(B) They tried to see nature unemotionally
(C) They worked toward a unified goal
(D) They idealized life

53. Most people did not like impressionistic painting
(A) before 1920
(B) between 1920 and 1930
(C) between 1930 and 1950
(D) after 1950

GO ON TO THE NEXT PAGE

Questions 54–60

Both tissue transplants and organ transplants are used in the treatment of disease. Tissue transplants include the transplanting of skin, bones, and the cornea of the eye; whereas organ transplanting includes replacing a kidney, heart, lung, or liver. Skin and cornea transplants are very common and successful, and have been performed for hundreds of years. In fact, there is evidence that skin transplants were done as early as 600 B.C. in India. Organ transplants, on the other hand, are quite recent. They are also more difficult to perform. Moreover, it is not always easy to find a suitable donor. Even if a healthy organ is found, the receiver's body may reject it. This is the major reason for problems with organ transplants.

The first heart transplant was performed by Dr. Christiaan Barnard in 1967 in South Africa. Many successful heart transplant operations have been performed since then. In 1982, Dr. Barney Clark was the first to receive an artificial heart. Research into organ transplants continues all the time. Doctors are continuing to find new ways to combat the problems, and to make transplants safer and more available to people who need them.

54. Which of the following is a tissue transplant?
(A) Liver
(B) Lung
(C) Bone
(D) Kidney

55. In 600 B.C., there were
(A) organ transplants
(B) skin transplants
(C) cornea replacements
(D) artificial hearts

56. A cornea is located in the
(A) heart
(B) skin
(C) bone
(D) eye

57. The most common problem with organ transplants is
(A) rejection of the organ
(B) finding a donor
(C) finding a healthy organ
(D) replacing the organ

58. Successful heart transplants have been performed since
(A) 600 B.C.
(B) 1967
(C) 1982
(D) 600 A.D.

59. The first heart transplant was
(A) received by Dr. Christiaan Barnard
(B) performed by Dr. Barney Clark
(C) performed in South Africa
(D) with an artificial heart

60. The best title for this passage is
(A) The Treatment of Disease
(B) The First Heart Transplants
(C) Successful Organ Transplants
(D) Transplants: Past and Present

THIS IS THE END OF SECTION 3. IF YOU FINISH BEFORE YOUR TIME IS UP, CHECK YOUR WORK ON SECTION 3 ONLY. DO NOT READ OR WORK ON ANY OTHER SECTION OF THE TEST. **STOP**

Answer Key for Practice Test II

SECTION 1: LISTENING COMPREHENSION

Part A

1. A	**6.** D	**11.** A	**16.** A
2. D	**7.** B	**12.** D	**17.** B
3. B	**8.** A	**13.** B	**18.** D
4. C	**9.** A	**14.** A	**19.** C
5. C	**10.** C	**15.** D	**20.** D

Part B

21. A	**26.** B	**31.** A
22. B	**27.** A	**32.** C
23. C	**28.** D	**33.** D
24. B	**29.** D	**34.** A
25. D	**30.** D	**35.** C

Part C

36. B	**41.** B	**46.** C
37. A	**42.** D	**47.** D
38. C	**43.** A	**48.** C
39. A	**44.** D	**49.** B
40. C	**45.** D	**50.** D

SECTION 2: STRUCTURE AND WRITTEN EXPRESSION

1. B	**11.** C	**21.** C	**31.** B
2. C	**12.** A	**22.** C	**32.** A
3. C	**13.** D	**23.** A	**33.** C
4. C	**14.** C	**24.** B	**34.** C
5. A	**15.** A	**25.** D	**35.** A
6. D	**16.** B	**26.** B	**36.** B
7. A	**17.** D	**27.** D	**37.** C
8. D	**18.** B	**28.** D	**38.** A
9. A	**19.** C	**29.** A	**39.** D
10. A	**20.** C	**30.** B	**40.** B

SECTION 3: VOCABULARY AND READING COMPREHENSION

1. D
2. B
3. A
4. A
5. D
6. A
7. C
8. A
9. D
10. C
11. B
12. D
13. A
14. D
15. A
16. D
17. D
18. A
19. B
20. D
21. B
22. C
23. D
24. A
25. D
26. C
27. A
28. D
29. A
30. C
31. B
32. D
33. C
34. A
35. A
36. C
37. D
38. B
39. D
40. B
41. B
42. D
43. C
44. B
45. C
46. D
47. A
48. D
49. C
50. B
51. A
52. B
53. A
54. C
55. B
56. D
57. A
58. B
59. C
60. D

Score Analysis Form for Practice Test II

Directions: Count the number of answers you have correct in Practice Test II, using the answer key on pages 427–428. Then use the chart on page 49 to figure out your converted score range. Fill in the rest of this form so you can compare it to your scores in Practice Test I.

	RAW SCORE		CONVERTED SCORE RANGE		APPROXIMATE SCORE RANGE
		(each)		(each)	
Listening Comprehension	____	____–____ × 10 =	____–____	÷ 3 =	____–____
Structure and Written Expression	____	____–____ × 10 =	____–____	÷ 3 =	____–____
Vocabulary and Reading Comprehension	____	____–____ × 10 =	____–____	÷ 3 =	____–____
TOTAL APPROXIMATE SCORE (add 3 approximate scores)					____–____

What is your best section out of the above three? ____________________

ANALYSIS OF EACH SECTION

1. Listening Comprehension

	Number Correct	Total	Percent Correct
Part A (Questions 1–20)	______	÷ 20	= ______%
Part B (Questions 21–35)	______	÷ 15	= ______%
Part C (Questions 36–50)	______	÷ 15	= ______%

Which part has the highest percentage of correct answers? __________

2. *Structure and Written Expression*

	Number Correct	Total	Percent Correct
Sentence Completion (Questions 1–15)	_______	÷ 15	= _______%
Error Identification (Questions 16–40)	_______	÷ 25	= _______%

Which section has the highest percentage of correct answers? _______

3. *Vocabulary and Reading Comprehension*

	Number Correct	Total	Percent Correct
Vocabulary (Questions 1–30)	_______	÷ 30	= _______%
Reading (Questions 31–60)	_______	÷ 30	= _______%

Which part has the highest percentage of correct answers? _______

Explanatory Answers

SECTION 1: LISTENING COMPREHENSION

The Listening Comprehension Tapescript for this test is on pages 637 to 641.

Part A

1. I'd rather go early than late.
(A) I want to go early.
(B) I like to be late.
(C) I hope you won't be early.
(D) I prefer to be late.

(A) Glance at the choices and summarize: I, early or late.
Testing point: restatement/modal. "I'd rather go early . . ." means "I want to go early."

2. If you go to the party, I'll go, too.
(A) I want to go less than you.
(B) I'll go if you can't go.
(C) I won't go even if you go.
(D) I'll go if you go.

(D) Glance at the choices and summarize: I, you, go.
Testing point: restatement/conditional. "If you go . . ., I'll go, too" means "I'll go if you go."

3. It looks like rain.
(A) It's raining.
(B) It's likely to rain.
(C) It looks wet.
(D) It likes rain.

(B) Glance at the choices and summarize: it, rain.
Testing point: restatement. "It looks like rain" means "It's likely to rain."

4. I ran into my old friend in town yesterday.
(A) I had an argument with my old friend yesterday.
(B) I passed my friend in town.
(C) I met my friend in town by accident.
(D) My friend and I had an accident yesterday.

(C) Glance at the choices and summarize: I, friend, accident. Testing point: restatement/idiom. "Run into somebody" means "meet somebody by accident."

5. Unlike her brother, Ann is open-minded.
(A) Ann is very intelligent.
(B) Ann doesn't like her brother.
(C) Ann is willing to listen to new ideas.
(D) Ann is like her brother.

(C) Glance at the choices and summarize: Ann, brother.
Testing point: restatement/vocabulary. "Open-minded" means "willing to listen to new ideas."

6. Come in a minute so I can give you a run-down on the class.
(A) I'd like to go running with you after class.
(B) Please run down to the class for me.
(C) Let's meet after class.
(D) Let me tell you about the class.

(D) Glance at the choices and summarize: you, class.
Testing point: restatement/idiom. "A run-down on the class" means "a brief talk about the class"

7. Not once has she missed a class this semester!
(A) She missed one class this semester.
(B) She hasn't missed any classes this semester.
(C) She's missed only a few classes this semester.
(D) She's missed many classes this semester.

(B) Glance at the choices and summarize: she, missed, class, semester.
Testing point: restatement/negative. "Not once" means "not any." Notice the inverted word order after "Not once."

8. The telephone is disconnected; Bill must have forgotten to pay the bill.
(A) Bill forgot to pay the bill, and the phone is not working.
(B) Bill paid the bill on time, but the phone is still not working.
(C) Bill forgot the phone was not working when he paid the bill.
(D) Bill forgot to connect the phone before he paid the bill.

(A) Glance at the choices and summarize: bill, phone, pay.
Testing point: restatement/vocabulary. "The telephone is *disconnected*" means the telephone is out of service, and implies "the telephone is not working."

9. Whatever she knows, she's not telling anyone.
(A) She's keeping a secret.
(B) She doesn't want to tell anyone about the accident to her nose.
(C) She doesn't know anything.
(D) She doesn't like to talk about her ideas.

(A) Glance at the choices and summarize: she, tell or talk.
Testing point: inference. "She is not telling . . ." implies "she is keeping a secret."

10. It takes a long time, but in the long run, it's well worth it.
(A) It takes a long time to run.
(B) It's worth it to run a long time in training.
(C) Your work will be worth the time eventually.
(D) An old well gets worse in time.

(C) Glance at the choices and summarize: time, worse or worth.
Testing point 1: restatement. In the first part of the sentence "It takes long time," "it" refers to "your work." In the second part of the sentence, "it's well worth it," the last "it" refers to the time that the work has taken.
Testing point 2: idiom. "In the long run" means "eventually."

11. This book is out-of-date.
(A) The information is old.
(B) The book is sold out.
(C) The quality is poor.
(D) There is no date on the book.

(A) Glance at the choices and summarize: book, old or sold.
Testing point: restatement/idiom. "Out-of-date" means "old." Its opposite is "up-to-date."

12. Having a car is by no means cheap.
(A) It seems cheap to buy a car.
(B) Cheap cars do not run well.
(C) It's convenient to have a car.
(D) It's expensive to have a car.

(D) Glance at the choices and summarize: car, cheap or expensive.
Testing point 1: idiom. "By no means" means "not at all." Testing point 2: inference. "By no means cheap" implies "expensive."

13. Although he's eighteen, he doesn't act very grown-up.
(A) He isn't growing anymore.
(B) He seems younger than eighteen.
(C) He is short for his age.
(D) He is almost eighteen.

(B) Glance at the choices and summarize: he, age.
Testing point 1: concession. "Although . . ., he doesn't . . ."
Testing point 2: vocabulary. "Grown-up" means "adult." A person above eighteen years old is considered to be grown-up.
Testing point 3: inference. "He doesn't act very grown-up" implies "he seems younger than eighteen."

14. Randy prefers pizza to tacos.
(A) Randy likes pizza better than tacos.
(B) Randy doesn't like tacos.
(C) Randy would like a piece of pizza.
(D) Randy likes to talk about pizza.

(A) Glance at the choices and summarize: Randy, likes, taco pizza, comparative.
Testing point: restatement/vocabulary. "Somebody *prefers* something *to* something" means "somebody thinks something is better than something."

15. Jim used to smoke a lot more.
(A) Jim is used to smoking.
(B) Jim likes to smoke when it's hot.
(C) Jim does not smoke anymore.
(D) Jim smoked more before.

(D) Glance at the choices and summarize: Jim, smoke.
Testing point: restatement/structure. "*Used to* smoke" means "smoked in the past" or "smoked before."

16. Exercise is a good remedy for depression.
(A) Exercising can reduce depression.
(B) Exercise can cause depression.
(C) Depression helps you exercise better.
(D) Depression can remind you to exercise.

(A) Glance at the choices and summarize: exercise, depression.
Testing point 1: restatement/vocabulary. A "remedy" is a cure or a way to make something better.
Testing point 2: inference. Reducing depression is good, so something that reduces depression can be called a remedy.

17. They are the same books except for their covers.
(A) They are different books, but they look alike.
(B) The covers are different.
(C) They cover different material.
(D) Some of the books have soft covers.

(B) Glance at the choices and summarize: covers, different or alike.
Testing point: inference. ". . . are the same . . . except for their covers" implies "the covers are different."

18. Mary had the salesman wrap the present.
(A) Mary asked the salesman to be present.
(B) Mary presented the wrapping.
(C) The salesman dropped the present.
(D) The salesman put paper around the present.

(D) Glance at the choices and summarize: Mary, salesman, present.
Testing point 1: restatement/structure. "To have somebody do something" means "to ask somebody to do something."
Testing point 2: vocabulary. "Wrap" means "put paper around something."

19. Never have I been so angry!
(A) I am really hungry!
(B) I have never been hungry!
(C) I am very angry!
(D) I'm never angry!

(C) Glance at the choices and summarize: I, hungry or angry.
Testing point 1: restatement/negative/inverted word order. "Never have I been so angry" means "I have never been so angry before."
Testing point 2: "I have never been so angry before" implies "I am very angry."

20. Jenny is smaller than her younger sister, Jane.
(A) Jenny is younger than Jane.
(B) Jane is smaller than Jenny.
(C) Jane is older than Jenny.
(D) Jane is bigger than Jenny.

(D) Glance at the choices and summarize: Jenny, Jane, comparative.
Testing point: inference. "Jenny is smaller than . . . Jane" implies "Jane is bigger than Jenny." Don't be confused by the words "younger sister." Younger can be bigger.

Part B

21. Man: Do you want to take a break now?
Woman: Yes! I'm starving!
What does the woman mean?
(A) She's hungry.
(B) She's tired.
(C) She's bored.
(D) She's thirsty.

(A) Glance at the choices and summarize: she is what?
Testing point: restatement/vocabulary. The word "starving" means "very hungry."

22. Woman: How's your class going?
Man: Terrible. It seems like the more the professor talks, the less I understand.
How does the man feel about the class?
(A) He wishes the professor would talk more.
(B) He doesn't always understand the professor.
(C) He thinks the professor has an accent.
(D) He thinks the professor talks too quietly.

(B) Glance at the choices and summarize: he, professor, talk.
Testing point 1: comparative. "The more . . ., the less . . ."
Testing point 2: inference. ". . . the less I understand" implies that he doesn't always understand.

23. Man: Shall we eat lunch out today?
Woman: Only if we split the bill.
What does the woman want to do?
(A) She wants to pay the bill.
(B) She wants Bill to pay for the meal.
(C) She wants to pay for her meal.
(D) She wants the man to pay.

(C) Glance at the choices and summarize: she, pays, bill.
Testing point 1: idiom. "Split the bill" means "everybody pays for his or her own meal."
Testing point 2: inference. "Only if" implies that she would like to eat lunch with the man if everybody pays his or her own bill, but she doesn't want him to pay for her meal.

24. Man: How's everything?
Woman: Fine, except for my sore throat.
What does the woman imply?
(A) Her drink tastes sour.
(B) Her throat hurts.
(C) She hasn't sold anything.
(D) She is very busy.

(B) Glance at the choices and summarize: she, what?
Testing point: vocabulary. "Sore throat" means "throat hurts."

25. Man: Hi, Mary. How're you doing?
Woman: Oh, it's been a long day!
What does the woman mean?
(A) She has had a nice day.
(B) She is sick.
(C) The daylight hours are long.
(D) She is tired.

(D) Glance at the choices and summarize: she, sick, tired, day.
Testing point: idiom. "It's been a long day" means "I am tired."

26. Woman: Jack, would you please check my mailbox while I'm gone?
Man: Sure, no problem.
What does the man mean?
(A) He will mail a check for her.
(B) He will pick up her mail.
(C) He will put a check in his mailbox.
(D) He will take a check from her mailbox.

(B) Glance at the choices and summarize: mail, check.
Testing point: vocabulary. "Check my mail" means "look in my mailbox and pick up my mail for me." The phrase "no problem" is a casual way of saying "of course I will."

27. Man: If you don't like it, you don't have to take it.
Woman: Thanks, but I like it.
What will the woman probably do?
(A) She will take it because she likes it.
(B) She will take it even though she doesn't like it.
(C) She won't take it because she doesn't like it.
(D) She won't take it even though she likes it.

(A) Glance at the choices and summarize: she, will or won't, take it, like it.
Testing point 1: contradiction. "But" indicates the woman doesn't agree with the man.
Testing point 2: inference. "But I like it" implies "she'll take it because she likes it."

28. Man: Would you like to have a piece of cake?
Woman: No, thanks. I'm on a diet.
What does the woman mean?
(A) She does not like cake.
(B) She is going to dive.
(C) She is afraid to diet.
(D) She wants to lose weight.

(D) Glance at the choices and summarize: she, dive, diet.
Testing point: inference. "On a diet" implies "she is restricting her food because she wants to lose weight."

29. Woman: What kind of dressing would you like?
Man: Italian, please.
Where does this conversation probably take place?
(A) In a dressing room
(B) In a bedroom
(C) In a department store
(D) In a restaurant

(D) Glance at the choices and summarize: location.
Testing point: inference/vocabulary. "Dressing" and "Italian" are related to "restaurant." The word "dressing" refers to a sauce, usually oil and vinegar, for a salad. The word "Italian" here refers to one type of salad dressing.

30. Woman: The deadline for computer registration is tomorrow.
Man: But I haven't decided which course to take yet.
What are the man and woman talking about?
(A) Buying a computer
(B) Getting directions
(C) Buying books
(D) Registering for classes

(D) Glance at the choices and summarize: doing something.
Testing point: inference. "Computer registration" means "registering for classes by computer." The words "deciding on a course" also refer to class registration.

31. Woman: Will you accept a collect call from Lisa?
Man: Yes, I will.
What does the man mean?
(A) He will pay for a call from Lisa.
(B) He will make a call to Lisa.
(C) He is collecting money for Lisa.
(D) He is correcting a call from Lisa.

(A) Glance at the choices and summarize: he, call, Lisa.
Testing point 1: vocabulary. "Collect call" means that the fee for a long distance call will be paid by the receiver, rather than the person who is making the call.
Testing point 2: inference. "Yes, I will" implies that the man will accept the collect call, therefore, he will pay for the call from Lisa.

32. Man: Hello. I'm interested in the rates for Triple S insurance.
Woman: All right. Have you had any tickets or accidents in the last three years?
What do we learn from this conversation?
(A) It is expensive to buy life insurance.
(B) Everyone should have health insurance.
(C) The man wants to buy car insurance.
(D) The man had an accident.

(C) Glance at the choices and summarize: insurance.
Testing point: inference. The man says, ""I am interested in the rates . . ." The word "rates" means "cost." We can infer that he wants to buy insurance.

33. Man: Dr. Smith, could you let me audit your class?
Woman: Let me see, I'll have to check the class enrollment list first.
What does the woman mean?
(A) She thinks it will be fine.
(B) She says it is impossible.
(C) She has to ask for permission.
(D) She doesn't know yet.

(D) Glance at the choices and summarize: what does she think?
Testing point: vocabulary. "Let me see" means that she hasn't decided yet. She needs more information before she can make a decision.

34. Man: You're wearing your glasses again!
Woman: I couldn't find my contact lenses.
What does the woman mean?
(A) She misplaced her contact lenses.
(B) She finds her old glasses better.
(C) She couldn't contact her optometrist.
(D) Her contact lenses are better.

(A) Glance at the choices and summarize: she, contact lenses.
Testing point: inference. "Couldn't find" implies "misplaced." The man's voice shows surprise, indicating that it is unusual to see the woman wearing glasses.

35. Woman: I don't think the job has to be done perfectly.
Man: Maybe not, but it's important that you do your best.
What does the man mean?
(A) One should write down anything important.
(B) Nobody can be the best.
(C) Do as well as you can.
(D) It's difficult to write correctly.

(C) Glance at the choices and summarize: write, best, well.
Testing point: restatement. "Do your best" is the same as "do as well as you can."

Part C

36. Where does this conversation probably take place?
(A) In a doctor's office
(B) In an exercise class
(C) In a dentist's office
(D) In a biology class

(B) This is an inference question. The first clue is that the woman begins by saying, "In this class . . ." From this statement, you can eliminate answer choices (A) and (C). The most likely choice is "exercise class," since the woman says she will demonstrate a type of exercise that might be different from other ways the students have been taught to exercise.

37. What does this woman mainly want to explain?
(A) How to stretch
(B) How to change ideas
(C) How to pull a tooth
(D) How to exhale

(A) This is a restatement question. The woman says, "What I want you to do is stretch your body . . ."

38. According to the man, what is painful?
(A) Gaining new concepts
(B) Releasing stress
(C) Stretching
(D) Pulling teeth

(C) This is a restatement question. The man says, "it always hurts to stretch."

39. With which statement would both speakers probably agree?
(A) It is difficult to learn something new.
(B) It always hurts to exercise.
(C) It hurts more to have a tooth pulled than it does to exercise.
(D) If you don't feel the pain of stretching, you need to stretch more.

(A) This is an inference question. The woman says, "It can be painful to gain a new concept." The man's ideas can be inferred by his comments to the woman about "no pain, no gain." This question can also be answered by elimination. Answer (B) is incorrect, because only the man says it always hurts to exercise. Answer (C) is incorrect, because neither speaker says that tooth pulling hurts more than exercise. Answer (D) is incorrect, because only the man says that you should feel pain while stretching.

40. What will happen next?
(A) The woman will pull a tooth.
(B) Everyone will go home.
(C) The woman will demonstrate a new way to exercise.
(D) The woman will discuss difficulties of learning.

(C) This is an inference question. At the end of the talk the woman says, "Now let's just try this new way of doing stretching exercises. Ready, everybody? Let's begin."

41. Who is the main speaker?
(A) Ana
(B) Ana's friend
(C) A clerk at the social security office
(D) A person from Spain

(B) This is an inference question. The speaker says, "She [Ana] is the woman I met at school last week." You can also answer this question by elimination. The answer cannot be (A), because the speaker is talking about Ana. The answer cannot be (C), because the speaker is also talking about a clerk. The answer cannot be (D), because there is no mention of anyone being from Spain.

42. Why was Ana embarrassed?
(A) Because she couldn't speak Spanish.
(B) Because her friend wasn't there to help her.
(C) Because she couldn't write very well.
(D) Because she didn't realize it wasn't English.

(D) This is an inference question. The clerk says to Ana, "I'm sorry I gave you the wrong form. This one is in Spanish." Ana then says that she couldn't believe she hadn't realized that and that she was embarrassed.

43. Why couldn't she first fill out the form?
(A) It was in Spanish.
(B) She couldn't read enough English.
(C) She hadn't been in the country long enough.
(D) She was too embarrassed.

(A) This is an inference question. The clerk says, "This form is in Spanish." We can infer that Ana is not able to read Spanish.

44. Why did the clerk say he was sorry?
(A) Because he couldn't help Ana.
(B) Because it was so difficult to understand the form.
(C) Because Ana's friend was not there.
(D) Because he gave her the wrong form.

(D) This is a restatement. The clerk says, "I'm sorry. I gave you the wrong form."

45. How does the speaker seem to feel about Ana?
(A) Jealous
(B) Angry
(C) Pleased
(D) Concerned

(D) This is an inference question. The speaker shows her concern when she says, "Poor Ana." There is nothing to indicate that she might be angry with Ana or jealous of Ana. She may be pleased with Ana, but this conversation doesn't demonstrate that clearly.

46. Who is the most likely speaker?
(A) A doctor
(B) A mechanic
(C) A professor
(D) A chemist

(C) This is an inference question. The speaker's first and last sentence indicate that this talk is a professor's lecture. He begins with, "Today I'd like to begin a discussion . . ." and he ends with, "we'll go into that new study more next time." Even though anyone could be saying these words, the professor is the most likely choice.

47. What is the speaker's main topic?
(A) Ultraviolet light
(B) The use of spray cans
(C) Air-conditioning systems
(D) Fluorocarbons and the ozone layer

(D) This is a restatement question. The speaker begins by saying, "First we'll touch on the relationship between fluorocarbons and the ozone layer."

48. What is the most important purpose of the ozone layer?
(A) Providing fluorocarbons
(B) Shielding the sun
(C) Protecting the earth
(D) Destroying chemicals

(C) This is a restatement question. The speaker says, ". . . the ozone layer is the protective shield around the earth. It is important to all life . . ."

49. What is the ozone layer made of?
(A) Fluorocarbons
(B) Oxygen
(C) Shields
(D) Ultraviolet light

(B) This is a restatement question. The speaker says, "Ozone itself, a form of oxygen, . . ."

50. What will the speaker probably discuss next?
(A) How to Make Air Conditioners with Fluorocarbons
(B) Harmful Effects of Ultraviolet Light
(C) The Makeup of the Ozone Layer
(D) The Sun as a Cause of Ozone Layer Depletion

(D) This is a following-possible-topic question. The speaker ends by saying, "There are, however, new studies linking the sun itself to the depletion of the ozone layer. We'll go into that new study more next time."

SECTION 2: STRUCTURE AND WRITTEN EXPRESSION

1. The population of cities in the Eastern and Northern areas of the United States is declining, while ________ Southern cities is growing.
(A) that in
(B) that of
(C) those of
(D) those in

(B) Testing point: pronoun agreement. The pronoun "*that*" refers to "the population." The sentence should be "The population of cities . . . is . . ., while *that of* Southern cities is . . ."

2. Some people find it surprising ________ his career as an actor in California.
(A) when Ronald Reagan began
(B) Ronald Reagan began
(C) that Ronald Reagan began
(D) to know Ronald Reagan

(C) Testing point: noun clause. The sentence needs a "that" clause with a subject + verb. The sentence should read like this: "Some people find it surprising *that subject + verb* . . ."

3. The travels of Marco Polo in the twelfth century would not have been so well known ________ for the book he wrote while in jail.
(A) it not have been
(B) is not been
(C) had it not been
(D) has not been

(C) Testing point: inverted verb order. "Had it not been" is the same as "if it had not been."

4. The Caspian Sea, a salt lake, is ________ any other lake in the world.
(A) largest
(B) the largest
(C) larger than
(D) the larger than

(C) Testing point: comparative. The words "any other lake" are a clue for a comparative structure.

5. At 3,810 meters above sea level in Bolivia stands Lake Titicaca, ________ in the world.
(A) the highest large lake
(B) highest large lake
(C) high largest lake
(D) the high largest lake

(A) Testing point: superlative. A superlative form needs the "est" word after "the." The sentence should be ". . . in Bolivia stands . . ., the highest large lake in the world."

6. ________ in an electric typewriter is the ability to correct spelling errors.
(A) There are many new features
(B) New features
(C) The new features
(D) One of the new features

(D) Testing point: subject/noun phrase. The verb "is" indicates the noun must be singular. Answers (A), (B), and (C) all have plural subjects. The sentence should read like this: "One of the new features in . . . is . . ."

7. Ballet dancers, ________ actors, must spend many hours a day practicing before a performance.
(A) like
(B) the like
(C) the same
(D) same as

(A) Testing point: like/unlike. The word "like" acts like a preposition. You could also say "dancers, unlike actors, ..." The words "like" or "unlike" come before a noun.

8. It is a sign ________ fall when the leaves on the trees begin to change color.
(A) for
(B) at
(C) to
(D) of

(D) Testing point: preposition. The phrase "of fall" means "of the fall season."

9. Bees have compound eyes ________ almost 6,000 tiny lenses.
(A) made of
(B) made in
(C) made on
(D) made up

(A) Testing point: preposition. "Made of" = "consisting of."

10. ________ the reactions of people with amnesia, scientists are learning more about the process of memory in the brain.
(A) By studying
(B) To study
(C) They study
(D) They're studying

(A) Testing point: adverb phrase. "Scientists are learning . . ." is the main sentence. The sentence needs an adverb phrase to describe *how* the scientists are learning. The sentence should be "By studying . . ., scientists are learning . . ."

11. The White House is where the president lives, and the Capitol Building is where ________.
(A) laws made
(B) the laws are making
(C) the laws are made
(D) are making the laws

(C) Testing point: passive voice. "The laws" are not the actor here, and must "be made" by someone. The second half of the sentence should read like this: "the Capitol . . . is where the laws are made."

12. High levels of hazardous waste ________ in soil near many nuclear defense facilities.
(A) have been measured
(B) has been measured
(C) is measuring
(D) are measuring

(A) Testing point: verb. The noun "High levels . . ." is plural, so the verb must start with "have" instead of "has." The subject "High levels of . . ." is not an actor, and must use the passive voice. The sentence should be "High levels of . . . have been measured in . . ."

13. Bigamy is a situation in which a man ________ two women at the same time.
(A) marries to
(B) is marry to
(C) married
(D) is married to

(D) Testing point: passive voice. The phrase "is married" is in the passive voice. Answer (A) would be correct as an active voice verb if it didn't have the word "to." The sentence should read: ". . . is a situation in which a man is married to two . . ."

14. ________ the rainfall was adequate this year, the apricot trees still did not produce a high yield.
(A) Since
(B) However
(C) Although
(D) Due to

(C) Testing point: adverb clause. ________ adequate . . ., . . . still did not . . ." indicates the sentence needs a word that shows contrast to begin the adverb clause. The word "although" is the only one to indicate a contrast correctly. The sentence should read: "Although . . . was adequate . . ., . . . still did not . . ."

15. Ludwig van Beethoven is considered one of the greatest composers ________.
(A) who ever lived
(B) he lived
(C) when living
(D) while he lived

(A) Testing point: noun clause. The sentence needs a clause to describe "composer." Answers (C) and (D) would be correct as adjective clauses if the main verb of the sentence were "was considered" instead of "is considered."

16. The research works of paleontologists comes
A B

to life with paintings and sculptures of dino-
C D

saurs.

(B) Testing point: singular/plural noun. "Work" is a mass noun that describes employment or physical or mental jobs. It does not take an "s" as a plural.

17. According to a *Newsweek* magazine poll
A

taken in 1986, 77 percent of Americans want
B

the U.S. and the Soviet Union to sign an arms
C

agreement limits nuclear weapons.
D

(D) Testing point: word form. The word "limits" should be "limiting," because it begins an adjective phrase that describes the arms agreement. The main verb of the sentence is "want."

18. In 1963, the Beatles, with their haircuts,
A

clothes, and joking, drew crowds of shrieking
B C D

teenagers.

(B) Testing point: parallel construction. "Haircuts," "clothes," and "joking" must all be parallel. The words "haircuts" and "clothes" describe objects, and the word "joking" describes a process. It should be changed to a parallel form: "jokes."

19. Conditions that are necessary for a successful
A B

business includes consumer demand and ade-
C D

quate supply.

(C) Testing point: verb agreement. The subject "conditions" is plural, so the main verb "include" must be plural. "Conditions" must be a plural noun, because there is no line under "are."

20. On New Year's Day, most Americans watch
A

football on TV, visiting friends, and relax
B C

around the house.
D

(C) Testing point: parallel construction. "Watch" and "relax" are verbs; "visiting" must be a verb form: "visit."

21. Scientists have been studying (A) the effects of (B) aspirin on lower (C) the instances of (D) heart attacks in people.

(C) Testing point: word form. After the preposition "on," you must use the gerund "lowering" to form an adverb phrase.

22. The more (A) you pull (B) on a square knot, the tightest (C) it gets (D).

(C) Testing point: comparative. "the more . . ., the tighter." Use a comparative form after both of the words "the."

23. The koto, a Japanese string instrument, consists in (A) a (B) long wooden (C) body and seven to thirteen strings (D).

(A) Testing point: preposition. The preposition "of" should follow "consist."

24. Much of (A) the beautifully (B) spring color in the mountain meadows comes (C) from (D) the flower of the wild lupine plant.

(B) Testing point: word form. Use an adjective, not an adverb, to modify the noun phrase "spring color." "Beautiful" is correct.

25. The earliest (A) suspension bridges in the United States were (B) built by (C) American building (D) James Finley.

(D) Testing point: word form. The words "by" and "James Finley" indicate that (D) needs a word that refers to a person. Use "builder," not "building."

26. Caterpillars have three pairs of (A) legs, two row (B) of eyes (C), and strong (D) jaws.

(B) Testing point: plural noun. "Two" is plural, so you must use "rows" instead of "row."

27. Cro-Magnon man, a human being who (A) lived about 35,000 years ago, was (B) about six feet tall, stood (C) straight, and with (D) a large brain and a high forehead.

(D) Testing point: parallel construction. ". . . was . . ., stood . . ., and ________ . . ." indicates (D) needs the past tense verb "had."

28. The boll weevil, a cotton-eating (A) insect, was a major reason (B) for the change from a one-crop economy (C) to diversified agricultural (D) in the U.S.

(D) Testing point: word form. "From . . . economy to . . . ________" indicates that (D) needs a noun instead of adjective. "Agriculture" is correct.

29. Scientists predict that there would be (A) an earthquake of great magnitude (B) in California within (C) the next (D) few years.

(A) Testing point: verb tense. ". . . predict that there ________ . . . within the next few years." The structure indicates (A) needs the future tense verb "will be."

30. The number of wild condors, an endangered species of (A) bird, have been (B) increasing steadily (C) this year because of (D) the work of scientists and environmentalists.

(B) Testing point: verb agreement. The subject is "the number," which is singular, so the verb (B) must use the singular form "has been . . ."

31. Since (A) the last explore (B) voyage into space, we have increased (C) our knowledge about (D) the planet Jupiter.

(B) Testing point: word form. You can use "explorer's voyage," "exploration voyage," or "explorative voyage," but not "explore."

32. Mahogany wood, what (A) is used for making (B) furniture, is resistant to (C) termites, and is (D) a beautiful color.

(A) Testing point: adjective clause. The word "which" must begin this nonrestrictive clause. Adjective clauses never begin with "what."

33. Muscular dystrophy is a disease of the (A) muscles, which commonly (B) afflicting (C) boys more than (D) girls.

(C) Testing point: verb tense. ". . . is a disease of . . ., which . . . __________ . . ." (C) needs the present tense verb "afflicts . . ."

34. Yellowstone National Park is well known for its beautiful (A) canyon, (B) its amazed (C) geysers, and its wild life. (D)

(C) Testing point: word form. "Amazing" is the correct word. It describes one's feelings about the geysers. The word "amazed" would describe feelings that the geysers would have about themselves (impossible).

35. Have (A) red leaves in the (B) fall, the poison oak plant is (C) easy (D) to see.

(A) Testing point: word form. This sentence begins with an adjective phrase. A gerund, "having," is correct here.

36. A (A) planetarium, with his (B) domed ceiling and many projectors, is capable of (C) showing the position of (D) the stars in any season.

(B) Testing point: pronoun. From the context, you know a planetarium is not a person; therefore, the corresponding pronoun cannot be "his." The correct word is "its."

37. Both (A) scientists and treasure seekers (B) are interesting in (C) uncovering (D) the mysteries of the sunken ship, the *Titanic*.

(C) Testing point: word form. The correct form is "interested." You can say, "People are interested in the *Titanic*," or "The *Titanic* is interesting."

38. Harvard University, that is (A) the oldest (B) American college, was (C) founded (D) in 1636.

(A) Testing point: adjective clause. A nonrestrictive clause cannot begin with "that." The correct word is "which."

39. Franz Schubert, the famous Austrian composer, was (A) first taught to play (B) the (C) violin and piano from (D) his father.

(D) Testing point: preposition. The correct answer is ". . . was taught . . . by his father." The preposition "by" follows "taught."

40. A few of (A) the works in art (B) of the French painter Cezanne are part of (C) the permanent collection of (D) the Museum of Modern Art in New York City.

(B) Testing point: prepositional phrase. The correct answer is "the works of art."

SECTION 3: VOCABULARY AND READING COMPREHENSION

1. Vincent Van Gogh is renowned for his post-impressionist paintings.
(A) regarded
(B) applauded
(C) accomplished
(D) famous

(D) The closest meaning for "renowned" is "famous." The other words are very close in meaning, however. "Regarded" means "respected"; "Applauded" means "praised"; and "accomplished" means "successful."

2. Extreme sunburn can cause small blisters on the skin.
(A) spots
(B) swellings
(C) wounds
(D) bites

(B) Blisters are raised bumps on the skin that contain fluid.

3. Natural occurrences such as hurricanes, earthquakes, and tornadoes can have catastrophic effects on people.
(A) disastrous
(B) killing
(C) categorical
(D) unimaginable

(A) "Catastrophic" and "disastrous" both mean "terrible."

4. Jane Goodall has written a new, comprehensive book on her study of the chimpanzees in Africa.
(A) complete
(B) factual
(C) festive
(D) illustrated

(A) "Comprehensive" also means "including a lot."

5. The earthworm is a segmented worm found in almost all parts of the world.
(A) plated
(B) round
(C) long
(D) sectional

(D) "Segmented" and "sectional" both mean that something is composed of separate pieces.

6. Ammonia is a chemical with a penetrating odor.
(A) smell
(B) flavor
(C) sting
(D) burn

(A) The word "odor" means "smell," but it commonly refers to an unpleasant smell.

7. After the American Civil War, the Southern armies were granted amnesty.
(A) punished
(B) frightened
(C) pardoned
(D) separated

(C) "Amnesty" and "pardon" both mean that the person does not receive punishment for breaking the law. This act is most commonly used for political offenses.

8. Amphibians like frogs and toads have moist skin.
(A) wet
(B) slimy
(C) sticky
(D) tough

(A) "Moist" means slightly wet, not dripping wet.

9. The Bay of Pigs invasion in 1961 resulted in severe criticism of President Kennedy by the American people.
(A) deep
(B) special
(C) tight
(D) harsh

(D) "Severe" and "harsh" also mean "stern" or "serious."

10. Coral is made by a small, sedentary animal that lives in the ocean.
(A) secluded
(B) hard-working
(C) immobile
(D) lively

(C) "Sedentary" usually means that someone or something is sitting. In this case it means that this animal cannot move.

11. Charles Darwin formulated his famous theory of evolution during his five-year cruise on the *Beagle*.
(A) expanded
(B) developed
(C) critiqued
(D) finished

(B) To "formulate" means to express something as a theory in a systematic way. The word "develop" refers to the same process.

12. By the end of the Crimean War, the name of Florence Nightingale was legendary.
(A) imaginary
(B) novel
(C) gratifying
(D) famous

(D) "Legendary" means being remembered as a legend or story that is told to many people. In order to be legendary, a person would first have to be famous.

13. A devastating earthquake in North America occurred in Alaska in 1964.
(A) damaging
(B) divisive
(C) crushing
(D) shocking

(A) "Devastating" means "causing much damage or destruction."

14. In many coastal areas of the U.S. there is a deficiency of sand, causing an erosion problem.
(A) quality
(B) propagation
(C) movement
(D) lack

(D) A "deficiency" means that there is not enough of something. A "lack of" means the same thing.

15. The increase in world population was negligible until around 1900.
(A) unimportant
(B) needless
(C) average
(D) misleading

(A) The word "negligible" means such a small amount of something that it isn't worth considering.

16. A credit card allows the user to receive credit at the time of a purchase.
(A) donate
(B) arbitrate
(C) reject
(D) obtain

(D) "Receive" and "obtain" both mean "to get."

17. Credit card holders can postpone payment on their purchases by accepting a monthly interest charge.
(A) provide
(B) decrease
(C) mail
(D) defer

(D) "Postpone" and "defer" both mean to put off or delay something until a later time.

18. William Faulkner, a brilliant American novelist, was awarded the 1949 Nobel Prize in literature.
(A) intelligent
(B) starry
(C) captive
(D) well-known

(A) In this sentence, "brilliant" means very intelligent or very talented. "Brilliant" commonly refers to anything that is very bright or sparkling.

19. When frost appears on a window, it often has a delicate and curious pattern.
(A) special
(B) strange
(C) fine
(D) cute

(B) Usually "curious" refers to someone who is very interested in learning or knowing something. In this sentence, however, it has the meaning of "strange, unusual, or rare." All these words refer to the fact that frost always has a unique pattern. It is never the same.

20. The American Dental Association cautions people not to neglect their teeth during their growing years.
(A) abuse
(B) damage
(C) disrupt
(D) disregard

(D) Both "neglect" and "disregard" mean "not pay attention to" or "ignore."

21. When the earth turns, the moon appears to rise in the east and set in the west.
(A) refers
(B) seems
(C) is likely
(D) is supposed

(B) Both "appear" and "seem" mean that something gives the impression of being true, whether it is true or not.

22. One goal of a physical fitness program is to maximize a person's strength and endurance.
(A) split
(B) distinguish
(C) increase
(D) combine

(C) To "maximize" is to make something the most it can be; to increase it to its maximum or to the highest degree.

23. Among the dangers of drilling for oil in the ocean is the problem of potential leaks.
(A) serious
(B) dangerous
(C) influential
(D) possible

(D) The word "potential" means the future possibility of something happening. It refers to an unrealized or undeveloped event, not an actual event.

24. Kangaroos give birth to babies that develop within their mother's pouches.
(A) abdominal sacks
(B) tender care
(C) range of hearing
(D) concealed nests

(A) A pouch is any kind of small bag or sack. Kangaroos have pouches on their abdomens.

25. Unicorns, dragons, and centaurs are all imaginary animals.
(A) magic
(B) unimportant
(C) pictorial
(D) unreal

(D) "Imaginary" means that something exists in the mind only; it is not real.

26. The Milky Way consists of about a hundred billion stars.
(A) is conscious of
(B) surrounds
(C) is composed of
(D) makes

(C) "Consists of" and "is composed of" both mean "is made up of" or "is formed of."

27. Blizzards in the high mountains can be dangerous for hikers and skiers.
(A) Snow storms
(B) High winds
(C) Avalanches
(D) Slippery ice

(A) A blizzard is a very heavy or severe snow storm.

28. To make raisins, the ripened grapes are usually picked by hand, placed on trays, and set in the sun for several days.
(A) dried
(B) cleaned
(C) crushed
(D) mature

(D) If fruit is ripe, it is ready to eat, fully developed, or fully grown; mature.

29. Of all the Olympic ski events, ski jumping is the most spectacular.
(A) striking
(B) dangerous
(C) appealing
(D) difficult

(A) The word "spectacular" refers to something being very unusual, possibly daring. "Striking" refers to something making an impression. In this sentence, ski jumping is spectacular because it makes an impression on your mind.

30. The central states in the U.S. are noted for their production of wheat and corn.
(A) applauded for
(B) informed of
(C) known for
(D) described by

(C) "Noted" means "distinguished," "well-known," or "famous."

31. Which of the following would be the most appropriate title for this passage?
(A) The Geodesic Dome
(B) An American Architect
(C) American Architecture
(D) Revolutionary Designs

(B) This passage is a general discussion of Fuller, so (B) is the best answer. Answer (A) doesn't refer to Fuller. Answer (C) is too general; the passage only discusses one type of architectural style. Answer (D) is also not appropriate, since only one type of design is discussed.

32. Which statement best describes the dome?
(A) It uses a lot of material, but takes less energy to construct than traditional structures.
(B) It takes a lot of energy to build.
(C) It is very spacious.
(D) It takes less material and energy than traditional structures.

(D) This is an inference question. The passage states that the dome follows the principle of getting maximum output from a minimum amount of material and energy. You can also choose the answer by elimination. Answers (A) and (B) are incorrect, because the passage states that the dome uses a minimum input of material and energy. Answer (C) is incorrect, because the passage doesn't discuss the idea of being spacious (having a lot of space).

33. A geodesic dome is closest in shape to
(A) a tube
(B) the end of a box
(C) a half of a ball
(D) the tip of a triangle

(C) This is an inference question. The word "spherical" means "ball-shaped."

34. Fuller wrote about his life in his book
(A) *Ideas and Integrities*
(B) *Utopia or Oblivion*
(C) *Nine Chains to the Moon*
(D) *Earth, Inc.*

(A) This is a restatement question. The passage states that *Ideas and Integrities* is an autobiography.

35. Clouds are formed from
(A) water vapor
(B) evaporation
(C) the hydrologic cycle
(D) groundwater

(A) This is a restatement. The passage states that water turns into vapor which then forms clouds.

36. Water returns to the earth by
(A) infiltration
(B) pollution
(C) precipitation
(D) evaporation

(C) This is a restatement. The passage states that water returns to the earth "in the form of precipitation."

37. Groundwater
(A) depends on seasonal rain
(B) comes from toxic waste
(C) is .05 percent of all water
(D) collects under the earth

(D) This is a restatement question. The passage states that "some of it [water] seeps into the ground through infiltration and collects under the earth's surface as groundwater."

38. The amount of groundwater is
(A) about 95 percent of all water
(B) less than 5 percent of all water
(C) .05 percent of above-ground water
(D) 95 percent of above-ground water

(B) This is another restatement/computation question. The passage states that 95 percent of all water is in the oceans, and that of the 5 percent on land, only .05 percent is above ground. The rest is underground. "The rest," then is a little less than 5 percent.

39. The supply of groundwater is getting low because of
(A) conservation
(B) toxic waste
(C) pollution
(D) population increase

(D) This is a restatement question. The passage states that "as the population increases and the need for water also increases, the groundwater . . . is getting dangerously low."

40. The best title for this passage is
(A) Water Conservation
(B) The Hydrologic Cycle
(C) Underground Water
(D) Polluted Groundwater

(B) The hydrologic cycle is mentioned in both the first and last sentences. That is the best clue for a title and a main idea. Answer (A) is only one aspect of the hydrologic cycle. Answer (C) is too narrow; it is also only one part of the hydrologic cycle. Answer (D) is only mentioned as one problem in the passage.

41. The Library of Congress
(A) is headed for destruction
(B) is fighting a battle
(C) is causing paper deterioration
(D) was built in the nineteenth century

(B) This is a restatement question. The first sentence of the passages states that the library is fighting a battle against paper deterioration.

42. According to this passage, libraries are trying to stop
- **(A)** the tearing of books
- **(B)** the yellowing of pages
- **(C)** the problem of air pollution
- **(D)** the deterioration of paper

(D) This is a restatement question. The words "fighting a battle" in the first sentence mean the same as "trying to stop" paper deterioration.

43. Before the nineteenth century,
- **(A)** most books crumbled
- **(B)** the industry used wood pulp
- **(C)** paper had less acid
- **(D)** thousands of books were deacidified

(C) This is an inference question. The passage states that in the nineteenth century, the paper industry began using chemically treated wood pulp to make paper, and that the chemical in this paper is causing the problem today. The passage also states earlier that the paper in books made before the last century was made from cotton and linen rags which are naturally low in acid.

44. We can assume from this passage that
- **(A)** cotton and linen rags are not good for making paper
- **(B)** calfskin is low in acid
- **(C)** wood pulp is expensive
- **(D)** microfilming is an inexpensive way to preserve old books

(B) This is an inference question. The passage states that cotton and linen rags are good for paper-making because they are naturally low in acid. The passage then states that the Gutenberg Bible, which was made of calfskin, is in remarkably good shape. We can infer from this that acid causes deterioration; therefore, calfskin must be low in acid.

45. Some countries in the world are
- **(A)** using calfskin for book production.
- **(B)** producing books from cotton and linen rags
- **(C)** doing research into methods of mass preservation
- **(D)** building treatment facilities

(C) This is an inference question. The passage states that the problem is one of global concern and that France, Canada, and Austria are all doing research into new methods of deacidification. The passage then states that a new method of mass preservation has been developed. We don't know who has developed this method, but we know that some countries are doing research.

46. A new technique in deacidification
- **(A)** uses microfilm to save books
- **(B)** will save the Gutenberg Bible
- **(C)** uses chemically treated wood pulp
- **(D)** can treat thousands of books at a time

(D) This is a restatement question. The passage states that "a new technology . . . allows for mass deacidification of thousands of books at the same time."

47. The best title for this passage is
- **(A)** Paper Deterioration
- **(B)** The Gutenberg Bible
- **(C)** Microfilming vs. Deacidification
- **(D)** Types of Paper Used in Bookmaking

(A) This topic is mentioned in both the first and last sentences of the passage. Answers (B) and (C) are too narrow; they are only one aspect of the information given in the passage. Answer (D) is not discussed. The passage doesn't discuss very much about the types of paper used in bookmaking.

48. Impressionism began with a small group of artists who wanted to
- **(A)** use light colors
- **(B)** fight the government
- **(C)** become scientists
- **(D)** show their paintings

(D) This is a restatement question. The second sentence states that the painters wanted to exhibit their paintings.

49. The first impressionists
- **(A)** supported the academic standards
- **(B)** began a new academy
- **(C)** did not like the academic standards
- **(D)** developed new official standards

(C) This is a restatement question. The passage states that the first impressionists were reacting against the academic standards of their time.

50. The early impressionist artists painted
- **(A)** with imagination
- **(B)** different subject matter
- **(C)** landscapes
- **(D)** diverse personalities

(B) This is a restatement question. The passage states that their subject matter was as diverse as their personalities.

51. What subject matter did Monet and Sisley usually paint?
- **(A)** Country scenes
- **(B)** Portraits
- **(C)** Skyscrapers
- **(D)** Animals in nature

(A) This is a restatement question. The passage states that Monet and Sisley painted landscapes.

52. Which of the following typifies the early impressionists?
(A) They had a romantic emphasis.
(B) They tried to see nature unemotionally.
(C) They worked toward a unified goal.
(D) They idealized life.

(B) This is an inference question. The passages states that the early impressionists rejected the role of imagination in art. They observed nature closely and painted with a scientific interest in visual phenomena. A characteristic of the scientific approach is not to let emotions affect one's views.

53. Most people did not like impressionistic painting
(A) before 1920
(B) between 1920 and 1930
(C) between 1930 and 1950
(D) after 1950

(A) This is a restatement question. The passage states that the works of impressionists were received with hostility until the 1920s.

54. Which of the following is a tissue transplant?
(A) Liver
(B) Lung
(C) Bone
(D) Kidney

(C) This is a restatement question. The passage states that tissue transplants include the transplanting of skin, bones, and the cornea of the eye.

55. In 600 B.C. there were
(A) organ transplants
(B) skin transplants
(C) cornea replacements
(D) artificial hearts

(B) This is a restatement question. The passage states, "there is evidence that skin transplants were done as early as 600 B.C."

56. A cornea is located in the
(A) heart
(B) skin
(C) bone
(D) eye

(D) This is an inference question. The passage mentions the cornea of the eye. You can infer, then, that the cornea is in the eye.

57. The most common problem with organ transplants is
(A) rejection of the organ
(B) finding a donor
(C) finding a healthy organ
(D) replacing the organ

(A) This is an inference/referent question. The passage states that even if a healthy organ is found, the receiver's body may reject it. The next sentence says, "This is the major reason for problems with organ transplants." The word "this" stands for the previous sentence: rejection of the organ.

58. Successful heart transplants have been performed since
(A) 600 B.C.
(B) 1967
(C) 1982
(D) 600 A.D.

(B) This is a restatement/referent question. The passage states that the first heart transplant was performed in 1967, and that many successful transplants have been performed since then. The word "then" is a referent that refers to the year 1967.

59. The first heart transplant was
(A) received by Dr. Christiaan Barnard
(B) performed by Dr. Barney Clark
(C) performed in South Africa
(D) with an artificial heart

(C) This is a restatement question. The passage states that the first heart transplant was performed in South Africa.

60. The best title for this passage is
(A) The Treatment of Disease
(B) The First Heart Transplants
(C) Successful Organ Transplants
(D) Transplants: Past and Present

(D) The best title for this passage is (D), because this title covers all the main information mentioned in the passage. Answer (A) is too general. The passage doesn't discuss the treatment of disease in general. Answers (B) and (C) are mentioned in part of the passage only.

Practice Test III
(Long Form)

NOTE: You will need the tape to do Section 1. If you do not have the tape, the tapescript for Section 1 is on pages 641 to 647. The answer key is on pages 481–482, and explanatory answers begin on page 486. Use the answer sheet for Practice Test III on page 451 to mark your answers.

ANSWER SHEET FOR PRACTICE TEST III

SECTION 1

1. (A) (B) (C) (D)
2. (A) (B) (C) (D)
3. (A) (B) (C) (D)
4. (A) (B) (C) (D)
5. (A) (B) (C) (D)
6. (A) (B) (C) (D)
7. (A) (B) (C) (D)
8. (A) (B) (C) (D)
9. (A) (B) (C) (D)
10. (A) (B) (C) (D)
11. (A) (B) (C) (D)
12. (A) (B) (C) (D)
13. (A) (B) (C) (D)
14. (A) (B) (C) (D)
15. (A) (B) (C) (D)
16. (A) (B) (C) (D)
17. (A) (B) (C) (D)
18. (A) (B) (C) (D)
19. (A) (B) (C) (D)
20. (A) (B) (C) (D)
21. (A) (B) (C) (D)
22. (A) (B) (C) (D)
23. (A) (B) (C) (D)
24. (A) (B) (C) (D)
25. (A) (B) (C) (D)
26. (A) (B) (C) (D)
27. (A) (B) (C) (D)
28. (A) (B) (C) (D)
29. (A) (B) (C) (D)
30. (A) (B) (C) (D)
31. (A) (B) (C) (D)
32. (A) (B) (C) (D)
33. (A) (B) (C) (D)
34. (A) (B) (C) (D)
35. (A) (B) (C) (D)
36. (A) (B) (C) (D)
37. (A) (B) (C) (D)
38. (A) (B) (C) (D)
39. (A) (B) (C) (D)
40. (A) (B) (C) (D)
41. (A) (B) (C) (D)
42. (A) (B) (C) (D)
43. (A) (B) (C) (D)
44. (A) (B) (C) (D)
45. (A) (B) (C) (D)
46. (A) (B) (C) (D)
47. (A) (B) (C) (D)
48. (A) (B) (C) (D)
49. (A) (B) (C) (D)
50. (A) (B) (C) (D)
51. (A) (B) (C) (D)
52. (A) (B) (C) (D)
53. (A) (B) (C) (D)
54. (A) (B) (C) (D)
55. (A) (B) (C) (D)
56. (A) (B) (C) (D)
57. (A) (B) (C) (D)
58. (A) (B) (C) (D)
59. (A) (B) (C) (D)
60. (A) (B) (C) (D)
61. (A) (B) (C) (D)
62. (A) (B) (C) (D)
63. (A) (B) (C) (D)
64. (A) (B) (C) (D)
65. (A) (B) (C) (D)
66. (A) (B) (C) (D)
67. (A) (B) (C) (D)
68. (A) (B) (C) (D)
69. (A) (B) (C) (D)
70. (A) (B) (C) (D)
71. (A) (B) (C) (D)
72. (A) (B) (C) (D)
73. (A) (B) (C) (D)
74. (A) (B) (C) (D)
75. (A) (B) (C) (D)
76. (A) (B) (C) (D)
77. (A) (B) (C) (D)
78. (A) (B) (C) (D)
79. (A) (B) (C) (D)
80. (A) (B) (C) (D)

SECTION 2

1. (A) (B) (C) (D)
2. (A) (B) (C) (D)
3. (A) (B) (C) (D)
4. (A) (B) (C) (D)
5. (A) (B) (C) (D)
6. (A) (B) (C) (D)
7. (A) (B) (C) (D)
8. (A) (B) (C) (D)
9. (A) (B) (C) (D)
10. (A) (B) (C) (D)
11. (A) (B) (C) (D)
12. (A) (B) (C) (D)
13. (A) (B) (C) (D)
14. (A) (B) (C) (D)
15. (A) (B) (C) (D)
16. (A) (B) (C) (D)
17. (A) (B) (C) (D)
18. (A) (B) (C) (D)
19. (A) (B) (C) (D)
20. (A) (B) (C) (D)
21. (A) (B) (C) (D)
22. (A) (B) (C) (D)
23. (A) (B) (C) (D)
24. (A) (B) (C) (D)
25. (A) (B) (C) (D)
26. (A) (B) (C) (D)
27. (A) (B) (C) (D)
28. (A) (B) (C) (D)
29. (A) (B) (C) (D)
30. (A) (B) (C) (D)
31. (A) (B) (C) (D)
32. (A) (B) (C) (D)
33. (A) (B) (C) (D)
34. (A) (B) (C) (D)
35. (A) (B) (C) (D)
36. (A) (B) (C) (D)
37. (A) (B) (C) (D)
38. (A) (B) (C) (D)
39. (A) (B) (C) (D)
40. (A) (B) (C) (D)
41. (A) (B) (C) (D)
42. (A) (B) (C) (D)
43. (A) (B) (C) (D)
44. (A) (B) (C) (D)
45. (A) (B) (C) (D)
46. (A) (B) (C) (D)
47. (A) (B) (C) (D)
48. (A) (B) (C) (D)
49. (A) (B) (C) (D)
50. (A) (B) (C) (D)
51. (A) (B) (C) (D)
52. (A) (B) (C) (D)
53. (A) (B) (C) (D)
54. (A) (B) (C) (D)
55. (A) (B) (C) (D)
56. (A) (B) (C) (D)
57. (A) (B) (C) (D)
58. (A) (B) (C) (D)
59. (A) (B) (C) (D)
60. (A) (B) (C) (D)

SECTION 3

1. (A) (B) (C) (D)
2. (A) (B) (C) (D)
3. (A) (B) (C) (D)
4. (A) (B) (C) (D)
5. (A) (B) (C) (D)
6. (A) (B) (C) (D)
7. (A) (B) (C) (D)
8. (A) (B) (C) (D)
9. (A) (B) (C) (D)
10. (A) (B) (C) (D)
11. (A) (B) (C) (D)
12. (A) (B) (C) (D)
13. (A) (B) (C) (D)
14. (A) (B) (C) (D)
15. (A) (B) (C) (D)
16. (A) (B) (C) (D)
17. (A) (B) (C) (D)
18. (A) (B) (C) (D)
19. (A) (B) (C) (D)
20. (A) (B) (C) (D)
21. (A) (B) (C) (D)
22. (A) (B) (C) (D)
23. (A) (B) (C) (D)
24. (A) (B) (C) (D)
25. (A) (B) (C) (D)
26. (A) (B) (C) (D)
27. (A) (B) (C) (D)
28. (A) (B) (C) (D)
29. (A) (B) (C) (D)
30. (A) (B) (C) (D)
31. (A) (B) (C) (D)
32. (A) (B) (C) (D)
33. (A) (B) (C) (D)
34. (A) (B) (C) (D)
35. (A) (B) (C) (D)
36. (A) (B) (C) (D)
37. (A) (B) (C) (D)
38. (A) (B) (C) (D)
39. (A) (B) (C) (D)
40. (A) (B) (C) (D)
41. (A) (B) (C) (D)
42. (A) (B) (C) (D)
43. (A) (B) (C) (D)
44. (A) (B) (C) (D)
45. (A) (B) (C) (D)
46. (A) (B) (C) (D)
47. (A) (B) (C) (D)
48. (A) (B) (C) (D)
49. (A) (B) (C) (D)
50. (A) (B) (C) (D)
51. (A) (B) (C) (D)
52. (A) (B) (C) (D)
53. (A) (B) (C) (D)
54. (A) (B) (C) (D)
55. (A) (B) (C) (D)
56. (A) (B) (C) (D)
57. (A) (B) (C) (D)
58. (A) (B) (C) (D)
59. (A) (B) (C) (D)
60. (A) (B) (C) (D)
61. (A) (B) (C) (D)
62. (A) (B) (C) (D)
63. (A) (B) (C) (D)
64. (A) (B) (C) (D)
65. (A) (B) (C) (D)
66. (A) (B) (C) (D)
67. (A) (B) (C) (D)
68. (A) (B) (C) (D)
69. (A) (B) (C) (D)
70. (A) (B) (C) (D)
71. (A) (B) (C) (D)
72. (A) (B) (C) (D)
73. (A) (B) (C) (D)
74. (A) (B) (C) (D)
75. (A) (B) (C) (D)
76. (A) (B) (C) (D)
77. (A) (B) (C) (D)
78. (A) (B) (C) (D)
79. (A) (B) (C) (D)
80. (A) (B) (C) (D)
81. (A) (B) (C) (D)
82. (A) (B) (C) (D)
83. (A) (B) (C) (D)
84. (A) (B) (C) (D)
85. (A) (B) (C) (D)
86. (A) (B) (C) (D)
87. (A) (B) (C) (D)
88. (A) (B) (C) (D)
89. (A) (B) (C) (D)
90 (A) (B) (C) (D)

1 1 1 1 1 1 1 1 1 1 1

SECTION 1
LISTENING COMPREHENSION
Time—approximately 50 minutes

In this section of the test, you will have an opportunity to demonstrate your ability to understand spoken English. There are three parts to this section, with special directions for each part.

Part A

Directions: For each question in Part A, you will hear a short sentence. Each sentence will be spoken just one time. The sentences you hear will not be written out for you. Therefore, you must listen carefully to understand what the speaker says.

After you hear a sentence, read the four choices in your test book, marked (A), (B), (C), and (D), and decide which one is closest in meaning to the sentence you heard. Then, on your answer sheet, find the number of the question and fill in the space that corresponds to the letter of the answer you have chosen. Fill in the space so that the letter inside the oval cannot be seen.

Example I

You will hear:

Sample Answer

Ⓐ Ⓑ   Ⓓ

You will read:

- **(A)** Mary outswam the others.
- **(B)** Mary ought to swim with them.
- **(C)** Mary and her friends swam to the island.
- **(D)** Mary's friends owned the island.

The speaker said, "Mary swam out to the island with her friends." Sentence (C), "Mary and her friends swam to the island," is closest in meaning to the sentence you heard. Therefore, you should choose answer (C).

Example II

You will hear:

Sample Answer

Ⓐ   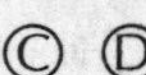 Ⓒ Ⓓ

You will read:

- **(A)** Please remind me to read this book.
- **(B)** Could you help me carry these books?
- **(C)** I don't mind if you help me.
- **(D)** Do you have a heavy course load this term?

The speaker said, "Would you mind helping me with this load of books?" Sentence (B), "Could you help me carry these books?" is closest in meaning to the sentence you heard. Therefore, you should choose answer (B).

GO ON TO THE NEXT PAGE

1. **(A)** Dora went to the bank at six o'clock.
   (B) Dora has to go to the bank right away.
   (C) Dora still has plenty of time to go to the bank.
   (D) Dora was afraid the bank would close earlier on Friday.

2. **(A)** The bus station is missing.
   (B) You have to wait for another bus.
   (C) There must be something wrong with the bus.
   (D) It's upsetting to miss the bus.

3. **(A)** He has many well-fitting clothes.
   (B) There are only a few clothes in the closet.
   (C) Some of the clothes in the closet fit him well.
   (D) He doesn't have any clothes that fit him well.

4. **(A)** The young man is hard on the equipment.
   (B) The young man won a scholarship.
   (C) Good characteristics made him a great success.
   (D) Difficulties in his life have had a positive end result.

5. **(A)** It's a difficult solution, isn't it?
   (B) Did you find the solution for the problem?
   (C) Do you want to think it over quietly?
   (D) You couldn't find the solution, could you?

6. **(A)** I suspect that the supervisor doesn't know how to do it.
   (B) I'm hesitant to ask the supervisor to help me do it.
   (C) I want to do it by myself.
   (D) I'll have the supervisor help me do it.

7. **(A)** They make the soft drinks in the supermarket.
   (B) The price of this drink is more reasonable in the supermarket.
   (C) This supermarket only sells soft drinks, not wine and beer.
   (D) You can buy soft drinks in every supermarket.

8. **(A)** George went to see a doctor for a special diet.
   (B) George was waiting for a special diet.
   (C) George monitored his weight carefully.
   (D) George lost weight every day because of the special diet.

9. **(A)** The elderly suffered from the hot weather.
   (B) Elderly people like warm temperatures.
   (C) The high temperature caused heavy humidity.
   (D) The weather doesn't always affect the elderly.

10. **(A)** The librarian will be at the reference desk tonight.
    (B) I'll work at the cafeteria instead of the library soon.
    (C) I'll work at the library tonight.
    (D) It wasn't easy to work at the library.

11. **(A)** Why couldn't you find these books on the shelf?
    (B) We don't know where to put these books.
    (C) The books should be put away first.
    (D) Why do you want to keep these books on the table?

12. **(A)** Richard gets a headache when he studies international business.
    (B) Richard took a language class instead of a business class.
    (C) Richard has strong background knowledge in business affairs.
    (D) Richard has an advantage in studying international affairs.

13. **(A)** No one likes these pictures.
    (B) Elderly people don't speak highly of these pictures.
    (C) Young people see more value in the old pictures.
    (D) The older people care a lot about the pictures.

14. **(A)** Everybody should drink water when driving in the summer.
    (B) The police will fine people who are drinking and driving.
    (C) Whoever gets a ticket should see or call the police.
    (D) People who speed on the highway will have to pay money to the police.

15. **(A)** He made a copy of the reference to take home.
    (B) He needs more references to get a loan.
    (C) He has references in his house.
    (D) He didn't have enough references at home.

GO ON TO THE NEXT PAGE

16. **(A)** There will be a big picnic Saturday night.
    (B) This restaurant is usually more crowded on Saturday nights.
    (C) Let's go to another restaurant; there are too many people here.
    (D) We don't usually eat at this restaurant on weekend evenings.

17. **(A)** The speech won't last long.
    (B) We'll have a speech after the reception.
    (C) The speech will be before the reception.
    (D) Someone is giving a speech at the reception.

18. **(A)** It doesn't matter whether we have rain or not.
    (B) It's impossible to have rain all the time.
    (C) It's nice to have rain this time of the year.
    (D) We don't usually have much rain now.

19. **(A)** He didn't take many classes in the first semester.
    (B) It's wise to take more classes in the beginning.
    (C) He did a better job on writing this semester than last semester.
    (D) He shouldn't sign up for too many classes.

20. **(A)** There is no reason to buy a watch like that.
    (B) This watch has a fair price.
    (C) The least expensive watch isn't always bad.
    (D) This is the most expensive watch I've ever seen.

21. **(A)** I didn't bring my wallet or my ticket.
    (B) Fortunately, I brought my wallet with me.
    (C) I don't have my ticket with me.
    (D) I didn't know I needed a ticket.

22. **(A)** He was wearing the old sweater for fun.
    (B) He likes the old sweater better than the new one.
    (C) He needs a new sweater.
    (D) He traded his sweater for a shirt.

23. **(A)** We wonder if we can visit our grandparents.
    (B) We enjoyed visiting Wyoming.
    (C) Our grandparents love their cabin in Wyoming.
    (D) We visited Wyoming and other places.

24. **(A)** We want the ring that is the best made.
    (B) We had plenty of water from this rain.
    (C) We should try to save water during dry weather.
    (D) A certain amount of water was saved this year.

25. **(A)** The maid will come late.
    (B) The mayor canceled his appointment.
    (C) The mail hasn't come yet.
    (D) Being late is maddening.

26. **(A)** She had a performance at 7 o'clock.
    (B) She went to the ballet class after dinner.
    (C) She taught a ballet class for seven girls.
    (D) She started learning ballet when she was a child.

27. **(A)** He is naive.
    (B) He is wise.
    (C) Why is he so foolish?
    (D) He'll fool you if you don't fool him.

28. **(A)** Shall we have a family get-together this year?
    (B) Do we have a nice family?
    (C) Our family doesn't belong in this union.
    (D) We have enough time to arrange a family reunion.

29. **(A)** This music doesn't attract me at all.
    (B) I learned to play music when I was in Massachusetts.
    (C) The music is familiar to me.
    (D) Only a child would like music like this.

30. **(A)** Gloria and her mother were doing Christmas shopping.
    (B) Gloria's mother sent her daughter a necklace.
    (C) Gloria doesn't like the necklace her mother gave her.
    (D) Gloria chose jewelry as a present.

GO ON TO THE NEXT PAGE

1 1 1 1 1 1 1 1 1 1 1

Part B

Directions: In Part B you will hear short conversations between two speakers. At the end of each conversation, a third person will ask a question about what was said. You will hear each conversation and question about it just one time. Therefore, you must listen carefully to understand what each speaker says. After you hear a conversation and the question about it, read the four possible answers in your test book and decide which one is the best answer to the question you heard. Then, on your answer sheet, find the number of the question and fill in the space that corresponds to the letter of the answer you have chosen.

Look at the following example.

You will hear:

Sample Answer

You will read:

(A) Present Professor Smith with a picture.
(B) Photograph Professor Smith.
(C) Put glass over the photograph.
(D) Replace the broken headlight.

From the conversation you learn that the woman thinks Professor Smith would like a photograph of the class. The best answer to the question "What does the woman think the class should do?" is (A), "Present Professor Smith with a picture." Therefore, you should choose answer (A).

GO ON TO THE NEXT PAGE

31. **(A)** Taking the summer classes
(B) Finding a summer job
(C) Waiting until later to decide
(D) Working and studying

32. **(A)** They weren't able to see the movie last night.
(B) They bought two tickets for today's movie.
(C) They enjoyed the beach more.
(D) They didn't go to the beach, but rented a video at home.

33. **(A)** Why is the man great?
(B) Why did the man say that?
(C) What kind of man is he?
(D) What happened to the man?

34. **(A)** They won't come if they don't call.
(B) She is sure that the people will come to the party.
(C) She will cancel the party since nobody called.
(D) There is plenty of food for all the people.

35. **(A)** It makes a big difference when she takes Physics 101.
(B) She doesn't need to take Physics 101.
(C) He doesn't know when the class will be offered.
(D) She can take Physics 101 any semester.

36. **(A)** He will fix the sink.
(B) He will ask someone to do the work.
(C) He will move into the apartment.
(D) He will buy a new sink.

37. **(A)** She is sorry that the man asked her.
(B) She is going to ask for a new number.
(C) She lost her phone number.
(D) She doesn't have a phone number at this time.

38. **(A)** He is nervous.
(B) He is disappointed.
(C) He is surprised.
(D) He is anxious.

39. **(A)** The woman should pay the fee at the library.
(B) The woman should wait in line.
(C) The woman should pay the fee at another office.
(D) The woman should pay by cash only.

40. **(A)** The typist has completed it already.
(B) He completed the typing himself.
(C) He'll need some help later on.
(D) He wants the woman to type more carefully.

41. **(A)** Wait for the next bus.
(B) Walk to the housing office.
(C) Ask someone else.
(D) Get on this bus.

42. **(A)** Students with a proper I.D. can check any book out.
(B) Only the students with special permission can check out reference books.
(C) Only professors can check out the reference books.
(D) The reference books are not allowed to be checked out.

43. **(A)** The convention was canceled.
(B) The convention was put off.
(C) The convention was held last Wednesday.
(D) The convention was overcrowded.

44. **(A)** Joan called about her business trip.
(B) Joan wants to send her card to us.
(C) Joan will mail us her new address.
(D) Joan's card was lost somewhere.

45. **(A)** It's taken her a long time to get a PhD degree.
(B) It's a piece of cake to receive a degree.
(C) She did it much quicker than other people working on the degree.
(D) She is still a graduate student.

46. **(A)** A money order
(B) The current time
(C) A telephone number
(D) Weather information

47. **(A)** The scores are not listed.
(B) You can read the scores yourself.
(C) The English department doesn't give out scores.
(D) The scores will be out tomorrow.

48. **(A)** The man doesn't know how to make a correction.
(B) The typewriter is broken.
(C) The man is learning how to change the ribbon.
(D) The man is asking why the typing error occurred.

GO ON TO THE NEXT PAGE

49. **(A)** Everything is completed.
(B) There is only one thing left to complete.
(C) No, it is not enough.
(D) That is the right one.

50. **(A)** He doesn't want sugar in his coffee.
(B) He doesn't want caffeine in his coffee.
(C) He doesn't want his coffee too hot.
(D) He doesn't want coffee yet.

51. **(A)** She has to wait in line to buy her textbook.
(B) She can borrow the textbook from the library.
(C) It's too late to buy the textbook now.
(D) She had the salesman order the book for her.

52. **(A)** She thinks a new way will take too long.
(B) She doesn't want to go the same way this time.
(C) She has changed her mind.
(D) She agrees with the man's idea.

53. **(A)** You should have turned the paper in yesterday.
(B) The paper is acceptable.
(C) The paper must be typed.
(D) The typing errors are not acceptable.

54. **(A)** She has a date tomorrow.
(B) She knows tomorrow is Tuesday.
(C) The book must be returned tomorrow.
(D) She'll become a bookkeeper tomorrow.

55. **(A)** He prefers to use the stairs.
(B) He doesn't know where the elevator is.
(C) He is in too much of a hurry to wait for the elevator.
(D) He uses elevators all the time.

GO ON TO THE NEXT PAGE

1 1 1 1 1 1 1 1 1 1 1

Part C

Directions: In this part of the test, you will hear short talks and conversations. After each of them you will be asked some questions. You will hear the talks and conversations and the questions about them just one time. They will not be written out for you. Therefore, you must listen carefully to understand what each speaker says.

After you hear a question, read the four possible answers in your test book and decide which one is the best answer to the question you heard. Then, on you answer sheet, find the number of the question and fill in the space that corresponds to the letter of the answer you have chosen.

Answer all questions on the basis of what is stated or implied in the talk or conversation.

Listen to this sample talk.
You will hear:
Now look at the following example.
You will hear:

You will read:

Sample Answer

(A) They are impossible to guide.
(B) They may go up in flames.
(C) They tend to leak gas.
(D) They are cheaply made.

The best answer to the question "Why are gas balloons considered dangerous?" is (B), "They may go up in flames." Therefore, you should choose answer (B).

Now look at the next example.
You will hear:

Sample Answer

You will read:

(A) Watch for changes in weather.
(B) Watch their altitude.
(C) Check for weak spots in their balloons.
(D) Test the strength of the ropes.

The best answer to the question "According to the speaker, what must balloon pilots be careful to do?" is (A), "Watch for changes in weather." Therefore, you should choose answer (A).

GO ON TO THE NEXT PAGE

56. **(A)** Julius Caesar
(B) A summer play
(C) A public lecture
(D) A Shakespeare festival

57. **(A)** Literature students
(B) The audience at a Shakespeare play
(C) Professional actors
(D) Community members

58. **(A)** Because there are actors from out of town
(B) Because they just read *Julius Caesar*
(C) Because there will be community talks
(D) Because the plays are in the summer

59. **(A)** An actor
(B) A chairman
(C) A librarian
(D) A teacher

60. **(A)** To help people understand the play
(B) To get financial support for the series
(C) To explain the grant
(D) To introduce the actors

61. **(A)** On Friday
(B) In two weeks
(C) At 7 P.M.
(D) Right after the library talk

62. **(A)** The lack of water
(B) The quality of water
(C) The cost of water
(D) The abundance of water

63. **(A)** Water their cars.
(B) Disconnect their washing machines.
(C) Wash their decks.
(D) Turn off their sprinkler systems.

64. **(A)** Use the sprinkler on Monday, Wednesday, or Friday.
(B) Water by hand.
(C) Water on Wednesdays.
(D) Don't water.

65. **(A)** Brushing teeth
(B) Washing clothes
(C) Watering grass
(D) Using dishwashers

66. **(A)** Fine citizens.
(B) Look for water sources.
(C) Ration water.
(D) Write new water rules.

67. **(A)** Paying $50
(B) Fining your neighbor
(C) Reusing washing machine water
(D) Taking baths instead of showers

68. **(A)** To see a friend
(B) To write his report
(C) Home
(D) To the library

69. **(A)** Because the building is noisy
(B) Because the library is closed
(C) Because the resource center is new
(D) Because the library is shaking

70. **(A)** In the community
(B) Outside the main library
(C) In the basement of the library
(D) Downtown

71. **(A)** World War II Fighter Pilots
(B) Protection for Endangered Species
(C) Dealing with the Shortage of Fossil Fuels
(D) The Results of Nuclear Testing

72. **(A)** Because cooperation is important for everyone
(B) Because money is an ancient tool
(C) Because all societies use money
(D) Because economics is a global issue

73. **(A)** He is angry about the change.
(B) He thinks that the hours are better than before.
(C) He thinks that it is necessary for now.
(D) He is disappointed because of his paper.

74. **(A)** 500
(B) 100
(C) 10
(D) 7

75. **(A)** A graduate student
(B) A teaching assistant
(C) A teacher
(D) The chancellor

76. **(A)** Cash
(B) A job
(C) A credential
(D) A letter

77. **(A)** Holding office hours
(B) Grading student work
(C) Directing labs
(D) Leading discussion sessions

GO ON TO THE NEXT PAGE

78. **(A)** Teaching assistants should get $100 more.
(B) Teaching assistants teach many classes.
(C) Teaching assistants are an important part of the school.
(D) Teaching assistants should work longer hours.

79. **(A)** They like the job.
(B) They meet many students.
(C) They need the money.
(D) It helps their studies.

80. **(A)** To get an award
(B) To meet the teaching assistant
(C) To show their support
(D) To give out prizes

THIS IS THE END OF THE LISTENING COMPREHENSION PART OF THIS TEST. The next part of the test is Section 2. Turn to the directions for Section 2 in your test book, read them, and begin work. Do not read or work on any other section of the test.

2 2 2 2 2 2 2 2 2 2 2

SECTION 2
STRUCTURE AND WRITTEN EXPRESSION
Time—35 minutes

This section is designed to measure your ability to recognize language that is appropriate for standard written English. There are two types of questions in this section, with special directions for each type.

Directions: Questions 1–23 are incomplete sentences. Beneath each sentence you will see four words or phrases, marked (A), (B), (C), and (D). Choose the one word or phrase that best completes the sentence. Then, on your answer sheet, find the number of the question and fill in the space that corresponds to the letter of the answer you have chosen. Fill in the space so that the letter inside the oval cannot be seen.

Example I

Vegetables are an excellent source ________ vitamins.

Sample Answer

● Ⓑ Ⓒ Ⓓ

(A) of
(B) has
(C) where
(D) that

The sentence should read, "Vegetables are an excellent source of vitamins." Therefore, you should choose answer (A).

Example II

________ in history when remarkable progress was made within a relatively short span of time.

Sample Answer

   Ⓓ

(A) Periods
(B) Throughout periods
(C) There have been periods
(D) Periods have been

The sentence should read, "There have been periods in history when remarkable progress was made within a relatively short span of time." Therefore, you should choose answer (C).

Now begin work on the questions.

GO ON TO THE NEXT PAGE

1. Fortunately, _________ single nation has to have the task of learning all we need to know about the ocean.
   (A) no
   (B) not
   (C) none
   (D) never

2. _________ some cultures, openness is considered in a very negative light.
   (A) From
   (B) In
   (C) At
   (D) On

3. _________, often of a religious character, were developed from fundamental African forms.
   (A) Ancient dancing of Egyptians
   (B) Ancient Egyptian dancing
   (C) Ancient Egyptian dance
   (D) Ancient Egyptian dances

4. _________, allowing the passage of nerve fibers and blood vessels.
   (A) Whenever microscopic canals embraced by the bone
   (B) The bone embraces many microscopic canals
   (C) Microscopic canals embraced by the bone
   (D) Whereas the bone embraced many microscopic canals

5. The troublesome tartar above the gumline _________ by careful toothbrushing.
   (A) can reduce
   (B) can be reduced significantly
   (C) is reducing significantly
   (D) to reduce

6. Of all the brass instruments, _________, since it mingles well with the woodwinds.
   (A) the French horn used
   (B) the French horn is useful the most
   (C) the French horn is the most useful
   (D) is the most useful French horn

7. _________ some satellites have retrograde motion is not yet understood.
   (A) Why
   (B) Whenever
   (C) What
   (D) Although

8. George Stephenson, an English engineer, _________ to haul coal from mines.
   (A) traveling engine that he constructed
   (B) constructed a traveling engine
   (C) which was constructed in a traveling engine
   (D) he was a constructor of traveling engines

9. In the type of _________ radio receivers, a signal is translated upward or downward in frequency.
   (A) used mixer in
   (B) mixer used
   (C) used in a mixer
   (D) mixer used in

10. Each subject of the speech was _________ carefully prepared that the keynote speaker received a great response from the audience.
   (A) as
   (B) so
   (C) such
   (D) very

11. The weather in the far north is not _________ it is near the Equator.
   (A) like humid as
   (B) as humid as
   (C) humid as
   (D) so humid that

12. _________ of several women's records in aviation, Ms. Savitskaya made over 500 parachute jumps.
   (A) Holder
   (B) Hold
   (C) To hold
   (D) Holds

GO ON TO THE NEXT PAGE

13. ________ protects copper from damage is its patina, a greenish surface film.

(A) There
(B) That
(C) Which
(D) What

14. Landslides, ________, and volcanic eruptions can all cause vibrations in the earth.

(A) that falling
(B) falling rocks
(C) rock is falling
(D) when rocks falling

15. When ________ people who irritated him, the columnist was bitter and even splenetic.

(A) in discussion
(B) his discussing
(C) he discussed
(D) he discuss

16. Vitamin E cream, a moisturizing emollient, ________ maintaining soft, healthy looking skin.

(A) having been used for
(B) used for
(C) has been used for
(D) having used for

17. Childless couples sometimes acquire ________ pets to whom they can give parental love.

(A) baby-sized
(B) size like a baby
(C) baby's size
(D) size of a baby

18. Encounters between people from different countries can result in misunderstandings ________ different conceptions about space.

(A) because they
(B) is because they
(C) is because their
(D) because of their

19. Having introduced the experimental and theoretical study of vibrational relaxation, ________ to examine the properties of methyl iodide.

(A) proceeding the author
(B) the author proceeded
(C) proceeded the author
(D) did the author proceed

20. Not until the 1960s, ________ at Hugnes Research Laboratories build the world's first working laser.

(A) Theodore Mainman
(B) while Theodore Mainman
(C) did Theodore Mainman
(D) Theodore Mainman did

21. After the election, ________ a new stage.

(A) the entering nation
(B) to enter the nation
(C) entering the nation
(D) the nation will enter

22. The national parks have interpretative centers ________ tourists can acquire information about the animals and trees.

(A) which
(B) where
(C) that
(D) there

23. More and more graduates of medical schools tend ________ on limited areas of their professions.

(A) to concentrate
(B) concentrate
(C) concentrated
(D) concentrating

GO ON TO THE NEXT PAGE

Directions: In questions 24–60 each sentence has four underlined words or phrases. The four underlined parts of the sentence are marked (A), (B), (C), and (D). Identify the one underlined word or phrase that must be changed in order for the sentence to be correct. Then, on your answer sheet, find the number of the question and fill in the space that corresponds to the letter of the answer you have chosen.

Example I

A ray of light passing through (A) the center (B) of a thin lens keep (C) its original (D) direction.

Sample Answer

Ⓐ Ⓑ ● Ⓓ

The sentence should read, "A ray of light passing through the center of a thin lens keeps its original direction." Therefore, you should choose answer (C).

Example II

The mandolin, a musical instrument (A) that has (B) strings, was probably copied from (C) the lute, a many (D) older instrument.

Sample Answer

Ⓐ Ⓑ Ⓒ ●

The sentence should read, "The mandolin, a musical instrument that has strings, was probably copied from the lute, a much older instrument." Therefore, you should choose answer (D).

Now begin work on the questions.

24. Wild creatures are energetic (A) in their (B) natural habitats (C) than in a zoo (D).

25. The social worker has such a (A) sympathetic, comfortably (B) manner that people like (C) to confide in (D) her.

26. Fire, the phenomenon of combustion as observed (A) in light, flame, and heat, it is (B) one of the basic (C) tools of mankind (D).

27. Organized (A) labor has fight (B) for and won protection and benefits (C) for its (D) worker-members.

28. Women's (A) liberation has supported (B) by many (C) men and by much of (D) society.

29. The capable (A) to use books in one's work (B) is (C) one characteristic of a scholar (D).

GO ON TO THE NEXT PAGE

30. Alike other turtles, marine turtles breathe air through their lungs and lay eggs
A B C D
on land.

31. The strong wind does a terrible noise when it blows through the antenna.
A B C D

32. Bacteria and germs are too tiny that they are invisible to the naked eye.
A B C D

33. Different kinds of turtles are uniquely adapt to living on land, in fresh water,
A B C
or in the ocean.
D

34. The field of laser spectroscopy has changed radically between the last decade.
A B C D

35. The surgeon and sanitary techniques applied by the Greeks were lost with the
A B C
deterioration of their civilization.
D

36. Smoking is not allowed in gas stations because there is too many easily ignited
A B C D
material in the vicinity.

37. Comets are apparently the more numerous bodies in the solar system except for
A B C D
small meteor fragments.

38. Benzene should be kept in tightly-capped bottles, because it is high volatile.
A B C D

39. The researchers systematic their information before writing the report.
A B C D

40. The use of standard spelling, correct grammar, and approving pronunciation
A B
indicates that a person is educated.
C D

41. Studies reveal that people who eat the great amount of salt suffer the most from
A B C D
hypertension.

42. The adult flea of both sexes eats only bleed and can survive away from its host for
A B C
weeks without eating.
D

43. In the American educated system, children go to school for twelve years.
A B C D

GO ON TO THE NEXT PAGE

44. It is impossible of an alcoholic to drink moderately.
A B C D

45. Recreation is any activity voluntarily engaged for self-satisfaction through
A B C
relaxation, fun, or the opportunity for expression.
D

46. Handicapped people frequently state that they feel isolated and other people avoid
A B C D
them.

47. Detection often find out the truth by gathering lots of unrelated information and
A B C
studying it.
D

48. Gas efficiency, secure, economical, and practical, today's cars are better than any
A B C D
produced before.

49. Byssinosis, known as one of the many lung diseases, are believed to be the result
A B
of years of exposure to fine cotton dust.
C D

50. The population problem around the world is complicated, since much people see
A B
benefits in having large families.
C D

51. Some people prefers urban living; others don't.
A B C D

52. The man claimed that the panacea he sold was good for alleviating stomachaches,
A B C
fever, and seasick.
D

53. People have to take precautions to both acts of sabotage and direct violence in
A B C
times of war.
D

54. The candidate spoke ambiguously on purpose so that people listen to him could
A B C
hear whatever they wanted to hear.
D

55. The lack of rain in the northern Africa caused severe scarcity of food.
A B C D

56. The political contestant's speech was filled with empty promise, platitudes, and
A B C
trite expressions.
D

GO ON TO THE NEXT PAGE

57. The economies of many OPEC nations is primarily oil-based.
(A = The; B = many; C = is; D = primarily)

58. People dream more when they enter to lighter phases of sleep.
(A = dream; B = they; C = enter to; D = lighter)

59. Studies conducted by Johns Hopkins University indicated that it was the husbands, not the wives, whose lives were shortened by the lost of their spouses.
(A = conducted; B = whose lives; C = shortened by; D = lost)

60. For minor cuts, scratches, and insect bitings, apply an antiseptic directly to the injury.
(A = For; B = bitings; C = directly; D = the injury)

THIS IS THE END OF SECTION 2. IF YOU FINISH BEFORE TIME IS UP, CHECK YOUR WORK ON SECTION 2 ONLY. DO NOT READ OR WORK ON ANY OTHER SECTION UNTIL YOUR TIME IS UP. **STOP**

3 3 3 3 3 3 3 3 3 3 3

SECTION 3
VOCABULARY AND READING COMPREHENSION
Time—65 minutes

This section is designed to measure your comprehension of standard written English. There are two types of questions in this section, with special directions for each type.

Directions: In questions 1–45 each sentence has an underlined word or phrase. Below each sentence are four other words or phrases, marked (A), (B), (C), and (D). You are to choose the one word or phrase that best keeps the meaning of the original sentence if it is substituted for the underlined word or phrase. Then, on your answer sheet, find the number of the question and fill in the space that corresponds to the letter you have choosen. Fill in the space so that the letter inside the oval cannot be seen.

Example:

Passenger ships and aircraft are often equipped with ship-to-shore or air-to-land radio telephones.

(A) highways
(B) railroads
(C) planes
(D) sailboats

Sample Answer

   Ⓓ

The best answer is (C), because "Passenger ships and planes are often equipped with ship-to-shore or air-to-land radio telephones" is closest in meaning to the original sentence. Therefore, you should choose answer (C).

Now begin work on the questions.

GO ON TO THE NEXT PAGE

1. The sixteenth century witnessed the creation of numerous types of Japanese ceramics.
   (A) was the judgment of
   (B) was the setting for
   (C) stood for
   (D) bypassed

2. Mass production yields vast quantities of goods for domestic and foreign use.
   (A) expanding
   (B) diverse
   (C) enormous
   (D) intense

3. The Smithsonian Institution houses administrative offices as well as museums.
   (A) shelters
   (B) builds
   (C) places
   (D) rents

4. In many parts of the world wild animals are practically nonexistent.
   (A) primitive
   (B) dangerous
   (C) undisturbed
   (D) undomesticated

5. Gold jewelry is as dazzling as it is expensive.
   (A) shocking
   (B) brilliant
   (C) colorful
   (D) valued

6. The earliest Islamic metal objects reveal past traditions in their decoration.
   (A) suggest
   (B) inherit
   (C) fabricate
   (D) display

7. The Japanese tea ceremony embodies a simple and direct spirit.
   (A) ghost
   (B) soul
   (C) feeling
   (D) solution

8. It is common to find a great number of museum items preserved in storage rooms.
   (A) featured
   (B) manufactured
   (C) prepared
   (D) protected

9. Most teachers spend considerable time planning lessons and correcting papers.
   (A) much
   (B) important
   (C) quality
   (D) excessive

10. Selected animals around the world are being studied for the purpose of preserving threatened species.
    (A) angry
    (B) harmful
    (C) endangered
    (D) menacing

11. The newly planned satellite flights will begin a new phase in the American space program.
    (A) system
    (B) season
    (C) stage
    (D) position

12. A deficiency in zinc can cause birth defects in rodents.
    (A) A lack of
    (B) An overdose of
    (C) An impurity in
    (D) A defect in

13. One of the mundane tasks in life is cleaning the house.
    (A) boring
    (B) manual
    (C) ordinary
    (D) necessary

14. Some people feel queasy when taking ocean trips.
    (A) nauseous
    (B) energized
    (C) confused
    (D) afraid

15. The U.S. park system employs hundreds of people each year to clear paths for visitors' use.
    (A) latrines
    (B) walkways
    (C) campsites
    (D) amphitheaters

16. Babies often like to hold fuzzy objects.
    (A) small and cute
    (B) clean and colorful
    (C) warm and cuddly
    (D) soft and fluffy

GO ON TO THE NEXT PAGE

17. A U.S. president has the power to veto a bill.
(A) enforce
(B) modify
(C) reject
(D) verify

18. Abraham Lincoln was born in a log cabin.
(A) an isolated
(B) a drafty
(C) a cozy
(D) a wooden

19. In San Francisco ferries are sometimes used to take people to work.
(A) cable cars
(B) boats
(C) subways
(D) trams

20. Today, in this global state, the English language has more variety of local expressions than it ever has had before.
(A) condition
(B) territory
(C) rank
(D) government

21. A pontil is a tool used to handle hot glass while it is being shaped during glassmaking.
(A) disposed of
(B) copied
(C) designed
(D) formed

22. English furniture made between 1714 and 1830 is called Georgian, after the reigning monarchs of that time.
(A) ruling
(B) historic
(C) winning
(D) scholarly

23. From the beginnings of history, literature has recorded the story of human dreams.
(A) processed
(B) transformed
(C) preserved
(D) reproduced

24. The Puritans, early American settlers, shared many of the same beliefs as the Pilgrims.
(A) divided
(B) enjoyed
(C) contributed
(D) had

25. The Roman Pantheon and the Colosseum represent two of the world's most durable examples of concrete architecture.
(A) are
(B) erected
(C) support
(D) belong to

26. Some plants can produce a chemical that stunts the growth of insects.
(A) increases
(B) halts
(C) releases
(D) submerges

27. The mountains around the Li River have lured poets and artists for centuries.
(A) intrigued
(B) mystified
(C) inspired
(D) attracted

28. Harsh arctic and desert environments have always posed great challenges to human life.
(A) Severe
(B) Barren
(C) Bright
(D) Exceptional

29. Human beings share a common heritage of a life cycle that includes trial and error, success, and failure.
(A) hierarchy
(B) inheritance
(C) mark
(D) problem

30. People have always dispersed across the Earth looking for arable land.
(A) pastoral
(B) fertilized
(C) plowable
(D) sufficient

31. The Northwest is an important area for the lumber industry.
(A) steel
(B) garment
(C) timber
(D) fishing

GO ON TO THE NEXT PAGE

32. It is possible that an emotional condition can trigger a physical reaction.
(A) cause
(B) diminish
(C) enhance
(D) supersede

33. Toddlers sometimes require special attention.
(A) Elderly people
(B) Babies
(C) Pets
(D) Houseplants

34. Minoan kings had such strong navies that they were able to build unfortified palaces.
(A) unprotected
(B) undeveloped
(C) unequaled
(D) unidentified

35. Tempe, Arizona was known as Hayden's Ferry when it was founded in 1872.
(A) discovered
(B) destroyed
(C) established
(D) built

36. Chester Alan Arthur, 21st president of the United States, was a handsome man with a ruddy complexion.
(A) broad shoulders
(B) red-colored skin
(C) a slight limp
(D) wavy hair

37. Automation has done away with much of the drudgery of work.
(A) uniqueness
(B) dirtiness
(C) unpleasantness
(D) slowness

38. Little Rock is the hub of the federal interstate highways that cross Arkansas.
(A) highpoint
(B) summit
(C) path
(D) center

39. In the 13th century there were thousands of castles in France.
(A) military ships
(B) fortified buildings
(C) acres of vineyards
(D) noble men and women

40. In the spring, one might see newly born animals taking their first wobbly steps.
(A) unsteady
(B) mincing
(C) baby
(D) tentative

41. Marion Anderson's European debut was triumphant.
(A) luxuriant
(B) disastrous
(C) victorious
(D) newsworthy

42. A sistrum is a rattle that was used in ancient Egypt.
(A) shaking device
(B) weapon
(C) cooking utensil
(D) water container

43. In his conquest of the Mediterranean, Alexander the Great seized many of the coastal cities held by the Russian navy.
(A) released
(B) captured
(C) surrounded
(D) segregated

44. A slaughterhouse is often in the vicinity of a meat-packing plant.
(A) An inspection house
(B) A barn
(C) A food processing house
(D) A butchering house

45. In some parts of the world, an everyday outfit consists of a colorful shirt and baggy pants.
(A) tight
(B) worn
(C) loose
(D) woven

GO ON TO THE NEXT PAGE

Directions: In the rest of this section you will read several passages. Each one is followed by several questions about it. For questions 46–90, you are to choose the one best answer, (A), (B), (C), or (D), to each question. Then, on your answer sheet, find the number of the question and fill in the space that corresponds to the letter of the answer you have chosen.

Answer all questions following a passage on the basis of what is stated or implied in that passage.

Read the following passage:

> The rattles with which a rattlesnake warns of its presence are formed by loosely interlocking hollow rings of hard skin, which make a buzzing sound when its tail is shaken. As a baby, the snake begins to firm its rattles from the button at the very tip of its tail. Thereafter, each time it sheds its skin, a new ring is formed. Popular belief holds that a snake's age can be told by counting the rings, but this idea is fallacious. In fact, a snake may lose its old skin as often as four times a year. Also, rattles tend to wear or break off with time.

Example I:

A rattlesnake's rattles are made of

(A) skin
(B) bone
(C) wood
(D) muscle

Sample Answer

   Ⓓ

According to the passage, a rattlesnake's rattles are made out of rings of hard skin. Therefore, you should choose answer (A).

Example II:

How often does a rattlesnake shed its skin?

(A) Once every four years
(B) Once every four months
(C) Up to four times every year
(D) Four times more often than other snakes

Sample Answer

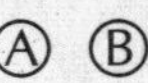 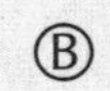  Ⓓ

The passage states that "a snake may lose its old skin as often as four times a year." Therefore, you should choose answer (C).

Now begin work on the questions.

GO ON TO THE NEXT PAGE

Questions 46-52

Harvesting ice sounds like a new concept, but actually it has been around for years. Scientists have been studying this idea as a possible solution to the problem of the world's dwindling fresh water supply. Ninety percent of the earth's fresh water is in the icecaps of Antarctica. If only 10 percent of that ice could be towed to civilization, it could provide water for 500 million people. But the problem, of course, is one of melting. How can a giant iceberg be towed across the sea without melting? The answer could lie in enclosing the floating ice in a huge cylindrical container made of a high-strength synthetic fabric. If the iceberg is nudged into the fabric container, which is opened at both ends, then the ends can be sealed and the sea water pumped out. After that it can be towed to civilization. The melting rate will be slowed down, and the synthetic cocoon will act as a holding tank for the water. Engineering this project, which might include a container up to one kilometer in length and 100 meters in diameter, would be a feat, but engineers say it is possible. After all, fishermen in north Australia sometimes use nets 8 kilometers long and 20 meters across.

46. Which of the following is the best title for this passage?

(A) The Earth's Dwindling Water Supply
(B) Icecaps of Antarctica
(C) A Solution to Fresh Water Needs
(D) A Synthetic Cocoon

47. Of all the earth's water, the icecaps of Antarctica contain

(A) 10 percent of the fresh water
(B) 10 percent of the salt water
(C) 90 percent of the fresh water
(D) 90 percent of the salt water

48. How does the author propose to transport the ice?

(A) By pulling it
(B) By chopping it
(C) By piping it
(D) By melting it

49. According to the passage, the purpose of the fabric container is to

(A) protect the ice
(B) diminish the speed of melting
(C) cause the ice to float
(D) pump out the sea water

50. In line 8 the word "nudged" is closest in meaning to

(A) imagined
(B) glued
(C) melted
(D) pushed

51. A "cocoon" (line 11) refers to

(A) protection against insects
(B) a tank in the boat
(C) a very large net
(D) a protective covering

52. The purpose of the last sentence is to

(A) reinforce the feasibility of the project
(B) compare fishermen to engineers
(C) contrast iceberg containers and fishing nets
(D) define the size of the container

GO ON TO THE NEXT PAGE

Questions 53-59

Though Paul Gauguin, himself, recognized both the "sensitive" and the "savage" as two opposing sides of his character, in his career as an artist he thought of himself as "the savage." He tended to disregard convention and abandon social responsibilities. He felt that only by renouncing the ordinary could he be the artist he wanted to be. He justified his quarreling with friends, his leaving his wife and children, and his promiscuity, because he believed it to be the only way his art could be liberated. In his attitude can be found seeds for art in the 20th century: the art of the primitive, of symbol, and of imagination. He wanted to escape from merely observing naturalism to using abstract color and form as conveyors of feeling. He wanted to free painting from all restrictions. He began to carry his art deep into the realm of myth and dream with the idea that mystery and enigma were essential to art.

53. What is the author's purpose in this passage?

(A) To compare two sides of Gauguin's character
(B) To describe Gauguin's relationship with his family
(C) To introduce the sensitivity in Gauguin's art
(D) To discuss the effects of the "savage" side of Gauguin's character

54. Which of the following is the best title for this passage?

(A) Gauguin's Escape
(B) Gauguin: Myth and Reality
(C) The Life of Paul Gauguin
(D) Attitude and Art

55. According to the passage, Gauguin

(A) divorced his wife
(B) lived alone
(C) liberated his family
(D) disregarded society's rules

56. Which of the following is NOT supported by the passage?

(A) Gauguin justified his behavior.
(B) Gauguin quarreled with his friends.
(C) Gauguin left his family.
(D) Gauguin promised to come back.

57. It can be inferred from the passage that the art of the coming century would be more

(A) colorful
(B) naturalistic
(C) symbolic
(D) complex

58. From the passage we can infer that Gauguin wanted to

(A) paint in a new way
(B) restrict forms of art
(C) make new friends
(D) liberate society

59. The best synonym for "savage" in this passage is

(A) cruel
(B) crude
(C) fierce
(D) untamed

GO ON TO THE NEXT PAGE

Questions 60-64

With increasing development and use of computer technology, there is a new disease to worry about. Computer "viruses," programs designed to sabotage computers, are infecting computers in corporations, homes, and universities. These viruses spread exponentially, much like biological contagion, and then disrupt the affected systems. The virus secretly attaches itself to other programs and can then delete or alter files. The damage is generally activated by using the computer's clock. Then, any program that is executed may be exposed to the virus, including programs spread through telephone connections. Because of the increasing incidents of virus infiltration, businesses and agencies are becoming wary of sharing software. Security policies need to be increased as immunity programs are being developed.

60. Which of the following is the best title of this passage?

(A) Be Aware
(B) Stop the Clock
(C) Deleting Files
(D) Sharing Software

61. The people most interested in reading this passage probably would be

(A) medical personnel
(B) computer users
(C) government workers
(D) health researchers

62. It is inferred that a company can best protect itself from the virus by

(A) keeping clean
(B) spreading programs by telephone
(C) setting the clock correctly
(D) not using shared software

63. The virus is

(A) a microbe
(B) an insect
(C) a disk
(D) a program

64. If the virus infects a computer, the result would probably be

(A) lost information
(B) a broken computer
(C) sick personnel
(D) dead telephones

GO ON TO THE NEXT PAGE

Questions 65-70

Though we think of Mount Vernon as George Washington's home, the site actually was granted to George Washington's great-grandfather in 1674. From George's great-grandfather, it was passed to George's father, then to his half-brother, and later, to George, eighty years after his great-grandfather had first received the land.

George acquired Mount Vernon in 1754, when he was twenty-two. He lived there until he died in 1799. Even though the main part of the home was constructed in 1735 by Washington's father, George made many changes, significantly enlarging and embellishing the estate. He carefully planned the arrangement of more than a dozen outbuildings. They were built close enough to the house to be useful, but far enough away not to intrude upon the beauty and tranquility of the surroundings. The outbuildings were built mainly for such tasks as weaving, spinning, curing meat, repairing shoes, and doing laundry. In addition to outbuildings, Washington designed three gardens: one for flowers, vegetables, and trees; another for fresh produce for the kitchen; and a third for botanical experimentation. George Washington died at Mount Vernon when he was only sixty-seven. He is buried in a tomb on the grounds of his beloved estate.

65. What is the best title for this passage?

(A) Family Ties
(B) Washington's Botanical Experiments
(C) A Beloved Estate
(D) The Outbuildings of Mount Vernon

66. George Washington acquired Mount Vernon

(A) in 1799
(B) in 1735
(C) from his grandfather
(D) at age twenty-two

67. According to the author, Mount Vernon seemed

(A) busy
(B) cozy
(C) peaceful
(D) exciting

68. When George acquired Mount Vernon, the main house was

(A) less than twenty years old
(B) about eighty years old
(C) too small for him
(D) used for jobs like spinning and weaving

69. The word "embellishing" in line 8 is closest in meaning to

(A) overseeing
(B) tearing down
(C) leaving out
(D) adding to

70. Which of the following statements about George Washington is best supported by this passage?

(A) He had strong connections with his family.
(B) He enjoyed housework.
(C) He liked to experiment with seeds and plants.
(D) He was busy conducting state business from his home.

GO ON TO THE NEXT PAGE

Questions 71-75

By adopting a few simple techniques, parents who read to their children can substantially increase their children's language development. It's surprising, but true. How parents talk to their children makes a big difference in the children's language development. If a parent encourages the child to actively respond to what the parent is reading, the child's language skills increase.

A study was done with two- to three-year-old children and their parents. Half of the thirty children participated in the experimental study; the other half acted as the control group. In the experimental group, the parents were given a two-hour training session in which they were taught to ask open-ended questions rather than yes/no questions. For example, the parent should ask, "What is the doggie doing?" rather than, "Is the doggie running away?" Experimental parents were also instructed in how to expand on their children's answers, how to suggest alternative possibilities, and how to praise correct answers.

At the beginning of the study, the children did not differ on measures of language development, but at the end of one month, the children in the experimental group tested 5.5 months ahead of the control group on a test of verbal expression and vocabulary. Nine months later, the children in the experimental group still showed an advance of 6 months over the children in the control group.

71. Which of the following can be inferred from this passage?

(A) Children who talk a lot are more intelligent.
(B) Parents who listen to their children can teach them more.
(C) Active children should read more.
(D) Verbal ability can easily be increased.

72. In line 2, what does "it's" refer to?

(A) Parents increasing children's language development
(B) Reading techniques being simple
(C) Parents reading to children
(D) Children's language development

73. According to the author, which of the following questions is the best type to ask children about reading?

(A) Do you see the elephant?
(B) Is the elephant in the cage?
(C) What animals do you like?
(D) Shall we go to the zoo?

74. What was the difference between the control group and the experimental group?

(A) The training parents received
(B) The age of the children
(C) The books that were read
(D) The number of children

75. What conclusion is best supported by this passage?

(A) Parents should be trained to read to their children.
(B) The more children read, the more intelligent they become.
(C) Children's language skills increase when they are required to respond actively.
(D) Children who read actively act six months older.

GO ON TO THE NEXT PAGE

Questions 76-83

When John James Audubon first began painting birds, most birds were drawn as though stuffed and fastened to wooden perches. Audubon took birds out of glass cages and gave them a semblance of life. His paintings still have a dramatic impact seldom achieved by wildlife painters. Audubon did not accomplish this from the comfort of his armchair. He spent much of his time roaming the countryside and observing nature. He passionately believed that nature must first be seen alive before it can be represented on paper. Audubon painted his subjects with painstaking accuracy. To him, nature was a continual life-and-death drama. His birds, for instance, never just sit there. They feed one another; they attack their prey; they care for their young. They are always portrayed in their natural habitats. Audubon's art seems composed equally of scientific accuracy and passionate vision. Even now, 150 years after he published *The Birds of America,* Audubon remains America's best-known wildlife artist. His art is hailed the world over as pioneering work. His prints are available now for between $800 and $7,500. That's not a bad investment and gives one a work of art that is also decoration.

76. The main purpose of this passage is to

(A) discuss Audubon's life
(B) give a background of painting in Audubon's time
(C) describe Audubon's painting techniques
(D) give an insight into Audubon's philosophy of painting

77. When Audubon "took birds out of glass cages" (line 2), he

(A) let the birds fly away unharmed.
(B) put the birds in a more natural place.
(C) painted them as if they were alive.
(D) nursed them back to life.

78. Before Audubon began painting, other wildlife painters

(A) stuffed birds
(B) drew still birds
(C) observed dead birds
(D) tied birds to branches

79. Audubon spent much of his time

(A) outside
(B) in his studio
(C) in his favorite chair
(D) looking at bird pictures

80. Which of the following would Audubon probably NOT paint?

(A) A bird feeding its babies.
(B) A bird eating a worm.
(C) A bird diving in the ocean.
(D) A bird singing in its cage.

81. Audubon

(A) is living now
(B) died recently
(C) lived in the 1800s
(D) lived in the 1700s

82. In line 12, the word "hailed" could best be substituted with

(A) published
(B) showered
(C) greeted
(D) praised

83. Audubon can best be characterized as

(A) an artist
(B) an author
(C) an environmentalist
(D) a scientist

GO ON TO THE NEXT PAGE

Question 84-90

But the most important role of the Library of Congress is to serve as the research and reference arm of Congress. The library provides legislators with the information they need to learn about the issues facing them. The library staff answers more than 450,000 queries a year, ranging from very simple requests to extremely complex issues. In addition, people on the library staff will prepare summaries of major legislation and bills to help Congress members stay abreast of daily legislation. The library staff includes people of all backgrounds, from civil engineers and oceanographers to experts in labor relations. Their most important function is to provide objective, unbiased information to Congress. They present all sides of issues, allowing the legislators to make up their own minds as to the effects of the issue involved. There is an additional department for foreign law. The Law Library answers congressional requests for analysis of foreign legislature and legal issues. The Law Library's legal specialists are proficient in fifty different languages.

84. What did the paragraph preceding this passage most likely discuss?

(A) Other libraries in the U.S.A.
(B) Other functions of the Library of Congress
(C) Other duties of legislators
(D) Other research organizations

85. The word "arm" in line 2 is closest in meaning to

(A) weapon
(B) limb
(C) branch
(D) support

86. The main job of the Library of Congress is to

(A) research information
(B) store books
(C) study law
(D) hire experts

87. Which of the following is NOT mentioned as a way that the library staff helps legislators?

(A) Preparing summaries
(B) Presenting their points of view
(C) Reading in foreign languages
(D) Keeping up-to-date

88. For whom is this passage most likely written?

(A) Congress members
(B) The public
(C) The library staff
(D) Lawyers

89. According to the passage, staff members

(A) present contrasting views
(B) ask the legislators for help
(C) give personal opinions
(D) are lawyers

90. The author is trying to be

(A) biased
(B) superficial
(C) informative
(D) cheerful

THIS IS THE END OF SECTION 3. IF YOU FINISH BEFORE TIME IS UP, CHECK YOUR WORK ON SECTION 3 ONLY. DO NOT READ OR WORK ON ANY OTHER SECTION OF THE TEST. **STOP**

Answer Key for Practice Test III

SECTION 1: LISTENING COMPREHENSION

Part A

1. C	**11.** C	**21.** C
2. B	**12.** D	**22.** C
3. D	**13.** D	**23.** B
4. D	**14.** B	**24.** C
5. A	**15.** C	**25.** C
6. A	**16.** B	**26.** D
7. B	**17.** C	**27.** B
8. C	**18.** D	**28.** A
9. A	**19.** D	**29.** C
10. C	**20.** B	**30.** D

Part B

31. B	**36.** B	**41.** A	**46.** C	**51.** D
32. A	**37.** D	**42.** D	**47.** B	**52.** A
33. A	**38.** C	**43.** B	**48.** A	**53.** C
34. D	**39.** C	**44.** B	**49.** A	**54.** C
35. D	**40.** A	**45.** A	**50.** B	**55.** A

Part C

56. D	**61.** B	**66.** A	**71.** A	**76.** A
57. A	**62.** A	**67.** C	**72.** D	**77.** A
58. B	**63.** D	**68.** D	**73.** C	**78.** C
59. B	**64.** B	**69.** B	**74.** C	**79.** C
60. A	**65.** D	**70.** C	**75.** D	**80.** C

SECTION 2: STRUCTURE AND WRITTEN EXPRESSION

1. A
2. B
3. D
4. B
5. B
6. C
7. A
8. B
9. D
10. B
11. B
12. A
13. D
14. B
15. C
16. C
17. A
18. D
19. B
20. C
21. D
22. B
23. A
24. A
25. B
26. B
27. B
28. B
29. A
30. A
31. B
32. A
33. B
34. C
35. A
36. C
37. B
38. D
39. B
40. B
41. C
42. B
43. B
44. B
45. B
46. D
47. A
48. A
49. B
50. B
51. B
52. D
53. B
54. C
55. B
56. B
57. C
58. C
59. D
60. B

SECTION 3: VOCABULARY AND READING COMPREHENSION

1. B
2. C
3. A
4. D
5. B
6. D
7. C
8. D
9. A
10. C
11. C
12. A
13. C
14. A
15. B
16. D
17. C
18. D
19. B
20. A
21. D
22. A
23. C
24. D
25. A
26. B
27. D
28. A
29. B
30. C
31. C
32. A
33. B
34. A
35. C
36. B
37. C
38. D
39. B
40. A
41. C
42. A
43. B
44. D
45. C
46. C
47. C
48. A
49. B
50. D
51. D
52. A
53. D
54. A
55. D
56. D
57. C
58. A
59. D
60. A
61. B
62. D
63. D
64. A
65. C
66. D
67. C
68. A
69. D
70. C
71. D
72. A
73. C
74. A
75. C
76. D
77. C
78. B
79. A
80. D
81. C
82. D
83. A
84. B
85. C
86. A
87. B
88. B
89. A
90. C

Score Analysis Form for Practice Test III

Directions: Count the number of answers you have correct in Practice Test III, using the answer key on pages 481–483. Then use the chart on page 49 (Long Form) to figure out your converted score range. Fill in the rest of this form so you can compare it to your scores in Practice Tests I and II.

	RAW SCORE		CONVERTED SCORE RANGE		APPROXIMATE SCORE RANGE
		(each)		(each)	
Listening Comprehension	____	____–____ × 10 =	____–____	÷ 3 =	____–____
Structure and Written Expression	____	____–____ × 10 =	____–____	÷ 3 =	____–____
Vocabulary and Reading Comprehension	____	____–____ × 10 =	____–____	÷ 3 =	____–____
TOTAL APPROXIMATE SCORE (add 3 approximate scores)					____–____

What is your best section out of the above three? ____________

ANALYSIS OF EACH SECTION

1. Listening Comprehension

	Number Correct	Total	Percent Correct
Part A (Questions 1–30)	______	÷ 30	= ______%
Part B (Questions 31–55)	______	÷ 25	= ______%
Part C (Questions 56–80)	______	÷ 25	= ______%

Which part has the highest percentage of correct answers? ______

2. Structure and Written Expression

	Number Correct	Total	Percent Correct
First Part (Questions 1–23)	______	÷ 23	= ______%
Second Part (Questions 24–60)	______	÷ 37	= ______%

Which section has the highest percentage of correct answers? ______

3. Vocabulary and Reading Comprehension

	Number Correct	Total	Percent Correct
Vocabulary (Questions 1–45)	______	÷ 45	= ______%
Reading (Questions 46–90)	______	÷ 45	= ______%

Which part has the highest percentage of correct answers? __________

Explanatory Answers

SECTION 1: LISTENING COMPREHENSION

The Listening Comprehension Tapescript for this test is on pages 641 to 647.

Part A

1. Dora doesn't need to hurry; the bank closes at six on Fridays.
   (A) Dora went to the bank at six o'clock.
   (B) Dora has to go to the bank right away.
   (C) Dora still has plenty of time to go to the bank.
   (D) Dora was afraid the bank would close earlier on Friday.

(C) Glance at the choices and summarize: Dora, bank, time. Testing point 1: inference. "Doesn't need to hurry" implies that she "has plenty of time." Testing point 2: vocabulary."Plenty of time" means "enough" or "as much as needed." Cultural information: most banks in the United States close later than usual on Fridays.

2. The bus you just missed was the wrong bus anyway.
   (A) The bus station is missing.
   (B) You have to wait for another bus.
   (C) There must be something wrong with the bus.
   (D) It's upsetting to miss the bus.

(B) Glance at the choices and summarize: bus, miss, wait, wrong. Testing point: inference. If you missed the bus, you must wait for another bus. The word "anyway" implies that the speaker is saying, "Don't worry. It doesn't matter if you missed that bus; it was not the bus you wanted."

3. He seems to have a lot of clothes in his closet, but none of them fit well.
   (A) He has many well-fitting clothes.
   (B) There are only a few clothes in the closet.
   (C) Some of the clothes in the closet fit him well.
   (D) He doesn't have any clothes that fit him well.

(D) Glance at the choices and summarize: he, clothes, fit. Testing point: restatement. "None . . . fit him well" means the same as "he doesn't have any . . . that fit him well."

4. Hardship has made the young man develop some good characteristics.
   (A) The young man is hard on the equipment.
   (B) The young man won a scholarship.
   (C) Good characteristics made him a great success.
   (D) Difficulties in his life have had a positive end result.

(D) Glance at the choices and summarize: young man, difficult, success. Testing point: restatement/vocabulary. "Hardship" means "difficulties." The words "end result" mean the same as "result in the end." The verb "has made" implies that the result has been positive at this time.

5. The solution to this problem is quite tricky, don't you think?
   (A) It's a difficult solution, isn't it?
   (B) Did you find the solution for the problem?
   (C) Do you want to think it over quietly?
   (D) You couldn't find the solution, could you?

(A) Glance at the choices and summarize: question, solution, you. Testing point 1: restatement/idiom. "Quite tricky" means "difficult." Testing point 2: question. "Don't you think?" and "isn't it?" both mean "Do you agree?"

6. Even the supervisor couldn't do it, I bet.
   (A) I suspect that the supervisor doesn't know how to do it.
   (B) I'm hesitant to ask the supervisor to help me do it.
   (C) I want to do it by myself.
   (D) I'll have the supervisor help me do it.

(A) Glance at the choices and summarize: I, supervisor, do. Testing point: restatement/vocabulary. "I bet" means "I suspect" or "I think." "Couldn't do it" means "doesn't know how to do it."

7. This soft drink will be much cheaper in the supermarket.
   (A) They make the soft drinks in the supermarket.
   (B) The price of this drink is more reasonable in the supermarket.
   (C) This supermarket only sells soft drinks, not wine and beer.
   (D) You can buy soft drinks in every supermarket.

(B) Glance at the choices and summarize: drinks, supermarket. Testing point: restatement/vocabulary. "Much cheaper" means "the price is more reasonable." The word "reasonable" means "not too much" or "a fair price."

8. George weighed himself every day when he was on his special diet.
   (A) George went to see a doctor for a special diet.
   (B) George was waiting for a special diet.
   (C) George monitored his weight carefully.
   (D) George lost weight every day because of the special diet.

(C) Glance at the choices and summarize: George, waiting, weight, diet. Testing point: restatement. "Weighed himself every day" means "monitored his weight carefully." The verb "to monitor" means "to watch," "to check," or "to keep track of something."

9. The high temperature and the heavy humidity gave the elderly a hard time.
   (A) The elderly suffered from the hot weather.
   (B) Elderly people like warm temperatures.
   (C) The high temperature caused heavy humidity.
   (D) The weather doesn't always affect the elderly.

(A) Glance at the choices and summarize: the elderly, weather. Testing point 1: restatement. "High temperature" means "hot weather." Testing point 2: idiom. ". . . a hard time" means "a difficult time." If you give someone a hard time, that person will suffer.

10. I'll volunteer at the library this evening.
   (A) The librarian will be at the reference desk tonight.
   (B) I'll work at the cafeteria instead of the library soon.
   (C) I'll work at the library tonight.
   (D) It wasn't easy to work at the library.

(C) Glance at the choices and summarize: library, work. Testing point: restatement. "To volunteer" means "to work without pay," or to be a "volunteer worker." "This evening" means the same as "tonight."

11. Why don't you put your books away before setting the table?
   (A) Why couldn't you find these books on the shelf?
   (B) We don't know where to put these books.
   (C) The books should be put away first.
   (D) Why do you want to keep these books on the table?

(C) Glance at the choices and summarize: question, books, shelf, table. Testing point 1: restatement/time sequence. "Do thing 1 before doing thing 2" means "thing 1 should be done first." Testing point 2: question word used as statement. "Why don't you do something?" means "you should do something."

12. Richard has a head start in studying international business with his bilingual background.
   (A) Richard gets a headache when he studies international business.
   (B) Richard took a language class instead of a business class.
   (C) Richard has strong background knowledge in business affairs.
   (D) Richard has an advantage in studying international affairs.

(D) Glance at the choices and summarize: Richard, class, business. Testing point: idiom. "Has a head start" means "has an advantage."

13. Older people often value family pictures more than young people do.
   (A) No one likes these pictures.
   (B) Elderly people don't speak highly of these pictures.
   (C) Young people see more value in the old pictures.
   (D) The older people care a lot about the pictures.

(D) Glance at the choices and summarize: elderly, young, old, pictures. Testing point: restatement/vocabulary. "Value something" means "care about something."

14. Whoever drinks and drives will get a ticket from the police.
   (A) Everybody should drink water when driving in the summer.
   (B) The police will fine people who are drinking and driving.
   (C) Whoever gets a ticket should see or call the police.
   (D) People who speed on the highway will have to pay money to the police.

(B) Glance at the choices and summarize: drink, police. Testing point 1: vocabulary/restatement. "Get a ticket" implies "pay a fine." The word "fine" means "payment of money as a punishment." Testing point 2: restatement. "Whoever drinks and drives" means "people who are drinking and driving."

15. He found the reference he needs at home.
- **(A)** He made a copy of the reference to take home.
- **(B)** He needs more references to get a loan.
- **(C)** He has references in his house.
- **(D)** He didn't have enough references at home.

(C) Glance at the choices and summarize: he, reference. Testing point: restatement. "He found the reference ... at home" means that the reference was in his house.

16. There ought to be more people in this restaurant on weekend evenings.
- **(A)** There will be a big picnic Saturday night.
- **(B)** This restaurant is usually more crowded on Saturday nights.
- **(C)** Let's go to another restaurant; there are too many people here.
- **(D)** We don't usually eat at this restaurant on weekend evenings.

(B) Glance at the choices and summarize: restaurant, Saturday. Testing point: inference/modal. "There ought to be more people" implies that the speaker is surprised that there are not many people. The inference is that usually there are more people. The word "crowded" means "full of people" or "many people." Even though the speaker says the plural "weekend evenings," he or she is only there on one night, Saturday.

17. We'll have a reception shortly after the speech.
- **(A)** The speech won't last long.
- **(B)** We'll have a speech after the reception.
- **(C)** The speech will be before the reception.
- **(D)** Someone is giving a speech at the reception.

(C) Glance at the choices and summarize: speech, reception, time. Testing point 1: restatement/time sequence. ". . . reception shortly after the speech" means ". . . speech before the reception." Testing point 2: vocabulary. "Shortly after" means "very soon after" or "in a little while."

18. We hardly have any rain this time of the year.
- **(A)** It doesn't matter whether we have rain or not.
- **(B)** It's impossible to have rain all the time.
- **(C)** It's nice to have rain this time of the year.
- **(D)** We don't usually have much rain now.

(D) Glance at the choices and summarize: it's, rain. Testing point 1: restatement/negative. ". . . hardly have any rain" means ". . . don't have much rain." Testing point 2: vocabulary. "This time of the year" means the same as "now."

19. He'll be better off taking fewer classes during the first semester.
- **(A)** He didn't take many classes in the first semester.
- **(B)** It's wise to take more classes in the beginning.
- **(C)** He did a better job on writing this semester than last semester.
- **(D)** He shouldn't sign up for too many classes.

(D) Glance at the choices and summarize: he, classes, many. Testing point 1: restatement/idiom. "To be better off" means "to be in a better position." Testing point 2: vocabulary. "Taking classes" refers to "signing up for classes."

20. That price for a watch like this is reasonable, to say the least.
- **(A)** There is no reason to buy a watch like that.
- **(B)** This watch has a fair price.
- **(C)** The least expensive watch isn't always bad.
- **(D)** This is the most expensive watch I've ever seen.

(B) Glance at the choices and summarize: watch, cheap, expensive. Testing point: restatement/vocabulary. The word "reasonable" means "fair" or "not too expensive." By saying "to say the least," the speaker implies that the price is probably very low for the value.

21. I'm sorry; I thought my ticket was in my wallet.
- **(A)** I didn't bring my wallet or my ticket.
- **(B)** Fortunately, I brought my wallet with me.
- **(C)** I don't have my ticket with me.
- **(D)** I didn't know I needed a ticket.

(C) Glance at the choices and summarize: wallet, ticket. Testing point: inference. "I thought my ticket was in my wallet" implies "I don't have my ticket with me."

22. The sweater he used to wear is too small for him this year.
- **(A)** He was wearing the old sweater for fun.
- **(B)** He likes the old sweater better than the new one.
- **(C)** He needs a new sweater.
- **(D)** He traded his sweater for a shirt.

(C) Glance at the choices and summarize: he, sweater, old, new. Testing point: inference. "The sweater he used to wear is too small" implies that he needs a new sweater because this one doesn't fit him.

23. We had a wonderful vacation in our grandparents' cabin in Wyoming.
(A) We wonder if we can visit our grandparents.
(B) We enjoyed visiting Wyoming.
(C) Our grandparents love their cabin in Wyoming.
(D) We visited Wyoming and other places.

(B) Glance at the choices and summarize: we, grandparents, visit. Testing point: restatement. ". . . had a wonderful vacation" means the same as "we enjoyed visiting."

24. We can't make rain, but we certainly can save water.
(A) We want the ring that is the best made.
(B) We had plenty of water from this rain.
(C) We should try to save water during dry weather.
(D) A certain amount of water was saved this year.

(C) Glance at the choices and summarize: we, rain, water. Testing point: inference. Since people can't make it rain, it is important to save the water we have. This implies that the speaker is worried about a lack of water.

25. The mailman is late today.
(A) The maid will come late.
(B) The mayor canceled his appointment.
(C) The mail hasn't come yet.
(D) Being late is maddening.

(C) Glance at the choices and summarize: maid, mayor, mail, late. Testing point: inference. "The mailman is late . . ." implies "the mail hasn't come yet." You may notice the similar sounds of "maid," "mayor," and "mail."

26. She started her ballet training at age seven.
(A) She had a performance at 7 o'clock.
(B) She went to the ballet class after dinner.
(C) She taught a ballet class for seven girls.
(D) She started learning ballet when she was a child.

(D) Glance at the choices and summarize: she, ballet, time. Testing point 1: restatement. "Started ballet training" means "started learning ballet." Testing point 2: restatement. "At age seven" is "when she was a child."

27. You cannot fool him.
(A) He is naive.
(B) He is wise.
(C) Why is he so foolish?
(D) He'll fool you if you don't fool him.

(B) Glance at the choices and summarize: he, wise, foolish. Testing point 1: vocabulary. The verb "to fool" means "to deceive" or "to cheat." Testing point 2: inference. "You cannot fool him" implies that he is so wise that it is impossible to deceive him.

28. Wouldn't it be nice to have a family reunion this fall?
(A) Shall we have a family get-together this year?
(B) Do we have a nice family?
(C) Our family doesn't belong in this union.
(D) We have enough time to arrange a family reunion.

(A) Glance at the choices and summarize: question, family. Testing point 1: restatement/question. "Wouldn't it be nice to do something" means "shall we do something." Testing point 2: vocabulary. "Family reunion" means "family get-together" or "a meeting or party with all extended family members (grandparents, aunts, uncles, cousins, etc.)." Testing point 3: vocabulary. "This fall" means "during the fall season of this year."

29. This music reminds me of my childhood in Massachusetts.
(A) This music doesn't attract me at all.
(B) I learned to play music when I was in Massachusetts.
(C) The music is familiar to me.
(D) Only a child would like music like this.

(C) Glance at the choices and summarize: music, me. Testing point: inference. If the music reminds you of something, it must be familiar to you.

30. Gloria bought a necklace for her mother as a Christmas gift.
(A) Gloria and her mother were doing Christmas shopping.
(B) Gloria's mother sent her daughter a necklace.
(C) Gloria doesn't like the necklace her mother gave her.
(D) Gloria chose jewelry as a present.

(D) Glance at the choices and summarize: Gloria, mother, necklace. Testing point: restatement/vocabulary. "Necklace" is one kind of jewelry; "gift" means "present."

Part B

31. Woman: I can't decide whether to take classes this summer or to find a summer job.
Man: I think you learn more by working, and you'll also make money for next semester.
What does the man suggest?
(A) Taking the summer classes
(B) Finding a summer job
(C) Waiting until later to decide
(D) Working and studying

(B) Glance at the choices and summarize: summer job, class. Testing point: inference. "Working" and "make money" imply that he thinks she should get a job.

32. Woman: Did you enjoy the movie last night?
Man: We couldn't get any tickets, so we went to the beach instead.
What does the man mean?
(A) They weren't able to see the movie last night.
(B) They bought two tickets for today's movie.
(C) They enjoyed the beach more.
(D) They didn't go to the beach, but rented a video at home.

(A) Glance at the choices and summarize: they, movie, beach. Testing point: inference. "Couldn't get tickets" implies "weren't able to see the movie."

33. Man: What a great man!
Woman: Why?
What does the woman want to know?
(A) Why is the man great?
(B) Why did the man say that?
(C) What kind of man is he?
(D) What happened to the man?

(A) Glance at the choices and summarize: why, what, man. Testing point: question. The word "why" relates directly to "Why is the man great?"

34. Man: I have no idea if they will come to the party or not.
Woman: Don't worry, we have enough food for all of them.
What does the woman mean?
(A) They won't come if they don't call.
(B) She is sure that the people will come to the party.
(C) She will cancel the party since nobody called.
(D) There is plenty of food for all the people.

(D) Glance at the choices and summarize: she, come, cancel, party. Testing point: restatement. "Enough food" is the same as "plenty of food."

35. Woman: I don't know if I should take Physics 101 this semester.
Man: It doesn't matter; that class is offered every semester.
What does the man say about the class?
(A) It makes a big difference when she takes Physics 101.
(B) She doesn't need to take Physics 101.
(C) He doesn't know when the class will be offered.
(D) She can take Physics 101 any semester.

(D) Glance at the choices and summarize: she, Physics 101. Testing point: inference. "That class is offered every semester" implies that she will be able to take the class any semester.

36. Woman: Mr. Day, I've just checked this apartment; the bathroom sink is leaking.
Man: OK, I'll have a maintenance man come over to fix it.
What will the man do?
(A) He will fix the sink.
(B) He will ask someone to do the work.
(C) He will move into the apartment.
(D) He will buy a new sink.

(B) Glance at the choices and summarize: he, sink. Testing point: restatement/structure. "To have someone fix it" means "to ask someone to do the work."

37. Man: May I have your phone number?
Woman: No, I haven't gotten one yet. Sorry.
What does the women mean?
(A) She is sorry that the man asked her.
(B) She is going to ask for a new number.
(C) She lost her phone number.
(D) She doesn't have a phone number at this time.

(D) Glance at the choices and summarize: she, phone number. Testing point: restatement. "I haven't gotten one yet" means that she doesn't have one. (It implies that she may get a phone number later.)

38. Woman: Louie, I'm going to give away these books. You can have them if you want.
Man: Are you sure?
What does the man imply?
(A) He is nervous.
(B) He is disappointed.
(C) He is surprised.
(D) He is anxious.

(C) Glance at the choices and summarize: feelings. Testing point: tone of voice. "Are you sure?" with a rising tone indicates surprise.

39. Woman: Excuse me, Sir, may I pay the bill for an overdue book here?
Man: No, pay at the cashier's office.
What do we learn from the conversation?
(A) The woman should pay the fee at the library.
(B) The woman should wait in line.
(C) The woman should pay the fee at another office.
(D) The woman should pay cash only.

(C) Glance at the choices and summarize: woman, pay, fee. Testing point: inference. ". . . pay . . . here?" "No, at . . . office" implies ". . . pay . . . at another office."

40. Woman: Do you want me to help you type your report?
Man: Thank you, but I already had the typist take care of it.
What does the man mean?
(A) The typist has completed it already.
(B) He completed the typing himself.
(C) He'll need some help later on.
(D) He wants the woman to type more carefully.

(A) Glance at the choices and summarize: typing, completed. Testing point 1: structure. "To have someone do something" means "to ask someone to do something." Testing point 2: vocabulary. "To take care of it" in this sentence means "to do" or "to complete."

41. Woman: Does this bus go to the housing office?
Man: No, but the next one does. Just wait for a few minutes.
What does the man suggest?
(A) Wait for the next bus.
(B) Walk to the housing office.
(C) Ask someone else.
(D) Get on this bus.

(A) Glance at the choices and summarize: wait, walk, bus. Testing point: restatement. "The next one does . . . wait for a few minutes." means the same as "wait for the next one."

42. Woman: I thought we could check out as many books as we need with a student I.D.
Man: That's right, but not those reference books.
What does the man mean?
(A) Students with a proper I.D. can check any book out.
(B) Only the students with special permission can check out reference books.
(C) Only professors can check out the reference books.
(D) The reference books are not allowed to be checked out.

(D) Glance at the choices and summarize: student, check out, books. Testing point: inference. "But not those reference books" implies "the reference books are not allowed to be checked out."

43. Man: Didn't you say you would go to the convention this morning?
Woman: Yes, but it was postponed until next Wednesday.
What does the woman mean?
(A) The convention was canceled.
(B) The convention was put off.
(C) The convention was held last Wednesday.
(D) The convention was overcrowded.

(B) Glance at the choices and summarize: convention, canceled, put off. Testing point: vocabulary. "Postponed" means "put off until later."

44. Man: What did Joan call for?
Woman: She wants our new address, so she can mail us her business card.
What does the woman mean?
(A) Joan called about her business trip.
(B) Joan wants to send her card to us.
(C) Joan will mail us her new address.
(D) Joan's card was lost somewhere.

(B) Glance at the choices and summarize: Joan, card. Testing point: restatement. "Mail us her . . . card" is the same as ". . . send her card to us."

45. Man: What? You've got your Ph.D. degree already?
Woman: Already? It's been six years!
What does the woman imply?
(A) It's taken her a long time to get a Ph.D degree.
(B) It's a piece of cake to receive a degree.
(C) She did it much quicker than other people working on the degree.
(D) She is still a graduate student.

(A) Glance at the choices and summarize: degree, time. Testing point: tone of voice. When the man says "already" he is implying that the time is earlier than he expected. When the woman repeats "already" and adds, "It's been six years," she implies that it has taken a long time to get a PhD degree.

46. Woman: May I help you?
Man: Yes, could you tell me the number of the local post office?
What does the man want?
(A) A money order
(B) The current time
(C) A telephone number
(D) Weather information

(C) Glance at the choices and summarize: time, order, number. Testing point: inference. When the man asks for a "number," he is referring to "a telephone number."

47. Man: Do you have the test scores?
Woman: No, but they are listed in the English department bulletin.
What does the woman imply?
(A) The scores are not listed.
(B) You can read the scores yourself.
(C) The English department doesn't give out scores.
(D) The scores will be out tomorrow..

(B) Glance at the choices and summarize: scores. Testing point: inference. "They" refers to "test scores." Since she says the scores are listed in the bulletin, she implies "you can read the scores yourself."

48. Man: How do you correct an error with this typewriter?
Woman: Just press the "correct" button.
What do we learn from this conversation?
(A) The man doesn't know how to make a correction.
(B) The typewriter is broken.
(C) The man is learning how to change the ribbon.
(D) The man is asking why the typing error occurred.

(A) Glance at the choices and summarize: correction, typewriter, type. Testing point: restatement. "How do you correct an error" has the same meaning as "how do you make a correction."

49. Man: Is there anything else that I have to do to complete this course?
Woman: No, that's it.
What does the woman mean?
(A) Everything is completed.
(B) There is only one thing left to complete.
(C) No, it is not enough.
(D) That is the right one.

(A) Glance at the choices and summarize: everything, one thing, complete. Testing point: idiom. "That's it" means "everything is completed" or "that's all there is."

50. Woman: How would you like your coffee?
Man: Decaffeinated, please.
What does the man mean?
(A) He doesn't want sugar in his coffee.
(B) He doesn't want caffeine in his coffee.
(C) He doesn't want his coffee too hot.
(D) He doesn't want coffee yet.

(B) Glance at the choices and summarize: coffee, doesn't want what? Testing point: vocabulary. "Decaffeinated" means "coffee with no caffeine."

51. Man: Have you gotten your textbook yet?
Woman: They are out of it in the bookstore, but they made a special order for me.
What does the woman mean?
(A) She has to wait in line to buy her textbook.
(B) She can borrow the textbook from the library.
(C) It's too late to buy the textbook now.
(D) She had the salesman order the book for her.

(D) Glance at the choices and summarize: she, textbook, buy. Testing point: inference. "They" refers to the salesman or the bookstore. "Special order" implies that she asked the salesman to order a book for her.

52. Man: Do you want to try a new way to get there?
Woman: Not this time; we don't have enough time.
What does the woman imply?
(A) She thinks a new way will take too long.
(B) She doesn't want to go the same way this time.
(C) She has changed her mind.
(D) She agrees with the man's idea.

(A) Glance at the choices and summarize: new way, same way. Testing point: inference. "Not this time" implies that she doesn't want to try something new at this time. She wants to get there quickly.

53. Man: Is this paper acceptable?
Woman: No, you have to type it.
What does the woman mean?
(A) You should have turned the paper in yesterday.
(B) The paper is acceptable.
(C) The paper must be typed.
(D) The typing errors are not acceptable.

(C) Glance at the choices and summarize: paper, typing. Testing point: restatement. "You have to type it" means the same as "it must be typed."

54. Man: What's the due date for this book?
Woman: Tomorrow.
What does the woman mean?
(A) She has a date tomorrow.
(B) She knows tomorrow is Tuesday.
(C) The book must be returned tomorrow.
(D) She'll become a bookkeeper tomorrow.

(C) Glance at the choices and summarize: book, tomorrow. Testing point: vocabulary. "Due date" means the date that a certain action must be taken. "Due date for the book" means "the date the book must be returned."

55. Woman: The elevator is over here.
Man: I know, but I like to walk up.
What does the man mean?
(A) He prefers to use the stairs.
(B) He doesn't know where the elevator is.
(C) He is in too much of a hurry to wait for the elevator.
(D) He uses elevators all the time.

(A) Glance at the choices and summarize: he, elevator. Testing point: inference. When the man says "I know," he implies that he knows where the elevator is, but he doesn't want to use the elevator. "But I like to walk up" implies that the man "prefers to use the stairs."

Part C

56. What is the speaker mainly discussing?
(A) Julius Caesar
(B) A summer play
(C) A public lecture
(D) A Shakespeare festival

(D) This is an inference question. The speaker discusses many aspects of the Shakespeare Festival. Answers (A), (B), and (C) are too narrow. They focus on only one aspect of the talk.

57. Who is most likely listening to this talk?
(A) Literature students
(B) The audience at a Shakespeare play
(C) Professional actors
(D) Community members

(A) This is an inference question. The speaker says, ". . . since we've just finished reading . . ." It is unlikely that an audience (answer B) would be addressed this way. Answer (C) is unlikely, since the speaker says, ". . . our own chair, Dr.Arthur Johnson" and ". . . our own college actors . . ." Answer (D) is unlikely because of the references to the college.

58. Why does the speaker think the listeners would be interested in the plays?
(A) Because there are actors from out of town
(B) Because they just read *Julius Caesar*
(C) Because there will be community talks
(D) Because the plays are in the summer

(B) This is a restatement question. The speaker says, ". . . since we've just finished reading *Julius Caesar*, I thought you'd be interested in going."

59. Who is Dr. Johnson?
(A) An actor
(B) A chairman
(C) A librarian
(D) A teacher

(B) This is a restatement question. The speaker says, ". . . our own chair, Dr. Arthur Johnson." The word "chair" is a short version of "chairman" or "chairwoman."

60. Why is Dr. Johnson giving a speech?
(A) To help people understand the play
(B) To get financial support for the series
(C) To explain the grant
(D) To introduce the actors

(A) This is an inference question. The speaker says, "Dr. Johnson will first give a brief introduction to the whole series and then discuss *Julius Caesar* in detail." You can infer from this that Dr. Johnson wants to help people understand the play.

61. When will the first play begin?
(A) On Friday
(B) In two weeks
(C) At 7 P.M.
(D) Right after the library talk

(B) This is a restatement question. In the final sentence, the speaker says that the first play will begin two weeks from Friday.

62. What is the main problem the speaker is referring to?
(A) The lack of water
(B) The quality of water
(C) The cost of water
(D) The abundance of water

(A) This is a restatement question. The speaker says in the first sentence, "Because of the severe drought . . ." The word"drought" means "a long period of time with a shortage of water."

63. What should people do on Monday?
(A) Water their cars.
(B) Disconnect their washing machines.
(C) Wash their decks.
(D) Turn off their sprinkler systems.

(D) This is an inference question. The speaker says, ". . . water rationing will go into effect on Monday . . . lawns cannot be watered with automatic sprinklers . . ." Since "a sprinkler system" (answer D) refers to an automatic sprinkler, you can infer that people must turn off their sprinkler systems.

64. If you have a lawn, what are your rules?
(A) Use the sprinkler on Monday, Wednesday, or Friday.
(B) Water by hand.
(C) Water on Wednesdays.
(D) Don't water.

(B) This is a restatement question. The speaker says, "You may water by hand . . ."

65. Which of the following was NOT mentioned by the speaker?
(A) Brushing teeth
(B) Washing clothes
(C) Watering grass
(D) Using dishwashers

(D) This is a negative restatement question. You can answer it by elimination. The speaker mentions brushing teeth, washing clothes, and watering grass. He does not mention using a dishwasher (though he does mention washing dishes by hand under running water).

66. What will the drought patrol crew do?
(A) Fine citizens.
(B) Look for water sources.
(C) Ration water.
(D) Write new water rules.

(A) This is a restatement question. The speaker says, ". . . a new drought patrol crew . . . will be looking for offenders . . . If you are caught, there will be a $50 fine." "A fine" is a sum of money to be paid as a penalty.

67. What does the speaker suggest?
(A) Paying $50
(B) Fining your neighbor
(C) Reusing washing machine water
(D) Taking baths instead of showers

(C) This is a restatement question. The speaker says, "when you wash your clothes, save the final rinse water to begin your next load."

68. When the man first speaks, where is he probably going?
(A) To see a friend
(B) To write his report
(C) Home
(D) To the library

(D) This is an inference question. The speaker says, "Are you heading over to the library, too?" The word "too" implies that he is going that way also. The idiom "heading over" means "going to" or "going in the direction of."

69. Why is the man surprised?
(A) Because the building is noisy.
(B) Because the library is closed.
(C) Because the resource center is new.
(D) Because the library is shaking.

(B) This is an inference question. The man's rising tone of voice as he says, "Closed already?" shows that he is surprised.

70. Where will the new resource center be?
(A) In the community
(B) Outside the main library
(C) In the basement of the library
(D) Downtown

(C) This is an inference question. The woman says, "They have to rebuild the basement . . ." From this you can infer that the new center will be located in the basement.

71. Which of the following topics would probably NOT be found in the new resource center?
(A) World War II Fighter Pilots
(B) Protection for Endangered Species
(C) Dealing with the Shortage of Fossil Fuels
(D) The Results of Nuclear Testing

(A) This is an inference question. The woman says that the new center is for projects that focus on global concerns in the 21st century. Answer (A) is the only topic that occurred at a definite time in the past. The other topics fit into a study of technology, the environment, and the arms build-up, and they affect the whole world. They will also be of concern during the next century.

72. Why does the man think that information for his research topic would be found in the new resource center?
   (A) Because cooperation is important for everyone
   (B) Because money is an ancient tool
   (C) Because all societies use money
   (D) Because economics is a global issue

(D) This is an inference question. The man says that his topic is increasing global economic cooperation and that this should be a 21st century concern. Answer (A) is too general; it doesn't mention economic cooperation.

73. How does the man feel about the library's new hours?
   (A) He is angry about the change.
   (B) He thinks that the hours are better than before.
   (C) He thinks that it is necessary for now.
   (D) He is disappointed because of his paper.

(C) This is an inference question. You can infer answer (C) when the man says, "I guess it's worth putting up with building noise and shortened hours for the time being." The phrase "the time being" means "now."

74. How many students will get awards?
   (A) 500
   (B) 100
   (C) 10
   (D) 7

(C) This is a restatement question. The first words of the talk are, "Ten graduate students . . ."

75. Who will give the awards?
   (A) A graduate student
   (B) A teaching assistant
   (C) A teacher
   (D) The chancellor

(D) This is a restatement question. The speaker says, "The chancellor will present . . ."

76. What will the winners receive?
   (A) Cash
   (B) A job
   (C) A credential
   (D) A letter

(A) This is a restatement question. The speaker says, ". . . a cash prize of $100 . . ."

77. Which of the following is NOT mentioned as a job for teaching assistants?
   (A) Holding office hours
   (B) Grading student work
   (C) Directing labs
   (D) Leading discussion sessions

(A) This is a negative restatement question. You can answer it by elimination. The speaker mentions "leading discussion groups, grading papers, and overseeing lab work." He does not mention holding office hours.

78. What did the chancellor say?
   (A) Teaching assistants should get $100 more.
   (B) Teaching assistants teach many classes.
   (C) Teaching assistants are an important part of the school.
   (D) Teaching assistants should work longer hours.

(C) This is a restatement question. The speaker says, "The chancellor has noted that teaching assistants are an integral part of our campus . . ." The word "integral" means "necessary in order to complete something"; in this sentence it means "important."

79. According to the speaker, why do most teaching assistants work?
   (A) They like the job.
   (B) They meet many students.
   (C) They need the money.
   (D) It helps their studies.

(C) This is a restatement question. The speaker says, "Most of them work . . . to help with the cost of their education.

80. Why should the listeners go to the ceremony?
   (A) To get an award
   (B) To meet the teaching assistants
   (C) To show their support
   (D) To give out prizes

(C) This is a restatement question. The speaker says, "Please come to the ceremony . . . to show your appreciation . . ."

SECTION 2: STRUCTURE AND WRITTEN EXPRESSION

1. Fortunately, _________ single nation has to have the task of learning all we need to know about the ocean.
(A) no
(B) not
(C) none
(D) never

(A) Testing point: no/not/none. Use "no" before a noun; use "not" to make a negative verb; use "none" as a negative noun; and use "never" to mean "at no time."

2. _________ some cultures, openness is considered in a very negative light.
(A) From
(B) In
(C) At
(D) On

(B) Testing point: preposition. "In some cultures" means the same as "inside."

3. _________, often of a religious character, were developed from fundamental African forms.
(A) Ancient dancing of Egyptians
(B) Ancient Egyptian dancing
(C) Ancient Egyptian dance
(D) Ancient Egyptian dances

(D) Testing point: noun phrase. The subject of the sentence is "dances." The nouns "Ancient" and "Egyptian" describe the kind of dancing. "Dances" is a plural noun; therefore, the plural verb "were" is needed.

4. _________, allowing the passage of nerve fibers and blood vessels.
(A) Whenever microscopic canals embraced by the bone
(B) The bone embraces many microscopic canals
(C) Microscopic canals embraced by the bone
(D) Whereas the bone embraced many microscopic canals

(B) Testing point: subject + verb. The sentence needs a main clause. "Allowing . . ." is an adverb phrase describing the canals.

5. The troublesome tartar above the gumline _________ by careful toothbrushing.
(A) can reduce
(B) can be reduced significantly
(C) is reducing significantly
(D) to reduce

(B) Testing point: passive voice. The sentence should be ". . . tartar . . . can be reduced significantly by . . ."

6. Of all the brass instruments, _________, since it mingles well with the woodwinds.
(A) the French horn used
(B) the French horn is useful the most
(C) the French horn is the most useful
(D) is the most useful French horn

(C) Testing point: subject + verb. The sentence needs a main clause. "Of all the brass" gives additional information about the French horn. The sentence should read, "Of all the . . . instruments, . . . horn . . . is the most useful, since . . ."

7. _________ some satellites have retrograde motion is not yet understood.
(A) Why
(B) Whenever
(C) What
(D) Although

(A) Testing point: "wh" word as subject. The main verb of the sentence is "is." All of the first six words tell what "is not understood."

8. George Stephenson, an English engineer, _________ to haul coal from mines.
(A) traveling engine that he constructed
(B) constructed a traveling engine
(C) which was constructed in a traveling engine
(D) he was a constructor of traveling engines

(B) Testing point: verb. The sentence needs a past tense verb and an object. The sentence should be "George Stephenson . . . constructed a traveling engine . . ."

9. In the type of _________ radio receivers, a signal is translated upward or downward in frequency.
(A) used mixer in
(B) mixer used
(C) used in a mixer
(D) mixer used in

(D) Testing point: word order. The sentence needs a noun and a past participle phrase to modify the noun "mixer."

10. Each subject of the speech was _________ carefully prepared that the keynote speaker received a great response from the audience.
(A) as
(B) so
(C) such
(D) very

(B) Testing point: purpose/reason. The word "that" is a clue to identify this testing point ("so . . . that . . ." Use "so" before an adjective or adverb; use "such" before a noun.

11. The weather in the far north is not _________ it is near the Equator.
(A) like humid as
(B) as humid as
(C) humid as
(D) so humid that

(B) Testing point: comparative "as . . . as." Two situations are compared in this type of sentence.

12. _________ of several women's records in aviation, Ms. Savitskaya made over 500 parachute jumps.
(A) Holder
(B) Hold
(C) To hold
(D) Holds

(A) Testing point: subject/noun phrase. The second part of the sentence, beginning with Ms. Savitskaya, is the main part. The first part is a description of Ms. Savitskaya. The comma is a clue that the first part is a phrase describing the person.

13. _________ protects copper from damage is its patina, a greenish surface film.
(A) There
(B) That
(C) Which
(D) What

(D) Testing point: "wh" word as subject. The main verb is the word "is." All the words before "is" describe "patina." The sentence should read, "What protects copper . . . is . . ."

14. Landslides, _________, and volcanic eruptions can all cause vibrations in the earth.
(A) that falling
(B) falling rocks
(C) rock is falling
(D) when rocks falling

(B) Testing point: parallel construction. The sentence should read, "Landslides, falling rocks, and volcanic eruptions can all cause . . ." The words "landslides" and "volcanic eruptions" are clues to the fact that the other word must be plural.

15. When _________ people who irritated him, the columnist was bitter and even splenetic.
(A) in discussion
(B) his discussing
(C) he discussed
(D) he discuss

(C) Testing point: adverb clause. The comma and the word "when" are clues that the first part of the sentence is a dependent clause describing "the columnist." The clause needs a subject and a verb.

16. Vitamin E cream, a moisturizing emollient, _________ maintaining soft, healthy looking skin.
(A) having been used for
(B) used for
(C) has been used for
(D) having used for

(C) Testing point: verb. The sentence should read, ". . . cream has been used for maintaining . . ." The word "cream" is a singular noun; therefore, the verb must start with the word "has." "Cream" is not an actor, so the verb must be in the passive voice.

17. Childless couples sometimes acquire _________ pets to whom they can give parental love.
(A) baby-sized
(B) size like a baby
(C) baby's size
(D) size of a baby

(A) Testing point: adjective. The sentence needs an adjective to modify the noun "pets." The hyphen means that both words stand for one idea. The two nouns "baby" and "size" are used to describe a type of pet.

18. Encounters between people from different countries can result in misunderstandings _________ different conceptions about space.
(A) because they
(B) is because they
(C) is because their
(D) because of their

(D) Testing point: cause/result. "Because of" is followed by a phrase (because of their different conceptions about space). The word "because" is followed by a clause (because they *have* different conceptions).

19. Having introduced the experimental and theoretical study of vibrational relaxation, _________ to examine the properties of methyl iodide.
(A) proceeding the author
(B) the author proceeded
(C) proceeded the author
(D) did the author proceed

(B) Testing point: subject + verb. Use the comma as a clue to indicate that the whole first part of the sentence is not the main sentence. It can be omitted while still keeping a grammatically correct sentence.

20. Not until the 1960s, ________ at Hugnes Research Laboratories build the world's first working laser.
(A) Theodore Mainman
(B) while Theodore Mainman
(C) did Theodore Mainman
(D) Theodore Mainman did

(C) Testing point: inverted verb. Use the words "not until" as a clue to inverted verb order. The sentence should read, "Not until . . ., did Theodore Mainman . . . build . . ."

21. After the election, ________ a new stage.
(A) the entering nation
(B) to enter the nation
(C) entering the nation
(D) the nation will enter

(D) Testing point: subject + verb. The sentence needs a noun and a future tense verb.

22. The national parks have interpretative centers ________ tourists can acquire information about the animals and trees.
(A) which
(B) where
(C) that
(D) there

(B) Testing point: adjective clause. "Interpretative centers" is a place; use "where" to describe the place.

23. More and more graduates of medical schools tend ________ on limited areas of their professions.
(A) to concentrate
(B) concentrate
(C) concentrated
(D) concentrating

(A) Testing point: infinitive. An infinitive follows the verb "tend."

24. Wild creatures are energetic in their natural
A B
habitats than in a zoo.
C D

(A) Testing point: omission of word. This is a comparative sentence. The correct sentence is "wild creatures are more energetic in . . . than in . . ."

25. The social worker has such a sympathetic,
A
comfortably manner that people like to con-
B C
fide in her.
D

(B) Testing point: word form. The correct sentence is "The social worker has . . . a *comfortable* manner. "Comfortable" is an adjective describing the kind of manner.

26. Fire, the phenomenon of combustion
as observed in light, flame, and heat,
A
it is one of the basic tools of mankind.
B C D

(B) Testing point: additional word. The word "it" is unnecessary, because it repeats the subject. The correct sentence is "Fire . . . is one of the . . ."

27. Organized labor has fight for and won protec-
A B
tion and benefits for its worker-members.
C D

(B) Testing point: verb tense. Both verbs must be in the same tense. The tense in this sentence is present perfect, as indicated by the word "has." The correct sentence is "Organized labor has fought for and won . . ."

28. Women's liberation has supported by many
A B C
men and by much of society.
D

(B) Testing point: verb tense. The verb should be in the passive form: "has been supported."

29. The capable to use books in one's work is one
A B C
characteristic of a scholar.
D

(A) Testing point: word form. The word "capable" is an adjective. This sentence needs a noun form: "capability."

30. Alike other turtles, marine turtles breathe air through their lungs and lay eggs on land.
(A = Alike; B = breathe; C = through their; D = lay eggs)

(A) Testing point: like/unlike/alike. The word "like" indicates a comparison between two things. It comes before a noun. The correct sentence is, "Like other turtles, marine turtles . . ."

31. The strong wind does a terrible noise when it blows through the antenna.
(A = The; B = does; C = when; D = through)

(B) Testing point: wrong word. The word should be "makes" not "does." The correct sentence is, "The . . . wind makes a . . . noise ..."

32. Bacteria and germs are too tiny that they are invisible to the naked eye.
(A = are too tiny; B = are invisible; C = to; D = naked)

(A) Testing point: so/such/so that. The clue for this sentence is the word "that." The correct sentence is, "Bacteria and germs are so tiny that . . ."

33. Different kinds of turtles are uniquely adapt to living on land, in fresh water, or in the ocean.
(A = turtles are; B = adapt; C = to living; D = or in the)

(B) Testing point: word form. This could also be called a passive voice testing point. The correct verb is the passive, "are uniquely adapted to ..." The meaning of "adapt" is that something is suitable or fit for a particular situation.

34. The field of laser spectroscopy has changed radically between the last decade.
(A = The field; B = has changed; C = between; D = decade)

(C) Testing point: wrong word. The correct word is "since" in this sentence. One clue is that the verb is in the present perfect tense. The word "since" often goes with the present perfect tense. It is also impossible to have something occur between the last decade (or decades), because there is no time between decades. A decade ends in December, and the next decade begins in January. A decade refers to any period of ten years, but it is commonly used to refer to a period such as January 1, 1960 to December 30, 1969.

35. The surgeon and sanitary techniques applied by the Greeks were lost with the deterioration of their civilization.
(A = surgeon; B = applied by; C = were lost; D = their)

(A) Testing point: word form. This sentence needs a word to describe "techniques." The correct form is "surgical." The sentence should be, "The surgical and sanitary techniques . . ."

36. Smoking is not allowed in gas stations, because there is too many easily ignited material in the vicinity.
(A = Smoking; B = there is; C = too many; D = ignited)

(C) Testing point: many/much. The sentence should be, "Smoking is not allowed . . . because there is too much easily ignited material . . ." Since the word "material" is a mass (uncountable) noun, the word "much" is used to describe it.

37. Comets are apparently the more numerous bodies in the solar system except for small meteor fragments.
(A = Comets; B = more; C = bodies; D = except for)

(B) Testing point: superlative. The word "the" is a clue. The sentence should be, "Comets are . . . the most numerous bodies in the solar system . . ."

38. Benzene should be kept (A) in tightly-capped (B) bottles, because it is (C) high (D) volatile.

(D) Testing point: word form. The word "volatile" needs an adjective to describe how volatile. The correct sentence is ". . . because it is highly volatile." The word "volatile" means "changes quickly from a gas to a vapor."

39. The researchers (A) systematic (B) their (C) information before writing (D) the report.

(B) Testing point: word form. The sentence needs a verb form: "systematize" or "systematized." This verb form means that the researchers developed a system.

40. The use of (A) standard spelling, correct grammar, and approving (B) pronunciation indicates (C) that a person is educated (D).

(B) Testing point: word form. The word "approved" is correct for this sentence. The sentence should be, "use of standard spelling . . . and approved pronunciation . . ." The meaning of "approved pronunciation" is that the pronunciation has been approved (accepted).

41. Studies reveal (A) that people who (B) eat the great (C) amount of salt suffer (D) the most from hypertension.

(C) Testing point: superlative. A clue here is the word "the." The sentence should be, ". . . people who eat the greatest amount of salt suffer the most . . ."

42. The adult flea of both sexes (A) eats only bleed (B) and can survive away from (C) its host for weeks without eating (D).

(B) Testing point: word form. This sentence needs a noun form: "blood." The word "bleed" is a verb. The correct sentence is, "The adult flea . . . eats only blood . . ."

43. In the American (A) educated (B) system, children go to school (C) for (D) twelve years.

(B) Testing point: word form. This sentence needs an adjective to describe the word "system." The correct word is "educational," which means "relating to education." The word "educated" can be a verb or an adjective. As an adjective, "educated" means that a person has education.

44. It is (A) impossible of (B) an alcoholic (C) to (D) drink moderately.

(B) Testing point: preposition. After the word "impossible," the word "for" is needed. The correct sentence is, "It is impossible for an alcoholic to . . ."

45. Recreation is any activity (A) voluntarily engaged (B) for self-satisfaction through (C) relaxation, fun, or the opportunity for expression (D).

(B) Testing point: omission of word. After the word "engaged" there must be a preposition, "in." The correct sentence is, "Recreation is any activity . . . engaged in for self-satisfaction . . ."

46. Handicapped (A) people frequently state (B) that they feel isolated (C) and other people (D) avoid them.

(D) Testing point: omission of word. The word "that" must be in this sentence to indicate the beginning of each clause that follows the word "state." The correct sentence is, "Handicapped people frequently state that they feel isolated and that other people . . ."

47. Detection (A) often find out the truth (B) by gathering lots of (C) unrelated information and studying it (D).

(A) Testing point: word form. The subject of this sentence should refer to a group of people: "detectives."

48. Gas efficiency (A), secure (B), economical, and practical (C), today's cars are better than any (D) produced before.

(A) Testing point: word form. This could also be called parallel construction. The first part of this sentence should consist of adjectives that describe the car. "Gas efficiency" is a noun form. The correct sentence is "Gas-efficient, secure, economical, and practical . . ." The phrase "gas-efficient" means that the car makes efficient use of gas; it doesn't waste gas.

49. Byssinosis, known as (A) one of the many lung diseases, are believed (B) to be the result of years of exposure (C) to (D) fine cotton dust.

(B) Testing point: verb agreement. The subject is "byssinosis," a singular noun, so the verb must be "is believed."

50. The population problem around the world is complicated (A), since much (B) people see benefits in having (C) large families (D).

(B) Testing point: many/much. The word "many" must come before "people," since "people" is a plural (countable) noun.

51. Some (A) people prefers (B) urban living (C); others don't (D).

(B) Testing point: verb agreement. Since "people" is plural, the verb must be "prefer."

52. The man claimed that the panacea he sold (A) was good (B) for alleviating (C) stomachaches, fever, and seasick (D).

(D) Testing point: parallel construction. The correct sentence is, ". . . stomachaches, fever, and seasickness." The word "seasickness" is a noun form. "Seasick" is an adjective.

53. People have to (A) take precautions to (B) both acts of (C) sabotage and direct violence in times (D) of war.

(B) Testing point: preposition. After the word "precaution" you need either the preposition "against" or the preposition "for."

54. The candidate spoke ambiguously (A) on purpose (B) so that people listen to (C) him could hear whatever (D) they wanted to hear.

(C) Testing point: word form. The correct word is "listening," which describes who the people are. The correct sentence is, "The candidate spoke . . . so that people listening to him could hear . . ."

55. The lack of rain in the northern Africa caused
A B C

severe scarcity of food.
D

(B) Testing point: article. The word "the" cannot come before the name "Africa." The correct sentence is, ". . . in northern Africa . . ."

56. The political contestant's speech

was filled with empty promise, platitudes,
A B

and trite expressions.
C D

(B) Testing point: singular/plural noun. The correct word is "promises."

57. The economies of many OPEC nations is
A B C

primarily oil-based.
D

(C) Testing point: verb agreement. Since the subject is "economies," the verb must be "are."

58. People dream more when they enter to lighter
A B C D

phases of sleep.

(C) Testing point: preposition. This testing point could also be "additional word." To correct this sentence, you could either leave out the word "to," or change "to" to "into." The sentence could be, ". . . when they enter lighter phrases . . ." or ". . . when they enter into lighter phases . . ."

59. Studies conducted by Johns Hopkins University
A

indicated that it was the husbands, not the

wives, whose lives were shortened by the lost
B C D

of their spouses.

(D) Testing point: word form. The correct word is "loss," not "lost." The sentence needs a noun form, ". . . the loss of their spouses."

60. For minor cuts, scratches, and insect bitings,
A B

apply an antiseptic directly to the injury.
C D

(B) Testing point: word form. The correct noun is "bites," not "bitings."

PART 3: VOCABULARY AND READING COMPREHENSION

1. The sixteenth century witnessed the creation of numerous types of Japanese ceramics.
(A) was the judgment of
(B) was the setting for
(C) stood for
(D) bypassed

(B) The word "witness" means "see," "observe," "give evidence of something," or "be the scene or setting of something." The meaning of this sentence is that many types of ceramics were created during the time of the sixteenth century.

2. Mass production yields vast quantities of goods for domestic and foreign use.
(A) expanding
(B) diverse
(C) enormous
(D) intense

(C) The word "vast" means "very large" or "immense." The word "enormous" also means "very large."

3. The Smithsonian Institution houses administration offices as well as museums.
(A) shelters
(B) builds
(C) places
(D) rents

(A) The word "house" is a verb in this sentence. It means "to provide a house or a shelter for something."

4. In many parts of the world wild animals are practically nonexistent.
(A) primitive
(B) dangerous
(C) undisturbed
(D) undomesticated

(D) "Wild" is the opposite of "domesticated" or "tame." It means "living in a natural condition." A wild animal is one that lives off the land with no food or care given by humans.

5. Gold jewelry is as dazzling as it is expensive.
(A) shocking
(B) brilliant
(C) colorful
(D) valued

(B) "Dazzling" refers to a very bright light or glare. In this sentence it means "brilliant" or "very bright."

6. The earliest Islamic metal objects reveal past traditions in their decoration.
(A) suggest
(B) inherit
(C) fabricate
(D) display

(D) "To reveal" means "to show, exhibit, or display" something.

7. The Japanese tea ceremony embodies a simple and direct spirit.
(A) ghost
(B) soul
(C) feeling
(D) solution

(C) The word "spirit" often means ghost or soul, but in this sentence it refers to an attitude or feeling about something.

8. It is common to find a great number of museum items preserved in storage rooms.
(A) featured
(B) manufactured
(C) prepared
(D) protected

(D) "Preserve" and "protect" both mean "to save from harm."

9. Most teachers spend considerable time planning lessons and correcting papers.
(A) much
(B) important
(C) quality
(D) excessive

(A) The word "considerable" can mean either "much" or "large." Answer (D) means "too much."

10. Selected animals around the world are being studied for the purpose of preserving threatened species.
(A) angry
(B) harmful
(C) endangered
(D) menacing

(C) "Threatened" generally means that there is an intention of giving harm or punishment to someone or something. In this sentence, "threatened" and "endangered" refer to the fact that there are some animals that are dying out completely. For some species, there is a danger that not one animal will survive, and their fate will be similar to the fate of the dinosaurs.

11. The newly planned satellite flights will begin a new phase in the American space program.
(A) system
(B) season
(C) stage
(D) position

(C) In this sentence, "phase" refers to a change in the cycle of development. A stage of development has the same meaning.

12. A deficiency in zinc can cause birth defects in rodents.
(A) A lack of
(B) An overdose of
(C) An impurity in
(D) A defect in

(A) "Deficiency" refers to a lack of something; something is missing; therefore, it is not complete.

13. One of the mundane tasks in life is cleaning the house.
(A) boring
(B) manual
(C) ordinary
(D) necessary

(C) The dictionary meaning of "mundane" is something that is of the world rather than of the spirit or heavens. This word also means "ordinary" or "practical." It is commonly used to refer to situations that do not change and are therefore boring. Being boring, however, is a result of being mundane; it is not a synonym. The word "manual" means "performed by hand."

14. Some people feel queasy when taking ocean trips.
(A) nauseous
(B) energized
(C) confused
(D) afraid

(A) "Queasy" and "nauseous" both refer to the feeling of an upset stomach that many people get while riding in a car, airplane, or boat.

15. The U.S. park system employs hundreds of people each year to clear paths for visitors' use.
(A) latrines
(B) walkways
(C) campsites
(D) amphitheaters

(B) A path is a place that is made for walking, such as a walkway in a park or garden. When it is in the woods, it is often called a trail.

16. Babies often like to hold fuzzy objects.
(A) small and cute
(B) clean and colorful
(C) warm and cuddly
(D) soft and fluffy

(D) "Fuzzy" refers to something that is covered with fuzz, which consists of loose light pieces of a substance like soft wool. "Fuzz" also refers to fine hairs or fibers that cover something. The word "cuddly" refers to something that is nice to embrace or hug.

17. A U.S. president has the power to veto a bill.
(A) enforce
(B) modify
(C) reject
(D) verify

(C) "Veto" refers to the power to prohibit something from being done. The president can prevent action by rejecting or prohibiting a bill, which then cannot become a law.

18. Abraham Lincoln was born in a log cabin.
(A) an isolated
(B) a drafty
(C) a cozy
(D) a wooden

(D) A "log" refers to the wood of a tree that has been cut down.

19. In San Francisco ferries are sometimes used to take people to work.
(A) cable cars
(B) boats
(C) subways
(D) trams

(B) A ferry is a boat that has the major purpose of transporting people or goods from one place to another, usually for only a short distance.

20. Today, in this global state, the English language has more variety of local expressions than it ever has had before.
(A) condition
(B) territory
(C) rank
(D) government

(A) The word "state" has many meanings. In this sentence, it refers to "a state of being," rather than a particular place. The meaning of the phrase "global state" is that the world is in the condition of being thought of as one world rather than as a series of separate countries.

21. A pontil is a tool used to handle hot glass while it is being shaped during glassmaking.
(A) disposed of
(B) copied
(C) designed
(D) formed

(D) "To shape" means "to form" or "to create." In this sentence the word refers to the physical form of the glass.

22. English furniture made between 1714 and 1830 is called Georgian, after the reigning monarchs of that time.
(A) ruling
(B) historic
(C) winning
(D) scholarly

(A) "To reign" means "to rule." A king or queen reigns over a country.

23. From the beginnings of history, literature has recorded the story of human dreams.
(A) processed
(B) transformed
(C) preserved
(D) reproduced

(C) The word "recorded" in this sentence refers to anything that is written down in a book. The act of writing preserves the information for a later time.

24. The Puritans, early American settlers, shared many of the same beliefs as the Pilgrims.
(A) divided
(B) enjoyed
(C) contributed
(D) had

(D) "To share" means "to divide something into portions" or "to use or enjoy something in common with others." In the sense of this sentence, however, ideas are shared, not objects. In order to keep the meaning of the sentence, the best choice is, "The Puritans had the same beliefs as the Pilgrims."

25. The Roman Pantheon and the Colosseum represent two of the world's most durable examples of concrete architecture.
(A) are
(B) erected
(C) support
(D) belong to

(A) The verb "to represent" can mean "to be," "to serve as," or "to stand as."

26. Some plants can produce a chemical that stunts the growth of insects.
(A) increases
(B) halts
(C) releases
(D) submerges

(B) When something has stunted growth it does not grow as much as it should. The growth is stopped or slowed down. "Halt" means "stop."

27. The mountains around the Li River have lured poets and artists for centuries.
(A) intrigued
(B) mystified
(C) inspired
(D) attracted

(D) "To lure" is to attract someone or tempt someone with something. In the sense of this sentence, people are attracted to (lured by) the beauty of the mountains.

28. Harsh arctic and desert environments have always posed great challenges to human life.
(A) Severe
(B) Barren
(C) Bright
(D) Exceptional

(A) "Harsh" means "severe" or "very rough." The word "barren" means "without vegetation." Being barren is a result of the harsh climate, not a synonym.

29. Human beings share a common heritage of a life cycle that includes trial and error, success, and failure.
(A) hierarchy
(B) inheritance
(C) mark
(D) problem

(B) The word "heritage" refers to something that is inherited or handed down from one's ancestors. "Tradition" has the same meaning.

30. People have always dispersed across the Earth looking for arable land.
(A) pastoral
(B) fertilized
(C) plowable
(D) sufficient

(C) If land is "arable," it means that it can be plowed.

31. The Northwest is an important area for the lumber industry.
(A) steel
(B) garment
(C) timber
(D) fishing

(C) "Lumber" and "timber" both refer to the wood from trees. "Timber" refers to the trees either before or after being cut. "Lumber" only refers to the tree after it is cut and sawn into beams for building. Timber is cut into lumber.

32. It is possible that an emotional condition can trigger a physical reaction.
(A) cause
(B) enhance
(C) diminish
(D) supersede

(A) "To trigger" means "to initiate" or "to set off." It is often used in scientific discussion, meaning that one action initiates or causes another action. The noun form "trigger" refers to the small lever on a gun that is pulled to shoot the gun.

33. Toddlers sometimes require special attention.
(A) Elderly people
(B) Babies
(C) Pets
(D) Houseplants

(B) "Toddlers" refers to babies or small children. A toddler is a small child who is just beginning to walk.

34. Minoan kings had such strong navies that they were able to build unfortified palaces.
(A) unprotected
(B) undeveloped
(C) unequaled
(D) unidentified

(A) A fort is a protected place. "Unfortified," then, means "unprotected."

35. Tempe, Arizona was known as Hayden's Ferry when it was founded in 1872.
(A) discovered
(B) destroyed
(C) established
(D) built

(C) "To found" comes from the word "foundation." It refers to the base or support of something. It is commonly used to mean "begin the construction," which has the same meaning as "to establish." The word "built" is not correct, since it doesn't necessarily give the idea of "beginning." Something can continue being built over a long period to time.

36. Chester Alan Arthur, 21st President of the United States, was a handsome man with a ruddy complexion.
(A) broad shoulders
(B) red-colored skin
(C) a slight limp
(D) wavy hair

(B) The word "ruddy" means "red" or "having a healthy red color." The word "complexion" refers to the skin.

37. Automation has done away with much of the drudgery of work.
(A) uniqueness
(B) dirtiness
(C) unpleasantness
(D) slowness

(C) "Drudgery" refers to work that is hard to do or unpleasant.

38. Little Rock is the hub of the federal interstate highways that cross Arkansas.
(A) highpoint
(B) summit
(C) path
(D) center

(D) A "hub" is the center of a wheel or the center of interest.

39. In the 13th century there were thousands of castles in France.
(A) military ships
(B) fortified buildings
(C) acres of vineyards
(D) noble men and women

(B) A castle is a large building or group of buildings with thick walls to keep out enemies. They were commonly built in the Middle Ages (the years 476 A.D. to 1450 A.D.).

40. In the spring, one might see newly born animals taking their first wobbly steps.
(A) unsteady
(B) mincing
(C) baby
(D) tentative

(A) "Wobbly" refers to being shaky or moving from side to side; not firm. "Tentative" means "done as a trial." The wobbly steps of a newly born animal might also be tentative steps, but "tentative" does not mean "wobbly."

41. Marion Anderson's European debut was triumphant.
   (A) luxuriant
   (B) disastrous
   (C) victorious
   (D) newsworthy

(C) "Triumphant" and "victorious" both mean "successful."

42. A sistrum is a rattle that was used in ancient Egypt.
   (A) shaking device
   (B) weapon
   (C) cooking utensil
   (D) water container

(A) The word "rattle" usually refers to a toy for babies that makes a noise when it is shaken.

43. In his conquest of the Mediterranean, Alexander the Great seized many of the coastal cities held by the Russian navy.
   (A) released
   (B) captured
   (C) surrounded
   (D) segregated

(B) "To seize" and "to capture" both mean "to take something by force." Usually it also means that it is taken suddenly.

44. A slaughterhouse is often in the vicinity of a meatpacking plant.
   (A) An inspection house
   (B) A barn
   (C) A food processing house
   (D) A butchering house

(D) "Slaughter" and "butcher" both refer to killing animals.

45. In some parts of the world, an everyday outfit consists of a colorful shirt and baggy pants.
   (A) tight
   (B) worn
   (C) loose
   (D) woven

(C) "Baggy pants" are loosely fitting pants.

46. Which of the following is the best title for this passage?
   (A) The Earth's Dwindling Water Supply
   (B) Icecaps of Antarctica
   (C) A Solution to Fresh Water Needs
   (D) A Synthetic Cocoon

(C) This is a main idea question. The second sentence of the passage states that scientists have been studying this idea as a solution to the world's dwindling fresh water supply. Answer (A) is too broad. This passage does not discuss a lot of the problem with water. Answer (B) is mentioned as a source of fresh water. Answer (D) is only mentioned as a name for the container.

47. Of all the earth's water, the icecaps of Antarctica contain
   (A) 10 percent of the fresh water
   (B) 10 percent of the salt water
   (C) 90 percent of the fresh water
   (D) 90 percent of the salt water

(C) This is a restatement question. The passage states that 90 percent of the earth's fresh water is in the icecaps of Antarctica.

48. How does the author propose to transport the ice?
   (A) By pulling it
   (B) By chopping it
   (C) By piping it
   (D) By melting it

(A) This is a restatement question. The passages states that the fabric container can be towed to civilization. "Towed" means "pulled."

49. According to the passage, the purpose of the fabric container is to
   (A) protect the ice
   (B) diminish the speed of melting
   (C) cause the ice to float
   (D) pump out the sea water

(B) This is a restatement question. The passage states that the melting rate will be slowed down.

50. In line 8 the word "nudged" is closest in meaning to
   (A) imagined
   (B) glued
   (C) melted
   (D) pushed

(D) This is a vocabulary question. The word "nudged" means "pushed" or "shoved."

51. A "cocoon" (line 11) refers to
(A) protection against insects
(B) a tank in the boat
(C) a very large net
(D) a protective covering

(D) A cocoon is a protective covering that certain insects, such as the larva form of a butterfly, form to protect themselves as they change shape. In this passage the word "cocoon" is used to mean the protective covering around the iceberg.

52. The purpose of the last sentence is to
(A) reinforce the feasibility of the project
(B) compare fishermen to engineers
(C) contrast iceberg containers and fishing nets
(D) define the size of the container

(A) The last sentence mentions the nets in Australia as an example, because those nets are even larger than the proposed nets in this passage. This is evidence that it is possible to construct such a big container.

53. What is the author's purpose in this passage?
(A) To compare two sides of Gauguin's character
(B) To describe Gauguin's relationship with his family
(C) To introduce the sensitivity in Gauguin's art
(D) To discuss the effects of the "savage" in Gauguin's character

(D) The first sentence introduces the "savage" side of Gauguin, and the rest of the passage gives examples of it.

54. Which of the following is the best title for this passage?
(A) Gauguin's Escape
(B) Gauguin: Myth and Reality
(C) The Life of Paul Gauguin
(D) Attitude and Art

(A) This is a main idea question. Answer (A) is the best choice, since the entire passage discusses Gauguin's escape from something. He is escaping from social responsibilities, from his wife and children, and from restrictions of painting styles. The other answers are too general or broad.

55. According to the passage, Gauguin
(A) divorced his wife
(B) lived alone
(C) liberated his family
(D) disregarded society's rules

(D) This is a restatement question. The passage states that Gauguin disregarded convention and abandoned social responsibilities. It says that he left his wife, but not that he divorced his wife.

56. Which of the following is NOT supported by the passage?
(A) Gauguin justified his behavior.
(B) Gauguin quarreled with his friends.
(C) Gauguin left his family.
(D) Gauguin promised to come back.

(D) This is a negative question. You can answer it by elimination. The passage states that Gauguin "justified his quarreling with friends, his leaving his wife and children and his promiscuity . . ." The passage does not state that Gauguin promised to come back.

57. It can be inferred from the passage that the art of the coming century would be more
(A) colorful
(B) naturalistic
(C) symbolic
(D) complex

(C) This is an inference question. The passage states, "In his attitude can be found seeds of art in the 20th century: the art of the primitive, of symbol . . ." From this we can infer answer (C).

58. From the passage we can infer that Gauguin wanted to
(A) paint in a new way
(B) restrict forms of art
(C) make new friends
(D) liberate society

(A) This is an inference question. We can infer that Gauguin wanted to paint in a new way by the comments in the passage, such as "disregard convention" and "his art could be liberated." This question can also be answered by elimination. Answer (B) is the opposite of what the passage states. Answer (C) is not correct, since nothing in the passage mentions his desire to have new friends. Answer (D) is incorrect, because he wanted to liberate art, not society.

59. The best synonym for "savage" in this passage is
(A) cruel
(B) crude
(C) fierce
(D) untamed

(D) This is a vocabulary question. The word "savage" refers to something that is wild, primitive, or untamed.

60. Which of the following is the best title of this passage?
(A) Be Aware
(B) Stop the Clock
(C) Deleting Files
(D) Sharing Software

(A) This is a main idea question. Answer (A) is the best choice, because the entire passage discusses the problems of viruses infecting computers. The first sentence says "There is a new disease to worry about." The three other answers are mentioned only as smaller topics of the main idea.

61. The people most interested in reading this passage probably would be
(A) medical personnel
(B) computer users
(C) government workers
(D) health researchers

(B) This is an inference question. Computer viruses infect computers, so the most likely interested people would be the users of computers. The other answers name people who might also be interested, but "computer users" is the best choice for "most interested."

62. It is inferred that a company can best protect itself from the virus by
(A) keeping clean
(B) spreading programs by telephone
(C) setting the clock correctly
(D) not using shared software

(D) This is an inference question. The passage states that businesses and agencies are becoming wary of sharing software. Answer (A) is not mentioned. Answer (B) is incorrect, because the passage says the virus can be spread by telephone connections. Setting the clock answer (C) is not mentioned as a prevention for computer viruses.

63. The virus is
(A) a microbe
(B) an insect
(C) a disk
(D) a program

(D) This is a restatement question. The second sentence of the passages states, "computer viruses, programs designed to . . ." The comma in this sentence gives you a clue that the words after the comma are a definition of the words before the comma.

64. If the virus infects a computer, the result would probably be
(A) lost information
(B) a broken computer
(C) sick personnel
(D) dead telephones

(A) This is an inference question. There are two words that give you the best clue to the answer: "sabotage" and "disrupt." The passage states that viruses sabotage computers; this could possibly result in answer (B), a broken computer. But further in the passage it states that the viruses "disrupt the affected systems." From this sentence you can infer answer (A), since "disrupt" doesn't mean "break." Answers (C) and (D) are not mentioned.

65. What is the best title for this passage?
(A) Family Ties
(B) Washington's Botanical Experiments
(C) A Beloved Estate
(D) The Outbuildings of Mount Vernon

(C) This is a main topic sentence. All of the paragraphs discuss Mount Vernon, and the last sentence uses the words "a beloved estate" to describe Mount Vernon.

66. George Washington acquired Mount Vernon
(A) in 1799
(B) in 1735
(C) from his grandfather
(D) at age twenty-two

(D) This is a restatement question. In the first sentence of the second paragraph, the passage states that George acquired Mount Vernon when he was twenty-two. Answer (C) is wrong, because the passage states that George acquired the estate from his half-brother, not his grandfather.

67. According to the author, Mount Vernon seemed
(A) busy
(B) cozy
(C) peaceful
(D) exciting

(C) This is an inference question. The passage states that the outbuildings of Mount Vernon are far enough away not to intrude upon the beauty and tranquility of the surroundings. The word "tranquility" means "peacefulness."

68. When George acquired Mount Vernon, the main house was
(A) less than twenty years old
(B) about eighty years old
(C) too small for him
(D) used for jobs like spinning and weaving

(A) This is a restatement/computation question. The passage states that George acquired the estate in 1754. The passage also states that the main part of the home was constructed in 1735. The year 1735 is nineteen years earlier than 1754. Answer (B) is incorrect, because the site was eighty years old, not the house.

69. The word "embellishing" in line 8 is closest in meaning to
(A) overseeing
(B) tearing down
(C) leaving out
(D) adding to

(D) This is a vocabulary question. The best way to guess the meaning of this word is to read the complete sentence in which it is used. "George made many changes, significantly enlarging and embellishing the estate." Three words are similar: "changes," "enlarging," and "embellishing." The passage then describes the building of rooms and places for weaving, spinning, etc. All of these are clues that "embellishing" means that something is added. The word "overseeing" means "supervising." George may have been doing this, but it is not a synonym for "embellish." Answers (B) and (C) both mean that something is taken away. They are opposite in meaning to the word "enlarging."

70. Which of the following statements about George Washington is best supported by this passage?
(A) He had strong connections with his family.
(B) He enjoyed housework.
(C) He liked to experiment with seeds and plants.
(D) He was busy conducting state business from his home.

(C) This is a support question. The best choice is (C), because the passage states that George designed three gardens, one of them for botanical experimentation. Answer (A) is possible, but not the best choice, since the only mention of family connections is that he inherited the land. There is no mention of his enjoying housework, so (B) is not a good choice. Housework means doing jobs in the house, such as cleaning. Nothing is mentioned about answer (D).

71. Which of the following can be inferred from this passage?
(A) Children who talk a lot are more intelligent.
(B) Parents who listen to their children can teach them more.
(C) Active children should read more.
(D) Verbal ability can easily be increased.

(D) This is an inference question. The final sentence of the first paragraph says, ". . . the child's language skills increase." The word "easily" in answer (D) is inferred, since the passages states that the only thing parents need to do is talk to their children.

72. In line 2, what does "it's" refer to?
(A) Parents increasing children's language development
(B) Reading techniques being simple
(C) Parents reading to children
(D) Children's language development

(A) This is a referent question. The word "it's" refers to the whole previous sentence, that parents who read to their children can increase their children's language development.

73. According to the author, which of the following questions is the best type to ask children about reading?
(A) Do you see the elephant?
(B) Is the elephant in the cage?
(C) What animals do you like?
(D) Shall we go to the zoo?

(C) This is an inference question. The passage states that parents should ask open-ended questions rather than yes/no questions.

74. What was the difference between the control group and the experimental group?
(A) The training parents received
(B) The age of the children
(C) The books that were read
(D) The number of children

(A) This is an inference question. The passage states that in the experimental group the parents were given a two-hour training session. You can infer that in the control group the parents were not given this training session.

75. What conclusion is best supported by this passage?
(A) Parents should be trained to read to their children.
(B) The more children read, the more intelligent they become.
(C) Children's language skills increase when they are required to respond actively.
(D) Children who read actively act six months older.

(C) This is a support question. Answer (C) is the best choice. The passage gives several examples of how the parents should respond to make the children think of their answers. The final sentence of the first sentence says that "If a parent encourages the child to actively respond . . ." You can infer that "actively responding" requires thinking. You can also answer this question by elimination. Answer (A) is incorrect, because the first paragraph says that parents need to talk to their children, not only read to them. Answer (B) is incorrect, since there is nothing mentioned about being intelligent. The children were tested on verbal expression and vocabulary. Answer (D) is incorrect, because this answer is stated as a general truth. The sentence in the passage is about one group of children who were tested nine months after the experiment. The passage does not say that all children will act six months older.

76. The main purpose of this passage is to
(A) discuss Audubon's life.
(B) give a background of painting in Audubon's time.
(C) describe Audubon's painting techniques.
(D) give an insight into Audubon's philosophy of painting.

(D) This is a main idea question. Answer (D) is correct, because the passage contains more than a discussion of painting techniques. It mentions Audubon's passion about observing nature and his feeling that nature was a continual life-and-death drama. Answer (A) is incorrect, because Audubon's life story is not discussed. Answer (B) is incorrect, because the passage is not about other people's painting.

77. When Audubon "took birds out of glass cages" (line 2), he
(A) let the birds fly away unharmed
(B) put the birds in a more natural place
(C) painted them as if they were alive
(D) nursed them back to life

(C) This is an inference question. The passage says that Audubon gave the birds a semblance of life. The word "semblance" means "appearance" or "resemblance." The words "as if" in the answer choice refer to the same idea. It means that Audubon painted the birds so that they would appear to be alive.

78. Before Audubon began painting, other wildlife painters
(A) stuffed birds
(B) drew still birds
(C) observed dead birds
(D) tied birds to branches

(B) This is an inference question. The first sentence states that "most birds were drawn as though stuffed and fastened to wooden perches." The inference here is that the birds looked as if they could not move. Answer (A) is incorrect, because the passage does not say that the painters stuffed the birds themselves. It says that the birds looked like they were stuffed. The word "stuffed" means "filled with a material such as cotton." Answer (D) is incorrect for the same reason as answer (A) The birds were not actually tied to branches. They were painted in a way that made them look like they were tied to branches.

79. Audubon spent much of his time
(A) outside
(B) in his studio
(C) in his favorite chair
(D) looking at bird pictures

(A) This is a restatement question. The passage states that Audubon spent much of his time roaming the countryside.

80. Which of the following would Audubon probably NOT paint?
(A) A bird feeding its babies.
(B) A bird eating a worm.
(C) A bird diving in the ocean.
(D) A bird singing in its cage.

(D) This is a negative question. The passages states that Audubon always portrayed birds in their natural habitats. Answer (D) describes a bird enclosed in a cage, not in its natural environment.

81. Audubon
(A) is living now
(B) died recently
(C) lived in the 1800s
(D) lived in the 1700s

(C) This is an inference/computation question. The passage states that it is now 150 years after he published his book. The answer then must be that he lived during the 1800s.

82. In line 12, the word "hailed" could best be substituted with
(A) published
(B) showered
(C) greeted
(D) praised

(D) This is a vocabulary question. "To hail" means "to call out in order to attract attention to something" or "to express approval." In this case "praised" is the closest in meaning. The word "hail" can also mean "greeting," but that meaning does not fit in this sentence. "Hail" is also the name for frozen raindrops or for something being thrown upon someone, usually violently.

83. Audubon can best be characterized as
(A) an artist
(B) an author
(C) an environmentalist
(D) a scientist

(A) This is an inference question. Even though Audubon wrote books and was interested in nature and science, the passage describes him primarily as an artist.

84. What did the paragraph preceding this passage most likely discuss?
(A) Other libraries in the U.S.A.
(B) Other functions of the Library of Congress
(C) Other duties of legislators
(D) Other research organizations

(B) This is a preceding possible topic question. Since the passage begins with the word "but," you can infer that the previous paragraph discussed an opposite topic. Answer (B) is the best guess, since the first sentence mentions the "role of the Library of Congress." The word "function" in answer (B) is similar to "role," so if the previous paragraph discussed other functions or roles, that would be an opposite topic.

85. The word "arm" in line 2 is closest in meaning to
(A) weapon
(B) limb
(C) branch
(D) support

(C) This is a vocabulary question. All of the above words can refer to "arm" in different contexts. The word "arm" here refers to something that is attached to something larger; in this case, the library is connected to the government.

86. The main job of the Library of Congress is to
(A) research information.
(B) store books.
(C) study law.
(D) hire experts.

(A) This is a restatement question. In the first sentence, the passage states that the library is the research and reference arm.

87. Which of the following is NOT mentioned as a way that the library staff helps legislators?
(A) Preparing summaries
(B) Presenting their points of view
(C) Reading in foreign languages
(D) Keeping up-to-date

(B) This is a negative question. The passage states that librarians do all of the above except (B). It states that the librarians present all sides of issues, not their own points of view. Answer (D) is a restatement of "staying abreast of daily legislation."

88. For whom is this passage most likely written?
(A) Congress members
(B) The public
(C) The library staff
(D) Lawyers

(B) This is an inference question. Answer (B) is most likely, since the other people mentioned probably already know more information than this passage gives.

89. According to this passage, staff members
(A) present contrasting views
(B) ask the legislators for help
(C) give personal opinions
(D) are lawyers

(A) This is an inference question. Since the passage states that the librarians present all sides of issues, you can infer that they will present contrasting views. Answer (B) is incorrect, because the passage says that the function of the staff members is to give information, not to ask for help. Answer (C) is incorrect, because it is the opposite of (A). Answer (D) is incorrect, because there is no mention of the staff being lawyers themselves.

90. The author is trying to be
(A) biased
(B) superficial
(C) informative
(D) cheerful

(C) This is an author's purpose question. The tone of the passage is one of help and information. The answer cannot be (A), because the author is giving a description of many kinds of jobs, not only one point of view. Even though the passage is short, the author does not seem to be superficial, which means giving only obvious and easily seen information. The author gives a lot of information that many people do not know. Answer (D) is incorrect, because there are no particular words that show cheerfulness.

Practice Test IV
(Long Form)

NOTE: You will need the tape to do Section 1. If you do not have the tape, the tapescript for Section 1 is on pages 647 to 653. The answer key is on pages 544–545, and explanatory answers begin on page 548. Use the answer sheet for Practice Test IV on page 515 to mark your answers.

ANSWER SHEET FOR PRACTICE TEST IV

SECTION 1

1. (A) (B) (C) (D)
2. (A) (B) (C) (D)
3. (A) (B) (C) (D)
4. (A) (B) (C) (D)
5. (A) (B) (C) (D)
6. (A) (B) (C) (D)
7. (A) (B) (C) (D)
8. (A) (B) (C) (D)
9. (A) (B) (C) (D)
10. (A) (B) (C) (D)
11. (A) (B) (C) (D)
12. (A) (B) (C) (D)
13. (A) (B) (C) (D)
14. (A) (B) (C) (D)
15. (A) (B) (C) (D)
16. (A) (B) (C) (D)
17. (A) (B) (C) (D)
18. (A) (B) (C) (D)
19. (A) (B) (C) (D)
20. (A) (B) (C) (D)
21. (A) (B) (C) (D)
22. (A) (B) (C) (D)
23. (A) (B) (C) (D)
24. (A) (B) (C) (D)
25. (A) (B) (C) (D)
26. (A) (B) (C) (D)
27. (A) (B) (C) (D)
28. (A) (B) (C) (D)
29. (A) (B) (C) (D)
30. (A) (B) (C) (D)
31. (A) (B) (C) (D)
32. (A) (B) (C) (D)
33. (A) (B) (C) (D)
34. (A) (B) (C) (D)
35. (A) (B) (C) (D)
36. (A) (B) (C) (D)
37. (A) (B) (C) (D)
38. (A) (B) (C) (D)
39. (A) (B) (C) (D)
40. (A) (B) (C) (D)
41. (A) (B) (C) (D)
42. (A) (B) (C) (D)
43. (A) (B) (C) (D)
44. (A) (B) (C) (D)
45. (A) (B) (C) (D)
46. (A) (B) (C) (D)
47. (A) (B) (C) (D)
48. (A) (B) (C) (D)
49. (A) (B) (C) (D)
50. (A) (B) (C) (D)
51. (A) (B) (C) (D)
52. (A) (B) (C) (D)
53. (A) (B) (C) (D)
54. (A) (B) (C) (D)
55. (A) (B) (C) (D)
56. (A) (B) (C) (D)
57. (A) (B) (C) (D)
58. (A) (B) (C) (D)
59. (A) (B) (C) (D)
60. (A) (B) (C) (D)
61. (A) (B) (C) (D)
62. (A) (B) (C) (D)
63. (A) (B) (C) (D)
64. (A) (B) (C) (D)
65. (A) (B) (C) (D)
66. (A) (B) (C) (D)
67. (A) (B) (C) (D)
68. (A) (B) (C) (D)
69. (A) (B) (C) (D)
70. (A) (B) (C) (D)
71. (A) (B) (C) (D)
72. (A) (B) (C) (D)
73. (A) (B) (C) (D)
74. (A) (B) (C) (D)
75. (A) (B) (C) (D)
76. (A) (B) (C) (D)
77. (A) (B) (C) (D)
78. (A) (B) (C) (D)
79. (A) (B) (C) (D)
80. (A) (B) (C) (D)

SECTION 2

1. (A) (B) (C) (D)
2. (A) (B) (C) (D)
3. (A) (B) (C) (D)
4. (A) (B) (C) (D)
5. (A) (B) (C) (D)
6. (A) (B) (C) (D)
7. (A) (B) (C) (D)
8. (A) (B) (C) (D)
9. (A) (B) (C) (D)
10. (A) (B) (C) (D)
11. (A) (B) (C) (D)
12. (A) (B) (C) (D)
13. (A) (B) (C) (D)
14. (A) (B) (C) (D)
15. (A) (B) (C) (D)
16. (A) (B) (C) (D)
17. (A) (B) (C) (D)
18. (A) (B) (C) (D)
19. (A) (B) (C) (D)
20. (A) (B) (C) (D)
21. (A) (B) (C) (D)
22. (A) (B) (C) (D)
23. (A) (B) (C) (D)
24. (A) (B) (C) (D)
25. (A) (B) (C) (D)
26. (A) (B) (C) (D)
27. (A) (B) (C) (D)
28. (A) (B) (C) (D)
29. (A) (B) (C) (D)
30. (A) (B) (C) (D)
31. (A) (B) (C) (D)
32. (A) (B) (C) (D)
33. (A) (B) (C) (D)
34. (A) (B) (C) (D)
35. (A) (B) (C) (D)
36. (A) (B) (C) (D)
37. (A) (B) (C) (D)
38. (A) (B) (C) (D)
39. (A) (B) (C) (D)
40. (A) (B) (C) (D)
41. (A) (B) (C) (D)
42. (A) (B) (C) (D)
43. (A) (B) (C) (D)
44. (A) (B) (C) (D)
45. (A) (B) (C) (D)
46. (A) (B) (C) (D)
47. (A) (B) (C) (D)
48. (A) (B) (C) (D)
49. (A) (B) (C) (D)
50. (A) (B) (C) (D)
51. (A) (B) (C) (D)
52. (A) (B) (C) (D)
53. (A) (B) (C) (D)
54. (A) (B) (C) (D)
55. (A) (B) (C) (D)
56. (A) (B) (C) (D)
57. (A) (B) (C) (D)
58. (A) (B) (C) (D)
59. (A) (B) (C) (D)
60. (A) (B) (C) (D)

SECTION 3

1. (A) (B) (C) (D)
2. (A) (B) (C) (D)
3. (A) (B) (C) (D)
4. (A) (B) (C) (D)
5. (A) (B) (C) (D)
6. (A) (B) (C) (D)
7. (A) (B) (C) (D)
8. (A) (B) (C) (D)
9. (A) (B) (C) (D)
10. (A) (B) (C) (D)
11. (A) (B) (C) (D)
12. (A) (B) (C) (D)
13. (A) (B) (C) (D)
14. (A) (B) (C) (D)
15. (A) (B) (C) (D)
16. (A) (B) (C) (D)
17. (A) (B) (C) (D)
18. (A) (B) (C) (D)
19. (A) (B) (C) (D)
20. (A) (B) (C) (D)
21. (A) (B) (C) (D)
22. (A) (B) (C) (D)
23. (A) (B) (C) (D)
24. (A) (B) (C) (D)
25. (A) (B) (C) (D)
26. (A) (B) (C) (D)
27. (A) (B) (C) (D)
28. (A) (B) (C) (D)
29. (A) (B) (C) (D)
30. (A) (B) (C) (D)
31. (A) (B) (C) (D)
32. (A) (B) (C) (D)
33. (A) (B) (C) (D)
34. (A) (B) (C) (D)
35. (A) (B) (C) (D)
36. (A) (B) (C) (D)
37. (A) (B) (C) (D)
38. (A) (B) (C) (D)
39. (A) (B) (C) (D)
40. (A) (B) (C) (D)
41. (A) (B) (C) (D)
42. (A) (B) (C) (D)
43. (A) (B) (C) (D)
44. (A) (B) (C) (D)
45. (A) (B) (C) (D)
46. (A) (B) (C) (D)
47. (A) (B) (C) (D)
48. (A) (B) (C) (D)
49. (A) (B) (C) (D)
50. (A) (B) (C) (D)
51. (A) (B) (C) (D)
52. (A) (B) (C) (D)
53. (A) (B) (C) (D)
54. (A) (B) (C) (D)
55. (A) (B) (C) (D)
56. (A) (B) (C) (D)
57. (A) (B) (C) (D)
58. (A) (B) (C) (D)
59. (A) (B) (C) (D)
60. (A) (B) (C) (D)
61. (A) (B) (C) (D)
62. (A) (B) (C) (D)
63. (A) (B) (C) (D)
64. (A) (B) (C) (D)
65. (A) (B) (C) (D)
66. (A) (B) (C) (D)
67. (A) (B) (C) (D)
68. (A) (B) (C) (D)
69. (A) (B) (C) (D)
70. (A) (B) (C) (D)
71. (A) (B) (C) (D)
72. (A) (B) (C) (D)
73. (A) (B) (C) (D)
74. (A) (B) (C) (D)
75. (A) (B) (C) (D)
76. (A) (B) (C) (D)
77. (A) (B) (C) (D)
78. (A) (B) (C) (D)
79. (A) (B) (C) (D)
80. (A) (B) (C) (D)
81. (A) (B) (C) (D)
82. (A) (B) (C) (D)
83. (A) (B) (C) (D)
84. (A) (B) (C) (D)
85. (A) (B) (C) (D)
86. (A) (B) (C) (D)
87. (A) (B) (C) (D)
88. (A) (B) (C) (D)
89. (A) (B) (C) (D)
90 (A) (B) (C) (D)

1 1 1 1 1 1 1 1 1 1 1

SECTION 1
LISTENING COMPREHENSION
Time—approximately 50 minutes

In this section of the test, you will have an opportunity to demonstrate your ability to understand spoken English. There are three parts to this section, with special directions for each part.

Part A

Directions: For each question in Part A, you will hear a short sentence. Each sentence will be spoken just one time. The sentences you hear will not be written out for you. Therefore, you must listen carefully to understand what the speaker says.

After you hear a sentence, read the four choices in your test book, marked (A), (B), (C), and (D), and decide which one is closest in meaning to the sentence you heard. Then, on your answer sheet, find the number of the question and fill in the space that corresponds to the letter of the answer you have chosen. Fill in the space so that the letter inside the oval cannot be seen.

Example I:

You will hear:

Sample Answer

You will read:

(A) Mary outswam the others.
(B) Mary ought to swim with them.
(C) Mary and her friends swam to the island.
(D) Mary's friends owned the island.

The speaker said, "Mary swam out to the island with her friends." Sentence (C), "Mary and her friends swam to the island," is closest in meaning to the sentence you heard. Therefore, you should choose answer (C).

Example II:

You will hear:

Sample Answer

You will read:

(A) Please remind me to read this book.
(B) Could you help me carry these books?
(C) I don't mind if you help me.
(D) Do you have a heavy course load this term?

The speaker said, "Would you mind helping me with this load of books?" Sentence (B), "Could you help me carry these books?" is closest in meaning to the sentence you heard. Therefore, you should choose answer (B).

GO ON TO THE NEXT PAGE

1. (A) There are many tape recorders on sale.
   (B) You paid a low price for the tape recorder.
   (C) Your tape recorder is not new, but it's clean.
   (D) The tape recorder you bought should help you study.

2. (A) He ran across his friend while walking in the hall.
   (B) He could see the pencil sharpener through the hall.
   (C) He was trying to find the pencil sharpener.
   (D) He walked around whenever he had time.

3. (A) I enjoy watermelon more than anybody else.
   (B) I bought more watermelon than anyone else.
   (C) Watermelon grows much faster than I expected.
   (D) Very few people in this area grow watermelon.

4. (A) She had a bad vacation.
   (B) Her vacation wasn't very interesting.
   (C) She really should take some time off.
   (D) She hasn't begun to plan her trip yet.

5. (A) You don't need these pants right now.
   (B) These pants are clean.
   (C) These pants are dry.
   (D) Don't wash these pants in water.

6. (A) This is enjoyable to look at.
   (B) What kind of view do you like the most?
   (C) That's a beautiful dress.
   (D) The view isn't as good as I expected.

7. (A) The answer should be altered.
   (B) All the answers are here.
   (C) All the answers will be given in the next class.
   (D) This answer could be correct, too.

8. (A) You should use your fork.
   (B) Why is the waitress so slow?
   (C) You should ask the waitress for another fork.
   (D) It would be nice to have some extra napkins.

9. (A) People drive quickly when they are in a hurry.
   (B) There were a lot of cars on the road after work.
   (C) People take turns driving on the highway.
   (D) The highway is better than the subway.

10. (A) I like cold drinks.
    (B) I'm glad I'm not as hot as I was.
    (C) I am glad he's not cruel to me any more.
    (D) I feel like having another Coke.

11. (A) Making a decision is easy when the time is right.
    (B) There is not much time left for him to hesitate.
    (C) He can't make up his mind when he has to make a decision.
    (D) He still has time to hesitate.

12. (A) He seldom shows anger.
    (B) He doesn't care what happens to him.
    (C) He was very angry when he had an accident.
    (D) He was very calm during the accident.

13. (A) The newborn panda looks awful.
    (B) A baby panda grows up fast.
    (C) The baby panda is really attractive.
    (D) A newborn panda needs special care.

14. (A) I don't want to use this topic.
    (B) I couldn't have changed my research subject earlier.
    (C) My thesis is almost finished.
    (D) I couldn't improve my thesis without help.

15. (A) There is only a week before finals.
    (B) We need a week to prepare for the school play.
    (C) School started a week ago.
    (D) School begins again next week.

16. (A) Sue applied for a new teaching job.
    (B) Sue has a friend in this course.
    (C) Sue is taking this course, too.
    (D) Sue will be the professor in this class.

17. (A) You'd better go to the cafeteria with someone else.
    (B) The cafeteria has inexpensive but good food.
    (C) The cafeteria is a nicer building than the library.
    (D) The cafeteria is a good place to go for several activities.

GO ON TO THE NEXT PAGE

18. (A) Everybody likes your new jacket very much.
    (B) Both you and the professors have to dress up.
    (C) You don't have to dress formally but professors do.
    (D) Neither professors nor students dress up.

19. (A) The empty box is good for used newspapers.
    (B) It's too late to buy today's newspaper.
    (C) The price of the newspaper has gone up.
    (D) We can get a newspaper here.

20. (A) They tested the new cars.
    (B) The new equipment needs more tests.
    (C) The tests of the new instruments were accurate.
    (D) We're having a test next week.

21. (A) I'd like to have more choices.
    (B) I have to take it.
    (C) You don't have to take it if you don't need it.
    (D) I have many other choices, don't I?

22. (A) Occasionally I take chances doing things.
    (B) Once I took a chance.
    (C) You should never take chances.
    (D) I rarely get chances to do things.

23. (A) I don't want to say bad things about my job.
    (B) I didn't mean what I said.
    (C) I've made up my mind to quit this job.
    (D) I can quit this job, even though it's mean.

24. (A) Jack likes to work with me.
    (B) Jack's driver's license was suspended.
    (C) Jack and I went on vacation together.
    (D) Jack took over for me when I was not here.

25. (A) Absence from this class may affect your grade.
    (B) The only requirement of this class is attendance.
    (C) Your grade depends solely on your final exam.
    (D) You can study the textbook at home for this class.

26. (A) I'm tired of looking for a place to eat.
    (B) Let's stop talking; it's lunch time now.
    (C) It's not a good idea to talk while eating.
    (D) Let's talk more over lunch.

27. (A) Jessica is active in the church to which she belongs.
    (B) Jessica was offered a role in the church play.
    (C) Jessica sings in the church choir.
    (D) Jessica invited a friend to her church last Sunday.

28. (A) That's just a part of my interest.
    (B) My sister doesn't like that at all.
    (C) My sister has the same tastes as I do.
    (D) My interests are different from my sister's.

29. (A) Mr. Jones doesn't want to retire from the committee.
    (B) Mr. Jones dressed formally at the committee meeting.
    (C) Mr. Jones is no longer the chairman.
    (D) Mr. Jones is a farmer.

30. (A) Nobody should make this kind of mistake.
    (B) You are excused this time, but no more.
    (C) You should excuse others for their errors.
    (D) Errors are correctable.

GO ON TO THE NEXT PAGE

1 1 1 1 1 1 1 1 1 1 1

Part B

Directions: In Part B you will hear short conversations between two speakers. At the end of each conversation, a third person will ask a question about what was said. You will hear each conversation and question about it just one time. Therefore, you must listen carefully to understand what each speaker says. After you hear a conversation and the question about it, read the four possible answers in your test book and decide which one is the best answer to the question you heard. Then, on your answer sheet, find the number of the question and fill in the space that corresponds to the letter of the answer you have chosen.

Look at the following example.

You will hear:

Sample Answer

● Ⓑ Ⓒ Ⓓ

You will read:

(A) Present Professor Smith with a picture.
(B) Photograph Professor Smith.
(C) Put glass over the photograph.
(D) Replace the broken headlight.

From the conversation you learn that the woman thinks Professor Smith would like a photograph of the class. The best answer to the question "What does the woman think the class should do?" is (A), "Present Professor Smith with a picture." Therefore, you should choose answer (A).

31. **(A)** In a travel agency
(B) In an airport
(C) In a bank
(D) In a government office

32. **(A)** He likes it.
(B) He thinks it has a good smell.
(C) He hopes it will be done at two.
(D) He thinks it's too dry.

33. **(A)** She thinks the explanations are difficult.
(B) The explanations will be added in a later edition.
(C) She thinks the book should include more information.
(D) The book includes an explanation of all the answers.

34. **(A)** Both editions are the same price now.
(B) The paperback book is on sale.
(C) The hardcover book is better quality; therefore, it costs more.
(D) The books are different, but the covers are the same.

35. **(A)** Become a representative of the class.
(B) Leave the class early.
(C) Take pictures.
(D) Give a presentation to the class.

36. **(A)** She would be willing to see the representative.
(B) She doesn't want to see the representative at the moment.
(C) She plans to see the representative later.
(D) She'll keep it in mind to arrange a time to see him.

37. **(A)** Reservations should be made early in the day.
(B) It is impossible to make reservations on Saturdays and Sundays.
(C) The restaurant has a branch nearby that makes reservations.
(D) The restaurant is being remodeled this weekend.

GO ON TO THE NEXT PAGE

38 (A) He talked to the consultant about the new program until two.
(B) The consultant was leaving at two.
(C) The consultant wanted to talk to him, too.
(D) He couldn't talk to the consultant before two.

39. (A) She lives far away.
(B) She has a new car.
(C) She wants the man to walk with her.
(D) Her car is close.

40. (A) She knows the movie was terrifying.
(B) She also liked the movie.
(C) She doesn't want to see the movie again.
(D) She knows the actor personally.

41. (A) There is not much manufacturing around here.
(B) Nothing can be mentioned.
(C) A big park is not far away from here.
(D) Industrial pollution is not severe in this area.

42. (A) You should not eat the skin.
(B) The fruit has not been washed yet.
(C) It's not good raw.
(D) The seeds are not good to eat.

43. (A) It was a careless comment.
(B) It was a boring activity.
(C) It was a compliment.
(D) It was a correction.

44. (A) She'll be gone a long time.
(B) She'll be back shortly.
(C) She has too much to do.
(D) She is taking her time.

45. (A) He isn't ready to show his pictures yet.
(B) The pictures are still being processed.
(C) He isn't ready to take pictures yet.
(D) He wants the woman to take a picture of him.

46. (A) Reading is more useful than watching TV.
(B) Watching TV is better than reading a newspaper.
(C) The newspaper is a good source for learning English.
(D) A combination of reading and listening is most effective.

47. (A) She will not make the decision for him.
(B) She'll help to make the decision only if he asks for it.
(C) He doesn't have to make the decision right now.
(D) He should consult with the woman about this decision.

48. (A) It was impossible for him to come to the party.
(B) He stayed home to study for his exam.
(C) Everybody was surprised by his attendance at the party.
(D) He had expected to come to the party for a long time.

49. (A) Her senior project is more important right now.
(B) She cares about her grade more than the man does.
(C) She couldn't even pass the exam for that class.
(D) She wants to be excellent in all her classes.

50. (A) She agrees that they met before.
(B) She met Professor Dean at the man's office.
(C) She denies the fact that they met before.
(D) She wants to meet the man at Professor Dean's seminar.

51. (A) Aunt Jane was angry.
(B) Aunt Jane was excited.
(C) Aunt Jane was disappointed.
(D) Aunt Jane was surprised.

52. (A) It's an informal party.
(B) She should wear something dressy.
(C) It's a cocktail party.
(D) She shouldn't wear pants.

53. (A) It runs better.
(B) It's likely to last longer.
(C) It's probably a bigger car.
(D) It's only a little more expensive.

54. (A) She will decide later.
(B) She doesn't care for either.
(C) She wants the man to decide.
(D) She doesn't want to go out.

55. (A) She doesn't like the fishing industry.
(B) The fish is not fresh enough.
(C) She is very tired.
(D) She feels uncomfortable at work.

GO ON TO THE NEXT PAGE

1 1 1 1 1 1 1 1 1 1 1

Part C

Directions: In this part of the test, you will hear short talks and conversations. After each of them, you will be asked some questions. You will hear the talks and conversations and the questions about them just one time. They will not be written out for you. Therefore, you must listen carefully to understand what each speaker says.

After you hear a question, read the four possible answers in your test book and decide which one is the best answer to the question you heard. Then, on your answer sheet, find the number of the question and fill in the space that corresponds to the letter of the answer you have chosen.

Answer all questions on the basis of what is stated or implied in the talk or conversation.

Listen to this sample talk.

You will hear:

Now look at the following example.

You will hear:

Sample Answer

  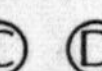

You will read:

(A) They are impossible to guide.
(B) They may go up in flames.
(C) They tend to leak gas.
(D) They are cheaply made.

The best answer to the question "Why are gas balloons considered dangerous?" is (B), "They may go up in flames." Therefore, you should choose answer (B).

Now look at the next example.

You will hear:

Sample Answer

  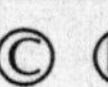

You will read:

(A) Watch for changes in weather.
(B) Watch their altitude.
(C) Check for weak spots in their balloons.
(D) Test the strength of the ropes.

The best answer to the question "According to the speaker, what must balloon pilots be careful to do?" is (A), "Watch for changes in weather." Therefore, you should choose answer (A).

GO ON TO THE NEXT PAGE

56. **(A)** A dormitory attendant
(B) A financial officer
(C) A housing coordinator
(D) Dr. Paulson

57. **(A)** New graduate students
(B) New undergraduate students
(C) Returning students
(D) High school students

58. **(A)** One student in each unit
(B) Two students in each unit
(C) Two students in each bedroom
(D) Four students in each unit

59. **(A)** Add your name to the waiting list.
(B) Sign up to move in right away.
(C) Go ask someone at the apartments.
(D) Go to the off-campus housing office.

60. **(A)** Find a house for you.
(B) Give you a list of rentals.
(C) Sign you up for family student housing.
(D) Add your name to a waiting list.

61. **(A)** Going to visit housing areas
(B) Going to see Dr. Paulson
(C) Listening to a talk on financial aid
(D) Filling out application forms

62. **(A)** Because he ran into the woman.
(B) Because he will get some money.
(C) Because his parents will pay for his room and board.
(D) Because he just got an application for a scholarship.

63. **(A)** They can't pay for her room.
(B) They will give her more money.
(C) They will come visit her.
(D) They live far away.

64. **(A)** She is a teaching assistant.
(B) She is on a work-study program.
(C) She works in an ice cream shop.
(D) She works in the financial aid office.

65. **(A)** Apply for a job.
(B) Get an application for aid.
(C) Ask her parents for money.
(D) Study harder.

66. **(A)** Because she didn't know about the job.
(B) Because she hadn't applied yet.
(C) Because all the jobs were filled.
(D) Because her class schedule was too busy.

67. **(A)** To the library
(B) To the bookstore
(C) To the ice cream shop
(D) To the financial aid office

68. **(A)** To tell people of an invitation
(B) To invite people to Harry's house
(C) To warn people of danger
(D) To describe an event

69. **(A)** An electrical blackout
(B) A storm
(C) A camping ban
(D) A shark attack

70. **(A)** Tomorrow
(B) Next week
(C) This afternoon
(D) Immediately

71. **(A)** Camp on the beach.
(B) Put wood over your windows.
(C) Leave town.
(D) Stay indoors.

72. **(A)** Tell your neighbors.
(B) Be patient.
(C) Take the loose wires off the street.
(D) Fix it as soon as possible.

73. **(A)** Listen to the radio.
(B) Leave town.
(C) Watch television.
(D) Contact your neighbor.

74. **(A)** An electrician
(B) The city mayor
(C) The harbor master
(D) A radio announcer

75. **(A)** A chemistry lab assistant
(B) A botany lecturer
(C) A landscape gardener
(D) An historian

76. **(A)** Their vascular system
(B) Their growth on rocks
(C) Their need for water
(D) Their being a land plant

77. **(A)** 300 years ago
(B) 9,000 B.C.
(C) The Carboniferous Period
(D) The Upper Devonian Period

GO ON TO THE NEXT PAGE

78. **(A)** In their structure
(B) In their size
(C) In their color
(D) In their reproductive system

79. **(A)** In a desert
(B) In a moist rock
(C) In a forest
(D) By water

80. **(A)** Up to 12 feet high
(B) Up to 20 feet high
(C) Up to 60 feet high
(D) Up to 100 feet high

THIS IS THE END OF THE LISTENING COMPREHENSION PART OF THE TEST. The next part of the test is Section 2. Turn to the directions for Section 2 in your test book, read them, and begin work. Do not read or work on any other section of the test.

GO ON TO THE NEXT PAGE

2 2 2 2 2 2 2 2 2 2 2

SECTION 2
STRUCTURE AND WRITTEN EXPRESSION
Time—35 minutes

This section is designed to measure your ability to recognize language that is appropriate for standard written English. There are two types of questions in this section, with special directions for each type.

Directions: Questions 1–23 are incomplete sentences. Beneath each sentence you will see four words or phrases, marked (A), (B), (C), and (D). Choose the one word or phrase that best completes the sentence. Then, on your answer sheet, find the number of the question and fill in the space that corresponds to the letter of the answer you have chosen. Fill in the space so that the letter inside the oval cannot be seen.

Example I:

Vegetables are an excellent source ________ vitamins.

(A) of
(B) has
(C) where
(D) that

Sample Answer

● Ⓑ Ⓒ Ⓓ

The sentence should read, "Vegetables are an excellent source of vitamins." Therefore, you should choose answer (A).

Example II:

________ in history when remarkable progress was made within a relatively short span of time.

(A) Periods
(B) Throughout periods
(C) There have been periods
(D) Periods have been

Sample Answer

Ⓐ Ⓑ ● Ⓓ

The sentence should read, "There have been periods in history when remarkable progress was made within a relatively short span of time." Therefore, you should choose answer (C).

Now begin work on the questions.

GO ON TO THE NEXT PAGE

1. In some states, a low-income tenant over sixty-two years old _________ in a rent-stabilized dwelling.
   (A) living
   (B) to live
   (C) can live
   (D) live

2. Tasty Mix Treat, _________ with milk,tastes so good that children will be clamoring for more.
   (A) blended
   (B) was blended
   (C) to blend
   (D) blending

3. A dog _________ on his owner's lap may refuse to eat from a bowl on the floor.
   (A) fed
   (B) is fed
   (C) was fed
   (D) to feed

4. To resist corrosion, _________ for today's car to prevent havoc caused by road salts, gravel, and other materials.
   (A) new coatings have been developed
   (B) having new coatings been developed
   (C) new coating developings
   (D) development of new coatings

5. _________ to Easter Egg Rock is tiring, yet stimulating.
   (A) All-day trips
   (B) An all-day boat trip
   (C) When boating all day
   (D) Now that all-day boat trips

6. The impact of two vehicles can cause a lot of _________ to both.
   (A) damage
   (B) damages
   (C) damaging
   (D) damagings

7. After the oil embargo, no longer _________ gas-guzzling cars as the cost of gasoline increased.
   (A) people could afford
   (B) that people could afford
   (C) could people afford
   (D) could afford

8. Yuen T. Lee received the 1986 Nobel Peace Prize in chemistry _________.
   (A) his crossed molecular beam reaction was successful
   (B) for his contribution to crossed molecular beam reactions
   (C) the excellence of his crossed molecular beam reactions
   (D) his molecular beam theory was historical

9. The greatest _________ between fresh water and sea water lies in its concentration of salt.
   (A) difference that
   (B) is a difference
   (C) difference is
   (D) difference

10. Not until the Enlightenment, 200 years ago, _________ the state's power to kill.
    (A) the societies seriously questioned
    (B) questioned seriously by societies
    (C) questioned by societies seriously
    (D) did societies seriously question

11. The electronic violin ought to be better than existing modern instruments, _________ the intermodulation distortion is virtually eliminated.
    (A) or
    (B) due
    (C) also
    (D) since

GO ON TO THE NEXT PAGE

12. _________ from France in 1803 was one of the greatest events in the history of the growth of the United States.
    (A) Purchasing of Louisiana
    (B) Louisiana Purchase
    (C) Purchased Louisiana
    (D) The purchase of the Louisiana Territory

13. Ancient mountains have been worn away by wind, rain, and _________.
    (A) with agents of erosion
    (B) other agents of erosion
    (C) for agents of erosion
    (D) to other agents of erosion

14. Ultrasound can be used to assess gestational age, to evaluate bleeding during pregnancy, and _________.
    (A) determining the location of the fetus
    (B) to determine the location of the fetus
    (C) which determined the location of the fetus
    (D) it is a determination of the fetus location

15. For years, researchers have tried to lower the antipsychotic drug dosage to a level _________ movement disorders, yet controls psychosis.
    (A) that they minimize
    (B) the minimum is
    (C) they minimizes
    (D) that minimizes

16. The details of the geological history of the Rocky Mountains have been lost _________ hundreds of millions of years.
    (A) on the passage for
    (B) during the passage of
    (C) in the passage
    (D) at the passage of

17. In China, acupuncture is used as an anesthesia, permitting patients to have major surgery _________.
    (A) while fully conscious
    (B) what is fully conscious
    (C) that fully consciousness
    (D) which is fully conscious

18. _________ as president, a candidate must win a majority of votes.
    (A) Having elected
    (B) Electing
    (C) To be elected
    (D) Elected

19. _________ numbers were created is not known.
    (A) When
    (B) After
    (C) Since
    (D) Before

20. Hair color is _________ characteristics to use in identifying people.
    (A) one of most obvious
    (B) obviously one of the most
    (C) one of the most obvious
    (D) one of the most obvious that is

21. It takes _________ car to get there.
    (A) a shorter time by subway than by
    (B) shorter time than by subway and by
    (C) by subway shorter time than
    (D) shorter time by subway than

22. _________ first place in the women's ten meter platform diving event, Xu Yianmei became China's first gold medal winner in the 1988 Summer Olympic Games in Seoul.
    (A) To win
    (B) Being won
    (C) Won
    (D) Having won

GO ON TO THE NEXT PAGE

23. The script has to ________ for a speech even though it's well-written.

(A) adapt to
(B) be adapted
(C) adapted
(D) adapt

Directions: In questions 24–60 each sentence has four underlined words or phrases. The four underlined parts of the sentence are marked (A), (B), (C), and (D). Identify the one underlined word or phrase that must be changed in order for the sentence to be correct. Then, on your answer sheet, find the number of the question and fill in the space that corresponds to the letter of the answer you have chosen.

Example I:

A ray of light passing through (A) the center (B) of a thin lens keep (C) its original (D) direction.

Sample Answer
Ⓐ Ⓑ ● Ⓓ

The sentence should read, "A ray of light passing through the center of a thin lens keeps its original direction." Therefore, you should choose answer (C).

Example II:

The mandolin, a musical instrument (A) that has (B) strings, was probably copied from (C) the lute, a many (D) older instrument.

Sample Answer
Ⓐ Ⓑ Ⓒ ●

The sentence should read, "The mandolin, a musical instrument that has strings, was probably copied from the lute, a much older instrument." Therefore, you should choose answer (D).

After you read the directions, begin work on the questions.

24. What (A) a strong defense is important to any country (B), it cannot be more important (C) than the livelihood of its (D) citizens.

25. "Order is Heaven's (A) first law," made (B) by the poet Alexander Pope (C), is painted on (D) the ceiling of the Library of Congress in Washington, D. C.

GO ON TO THE NEXT PAGE

26. As a result of the Women's Rights Movement, women around the world now holds
A B
positions that were once restricted to men.
C D

27. Whether or not a divorced person is entitled to share of his or her spouse's pension
A B C
has to be decided by the court.
D

28. Some people believe that printing does as much harm like good, since it brings out
A B C
falsehood as much as truth.
D

29. Comets can burst into fragments that fly upon in fiery orbits of their own.
A B C D

30. If the information in a report does not make sense, it may be necessary to check
A B C
the statistical.
D

31. Toledo, locating in the center of Spain, is encircled by the Tagus River.
A B C D

32. In some cultures, openness and directness seem rude, childish, and destructive
A B C D
naive.

33. Surgical apparatus has to be capable of great precise.
A B C D

34. Each chapter contains a few appendix, which give additional details as supple-
A B C D
ments to the text.

35. The dove nurtured her young until them were old enough to hunt for themselves.
A B C D

36. When a person from a contact culture moves in closer, a person from a
A
noncontact culture may feel the needy to back off.
B C D

37. As they grow older, children taught not to rely on their parents.
A B C D

38. Too many polished rice in one's diet could cause beriberi, a painful nerve disease.
A B C D

39. Drivers have the responsibility not endangering the lives of people and of animals
A B C
on the road.
D

GO ON TO THE NEXT PAGE

40. The cabin is certainly not luxuriously, but it is very practical and comfortable.
A B C D

41. Unfortunately, jogging nor dieting, carried to extremes, can be harmful.
A B C D

42. The letter that was sent by special delivery must be importance.
A B C D

43. What happens during a person's formulate years may affect the rest of that person's life.
A B C D

44. The gerund in English is normally formed by adding "ing" to the basically form of the verb.
A B C D

45. The camera must be focused good, otherwise the picture will be blurred.
A B C C

46. People tend to become irritate and short-tempered whenever they get overtired.
A B C D

47. A mule is a animal that is neither a horse nor a donkey, but a combination of the two.
A B C D

48. People living in cities are often sophisticated than people in rural areas.
A B C D

49. Disneyworld was built on 27,400 acres of in part swamp land in central Florida.
A B C D

50. Soaring medicinally costs have a direct influence on the cost of other merchandise.
A B C D

51. In addition to save on gas, the modern car is designed to save on maintenance and repair expenses.
A B C D

52. Edward Hall, a professor of anthropology, first commented on people's strong feelings about personnel space.
A B C D

53. Education trains a student to see things as it is, to disentangle a skein of thought.
A B C D

54. Before the middle of the eighteenth century, there were none public libraries in the United States.
A B C D

55. The nucleus of an ordinary comet is a mile but two in diameter.
A B C D

GO ON TO THE NEXT PAGE

56. George Gershwin believed that music should express the thoughts and feelings of
A: believed that; B: should express; C: their own time; D: in

their own time in history.

57. Some senior citizens have to cope with arthritis and other physical difficulties of
A: cope with; B: other; C: physical difficulties; D: aged

aged, in addition to psychological and social problems.

58. It has been estimated that in a few years, twelve percents of Canadians will be
A: in a few years; B: twelve percents; C: Canadians; D: senior citizens

senior citizens.

59. Many museum exhibits encourage you to investigate further through microscopes,
A: exhibits; B: further; C: through; D: even telescoping

magnifiers, and even telescoping.

60. The workers repairing the road surface are wearing specially jackets for easy
A: repairing; B: surface; C: specially; D: for

identification.

THIS IS THE END OF SECTION 2. CHECK YOUR WORK ON SECTION 2 ONLY. DO NOT READ OR WORK ON ANY OTHER SECTION OF THE TEST UNTIL YOUR TIME IS UP. **STOP**

3 3 3 3 3 3 3 3 3 3 3

SECTION 3
VOCABULARY AND READING COMPREHENSION
Time—65 minutes

This section is designed to measure your comprehension of standard written English. There are two types of questions in this section, with special directions for each type.

Directions: In questions 1–45 each sentence has an underlined word or phrase. Below each sentence are four other words or phrases, marked (A), (B), (C), and (D). You are to choose the one word or phrase that best keeps the meaning of the original sentence if it is substituted for the underlined word or phrase. Then, on your answer sheet, find the number of the question and fill in the space that corresponds to the letter you have chosen. Fill in the space so that the letter inside the oval cannot be seen.

Example:

Passenger ships and aircraft are often equipped with ship-to-shore or air-to-land radio telephones.

(A) highways
(B) railroads
(C) planes
(D) sailboats

Sample Answer

Ⓐ Ⓑ ● Ⓓ

The best answer is (C) because "Passenger ships and planes are often equipped with ship-to-shore or air-to-land radio telephones" is closest in meaning to the original sentence. Therefore, you should choose answer (C).

Now begin work on the questions.

GO ON TO THE NEXT PAGE

1. Scientific probes have searched for life beyond the earth.
   (A) over
   (B) outside of
   (C) surpassing
   (D) exceeding

2. A beam of light contains all the colors of the rainbow.
   (A) speck
   (B) signal
   (C) stream
   (D) crosspiece

3. Because of Nicolaus Copernicus' writings in the 15th century, people began to take a fresh interest in astronomy.
   (A) bright
   (B) cool
   (C) bold
   (D) new

4. The ancestors of Australian aborigines settled in Australia more than 30,000 years ago.
   (A) became calm
   (B) made an agreement
   (C) became restless
   (D) became established

5. Many people consider automobiles to be essential to American life.
   (A) critical
   (B) accessible
   (C) necessary
   (D) advantageous

6. Icarus and Daedalus are familiar from one of the earliest legends of flying.
   (A) stories
   (B) histories
   (C) epics
   (D) heroes

7. Saint Thomas Aquinas had a powerful influence on the thinking of his time.
   (A) effect
   (B) critique
   (C) affection
   (D) domination

8. Food that is considered a delicacy in one culture may be abhorred in another.
   (A) basic
   (B) special
   (C) satisfactory
   (D) plentiful

9. The ancient Romans built huge aqueducts that ran through tunnels and over bridges.
   (A) impressive
   (B) solid
   (C) large
   (D) high

10. More than 3,000 years ago, ancient people stumbled upon the fact that some molds could cure disease.
   (A) disputed
   (B) were disillusioned by
   (C) learned by experimentation
   (D) discovered by accident

11. On the tip of a fly's proboscis is a spongy pad.
   (A) an absorbent
   (B) an elastic
   (C) a firm
   (D) a damp

12. Vision is one of the five basic senses of animals in the animal kingdom.
   (A) accurate
   (B) exceptional
   (C) fundamental
   (D) beneficial

13. Insects are attracted to flowers that reflect ultraviolet light.
   (A) affected by
   (B) inspiring to
   (C) perplexed by
   (D) drawn towards

14. An earthworm is built up of a number of segments.
   (A) plumes
   (B) sections
   (C) pods
   (D) trunks

15. A bat uses a sonar device to orient itself to its surrounding world.
   (A) determine its position in
   (B) become impressed with
   (C) form an opinion of
   (D) guard against

16. Baby animals imitate their parents.
   (A) desire
   (B) copy
   (C) disrupt
   (D) arouse

GO ON TO THE NEXT PAGE

17. Some medicines should be dissolved before they are taken.
(A) boiled
(B) sweetened
(C) prepared with food
(D) mixed with a liquid

18. A simple society is based on an exchange of goods and services.
(A) a cycle
(B) a harmony
(C) a trade
(D) a collection

19. Most advanced countries have compulsory education.
(A) considerable
(B) required
(C) elaborate
(D) high-powered

20. Graphic displays of human organs are upsetting to some people.
(A) Clearly drawn
(B) Illicitly displayed
(C) Grave
(D) Grueling

21. In 1962 James Meredith made his first attempt at enrolling at the University of Mississippi.
(A) appeal
(B) try
(C) headway
(D) overthrow

22. A river begins with a trickle of water flowing over some pebbles.
(A) dripping irregularly
(B) splashing haphazardly
(C) running roughly
(D) moving smoothly

23. A bad winter storm can paralyze an urban area.
(A) immobilize
(B) evacuate
(C) isolate
(D) stabilize

24. Sunglasses come in many different colors, shapes, and strengths.
(A) circulate
(B) are discovered
(C) take part
(D) can be found

25. In 1605 the Mughal Empire ruled most of India.
(A) separated
(B) employed
(C) controlled
(D) influenced

26. There is evidence that Marco Polo traveled extensively in India and South East Asia as well as China.
(A) widely
(B) incredibly
(C) imperceptibly
(D) hygienically

27. Many people feel that it is common to go through a crisis period in midlife.
(A) time of domination
(B) time of change
(C) laborious time
(D) celebration

28. Jack London was a bold, rugged adventurer.
(A) fearless
(B) ambitious
(C) astute
(D) bizarre

29. Smoking cigarettes is often seen as an addiction.
(A) thought of
(B) taken care of
(C) experienced
(D) imagined

30. The gruesome details of Edgar Allan Poe's stories often stick in people's minds.
(A) gratifying
(B) exhilarating
(C) fiery
(D) horrible

31. Greek myths are prime sources of mythology for the western world.
(A) effective
(B) chief
(C) curious
(D) elaborated

32. Helen Keller explored the faces of people and animals by touch.
(A) inscribed
(B) isolated
(C) remembered
(D) examined

GO ON TO THE NEXT PAGE

33. Rudyard Kipling was fascinated by the customs and people of India.

(A) frightened
(B) influenced
(C) attracted
(D) overwhelmed

34. Many famous people are unremarkable as children.

(A) alert
(B) acclaimed
(C) ordinary
(D) delicate

35. Henry Wadsworth Longfellow is undoubtedly one of America's best-loved poets.

(A) practically
(B) certainly
(C) persistently
(D) relatively

36. A diminutive dancer can charm an audience.

(A) graceful
(B) tiny
(C) playful
(D) clever

37. Earthquakes occur at the boundaries of the earth's crust.

(A) happen
(B) originate
(C) appear
(D) diffuse

38. The ozone layer blocks ultraviolet radiation.

(A) contains
(B) disrupts
(C) penetrates
(D) obstructs

39. Many animals thrive in the Serengeti Plain.

(A) burrow
(B) persist
(C) flourish
(D) gather

40. Black sand is formed from volcanic glass ground by the action of the waves.

(A) soiled
(B) crushed
(C) gathered
(D) flooded

41. Getting caught in a dust storm can be frightening.

(A) typhoon with strong winds
(B) heavy rain with thunder and lightning
(C) wind carrying clouds of fine dry earth
(D) tornado with spiraling winds

42. The Himalayas remain the world's highest mountains because they are still rising.

(A) accentuate
(B) belong to
(C) stay behind
(D) continue to be

43. A good leader can anticipate people's responses.

(A) expect
(B) understand
(C) encourage
(D) sympathize with

44. When viewed from a new angle, the surprising often becomes understandable.

(A) recorded
(B) considered
(C) verified
(D) reassured

45. Some people won't let a shaggy dog into their home.

(A) dirty
(B) noisy
(C) hairy
(D) smelly

GO ON TO THE NEXT PAGE

Directions: In the rest of this section you will read several passages. Each one is followed by several questions about it. For questions 46–90, you are to choose the one best answer, (A), (B), (C), or (D), to each question. Then, on your answer sheet, find the number of the question and fill in the space that corresponds to the letter of the answer you have chosen.

Answer all questions following a passage on the basis of what is stated or implied in that passage.

Read the following passage:

The rattles with which a rattlesnake warns of its presence are formed by loosely interlocking hollow rings of hard skin, which make a buzzing sound when its tail is shaken. As a baby, the snake begins to firm its rattles from the button at the very tip of its tail. Thereafter, each time it sheds its skin, a new ring is formed. Popular belief holds that a snake's age can be told by counting the rings, but this idea is fallacious. In fact, a snake may lose its old skin as often as four times a year. Also, rattles tend to wear or break off with time.

Example I:

A rattlesnake's rattles are made of

(A) skin
(B) bone
(C) wood
(D) muscle

Sample Answer

   Ⓓ

According to the passage, a rattlesnake's rattles are made out of rings of hard skin. Therefore, you should choose answer (A).

Example II:

How often does a rattlesnake shed its skin?

(A) Once every four years
(B) Once every four months
(C) Up to four times every year
(D) Four times more often than other snakes

Sample Answer

   Ⓓ

The passage states that "a snake may lose its old skin as often as four times a year." Therefore, you should choose answer (C).

Now begin work on the questions.

GO ON TO THE NEXT PAGE

Questions 46-51

Chronic disability is surprisingly common in the United States. More than 12 percent of civilian, noninstitutionalized Americans are limited in their activities due to chronic health conditions. And of these 12 percent, about half of them are afflicted with heart conditions, arthritis, and rheumatism. Other common disabling conditions include impairments of the back or spine, lower extremities, and hips; mental and nervous conditions; visual impairments; and hypertension.

Disabling conditions vary with age. Among those who are seventeen to forty-four years of age, the major disabler is impairment of the back or spine, and among people forty-four years and over it is heart disease. Although people at all ages are vulnerable to disability, the aged are most affected. With age, the rate of acute and chronic disabling conditions increases dramatically. Between the ages of seventeen and forty-four, 7 percent of the population have some chronic illness or disability. Between the ages of forty-five and sixty-five, the rate increases to about 19 percent, and in people sixty-five and over, it is over 46 percent.

Chronic disability also varies with family income. Chronic limitation of activity is most prevalent among low-income families. This relationship between disability and poverty tends to be cyclical. The poor get sick more frequently, seek and receive less medical treatment, take longer to recover, and suffer more from disabling conditions than those with higher incomes.

46. Which of the following is the most common chronic health condition?

(A) Back disorder
(B) Heart condition
(C) Visual impairment
(D) Hypertension

47. Impairment of the spine is most common among which group?

(A) people of ages 17–44
(B) 12 percent of the population
(C) 50 percent of disabled people
(D) 7 percent of the population

48. Which area of the body contains the spine?

(A) the lower extremities
(B) the internal organs
(C) the head
(D) the back

49. The words "afflicted with" in lines 3–4 can best be substituted with which of the following?

(A) infected by
(B) suffering with
(C) destroyed by
(D) reacting against

50. Which of the following conclusions is best supported by the passage?

(A) Aged people have more tension than younger people.
(B) Poor people are not as likely to take care of their health.
(C) Back problems are a major disabler for most people.
(D) Fifty percent of the population get heart disease.

51. What does the author mean by the words "tends to be cyclical" in line 17?

(A) One thing often causes the other.
(B) There is a relationship between getting treated and being disabled.
(C) The sicker one is, the more it costs for medical care.
(D) There is a cycle of rising costs for poorer people.

GO ON TO THE NEXT PAGE

Questions 52–58

The life of the sea otter, known to some people as a "floating teddy bear" and to scientists as *Enhydra lutris*, has not been easy, conservationists say. Their population off the California coast diminished from 18,000 in 1800 to 1,724 in 1988. In the 19th century, they were brought to the brink of extinction by American, Russian, and Spanish fur traders. But in 1938 a rancher spotted several of the small furry animals floating on their backs, their usual position, off the coast of California. Since then, their numbers have slowly multiplied. The problem now is not that people hunt them for their furs but that the sea otters are at odds with the commercial shellfish industry. Many people in the shellfish industry want to get rid of the otters because they eat the very things that the industry wants: clams, abalone, lobster, crabs, and sea urchins.

Another danger for the sea otter comes from the oil industry. Sea otters have no insulating layer of blubber to keep them warm in 50-degree waters. What keeps them warm is their long, thick fur. This fur must be kept fluffy and full of air bubbles in order to keep water from coming in direct contact with the otter's skin. If there is an oil spill, as has been common in recent years, the oil could mat the sea otter's fur, which would cause death by freezing within hours. As a result, conservationists are now concerned about what might happen if a large number of sea otters and an oil slick meet.

52. Which of the following is the best title for this passage?
(A) Sea Otters: A Conservationist's Concern
(B) Oil Slicks
(C) Sea Otters and Their Fur
(D) The Life of the Sea Otter

53. A sea otter is
(A) a furry animal
(B) a teddy bear
(C) a shellfish
(D) a sea bird

54. What happened to sea otters in the 19th century?
(A) The numbers of sea otters increased.
(B) The shellfish industry caused the extinction of sea otters.
(C) Conservationists protected the sea otters.
(D) Sea otters were killed for their fur.

55. The word "spotted" in line 5 could best be substituted by which of the following?
(A) Shot
(B) Recorded
(C) Saw
(D) Caught

56. According to the passage, what protects sea otters from the cold?
(A) Extra fat
(B) Insulation
(C) Matted coats
(D) Fluffy fur

57. Which of these would be a problem for sea otters?
(A) Warm weather
(B) Tangled hair
(C) Bubbly water
(D) Shellfish

58. What major problem are the conservationists concerned about?
(A) Freezing weather
(B) An accident by the oil industry
(C) Oily skin
(D) Air bubbles coming in contact with the sea otter's skin

GO ON TO THE NEXT PAGE

Questions 59–64

When John Muir, at twenty-nine, left his job as a machinist, he acted with his typical independence by walking to Florida, a distance of about a thousand miles. He chose the wildest ways, as he felt the need to give himself to the natural world. He felt that life was too precious to be devoted to machines. As he later put it, he could have become a millionaire but he chose to become a tramp. And, as it turned out, a millionaire's life could not have produced the effect that John Muir's life has had on the American landscape.

After his walk to Florida, Muir eventually found himself in California where he became entranced by Yosemite Valley. There he began his career as a nature essayist and conservationist. He also explored the mountains extensively and traveled to other wild areas, including Alaska. His life fell into a single-developing pattern of devotion to all things natural.

Besides independence, endurance and joy were a large part of Muir's character. He would set off for a mountain trek with very few belongings and only a little food. These would last him for weeks of climbing and exploring. Wherever he looked, he saw beauty and he felt joy. He felt as if the beauty was evidence of a divine presence, and eventually, in his own mind, the line between the divine and nature became blurred. Muir was one of the first voices in favor of the wild in a time better known for the destruction and exploitation of nature. He was born 150 years ago, but groves of sequoia redwood trees still grow because of his love and work.

59. John Muir walked to Florida because
(A) Florida was wild.
(B) Florida was far away.
(C) he was poor.
(D) he was independent.

60. From the passage we can infer that John Muir was
(A) lonely
(B) rich
(C) friendly
(D) dedicated

61. John Muir devoted his life to
(A) natural things
(B) wild animals
(C) climbing trees
(D) the divine

62. According to the passage, which of the following would best describe Muir?
(A) He didn't separate God and nature.
(B) He became a tramp because he didn't like people.
(C) He loved painting landscapes to show the beauty of nature.
(D) He enjoyed seeing how far he could walk in the wild.

63. According to this passage, John Muir lived
(A) in Florida
(B) a lonely life
(C) with people concerned about the environment
(D) in a time when people didn't care about conservation

64. When Muir felt joy about nature what would he have been most likely to do?
(A) Write
(B) Talk
(C) Sing
(D) Hike

GO ON TO THE NEXT PAGE

Questions 65–71

Over four hundred years after his death, scholars are still unraveling the mysteries of Michelangelo's art. Recently one mystery that was revealed was that his famous drawing of a pensive Cleopatra included a hidden drawing of a different Cleopatra on the reverse side. This hidden Cleopatra shows a tormented women, whose eyes stare out at the viewer and whose mouth is open, screaming in horror. The two images, drawn on two sides of the same paper, can be viewed simultaneously. Another mystery concerns Michelangelo's architectural plan for the dome of St. Peter's Basilica in Rome. Some scholars believe that the model he built between 1558 and 1561 shows the dome as he intended it for St. Peter's. Other scholars believe that he changed his mind and decided to elevate the dome in the way it is today. A third mystery about one of the greatest artists who ever lived was why he destroyed hundreds or thousands of his drawings before he died. Did he feel that they were unimportant? Did he want posterity to see only his finished products?

65. It can be inferred from the passage that the most unusual aspect of the Cleopatra drawing is that
(A) the figure is screaming
(B) the figure is tormented
(C) the drawing was hidden
(D) the drawing is backwards

66. The word "pensive" in line 3 can best be substituted by
(A) thoughtful
(B) angry
(C) happy
(D) anxious

67. Scholars disagree about
(A) when St. Peter's Basilica was built
(B) what kind of dome Michelangelo wanted
(C) who elevated the dome of St. Peter's
(D) who built the model

68. The dome of St. Peter's Basilica is
(A) a mosaic
(B) destroyed
(C) a model
(D) raised

69. According to this passage, Michelangelo is
(A) screaming in horror
(B) one of the greatest artists in the world
(C) a private person
(D) the most famous architect in Rome

70. Why did Michelangelo destroy so many drawings before he died?
(A) Nobody knows.
(B) They were unimportant.
(C) They were only drafts of later material.
(D) He had changed the drawings.

71. Which of the following is the best restatement of the final question in this passage (lines 12–13)
(A) Did he want his compatriots to judge only his final works of art?
(B) Did he want his position as an artist to be based on all of his productions?
(C) Did he want Roman society to see only his best work?
(D) Did he want future generations to judge him only by his completed work?

GO ON TO THE NEXT PAGE

Questions 72–76

The difference between holographic optics and conventional optics is similar to the difference between thinking of light as a wave and light as a particle. Traditional glass lenses treat light as a particle; they work by refraction. When the light meets glass or plastic, it bends at an angle. It is as though light were composed of rays of particles that enter a lens on one side, become bent by the glass, and then leave the lens on the other side.

Holography is based on diffraction, rather than refraction. Think of the light as a wave. When the wave strikes objects, it sets up different wave patterns. When light enters a holographic lens, it forms an interference pattern and is sent off in several directions. The holographic lens itself is only a block of plastic covered with microscopic valleys and ridges. A computer can calculate the pattern for the surface and manipulate light in any way that can be imagined.

72. This passage is mainly about
- **(A)** a new form of eyeglasses
- **(B)** types of camera lenses
- **(C)** a new way to take pictures
- **(D)** the science of light

73. According to the passage, what happens when light meets glass or plastic?
- **(A)** It gets brighter.
- **(B)** It changes direction.
- **(C)** It moves faster.
- **(D)** It stops moving.

74. In this passage, what does the author mean by the word "wave"?
- **(A)** A ridge of sea water
- **(B)** A way to say goodbye
- **(C)** A way of moving
- **(D)** A curve of hair

75. What is the main purpose of this passage?
- **(A)** To argue a point
- **(B)** To invent a term
- **(C)** To point out a similarity
- **(D)** To explain a difference

76. In line 11, the word "ridges" could best be replaced by
- **(A)** crests
- **(B)** slopes
- **(C)** gullies
- **(D)** grooves

GO ON TO THE NEXT PAGE

Questions 77–83

Are the 80s and 90s the era of color? According to some people, they are. Now you can buy radios and electric fans in lavender and pink. Restaurants have an emphasis on flowers and colorful plates. Cars are coming out in pink and aqua. Even bathroom fixtures are being made in "honeydew" and "blond." Part of the importance of the color of an object is that the color affects the way one feels about it. You want a vacuum cleaner to look light and easy, which is why it may be colored in pastels and light colors. But gardening equipment and athletic equipment you want to look powerful. You would never find a lawn mower in pink, but red would be fine. Not very long ago, sheets were always white, and refrigerators commonly came in colors like "Old Gold," "Avocado Green," and "Coppertone." Now those are thought of as old-fashioned. Popular colors change, because fashion influences everything. In fact, new colors often spring from the fashion industry. It's a lot cheaper to make a blouse or skirt than a sofa. After people get used to seeing new colors on clothing or towels, they are ready to accept those colors in carpeting, refrigerators, or cars. Color-analysis consultants have been very successful in recent years. People want to choose the most flattering colors for makeup and clothing. Some car designers are even saying that people may begin buying cars of the color that goes with their skin coloring. This sounds too extreme. It's hard to believe that people are that impressionable.

77. The best title for this passage is
(A) Popular Colors
(B) Color Consultants
(C) The Success of Color
(D) Flattering Colors

78. According to the passage, which of the following is not popular now?
(A) "Coppertone"
(B) Pastels
(C) Colorful cars
(D) Color consultants

79. According to the passage, why would red be a good color for a lawn mower?
(A) Because it's strong
(B) Because it's cheap
(C) Because it's light
(D) Because it's a pastel

80. How does the author probably feel about the topic of this passage?
(A) Excited
(B) Envious
(C) Skeptical
(D) Bored

81. In this passage, which of the following are NOT used as names for colors?
(A) Hair color
(B) Fruits
(C) Minerals
(D) Drinks

82. Why does the author say, "It's cheaper to make a skirt than a sofa"?
(A) As an illustration
(B) As a reason
(C) As a summary
(D) As a definition

83. According to this passage, before people will buy expensive things in new colors, they must
(A) be sure that the colors are popular
(B) see if the color matches their skin color
(C) talk to a color-analyst consultant
(D) become familiar with the color on cheaper items

GO ON TO THE NEXT PAGE

Questions 84–90

They remind astronomers of the death of mythic Icarus, killed after the wax holding together his homemade wings melted when he flew too close to the sun. But instead of a Greek myth, this "Icarus" is a comet. On rare occasions, astronomers have observed comets passing so near the sun that the heat has caused them to break up or even disappear altogether. Over the centuries only a dozen or so of these "sun-grazers" have been discovered with telescopes. Now, artificial satellites have turned up two or three more. These comets were probably once part of a single comet, which at one time passed so close to the sun that it fragmented. Centuries ago, the original discoverer, Heinrich Kreutz, determined that this type of comet circled the sun in a clockwise direction, with an orbit tilted at about forty degrees. The newly-found sun-grazers seem to fit in with those of the Kreutz group. Their present orbits suggest that some of the initial fragments split again in subsequent trips past the sun.

84. The best title for this passage is
- **(A)** The Mythic Icarus
- **(B)** Comets Near the Sun
- **(C)** Tilted Orbits
- **(D)** The Kreutz Group

85. The word "they" in line 1 refers to
- **(A)** comets
- **(B)** people
- **(C)** wings
- **(D)** astronomers

86. What is a "sun-grazer"?
- **(A)** A comet
- **(B)** An astronomer
- **(C)** A telescope
- **(D)** An orbit

87. Why did the comet become fragmented?
- **(A)** It flew too fast.
- **(B)** It became too hot.
- **(C)** It melted.
- **(D)** It hit the sun.

88. The word "tilted" in line 10 could be substituted best by
- **(A)** measured
- **(B)** slanted
- **(C)** encountered
- **(D)** poised

89. Which of the following is NOT true about the recently discovered sun-grazers?
- **(A)** They were part of a single comet.
- **(B)** They travel clockwise.
- **(C)** They were discovered by Heinrich Kreutz.
- **(D)** They have made trips around the sun.

90. The story of Icarus is used to
- **(A)** clarify a fact
- **(B)** summarize an idea
- **(C)** define a concept
- **(D)** add interest

THIS IS THE END OF SECTION 3. IF YOU FINISH BEFORE YOUR TIME IS UP, CHECK YOUR WORK ON SECTION 3 ONLY. DO NOT READ OR WORK ON ANY OTHER SECTION OF THE TEST. **STOP**

Answer Key for Practice Test IV

SECTION 1: LISTENING COMPREHENSION

Part A

1. B	**6.** A	**11.** C	**16.** D	**21.** B	**26.** D
2. C	**7.** D	**12.** A	**17.** D	**22.** A	**27.** A
3. A	**8.** C	**13.** C	**18.** D	**23.** C	**28.** D
4. C	**9.** B	**14.** A	**19.** B	**24.** D	**29.** C
5. D	**10.** B	**15.** D	**20.** B	**25.** A	**30.** A

Part B

31. C	**36.** A	**41.** A	**46.** D	**51.** A
32. A	**37.** B	**42.** A	**47.** A	**52.** A
33. D	**38.** D	**43.** A	**48.** C	**53.** B
34. A	**39.** D	**44.** B	**49.** A	**54.** C
35. D	**40.** B	**45.** B	**50.** A	**55.** D

Part C

56. C	**61.** C	**66.** D	**71.** A	**76.** A
57. A	**62.** B	**67.** D	**72.** B	**77.** C
58. D	**63.** A	**68.** C	**73.** A	**78.** D
59. A	**64.** C	**69.** B	**74.** D	**79.** A
60. B	**65.** B	**70.** C	**75.** B	**80.** C

SECTION 2: STRUCTURE AND WRITTEN EXPRESSION

1. C	**11.** D	**21.** A	**31.** A	**41.** A	**51.** A
2. A	**12.** D	**22.** D	**32.** D	**42.** D	**52.** D
3. A	**13.** B	**23.** B	**33.** D	**43.** B	**53.** C
4. A	**14.** B	**24.** A	**34.** B	**44.** D	**54.** C
5. B	**15.** D	**25.** B	**35.** B	**45.** B	**55.** C
6. A	**16.** B	**26.** B	**36.** C	**46.** B	**56.** C
7. C	**17.** A	**27.** C	**37.** B	**47.** A	**57.** D
8. B	**18.** C	**28.** B	**38.** A	**48.** C	**58.** B
9. D	**19.** A	**29.** C	**39.** A	**49.** C	**59.** D
10. D	**20.** C	**30.** D	**40.** B	**50.** B	**60.** C

SECTION 3: VOCABULARY AND READING COMPREHENSION

1. B	**11.** A	**21.** B	**31.** B	**41.** C	**51.** A	**61.** A	**71.** D	**81.** D
2. C	**12.** C	**22.** D	**32.** D	**42.** D	**52.** A	**62.** A	**72.** D	**82.** B
3. D	**13.** D	**23.** A	**33.** C	**43.** A	**53.** A	**63.** D	**73.** B	**83.** D
4. D	**14.** B	**24.** D	**34.** C	**44.** B	**54.** D	**64.** A	**74.** C	**84.** B
5. C	**15.** A	**25.** C	**35.** B	**45.** C	**55.** C	**65.** C	**75.** D	**85.** A
6. A	**16.** B	**26.** A	**36.** B	**46.** B	**56.** D	**66.** A	**76.** A	**86.** A
7. A	**17.** D	**27.** B	**37.** A	**47.** A	**57.** B	**67.** B	**77.** C	**87.** B
8. B	**18.** C	**28.** A	**38.** D	**48.** D	**58.** B	**68.** D	**78.** A	**88.** B
9. C	**19.** B	**29.** A	**39.** C	**49.** B	**59.** D	**69.** B	**79.** A	**89.** C
10. D	**20.** A	**30.** D	**40.** B	**50.** B	**60.** D	**70.** A	**80.** C	**90.** D

Score Analysis Form for Practice Test IV

Directions: Count the number of answers you have correct in Practice Test IV, using the answer key on pages 544–545. Then use the chart on page 49 (Long Form) to figure out your converted score range. Fill in the rest of this form so you can compare it to your scores in Practice Test III.

	RAW SCORE		(each)	CONVERTED SCORE RANGE	(each)	APPROXIMATE SCORE RANGE
Listening Comprehension	____	____–____	× 10 =	____–____	÷ 3 =	____–____
Structure and Written Expression	____	____–____	× 10 =	____–____	÷ 3 =	____–____
Vocabulary and Reading Comprehension	____	____–____	× 10 =	____–____	÷ 3 =	____–____
TOTAL APPROXIMATE SCORE (add 3 approximate scores)						____–____

What is your best section out of the above three? ____________

ANALYSIS OF EACH SECTION

1. Listening Comprehension

	Number Correct	Total		Percent Correct
Part A (Questions 1–30)	______	÷ 30	=	______%
Part B (Questions 31–55)	______	÷ 25	=	______%
Part C (Questions 56–80)	______	÷ 25	=	______%

Which part has the highest percentage of correct answers? __________

2. *Structure and Written Expression*

	Number Correct	Total	Percent Correct
First Part (Questions 1–23)	______	÷ 23	= ______%
Second Part (Questions 24–60)	______	÷ 37	= ______%

Which part has the highest percentage of correct answers? __________

3. *Vocabulary and Reading Comprehension*

	Number Correct	Total	Percent Correct
Vocabulary (Questions 1–45)	______	÷ 45	= ______%
Reading (Questions 46–90)	______	÷ 45	= ______%

Which part has the highest percentage of correct answers? __________

Explanatory Answers

SECTION 1: LISTENING COMPREHENSION

The Listening Comprehension Tapescript for this test is on pages 647 to 653.

Part A

1. You got a good deal when you bought this tape recorder at the clearance sale.
   (A) There are many tape recorders on sale.
   (B) You paid a low price for the tape recorder.
   (C) Your tape recorder is not new, but it's clean.
   (D) The tape recorder you bought should help you study.

(B) Glance at the choices and summarize: tape recorder.
Testing point 1: restatement/vocabulary. The word "deal" refers to a business transaction, a trade, or a negotiation.
Testing point 2: vocabulary. "You got a good deal ... at the clearance sale" means that you paid a low price for something.
Cultural knowledge: "clearance sale" refers to a sale that a store has in order to clear out or get rid of merchandise by selling it at a cheaper price.

2. He walked around the hall looking for a pencil sharpener.
   (A) He ran across his friend while walking in the hall.
   (B) He could see the pencil sharpener through the hall.
   (C) He was trying to find the pencil sharpener.
   (D) He walked around whenever he had time.

(C) Glance at the choices and summarize: he, pencil, sharpener.
Testing point: restatement/idiom. "To walk around" refers to walking in a general area rather than walking to a particular destination. "Looking for something" means "trying to find something."

3. Nobody likes watermelon more than I do.
   (A) I enjoy watermelon more than anybody else.
   (B) I bought more watermelon than anyone else.
   (C) Watermelon grows much faster than I expected.
   (D) Very few people in this area grow watermelon.

(A) Glance at the choices and summarize: I, watermelon, comparative.
Testing point: restatement/inference. "Nobody likes ... more than I do" implies "I enjoy ... more than anybody else."

4. She needs a vacation badly.
   (A) She had a bad vacation.
   (B) Her vacation wasn't very interesting.
   (C) She really should take some time off.
   (D) She hasn't begun to plan her trip yet.

(C) Glance at the choices and summarize: she, vacation.
Testing point 1: restatement/idiom. "To need something badly" means "to need something very much." The idiom "to take time off" means "to take a vacation or a break."
Testing point 2: inference. If she needs a vacation very much, she should take time off from her work.

5. These pants require dry cleaning.
   (A) You don't need these pants right now.
   (B) These pants are clean.
   (C) These pants are dry.
   (D) Don't wash these pants in water.

(D) Glance at the choices and summarize: pants, clean, dry.
Testing Point 1: restatement (opposite). The opposite of "require dry cleaning" is "don't wash ... in water."
Testing point 2: vocabulary. The words "dry cleaning" refer to a process of cleaning that uses chemicals instead of water.

6. What a beautiful view!
   (A) This is enjoyable to look at.
   (B) What kind of view do you like the most?
   (C) That's a beautiful dress.
   (D) The view isn't as good as I expected.

(A) Glance at the choices and summarize: view, beautiful. Testing point: restatement. "What a beautiful view!" means "the view is enjoyable to look at." "This" refers to "the view."

7. This could be an alternative answer.
   (A) The answer should be altered.
   (B) All the answers are here.
   (C) All the answers will be given in the next class.
   (D) This answer could be correct, too.

(D) Glance at the choices and summarize: answers, all. Testing point: restatement/vocabulary. "Alternative answer" means "another possible correct answer."

8. Why not ask the waitress to give you an extra fork?
   (A) You should use your fork.
   (B) Why is the waitress so slow?
   (C) You should ask the waitress for another fork.
   (D) It would be nice to have some extra napkins.

(C) Glance at the choices and summarize: fork, waitress.
Testing point 1: restatement/question. "Why not...?" means "you should ..."
Testing point 2: vocabulary. "An extra fork" means "another fork."

9. There was bumper-to-bumper traffic during the rush hour.
   (A) People drive quickly when they are in a hurry.
   (B) There were a lot of cars on the road after work.
   (C) People take turns driving on the highway.
   (D) The highway is better than the subway.

(B) Glance at the choices and summarize: drive, hurry, highway.
Testing point 1: restatement/idiom/inference. "Bumper-to-bumper traffic" refers to "many cars."
Testing point 2: vocabulary. "A bumper" is the steel bar on the front and back of a car that lessens the effect of a collision.

10. It feels good to be cool again.
   (A) I like cold drinks.
   (B) I'm glad I'm not so hot.
   (C) I am glad he's not cruel to me any more.
   (D) I feel like having another Coke.

(B) Glance at the choices and summarize: I, cold drinks, hot. Testing point: restatement/vocabulary. "Cool" is similar to "not hot." "It feels good" is similar to "I'm glad."

11. When the time comes to decide, he still hesitates.
   (A) Making a decision is easy when the time is right.
   (B) There is not much time left for him to hesitate.
   (C) He can't make up his mind when he has to make a decision.
   (D) He still has time to hesitate.

(C) Glance at the choices and summarize: make decision, time, hesitate.
Testing point: restatement/vocabulary. "Hesitate" means "stop or pause before making a decision" or "show uncertainty or unwillingness." The idiom "make up one's mind" means "come to a decision."

12. Only occasionally does he express his anger.
   (A) He seldom shows anger.
   (B) He doesn't care what happens to him.
   (C) He was very angry when he had an accident.
   (D) He was very calm during the accident.

(A) Glance at the choices and summarize: he, angry, calm.
Testing point: restatement/vocabulary. "Occasionally" means "seldom"; "express" means "show." Notice the inverted verb order after "only occasionally."

13. The newborn panda is awfully cute.
   (A) The newborn panda looks awful.
   (B) A baby panda grows up fast.
   (C) The baby panda is really attractive.
   (D) A newborn panda needs special care.

(C) Glance at the choices and summarize: newborn panda.
Testing point: restatement/vocabulary. "Awfully" means "extremely" or "really" or "very." "Cute" is similar to "attractive."

14. I'm going to change the topic of my thesis.
- **(A)** I don't want to use this topic.
- **(B)** I couldn't have changed my research subject earlier.
- **(C)** My thesis is almost finished.
- **(D)** I couldn't improve my thesis without help.

(A) Glance at the choices and summarize: topic, thesis.
Testing point: restatement/vocabulary. "I'm going to change ..." implies "I don't want to use ..." Background Information: a thesis is a statement or discussion of a theory with supporting arguments that is submitted for a university degree.

15. The new semester will start in one week.
- **(A)** There is only a week before finals.
- **(B)** We need a week to prepare for the school play.
- **(C)** School started a week ago.
- **(D)** School begins again next week.

(D) Glance at the choices and summarize: school, week.
Testing point: restatement. "The new semester" refers to "school."

16. Sue will be teaching this course this semester.
- **(A)** Sue applied for a new teaching job.
- **(B)** Sue has a friend in this course.
- **(C)** Sue is taking this course, too.
- **(D)** Sue will be the professor in this class.

(D) Glance at the choices and summarize: Sue, course.
Testing point: restatement/vocabulary. Since "Sue will be teaching," it means that "Sue is the professor."

17. The cafeteria is a place where you can eat, relax, and talk to people.
- **(A)** You'd better go to the cafeteria with someone else.
- **(B)** The cafeteria has inexpensive but good food.
- **(C)** The cafeteria is a nicer building than the library.
- **(D)** The cafeteria is a good place to go for several activities.

(D) Glance at the choices and summarize: cafeteria.
Testing point: restatement/vocabulary. The words "eat, relax, and talk" mean the same as "several activities."

18. You can wear informal clothes to class; even professors do.
- **(A)** Everybody likes your new jacket very much.
- **(B)** Both you and the professors have to dress up.
- **(C)** You don't have to dress formally but professors do.
- **(D)** Neither professors nor students dress up.

(D) Glance at the choices and summarize: everybody, both, neither ... nor, dress up.
Testing point 1: restatement/vocabulary. The phrase "dress up" means "to put on special clothes or one's best clothes."
Testing point 2: structure. "Even professors do" means "even professors wear informal clothes." The meaning is the same as the opposite statement, "Neither professors nor students dress up."

19. All of today's newspapers are gone; the box is empty.
- **(A)** The empty box is good for used newspapers.
- **(B)** It's too late to buy today's newspaper.
- **(C)** The price of the newspaper has gone up.
- **(D)** We can get a newspaper here.

(B) Glance at the choices and summarize: newspaper.
Testing point: inference. "All of today's newspapers are gone" means that all the newspapers have been sold. The sentence implies "It's too late to buy today's newspaper."

20. The accuracy of the new equipment still needs to be tested.
- **(A)** They tested the new cars.
- **(B)** The new equipment needs more tests.
- **(C)** The tests of the new instruments were accurate.
- **(D)** We're having a test next week.

(B) Glance at the choices and summarize: test, equipment.
Testing point: restatement/vocabulary. "... still needs to be tested" means "needs more tests."

21. I'll take it; I don't have any other choice.
- **(A)** I'd like to have more choices.
- **(B)** I have to take it.
- **(C)** You don't have to take it if you don't need it.
- **(D)** I have many other choices, don't I?

(B) Glance at the choices and summarize: I, have to, choice.
Testing point: inference. "I don't have any other choices" implies "I have to" or "I must" do it.

22. Only once in a while do I take chances.
(A) Occasionally I take chances doing things.
(B) Once I took a chance.
(C) You should never take chances.
(D) I rarely get chances to do things.

(A) Glance at the choices and summarize: occasionally, never, rarely, take chances.
Testing point: restatement/idiom. "Only once in a while" means "occasionally." "To take a chance" means "to risk." Notice the inverted verb order after "only once in a while ..."

23. I'll quit this job; I mean it.
(A) I don't want to say bad things about my job.
(B) I didn't mean what I said.
(C) I've made up my mind to quit this job.
(D) I can quit this job, even though it's mean.

(C) Glance at the choices and summarize: I, job, quit.
Testing point: restatement/vocabulary. "I mean it" means "I have made up my mind" or "I have come to a decision."

24. Jack was the substitute while I was on my trip.
(A) Jack likes to work with me.
(B) Jack's driver's license was suspended.
(C) Jack and I went on vacation together.
(D) Jack took over for me when I was not here.

(D) Glance at the choices and summarize: Jack, I, restatement.
Testing point 1: vocabulary. The word "substitute" refers to someone who does someone else's job for a while.
Testing point 2: vocabulary. "Took over" is the past tense of "to take over," which means "to do someone else's job."

25. Attendance is one of the requirements of this class.
(A) Absence from this class may affect your grade.
(B) The only requirement of this class is attendance.
(C) Your grade depends solely on your final exam.
(D) You can study the textbook at home for this class.

(A) Glance at the choices and summarize: class, requirement, attendance.
Testing point 1: inference/vocabulary. "Attendance" is the opposite of "absence."
Testing point 2: inference. "Attendance is one of the requirements of this class" implies "absence from this class may affect your grade" or "if you are not in class, you may receive a lower grade." The word "grade" is also referred to as "mark" or "score."

26. Why don't we have lunch together so that we can talk about it more?
(A) I'm tired of looking for a place to eat.
(B) Let's stop talking; it's lunch time now.
(C) It's not a good idea to talk while eating.
(D) Let's talk more over lunch.

(D) Glance at the choices and summarize: place to eat, lunch time, talk.
Testing point 1: restatement/question. "Why not ...?" means "let's ..."
Testing point 2: vocabulary. The phrase "over lunch" means "while we eat lunch."

27. Jessica is very involved in her church activities.
(A) Jessica is active in the church to which she belongs.
(B) Jessica was offered a role in the church play.
(C) Jessica sings in the church choir.
(D) Jessica invited a friend to her church last Sunday.

(A) Glance at the choices and summarize: Jessica, church. Testing point: restatement/idiom. "To be very involved in" means "to be active in."

28. That's what my sister is interested in, not me.
(A) That's just a part of my interest.
(B) My sister doesn't like that at all.
(C) My sister has the same tastes as I do.
(D) My interests are different from my sister's.

(D) Glance at the choices and summarize: interest, sister.
Testing point: inference. "That's what my sister is interested in, not me" implies "my interests are different from my sister's."

29. Mr. Jones was the former chair of the committee.
(A) Mr. Jones doesn't want to retire from the committee.
(B) Mr. Jones dressed formally at the committee meeting.
(C) Mr. Jones is no longer the chairman.
(D) Mr. Jones is a farmer.

(C) Glance at the choices and summarize: Mr. Jones, committee.
Testing point 1: vocabulary. "Former president" means "previous president" or "no longer president." The phrase "no longer" means "not any more."
Testing point 2: vocabulary. The word "chair" is a short form for "chairman" or "chairwoman."

30. There is no excuse for this kind of error.
(A) Nobody should make this kind of mistake.
(B) You are excused this time, but no more.
(C) You should excuse others for their errors.
(D) Errors are correctable.

(A) Glance at the choices and summarize: mistake, error, excused.
Testing point: inference. "... no excuse for ..." implies "there is no way to defend or explain your actions." Therefore, it is bad to make that kind of mistake.

Part B

31. Man: Hello, I'd like to buy a hundred dollar money order.
Woman: OK. Do you have an account here?
Where does this conversation most likely take place?
(A) In a travel agency
(B) In an airport
(C) In a bank
(D) In a government office

(C) Glance at the choices and summarize: location.
Testing point: inference. "Money order" and "account number" are words related to business in a bank.

32. Woman: This muffin smells good.
Man: Tastes good, too.
What is the man's comment about the muffin?
(A) He likes it.
(B) He thinks it has a good smell.
(C) He hopes it will be done at two.
(D) He thinks it's too dry.

(A) Glance at the choices and summarize: he, think, like.
Testing point: inference. "Tastes good too" implies "he likes it."

33. Man: I don't understand why this study book doesn't provide an explanation of the answers.
Woman: But it does!
What does the woman say about the study book?
(A) She thinks the explanations are difficult.
(B) The explanations will be added in a later edition.
(C) She thinks the book should include more information.
(D) The book includes an explanation of all the answers.

(D) Glance at the choices and summarize: she, think, explanation, book.
Testing point: contradiction. "But" indicates that the woman doesn't agree with the man's opinion. "It does" means that the book does provide an explanation of the answers.

34. Woman: Do you have the paperback edition of this book?
Man: Yes, we do, but the hardcover is on sale for the same price as the paperback.
What do we learn about the book from the man?
(A) Both editions are the same price now.
(B) The paperback book is on sale.
(C) The hardcover book is better quality; therefore, it costs more.
(D) The books are different, but the covers are the same.

(A) Glance at the choices and summarize: book, the same, different.
Testing point: the same as. "The hardcover is on sale for the same price as the paperback" means "both editions are the same price."

35. Woman: Why are you going to school so early?
Man: I have to practice using the slide projector and prepare my presentation for class today.
What will the man do in class?
(A) Become a representative of the class.
(B) Leave the class early.
(C) Take pictures.
(D) Give a presentation to the class.

(D) Glance at the choices and summarize: class.
Testing point: inference. "Prepare my presentation for class" implies he will give a presentation to the class.

36. Man: Would you mind seeing our representative?
Woman: I wouldn't mind at all.
What does the woman mean?
(A) She would be willing to see the representative.
(B) She doesn't want to see the representative at the moment.
(C) She plans to see the representative later.
(D) She'll keep it in mind to arrange a time to see him.

(A) Glance at the choices and summarize: see, representative.
Testing point: idiom. "Wouldn't mind" means the same as "be willing to."

37. Man: I would like to make a reservation for dinner for four tonight.
Woman: I'm sorry, sir. We don't take reservations on weekends.
What does the woman mean?
(A) Reservations should be made early in the day.
(B) It is impossible to make reservations on Saturdays and Sundays.
(C) The restaurant has a branch nearby that makes reservations.
(D) The restaurant is being remodeled this weekend.

(B) Glance at the choices and summarize: reservations, restaurant.
Testing point: inference. "We don't take reservations" implies "it's impossible to make reservations"; "on the weekends" means "on Saturdays and Sundays."

38. Woman: Did you talk to the consultant about the new program?
Man: No, he's at lunch until two.
What does the man mean?
(A) He talked to the consultant about the new program until two.
(B) The consultant was leaving at two.
(C) The consultant wanted to talk to him, too.
(D) He couldn't talk to the consultant before two.

(D) Glance at the choices and summarize: consultant, two, too.
Testing point: inference. "He's at lunch until two" implies "the consultant won't be here before two"; therefore, "he couldn't talk to the consultant before two."

39. Man: It's getting dark. Do you want me to walk you to your car?
Woman: No, thanks, it's not far.
What does the woman mean?
(A) She lives far away.
(B) She has a new car.
(C) She wants the man to walk with her.
(D) Her car is close.

(D) Glance at the choices and summarize: she, far away, close.
Testing point: restatement. In the phrase "it's not far," "it" refers to "her car." "Not far" has the same meaning as "it's close."

40. Man: This movie is terrific!
Woman: I know.
What does the woman mean?
(A) She knows the movie was terrifying.
(B) She also liked the movie.
(C) She doesn't want to see the movie again.
(D) She knows the actor personally.

(B) Glance at the choices and summarize: she, like, knows, movie.
Testing point: inference. "I know" implies that she agrees with the man's opinion about the movie.

41. Woman: Is there any industry in this area?
Man: Only a small amount; nothing big.
What does the man mean?
(A) There is not much manufacturing around here.
(B) Nothing can be mentioned.
(C) A big park is not far away from here.
(D) Industrial pollution is not severe in this area.

(A) Glance at the choices and summarize: manufacturing, park, industrial, pollution.
Testing point 1: restatement. "Only a small amount of industry" means the same as "not much manufacturing."
Testing point 2: vocabulary. Another way of saying "in this area" is "around here."

42. Man: Can I eat this fruit like it is?
Woman: No, you have to peel it first.
What does the woman mean?
(A) You should not eat the skin.
(B) The fruit has not been washed yet.
(C) It's not good raw.
(D) The seeds are not good to eat.

(A) Glance at the choices and summarize: fruit, eat, not good.
Testing point 1: vocabulary. "Peel" means to take the skin off.
Testing point 2: inference. "You have to peel it" implies "you shouldn't eat the skin."

43. Woman: I'm still upset about Frank's remark.
Man: Yes. It was a thoughtless thing to say.
What does the man mean?
(A) It was a careless comment.
(B) It was a boring activity.
(C) It was a compliment.
(D) It was a correction.

(A) Glance at the choices and summarize: careless, boring, compliment, correction.
Testing point: vocabulary. The word "thoughtless" means "careless" or "unthinking"; "inconsiderate of other people." A remark is a brief comment.

44. Man: What time will you be back?
Woman: Oh, it shouldn't take me too long.
What does the woman mean?
(A) She'll be gone a long time.
(B) She'll be back shortly.
(C) She has too much to do.
(D) She is taking her time.

(B) Glance at the choices and summarize: long time, shortly, too much, time.
Testing point: restatement. The negative sentence, "it shouldn't take me too long," also means the positive, "it should take a short time." The word "shortly" means "in a short time" or "soon."

45. Woman: How are the pictures you took in New York? I can't wait to see them.
Man: They're not ready yet.
What does the man mean?
(A) He isn't ready to show his pictures yet.
(B) The pictures are still being processed.
(C) He isn't ready to take pictures yet.
(D) He wants the woman to take a picture of him.

(B) Glance at the choices and summarize: she, pictures, ready.
Testing point: inference. In the sentence, "they're not ready yet," "they" refers to "the pictures." The processing or developing is not finished yet.

46. Woman: Watching the news on TV is a good way to learn English.
Man: It's especially helpful when you check the same information in the newspaper.
What does the man mean?
(A) Reading is more useful than watching TV.
(B) Watching TV is better than reading a newspaper.
(C) The newspaper is a good source for learning English.
(D) A combination of reading and listening is most effective.

(D) Glance at the choices and summarize: newspaper, reading, watching TV.
Testing point 1: inference. "Watching news on TV" and "check the same information in the newspaper" is the same as "a combination of reading and listening."
Testing point 2: restatement. "It's especially helpful" is similar to "is most effective."

47. Man: I don't know what to do.
Woman: You have to make your own decision, and there is not much time left.
What does the woman imply?
(A) She will not make the decision for him.
(B) She'll help to make the decision only if he asks for it.
(C) He doesn't have to make the decision right now.
(D) He should consult with the woman about this decision.

(A) Glance at the choices and summarize: she, make decision.
Testing point: inference. "You have to make your own decision" implies "she won't make the decision for him."

48. Woman: Nobody expected that he would be able to come to the party.
Man: But he did.
What can we learn from the conversation?
(A) It was impossible for him to come to the party.
(B) He stayed home to study for his exam.
(C) Everybody was surprised by his attendance at the party.
(D) He had expected to come to the party for a long time.

(C) Glance at the choices and summarize: come, party, surprised.
Testing point: contradiction. "But he did" refers to "he did come to the party" even though "nobody expected that he would be able to come to the party." Therefore, everybody was surprised.

49. Man: I hope I get an "A" in this class.
Woman: I don't think I'll do very well; I have to spend most of my time on my senior project.
What does the woman mean?
(A) Her senior project is more important right now.
(B) She cares about her grade more than the man does.
(C) She couldn't even pass the exam for that class.
(D) She wants to be excellent in all her classes.

(A) Glance at the choices and summarize: comparative, exam, project.
Testing point: inference. "I have to spend most of my time on my senior project" implies that her senior project is more important.

50. Man: I think I've met you somewhere before.
Woman: Yes! At Professor Dean's seminar.
What does the woman mean?
(A) She agrees that they met before.
(B) She met Professor Dean at the man's office.
(C) She denies the fact that they met before.
(D) She wants to meet the man at Professor Dean's seminar.

(A) Glance at the choices and summarize: she, met professor.
Testing point: inference. "Yes" implies that she agrees when the man says "I've met you before."

51. Man: How was your afternoon with Aunt Jane?
Woman: Oh, I couldn't believe it! She was in a rage. She flew off the handle at every little thing.
What does the woman mean?
(A) Aunt Jane was angry.
(B) Aunt Jane was excited.
(C) Aunt Jane was disappointed.
(D) Aunt Jane was surprised.

(A) Glance at the choices and summarize: Aunt Jane, feelings.
Testing point: idiom. "In a rage" means "very angry." "To fly off the handle" also means "to show anger."

52. Woman: What do you think I should wear to the party tonight?
Man: Oh, I don't know. It's not too fancy.
What does the man mean?
(A) It's an informal party.
(B) She should wear something dressy.
(C) It's a cocktail party.
(D) She shouldn't wear pants.

(A) Glance at the choices and summarize: party, dress.
Testing point: vocabulary. "Not too fancy" means it's an informal party.

53. Woman: I can't decide whether to buy that expensive new car or the cheaper used car.
Man: I'd get the new one. It's better in the long run.
Why would the man buy the more expensive car?
(A) It runs better.
(B) It's likely to last longer.
(C) It's probably a bigger car.
(D) It's only a little more expensive.

(B) Glance at the choices and summarize: better, more expensive, bigger.
Testing point: idiom. "In the long run" means "in the future." The verb "to last" means "to go on" or "to continue."

54. Man: Shall we go out for Mexican food or Chinese food tonight?
Woman: I don't care. It's up to you.
What does the woman mean?
(A) She will decide later.
(B) She doesn't care for either.
(C) She wants the man to decide.
(D) She doesn't want to go out.

(C) Glance at the choices and summarize: she, decide.
Testing point: idiom. "It's up to you" means "you decide."

55. Man: How's your new job going?
Woman: Not so well. I feel like a fish out of water in that job.
What does the woman mean?
(A) She doesn't like the fishing industry.
(B) The fish is not fresh enough.
(C) She is very tired.
(D) She feels uncomfortable at work.

(D) Glance at the choices and summarize: she, feels, fish.
Testing point: idiom. "Feel like a fish out of water" implies "she feels uncomfortable."

Part C

56. Who is the most likely speaker of this talk?
(A) A dormitory attendant
(B) A financial officer
(C) A housing coordinator
(D) Dr. Paulson

(C) This is an inference question. SInce the speaker begins by saying she will discuss student housing, the best guess is "a housing coordinator." Answer (D) must be incorrect, because the speaker mentions Dr. Paulson. Answer (A), a dormitory attendant, probably would not be discussing all types of housing. There is no clue that leads to the speaker being a financial speaker.

57. Who is probably listening to this talk?
(A) New graduate students
(B) New undergraduate students
(C) Returning students
(D) High school students

(A) This is an inference question. The speaker begins by saying that she will talk about graduate student housing, so you can infer that the students are new graduate students. The speaker does not mention undergraduate housing. Returning students or high school students would probably not need this information.

58. How many students can live in one unit for single graduate students?
(A) One student in each unit
(B) Two students in each unit
(C) Two students in each bedroom
(D) Four students in each unit

(D) This is a restatement question. The speaker says that four students share a dining and a living room, kitchen, bathrooms, and bedrooms.

59. If you want to move into the family student housing, what should you do?
(A) Add your name to the waiting list.
(B) Sign up to move in right away.
(C) Go ask someone at the apartments.
(D) Go to the off-campus housing office.

(A) This is a restatement question. The speaker says that students should come in if they want to add their names to the list, since the family student housing complex is full.

60. What will the off-campus housing office do for you?
(A) Find a house for you.
(B) Give you a list of rentals.
(C) Sign you up for family student housing.
(D) Add your name to a waiting list.

(B) This is a restatement question. The speaker says that you can find a lot of rentals listed in the housing office. She does not say that the people in the office will find a house for you.

61. What will the listeners be doing next?
(A) Going to visit housing areas
(B) Going to see Dr. Paulson
(C) Listening to a talk on financial aid
(D) Filling out application forms

(C) This is an inference question. The speaker says that she will turn the meeting over to Dr. Paulson, who will explain some things about financial aid programs. You infer that students will be listening to this talk.

62. Why is the man excited?
(A) Because he ran into the woman.
(B) Because he will get some money.
(C) Because his parents will pay for his room and board.
(D) Because he just got an application for a scholarship.

(B) This is an inference question. The man says, "I just got my scholarship approved!" His voice indicates that he is excited. Since his scholarship is now approved, you can infer that he will be receiving money.

63. What does the woman say about her parents?
(A) They can't pay for her room.
(B) They will give her more money.
(C) They will come visit her.
(D) They live far away.

(A) This is a restatement question. The woman says, "My folks can't pay my room and board this year."

64. What does the woman do besides her studies?
(A) She is a teaching assistant.
(B) She is on a work-study program.
(C) She works in an ice cream shop.
(D) She works in the financial aid office.

(C) This is an inference question. The woman says, "Working part time in the ice cream store doesn't pay enough to live on." From this statement we can infer that she works in an ice cream store.

65. What does the man suggest that the woman do?
(A) Apply for a job.
(B) Get an application for aid.
(C) Ask her parents for money.
(D) Study harder.

(B) This is an inference question. The man says, "I'd go over there right now. The deadline for new applications is next Friday." When he says, "I'd go over . . ." he is suggesting that she go to the financial aid office."

66. Why couldn't the woman be a teaching assistant?
(A) Because she didn't know about the job.
(B) Because she hadn't applied yet.
(C) Because all the jobs were filled.
(D) Because her class schedule was too busy.

(D) This is a restatement question. The woman says, "I couldn't do it this year because of my schedule."

67. Where will the woman go next?
(A) To the library
(B) To the bookstore
(C) To the ice cream shop
(D) To the financial aid office

(D) This is a restatement question. The woman says, "I'll drop by the financial aid office now." The phrase "drop by" means "go somewhere for a short time."

68. What is the main reason for making this announcement?
(A) To tell people of an invitation
(B) To invite people to Harry's house
(C) To warn people of danger
(D) To describe an event

(C) This is an inference question. The announcer says that the people should get prepared for the hurricane. We can infer that it is dangerous from the man's advice.

69. What is coming?
(A) An electrical blackout
(B) A storm
(C) A camping ban
(D) A shark attack

(B) This is a restatement question. The man says, "Hurricane Harry has changed its course and is now heading straight for the mainland." A hurricane is a big wind storm.

70. When is it coming?
(A) Tomorrow
(B) Next week
(C) This afternoon
(D) Immediately

(C) This is a restatement question. The man says, "The hurricane should arrive at about 3 P.M. this afternoon."

71. According to the announcement, which of the following is something you should NOT do?
(A) Camp on the beach.
(B) Put wood over your windows.
(C) Leave town.
(D) Stay indoors.

(A) This is a negative restatement question. The man states "No camping on the beach is allowed."

72. If your electricity goes out, what should you do?
(A) Tell your neighbors.
(B) Be patient.
(C) Take the loose wires off the street.
(D) Fix it as soon as possible.

(B) This is a restatement question. The man says, "If your electricity goes out, be patient."

73. What does the speaker suggest?
(A) Listen to the radio.
(B) Leave town.
(C) Watch television.
(D) Contact your neighbor.

(A) This is a restatement question. The man says, "Keep your radio tuned to this station."

74. Who is making this announcement?
(A) An electrician
(B) The city mayor
(C) The harbor master
(D) A radio announcer

(D) This is an inference question. The man says, "Keep your radio tuned to this station," so you can infer that he is a radio announcer.

75. Who is the most likely speaker?
(A) A chemistry lab assistant
(B) A botany lecturer
(C) A landscape gardener
(D) An historian

(B) This is an inference question. The speaker is discussing ferns and mosses, which are both botany subjects, since botany is the study of plants.

76. What is one difference between ferns and mosses?
(A) Their vascular system
(B) Their growth on rocks
(C) Their need for water
(D) Their being a land plant

(A) This is an inference question. The speaker says "... we discussed the difference between ferns and mosses. The ferns developed a vascular system . . ." From this statement we can infer that the mosses did not develop a vascular system.

77. When was the "Age of Ferns"?
(A) 300 years ago
(B) 9,000 B.C.
(C) The Carboniferous Period
(D) The Upper Devonian Period

(C) This is a restatement question. The speaker says, "... there are so many remains of fernlike plants in the Carboniferous Period that this period has been termed the Age of Ferns."

78. How does the speaker say that seed ferns are similar to true ferns?
(A) In their structure
(B) In their size
(C) In their color
(D) In their reproductive system

(D) This is a restatement question. The speaker says, "But even though these seed ferns were primitive in structure, they were quite similar to the ferns of today in their methods of reproduction."

79. Where would a fern be least likely to live?
(A) In a desert
(B) In a moist rock
(C) In a forest
(D) By water

(A) This is an inference question. The speaker says that ferns flourish in woods, meadows, and near rivers. Since all these places are wet, cool, or grassy, you can eliminate them and choose answer (A).

80. How tall can ferns grow?
(A) Up to 12 feet high
(B) Up to 20 feet high
(C) Up to 60 feet high
(D) Up to 100 feet high

(C) This is a restatement question. The speaker says, "... there can be trees of up to 60 feet in height."

SECTION 2: STRUCTURE AND WRITTEN EXPRESSION

1. In some states, a low-income tenant over sixty-two years old ________ in a rent-stabilized dwelling.
(A) living
(B) to live
(C) can live
(D) live

(C) Testing point: verb. Answer (A) is incorrect, because there is no form of "to be" with "living." Answer (B) is incorrect, because the sentence needs a main verb, not an infinitive. Answer (D) is incorrect, because the noun "tenant" is singular. The sentence should read "... a low-income tenant . . . can live in a . . ."

2. Tasty Mix Treat, ________ with milk, tastes so good that children will be clamoring for more.
(A) blended
(B) was blended
(C) to blend
(D) blending

(A) Testing point: adjective phrase. The past participle is used to form an adjective phrase, which describes the "treat."

3. A dog ________ on his owner's lap may refuse to eat from a bowl on the floor.
(A) fed
(B) is fed
(C) was fed
(D) to feed

(A) Testing point: adjective phrase. The past participle "fed" is used to form the adjective phrase.

4. To resist corrosion, ________ for today's car to prevent havoc caused by road salts, gravel, and other materials.
(A) new coatings have been developed
(B) having new coatings been developed
(C) new coating developings
(D) development of new coatings

(A) Testing point: subject + verb. The sentence needs a noun and a passive voice verb. The sentence should read "To resist . . ., new coatings have been developed for . . ." Use the comma as a clue to read the sentence without the first three words to see if it makes sense.

5. ________ to Easter Egg Rock is tiring, yet stimulating.
(A) All-day trips
(B) An all-day boat trip
(C) When boating all day
(D) Now that all-day boat trips

(B) Testing point: noun. The sentence needs a noun phrase. Since the main verb is singular, the noun also must be singular.

6. The impact of two vehicles can cause a lot of ________ to both.
(A) damage
(B) damages
(C) damaging
(D) damagings

(A) Testing point: noun. The word "damage" is an abstract noun, also called an uncountable or a mass noun.

7. After the oil embargo, no longer ________ gas-guzzling cars as the cost of gasoline increased.
(A) people could afford
(B) that people could afford
(C) could people afford
(D) could afford

(C) Testing point: inverted verb. The sentence should read ". . . no longer could people afford . . ." Use the words "no longer" as a clue.

8. Yuen T. Lee received the 1986 Nobel Peace Prize in chemistry ________.
(A) his crossed molecular beam reaction was successful
(B) for his contribution to crossed molecular beam reactions
(C) the excellence of his crossed molecular beam reactions
(D) his molecular beam theory was historical

(B) Testing point: prepositional phrase. The sentence should be "Yuen T. Lee received the . . . prize for his contribution to . . ."

9. The greatest ________ between fresh water and sea water lies in its concentration of salt.
(A) difference that
(B) is a difference
(C) difference is
(D) difference

(D) Testing point: noun. "The greatest difference between . . ." "Difference between" precedes two nouns.

10. Not until the Enlightenment, 200 years ago, ________ the state's power to kill.
(A) the societies seriously questioned
(B) questioned seriously by societies
(C) questioned by societies seriously
(D) did societies seriously question

(D) Testing point: inverted verb. "Not until . . . did societies seriously question . . ." Use the words "not until" as a clue.

11. The electronic violin ought to be better than existing modern instruments, ________ the intermodulation distortion is virtually eliminated.
(A) or
(B) due
(C) also
(D) since

(D) Testing point: cause/result. The word "since" introduces the reason that the electronic violin is better.

12. ________ from France in 1803 was one of the greatest events in the history of the growth of the United States.
(A) Purchasing of Louisiana
(B) Louisiana Purchase
(C) Purchased Louisiana
(D) The purchase of the Louisiana Territory

(D) Testing point: noun phrase. The word "purchase" is the subject of the sentence. "The purchase of . . . was . . ."

13. Ancient mountains have been worn away by wind, rain, and ________.
(A) with agents of erosion
(B) other agents of erosion
(C) for agents of erosion
(D) to other agents of erosion

(B) Testing point: parallel construction. "By wind, rain, and . . . agents . . ." Answer (B) is correct, since it is the only phrase that correctly follows the preposition "by."

14. Ultrasound can be used to assess gestational age, to evaluate bleeding during pregnancy, and ________.
(A) determining the location of the fetus
(B) to determine the location of the fetus
(C) which determined the location of the fetus
(D) it is a determination of the fetus location

(B) Testing point: parallel construction. ". . . to assess . . ., to evaluate . . ., and to determine . . ."

15. For years, researchers have tried to lower the antipsychotic drug dosage to a level ________ movement disorders, yet controls psychosis.
(A) that they minimize
(B) the minimum is
(C) they minimizes
(D) that minimizes

(D) Testing point: noun clause. The noun clause beginning with "that" describes "level": "to a level that minimizes . . ."

16. The details of the geological history of the Rocky Mountains have been lost ________ hundreds of millions of years.
(A) on the passage for
(B) during the passage of
(C) in the passage
(D) at the passage of

(B) Testing point: prepositional phrase. "During the passage of . . . years." Answer (C) would be correct if it had the word "of" after "passage." Both "in" and "during" indicate time.

17. In China, acupuncture is used as an anesthesia, permitting patients to have major surgery ________.
(A) while fully conscious
(B) what is fully conscious
(C) that fully consciousness
(D) which is fully conscious

(A) Testing point: adverb phrase. The words "while fully conscious" describe the patients' condition at the time of surgery. ". . . to have major surgery while fully conscious."

18. ________ as president, a candidate must win a majority of votes.
(A) Having elected
(B) Electing
(C) To be elected
(D) Elected

(C) Testing point: infinitive/gerund/participle. The infinitive phrase is used to show purpose. "To be elected as . . ., . . . must win . . ."

19. ________ numbers were created is not known.
(A) When
(B) After
(C) Since
(D) Before

(A) Testing point: "wh" word as subject. The main verb of the sentence is the word "is." The complete subject is "when numbers were created."

20. Hair color is ________ characteristics to use in identifying people.
(A) one of most obvious
(B) obviously one of the most
(C) one of the most obvious
(D) one of the most obvious that is

(C) Testing point: superlative. ". . . is one of the most . . . characteristics to . . ."

21. It takes ________ car to get there.
(A) a shorter time by subway than by
(B) shorter time than by subway and by
(C) by subway shorter time than
(D) shorter time by subway than

(A) Testing point: comparative. "It takes a shorter . . . by . . . than by . . ."

22. ________ first place in the women's ten meter platform diving event, Xu Yianmei became China's first gold medal winner in the 1988 Summer Olympic Games in Seoul.
(A) To win
(B) Being won
(C) Won
(D) Having won

(D) Testing point: infinitive/gerund/participle. The word "having" begins an adjective phrase that indicates a cause. Answer (A) is incorrect, because an infinitive indicates a purpose (future) rather than a cause (past). "Having won . . ., Xu Yianmei became . . ."

23. The script has to ________ for a speech even though it's well-written.
(A) adapt to
(B) be adapted
(C) adapted
(D) adapt

(B) Testing point: passive voice. "Be adapted" is a passive verb. The active sentence would be "somebody must adapt (change) the speech." The words "has to" mean the same as the modal "must."

24. What a strong defense is important to
A
any country, it cannot be more important than
B C
the livelihood of its citizens.
D

(A) Testing point: adjective/adverb clause. This sentence begins with an adverb clause, so it cannot begin with the word "what." The correct sentence is "Although a strong defense is important . . ."

25. "Order is Heaven's first law," made by the
A B
poet Alexander Pope, is painted on the ceiling
C D
of the Library of Congress in Washington, D. C.

(B) Testing point: wrong word. The correct word in this sentence is "written." The sentence should be ". . ., written by the poet Alexander Pope, . . ."

26. As a result of the Women's Rights Movement,
A
women around the world now holds positions
B
that were once restricted to men.
C D

(B) Testing point: verb agreement. Since the subject is plural, "women," the verb must be "hold."

27. Whether or not a divorced person is entitled
A B
to share of his or her spouse's pension has to
C
be decided by the court.
D

(C) Testing point: this testing point could be either omission of word, additional word, or preposition. There are two ways to correct the sentence: 1) add the word "a": ". . . entitled to a share of . . . spouse's . . ." and 2) omit the preposition "of": "entitled to share . . . spouse's . . ." In sentence 1, the word "share" is a noun. In sentence 2, the word "share" is a verb. Both are correct.

28. Some people believe that printing does as
A
much harm like good, since it brings out
B C
falsehood as much as truth.
D

(B) Testing point: comparative. The correct sentence is ". . . printing does as much harm as good . . ." The clue is "as . . . as."

29. Comets can burst into fragments that fly upon
A B C
in fiery orbits of their own.
D

(C) Testing point: preposition. The word "upon" should be changed to "out" or "away." The sentence should be ". . . fragments that fly out . . ."

30. If the information in a report does not make
A
sense, it may be necessary to check the
B C
statistical.
D

(D) Testing point: word form. The word "statistics" is a noun form; "statistical" is an adjective. This sentence needs a noun.

31. Toledo, locating in the center of Spain, is
A B
encircled by the Tagus River.
C D

(A) Testing point: word form. The correct word is "located." It begins the phrase that describes the city, Toledo.

32. In some cultures, openness and directness
A
seem rude, childish, and destructive naive.
B C D

(D) Testing point: word form. The correct word is the adverb form "destructively." It modifies "naive."

33. Surgical apparatus has to be capable of great
A B C
precise.
D

(D) Testing point: word form. The sentence should end with a noun. The correct form is "precision."

34. Each chapter contains (A) a few appendix, (B) which (C) give additional details as (D) supplements to the text.

(B) Testing point: singular/plural noun. The plural form of this word is "appendices" or "appendixes."

35. The dove nurtured her young (A) until them (B) were old enough (C) to hunt for themselves. (D)

(B) Testing point: pronoun. The correct pronoun in this sentence is "they." It is the subject of the verb "were."

36. When a person from a contact culture moves in closer, (A) a person from a noncontact (B) culture may feel the needy (C) to back off. (D)

(C) Testing point: word form. The noun "need" is correct in this sentence. The word "needy" refers to people who need things, i.e., poor people. The noun "need" means "the necessity."

37. As they grow older, children (A) taught (B) not to (C) rely on their (D) parents.

(B) Testing point: verb tense; passive voice. The correct sentence is ". . . children *are* taught . . ."

38. Too many (A) polished (B) rice in one's diet could cause (C) beriberi, a (D) painful nerve disease.

(A) Testing point: many/much. Since "rice" is an uncountable noun, you must use "much."

39. Drivers have the responsibility not endangering (A) the lives (B) of people and of (C) animals on (D) the road.

(A) Testing point: infinitive/gerund. The infinitive form must follow "not" in this sentence. The correct sentence is "Drivers have the responsibility not to endanger the lives of . . ."

40. The cabin is certainly (A) not luxuriously, (B) but it (C) is very practical (D) and comfortable.

(B) Testing point: word form. The correct form in this sentence is "luxurious," an adjective that describes the cabin.

41. Unfortunately, jogging nor (A) dieting, (B) carried (C) to extremes, (D) can be harmful.

(A) Testing point: conjunction. The correct conjunction in this sentence is "or" or "and." You cannot use "nor" unless the sentence is negative or you use the word "neither."

42. The letter that (A) was sent (B) by special delivery (C) must be importance. (D)

(D) Testing point: word form. The correct word is an adjective form: "important." The word "important" describes the letter.

43. What (A) happens during a person's formulate (B) years may affect (C) the rest of that (D) person's life.

(B) Testing point: word form. This sentence needs an adjective to describe "years." The adjective form is "formulative." The word "formulate" is a verb.

44. The gerund (A) in English is normally formed (B) by adding "ing" to (C) the basically (D) form of the verb.

(D) Testing point: word form. This sentence needs an adjective to describe the noun "form." The correct adjective form is "basic."

45. The camera must be focused (A) good, (B) otherwise (C) the picture will be blurred (D).

(B) Testing point: wrong word. The correct word is the adverb "well" to describe how the camera is focused. The word "good" is an adjective.

46. People tend to (A) become irritate (B) and short-tempered (C) whenever they get overtired (D).

(B) Testing point: word form. The correct word is an adjective form, "irritated." The word "irritate" is a verb. The correct sentence is "People tend to become irritated . . ."

47. A mule is a (A) animal that (B) is neither a horse nor a donkey, (C) but (D) a combination of the two.

(A) Testing point: article. Before a noun that begins with a vowel you must use the article "an" instead of "a."

48. People living (A) in cities are (B) often sophisticated (C) than people in rural areas (D).

(C) Testing point: omission of word. This is a comparative sentence. The word "more" is left out. One clue that this is a comparison is the word "than." The correct sentence is "People living in cities are often more sophisticated than people in . . ."

49. Disneyworld was built (A) on 27,400 acres of (B) in part (C) swamp land in central (D) Florida.

(C) Testing point: additional word. The word "in" is not necessary. The correct sentence is ". . . was built on . . . acres of part swamp land . . ." The meaning is that only part of the land was a swamp area.

50. Soaring (A) medicinally (B) costs have a direct (C) influence on the cost of other merchandise (D).

(B) Testing point: word form. The sentence needs an adjective to describe the subject "costs." In this sentence the noun form is used as an adjective to tell what type of costs. The correct sentence is "Soaring medicine costs have . . ." The word "soaring" means "flying" or "rising."

51. In addition to save (A) on gas, (B) the modern car is designed (C) to save on (D) maintenance and repair expenses.

(A) Testing point: infinitive/gerund. After the phrase, "in addition to," you must use the gerund "saving." The sentence should be "In addition to saving on gas, the modern car . . ."

52. Edward Hall, a professor of anthropology, first commented on (A) people's strong feelings (B) about (C) personnel (D) space.

(D) Testing point: wrong word. The word "personnel" means "people employed in a business." The correct word here should be "personal," meaning "individual" or "private."

53. Education trains a student to see things as it is,
A B C
to disentangle a skein of thought.
D

(C) Testing point: pronoun + verb. The correct sentence is "Education trains a student to see things as they are . . ." The pronoun must be "they," because it refers to the plural word "things."

54. Before the middle of the eighteenth century,
A
there were none public libraries in the United
B C D
States.

(C) Testing point: no/not/none. The word "no" goes before the noun "libraries." The correct sentence is "Before . . ., there were no public libraries . . ."

55. The nucleus of an ordinary comet is a mile
A B
but two in diameter.
C D

(C) Testing point: conjunction. The sentence should be "the nucleus . . . is a mile *or* two in diameter." The word "or" connects the idea of one mile or two miles.

56. George Gershwin believed that music
A
should express the thoughts, and feelings of
B
their own time in history.
C D

(C) Testing point: pronoun. This pronoun should be singular, not plural. In this sentence the best word to use is "one" instead of "their." The sentence should be "George Gershwin believed that music should express the thoughts . . . of one's own time . . ." The word "one" refers to anyone.

57. Some senior citizens have to cope with arthri-
A
tis and other physical difficulties of aged, in
B C D
addition to psychological and social problems.

(D) Testing point: there are three possible testing points in this sentence: word form, gerund, or omission of word. The word here must be a noun form. There are two ways to correct this sentence: 1) add the word "the" before the noun "aged," ". . . difficulties of the aged . . ." and 2) change "aged" to the gerund form "aging." The sentence would then be ". . . difficulties of aging . . ."

58. It has been estimated that in a few years,
A
twelve percents of Canadians will be
B C
senior citizens.
D

(B) Testing point: singular/plural noun. The word "percent" does not have an "s," because the number twelve refers to twelve parts of one whole.

59. Many museum exhibits encourage you to in-
A
vestigate further through microscopes, magni-
B C
fiers, and even telescoping.
D

(D) Testing point: parallel construction. The words "microscopes" and "magnifiers" are plural nouns, so the word "telescopes" is the correct form. Use the commas and the word "and" as a clue to parallel construction: __________, __________, and __________.

60. The workers repairing the road surface are
A B
wearing specially jackets for easy identifica-
C D
tion.

(C) Testing point: word form. The word "jackets" needs an adjective to describe the type of jacket, not an adverb. The correct word would be "special."

SECTION 3: VOCABULARY AND READING COMPREHENSION

1. Scientific probes have searched for life beyond the earth.
(A) over
(B) outside of
(C) surpassing
(D) exceeding

(B) The words "beyond" and "outside of" in this sentence both refer to someplace away from the earth. The word "over" means "above" or "at a higher level." Since the earth is round and space is infinite, this word is not correct. "Surpassing" means "better than," and "exceeding" means "more than."

2. A beam of light contains all the colors of the rainbow.
(A) speck
(B) signal
(C) stream
(D) crosspiece

(C) The words "beam" and "stream" both refer to something that is long and narrow.

3. Because of Nicolaus Copernicus' writings in the 15th century, people began to take a fresh interest in astronomy.
(A) bright
(B) cool
(C) bold
(D) new

(D) "Fresh" refers to something that is newly made, new, or different.

4. The ancestors of Australian aborigines settled in Australia more than 30,000 years ago.
(A) became calm
(B) made an agreement
(C) became restless
(D) became established

(D) "To settle" and "to become established" both mean "to plan on staying permanently."

5. Many people consider automobiles to be essential to American life.
(A) critical
(B) accessible
(C) necessary
(D) advantageous

(C) "Essential" and "necessary" both mean "very important," "fundamental," or "basic."

6. Icarus and Daedalus are familiar from one of the earliest legends of flying.
(A) stories
(B) histories
(C) epics
(D) heroes

(A) A legend is a story that has been handed down from generation to generation, and that is thought by some to be true, though the truth can never be proven.

7. Saint Thomas Aquinas had a powerful influence on the thinking of his time.
(A) effect
(B) critique
(C) affection
(D) domination

(A) "To have influence" over someone or something means that you have a strong effect on that person or thing.

8. Food that is considered a delicacy in one culture may be abhorred in another.
(A) basic
(B) special
(C) satisfactory
(D) plentiful

(B) A delicacy is something that is unusually good; often it refers to something to eat that is delicious and hard to get.

9. The ancient Romans built huge aqueducts that ran through tunnels and over bridges.
(A) impressive
(B) solid
(C) large
(D) high

(C) The word "huge" is commonly used as a synonym for "very large."

10. More than 3,000 years ago, ancient people stumbled upon the fact that some molds could cure disease.
(A) disputed
(B) were disillusioned by
(C) learned by experimentation
(D) discovered by accident

(D) "To stumble upon" something means that you find it without looking.

11. On the tip of a fly's proboscis is a spongy pad.
(A) an absorbent
(B) an elastic
(C) a firm
(D) a damp

(A) A sponge is a sea animal made of material that absorbs water easily. "Sponge" also refers to any material that also has this ability to absorb water easily. In this sentence, the pad is something that can absorb water easily. Answer (D), "damp," which means "a little wet," is a result of what happens when water is near a sponge.

12. Vision is one of the five basic senses of the animal kingdom.
(A) accurate
(B) exceptional
(C) fundamental
(D) beneficial

(C) "Fundamental" and "basic" both mean "supporting" or "essential."

13. Insects are attracted to flowers that reflect ultraviolet light.
(A) affected by
(B) inspiring to
(C) perplexed by
(D) drawn towards

(D) "Attracted" and "drawn toward" both mean that you want to approach something.

14. An earthworm is built up of a number of segments.
(A) plumes
(B) sections
(C) pods
(D) trunks

(B) "Segment" and "section" both refer to something that comes in several pieces.

15. A bat uses a sonar device to orient itself to its surrounding world.
(A) determine its position in
(B) become impressed with
(C) form an opinion of
(D) guard against

(A) "To orient" means "to become adjusted to one's situation."

16. Baby animals imitate their parents.
(A) desire
(B) copy
(C) disrupt
(D) arouse

(B) "To imitate" and "to copy" both mean that someone is trying to do the same thing as someone else.

17. Some medicines should be dissolved before they are taken.
(A) boiled
(B) sweetened
(C) prepared with food
(D) mixed with a liquid

(D) "To dissolve" means to put something into a liquid until it disintegrates or becomes a liquid.

18. A simple society is based on an exchange of goods and services.
(A) a cycle
(B) a harmony
(C) a trade
(D) a collection

(C) "To exchange" means to give one thing in order to get another thing.

19. Most advanced countries have compulsory education.
(A) considerable
(B) required
(C) elaborate
(D) high-powered

(B) "Compulsory education" means that the law requires children to go to school. They cannot legally choose to stay home or to work.

20. Graphic displays of human organs are upsetting to some people.
(A) Clearly drawn
(B) Illicitly displayed
(C) Grave
(D) Grueling

(A) The word "graphic" refers to something being drawn or described in careful detail.

21. In 1962 James Meredith made his first attempt at enrolling at the University of Mississippi.
(A) appeal
(B) try
(C) headway
(D) overthrow

(B) "To attempt" is to try to do something.

22. A river begins with a trickle of water flowing over some pebbles.
(A) dripping irregularly
(B) splashing haphazardly
(C) running roughly
(D) moving smoothly

(D) "To flow" means to move steadily and smoothly.

23. A bad winter storm can paralyze an urban area.
(A) immobilize
(B) evacuate
(C) isolate
(D) stabilize

(A) "To paralyze" and "to immobilize" both mean "to stop movement of something."

24. Sunglasses come in many different colors, shapes, and strengths.
(A) circulate
(B) are discovered
(C) take part
(D) can be found

(D) "To come" in this sentence has the meaning of "to appear," which is also the meaning of "can be found."

25. In 1605 the Mughal Empire ruled most of India.
(A) separated
(B) employed
(C) controlled
(D) influenced

(C) A ruler controls a country; "to be ruled" is therefore "to be controlled."

26. There is evidence that Marco Polo traveled extensively in India and South East Asia as well as China.
(A) widely
(B) incredibly
(C) imperceptibly
(D) hygienically

(A) "Extensively" and "widely" both refer to covering a large area or a long distance.

27. Many people feel that it is common to go through a crisis period in midlife.
(A) time of domination
(B) time of change
(C) laborious time
(D) celebration

(B) The word "crisis" refers to a change; a critical time when the future is unpredictable.

28. Jack London was a bold, rugged adventurer.
(A) fearless
(B) ambitious
(C) astute
(D) bizarre

(A) "Bold" and "fearless" both mean that a person is not afraid.

29. Smoking cigarettes is often seen as an addiction.
(A) thought of
(B) taken care of
(C) experienced
(D) imagined

(A) "To see" can mean "to get knowledge of," "to view," or "to get an impression of." All of these definitions also apply to "think of."

30. The gruesome details of Edgar Allan Poe's stories often stick in people's minds.
(A) gratifying
(B) exhilarating
(C) fiery
(D) horrible

(D) "Gruesome" and "horrible" both refer to something that causes fear.

31. Greek myths are prime sources of mythology for the western world.
(A) effective
(B) chief
(C) curious
(D) elaborated

(B) "Prime" means "first in authority" or "most important." "Chief" means the same thing in this sentence.

32. Helen Keller explored the faces of people and animals by touch.
(A) inscribed
(B) isolated
(C) remembered
(D) examined

(D) "To explore" is "to examine" or "to look at closely."

33. Rudyard Kipling was fascinated by the customs and people of India.
(A) frightened
(B) influenced
(C) attracted
(D) overwhelmed

(C) "Fascinated" and "attracted" both mean to get the attention of someone by the use of delightful qualities.

34. Many famous people are unremarkable as children.
(A) alert
(B) acclaimed
(C) ordinary
(D) delicate

(C) "Unremarkable" means that there is nothing special or unusual to say about something.

35. Henry Wadsworth Longfellow is undoubtedly one of America's best-loved poets.
(A) practically
(B) certainly
(C) persistently
(D) relatively

(B) "Undoubtedly" means the same as "without a doubt" or "certainly."

36. A diminutive dancer can charm an audience.
(A) graceful
(B) tiny
(C) playful
(D) clever

(B) "Diminutive" and "tiny" both mean "very small."

37. Earthquakes occur at the boundaries of the earth's crust.
(A) happen
(B) originate
(C) appear
(D) diffuse

(A) "To occur" and "to happen" both mean "to exist" or "to take place."

38. The ozone layer blocks ultraviolet radiation.
(A) contains
(B) disrupts
(C) penetrates
(D) obstructs

(D) "To block" and "to obstruct" both mean "to stop."

39. Many animals thrive in the Serengeti Plain.
(A) burrow
(B) persist
(C) flourish
(D) gather

(C) "To thrive" and "to flourish" both mean "to grow vigorously" or "to succeed."

40. Black sand is formed from volcanic glass ground by the action of the waves.
(A) soiled
(B) crushed
(C) gathered
(D) flooded

(B) The word "ground" in this sentence is the past tense and past participle of the verb "to grind," which means "to crush into tiny bits or particles."

41. Getting caught in a dust storm can be frightening.
(A) typhoon with strong winds
(B) heavy rain with thunder and lightning
(C) wind carrying clouds of fine dry earth
(D) tornado with spiraling winds

(C) "Dust" is very fine dry powdery earth. Dust storms are frequent in desert areas.

42. The Himalayas remain the world's highest mountains, because they are still rising.
(A) accentuate
(B) belong to
(C) stay behind
(D) continue to be

(D) The word "remain" usually means "stay." In this sentence, however, it means "to continue to exist" or "to endure."

43. A good leader can anticipate people's responses.
(A) expect
(B) understand
(C) encourage
(D) sympathize with

(A) "To anticipate" and "to expect" both mean "to think about something before it happens."

44. When viewed from a new angle, the surprising often becomes understandable.
(A) recorded
(B) considered
(C) verified
(D) reassured

(B) "To view" means "to look at" or "to think about." "To consider" has the same meaning.

45. Some people won't let a shaggy dog into their home.
(A) dirty
(B) noisy
(C) hairy
(D) smelly

(C) "Shaggy" means "covered with long, coarse hair."

46. Which of the following is the most common chronic health condition?
(A) Back disorder
(B) Heart condition
(C) Visual impairment
(D) Hypertension

(B) This is a restatement question. The passage says that heart conditions, arthritis, and rheumatism afflict approximately half of all disabled people. The other answer choices are mentioned, but not as the most common condition.

47. Impairment of the spine is most common among which group?
- **(A)** People of ages 17–44
- **(B)** 12 percent of the population
- **(C)** 50 percent of disabled people
- **(D)** 7 percent of the population

(A) This is a restatement question. The passage says, "Among those who are seventeen to forty-four years of age, the major disabler is impairment of the back or spine."

48. Which area of the body contains the spine?
- **(A)** The lower extremities
- **(B)** The internal organs
- **(C)** The head
- **(D)** The back

(D) This is an inference question. If you don 't know the meaning of "spine," you can infer that it is in "the back," since the passage says "back or spine." When two words are separated with "or," it often means that the second word is a definition of the first word.

49. The words "afflicted with" in lines 3–4 can best be substituted with which of the following?
- **(A)** infected by
- **(B)** suffering with
- **(C)** destroyed by
- **(D)** reacting against

(B) This is a vocabulary question. "To afflict" means to cause pain or suffering or distress.

50. Which of the following conclusions is best supported by the passage?
- **(A)** Aged people have more tension than younger people.
- **(B)** Poor people are not as likely to take care of their health.
- **(C)** Back problems are a major disabler for most people.
- **(D)** Fifty percent of the population get heart disease.

(B) This is a support question. Answer (B) is the best answer since the passage states, "The poor . . . seek and receive less medical treatment . . . " The words "seek . . . less" mean that they are less likely to look for and get treatment. Answer (A) is incorrect, because there is no mention of aged people having more tension. The passage says that aged people are most vulnerable to disability. Answer (C) is incorrect, because back problems are mentioned as being problems for less than 50 percent of all disabled people. Answer (D) is incorrect because the passage states that 50 percent of disabled people get heart disease, not 50 percent of all people.

51. What does the author mean by the words "tends to be cyclical" in line 17?
- **(A)** One thing often causes the other.
- **(B)** There is a relationship between getting treated and being disabled.
- **(C)** The sicker one is, the more it costs for medical care.
- **(D)** There is a cycle of rising costs for poorer people.

(A) The word "cyclical" means that something occurs in cycles or that events tend to recur in the same sequence. In this sentence, the meaning is that disability often causes poverty and that the poverty then often increases disability, since the poor people aren't able to get good medical care.

52. Which of the following is the best title for this passage?
- **(A)** Sea Otters: A Conservationist's Concern
- **(B)** Oil Slicks
- **(C)** Sea Otters and Their Fur
- **(D)** The Life of the Sea Otter

(A) The best clue to the answer to this question is that both the first and the last sentences of the passage mention conservationists. Answer (B) is too general; oil slicks are not discussed in detail. Answer (C) is too narrow. The fur of the sea otter is only mentioned as an example of the problem for sea otters. Answer (D) is too general. The life cycle of the sea otter is not discussed.

53. A sea otter is
- **(A)** a furry animal
- **(B)** a teddy bear
- **(C)** a shellfish
- **(D)** a sea bird

(A) This is an inference question. A sea otter is described as having "long, thick fur." Answer (B) is incorrect, because the name "floating teddy bear" is put in quotation marks. This means that it is a name, but not a definition. Sea otters eat shellfish, so the answer cannot be (C). A bird answer (D) has feathers, not fur.

54. What happened to sea otters in the 19th century?
- **(A)** The numbers of sea otters increased.
- **(B)** The shellfish industry caused the extinction of sea otters.
- **(C)** Conservationists protected the sea otters.
- **(D)** Sea otters were killed for their fur.

(D) This is an inference question. The passage states that sea otters were "brought to the brink of extinction by . . . fur traders." The words "to the brink of extinction" mean that almost all of them were killed. Since fur traders were doing the killing you can infer that they were killing the otters in order to sell their fur.

55. The word "spotted" in line 5 could best be substituted by which of the following?
(A) Shot
(B) Recorded
(C) Saw
(D) Caught

(C) This is a vocabulary question. One meaning of the verb "to spot" is "to see."

56. According to the passage, what protects sea otters from the cold?
(A) Extra fat
(B) Insulation
(C) Matted coats
(D) Fluffy fur

(D) This is a restatement question. The passage states, "What keeps them warm is their long, thick fur."

57. Which of these would be a problem for sea otters?
(A) Warm weather
(B) Tangled hair
(C) Bubbly water
(D) Shellfish

(B) This is an inference question. The passage states that their fur must be kept fluffy and full of air bubbles. If hair is tangled, it means that it is twisted together in chunks. Tangled hair could not be fluffy or full of air bubbles.

58. What major problem are the conservationists concerned about?
(A) Freezing weather
(B) An accident by the oil industry
(C) Oily skin
(D) Air bubbles coming in contact with the sea otter's skin

(B) This is a restatement question. The passage states, "Another danger for the sea otter comes from the oil industry." Also the final sentence of the passage repeats the concern: "Conservationists are now additionally concerned because of what might happen if a large number of sea otters and an oil slick meet."

59. John Muir walked to Florida because
(A) Florida was wild.
(B) Florida was far away.
(C) he was poor.
(D) he was independent.

(D) This is an inference question. The passage states that John Muir "acted with his typical independence by walking to Florida." We can infer then that Muir was independent.

60. From the passage we can infer that John Muir was
(A) lonely
(B) rich
(C) friendly
(D) dedicated

(D) This is an inference question. Muir's dedication is shown by the statement, "His life fell into a single-developing pattern of devotion to all things natural."

61. John Muir devoted his life to
(A) natural things
(B) wild animals
(C) climbing trees
(D) the divine

(A) This is a restatement question. The answer is in the same sentence as the above question. "His life fell into a single-developing pattern of devotion to all things natural."

62. According to the passage, which of the following would best describe Muir?
(A) He didn't separate God and nature.
(B) He became a tramp, because he didn't like people.
(C) He loved painting landscapes to show the beauty of nature.
(D) He enjoyed seeing how far he could walk in the wild.

(A) This is a restatement question. The passages states, ". . . eventually, in his own mind, the line between the divine and nature became blurred." The meaning of this is that he did not make a distinction between the divine (God) and nature.

63. According to this passage, John Muir lived
(A) in Florida
(B) alone
(C) with people concerned about the environment
(D) in a time when people didn't care about conservation

(D) This is a restatement question. The passage states, "Muir was one of the first voices in favor of the wild in a time better known for the destruction and exploitation of nature." This is the opposite of caring about conservation.

64. When Muir felt joy about nature what would he have been most likely to do?
(A) write
(B) talk
(C) sing
(D) hike

(A) This is an inference question. The passage states that Muir began his career as a nature essayist. This means that he wrote about nature. Answer (B) is not correct, because there is nothing written about him talking. In fact the opposite feeling is given. He was very independent and often went out alone. There is a mention of "voice" in Line 18, but this voice refers to his writing and his ideas, not necessarily his speaking. Answer (C) is incorrect, since there is no mention of him singing. Answer (D) is a possible inference, since we know that he liked to walk alone in the wilderness. However, it is more likely that the joy he felt was *because* of his walking. The question asks for what Muir would do as a result of the joy he felt.

65. It can be inferred from the passage that the most unusual aspect of the Cleopatra drawing is that
(A) the figure is screaming
(B) the figure is tormented
(C) the drawing was hidden
(D) the drawing is backwards

(C) This is an inference question. The passage states that one mystery that was revealed was that his famous drawing of a pensive Cleopatra included a hidden drawing. Answers (A) and (B) describe the hidden drawing, but these are not as unusual or interesting as the fact that the drawing was hidden. Answer (D) is incorrect, because the drawing wasn't backwards; the drawing was on the reverse side of the painting.

66. The word "pensive" in line 3 can best be substituted by
(A) thoughtful
(B) angry
(C) happy
(D) anxious

(A) This is a vocabulary question. "Pensive" means "to think deeply or seriously."

67. Scholars disagree about
(A) when St. Peter's Basilica was built
(B) what kind of dome Michelangelo wanted
(C) who elevated the dome of St. Peter's
(D) who built the model

(B) This is an inference question. The passage states that another mystery concerns the plan for the dome. Some scholars believe that the model he built shows the dome as he intended it. Other scholars believe that he changed his mind.

68. The dome of St. Peter's Basilica is
(A) a mosaic
(B) destroyed
(C) a model
(D) raised

(D) This is an inference question. The passage states, ". . . to elevate the dome in the way it is today." From this you can infer that the dome is elevated, which means raised.

69. According to this passage, Michelangelo is
(A) screaming in horror
(B) one of the greatest artists in the world
(C) a private person
(D) the most famous architect in Rome

(B) This is a restatement question. The passage states, "A third mystery about one of the greatest artists who ever lived . . ." This sentence is referring to Michelangelo.

70. Why did Michelangelo destroy so many drawings before he died?
(A) Nobody knows.
(B) They were unimportant.
(C) They were only drafts of later material.
(D) He had changed the drawings.

(A) This is an inference question. The passage states, "A third mystery . . . is why he destroyed hundreds or thousands of his drawings before he died." Since this is a mystery, you can infer that nobody knows that answer.

71. Which of the following is the best restatement of the final question in this passage (lines 12-13)?
(A) Did he want his compatriots to judge only his final works of art?
(B) Did he want his position as an artist to be based on all of his productions?
(C) Did he want Roman society to see only his best work?
(D) Did he want future generations to judge him only by his completed work?

(D) The word "posterity" means "future generations." The words "finished products" are restated as "completed work."

72. This passage is mainly about
(A) a new form of eyeglasses
(B) types of camera lenses
(C) a new way to take pictures
(D) the science of light

(D) The first sentence of this passage mentions light as a wave and light as a particle. This is the best clue to the idea that this passage is about the science of light.

73. According to the passage, what happens when light meets glass or plastic?
(A) It gets brighter.
(B) It changes direction.
(C) It moves faster.
(D) It stops moving.

(B) This is a restatement question. The passage states, ". . . light . . . bends at an angle." If something bends, it must change direction.

74. In this passage, what does the author mean by the word "wave"?
(A) A ridge of sea water
(B) A way to say goodbye
(C) A way of moving
(D) A curve of hair

(C) This is a vocabulary/inference question. The passage uses the word "wave" several times to refer to the way something moves.

75. What is the main purpose of this passage?
(A) To argue a point
(B) To invent a term
(C) To point out a similarity
(D) To explain a difference

(D) This is an author's purpose question. The first sentence gives the purpose. The first paragraph describes conventional optics, and the second paragraph explains holographic optics.

76. In line 11, the word "ridges" could best be replaced by
(A) crests
(B) slopes
(C) gullies
(D) grooves

(A) The words "ridges" and "crests" both refer to the high points of something. "Slopes" refer to the side or edge of something that is going up or down. "Gullies" and "grooves" both refer to the low point of something. Imagine a hill. The top is the ridge, the side is the slope, and the bottom is the gully.

77. The best title for this passage is
(A) Popular Colors
(B) Color Consultants
(C) The Success of Color
(D) Flattering Colors

(C) The entire passage gives examples of how successful the use of color is. Answer (A) is not correct, because the idea of which colors are popular is only a part of this passage. Answers (B) and (D) are examples of the success of color.

78. According to the passage, which of the following is not popular now?
(A) "Coppertone"
(B) Pastels
(C) Colorful cars
(D) Color consultants

(A) This is a restatement question. The passage mentions "Coppertone" and then states, "Now those are thought of as old-fashioned."

79. According to the passage, why would red be a good color for a lawn mower?
(A) Because it's strong.
(B) Because it's cheap.
(C) Because it's light.
(D) Because it's a pastel.

(A) This is an inference question. The passage says that you want garden equipment to look powerful. Then it says that you'd never find a lawn mower in pink, but red would be fine. "Powerful" is similar in meaning to "strong."

80. How does the author probably feel about the topic of this passage?
(A) Excited
(B) Envious
(C) Skeptical
(D) Bored

(C) This is an author's purpose question. At the end of the passage, the author says, "It's hard to believe that people are that impressionable." This indicates a feeling of skepticism. A "skeptic" is a person who doubts or questions an idea. The author shows this by the words "It's hard to believe . . ."

81. In this passage, which of the following are NOT used as names for colors?
(A) Hair color
(B) Fruits
(C) Minerals
(D) Drinks

(D) This is a negative question. You can answer it by elimination. The passage mentions blond (a word for hair color), honeydew and avocado (fruits), and copper and gold (minerals). There is no mention of any kind of drink.

82. Why does the author say, "It's cheaper to make a skirt than a sofa?"
(A) As an illustration
(B) As a reason
(C) As an summary
(D) As a definition

(B) This is an author's purpose question. This sentence is used as a reason that new colors first come out in the fashion industry. "Fashion" here refers to the popular style of clothes. The meaning is that because it is cheaper to make a skirt than a sofa, it is less of a risk to try something new with a skirt.

83. According to this passage, before people will buy expensive things in new colors, they must
(A) be sure that the colors are popular
(B) see if the color matches their skin color
(C) talk to a color-analyst consultant
(D) become familiar with the color on cheaper items

(D) This is an inference question. The answer is similar to question 82. The passage states, "After people get used to seeing new colors on clothing or towels, they are ready to accept those colors in carpeting, refrigerators, or cars." Clothes and towels are cheaper than carpet, refrigerators, or cars.

84. The best title for this passage is
(A) The Mythic Icarus
(B) Comets Near the Sun
(C) Tilted Orbits
(D) The Kreutz Group

(B) Answer (B) is the best answer, since all of the passage discusses something that happened close to the sun. Answer (A) is not correct, because it is not the main information in the passage. Answer (C) is not correct, because tilted orbits are mentioned as only one aspect of these comets. Answer (D) is not correct, since the Kreutz group is only mentioned as the first-discovered comets of this type.

85. The word "they" in line 1 refers to
(A) comets
(B) people
(C) wings
(D) astronomers

(A) This is a referent question. To find the answer you must read ahead in the passage to the next possible noun. The second sentence mentions comets, so this is the best answer.

86. What is a "sun-grazer"?
(A) A comet
(B) An astronomer
(C) A telescope
(D) An orbit

(A) This is an inference/referent question. The passage says, "These sun-grazers . . ." after mentioning the word "comets." You can then infer that "sun-grazer" is being used as another name for a particular type of comet.

87. Why did the comet become fragmented?
(A) It flew too fast.
(B) It became too hot.
(C) It melted.
(D) It hit the sun.

(B) This is an inference question. The passage states, ". . . comets passing so near the sun that the heat caused them to break up . . ." Answer (A) is incorrect, because the speed of travel is not mentioned. Answer (C) is incorrect, because "melting" is only one reaction to becoming too hot. Some things might explode rather than melt. Answer (D) is incorrect, because there is no mention of actually touching the sun.

88. The word "tilted" in line 10 could be substituted best by
(A) measured
(B) slanted
(C) encountered
(D) poised

(B) This is a vocabulary question. The word "tilt" means "to slope, slant, or tip in one direction." The earth lies in a tilted position.

89. Which of the following is NOT true about the recently discovered sun-grazers?
(A) They were part of a single comet.
(B) They travel clockwise.
(C) They were discovered by Heinrich Kreutz.
(D) They have made trips around the sun.

(C) This is a negative question. You can answer it by elimination. The passage says that the comets were probably once part of a single comet, that they circled the sun in a clockwise direction, and that they may split again in subsequent trips past the sun. They were not discovered by Heinrich Kreutz, however. He discovered the first sun-grazers, not the new ones that are discussed in this passage.

90. The story of Icarus is used to
  (A) clarify a fact
  (B) summarize an idea
  (C) define a concept
  (D) add interest

(D) This is an inference question. The answer cannot be (A) or (B), because clarification and summarizing come after a concept is discussed. Answer (C) must be incorrect, because there is no definition of a concept in this story of Icarus. Answer (D) is correct, since the story of Icarus is interesting, and also the idea of flying close to the sun introduces the discovery of these comets that çame close to the sun.

Practice Test V

Post Test (Short Form)

NOTE: You will need the tape to do Section 1. If you do not have the tape, the tapescript for Section 1 is on pages 653 to 657 The answer key is on pages 600–601 and explanatory answers begin on page 606. Use the answer sheet for Practice Test V on page 577 to mark your answers.

ANSWER SHEET FOR PRACTICE TEST V

Section 1: Listening Comprehension

1	2	3	4	5	6	7	8	9	10	11	12	13	14	15	16	17	18	19	20	21	22	23	24	25	26	27	28	29	30	31	32	33	34	35	36	37	38	39	40	41	42	43	44	45	46	47	48	49	50
A	A	A	A	A	A	A	A	A	A	A	A	A	A	A	A	A	A	A	A	A	A	A	A	A	A	A	A	A	A	A	A	A	A	A	A	A	A	A	A	A	A	A	A	A	A	A	A	A	A
B	B	B	B	B	B	B	B	B	B	B	B	B	B	B	B	B	B	B	B	B	B	B	B	B	B	B	B	B	B	B	B	B	B	B	B	B	B	B	B	B	B	B	B	B	B	B	B	B	B
C	C	C	C	C	C	C	C	C	C	C	C	C	C	C	C	C	C	C	C	C	C	C	C	C	C	C	C	C	C	C	C	C	C	C	C	C	C	C	C	C	C	C	C	C	C	C	C	C	C
D	D	D	D	D	D	D	D	D	D	D	D	D	D	D	D	D	D	D	D	D	D	D	D	D	D	D	D	D	D	D	D	D	D	D	D	D	D	D	D	D	D	D	D	D	D	D	D	D	D

Section 2: Structure and Written Expression

1	2	3	4	5	6	7	8	9	10	11	12	13	14	15	16	17	18	19	20	21	22	23	24	25	26	27	28	29	30	31	32	33	34	35	36	37	38	39	40
A	A	A	A	A	A	A	A	A	A	A	A	A	A	A	A	A	A	A	A	A	A	A	A	A	A	A	A	A	A	A	A	A	A	A	A	A	A	A	A
B	B	B	B	B	B	B	B	B	B	B	B	B	B	B	B	B	B	B	B	B	B	B	B	B	B	B	B	B	B	B	B	B	B	B	B	B	B	B	B
C	C	C	C	C	C	C	C	C	C	C	C	C	C	C	C	C	C	C	C	C	C	C	C	C	C	C	C	C	C	C	C	C	C	C	C	C	C	C	C
D	D	D	D	D	D	D	D	D	D	D	D	D	D	D	D	D	D	D	D	D	D	D	D	D	D	D	D	D	D	D	D	D	D	D	D	D	D	D	D

Section 3: Vocabulary and Reading Comprehension

1	2	3	4	5	6	7	8	9	10	11	12	13	14	15	16	17	18	19	20	21	22	23	24	25	26	27	28	29	30	31	32	33	34	35	36	37	38	39	40	41	42	43	44	45	46	47	48	49	50	51	52	53	54	55	56	57	58	59	60
A	A	A	A	A	A	A	A	A	A	A	A	A	A	A	A	A	A	A	A	A	A	A	A	A	A	A	A	A	A	A	A	A	A	A	A	A	A	A	A	A	A	A	A	A	A	A	A	A	A	A	A	A	A	A	A	A	A	A	A
B	B	B	B	B	B	B	B	B	B	B	B	B	B	B	B	B	B	B	B	B	B	B	B	B	B	B	B	B	B	B	B	B	B	B	B	B	B	B	B	B	B	B	B	B	B	B	B	B	B	B	B	B	B	B	B	B	B	B	B
C	C	C	C	C	C	C	C	C	C	C	C	C	C	C	C	C	C	C	C	C	C	C	C	C	C	C	C	C	C	C	C	C	C	C	C	C	C	C	C	C	C	C	C	C	C	C	C	C	C	C	C	C	C	C	C	C	C	C	C
D	D	D	D	D	D	D	D	D	D	D	D	D	D	D	D	D	D	D	D	D	D	D	D	D	D	D	D	D	D	D	D	D	D	D	D	D	D	D	D	D	D	D	D	D	D	D	D	D	D	D	D	D	D	D	D	D	D	D	D

Date Taken ____________________

Number Correct
Section 1 ________
Section 2 ________
Section 3 ________

1 1 1 1 1 1 1 1 1 1 1

SECTION 1
LISTENING COMPREHENSION
Time—approximately 35 minutes

In this section of the test, you will have an opportunity to demonstrate your ability to understand spoken English. There are three parts to this section, with special directions for each part.

Part A

Directions: For each question in Part A, you will hear a short sentence. Each sentence will be spoken just one time. The sentences you hear will not be written out for you. Therefore, you must listen carefully to understand what the speaker says.

After you hear a sentence, read the four choices in your test book, marked (A), (B), (C), and (D), and decide which one is closest in meaning to the sentence you heard. Then, on your answer sheet, find the number of the question and fill in the space that corresponds to the letter of the answer you have chosen. Fill in the space so that the letter inside the oval cannot be seen.

Example I:

You will hear:

Sample Answer

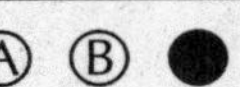

You will read:

(A) Mary outswam the others.
(B) Mary ought to swim with them.
(C) Mary and her friends swam to the island.
(D) Mary's friends owned the island.

The speaker said, "Mary swam out to the island with her friends." Sentence (C), "Mary and her friends swam to the island," is closest in meaning to the sentence you heard. Therefore, you should choose answer (C).

Example II:

You will hear:

Sample Answer

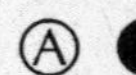

You will read:

(A) Please remind me to read this book.
(B) Could you help me carry these books?
(C) I don't mind if you help me.
(D) Do you have a heavy course load this term?

The speaker said, "Would you mind helping me with this load of books?" Sentence (B), "Could you help me carry these books?" is closest in meaning to the sentence you heard. Therefore, you should choose answer (B).

1. (A) The train is early.
   (B) You missed the train.
   (C) You must hurry.
   (D) You hurry too much.

2. (A) Grandma should enjoy the weather this fall.
   (B) Grandma should walk slowly so she doesn't fall.
   (C) Because of her fall, Grandma should rest more.
   (D) Since Grandma did so much work in the fall, she should rest this winter.

3. (A) John has already left for the party.
   (B) John will arrive after the director has left.
   (C) John will leave before the director comes.
   (D) The director has already gone to the party.

4. (A) Sandra didn't have enough time to finish the work.
   (B) There was no clock in Sandra's room.
   (C) It took more time than she thought to finish.
   (D) Sandra finished the work quickly.

5. (A) The front door is for the handicapped only.
   (B) You can use the back door if the front door is locked.
   (C) The disabled can use the back door if necessary.
   (D) I left your cap by the red door.

6. (A) Representing the entire class, the student gave a talk.
   (B) The class discussed whether or not the project should be presented.
   (C) The class didn't like the student's project.
   (D) The class discussed the student's project.

7. (A) At one time, Jenny wished she could be an Olympic winner.
   (B) Jenny almost won the gold medal in gymnastics.
   (C) Jenny used to be a very good gymnast.
   (D) Jenny took part in the gymnastics event in the Olympics.

8. (A) You have to move to the left.
   (B) Watch out! The track is on your right.
   (C) If you continue on the right side, you'll get there.
   (D) You are doing all right, so far.

9. (A) Mr. Wilson retired when he got rich.
   (B) Mr. Wilson could stop working, because he has enough money.
   (C) Rich people don't have to work anymore.
   (D) Health is more important than wealth.

10. (A) The black clothes fit you better than the white clothes.
    (B) The white clothes fit you better than the black clothes.
    (C) It's more appropriate to wear white clothes than black clothes in the summertime.
    (D) Your black clothes have gotten too tight to wear in the summer.

11. (A) They resigned their jobs.
    (B) They were starting to build.
    (C) They finished the plans early.
    (D) They were beginning to work on the design.

12. (A) The asteroids were large.
    (B) They were large planets.
    (C) They were too small to be called planets.
    (D) Planets are all small.

13. (A) You should do more because I have to rest.
    (B) I will cook the rice if you cook everything else.
    (C) I will do everything that you don't do.
    (D) Since you have to rest, I will prepare everything.

14. (A) His determination was the most important reason that he succeeded.
    (B) He was determined to get the key.
    (C) It was impossible for him to be successful.
    (D) He was difficult to work with.

15. (A) The computer room is very crowded.
    (B) Computer science has been applied to many fields.
    (C) Many people are studying computer science.
    (D) Computer technology is developing very quickly.

16. (A) I want to know what it costs.
    (B) I want to buy a coat that fits me.
    (C) I want it, but it's too expensive.
    (D) I'll buy it at any price.

GO ON TO THE NEXT PAGE

17. (A) My uncle is a famous speaker.
    (B) I've heard my uncle's lectures.
    (C) My uncle's lecture was excellent.
    (D) I don't know my uncle very well.

18. (A) George stopped going to class, because he didn't like it.
    (B) George couldn't take the class, since he had another class at the same time.
    (C) The class was about conflicts of schedule.
    (D) George needed another class in his busy schedule.

19. (A) We should have gone to the beach on a warmer day.
    (B) Today was not a good day for me to go to the beach.
    (C) The weather is just right for the beach today.
    (D) This beach is not good enough to go to.

20. (A) I can't work any faster.
    (B) I will work faster.
    (C) I am not able to work.
    (D) It's bad to work too fast.

GO ON TO THE NEXT PAGE

1 1 1 1 1 1 1 1 1 1 1

Part B

<u>Directions:</u> In Part B you will hear short conversations between two speakers. At the end of each conversation, a third person will ask a question about what was said. You will hear each conversation and question about it just one time. Therefore, you must listen carefully to understand what each speaker says. After you hear a conversation and the question about it, read the four possible answers in your test book and decide which <u>one</u> is the best answer to the question you heard. Then, on your answer sheet, find the number of the question and fill in the space that corresponds to the letter of the answer you have chosen.

Look at the following example.

You will hear:

Sample Answer

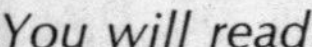

You will read:

(A) Present Professor Smith with a picture.
(B) Photograph Professor Smith.
(C) Put glass over the photograph.
(D) Replace the broken headlight.

From the conversation you learn that the woman thinks Professor Smith would like a photograph of the class. The best answer to the question "What does the woman think the class should do?" is (A), "Present Professor Smith with a picture." Therefore, you should choose answer (A).

21. **(A)** She will not say what the boss will do.
(B) The boss will not do anything.
(C) Don't tell the boss the bad news.
(D) She doesn't know what he will do.

22. **(A)** She wants him to stay longer.
(B) She wishes he had left sooner.
(C) She knows he must go soon.
(D) She wants him to go now.

23. **(A)** In a post office
(B) In a department store
(C) At a bank
(D) In a grocery store

24. **(A)** Three hours if working by hand
(B) A minimum of three hours
(C) Three hours at the maximum
(D) Three hours, more or less

25. **(A)** He wants to wait until the class is full.
(B) He will wait for the list.
(C) He hopes someone will drop the class.
(D) He is late and there are no more chairs.

26. **(A)** She doesn't know if the library is open.
(B) She doesn't know what time they must leave the hotel.
(C) She doesn't know how much they must pay.
(D) She doesn't know what food to order.

27. **(A)** He should go first and she will catch up to him later.
(B) She will go have coffee and then do her work.
(C) She will do her work instead of having coffee.
(D) She will do her work at the coffee house.

GO ON TO THE NEXT PAGE

28. (A) A room with a balcony
(B) A room with two beds
(C) A room and transportation
(D) A room and meals

29. (A) In a clothes store
(B) In a shoe store
(C) In a gymnasium
(D) At a swimming pool

30. (A) Go to the gym and work out.
(B) Be calm and patient.
(C) Listen carefully to John.
(D) Do the easiest thing.

31. (A) She has a strong opinion.
(B) She likes the man a lot.
(C) She wants to choose.
(D) She doesn't care which kind they get.

32. (A) She lost her job.
(B) She mislaid her money.
(C) She got divorced.
(D) She's in the hospital.

33. (A) He will call Pete before he goes home.
(B) He will call Pete after he gets home.
(C) He called Pete at home.
(D) He will call Pete tomorrow.

34. (A) She doesn't want pumpkin or apple.
(B) She can't decide; she likes them both.
(C) She doesn't know the difference between pumpkin and apple pie.
(D) She likes pumpkin pie better than apple pie.

35. (A) Bill has to pay $54.
(B) It is a little more than $54.
(C) It is a little less than $54.
(D) The whole bill is $54.

36. (A) A nurse
(B) A dentist
(C) A patient
(D) An assistant

37. (A) Just before pulling a tooth
(B) Just after pulling a tooth
(C) At a consultation about pulling a tooth
(D) While another person is pulling a tooth

38. (A) For a half hour
(B) For a few hours
(C) Until tomorrow
(D) Until the swelling goes down

39. (A) Rinse your mouth.
(B) Take aspirin.
(C) Sleep.
(D) Put ice on your cheek.

40. (A) Tonight
(B) In a half hour
(C) Tomorrow
(D) In four or five hours

GO ON TO THE NEXT PAGE

1 1 1 1 1 1 1 1 1 1 1

Part C

Directions: In this part of the test, you will hear short talks and conversations. After each of them you will be asked some questions. You will hear the talks and conversations and the questions about them just one time. They will not be written out for you. Therefore, you must listen carefully to understand what each speaker says.

After you hear a question, read the four possible answers in your test book and decide which one is the best answer to the question you heard. Then, on your answer sheet, find the number of the question and fill in the space that corresponds to the letter of the answer you have chosen.

Answer all questions on the basis of what is stated or implied in the talk or conversation.

Listen to this sample talk.

You will hear:

Now look at the following example.

You will hear:

You will read:

(A) They are impossible to guide.
(B) They may go up in flames.
(C) They tend to leak gas.
(D) They are cheaply made.

Sample Answer

  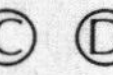

The best answer to the question "Why are gas balloons considered dangerous?" is (B), "They may go up in flames." Therefore, you should choose answer (B).

Now look at the next example.

You will hear:

Sample Answer

You will read:

(A) Watch for changes in weather.
(B) Watch their altitude.
(C) Check for weak spots in their balloons.
(D) Test the strength of the ropes.

The best answer to the question "According to the speaker, what must balloon pilots be careful to do?" is (A), "Watch for changes in weather." Therefore, you should choose answer (A).

GO ON TO THE NEXT PAGE

41. (A) It is normal.
 (B) It should stop in a half hour.
 (C) It is not bleeding.
 (D) There will be a lot of bleeding.

42. (A) Angry
 (B) Worried
 (C) Helpful
 (D) Excited

43. (A) New students
 (B) Returning students
 (C) Faculty
 (D) Staff

44. (A) Children
 (B) Cooking
 (C) Spouses
 (D) Single students

45. (A) Coed dorms
 (B) Married student apartments
 (C) The international houses
 (D) Spanish House

46. (A) Visit the housing they like.
 (B) Move into the housing.
 (C) Fill out forms.
 (D) Buy a meal ticket.

47. (A) It was exciting.
 (B) It was lonely.
 (C) It was dull.
 (D) It was too busy.

48. (A) Two days
 (B) A week
 (C) Three days
 (D) A month

49. (A) Sorting through papers
 (B) Meeting people
 (C) Giving a presentation
 (D) Getting a rest

50. (A) Discuss her project.
 (B) Have tea.
 (C) Fly away for three days.
 (D) Go to a conference.

THIS IS THE END OF THE LISTENING COMPREHENSION PART OF THIS TEST. The next part of the test is Section 2. Turn to the directions for Section 2 in your test book, read them, and begin work. Do not read or work on any other section of the test.

GO ON TO THE NEXT PAGE

2 2 2 2 2 2 2 2 2 2 2

SECTION 2
STRUCTURE AND WRITTEN EXPRESSION
Time—25 minutes

This section is designed to measure your ability to recognize language that is appropriate for standard written English. There are two types of questions in this section, with special directions for each type.

Directions: Questions 1–15 are incomplete sentences. Beneath each sentence you will see four words or phrases, marked (A), (B), (C), and (D). Choose the one word or phrase that best completes the sentence. Then, on your answer sheet, find the number of the question and fill in the space that corresponds to the letter of the answer you have chosen. Fill in the space so that the letter inside the oval cannot be seen.

Example I:

Vegetables are an excellent source ________ vitamins.

(A) of
(B) has
(C) where
(D) that

Sample Answer

● Ⓑ Ⓒ Ⓓ

The sentence should read, "Vegetables are an excellent source of vitamins." Therefore, you should choose answer (A).

Example II:

________ in history when remarkable progress was made within a relatively short span of time.

(A) Periods
(B) Throughout periods
(C) There have been periods
(D) Periods have been

Sample Answer

Ⓐ Ⓑ ● Ⓓ

The sentence should read, "There have been periods in history when remarkable progress was made within a relatively short span of time." Therefore, you should choose answer (C).

After you read the directions, begin work on the questions.

GO ON TO THE NEXT PAGE

1. Even though woodpeckers ________ as a nuisance to many people, they are actually helpful, since they feed on harmful insects.

(A) are seen
(B) which are seen
(C) being seen
(D) to be seen

2. The first clock, made nearly a thousand years ago, had neither a face nor hands, ________ that rang each hour.

(A) it had bells
(B) rather than bells
(C) though bells
(D) but it had bells

3. ________ on the floor of the ocean is a big farming industry.

(A) Oysters raising
(B) Oysters are raised
(C) The raising of oysters
(D) The oysters raised

4. A barbershop ________ a red and white striped pole.

(A) what symbolizes
(B) is symbolized by
(C) is symbolized to
(D) was symbolized

5. ________ as beasts of burden by the Indians in the Andes Mountains.

(A) Using llamas
(B) Llamas are used
(C) Llamas use
(D) There are llamas

6. The moon, ________ no air around it, grows extremely hot in the daytime and extremely cold at night.

(A) which has
(B) has
(C) having had
(D) what has

7. Even though they are not liquid, cottage cheese, sour cream, and yogurt are sold ________ liquid measurements.

(A) to
(B) for
(C) over
(D) by

8. To plant rice, farmers, ________, set young plants in the mud.

(A) they wade with bare feet in the water
(B) water wading in their bare feet
(C) wading in the water in their bare feet
(D) whose bare feet wading in the water

9. ________, farmers cut holes in the bark of maple trees.

(A) Maple syrup is collected
(B) To collect maple syrup
(C) The collection of maple syrup
(D) When collect maple syrup

10. The boll weevil, an insect ________ cotton plants, is native to Central America.

(A) destroys
(B) to destroy
(C) has destroyed
(D) that destroys

11. ________ humans, toads have tongues fastened at the front of their mouths, which allow them to catch insects.

(A) Not the same
(B) Unlike
(C) Except for
(D) Dislike

12. ________ on a hot fire is a delicacy in many parts of the world.

(A) Lamb roasted
(B) Roasted
(C) Lambs roast
(D) Lambs

GO ON TO THE NEXT PAGE

13. ________ determines a good meal varies from country to country.

(A) Which
(B) Why
(C) What
(D) How

14. ________, the pecan is the second most popular nut in the United States.

(A) The rich food
(B) Food is rich
(C) To be rich
(D) A rich food

15. More ivory is obtained from elephants in Africa ________ elephants in Asia.

(A) rather than
(B) more than
(C) than from
(D) as well as

Directions: In questions 16–40 each sentence has four underlined words or phrases. The four underlined parts of the sentence are marked (A), (B), (C), and (D). Identify the one underlined word or phrase that must be changed in order for the sentence to be correct. Then, on your answer sheet, find the number of the question and fill in the space that corresponds to the letter of the answer you have chosen.

Example 1:

A ray of light passing through (A) the center (B) of a thin lens keep (C) its original (D) direction

Sample Answer

Ⓐ Ⓑ ● Ⓓ

The sentence should read, "A ray of light passing through the center of a thin lens keeps its original direction." Therefore, you should choose answer (C).

Example II:

The mandolin, a musical instrument (A) that has (B) strings, was probably copied from (C) the lute, a many (D) older instrument.

Sample Answer

Ⓐ Ⓑ Ⓒ ●

The sentence should read, "The mandolin, a musical instrument that has strings, was probably copied from the lute, a much older instrument." Therefore, you should choose answer (D).

After you read the directions, begin work on the questions.

16. One of the most important discovery (A) of the nineteenth century was (B) a method of using (C) natural gas for cooking and heating (D).

GO ON TO THE NEXT PAGE

17. The Netherlands, a country with much of the land lying lower than sea level, have
A B C
a system of dikes and canals for controlling water.
D

18. Davy Crockett, a famed American pioneer, was known for his hunting, trapping,
A B
tell stories, and quick wit.
C D

19. The movement of ocean waves can be compared to the waves caused by the wind
A B C
in a field or grass.
D

20. Milk, often considered a nearly perfect food, contains fat, sweet, and protein.
A B C D

21. Only after they themselves become parents, do people realize the difficulties
A B C
of raised children.
D

22. Aviators, fishing, and sailors are among those who rely on weather predictions.
A B C D

23. Mohandas K. Gandhi, who was called Mahatma, lived a noble life of fasting and
A
poverty in order to work for peaceful and independence.
B C D

24. Soybean, which sometimes grow seven feet tall, have thick, woody stems.
A B C D

25. When settling the old west in pioneer times, American families building their
A B C
homes from split logs.
D

26. A Venus' Flytrap is a small plant that have leaves that snap together like traps.
A B C D

27. *The Last of the Mohicans* are a famous book about frontier life by the American
A B C D
author James Fenimore Cooper.

28. The Treaty of Ghent, signed in 1814, ends the last war between England and the
A B C D
United States.

29. In the year 500, ancient Greece was reaching its highest level of civilization, with
A B
great achievements in the fields of art, architecture, politic, and philosophy.
C D

GO ON TO THE NEXT PAGE

30. A fever, the elevations of body temperature above 98.6° F, is considered to be a
A B C
symptom of a disorder rather than a disease in itself.
D

31. Lacrosse is a ballgame played on a field outdoors similar soccer.
A B C D

32. The manufactural of ice cream in the United States on a commercial scale began
A B C D
in 1851.

33. People with two family members which suffer heart attacks before fifty-five
A B
are likely to have early heart attacks themselves.
C D

34. Children's games, which are amusements involve more than one individual,
A
appear to be a cultural universal.
B C D

35. During times of war, political groups will sometimes kidnap foreign diplomats and
keep them as hostages until the government meets certain demanding.
A B C D

36. The first year of a child's life is characterized in rapid physical growth.
A B C D

37. A fair trial is guarantee by the American Constitution.
A B C D

38. Since ancient times, water from rivers and smaller streams are used for irrigation.
A B C D

39. Khaki is a cloth made in linen or cotton and dyed a dusty color.
A B C D

40. The symptom of leukemia include weakness, a general ill feeling, and fever.
A B C D

THIS IS THE END OF SECTION 2. CHECK YOUR WORK ON SECTION 2 ONLY. DO NOT READ OR WORK ON ANY OTHER SECTION OF THE TEST UNTIL YOUR TIME IS UP. **STOP**

3 3 3 3 3 3 3 3 3 3 3

SECTION 3
VOCABULARY AND READING COMPREHENSION
Time—45 minutes

This section is designed to measure your comprehension of standard written English. There are two types of questions in this section, with special directions for each type.

Directions: In questions 1–30 each sentence has an underlined word or phrase. Below each sentence are four other words or phrases, marked (A), (B), (C), and (D). You are to choose the one word or phrase that best keeps the meaning of the original sentence if it is substituted for the underlined word or phrase. Then, on your answer sheet, find the number of the question and fill in the space that corresponds to the letter you have choosen. Fill in the space so that the letter inside the oval cannot be seen.

Example:

Passenger ships and aircraft are often equipped with ship-to-shore or air-to-land radio telephones.

(A) highways
(B) railroads
(C) planes
(D) sailboats

Sample Answer

Ⓐ Ⓑ ● Ⓓ

The best answer is (C), because "Passenger ships and planes are often equipped with ship-to-shore or air-to-land radio telephones" is closest in meaning to the original sentence. Therefore, you should choose answer (C).

After you read the directions, begin work on the questions.

GO ON TO THE NEXT PAGE

1. Produce is commonly shipped across the United States in large crates.
   (A) wooden boxes
   (B) box cars
   (C) trucks
   (D) quantities

2. Because of the baby boom of the 1980s, preschools in the U.S. have proliferated.
   (A) changed in philosophy
   (B) increased in numbers
   (C) become more crowded
   (D) become more expensive

3. Even though he was obese, Oliver Hardy gained fame as a comedian.
   (A) dying
   (B) crazy
   (C) unhappy
   (D) fat

4. Crimes against property have risen in the U.S. and other urbanized countries.
   (A) rich
   (B) large
   (C) multicultural
   (D) metropolitan

5. Raccoons and dormice are examples of animals that hibernate several months of the year.
   (A) sleep
   (B) fast
   (C) lose hair
   (D) store food

6. The California condor has become scarce during this century.
   (A) easily frightened
   (B) prone to disease
   (C) fewer in numbers
   (D) difficult to catch

7. Charles Darwin and A.R. Wallace published their ideas on evolution simultaneously in 1858.
   (A) in the same book
   (B) for the same people
   (C) on the same topic
   (D) at the same time

8. In coastal areas where there is an abundance of fish, the fishing industry prospers.
   (A) more than sufficient quantity
   (B) a wide variety
   (C) a unique type
   (D) a common diet

9. There is a common superstition that a ring around the moon means that rain will come soon.
   (A) attitude
   (B) speculation
   (C) belief
   (D) approach

10. Political refugees often find sanctuary in churches.
   (A) happiness
   (B) protection
   (C) peace
   (D) charity

11. Many pesticides are available for insects like termites and cockroaches.
   (A) poisons
   (B) deterrents
   (C) sprays
   (D) medicines

12. Children like to play games in vacant lots.
   (A) wooded areas
   (B) schoolyards
   (C) empty plots of ground
   (D) open houses

13. If you are going to be in a swamp area, you should take a mosquito repellent.
   (A) marsh
   (B) jungle
   (C) savanna
   (D) tropical

14. Ralph Nader is an advocate of consumer rights.
   (A) an opponent of
   (B) a believer in
   (C) a politician for
   (D) a supporter of

15. A backyard swimming pool can be a hazard for small children.
   (A) pleasure
   (B) disaster
   (C) danger
   (D) thrill

16. When the New York Giants lost the football game, the citizens of New York were abject.
   (A) surprised
   (B) disgusted
   (C) relieved
   (D) depressed

GO ON TO THE NEXT PAGE

17. Canada is a vast country in terms of its area.
(A) except for
(B) with regard to
(C) in spite of
(D) because of

18. Tenzing Norkay and Sir Edmund Hillary were the first people to scale Mount Everest.
(A) climb
(B) camp on
(C) discover
(D) survive on

19. At a high temperature, evaporation is more rapid than at a lower temperature.
(A) increase in a liquid
(B) decreased energy of molecules
(C) change of a solid into a liquid
(D) change of liquid into vapor

20. A huge mountain chain in Europe is formed by linking the Alps, the Pyrenees, the Balkans, the Caucasus, and the Carpathians.
(A) dividing
(B) surpassing
(C) surrounding
(D) joining

21. John Foster Dulles achieved recognition in the U.S. as an international lawyer in the 1930s.
(A) fought for
(B) gained
(C) wrote about
(D) chose

22. In 1936, Edward VIII renounced his title to the British throne to marry Wallis Warfield Simpson.
(A) gave up
(B) threw away
(C) let down
(D) put in

23. Many children looked emaciated during the drought.
(A) sick
(B) unhappy
(C) thin
(D) lonely

24. An increasing number of women in the 1980s delayed marriage and childbirth in order to launch their careers.
(A) postpone
(B) expand
(C) begin
(D) participate in

25. According to Carl Sagan, the Earth is a tiny and fragile world that needs to be cherished.
(A) explored
(B) valued
(C) unified
(D) developed

26. In certain areas of many cities, it is against the law to loiter.
(A) throw paper
(B) stand around
(C) join a mob
(D) carry a weapon

27. During the 1980s, women entered the work force in droves.
(A) seriously
(B) fervently
(C) in large numbers
(D) in management positions

28. Taking some kinds of medicine will cause your body to retain fluids.
(A) sustain
(B) inject
(C) lose
(D) keep

29. Down pillows are very popular.
(A) Floor
(B) Beanbag
(C) Feather
(D) Polyester

30. In most public buildings, ramps are installed for handicapped people.
(A) sloped walkways
(B) safe handrails
(C) low telephones
(D) wide doorways

GO ON TO THE NEXT PAGE

Directions: In the rest of this section you will read several passages. Each one is followed by several questions about it. For questions 31–60, you are to choose the one best answer, (A), (B), (C), or (D), to each question. Then, on your answer sheet, find the number of the question and fill in the space that corresponds to the letter of the answer you have chosen.

Answer all questions following a passage on the basis of what is stated or implied in that passage.

Read the following passage:

The rattles with which a rattlesnake warns of its presence are formed by loosely interlocking hollow rings of hard skin, which make a buzzing sound when its tail is shaken. As a baby, the snake begins to form its rattles from the button at the very tip of its tail. Thereafter, each time it sheds its skin, a new ring is formed. Popular belief holds that a snake's age can be told by counting the rings, but this idea is fallacious. In fact, a snake may lose its old skin as often as four times a year. Also, rattles tend to wear or break off with time.

Example I:

A rattlesnake's rattles are made of

(A) skin
(B) bone
(C) wood
(D) muscle

Sample Answer

According to the passage, a rattlesnake's rattles are made out of rings of hard skin. Therefore, you should choose answer (A).

Example II:

How often does a rattlesnake shed its skin?

(A) Once every four years.
(B) Once every four months.
(C) Up to four times every year
(D) Four times more often than other snakes

Sample Answer

The passage states that "a snake may lose its old skin as often as four times a year." Therefore, you should choose answer (C).

After you read the directions, begin work on the questions.

GO ON TO THE NEXT PAGE

Questions 31–34

Halley's comet has become the best observed comet in history, but the information that has been gathered is only the beginning of what is needed to understand this comet, one of the most primitive bodies in the solar system. During the recent appearance of Halley's comet, a research corps of over 1,000 professional astronomers gathered data around the world. The data revealed intriguing new information. For the first time ever, European and Soviet spacecraft have photographed the comet's center.

In spite of close-up photos revealing one of the oddest-looking objects in the solar system, comet scientists still can't decide how fast Halley's nucleus spins. Some experts believe it spins once every 2.2 days, some determine the spin to be once in 7.4 days, and other scientists suggest that the comet exhibits both motions superimposed together.

Astronomers monitor Halley each time it comes close enough to the earth, so that we can see the bright cloud of vaporized dust and gas that forms its tail. It is easiest to get a clear look at the comet when it is far away from the sun so that its activity dies down.

31. The word "primitive" in line 3 means
(A) mysterious
(B) singular
(C) ancient
(D) simple

32. According to this passage, scientists are puzzled about
(A) why we see a cloud of dust and gas
(B) how quickly the central part of the comet turns
(C) what the tail consists of
(D) when Halley will return

33. The passage implies that many scientists think that Halley's comet is
(A) strange-looking
(B) misunderstood
(C) dirty
(D) dying

34. It is easiest to see Halley when
(A) it is dead
(B) it has less activity
(C) it is closer to the sun
(D) it is active

GO ON TO THE NEXT PAGE

Questions 35–40

Compact discs (CD's) have revolutionized the music industry with their surprisingly realistic sound. The six-inch discs look like thin, plastic sandwiches with aluminum in the center. They have digitally recorded material that is read by laser beams, so the sound has none of the crackling of vinyl records. CD's are also virtually indestructible, and they are lighter and smaller than conventional records (LP's). CD's are becoming more widely available than LP's: they are sold in electronics and video stores that haven't formerly carried records or cassettes. Many record stores are now cutting their prices on LP's to make room for the new CD's.

There has been a phenomenal growth in the sale of CD's. Sales were up almost 150 percent in the first half of 1986 as compared to the first half of 1985. Although fewer than 6 million CD's were sold in the U.S. in 1984, there were approximately 50 million sold in 1986. It is likely that the sales would have been even higher were it not for the price; CD's cost nearly twice as much as LP's. In the near future, however, prices should lower as more production facilities open.

35. The main appeal of CD's is their
(A) price
(B) size
(C) sound
(D) availability

36. The author refers to CD's as "sandwiches," because they
(A) are light
(B) are small
(C) are layered
(D) don't crackle

37. This passage states that it is difficult to
(A) play a CD
(B) produce a CD
(C) record a CD
(D) destroy a CD

38. According to the passage, many record stores are currently
(A) lowering CD prices
(B) raising LP prices
(C) lowering LP prices
(D) raising CD prices

39. According to this passage, which one of the following is true?
(A) Different kinds of stores are selling CD's.
(B) More CD's are available than LP's.
(C) Stores are selling more CD's than LP's.
(D) Stores are losing money on their LP's.

40. The author's main purpose is to
(A) tell how CD's are made
(B) discuss the growth of CD's
(C) compare CD's and LP's
(D) describe the technology that produces CD's

GO ON TO THE NEXT PAGE

Questions 41–46

A national political struggle is continuing over the issue of protection for the remnants of vast ancient forests that once covered the northwestern areas of the United States. These old forests, called "old growth," contain trees from 200 to 1,200 years old. There are now about 6 million acres of virgin forest in Washington and Oregon, only about one-tenth of what existed before the 1800s. This old growth contains some of the most valuable timber in the nation, but its economic worth is also contained in its water, wildlife, scenery, and recreational facilities.

Conservationists want the majority of existing old growth protected from harvesting. They emphasize the vital relationship between old growth and the health of the forest's ecosystem. They cite studies that show that both downed and standing old trees store and release nutrients necessary to younger trees.

On the other hand, much of the Northwest's economy is developed around the logging industry. Trees are cut down to make wood products, and many mills are geared for old-growth industry. In recent years, 500 acres of old growth have been logged, including trees up to 500 years old and eight feet in diameter. Although the U.S. Forest Service wrestles with the problem of how much of the forest to save, the harvesting of timber continues. The district office refuses to remove any of the old growth from timber production. The struggle is continuing at the national level, with strong proponents on both sides.

41. The best title for this passage is
(A) Ancient Forests of the Northwest
(B) The U.S. Forest Service
(C) The Harvesting of Old-Growth Timber
(D) The Wood-Based Economy of the Northwest

42. According to this passage, conservationists would agree that
(A) old-growth trees are not necessary for the health of the forest
(B) fallen trees should not be taken away
(C) most of the old-growth trees do not need protection
(D) young trees should not be logged

43. The struggle is between
(A) Oregon and Washington
(B) Oregon and the U.S. Forest Service
(C) conservationists and the logging industry
(D) conservationists and the state of Oregon

44. Before the 1800s
(A) there were six million trees
(B) old growth was not cut down
(C) the trees had more economic value
(D) there were more virgin forests

45. Studies show that young trees gain nutrients from
(A) wildlife
(B) virgins
(C) old trees
(D) wood products

46. According to this passage, the economy of the Northwest is dependent on
(A) the U.S. Forest Service
(B) harvesting trees
(C) ancient forests
(D) the forest ecosystem

GO ON TO THE NEXT PAGE

Questions 47–53

Indian and Inuit artists in Canada are now benefiting from a resurgence of interest in their art. More and more retail stores are opening up all the time as the quality of the art increases. In the west coast province of British Columbia alone, there are over 2,000 Indians making their living by producing arts and crafts. This resurgence has come at a good time. During the 1970s, there was a large demand for soapstone carvings, but this demand had the effect of inundating the market with mediocre work. Then, in the early 1980s, there was an economic slump in the industrial world. These two factors resulted in slow sales. Now, however, the new enthusiasm for both Inuit and Indian art has stimulated higher quality work.

Both Indians and Inuit have far more artists per capita than do nonnative Canadians. One reason for this is that their cultures had no written language before the arrival of white people. Instead, they expressed their culture and beliefs through carvings, drawings, and baskets. Art became a way of life. A second reason for the large numbers of artists is economic. Indians have been selling their arts and crafts for hundreds of years, from as early as the 17th century. A third contributing factor is that art has historically been an absorbing occupation for the Inuit when the weather has been too cold to leave the shelter.

47. Because of the large demand for soapstone carvings in the 1970s,
(A) a lot of poor quality art was for sale
(B) people were more enthusiastic
(C) the markets were empty
(D) artists worked indoors

48. In the early 1980s
(A) more retail stores opened
(B) there was renewed interest in Indian and Inuit art
(C) less art was sold
(D) the economy expanded

49. According to the passage, the quality of Inuit and Indian art has improved because of
(A) the rise in the sale of soapstone carvings
(B) new interest in their art
(C) the slow sales of the early 1980s
(D) the economic slump

50. According to this author, "Inuit" refers to
(A) a native Canadian
(B) an Indian
(C) a soapstone artist
(D) a nonnative Canadian

51. Indians began selling their art
(A) in the 1970s
(B) in the early 1980s
(C) in the 17th century
(D) recently

52. According to this passage, both Inuit and Indians
(A) have no written language
(B) live in the snow
(C) are nonnative Canadians
(D) expressed their culture through art

53. The best title for this passage is
(A) New Interest in Indian and Inuit Art
(B) The Rise and Fall of Inuit Art
(C) Soapstone Carvings
(D) Indian vs. Inuit Art

GO ON TO THE NEXT PAGE

Questions 54–60

The excellence of ancient Chinese bronze casting has never been equaled. Though the earliest bronzes predated the Shang dynasty (1523 B.C.–1028 B.C.), general use in state worship rituals by the ruling elite became common early in that period. Towards the end of the Shang dynasty, bronze vessels were also used in private rituals. After that, and up to 220 A.D., bronze vessels were widely used as utensils for daily life.

The Chinese made bronzes by methods that differed greatly from those used in ancient Mesopotamia and Greece. Instead of cold-working the alloy to make the shapes and designs, they used a direct-casting process. In this process, clay molds were assembled around a clay core. The mold sections contained a negative image of the design that had been carved directly into the clay. To make the vessel, the hot molten alloy (a combination of tin and copper) was poured into the mold assembly and left to cool. The finished vessel required no more carving.

The decoration of the vessels developed through the years. Early designs had a narrow band of geometric designs, and later designs had complex patterns covering the entire vessel. Often the design included stylized dragons, birds, or snakes. Inscriptions of ancient script were also cast into vessels, with inlaid gold and silver adding contrasting color to the designs.

Both the direct-casting process and the intricacy of the design added to the excellence of Chinese bronzes.

54. This passage mainly discusses the
(A) excellence of Chinese bronze vessels
(B) techniques of producing bronze
(C) types of decorations on bronze vessels
(D) time period of the use of bronze vessels

55. It can be inferred from this passage that
(A) commoners shared in worship services with the elite
(B) Chinese script was understood by most people
(C) dragons, birds, and snakes were feared
(D) the direct-casting process is superior to cold-working the alloy

56. The earliest bronzes were made
(A) before 1523 B.C.
(B) between 1523 B.C. and 1028 B.C.
(C) just after 1028 B.C.
(D) around 220 A.D.

57. Around 1525 B.C., bronze vessels probably were used most commonly
(A) in private family rituals
(B) for drinking wine
(C) in official ceremonies
(D) as common eating bowls

58. Which of the following was not used in design?
(A) Writing
(B) Landscapes
(C) Animals
(D) Precious metals

59. What must happen to all vessels before they are complete?
(A) The gold and silver must be inlaid.
(B) The negative image must be carved.
(C) The alloy in the mold must have cooled.
(D) The ancient inscriptures must be cast.

60. What does "band" mean in line 14?
(A) A musical group
(B) A picture of ancient instruments
(C) A complete covering
(D) A strip around the edge

THIS IS THE END OF SECTION 3. IF YOU FINISH BEFORE YOUR TIME IS UP, CHECK YOUR WORK ON SECTION 3 ONLY. DO NOT READ OR WORK ON ANY OTHER SECTION OF THE TEST. **STOP**

Answer Key for Practice Test V

SECTION 1: LISTENING COMPREHENSION

Part A

1. C	**6.** D	**11.** B	**16.** D
2. C	**7.** A	**12.** A	**17.** A
3. B	**8.** D	**13.** C	**18.** B
4. D	**9.** B	**14.** A	**19.** C
5. C	**10.** C	**15.** C	**20.** A

Part B

21. D	**26.** B	**31.** D
22. A	**27.** C	**32.** A
23. B	**28.** D	**33.** B
24. D	**29.** A	**34.** B
25. C	**30.** B	**35.** D

Part C

36. B	**41.** A	**46.** C
37. B	**42.** C	**47.** D
38. B	**43.** A	**48.** C
39. D	**44.** D	**49.** B
40. C	**45.** D	**50.** A

SECTION 2: STRUCTURE AND WRITTEN EXPRESSION

1. A	**11.** B	**21.** D	**31.** D
2. D	**12.** A	**22.** B	**32.** A
3. C	**13.** C	**23.** C	**33.** B
4. B	**14.** D	**24.** A	**34.** A
5. B	**15.** C	**25.** C	**35.** D
6. A	**16.** A	**26.** B	**36.** C
7. D	**17.** C	**27.** A	**37.** C
8. C	**18.** C	**28.** B	**38.** C
9. B	**19.** D	**29.** D	**39.** B
10. D	**20.** D	**30.** A	**40.** A

SECTION 3: VOCABULARY AND READING COMPREHENSION

1. A
2. B
3. D
4. D
5. A
6. C
7. D
8. A
9. C
10. B
11. A
12. C
13. A
14. D
15. C
16. D
17. B
18. A
19. D
20. D
21. B
22. A
23. C
24. C
25. B
26. B
27. C
28. D
29. C
30. A
31. D
32. B
33. A
34. B
35. C
36. C
37. D
38. C
39. A
40. B
41. C
42. B
43. C
44. D
45. C
46. B
47. A
48. C
49. B
50. A
51. C
52. D
53. A
54. A
55. D
56. A
57. C
58. B
59. C
60. D

Score Analysis Form for Practice Test V

Directions: Count the number of answers you have correct in Practice Test V, using the answer key on page 600. Then use the chart on page 49 (short form) to figure out your converted score range. Fill in the rest of this form so you can compare it to your scores in the previous practice tests.

	RAW SCORE	CONVERTED SCORE RANGE (each)	APPROXIMATE SCORE RANGE (each)
Listening Comprehension	____	____–____ × 10 = ____–____	÷ 3 = ____–____
Structures and Written Expression	____	____–____ × 10 = ____–____	÷ 3 = ____–____
Vocabulary and Reading Comprehension	____	____–____ × 10 = ____–____	÷ 3 = ____–____
TOTAL APPROXIMATE SCORE (add 3 approximate scores)			____–____

What is your best section out of the above three? ______________________

ANALYSIS OF EACH SECTION

1. Listening Comprehension

	Number Correct	Total	Percent Correct
Part A (Questions 1–20)	______	÷ 20	= ______%
Part B (Questions 21–35)	______	÷ 15	= ______%
Part C (Questions 36–50)	______	÷ 15	= ______%

Which part has the highest percentage of correct answers? __________

2. *Structure and Written Expression*

	Number Correct	Total	Percent Correct
Sentence Completion (Questions 1–15)	______	÷ 15	= ______%
Error Correction (Questions 16–40)	______	÷ 25	= ______%

Which part has the highest percentage of correct answers? __________

3. *Vocabulary and Reading Comprehension*

	Number Correct	Total	Percent Correct
Vocabulary (Questions 1–30)	______	÷ 30	= ______%
Reading (Questions 31–60)	______	÷ 30	= ______%

Which part has the highest percentage of correct answers? __________

Now that you have taken all the practice tests, turn to page 000 and fill in the Self-Evaluation Checklist 2. Then turn back to pages 000–000 and compare your responses to Checklist 1 to see if your test-taking strategies and TOEFL skills have improved.

SELF-EVALUATION CHECKLIST 2

Directions: Complete this checklist after you have taken Test V, the Post Test. Read each statement and circle the number of the response that you feel is most true. Do not spend very much time on any particular statement, but mark the first response you think of. Be honest. You are the only person to see the results.

Circle your answers based on Listening Comprehension only.

Key: 1 = Never 2 = Rarely 3 = Sometimes 4 = Usually 5 = Always

1. I understood what the speaker said. 1 2 3 4 5
2. I read the four choices in Part A and B before I heard the tape. 1 2 3 4 5
3. I stopped thinking about a difficult question in order to focus on the next question. 1 2 3 4 5

Circle your answers based on Structure and Written Expression only.

4. I paid more attention to the grammar than to the meaning of each word. 1 2 3 4 5
5. I used my knowledge of testing points to help me choose the answer. 1 2 3 4 5
6. I didn't spend time trying to correct the incorrect words in the Error Identification part; I just identified them. 1 2 3 4 5

Circle your answers based on Vocabulary and Reading Comprehension only.

7. I paid close attention to the context of the vocabulary words before I marked the answers, even if the vocabulary words were familiar to me. 1 2 3 4 5
8. I paid close attention to the first and last sentences of the reading passages. 1 2 3 4 5
9. I used techniques of skimming and scanning to help me find answers quickly. 1 2 3 4 5

Circle your answers based on General Strategies.

10. I left difficult questions unanswered and went back to them later. 1 2 3 4 5

11. I guessed at answers when I didn't know them. 1 2 3 4 5

12. I filled in all the answer blanks even if I didn't know the answers. 1 2 3 4 5

Add all your circled numbers.
YOUR TOTAL SCORE: ______
Total possible score: 60.

What Does Your Score Mean?

Compare this score with your score from Checklist 1 on pages 53–54. If your score is higher, it means that you have learned better test-taking strategies. Good for you! The authors of this book hope you do well on the TOEFL!

Explanatory Answers

SECTION 1: LISTENING COMPREHENSION

Part A

1. You'll miss the train unless you hurry.
(A) The train is early.
(B) You missed the train.
(C) You must hurry.
(D) You hurry too much.

(C) Glance at the choices and summarize: you, hurry, train.
Testing point: inference. "You'll miss the train unless you hurry" implies "you must hurry, or you will be late for the train."

2. We all think Grandma should take it easy after her fall.
(A) Grandma should enjoy the weather this fall.
(B) Grandma should walk slowly so she doesn't fall.
(C) Because of her fall, Grandma should rest more.
(D) Since Grandma did so much work in the fall, she should rest this winter.

(C) Glance at the choices and summarize: Grandma, fall, because, since.
Testing point 1: restatement/idiom. "Take it easy" means "rest."
Testing point 2: vocabulary. "Fall" means "drop down to the ground."

3. By the time John gets to the party, the director will have already gone.
(A) John has already left for the party.
(B) John will arrive after the director has left.
(C) John will leave before the director comes.
(D) The director has already gone to the party.

(B) Glance at the choices and summarize: John, party, director.
Testing point: restatement/structure. "By the time John gets to the party, the director will have already gone" means "the director will get to the party before John, and he will leave before John arrives." The verb is in the future perfect tense.

4. Sandra finished the work in no time at all.
(A) Sandra didn't have enough time to finish the work.
(B) There was no clock in Sandra's room.
(C) It took more time than she thought to finish.
(D) Sandra finished the work quickly.

(D) Glance at the choices and summarize: Sandra, work, time.
Testing point: restatement/idiom. "In no time" means "quickly."

5. There is a door for the handicapped in the rear.
(A) The front door is for the handicapped only.
(B) You can use the back door if the front door is locked.
(C) The disabled can use the back door if necessary.
(D) I left your cap by the red door.

(C) Glance at the choices and summarize: front door, back door, handicapped.
Testing point 1: restatement/vocabulary. "Door . . . in the rear" means "back door." The word "handicapped" means "disabled people." This sentence infers that there is a special door that is wide enough for a wheelchair or a door that does not have stairs in front of it.

6. One student presented a project that was discussed by the whole class.
(A) Representing the entire class, the student gave a talk.
(B) The class discussed whether or not the project should be presented.
(C) The class didn't like the student's project.
(D) The class discussed the student's project.

(D) Glance at the choices and summarize: class, student, project.
Testing point: restatement. "One student presented . . . was discussed by . . . class" is the same as "the class discussed the student's project."

7. Jenny once dreamed of being an Olympic gold medal winner in gymnastics.
(A) At one time, Jenny wished she could be an Olympic winner.
(B) Jenny almost won the gold medal in gymnastics.
(C) Jenny used to be a very good gymnast.
(D) Jenny took part in the gymnastics event in the Olympics.

(A) Glance at the choices and summarize: Jenny, gymnast, Olympics.
Testing point 1: restatement/idiom. "Once dreamed of being . . ." means "at one time in the past, Jenny wished . . ."
Testing point 2: vocabulary. "Gold medal" refers to the highest award given.

8. You're on the right track.
(A) You have to move to the left.
(B) Watch out! The track is on your right.
(C) If you continue on the right side, you'll get there.
(D) You are doing all right, so far.

(D) Glance at the choices and summarize: you, left, right.
Testing point: restatement/idiom. "To be on the right track" means "to be doing the right thing." "So far" means "up to this time."

9. Mr. Wilson is wealthy enough to retire.
(A) Mr. Wilson retired when he got rich.
(B) Mr. Wilson could stop working, because he has enough money.
(C) Rich people don't have to work anymore.
(D) Health is more important than wealth.

(B) Glance at the choices and summarize: Mr. Wilson, work, retired, rich.
Testing point 1: restatement/vocabulary. "Retire" means "stop working."
Testing point 2: vocabulary. "Wealthy enough" is the same as "has enough money."

10. Black clothes are not as fit to wear in summer as white clothes.
(A) The black clothes fit you better than the white clothes.
(B) The white clothes fit you better than the black clothes.
(C) It's more appropriate to wear white clothes than black clothes in the summertime.
(D) Your black clothes have gotten too tight to wear in the summer.

(C) Glance at the choices and summarize: black clothes, white clothes, comparative.
Testing point 1: restatement/vocabulary.
The verb "to be fit" means "to be appropriate" or "to be proper."
Testing point 2: comparative. "Black clothes are not as fit to wear in summer as white clothes" implies "it's more appropriate to wear white clothes than black clothes in the summertime."

11. The design was complete, but the construction had just begun.
(A) They resigned their jobs.
(B) They were starting to build.
(C) They finished the plans early.
(D) They were beginning to work the design.

(B) Glance at the choices and summarize: job, starting, finished.
Testing point 1: restatement/structure. The past perfect tense "had just begun" means "they were starting."
Testing point 2: vocabulary. "Construction" means "building."

12. The asteroids were large enough to be called small planets.
(A) The asteroids were large.
(B) They were large planets.
(C) They were too small to be called planets.
(D) Planets are all small.

(A) Glance at the choices and summarize: planets, large, small.
Testing point: restatement. Don't be confused by "to be called small planets." The asteroids were still large. The sentence implies that asteroids are usually smaller than planets, but in this case the asteroids were very large.

13. If you do this part, I'll take care of the rest.
(A) You should do more because I have to rest.
(B) I will cook the rice if you cook everything else.
(C) I will do everything that you don't do.
(D) Since you have to rest, I will prepare everything.

(C) Glance at the choices and summarize: do, everything.
Testing point 1: restatement/idiom. "I'll take care of . . ." means "I'll do . . ."
Testing point 2: vocabulary. "The rest" means "everything else."

14. His determination to do what seemed impossible was the key to his success.
(A) His determination was the most important reason that he succeeded.
(B) He was determined to get the key.
(C) It was impossible for him to be successful.
(D) He was difficult to work with.

(A) Glance at the choices and summarize: determination, successful, difficult.
Testing point: vocabulary. "Key to something" means "the most important reason or information about something."

15. Classes in computer science are becoming overcrowded.
(A) The computer room is very crowded.
(B) Computer science has been applied to many fields.
(C) Many people are studying computer science.
(D) Computer technology is developing very quickly.

(C) Glance at the choices and summarize: computer science, many.
Testing point: inference/vocabulary. "Overcrowded" means "too many people." If the classes are overcrowded, it means that many people are studying computer science.

16. I want it, no matter what it costs.
(A) I want to know what it costs.
(B) I want to buy a coat that fits me.
(C) I want it, but it's too expensive.
(D) I'll buy it at any price.

(D) Glance at the choices and summarize: cost, fit, expensive.
Testing point: restatement. "No matter what it costs" means "I don't care what it costs."

17. My uncle is a well-known lecturer.
(A) My uncle is a famous speaker.
(B) I've heard my uncle's lectures.
(C) My uncle's lecture was excellent.
(D) I don't know my uncle very well.

(A) Glance at the choices and summarize: uncle, lecture, speaker.
Testing point 1: restatement/vocabulary. "Well-known" means "famous."
Testing point 2: vocabulary. A lecturer is a speaker.

18. George dropped the class because of a schedule conflict.
(A) George stopped going to class, because he didn't like it.
(B) George couldn't take the class, since he had another class at the same time.
(C) The class was about conflicts of schedule.
(D) George needed another class in his busy schedule.

(B) Glance at the choices and summarize: George, class, schedule.
Testing point 1: restatement/vocabulary. "To drop a class" means "to decide not to take a class after signing up for that class."
Testing point 2: vocabulary. "Schedule conflict" means "another class or activity at the same time."

19. We couldn't have gone to the beach on a better day.
(A) We should have gone to the beach on a warmer day.
(B) Today was not a good day for me to go to the beach.
(C) The weather is just right for the beach today.
(D) This beach is not good enough to go to.

(C) Glance at the choices and summarize: beach, weather.
Testing point: inference. "We couldn't have . . . on a better day" implies "the weather is just perfect" or "the weather could not be better; it is the best."

20. I'm working as fast as I can.
(A) I can't work any faster.
(B) I will work faster.
(C) I am not able to work.
(D) It's bad to work too fast.

(A) Glance at the choices and summarize: work, faster.
Testing point: inference. "I'm working as fast as I can" implies "I can't work any faster."

Part B

21. Man: What do you think the boss will do when we tell him the bad news?
Woman: Oh, you can never tell with him!
What does the woman mean?
(A) She will not say what the boss will do.
(B) The boss will not do anything.
(C) Don't tell the boss the bad news.
(D) She doesn't know what he will do.

(D) Glance at the choices and summarize: she, boss. Testing point: idiom. "You can never tell" means "no one knows."

22. Man: Well, I'll be leaving now.
Woman: Must you go so soon?
How does the woman feel?
(A) She wants him to stay longer.
(B) She wishes he had left sooner.
(C) She knows he must go soon.
(D) She wants him to go now.

(A) Glance at the choices and summarize: she, longer, sooner, go.
Testing point: inference. "Must you go so soon?" can also be stated as "Do you have to leave now?" This woman's response implies "Please stay longer."

23. Woman: Would you like this gift-wrapped?
Man: Thanks, I would.
Where does this conversation take place?
(A) In a post office
(B) In a department store
(C) At a bank
(D) In a grocery store

(B) Glance at the choices and summarize: location. Testing point: location. Among the four choices, "in a department store" is the most likely place, since department stores in the U.S. will often wrap the merchandise you buy as a gift. Post offices, grocery stores, and banks never wrap gifts.

24. Man: How long do you think it will take to finish this job?
Woman: Offhand, I'd say three hours.
What does the woman mean?
(A) Three hours if working by hand
(B) A minimum of three hours
(C) Three hours at the maximum
(D) Three hours, more or less

(D) Glance at the choices and summarize: three hours.
Testing point: idiom. "Offhand" means "more or less."

25. Woman: I'm sorry. The class is full.
Man: Well, could I be put on the waiting list?
What does the man imply?
(A) He wants to wait until the class is full.
(B) He will wait for the list.
(C) He hopes someone will drop the class.
(D) He is late and there are no more chairs.

(C) Glance at the choices and summarize: he, wait, class.
Testing point: inference. "Could I be put on the waiting list?" means "May I add my name to a list of people that you might take in the class later?" The man hopes that someone will drop (leave) the class so that there is room for him.

26. Man: What time do we have to check out of the room?
Woman: I'm not sure. Let's ask at the front desk.
What does the woman mean?
(A) She doesn't know if the library is open.
(B) She doesn't know what time they must leave the hotel.
(C) She doesn't know how much they must pay.
(D) She doesn't know what food to order.

(B) Glance at the choices and summarize: she doesn't know, library, hotel, pay.
Testing point 1: idiom. "Check out" means "pay for the room and leave."
Testing point 2: inference. "I'm not sure" means "I don't know." She implies that she doesn't know what time they must leave.

27. Man: Would you like to go have coffee?
Woman: Thanks, but I have some work I have to catch up on.
What does the woman mean?
(A) He should go first, and she will catch up to him later.
(B) She will go have coffee and then do her work.
(C) She will do her work instead of having coffee.
(D) She will do her work at the coffee house.

(C) Glance at the choices and summarize: she, work, coffee.
Testing point: idiom. "Catch up on" means "to have some work that is not finished yet." She implies that she must finish her work, so she can not stop to go drink coffee someplace.

28. Woman: How much is a dorm room?
Man: It's $500 a month for room and board.
What do you get for $500?
(A) A room with a balcony
(B) A room with two beds
(C) A room and transportation
(D) A room and meals

(D) Glance at the choices and summarize: room.
Testing point: idiom. "Room and board" means "room and meals."

29. Woman: May I try these clothes on?
Man: Yes, but no more than three items are allowed in the dressing room.
Where does this conversation take place?
(A) In a clothes store
(B) In a shoe store
(C) In a gymnasium
(D) At a swimming pool

(A) Glance at the choices and summarize: location.
Testing point: location. "Try these clothes on" indicates "in a clothes store." In a shoe store, you would try on shoes, not clothes. In a gym or pool area, you would "put on," not "try on."

30. Woman: I'm really angry at John. He never listens to me.
Man: Take it easy, Ellen. Things will work out.
What does the man imply?
(A) Go to the gym and work out.
(B) Be calm and patient.
(C) Listen carefully to John.
(D) Do the easiest thing.

(B) Glance at the choices and summarize: work out, calm, the easiest.
Testing point: idiom. "Take it easy" means "relax," "be calm," or "don't get upset."

31. Man: Would you like chocolate or butter brickle ice cream?
Woman: You choose. I like them both.
What does the woman mean?
(A) She has a strong opinion.
(B) She likes the man a lot.
(C) She wants to choose.
(D) She doesn't care which kind they get.

(D) Glance at the choices and summarize: she, likes, chooses.
Testing point: inference. "You choose, I like them both" implies "she doesn't care which kind she gets."

32. Man: Did you hear that Ann got laid off?
Woman: No, that's terrible.
What do we learn about Ann?
(A) She lost her job.
(B) She mislaid her money.
(C) She got divorced.
(D) She's in the hospital.

(A) Glance at the choices and summarize: she, lost job, divorced.
Testing point: idiom. "Laid off" means "lost her job" or "got fired from her job."

33. Woman: Have you called Pete yet?
Man: I'll call him as soon as I get home.
What does the man mean?
(A) He will call Pete before he goes home.
(B) He will call Pete after he gets home.
(C) He called Pete at home.
(D) He will call Pete tomorrow.

(B) Glance at the choices and summarize: he, call, Pete.
Testing point: restatement. "As soon as I get home" is similar to "after he gets home."

34. Man: Which kind of pie do you want?
Woman: I don't know. I like pumpkin as well as apple.
What does the woman mean?
(A) She doesn't want pumpkin or apple.
(B) She can't decide; she likes them both.
(C) She doesn't know the difference between pumpkin and apple pie.
(D) She likes pumpkin pie better than apple pie.

(B) Glance at the choices and summarize: she, both, pie.
Testing point: restatement. "I like pumpkin as well as apple" is the same as "I like them both in the same way."

35. Woman: How much is the bill?
Man: All in all, it comes to $54.00.
What does the man mean?
(A) Bill has to pay $54.
(B) It is a little more than $54.
(C) It is a little less than $54.
(D) The whole bill is $54.

(D) Glance at the choices and summarize: $54, less or more.
Testing point: idiom. "All in all" means "considering everything" or "the whole thing."

Part C

36. Who is probably speaking?
(A) A nurse
(B) A dentist
(C) A patient
(D) An assistant

(B) This is an inference question. Since the speaker begins by saying, "Now that I've extracted your tooth . . .," the best inference is that he is a dentist.

37. When is the man speaking?
(A) Just before pulling a tooth
(B) Just after pulling a tooth
(C) At a consultation about pulling a tooth
(D) While another person is pulling a tooth

(B) This is an inference question. The first sentence gives the answer. "Now that I've extracted your tooth . . ."

38. How long will the person's mouth be numb?
(A) For a half hour
(B) For a few hours
(C) Until tomorrow
(D) Until the swelling goes down

(B) This is a restatement question. The speaker says, "The numbness will wear off after a few hours." The word "numb" means that you cannot feel anything. We infer that the dentist gave an injection to the patient so that the patient could not feel the pain of pulling out the tooth. The phrase "wear off" means that the numb feeling will go away, and the person will feel things in the normal way.

39. What does he say is the most important thing to do?
(A) Rinse your mouth.
(B) Take aspirin.
(C) Sleep.
(D) Put ice on your cheek.

(D) This is a restatement question. The speaker says, "Now, the most important thing to remember is to apply ice to your cheek immediately when you get home."

40. When does he say to rinse with salt water?
(A) Tonight
(B) In a half hour
(C) Tomorrow
(D) In four or five hours

(C) This is a restatement question. The speaker says, "Tomorrow you should rinse your mouth . . ."

41. What does the speaker say about bleeding?
(A) It is normal.
(B) It should stop in a half hour.
(C) It is not bleeding.
(D) There will be a lot of bleeding.

(A) This is a restatement question. The speaker says, "A little bleeding is normal . . ."

42. What kind of person does the speaker seem to be?
(A) Angry
(B) Worried
(C) Helpful
(D) Excited

(C) This is an inference question. The speaker seems helpful when he says, "Call me anytime . . ."

43. Who is the speaker addressing?
(A) New students
(B) Returning students
(C) Faculty
(D) Staff

(A) This is a restatement question. The speaker begins by saying, ". . . I'd like to welcome all of you new students . . ."

44. What do the married student apartments not allow?
(A) Children
(B) Cooking
(C) Spouses
(D) Single students

(D) This is an inference question. The speaker says, "The married student apartments are for married students only." We can infer from this that no single students can live there. You can also answer this by elimination. The speaker mentions that children are allowed and that the apartments have kitchens. A spouse is the husband or wife of a married person, so this person must be allowed to live there.

45. Which place has no more room for students?
(A) Coed dorms
(B) Married student apartments
(C) The international houses
(D) Spanish House

(D) This is a restatement question. The speaker says, "I think that Spanish House is full . . ." The term "coed dorms" means that both men and women live in the same dormitory building.

46. What will the audience probably do next?
(A) Visit the housing they like.
(B) Move into the housing.
(C) Fill out forms.
(D) Buy a meal ticket.

(C) This is an inference question. The speaker ends by saying, "I'll pass out these applications now and answer your individual questions." From this we can infer that the listeners will fill out the forms.

47. How does the woman first describe the conference?
(A) It was exciting.
(B) It was lonely.
(C) It was dull.
(D) It was too busy.

(D) This is an inference question. The woman says, "I felt so rushed all the time." If she felt rushed, we can assume that she meant that she was very busy at the conference.

48. How long was the woman gone?
(A) Two days
(B) A week
(C) Three days
(D) A month

(C) This is a restatement question. The man says, "You spend all that money to fly away for three days . . ."

49. What was the most important part of the conference for the woman?
(A) Sorting through papers
(B) Meeting people
(C) Giving a presentation
(D) Getting a rest

(B) This is a restatement question. The woman says, "Actually, one of the best things about the conference was the people I talked to."

50. What will the woman do when she meets her new friend?
(A) Discuss her project.
(B) Have tea.
(C) Fly away for three days.
(D) Go to a conference.

(A) This is an inference question. The woman says, "We made plans to meet again next month to compare notes." From this statement we can infer that "compare notes" means that the woman will discuss her project.

SECTION 2: STRUCTURE AND WRITTEN EXPRESSION

1. Even though woodpeckers ________ as a nuisance to many people, they are actually helpful, since they feed on harmful insects.
(A) are seen
(B) which are seen
(C) being seen
(D) to be seen

(A) Testing point: passive voice. The active sentence would be "people see woodpeckers as . . ." The sentence should be ". . . woodpeckers are seen as . . ."

2. The first clock, made nearly a thousand years ago, had neither a face nor hands, ________ that rang each hour.
(A) it had bells
(B) rather than bells
(C) though bells
(D) but it had bells

(D) Testing point: conjunction using the word "but." The word "but" shows the connection between the two parts of the sentence. The sentence should read ". . . had neither . . . nor . . ., but it had . . ."

3. ________ on the floor of the ocean is a big farming industry.
(A) Oysters raising
(B) Oysters are raised
(C) The raising of oysters
(D) The oysters raised

(C) Testing point: noun phrase. The gerund "raising" forms a noun phrase. The sentence needs a noun phrase, not another sentence. Since the main verb is the word "is," the sentence should be "The raising of . . . is a . . . industry."

4. A barbershop ________ a red and white striped pole.
(A) what symbolizes
(B) is symbolized by
(C) is symbolized to
(D) was symbolized

(B) Testing point: passive voice/preposition. The sentence needs a passive voice verb which has to be present tense, because the subject is not an actor, and a general fact is being expressed.

5. ________ as beasts of burden by the Indians in the Andes Mountains.
(A) Using llamas
(B) Llamas are used
(C) Llamas use
(D) There are llamas

(B) Testing point: subject + verb/passive voice. The sentence needs a "subject + verb." Even if you don't know the word "llamas," you still can decide to use a passive voice by the clue word "as"; "be used as."

6. The moon, ________ no air around it, grows extremely hot in the daytime and extremely cold at night.
(A) which has
(B) has
(C) having had
(D) what has

(A) Testing point: adjective clause. The sentence needs a nonrestrictive clause to describe the moon, which must start with the word "which," not "what."

7. Even though they are not liquid, cottage cheese, sour cream, and yogurt are sold ________ liquid measurements.
(A) to
(B) for
(C) over
(D) by

(D) Testing point: preposition. "Sold by . . . measurements."

8. To plant rice, farmers, ________, set young plants in the mud.
(A) they wade with bare feet in the water
(B) water wading in their bare feet
(C) wading in the water in their bare feet
(D) whose bare feet wading in the water

(C) Testing point: adjective phrase. The sentence needs an adjective phrase, rather than a clause or another sentence. Use the commas as clues. The first comma indicates a phrase that can be omitted while still keeping a grammatically correct sentence. The next two commas indicate a phrase that can also be omitted from the sentence. It cannot be a clause (subject + verb). Answers (A) and (D) are incorrect, because they have subjects. Answer (B) is incorrect, because it is the wrong word order.

9. ________, farmers cut holes in the bark of maple trees.
(A) Maple syrup is collected
(B) To collect maple syrup
(C) The collection of maple syrup
(D) When collect maple syrup

(B) Testing point: infinitive. The sentence needs an infinitive phrase to show purpose. "To collect . . ." means "in order to collect . . ."

10. The boll weevil, an insect ________ cotton plants, is native to Central America.
(A) destroys
(B) to destroy
(C) has destroyed
(D) that destroys

(D) Testing point: adjective clause. The sentence needs a clause to describe the noun "insect." You must use "that" to begin the clause, because you can not use two main verbs in one sentence.

11. ________ humans, toads have tongues fastened at the front of their mouths, which allow them to catch insects.
(A) Not the same
(B) Unlike
(C) Except for
(D) Dislike

(B) Testing point: like/unlike. "Unlike" is a comparative form used before a noun. The sentence should be "Unlike . . ., toads have . . ."

12. ________ on a hot fire is a delicacy in many parts of the world.
(A) Lamb roasted
(B) Roasted
(C) Lambs roast
(D) Lambs

(A) Testing point: noun + participle. The sentence needs a noun and an adverbial phrase to be the main subject. The sentence should read "Lamb roasted on . . . is a . . ." It means the same as "lamb that is roasted . . ." The main subject must be "lamb," an uncountable (mass) noun, because the verb is singular; "is."

13. ________ determines a good meal varies from country to country.
(A) Which
(B) Why
(C) What
(D) How

(C) Testing point: "wh" word as subject. The main verb is "varies." The sentence should read "What determines a . . . varies . . ."

14. ________, the pecan is the second most popular nut in the United States.
(A) The rich food
(B) Food is rich
(C) To be rich
(D) A rich food

(D) Testing point: adjective phrase. "A rich food" is an appositive of the subject noun "the pecan." An appositive is a phrase or word that renames a noun or describes a noun.

15. More ivory is obtained from elephants in Africa ________ elephants in Asia.
(A) rather than
(B) more than
(C) than from
(D) as well as

(C) Testing point: comparative. The sentence should be "More . . . is obtained from . . . than from . . ."

16. One of the most important <u>discovery</u> (A) of the nineteenth century <u>was</u> (B) a method <u>of using</u> (C) natural gas for cooking and <u>heating</u> (D).

(A) Testing point: singular/plural noun. After the phrase "one of the most," the noun must be plural. The correct sentence should be "One of the most important discoveries of . . ."

17. The Netherlands, a country with <u>much of the</u> (A) land <u>lying</u> (B) lower than sea level, <u>have</u> (C) a system of dikes and canals <u>for controlling</u> (D) water.

(C) Testing point: verb agreement. Even though the country "The Netherlands" ends with an "s," it is singular. The correct sentence is "The Netherlands, a country . . ., has a system of . . ." This is similar to "the United States is . . ."

18. Davy Crockett, a <u>famed</u> (A) American pioneer, was <u>known for</u> (B) his hunting, trapping, <u>tell stories</u> (C), and <u>quick wit</u> (D).

(C) Testing point: parallel construction. The correct sentence should be ". . . hunting, trapping, storytelling, and quick wit." In this way, all the parallel words are written as noun forms.

19. The <u>movement of</u> (A) ocean waves <u>can be compared</u> (B) to the waves <u>caused by</u> (C) the wind in a <u>field or grass</u> (D).

(D) Testing point: conjunction. The word "or" is incorrect, because "field" and "grass" refer to the same thing. The word "a" is a clue. The word "a" refers to one thing: a field <u>of</u> grass.

20. Milk, often considered a <u>nearly perfect</u> (A) food, <u>contains</u> (B) <u>fat</u> (C), <u>sweet</u> (D), and protein.

(D) Testing point: wrong word. The word "sweet" should be changed to "sugar." "Sweet" is usually used as an adjective. When the word "sweet" is used as a noun, it means "candy" or something sweet to eat. This sentence needs a word that describes something that food is composed of, not something to eat.

21. Only after they <u>themselves</u> (A) <u>become</u> (B) parents, <u>do</u> (C) people realize the difficulties <u>of raised</u> (D) children.

(D) Testing point: word form. After the preposition "of," a noun form must be used. The gerund "raising" would be correct in this sentence.

22. Aviators (A), fishing (B), and sailors are among those who (C) rely on (D) weather predictions.

(B) Testing point: wrong word. The first three main words are all the same parts of speech (nouns), but "fishing" is an activity and the others are people. The correct word is "fishermen."

23. Mohandas K. Gandhi, who was called Mahatma, lived a noble life of fasting (A) and poverty (B) in order to work for peaceful (C) and independence (D).

(C) Testing point: parallel construction. After the word "for," a noun must be used here. The word "peace" is the correct form. The word "independence" is already correct as another noun. There is no way to change "independence" to another correct form.

24. Soybean (A), which sometimes (B) grow seven feet tall, have (C) thick, woody (D) stems.

(A) Testing point: the subject must be plural, because the verb is "have." The correct sentence is "Soybeans, which . . ., have thick, woody stems."

25. When settling (A) the old west in pioneer times (B), American families building (C) their homes from split (D) logs.

(C) Testing point: verb tense. This sentence should be in the past tense, because it begins with "when settling . . . in pioneer times." The verb should be "built." Even if the sentence were not in the past tense, the verb "building" would be incorrect.

26. A Venus' Flytrap is a (A) small plant that have (B) leaves that snap (C) together like (D) traps.

(B) Testing point: verb agreement. Since the subject is singular: ". . . Flytrap . . .," the verb must be "has."

27. *The Last of the Mohicans* are (A) a (B) famous book about frontier (C) life by the (D) American author James Fenimore Cooper.

(A) Testing point: verb agreement. The name of the book is *The Last of the Mohicans*. It is one name, a singular noun, so the verb must be "is."

28. The Treaty of Ghent, signed in (A) 1814, ends (B) the (C) last (D) war between England and the United States.

(B) Testing point: verb tense. The sentence is referring to a past event, so the verb must be in the past tense. The correct verb is "ended."

29. In the year 500, ancient Greece was reaching (A) its highest level of (B) civilization, with great achievements in the fields of art (C), architecture, politic (D), and philosophy.

(D) Testing point: parallel construction/word form. The word "politic" should be "politics." The word "politics" is a noun that refers to the science of government. The word "politic" is an adjective that means "showing good judgment." This sentence needs a noun to fit with "architecture" and "philosophy."

30. A fever, the elevations (A) of body temperature above 98.6° F, is considered (B) to be (C) a symptom of a disorder rather than a disease in itself (D).

(A) Testing point: singular/plural noun. Since the sentence begins with the singular noun, "a fever," the next word that describes it must also be singular. The correct sentence is "A fever, the elevation of body temperature . . ."

31. Lacrosse is a ballgame played on (A) a field (B) outdoors (C) similar (D) soccer.

(D) Testing point: omission of word. After the word "similar," you must have the word "to." The correct sentence is "Lacrosse is . . . similar to soccer."

32. The manufactural (A) of ice cream in the United States on (B) a commercial (C) scale (D) began in 1851.

(A) Testing point: word form. The sentence needs a noun to begin it. The correct sentence is "The manufacture of ice cream . . . began in 1851."

33. People with two family members (A) which (B) suffer heart attacks before fifty-five are likely to (C) have early heart attacks themselves (D).

(B) Testing point: adjective clause. The word "which" is incorrect, because the clause refers to family members. For people, the word must be "who." The correct sentence is, "People with two family members who suffer . . . are likely to . . ."

34. Children's games, which are amusements involve (A) more than one individual, appear (B) to be a cultural (C) universal (D).

(A) Testing point: word form. The word "involve" should be "involving," because it begins a phrase describing "amusements." The correct sentence is "Children's games, which are amusements involving more than one . . ., appear to be . . ." The word "universal" can be an adjective or a noun. In this sentence it is a correct noun meaning "a general, predictable concept."

35. During times of war, political groups will sometimes kidnap foreign diplomats and keep (A) them as hostages (B) until the government meets (C) certain demanding (D).

(D) Testing point: word form. The last word of this sentence must be a noun form, because it is an object of the verb "meets." The correct sentence is, ". . . until the government meets certain demands."

36. The first year of a child's life is (A) characterized (B) in (C) rapid physical (D) growth.

(C) Testing point: preposition. After "characterized," you must use the preposition "by."

37. A fair (A) trial (B) is guarantee (C) by the (D) American Constitution.

(C) Testing point: passive voice. The verb is "is guaranteed." One clue to this are the words, "by the . . ." The active sentence would be "The American Constitution guarantees a fair trial."

38. Since ancient times, (A) water from rivers and smaller (B) streams are (C) used for (D) irrigation.

(C) Testing point: verb tense. A clue for this sentence is the word "since," which is often used with the present perfect tense. The correct sentence is "Since ancient times, water . . . has been used for irrigation."

39. Khaki is a cloth (A) made in linen (B) or cotton and dyed (C) a dusty (D) color.

(B) Testing point: preposition. The correct preposition is "of." The sentence should be "Khaki is a cloth made of linen . . ." The word "linen" refers to a type of cloth made from a fiber called "flax."

40. The symptom of leukemia include weakness, a general ill feeling, and fever.
(symptom = A, of = B, weakness = C, feeling = D)

(A) Testing point: singular/plural noun. Since the verb is "include," the noun must be plural. The correct sentence is "The symptoms of leukemia include . . ."

SECTION 3: VOCABULARY AND READING COMPREHENSION

1. Produce is commonly shipped across the United States in large crates.
- **(A)** wooden boxes
- **(B)** box cars
- **(C)** trucks
- **(D)** quantities

(A) A crate is any kind of large box made of slats of wood, usually used for shipping or packing things to be stored.

2. Because of the baby boom of the 1980s, preschools in the U.S. have proliferated.
- **(A)** changed in philosophy
- **(B)** increased in numbers
- **(C)** become more crowded
- **(D)** become more expensive

(B) To proliferate means to grow rapidly by multiplying. It can also mean to reproduce.

3. Even though he was obese, Oliver Hardy gained fame as a comedian.
- **(A)** dying
- **(B)** crazy
- **(C)** unhappy
- **(D)** fat

(D) Obese means very fat.

4. Crimes against property have risen in the U.S. and other urbanized countries.
- **(A)** rich
- **(B)** large
- **(C)** multicultural
- **(D)** metropolitan

(D) An urban area is a city area, as opposed to a country area.

5. Raccoons and dormice are examples of animals that hibernate several months of the year.
- **(A)** sleep
- **(B)** fast
- **(C)** lose hair
- **(D)** store food

(A) To hibernate is to sleep during the winter months of the year.

6. The California condor has become scarce during this century.
- **(A)** easily frightened
- **(B)** prone to disease
- **(C)** fewer in numbers
- **(D)** difficult to catch

(C) Something that is scarce is not common or not plentiful.

7. Charles Darwin and A.R. Wallace published their ideas on evolution simultaneously in 1858.
- **(A)** in the same book
- **(B)** for the same people
- **(C)** on the same topic
- **(D)** at the same time

(D) "Simultaneous" means "occurring or existing at the same time."

8. In coastal areas where there is an abundance of fish, the fishing industry prospers.
- **(A)** more than sufficient quantity
- **(B)** a wide variety
- **(C)** a unique type
- **(D)** a common diet

(A) "Abundance" means "plenty" or "a great deal of."

9. There is a common superstition that a ring around the moon means that rain will come soon.
(A) attitude
(B) speculation
(C) belief
(D) approach

(C) A superstition is a belief or attitude that is inconsistent with known laws.

10. Political refugees often find sanctuary in churches.
(A) happiness
(B) protection
(C) peace
(D) charity

(B) A sanctuary is a place of refuge or protection; a place that protects someone from receiving punishment.

11. Many pesticides are available for insects like termites and cockroaches.
(A) poisons
(B) deterrents
(C) sprays
(D) medicines

(A) A pesticide is an insect killer. The pesticide can come in the form of a spray. It is also a deterrent, but the word "deterrent" is not a synonym for "pesticide." It is a result of the use of a pesticide. A medicine is for curing someone or something. A pesticide is for killing.

12. Children like to play games in vacant lots.
(A) wooded areas
(B) schoolyards
(C) empty plots of ground
(D) open houses

(C) The word "vacant" means "empty." The word "lot" in this sentence refers to an area of land that has been set aside as a building site for a new home.

13. If you are going to be in a swamp area, you should take a mosquito repellent.
(A) marsh
(B) jungle
(C) savanna
(D) tropical

(A) A swamp is a piece of wet, spongy land; a marsh.

14. Ralph Nader is an advocate of consumer rights.
(A) an opponent of
(B) a believer in
(C) a politician for
(D) a supporter of

(D) An advocate is a person who supports another person by speaking for them and for their beliefs.

15. A backyard swimming pool can be a hazard for small children.
(A) pleasure
(B) disaster
(C) danger
(D) thrill

(C) A hazard is anything that is dangerous or risky.

16. When the New York Giants lost the football game, the citizens of New York were abject.
(A) surprised
(B) disgusted
(C) relieved
(D) depressed

(D) "Abject" means "miserable." The closest meaning above is "depressed."

17. Canada is a vast country in terms of its area.
(A) except for
(B) with regard to
(C) in spite of
(D) because of

(B) Both "in terms of" and "with regard to" are used to focus on one aspect of something. In this case, the meaning is that Canada is vast (large) if one thinks about its area.

18. Tenzing Norkay and Sir Edmund Hillary were the first people to scale Mount Everest.
(A) climb
(B) camp on
(C) discover
(D) survive on

(A) "To scale" and "to climb" both mean to get to the top of the mountain by using ropes.

19. At a high temperature, evaporation is more rapid than at a lower temperature.
(A) increase in a liquid
(B) decreased energy of molecules
(C) change of a solid into a liquid
(D) change of liquid into vapor

(D) Water evaporates into steam as it boils.

20. A huge mountain chain in Europe is formed by linking the Alps, the Pyrenees, the Balkans, the Caucasus, and the Carpathians.
(A) dividing
(B) surpassing
(C) surrounding
(D) joining

(D) "To link" is to attach things together with chains, loops, or rings. In this sentence, it means "connect" or "join."

21. John Foster Dulles achieved recognition in the U.S. as an international lawyer in the 1930s.
(A) fought for
(B) gained
(C) wrote about
(D) chose

(B) "To achieve" usually means "to accomplish something successfully." In this sentence, it also means "to get" or "to gain."

22. In 1936, Edward VIII renounced his title to the British throne to marry Wallis Warfield Simpson.
(A) gave up
(B) threw away
(C) let down
(D) put in

(A) "To renounce" is to "give up," usually with a formal public statement. In this sentence, the meaning is that Edward VIII announced that he would not be the king of England even though he was the person who was supposed to be the next king.

23. Many children looked emaciated during the drought.
(A) sick
(B) unhappy
(C) thin
(D) lonely

(C) "To be emaciated" is to be very thin because of starvation.

24. An increasing number of women in the 1980s delayed marriage and childbirth in order to launch their careers.
(A) postpone
(B) expand
(C) begin
(D) participate in

(C) "To launch" is to begin or start something new.

25. According to Carl Sagan, the Earth is a tiny and fragile world that needs to be cherished.
(A) explored
(B) valued
(C) unified
(D) developed

(B) "To cherish" is to take care of something carefully and tenderly, because it is of much value. We cherish the things that we love.

26. In certain areas of many cities, it is against the law to loiter.
(A) throw paper
(B) stand around
(C) join a mob
(D) carry a weapon

(B) "To loiter" is to either walk slowly, stopping often, or to stand around doing very little.

27. During the 1980s, women entered the work force in droves.
(A) seriously
(B) fervently
(C) in large numbers
(D) in management positions

(C) "Droves" refers to a large number or a group or a crowd of people together.

28. Taking some kinds of medicine will cause your body to retain fluids.
(A) sustain
(B) inject
(C) lose
(D) keep

(D) "Retain" means "to continue to have something" or "to hold or keep" something.

29. Down pillows are very popular.
(A) Floor
(B) Beanbag
(C) Feather
(D) Polyester

(C) "Down" is the name of the very soft and tiny feathers of a young bird, such as a duck or a goose.

30. In most public buildings, ramps are installed for handicapped people.
(A) sloped walkways
(B) safe handrails
(C) low telephones
(D) wide doorways

(A) A ramp is used for pushing or guiding something up a slope; it is often used instead of stairs or steps.

31. The word "primitive" in line 3 means
(A) mysterious
(B) singular
(C) ancient
(D) simple

(D) This is a vocabulary question. "Primitive" means "simple" or "undeveloped" or "in an early stage of development."

32. According to this passage, scientists are puzzled about
(A) why we see a cloud of dust and gas
(B) how quickly the central part of the comet turns
(C) what the tail consists of
(D) when Halley will return

(B) This is a restatement question. The passage states, ". . . scientists still can't decide how fast Halleys' nucleus spins."

33. The passage implies that many scientists think that Halley's comet is
(A) strange-looking
(B) misunderstood
(C) dirty
(D) dying

(A) This is an inference question. The passage says that the comet is "one of the oddest-looking objects in the solar system." The word "odd" means "strange."

34. It is easiest to see Halley when
(A) it is dead
(B) it has less activity
(C) it is closer to the sun
(D) it is active

(B) This is a restatement question. The final sentence of the passage states, "It is easiest to get a clear look at the comet when it is far away from the sun so that its activity dies down." In this sentence "dies down" means "less."

35. The main appeal of CD's is their
(A) price
(B) size
(C) sound
(D) availability

(C) This is an inference question. The passage says that CD's have "surprisingly realistic sound." Since this is mentioned first, it is the best choice for "main appeal." Answer (A) is incorrect, because the price of CD's is more than the price of LP's, so that cannot be an appeal. Answer (B) is incorrect, since their size is mentioned as an additional appeal, not the main appeal. Answer (D) is incorrect, because their availability is not mentioned as being a main appeal. The passage only states that they are becoming more available.

36. The author refers to CD's as "sandwiches," because they
(A) are light
(B) are small
(C) are layered
(D) don't crackle

(C) This is an inference question. Since sandwiches are composed of two layers of bread with filling in between, you can infer that compact discs are also made up of layers.

37. This passage states that it is difficult to
(A) play a CD
(B) produce a CD
(C) record a CD
(D) destroy a CD

(D) This is a restatement question. The passage states that CD's are virtually indestructible. That means that it is almost impossible to destroy them.

38. According to the passage, many record stores are currently
(A) lowering CD prices
(B) raising LP prices
(C) lowering LP prices
(D) raising CD prices

(C) This is a restatement question. The passage says, "Many record stores are now cutting their prices on LP's . . ." The phrase "cut their price" means "lower their price."

39. According to this passage, which one of the following is true?
(A) Different kinds of stores are selling CD's.
(B) More CD's are available than LP's.
(C) Stores are selling more CD's than LP's.
(D) Stores are losing money on their LP's.

(A) This is a restatement question. The passage says, "CD's are becoming more widely available than LP's: they are sold in electronics and video stores that haven't formerly carried records or cassettes." The other answer choices are all false, according to this passage.

40. The author's main purpose is to
(A) tell how CD's are made
(B) discuss the growth of CD's
(C) compare CD's and LP's
(D) describe the technology that produces CD's

(B) This is an author's purpose question. You can infer answer (B) even though the main information about growth is given in the second paragraph, since all of the other answer choices are only discussed briefly.

41. The best title for this passage is
(A) Ancient Forests of the Northwest
(B) The US Forest Service
(C) The Harvesting of Old-Growth Timber
(D) The Wood-Based Economy of the Northwest

(C) Answer (C) is the best choice, since most of the passage is discussing old-growth timber. All the other answer choices are too general. The passage does not discuss any of them as much as it discusses answer (C).

42. According to this passage, conservationists would agree that
(A) old-growth trees are not necessary for the health of the forest
(B) fallen trees should not be taken away
(C) most of the old-growth trees do not need protection
(D) young trees should not be logged

(B) This is an inference question. The passage states that "both downed and standing old trees store and release nutrients necessary to younger trees." The words "downed trees" mean "trees that have fallen down." Answers (A) and (C) are incorrect, because they are the opposite of what the passage says. Answer (D) is incorrect, since the passage does not say how the conservationists feel about the young trees being logged. You might infer that they do not want the young trees logged (cut down), but you can't answer it "according to the passage."

43. The struggle is between
(A) Oregon and Washington
(B) Oregon and the U.S. Forest Service
(C) conservationists and the logging industry
(D) conservationists and the state of Oregon

(C) This is an inference question. The second paragraph is about the conservationists' feelings. The third paragraph is about the logging industry's feelings. The two points of view are opposite.

44. Before the 1800s
(A) there were six million trees
(B) old growth was not cut down
(C) the trees had more economic value
(D) there were more virgin forests

(D) This is a restatement question. The passage states, "There are now about 6 million acres of virgin forest . . . only about one-tenth of what existed before the 1800s."

45. Studies show that young trees gain nutrients from
(A) wildlife
(B) virgins
(C) old trees
(D) wood products

(C) This is a restatement question. The passage states, ". . . old trees store and release nutrients necessary to younger trees."

46. According to this passage the economy of the Northwest is dependent on
(A) the U.S. Forest Service
(B) harvesting trees
(C) ancient forests
(D) the forest ecosystem

(B) This is a restatement question. The passage states, ". . . much of the Northwest's economy is developed around the logging industry." The logging industry consists of "harvesting trees."

47. Because of the large demand for soapstone carvings in the 1970s
(A) a lot of poor quality art was for sale
(B) people were more enthusiastic
(C) the markets were empty
(D) artists worked indoors

(A) This is a restatement question. The passage states that "this demand had the effect of inundating the market with mediocre work." The word "inundating" means "flooding." In this sentence it means that there was a lot of art for sale. The word "mediocre" means "not very good" or "ordinary."

48. In the early 1980s
(A) more retail stores opened
(B) there was a renewed interest in Indian and Inuit art
(C) less art was sold
(D) the economy expanded

(C) This is a restatement question. The passage states, "These two factors resulted in slow sales." The words "slow sales" mean that they were not selling much art.

49. According to the passage, the quality of Indian and Inuit art has improved because of
(A) the rise in the sale of soapstone carvings
(B) new interest in their art
(C) the slow sales of the early 1980s
(D) the economic slump

(B) This is a restatement question. The passage states that "new enthusiasm . . . has stimulated higher quality work."

50. According to this author, "Inuit" refers to
(A) a native Canadian
(B) an Indian
(C) a soapstone artist
(D) a nonnative Canadian

(A) This is an inference question. It may be easiest to answer it by elimination. Answer (B) cannot be correct, since the passage says, "Inuit and Indian." Answer (C) cannot be correct, since the passage does not say that all Inuits are soapstone artists. Answer (D) cannot be correct, since the passage says, "Inuits have far more artists . . . than nonnative Canadians." Therefore, an Inuit must be a native Canadian.

51. Indians began selling their art
(A) in the 1970s
(B) in the early 1980s
(C) in the 17th century
(D) recently

(C) This is a restatement question. The passage states that "Indians have been selling their arts and crafts . . . as early as the 17th century."

52. According to this passage, both Inuit and Indians
(A) have no written language
(B) live in the snow
(C) are nonnative Canadians
(D) expressed their culture through art

(D) This is a restatement question. The passage says, ". . . they expressed their culture and beliefs through carvings, drawings, and baskets. Art became a way of life." Answer (A) was only true in the past. Answer (B) is only true in some times of the year. Answer (C) is the opposite of the truth; they are native Canadians.

53. The best title for this passage is
(A) New Interest in Indian and Inuit Art
(B) The Rise and Fall of Inuit Art
(C) Soapstone Carvings
(D) Indian vs. Inuit Art

(A) Answer (A) is the best choice, because the first sentence mentions the resurgence of interest in Indian and Inuit art. Answers (B) and (C) are too narrow; they only mention part of what was discussed. Answer (D) is incorrect, since the two kinds of art are not compared.

54. This passage mainly discusses the
(A) excellence of Chinese bronze vessels
(B) techniques of producing bronze
(C) types of decorations on bronze vessels
(D) time period of the use of bronze vessels

(A) The first sentence and the last sentence mention the excellence of ancient Chinese bronze casting. Answer choices (B) and (C) are mentioned as examples of the excellence.

55. It can be inferred from this passage that
(A) commoners shared in worship services with the elite
(B) Chinese script was understood by most people
(C) dragons, birds, and snakes were feared
(D) the direct-casting process is superior to cold-working the alloy

(D) This can be inferred from the statement, "Instead of cold-working the alloy to make the shapes and designs, they used a direct-casting process." We infer that this is a better process, since the whole passage is about the excellence of the method. Answer (A) is incorrect, because the opposite is inferred. There is no mention of anything to infer either (C) or (D).

56. The earliest bronzes were made
(A) before 1523 B.C.
(B) between 1523 B.C. and 1028 B.C.
(C) just after 1028 B.C.
(D) around 220 A.D.

(A) This is a restatement question. The passage states that the earliest bronzes predated the Shang dynasty (1523 B.C.–1028 B.C.). The word "predated" means "came before."

57. Around 1525 B.C., bronze vessels probably were used most commonly
(A) in private family rituals
(B) for drinking wine in official ceremonies
(C) in official ceremonies
(D) as common eating bowls

(C) This is an inference question. The passage states that "general use in state worship rituals by the ruling elite became common early in that period [Shang dynasty 1523 B.C.–1028 B.C.]." A worship ritual is an official ceremony.

58. Which of the following was not used in design?
(A) Writing
(B) Landscapes
(C) Animals
(D) Precious metals

(B) This is a negative question. You answer it by elimination. The passage mentions using inscriptions (writing), dragons, birds, and snakes (animals), and gold and silver (precious metals). There is no mention of landscapes.

59. What must happen to all vessels before they are complete?
(A) The gold and silver must be inlaid.
(B) The negative image must be carved.
(C) The alloy in the mold must have cooled.
(D) The ancient inscriptures must be cast.

(C) This is a restatement question. The passage states that "the hot molten alloy . . . was poured into the mold assembly and left to cool." Therefore, all vessels must be cooled. The other answer choices are necessary for some vessels only, not all vessels.

60. What does "band" mean in line 14?
(A) A musical group
(B) A picture of ancient instruments.
(C) A complete covering
(D) A strip around the edge

(D) The words "band" and "strip" both refer to a flat, thin piece of material covering something.

Tapescripts

Tapescripts for Listening Comprehension Tests

Pretest, pages 74–76

PART A: SENTENCES

TO THE READER: Read each sentence, pausing 12 seconds after each one.

1. It feels good to swim in the pool.
2. Be sure to pick up the litter when you leave.
3. I feel down in the dumps today.
4. If anyone can stick to her diet, Mary can!
5. Although I look ready to go, I haven't packed yet.

PART B: CONVERSATIONS

TO THE READER: Pause 12 seconds after each question.

6. *Man:* Isn't it a long drive to the camping site?

Woman: It's not too far, but the road is narrow and winding.

What does the woman mean?

7. *Man:* Excuse me, ma'am. I'd like to send some flowers to my friend.

Woman: O.K. We have this arrangement on sale today.

Where does this conversation take place?

8. *Woman:* Jim, you really did a good job on that report for the committee.

Man: I did?

What do we learn about the man?

9. *Woman:* It's too bad Tom couldn't go to the movie last night.

Man: But he did.

What does the man say about Tom?

10. *Man:* I've just heard the news!

Woman: Yes, I'm thrilled about getting accepted to the program!

How does the woman feel?

PART C: TALKS

Questions 11–15 are based on the following talk. (MALE VOICE)

Before we go on to our main discussion of the new dorm rules, I'd like to make an announcement. Since all of you are taking writing classes, you may be interested in the peace essay contest. This contest is sponsored by the U.S. Institute of Peace, which is an independent institution created and funded by Congress. The prizes are in the form of scholarships. First place is a scholarship of $5000, second place is $2500, and third place is $1000. Your essay must be no more than 1500 words long and it must focus on the significance of the recent international peace accord. I have some brochures that give

complete information on the contest and include application blanks. If you're interested, see me after the meeting.
TO THE READER: Pause 12 seconds after each question.

11. Which of the following applies to all of the people listening to this talk?
12. Who is the most likely speaker of this talk?
13. What is the main topic of this talk?
14. What will the speaker probably discuss next?
15. Where did this talk most likely occur?

Exercise 1, page 93

EXAMPLE:

He ate too much.

1. What a terrible mistake!
2. This book is up-to-date.
3. You should have finished your work on time.
4. The trip will take less time on the train than the bus.
5. Why not ask the manager for a refund?
6. *Man:* Will that be cash or charge?

Woman: I'd like to charge this dress.

Where does this conversation most likely take place?

7. *Man:* What's taking you so long?

Woman: Don't worry. I'll be ready in a minute.

What does the woman imply?

8. *Woman:* That was a great speech!

Man: Wasn't it!

How does the man feel about the speech?

9. *Woman:* Working on this play was fun!

Man: Seeing it was too.

What does the man mean?

10. *Woman:* I don't know why the buses aren't running today.

Man: But they are!

What does the man mean?

Drills 1 to 6, pages 133–138

DRILL 1: SENTENCES

TO THE READER: Pause 12 seconds after each sentence.

1. Can you tell me where the restroom is?
2. It seems less likely that David will catch a cold if he keeps exercising regularly.
3. Scratch paper and pencils are on the table next to the card catalog.

4. Tom's sister visited him in San Francisco last month.
5. Neither Bill nor Cindy cares about chocolate cake.
6. Shall we go to the park to relax for a while?
7. The doctor said Tony's earache was caused by the wind.
8. Judy didn't go to the machine shop to see if she got the new job.
9. Pat is doing her homework in the classroom where it's quiet.
10. All of Lisa's sculptures are great. I don't know which one to choose.

DRILL 2: SENTENCES

TO THE READER: Pause 12 seconds after each sentence.

1. Wearing flowers makes her more beautiful.
2. The project I just completed this quarter is a part of my thesis.
3. Two women were sent to the hospital after the car accident.
4. Scientists have spent over two decades studying acid rain.
5. We moved to Los Angeles from New York before our child was born last summer.
6. Gail examined the leaf with the microscope that belongs to Ann's group.
7. I was late to the seminar because I got lost on my way to the hotel.
8. Professor Smith graded the final in the morning, and posted the scores in the afternoon.
9. Sam was selected to be treasurer of the graduate association.
10. It is hard to remember every word if you read it only once.

DRILL 3: CONVERSATIONS

TO THE READER: Pause 12 seconds after each question.

1. *Man:* Did Joan take her umbrella today?

Woman: No. it's still downstairs.

What does the woman mean?

2. *Man:* It's hard to believe that Susan has already finished her homework.

Woman: Well, she copied Jack's homework and made a few changes.

What does the woman say about Susan?

3. *Woman:* Would you like to have a cup of tea?

Man: No, thanks. I just had some lemonade.

What did the man have?

4. *Woman:* How do you like the car I just bought?

Man: Well, it seems to run well, but I think it needs a new paint job.

What does the man think about the car?

5. *Man:* Would you take these books to the closet please?

Woman: Sure.

Where will the woman take the books?

6. *Man:* Did Pam sell her new painting?

Woman: No, but she is sure she can sell it any time she wants.

What does the woman imply?

7. *Woman:* I got my ticket at the travel agency near Broadway.

   Man: Oh. What time will you arrive at JFK airport?

   What do we learn from this conversation?

8. *Woman:* The space shuttle is taking off tomorrow.

   Man: I know. This is another routine mission; its first flight was six years ago.

   What are the man and woman discussing?

9. *Woman:* Party of two?

   Man: No, five. Three others are coming later.

   Where does this conversation take place?

10. *Woman:* There is no way around it.

    Man: Oh, yes, there is.

    What does the man mean?

DRILL 4: CONVERSATIONS

TO THE READER: Pause 12 seconds after each question.

1. *Woman:* Now it's your turn.

   Man: Thanks.

   What do we learn about the man?

2. *Man:* Are you free to meet now or would this afternoon be better?

   Woman: Either time is all right.

   What are the man and woman doing?

3. *Man:* May I speak to Alvin?

   Woman: Hang on just a minute, please.

   What does the woman mean?

4. *Woman:* What in the book interested you the most?

   Man: Nothing specific, but I liked it overall.

   What does the man mean?

5. *Woman:* Is it OK if I park here?

   Man: No, it's a driveway.

   What does the man mean?

6. *Man:* I told John to be here at 10:30.

   Woman: How come?

   What does the woman want to know?

7. *Man:* Could you tell me the scheduled departure for Chicago?

   Woman: At 15 minutes after each hour there is a bus leaving this station.

   Where does this conversation probably take place?

8. *Woman:* How do you like it cut?

Man: Not too short. Leave it long in front.

Where does this conversation probably take place?

9. *Man:* Are you going to apply to medical school this year?

Woman: I might, but it all depends on my test score.

What does the woman mean?

10. *Man:* Where is your savings account?

Woman: I don't have a savings account, but I have a checking account.

What are the two people discussing?

DRILL 5: TALKS

Questions 1–4 are based on the following conversation.

Man: Hi, Joanie. Where are you going?

Woman: Oh, hi, Paul. I'm on my way to the library.

Man: Oh yeah? I just wondered if you wanted to go to a movie with me.

Woman: I'd love to, but I can't. I can't believe this semester. I only have three classes, but in all of them I have lots of reading, term papers, reports, and essay exams. It's incredible! I feel like I'll never get through everything.

Man: That's terrible. I felt like that last year, but this semester seems easy now. I spend a lot of time in class, but most of it is in labs doing experiments. I don't have all those term papers this time. But can't I talk you into going to the show anyway? I've heard that the movie over at the East Auditorium is really good. It's a murder mystery.

Woman: Oh, now I'm sure I won't go. I might go to a comedy, but I hate to see murders!

TO THE READER: Pause 12 seconds after each question.

1. Where is the woman going?
2. How does the woman feel about her classes?
3. Which best describes the man's feeling about his classes?
4. Which best describes the woman's feelings about going to the movie?

Questions 5–8 are based on the following announcement.

(MALE VOICE)

Graduation ceremonies will be held on Saturday, June 10 this year. All graduating seniors must order their caps and gowns by May 15 in the Student Activities Office. The form will ask you for your height and your cap size. If you don't know your cap size, you can measure the widest part of your head just above your ears. The office has a tape measure for you to use. The rental fee for the caps and gowns is $15, and you must pay that fee when you submit your order blank. You will be able to pick up your caps and gowns a few days before the ceremony, and you must return them by 5 P.M. on June 10, right after the ceremony.

TO THE READER: Pause 12 seconds after each question.

5. What will happen on June 10?
6. Who must order caps and gowns?
7. What is this announcement mainly about?
8. What will the students do with their caps and gowns?

DRILL 6: TALKS

Questions 1–4 are based on the following talk.

(FEMALE VOICE)

During these last five minutes of class I'd like to remind you of the field trip on Thursday. Meet at 3 P.M. in the parking lot outside the gym so we can carpool. I handed out directions to the museum yesterday, so if you didn't get one, see me after class. I think you'll find that the exhibit complements our study of Impressionism. You'll see examples of art from the early period, around 1875, and up to the turn of the century. Don't forget to take notes for your reports. You need to turn them in by next Tuesday. Remember, you can either do an in-depth analysis of one painting or you can choose several to discuss and contrast. You should find the exhibit excellent. I was there last week and I thoroughly enjoyed it.

TO THE READER: Pause 12 seconds after each question.

1. What is the speaker's main purpose in this talk?
2. How will the students get to the museum?
3. What did the speaker do yesterday?
4. What period are the paintings from?

Questions 5–8 are based on the following talk.

(MALE VOICE)

While we're discussing the early part of this century, I'd like to spend a few moments on the National Park System. The U.S. Department of the Interior established the National Park Service in 1916 in order to consolidate the administration of the 37 national parks and monuments it had then. This new National Park Service was instructed by an act of Congress to conserve and protect the natural and historic objects so that they could be enjoyed by future generations. The parks were classified into four groups: natural, historical, recreational, and cultural areas. I'm sure that many of you have been to some of the most famous, like Yellowstone and the Grand Canyon, but did you know that we now have over 300 separate parks, monuments, sites, and memorials? Yellowstone, which was established back in 1872, is certainly beautiful, but so are the others. If you have time sometime, try visiting some of the less well-known parks, like Platt in Oklahoma, or Hot Springs in Arkansas. Our national park system is probably the most extensive in the world. It's an important part of our continuing history.

TO THE READER: Pause 12 seconds after each question.

5. What is the main idea of this talk?
6. What happened in 1872?
7. How many parks, monuments, and sites are there now?
8. What does the speaker suggest that people do?

Practice Test I, pages 359–380

Part A

Example 1:

Mary swam out to the island with her friend.

Example 2:

Would you mind helping me with this load of books?

TO THE READER: Pause twelve seconds after each question.

1. Is the airport located around here?
2. Send me the information as soon as possible.
3. Jane followed in her mother's footsteps by teaching disabled children.
4. The kids can go to school by foot.
5. Sam looks cool and confident.
6. It was a winding and muddy road.
7. Alan never neglects to rehearse before his performance.
8. Diane's allergy has gone from bad to worse.
9. It's going to be all right.
10. Did you two give up the class?
11. I'm sorry; I thought you were a friend of mine.
12. He acts like an adult, but he is only a junior high school student.
13. Dr. Stevenson will probably be elected as the department chair this year, won't she?
14. Are you sure you have a reservation for dinner?
15. Sam ordered cheese cake for dessert this time, although he likes apple pie better.
16. Often we learn more from failure than from success.
17. If he were not a dreamer, he wouldn't have gone this far.
18. Simon shouldn't expect to know everything on the test.
19. You know I don't like chocolate.
20. She recovered faster than the doctor predicted.

Part B

Example:

Man: Professor Smith is going to retire soon. What kind of gift shall we give her?

Woman: I think she'd like to have a photograph of our class.

What does the woman think the class should do?

TO THE READER: Read the sentences below. Pause twelve seconds after each question.

21. *Woman:* Thanks for the help.

Man: No problem.

What does the man mean?

22. *Woman:* I can't get through to this number.

Man: You must first dial one.

What do we learn from this conversation?

23. *Woman:* Did you mow the lawn?

Man: I had the neighbor boy take care of it.

What does the man mean?

24. *Woman:* Are there any dogs around?

Man: No, they're not allowed in this complex.

What do we learn from the conversation?

25. *Man:* This one is much cheaper.

Woman: But it may not last as long.

What does the woman imply?

26. *Man:* Did you ever get in touch with your friend?

Woman: No, when I called, all I got was a recorded message.

What did the woman do?

27. *Man:* Are you sure?

Woman: Of course I am.

What does the woman mean?

28. *Woman:* Could you OK this request for me?

Man: Sure, may I use your pen?

What does the man need to do?

29. *Woman:* Is it possible to see the apartment before we rent it?

Man: You bet, it's vacant.

What does the man mean?

30. *Man:* You left your lights on!

Woman: Oh, thanks a lot.

What do we learn from the conversation?

31. *Woman:* Tim missed the deadline for the assignment again.

Man: He's got to adjust his study habits in order to survive at the university.

What do we learn about Tim?

32. *Man:* Is there anyone available to help make a copy of my VCR tape?

Woman: No, not until tomorrow. But you can do it yourself by following the instructions on the machine.

What does the woman mean?

33. *Woman:* How do you like your new computer?

Man: I've just put it together, but I really haven't tried to use it yet.

What does the man mean?

34. *Woman:* The bookstore has run out of the textbook assigned by Dr. Martin.

Man: He didn't expect so many students to take his class this semester.

What do we learn about this situation?

35. *Woman:* It takes too much time to cook; I wish I had more time to study.

Man: Why don't you eat at the university cafeteria? It's not too expensive.

What does the man suggest?

Part C

Sample Talk:

Balloons have been used for about a hundred years. There are two kinds of sport balloons: gas and hot air. Hot air balloons are safer than gas balloons, which may catch fire. Hot air balloons are preferred by most balloonists in the United States because of their safety. They are also cheaper and easier to manage than gas balloons. Despite the ease of operating a balloon, pilots must watch the weather carefully. Sport balloon flights are best in the morning or early afternoon when the wind is light.

Example 1:

Why are gas balloons considered dangerous?

Example 2:

According to the speaker, what must balloon pilots be careful to do?

Questions 36 through 40 are based on the following announcement made at the beginning of a university class.
(MALE VOICE)

Hi. My name is John. I'm your teaching assistant for Chemistry 1A, Professor Smith's class. Let me explain a little about this lab section. It's a required meeting, twice a week. I expect you to do all the experiments and keep the results in your lab notebook. I'll collect the notebooks every two weeks. You'll be graded on your lab notebooks, your attendance, and quizzes. But the most important information I want to give you today is about the safety procedures.

First of all, you must wear shoes that cover your feet in the lab. That means you can't wear thongs or sandals. Tennis shoes are OK. Also, don't wear clothes that have loose baggy parts, like long scarves and necklaces or loose belts. They could get caught in something or fall into a liquid.

Another important safety precaution is cleaning up. Be sure to put the waste in the correct containers. We can't mix liquid with paper. This is extremely important. I don't want any fires in this room.

You are responsible for washing out your own lab equipment and putting it away. If you don't do this, I will deduct points from your grades. I'm not going to clean up after you.

OK. That's about all for this meeting. Our first regular class will be next week. Be sure to get a lab notebook before then. Also, let Professor Smith know that you are attending this section.

TO THE READER: Pause 12 seconds after each question.

36. Who is the speaker of this talk?
37. How often does this class meet?
38. What is the main purpose of the speaker's talk?
39. Which of the following can be worn in the lab?
40. What must the students do before the next class?

Questions 41 through 45 are based on the following conversation.

Man: Did you see the play "A Midsummer Night's Dream" last night?

Woman: Yes, it was excellent. I really like Shakespeare.

Man: I do, too. You know, I'm taking a class in Shakespeare now. Did you know that a lot of people are saying that Shakespeare isn't the man we think he was?

Woman: Well, I've heard something about that, but I can't remember exactly what people are saying. What have you heard?

Man: Well, my professor was just discussing this yesterday. In most books it is written that Shakespeare was born in Stratford-on-Avon.

Woman: Yeah, I know that.

Man: But for this man who was called Shakespeare, or Shagsper, or something that sounds like that, there is no evidence that he was literate. There are a few signatures that are written like an illiterate man and there is nothing else—not a single letter, not a single clue that he might have been a writer. And his parents were illiterate and so were his daughters! In addition there is no evidence that he owned a single book or that he ever went to school. In fact there is no evidence that there even was a school in the little village of Stratford.

Woman: Wow, what a mystery. I didn't know all that. So what does your professor say about who wrote the plays?

Man: Well, one likely candidate is the Earl of Oxford, but nobody knows for sure. The Earl was a lord and a leading member of the court, so he couldn't sign his name to his own work. It seems possible that the Earl of Oxford, whose name was Edward de Vere, might have used William Shakespeare's name to fool people.

Woman: But what about this Shakespeare then? Wouldn't he know his name was being used?

Man: Yes. So now some people are saying that the Earl of Oxford gave money to Shakespeare to keep him quiet. And that's the money that he used to build the house that tourists all go to now in Stratford!

Woman: What a story. I wonder if it's true? I think I'll go read more about the Earl of Oxford!

TO THE READER: Pause 12 seconds after each question.

41. What is the main topic of this conversation?
42. What led to this conversation?
43. According to the conversation, who might have written the Shakespeare plays?
44. According to the conversation, what do tourists do?
45. What is the woman interested in doing now?

Questions 46 through 50 are based on the following lecture.
(FEMALE VOICE)

I just want to introduce the next area we'll cover: the food chain. Food chains are divided into three types. The first one is the predator chain, in which larger animals feed on smaller animals, such as when a bird eats a fish. The second is the parasite chain, in which smaller animals live off larger animals, such as a tapeworm living in a cat's intestines. And the third type is the saprophytic chain in which a microorganism feeds off dead matter.

In each type of chain, potential energy is lost at each level. Let's take the example of a green plant. It gets energy from the sun by photosynthesis, but can use only about

2 or 3 percent of the energy that falls on it. The plant is then eaten by a rabbit, but the rabbit can use only about 10 percent of the potential energy of the plant. The rabbit is then eaten by a fox, which can use about 12–15 percent of the energy from the rabbit. And finally, the fox is eaten by a mountain lion. As you can see, at each step the percentage of energy obtained increases, but all in all, a great deal of energy is lost at each step.

That's all for today. Read the next chapter in your books. We'll go on with more about the food chain next time.

TO THE READER: Pause 12 seconds after each question.

46. What is the major topic of this lecture?
47. Which of the following is an example of a predator chain?
48. How much of the potential energy from the sun can a plant use?
49. What happens at each step of the food chain?
50. What is eaten in a saprophytic chain?

Practice Test II, pages 403–426

Part A

Example 1:

Mary swam out to the island with her friend.

Example 2:

Would you mind helping me with this load of books?

TO THE READER: Pause twelve seconds after each question.

1. I'd rather go early than late.
2. If you go to the party, I'll go, too.
3. It looks like rain.
4. I ran into my old friend in town yesterday.
5. Unlike her brother, Ann is open-minded.
6. Come in a minute so I can give you a run-down on the class.
7. Not once has she missed a class this semester!
8. The telephone is disconnected; Bill must have forgotten to pay the bill.
9. Whatever she knows, she's not telling anyone.
10. It takes a long time, but in the long run, it's well worth it.
11. This book is out-of-date.
12. Having a car is by no means cheap.
13. Although he's eighteen, he doesn't act very grown-up.
14. Randy prefers pizza to tacos.
15. Jim used to smoke a lot more.
16. Exercise is a good remedy for depression.
17. They are the same books except for their covers.
18. Mary had the salesman wrap the present.
19. Never have I been so angry!
20. Jenny is smaller than her younger sister, Jane.

Part B

Example:

Man: Professor Smith is going to retire soon. What kind of gift shall we give her?

Woman: I think she'd like to have a photograph of our class.

What does the woman think the class should do?

TO THE READER: Read the sentences below. Pause twelve seconds after each question.

21. *Man:* Do you want to take a break now?

Woman: Yes! I'm starving!

What does the woman mean?

22. *Woman:* How's your class going?

Man: Terrible. It seems like the more the professor talks, the less I understand.

How does the man feel about the class?

23. *Man:* Shall we eat lunch out today?

Woman: Only if we split the bill.

What does the woman want to do?

24. *Man:* How's everything?

Woman: Fine, except for my sore throat.

What does the woman imply?

25. *Man:* Hi, Mary. How're you doing?

Woman: Oh, it's been a long day!

What does the woman mean?

26. *Woman:* Jack, would you please check my mailbox while I'm gone?

Man: Sure, no problem.

What does the man mean?

27. *Man:* If you don't like it, you don't have to take it.

Woman: Thanks, but I like it.

What will the woman probably do?

28. *Man:* Would you like to have a piece of cake?

Woman: No, thanks. I'm on a diet.

What does the woman mean?

29. *Woman:* What kind of dressing would you like?

Man: Italian, please.

Where does this conversation probably take place?

30. *Woman:* The deadline for computer registration is tomorrow.

Man: But I haven't decided which course to take yet.

What are the man and woman talking about?

31. *Woman:* Will you accept a collect call from Lisa?

Man: Yes, I will.

What does the man mean?

32. *Man:* Hello. I'm interested in the rates for Triple S insurance.

Woman: All right. Have you had any tickets or accidents in the last three years?

What do we learn from this conversation?

33. *Man:* Dr. Smith, could you let me audit your class?

Woman: Let me see. I'll have to check the class enrollment list first.

What does the woman mean?

34. *Man:* You're wearing your glasses again!

Woman: I couldn't find my contact lenses.

What does the woman mean?

35. *Woman:* I don't think the job has to be done perfectly.

Man: Maybe not, but it's important that you do your best.

What does the man mean?

Part C

Sample Talk:

Balloons have been used for about a hundred years. There are two kinds of sport balloons: gas and hot air. Hot air balloons are safer than gas balloons, which may catch fire. Hot air balloons are preferred by most balloonists in the United States because of their safety. They are also cheaper and easier to manage than gas balloons. Despite the ease of operating a balloon, pilots must watch the weather carefully. Sport balloon flights are best in the morning or early afternoon when the wind is light.

Example 1:

Why are gas balloons considered dangerous?

Example 2:

According to the speaker, what must balloon pilots be careful to do?

Questions 36 through 40 are based on the following dialogue:

Woman: Good afternoon. In today's class, I want to discuss and demonstrate one of the principles of relaxation exercise. This might be different from other ways you've been taught to exercise. What I want you to do is this: stretch your body to the point where you feel a little pull. Then stop stretching, but keep the same posture and exhale deeply. By doing this, you will allow your body to release the stress and reduce the resistance. Then you will be able to stretch further, relax, and have no pain.

Man: But Mrs. Jones, I've done exercises all my life, and for me it always hurts to stretch. In fact, if I don't feel any pain, I feel that I'm not stretching enough. You know the old saying, "No pain, no gain!"

Woman: Oh yes, I'm well aware of that saying, and, in fact, I agree with it. But let's look at this saying in another way. "No pain, no gain." It can be painful to gain a new concept. Sometimes, it's even more painful to change your ideas than it is to have a tooth pulled. Now let's just try this new way of doing stretching exercises. Ready, everybody? Let's begin.

TO THE READER: Pause twelve seconds after each question.

36. Where does this conversation probably take place?
37. What does this woman mainly want to explain?
38. According to the man, what is painful?
39. With which statement would both speakers probably agree?
40. What will happen next?

Questions 41 through 45 are based on the following conversation. The woman has just returned from being with her friend, Ana, who is new to the United States.

Woman: Poor Ana!

Man: Who's Ana?

Woman: Oh, she's the woman I met at school last week. She just arrived in this country about a week ago. I told her I would help her learn her way around, and today she was told she needed to apply for a Social Security card. So I took her to the Social Security office this afternoon.

Man: That was nice of you.

Woman: But wait until you hear what happened!

Man: What happened?

Woman: Well, I dropped Ana off at the Social Security office. I decided not to wait with her because there were so many people waiting in line, and I told her I would come back in an hour.

Man: And?

Woman: And when I came back, she told me this story. She waited for a long time in line, and when she got to the front of the line, the clerk gave her a form to fill out. She sat down to fill it out, but when she read it, she couldn't figure out how to answer the questions. She couldn't make any sense out of it. She sat there for ages, feeling terrible. She has studied English for several years, but she realized that she had never learned to read a form like this. So she sat there for a long time, hoping I would come back to help her. But I wasn't back yet, so she finally went up to the clerk, and asked for help in filling out the form. He looked at the form quickly and then said, "Oh, I'm sorry. I gave you the wrong form. This one is in Spanish! Here, take a new form." Ana told me that she couldn't believe that she hadn't realized that. She was really embarrassed. But she sat down and filled it out quickly. It really wasn't any problem for her at all. When I arrived, she told me it was one of the most embarrassing things she has done here!

TO THE READER: Pause 12 seconds after each question.

41. Who is the main speaker?
42. Why was Ana embarrassed?
43. Why couldn't she first fill out the form?
44. Why did the clerk say he was sorry?
45. How does the speaker seem to feel about Ana?

Questions 46 through 50 are based on the following talk:

(MALE VOICE)

Today I'd like to begin a discussion on the problem of the heating up of the earth. First we'll touch on the relationship between fluorocarbons and the ozone layer. You probably remember that the ozone layer is the protective shield around the earth. It is important to all life, because it filters out harmful ultraviolet light from the sun. Ozone itself, a form of oxygen, is regularly made by the action of the sun in the upper atmosphere. It is also regularly destroyed by natural chemical processes. The problem now is that too much of the ozone layer is being destroyed. Scientists suspect that certain chemicals, such as fluorocarbons, are contributing to this depletion of the ozone layer. And how do we use fluorocarbons? The most common uses are in spray cans and automobile cooling systems. The chemical pollution from these fluorocarbons can account for some of the ozone losses that have been reported. There are, however, new studies linking the sun itself to the depletion of the ozone layer. We'll go into that new study more next time.

TO THE READER: Pause twelve seconds after each question.

46. Who is the most likely speaker?
47. What is the speaker's main topic?
48. What is the most important purpose of the ozone layer?
49. What is the ozone layer made of?
50. What will the speaker probably discuss next?

Practice Test III, pages 449–480

Part A

Example 1:

Mary swam out to the island with her friend.

Example 2:

Would you mind helping me with this load of books?

TO THE READER: Pause twelve seconds after each question.

1. Dora doesn't need to hurry; the bank closes at six on Fridays.
2. The bus you just missed was the wrong bus anyway.
3. He seems to have a lot of clothes in his closet, but none of them fit well.
4. Hardship has made the young man develop some good characteristics.
5. The solution to this problem is quite tricky, don't you think?
6. Even the supervisor couldn't do it, I bet.
7. This soft drink will be much cheaper in the supermarket.
8. George weighed himself every day when he was on his special diet.
9. The high temperature and heavy humidity give the elderly a hard time.
10. I'll volunteer at the library this evening.
11. Why don't you put your books away before setting the table?

12. Richard has a head start in studying international business with his bilingual background.
13. Older people often value family pictures more than young people do.
14. Whoever drinks and drives will get a ticket from the police.
15. He found the reference he needs at home.
16. There ought to be more people in this restaurant on weekend evenings.
17. We'll have a reception shortly after the speech.
18. We hardly have any rain this time of the year.
19. He'll be better off taking fewer classes during the first semester.
20. That price for a watch like this is reasonable, to say the least.
21. I'm sorry; I thought my ticket was in my wallet.
22. The sweater he used to wear is too small for him this year.
23. We had a wonderful vacation in our grandparents' cabin in Wyoming.
24. We can't make rain, but we certainly can save water.
25. The mailman is late today.
26. She started her ballet training at age seven.
27. You cannot fool him.
28. Wouldn't it be nice to have a family reunion this fall?
29. This music reminds me of my childhood in Massachusetts.
30. Gloria bought a necklace for her mother as a Christmas gift.

Part B

Example:

Man: Professor Smith is going to retire soon. What kind of gift shall we give her?
Woman: I think she'd like to have a photograph of our class.

What does the woman think the class should do?

TO THE READER: Read the sentences below. Pause twelve seconds after each question.

31. *Woman:* I can't decide whether to take classes this summer or to find a summer job.

Man: I think you learn more by working, and you'll also make money for next semester.

What does the man suggest?

32. *Woman:* Did you enjoy the movie last night?

Man: We couldn't get any tickets, so we went to the beach instead.

What does the man mean?

33. *Man:* What a great man!

Woman: Why?

What does the woman want to know?

34. *Man:* I have no idea if they will come to the party or not.

Woman: Don't worry, we have enough food for all of them.

What does the woman mean?

35. *Woman:* I don't know if I should take Physics 101 this semester.

Man: It doesn't matter; that class is offered every semester.

What does the man say about the class?

36. *Woman:* Mr. Day, I've just checked this apartment; the bathroom sink is leaking.

Man: OK, I'll have a maintenance man come over to fix it.

What will the man do?

37. *Man:* May I have your phone number?

Woman: No, I haven't gotten one yet. Sorry.

What does the woman mean?

38. *Woman:* Louie, I'm going to give away these books. You can have them if you want.

Man: Are you sure?

What does the man imply?

39. *Woman:* Excuse me, Sir, may I pay the bill for an overdue book here?

Man: No, pay at the cashier's office.

What do we learn from the conversation?

40. *Woman:* Do you want me to help you type your report?

Man: Thank you, but I already had the typist take care of it.

What does the man mean?

41. *Woman:* Does this bus go to the housing office?

Man: No, but the next one does. Just wait for a few minutes.

What does the man suggest?

42. *Woman:* I thought we could check out as many books as we need with a student I.D.

Man: That's right, but not those reference books.

What does the man mean?

43. *Man:* Didn't you say you would go to the convention this morning?

Woman: Yes, but it was postponed until next Wednesday.

What does the woman mean?

44. *Man:* What did Joan call for?

Woman: She wants our new address, so she can mail us her business card.

What does the woman mean?

45. *Man:* What? You've got your Ph.D. degree already?

Woman: Already? It's been six years!

What does the woman imply?

46. *Woman:* May I help you?

Man: Yes, could you tell me the number of the local post office?

What does the man want?

47. *Man:* Do you have the test scores?

Woman: No, but they are listed in the English department bulletin.

What does the woman imply?

48. *Man:* How do you correct an error with this typewriter?

Woman: Just press the "correct" button.

What do we learn from this conversation?

49. *Man:* Is there anything else that I have to do to complete this course?

Woman: No that's it.

What does the woman mean?

50. *Woman:* How would you like your coffee?

Man: Decaffeinated, please.

What does the man mean?

51. *Man:* Have you gotten your textbook yet?

Woman: They are out of it in the bookstore, but they made a special order for me.

What does the woman mean?

52. *Man:* Do you want to try a new way to get there?

Woman: Not this time; we don't have enough time.

What does the woman imply?

53. *Man:* Is this paper acceptable?

Woman: No, you have to type it.

What does the woman mean?

54. *Man:* What's the due date for this book?

Woman: Tomorrow.

What does the woman mean?

55. *Woman:* The elevator is over here.

Man: I know, but I like to walk up.

What does the man mean?

PART C

Sample Talk:

Balloons have been used for about a hundred years. There are two kinds of sport balloons: gas and hot air. Hot air balloons are safer than gas balloons, which may catch fire. Hot air balloons are preferred by most balloonists in the United States because of their safety. They are also cheaper and easier to manage than gas balloons. Despite the ease of operating a balloon, pilots must watch the weather carefully. Sport balloon flights are best in the morning or early afternoon when the wind is light.

Example 1:

Why are gas balloons considered dangerous?

Example 2:

According to the speaker, what must balloon pilots be careful to do?

Questions 56-61 are based on the following talk.

(FEMALE VOICE)

This summer the Shakespeare Festival will feature four plays that focus on Roman history, and since we've just finished reading *Julius Caesar*, I thought you'd be interested in going. The performances should be excellent. Besides our own college actors, there will be actors coming from New York, Los Angeles, Chicago, and London. The festival has received a grant from the National Endowment for the Humanities to support the plays, as well as a series of events to increase the public's appreciation of the plays. One of the events I hope you can go to is a public lecture by our own chair, Dr. Arthur Johnson. That will be two weeks from Wednesday at 7 P.M. in the community room downtown at the public library. Dr. Johnson will first give a brief introduction to the whole series, and then discuss *Julius Caesar* in detail. Tickets for the whole series are on sale now at the campus box office. The first play will begin two weeks from Friday.

TO THE READER: Pause 12 seconds after each question.

56. What is the speaker mainly discussing?
57. Who is most likely listening to this talk?
58. Why does the speaker think the listeners would be interested in the plays?
59. Who is Dr. Johnson?
60. Why is Dr. Johnson giving a speech?
61. When will the first play begin?

Questions 62-67 are based on the following announcement.

(MALE VOICE)

Because of the severe drought which has continued this year, water rationing will go into effect on Monday. Lawns cannot be watered with automatic sprinklers; driveways, porches, and decks cannot be hosed down. You may water by hand, but only on even-numbered days. Cars can be washed on Wednesdays only. The city has hired a new drought patrol crew, which will be looking for offenders. If you are caught, there will be a $50 fine for the first offense and a $100 fine for the second offense. We realize that this is strict, but the drought has affected us dramatically. We ask your cooperation in conserving water. Besides the drought rules, we ask that you be prudent in your household water use. Turn off the faucet while you brush your teeth. Take short showers; you might even consider turning off the water as you soap up. Don't wash dishes under running water, and when you wash your clothes, save the final rinse water to begin your next load. Thank you for listening. Let's all work together to save our community's water.

TO THE READER: Pause 12 seconds after each question.

62. What is the main problem the speaker is referring to?
63. What should people do on Monday?
64. If you have a lawn, what are your rules?
65. Which of the following was NOT mentioned by the speaker?
66. What will the drought patrol crew do?
67. What does the speaker suggest?

Questions 68-73 are based on the following conversation between two students:

Man: Hi, Joannie. Are you heading over to the library, too?

Woman: No, it's closed now.

Man: Closed already? It's still early!

Woman: I know. Didn't you hear about the new hours? They're only open for a half day now.

Man: What's going on?

Woman: I heard that they are putting in a new special resource center. They have to rebuild the basement, and the whole library shakes when they begin using their tools.

Man: Oh, well. I guess it's just as well that they're closed then. What do you know about the new resource center? What's it for?

Woman: I think it's for projects that focus on global concerns in the 21st century. They're trying to attract community people as well as students who need resources concerning new technology, the environment, the arms build-up, and such.

Man: That sounds great. I wish it were ready now. I'm doing a report on increasing global economic cooperation. That should be a 21st century concern. I've been spending a lot of time in different sections of the main library looking up material. This new center should be excellent. I guess it's worth putting up with building noise and shortened hours for the time being.

TO THE READER: Pause 12 seconds after each question.

68. When the man first speaks, where is he probably going?
69. Why is the man surprised?
70. Where will the new resource center be?
71. Which of the following topics would probably NOT be found in the new resource center?
72. Why does the man think that information for his research topic would be found in the new resource center?
73. How does the man feel about the library's new hours?

Questions 74–80 are based on the following announcement.

(MALE VOICE)

Ten graduate students who have served as teaching assistants this year have been nominated to receive awards for outstanding teaching. They were chosen from out of approximately 500 teaching assistants. There will be a ceremony on Tuesday evening at 7:30 to honor them. The chancellor will present each of the winners with a cash prize of $100 and a certificate commending them. The chancellor has noted that teaching assistants are an integral part of our campus, and that the quality of undergraduate education has been improved by the quality of our teaching assistants. They work long hours leading discussion groups, grading papers, and overseeing lab work. Most of them work as teaching assistants to help with the cost of their education. Please come to the ceremony on Tuesday to show your appreciation of these hard-working students.

TO THE READER: Pause 12 seconds after each question.

74. How many students will get awards?
75. Who will give the awards?
76. What will the winners receive?
77. Which of the following is NOT mentioned as a job for teaching assistants?
78. What did the chancellor say?
79. According to the speaker, why do most teaching assistants work?
80. Why should the listeners go to the ceremony?

Practice Test IV, pages 513–543

Part A

Example 1:

Mary swam out to the island with her friend.

Example 2:

Would you mind helping me with this load of books?

TO THE READER: Pause twelve seconds after each question.

1. You got a good deal when you bought this tape recorder at the clearance sale.
2. He walked around the hall looking for a pencil sharpener.
3. Nobody likes watermelon more than I do.
4. She needs a vacation badly.
5. These pants require dry cleaning.
6. What a beautiful view!
7. This could be an alternative answer.
8. Why not ask the waitress to give you an extra fork?
9. There was bumper-to-bumper traffic during the rush hour.
10. It feels good to be cool again.
11. When the time comes to decide, he still hesitates.
12. Only occasionally does he express his anger.
13. The newborn panda is awfully cute.
14. I'm going to change the topic of my thesis.
15. The new semester will start in one week.
16. Sue will be teaching this course this semester.
17. The cafeteria is a place where you can eat, relax, and talk to people.
18. You can wear informal clothes to class; even professors do.
19. All of today's newspapers are gone; the box is empty.
20. The accuracy of the new equipment still needs to be tested.
21. I'll take it; I don't have any other choice.
22. Only once in a while do I take chances.
23. I'll quit this job; I mean it.
24. Jack was the substitute while I was on my trip.

25. Attendance is one of the requirements of this class.
26. Why don't we have lunch together so that we can talk about it more?
27. Jessica is very involved in her church activities.
28. That's what my sister is interested in, not me.
29. Mr. Jones was the former chair of the committee.
30. There is no excuse for this kind of error.

Part B

Example:

Man: Professor Smith is going to retire soon. What kind of gift shall we give her?

Woman: I think she'd like to have a photograph of our class.

What does the woman think the class should do?

TO THE READER: Read the sentences below. Pause twelve seconds after each question.

31. *Man:* Hello, I'd like to buy a hundred dollar money order.

Woman: OK. Do you have an account here?

Where does this conversation most likely take place?

32. *Woman:* This muffin smells good.

Man: Tastes good, too.

What is the man's comment about the muffin?

33. *Man:* I don't understand why this study book doesn't provide an explanation of the answers.

Woman: But it does!

What does the woman say about the study book?

34. *Woman:* Do you have the paperback edition of this book?

Man: Yes, we do, but the hardcover is on sale for the same price as the paperback.

What do we learn about the book from the man?

35. *Woman:* Why are you going to school so early?

Man: I have to practice using the slide projector and prepare my presentation for class today.

What will the man do in class?

36. *Man:* Would you mind seeing our representative?

Woman: I wouldn't mind at all.

What does the woman mean?

37. *Man:* I would like to make a reservation for dinner for four tonight.

Woman: I'm sorry, sir. We don't take reservations on weekends.

What does the woman mean?

38. *Woman:* Did you talk to the consultant about the new program?

Man: No, he's at lunch until two.

What does the man mean?

39. *Man:* It's getting dark. Do you want me to walk you to your car?

Woman: No, thanks, it's not far.

What does the woman mean?

40. *Man:* That movie was terrific!

Woman: I know.

What does the woman mean?

41. *Woman:* Is there any industry in this area?

Man: Only a small amount; nothing big.

What does the man mean?

42. *Man:* Can I eat this fruit like it is?

Woman: No, you have to peel it first.

What does the woman mean?

43. *Woman:* I'm still upset about Frank's remark.

Man: Yes. It was a thoughtless thing to say.

What does the man mean?

44. *Man:* What time will you be back?

Woman: Oh, it shouldn't take me too long.

What does the woman mean?

45. *Woman:* How are the pictures you took in New York? I can't wait to see them.

Man: They're not ready yet.

What does the man mean?

46. *Woman:* Watching the news on TV is a good way to learn English.

Man: It's especially helpful when you check the same information in the newspaper.

What does the man mean?

47. *Man:* I don't know what to do.

Woman: You have to make your own decision, and there is not much time left.

What does the woman imply?

48. *Woman:* Nobody expected that he would be able to come to the party.

Man: But he did.

What can we learn from the conversation?

49. *Man:* I hope I get an "A" in this class.

Woman: I don't think I'll do very well; I have to spend most of my time on my senior project.

What does the woman mean?

50. *Man:* I think I've met you somewhere before.

Woman: Yes! At Professor Dean's seminar.

What does the woman mean?

51. *Man:* How was your afternoon with Aunt Jane?

Woman: Oh, I couldn't believe it! She was in a rage. She flew off the handle at every little thing.

What does the woman mean?

52. *Woman:* What do you think I should wear to the party tonight?

Man: Oh, I don't know. It's not too fancy.

What does the man mean?

53. *Woman:* I can't decide whether to buy that expensive new car or the cheaper used car.

Man: I'd get the new one. It's better in the long run.

Why would the man buy the more expensive car?

54. *Man:* Shall we go out for Mexican food or Chinese food tonight?

Woman: I don't care. It's up to you.

What does the woman mean?

55. *Man:* How's your new job going?

Woman: Not so well. I feel like a fish out of water in that job.

What does the woman mean?

Part C

Sample Talk:

Balloons have been used for about a hundred years. There are two kinds of sport balloons: gas and hot air. Hot air balloons are safer than gas balloons, which may catch fire. Hot air balloons are preferred by most balloonists in the United States because of their safety. They are also cheaper and easier to manage than gas balloons. Despite the ease of operating a balloon, pilots must watch the weather carefully. Sport balloon flights are best in the morning or early afternoon when the wind is light.

Example 1:

Why are gas balloons considered dangerous?

Example 2:

According to the speaker, what must balloon pilots be careful to do?

Questions 56-61 are based on the following talk.

(FEMALE VOICE)

Good morning students and welcome to the university. I'd like to begin with some information about graduate student housing, and then turn this session over to Dr. Paulson, who will explain some of the financial support services we offer to graduate students.

First of all, I hope you're getting settled into your new surroundings without too much difficulty. I know that several of you have moved into our new unit for single graduate students. It's located on the west side of campus. In this building, four students share a dining and living room, kitchen, two bathrooms, and four single bedrooms. We do have a few more empty rooms, so if you're interested in moving in, let me know right away.

If you haven't visited the family student housing complex, be sure to go take a look at it. This small community has two-bedroom unfurnished apartments. They are on the south side of campus, near the bus stop for the town center. All apartments are full now, and we have a waiting list for next year. Come see me if you want to add your name to the list. You should apply as soon as possible for next year.

If you want to live off campus and are still looking for a house, be sure to check out the off-campus housing office. You'll find a lot of rentals listed there.

Now let me turn this over to Dr. Paulson. He will explain some things about financial aid programs.

TO THE READER: Pause 12 seconds after each question.

56. Who is the most likely speaker of this talk?
57. Who is probably listening to this talk?
58. How many students can live in one unit for single graduate students?
59. If you want to move into the family student housing, what should you do?
60. What will the off-campus housing office do for you?
61. What will the listeners be doing next?

Questions 62–67 are based on the following conversation between two university students.

Man: Hey, Joannie. I'm really excited!

Woman: What's happening?

Man: I just got my scholarship approved! I'll be getting the money at the first of next month.

Woman: That's fantastic! I was going to apply for a scholarship this year, but I figured that my grades weren't good enough.

Man: Have you been to the financial aid office? They have a list of about ten different kinds of scholarships. And only some of them are based on grades. Others are based on financial need. And there are work-study programs, too.

Woman: Maybe I should go over there. My folks can't pay my room and board this year, and my money is really low. Working part time in the ice cream store doesn't pay enough to live on.

Man: Yeah, I'd go over right now. The deadline for new applications is next Friday. You'll probably be able to get something. It's easier for graduate students, too. And have you talked to your department about being a teaching assistant?

Woman: Yes, I already did that. I couldn't do it this year because of my schedule. But I might be able to next year. Anyway, I'll drop by the financial aid office now. I'm going that way anyway. Bye.

Man: See you later.

TO THE READER: Pause 12 seconds after each question.

62. Why is the man excited?
63. What does the woman say about her parents?
64. What does the woman do besides her studies?
65. What does the man suggest that the woman do?
66. Why couldn't the woman be a teaching assistant?
67. Where will the woman go next?

Questions 68–74 are based on the following announcement.

(MALE VOICE)

We've just received word that Hurricane Harry has changed its course, and is now heading straight for the mainland. We expect to have winds of over 150 miles per hour. The hurricane should arrive at about 3 P.M. this afternoon. Please get prepared for it. Board up your windows as much as possible. Tie your boats down well. No camping is allowed on the beach; it's too dangerous. If you are planning to leave for the day, try to get out of town before 3. For those of you staying in town, stay indoors and out of your car.

After the hurricane dies down, be careful of loose electric wires. The electric company will be out repairing the wires as soon as possible. Don't touch any wires on the ground. If your electricity goes out, be patient. You can be assured that the electric company will be working as quickly as possible to restore it. Keep your radio tuned to this station for more information. Thank you.

TO THE READER: Pause 12 seconds after each question.

68. What is the main reason for making this announcement?
69. What is coming?
70. When is it coming?
71. According to the announcement, which of the following is something you should NOT do?
72. If your electricity goes out, what should you do?
73. What does the speaker suggest?
74. Who is making this announcement?

Questions 75–80 are based on the following lecture.

(FEMALE VOICE)

Let's continue today with a discussion of the development of ferns. As you may remember, in the last lecture we discussed the difference between ferns and mosses. Ferns developed a vascular system and began a line of many different vascular plants, which include ferns as well as conifers and flowering plants.

One of the amazing things about ferns is their large family. They include about 9,000 or so species, and they are classified—along with the conifers, flowering plants, and certain other groups—in the largest subdivision of vascular plants.

Another interesting thing about ferns is their age. They are among the oldest groups of living land plants. Fossils of early ferns are found in the rocks of the Upper Devonian period, about 300 million years ago, and there are so many remains of fernlike plants in the Carboniferous that this period has been called the "Age of Ferns." However, most of these fern-like plants of the Carboniferous Period were not true ferns, but seed ferns. You may remember that the difference between true ferns and seed ferns is in their structure. But even though these seed ferns were primitive in structure, they were quite similar to the ferns of today in their methods of reproduction.

In addition to their large numbers and their age, it is interesting to note how widely they are distributed. They can live in places as different as the moist tropics and the Arctic Circle. But they are especially abundant in the tropical rain forests on foggy mountainsides. They also flourish around here in the woods, meadows, along roadsides, and near rivers. You've probably seen small- or medium-sized ferns, but in the tropics they can be trees of up to 60 feet in height with leaves up to 12 feet long.

TO THE READER: Pause 12 seconds after each question.

75. Who is the most likely speaker?
76. What is one difference between ferns and mosses?
77. When was the "Age of Ferns"?
78. How does the speaker say that seed ferns are similar to true ferns?
79. Where would a fern be least likely to live?
80. How tall can ferns grow?

Practice Test V, pages 575–599

Part A

Example 1:

Mary swam out to the island with her friend.

Example 2:

Would you mind helping me with this load of books?

TO THE READER: Pause twelve seconds after each question.

1. You'll miss the train unless you hurry.
2. We all think Grandma should take it easy after her fall.
3. By the time John gets to the party, the director will have already gone.
4. Sandra finished the work in no time at all.
5. There is a door for the handicapped in the rear.
6. One student presented a project that was discussed by the whole class.
7. Jenny once dreamed of being an Olympic gold medal winner in gymnastics.
8. You're on the right track.
9. Mr. Wilson is wealthy enough to retire.
10. Black clothes are not as fit to wear in summer as white clothes.
11. The design was complete, but the construction had just begun.
12. The asteroids were large enough to be called small planets.
13. If you do this part, I'll take care of the rest.
14. His determination to do what seemed impossible was the key to his success.
15. Classes in computer science are becoming overcrowded.

16. I want it, no matter what it costs.
17. My uncle is a well-known lecturer.
18. George dropped the class because of a schedule conflict.
19. We couldn't have gone to the beach on a better day.
20. I'm working as fast as I can.

Part B

Example:

Man: Professor Smith is going to retire soon. What kind of gift shall we give her?

Woman: I think she'd like to have a photograph of our class.

What does the woman think the class should do?

TO THE READER: Read the sentences below. Pause twelve seconds after each question.

21. *Man:* What do you think the boss will do when we tell him the bad news?

Woman: Oh, you can never tell with him!

What does the woman mean?

22. *Man:* Well, I'll be leaving now.

Woman: Must you go so soon?

How does the woman feel?

23. *Woman:* Would you like this gift-wrapped?

Man: Thanks, I would.

Where does this conversation take place?

24. *Man:* How long do you think it will take to finish this job?

Woman: Off-hand, I'd say three hours.

What does the woman mean?

25. *Woman:* I'm sorry. The class is full.

Man: Well, could I be put on the waiting list?

What does the man imply?

26. *Man:* What time do we have to check out of the room?

Woman: I'm not sure. Let's ask at the front desk.

What does the woman mean?

27. *Man:* Would you like to go have some coffee?

Woman: Thanks, but I have some work I have to catch up on.

What does the woman mean?

28. *Woman:* How much is a dorm room?

Man: It's $500 a month for room and board.

What do you get for $500?

29. *Woman:* May I try these clothes on?

Man: Yes, but no more than three items are allowed in the dressing room.

Where does this conversation take place?

30. *Woman:* I'm really angry at John. He never listens to me.

Man: Take it easy, Ellen. Things will work out.

What does the man imply?

31. *Man:* Would you like chocolate or butter brickle ice cream?

Woman: You choose. I like them both.

What does the woman mean?

32. *Man:* Did you hear that Ann got laid off?

Woman: No, that's terrible.

What do we learn about Ann?

33. *Woman:* Have you called Pete yet?

Man: I'll call him as soon as I get home.

What does the man mean?

34. *Man:* Which kind of pie do you want?

Woman: I don't know. I like pumpkin as well as apple.

What does the woman mean?

35. *Woman:* How much is the bill?

Man: All in all, it comes to $54.00.

What does the man mean?

Part C

Sample Talk:

Balloons have been used for about a hundred years. There are two kinds of sport balloons: gas and hot air. Hot air balloons are safer than gas balloons, which may catch fire. Hot air balloons are preferred by most balloonists in the United States because of their safety. They are also cheaper and easier to manage than gas balloons. Despite the ease of operating a balloon, pilots must watch the weather carefully. Sport balloon flights are best in the morning or early afternoon when the wind is light.

Example 1:

Why are gas balloons considered dangerous?

Example 2:

According to the speaker, what must balloon pilots be careful to do?

Questions 36 through 42 are based on the following talk.

(MALE VOICE)

Now that I've extracted your tooth, I want to give you some words of advice. Remember that this is surgery. You need to go home and rest for the rest of the day. You shouldn't do your regular work. Since you're adult, it might take you longer to heal than if you were a child. The numbness will wear off after a few hours, and if it's painful after that, you should take two aspirins.

Now, the most important thing to remember is to apply ice to your cheek immediately when you get home. This will keep the swelling down. You can use an ice bag or put chopped ice in a towel. Hold it on your cheek over the extraction area for twenty minutes, and then take it off for twenty minutes. Keep this up for four or five hours.

Secondly, don't rinse your mouth today. Tomorrow you should rinse your mouth gently every three or four hours with salt water. Put about a quarter of a teaspoon of salt in a glass of warm water. Continue this rinsing for several days.

Don't be alarmed if there is some bleeding this morning. A little bleeding is normal following an extraction. I've put gauze pads over the extraction, and I will give you some to take home. Change the pads about a half hour after you get home.

That's all you need to do. Call me anytime if you have a lot of bleeding or pain. And remember to apply ice right away.

TO THE READER: Pause twelve seconds after each question.

36. Who is probably speaking?
37. When is the man speaking?
38. How long will the person's mouth be numb?
39. What does he say is the most important thing to do?
40. When does he say to rinse with salt water?
41. What does the speaker say about bleeding?
42. What kind of person does the speaker seem to be?

Questions 43 through 46 are based on the following talk.

(FEMALE VOICE)

Good morning. First I'd like to welcome all of you new students to this workshop on student housing. I'll go through the information about types of housing available for the fall and later hand out application blanks. Then, if you have any questions, feel free to ask me.

There are three main types of housing here for you to choose from: the student dorms, the married student apartments, and the international houses. As of now, there is some space available in each type, but they are filling up fast. You should get your application in as soon as possible. Let me explain some of the main features of each type of housing.

The student dorms are for any student. We have men's dorms, women's dorms, and coed dorms. In the coed dorms there is one large bathroom and shower area for both sexes to use. Most of the rooms have two beds, two closets, and two desks. We also have a few triples, and a few single suites, but I